Śrī Caitanya-caritāmṛta

BOOKS by
His Divine Grace A.C. Bhaktivedanta Swami Prabhupāda

Bhagavad-gītā As It Is
Śrīmad-Bhāgavatam, Cantos 1-4 (13 Vols.)
Śrī Caitanya-caritāmṛta (3 Vols.)
Teachings of Lord Caitanya
The Nectar of Devotion
Śrī Īśopaniṣad
Easy Journey to Other Planets
Kṛṣṇa Consciousness: The Topmost Yoga System
Kṛṣṇa, The Supreme Personality of Godhead (2 Vols.)
Transcendental Teachings of Prahlād Mahārāja
Transcendental Teachings of Caitanya Mahāprabhu
Kṛṣṇa, the Reservoir of Pleasure
The Perfection of Yoga
Beyond Birth and Death
On the Way to Kṛṣṇa
Rāja-vidyā: The King of Knowledge
Elevation to Kṛṣṇa Consciousness
Lord Caitanya in Five Features
Back to Godhead Magazine (Founder)

A complete catalogue is available upon request.

Bhaktivedanta Book Trust
3764 Watseka Ave.
Los Angeles, Calif. 90034

All Glory to Śrī Guru and Gaurāṅga

ŚRĪ CAITANYA-CARITĀMṚTA

of Kṛṣṇadāsa Kavirāja Gosvāmī

Ādi-līlā

Volume Two

"LORD CAITANYA MAHĀPRABHU
in the
RENOUNCED ORDER OF LIFE"

with the original Bengali text, Roman transliterations, synonyms, translation and elaborate purports

by

HIS DIVINE GRACE

A.C. Bhaktivedanta Swami Prabhupāda

Founder-Ācārya of the International Society for Krishna Consciousness

THE BHAKTIVEDANTA BOOK TRUST
New York · Los Angeles · London · Bombay

Readers interested in the subject matter of this book
are invited by the International Society for Krishna Consciousness
to correspond with its Secretary.

International Society for Krishna Consciousness
3959 Landmark Street
Culver City, California 90230

Library of Congress Catalogue Card Number: 73-93206
International Standard Book Number: 0-912776-51-X

Printed in the United States of America

Contents

Introduction		vii
Chapter 7	Lord Caitanya in Five Features	1
Chapter 8	The Author's Receiving the Orders of the Authorities, Kṛṣṇa and Guru	157
Chapter 9	The Tree of Devotional Service	213
Chapter 10	The Main Trunk of the Caitanya Tree, Its Branches and Its Sub-branches	251
Chapter 11	The Expansions of Lord Nityānanda	353
References		391
Glossary		393
Bengali Pronunciation Guide		397
Map of Bengal		399
General Index		401

Introduction

"HARE KṚṢṆA" has become a household phrase in cities, towns and villages throughout the world, fulfilling a prophecy made almost five hundred years ago by Lord Śrī Caitanya Mahāprabhu. From Los Angeles to London, from Bombay to Buenos Aires, from Pittsburgh and Melbourne to Paris and even Moscow, people of all ages, colors, creeds and faiths are feeling the bliss of the dynamic *yoga* system called "Kṛṣṇa consciousness."

This Kṛṣṇa consciousness movement began in full force some five hundred years ago, when Lord Śrī Caitanya Mahāprabhu, an incarnation of Kṛṣṇa (God), flooded the subcontinent of India with the chanting of the *mantra* Hare Kṛṣṇa, Hare Kṛṣṇa, Kṛṣṇa Kṛṣṇa, Hare Hare/ Hare Rāma, Hare Rāma, Rāma Rāma, Hare Hare. To reveal the secret of what real love is, Kṛṣṇa came to earth five hundred years ago in the guise of His own devotee—as Lord Caitanya Mahāprabhu. With His chief associates —Nityānanda, Advaita, Gadādhara and Śrīvāsa—He taught how to develop love of Godhead simply by chanting Hare Kṛṣṇa and dancing in ecstasy.

Śrī Caitanya-caritāmṛta, which was written by the great saint Kṛṣṇadāsa Kavirāja Gosvāmī shortly after Lord Caitanya's disappearance, vividly describes Lord Caitanya's blissful pastimes and probes deeply into His profound spiritual philosophy.

The translations and purports, the explanations of the verses, are the work of His Divine Grace A.C. Bhaktivedanta Swami Prabhupāda, author of *Bhagavad-gītā As It Is; The Nectar of Devotion; Kṛṣṇa, the Supreme Personality of Godhead* (first published in 1970 with the kind help of Mr. George Harrison); and numerous other books about *yoga* and self-realization.

Although this is the second volume of *Śrī Caitanya-caritāmṛta,* one need not have read Volume One to understand and appreciate this book. Śrīla Prabhupāda remarks that such a spiritual work is like sugar, for wherever you begin tasting it you will surely enjoy its sweetness.

His Divine Grace
A.C. BHAKTIVEDANTA SWAMI PRABHUPĀDA
Founder-Ācārya of the International Society for Krishna Consciousness

ŚRĪLA BHAKTISIDDHĀNTA SARASVATĪ GOSVĀMĪ MAHĀRĀJA
the spiritual master of
His Divine Grace A.C. Bhaktivedanta Swami Prabhupāda
and foremost scholar and devotee in the recent age.

Plate 1 *The supreme energetic, the Personality of Godhead, manifesting in five kinds of pastimes, appears as the Pañca-tattva.* *(p. 5)*

Plate 2 *Among the many transcendental lovers of Kṛṣṇa, the* gopīs *[cowherd girls of Vṛndāvana] are the best, and among the* gopīs *Śrīmatī Rādhārāṇī is the best.* (*p. 15*)

Plate 3 *Lord Caitanya and His associates danced again and again and thus made it easier to drink nectarean love of Godhead.* (*p. 17*)

Plate 4 *Prakāśānanda Sarasvatī, seeing Śrī Caitanya Mahāprabhu in an unclean place, caught Him by the hand and seated Him with great respect in the midst of the assembly.* (*p. 49*)

Plate 5 *After the Māyāvādī* sannyāsīs *heard Lord Caitanya, their minds changed, and they began to chant the holy name of Kṛṣṇa.* (*p.* 141)

Plate 6 *Whenever the crowds were too great, Śrī Caitanya Mahāprabhu stood up, raised His hands and chanted "Hari! Hari!" to which all the people again responded, filling both the land and sky with the vibration.* *(p. 149)*

Plate 7 *In the temple of Govindajī, thousands of servitors always render service to the Lord, who is seated on a golden throne bedecked with jewels.* (p. 196)

Plate 8 *After seeing Madana-mohana, Kṛṣṇadāsa Kavirāja Gosvāmī accepted the garland of order from the temple priest.* (*p. 208*)

Plate 9 *While chanting the Hare Kṛṣṇa* mantra *in Benapola, Haridāsa Ṭhākura was personally tested by Māyādevī herself.* (p. 276)

Plate 10 *After the passing of Haridāsa Ṭhākura, Lord Caitanya took his body and danced with it in great ecstasy.* (*p. 277*)

Plate 11 *Lord Caitanya exhibited His Varāha form in the house of Murāri Gupta, the twenty-first branch of the Śrī Caitanya tree.* (p. 279)

Plate 12 *Śacīmātā saw that the foodstuffs had actually been eaten by Śrī Caitanya Mahāprabhu, even though He was far away.* (p. 285)

Plate 13 *Lord Caitanya embraced Sanātana, accepting his body as spiritual.* (*p. 305*)

Plate 14 *"I saw that Lord Caitanya Mahāprabhu was entering the body of Jagannātha and again coming out of His body."* (*p. 339*)

Ādi-Līlā

CHAPTER 7

TEXT 1

অগত্যেকগতিং নত্বা হীনার্থাধিকসাধকম্‌ ।
শ্রীচৈতন্যং লিখ্যতেঽস্য প্রেমভক্তিবদান্যতা ॥ ১ ॥

agaty-eka-gatiṁ natvā
hīnārthādhika-sādhakam
śrī-caitanyaṁ likhyate 'sya
prema-bhakti-vadānyatā

SYNONYMS

agati—of the most fallen; *eka*—the only one; *gatim*—destination; *natvā*—after offering obeisances; *hīna*—inferior; *artha*—interest; *adhika*—greater than that; *sādhakam*—who can render; *śrī-caitanyam*—unto Lord Śrī Caitanya; *likhyate*—is being written; *asya*—of the Lord, Śrī Caitanya Mahāprabhu; *prema*—love; *bhakti*—devotional service; *vadānyatā*—magnanimity.

TRANSLATION

Let me first offer my respectful obeisances unto Lord Caitanya Mahāprabhu, who is the ultimate goal of life for one bereft of all possessions in this material world and is the only meaning for one advancing in spiritual life. Thus let me write about His magnanimous contribution of devotional service in love of God.

PURPORT

A person in the conditional stage of material existence is in an atmosphere of helplessness, but the conditioned soul, under the illusion of *māyā,* or the external energy, thinks that he is completely protected by his country, society, friendship and love, not knowing that at the time of death none of these can save him. The laws of material nature are so strong that none of our material possessions can save us from the cruel hands of death. In *Bhagavad-gītā* (13.9) it is stated, *janma-mṛtyu-jarā-vyādhi-duḥkha-doṣānudarśanam:* one who is actually advancing must always consider the four principles of miserable life, namely, birth, death, old age and disease. One cannot be saved from all these miseries unless he takes shelter of the lotus feet of the Lord. Śrī Caitanya Mahāprabhu is therefore the only shelter for all conditioned souls. An intelligent person, therefore, does not put his faith in any material possessions, but completely takes shelter of the lotus feet of the Lord. Such a person is called *akiñcana,* or one who does not possess anything in this material world. The Supreme Personality of Godhead is also known as Akiñcana-gocara, for He can be achieved by a person who does not put his faith in material possessions. Therefore, for the fully surrendered soul who has no material possessions on which to depend, Lord Śrī Caitanya Mahāprabhu is the only shelter. Everyone depends upon *dharma* (religiosity), *artha* (economic development), *kāma* (sense gratification) and ultimately *mokṣa* (salvation), but Śrī Caitanya Mahāprabhu, due to His magnanimous character, can give more than salvation. Therefore in this verse the words *hīnārthādhika-sādhakam* indicate that although by material estimation salvation is of a quality superior to the inferior interests of religiosity, economic development and sense gratification, above salvation there is the position of devotional service and transcendental love for the Supreme Personality of Godhead. Śrī Caitanya Mahāprabhu is the bestower of this great benediction. Śrī Caitanya Mahāprabhu said, *premā pumartho mahān:* "Love of Godhead is the ultimate benediction for all human beings." Śrīla Kṛṣṇadāsa Kavirāja Gosvāmī, the author of *Caitanya-caritāmṛta,* therefore first offers his respectful obeisances unto Lord Caitanya Mahāprabhu before describing His magnanimity in bestowing love of Godhead.

TEXT 2

জয় জয় মহাপ্রভু শ্রীকৃষ্ণচৈতন্য ।
তাঁহার চরণাশ্রিত, সেই বড় ধন্য ॥ ২ ॥

jaya jaya mahāprabhu śrī-kṛṣṇa-caitanya
tāṅhāra caraṇāśrita, sei baḍa dhanya

SYNONYMS

jaya—all glories; *jaya*—all glories; *mahāprabhu*—unto the Supreme Lord; *śrī-kṛṣṇa-caitanya*—of the name Śrī Kṛṣṇa Caitanya; *tāṅhāra*—of His; *caraṇa-āśrita*—one who has taken shelter of the lotus feet; *sei*—he; *baḍa*—is very; *dhanya*—glorified.

TRANSLATION

Let me offer glorification to the Supreme Lord Śrī Caitanya Mahāprabhu. One who has taken shelter of His lotus feet is the most glorified person.

PURPORT

Prabhu means master. Śrī Caitanya Mahāprabhu is the supreme master of all masters; therefore He is called Mahāprabhu. Any person who takes shelter of Śrī Kṛṣṇa Caitanya Mahāprabhu is most glorified because by the mercy of Śrī Caitanya Mahāprabhu he is able to get promotion to the platform of loving service to the Lord, which is transcendental to salvation.

TEXT 3

পূর্বে গুর্বাদি ছয় তত্ত্বে কৈল নমস্কার ।
গুরুতত্ত্ব কহিয়াছি, এবে পাঁচের বিচার ॥ ৩ ॥

pūrve gurv-ādi chaya tattve kaila namaskāra
guru-tattva kahiyāchi, ebe pāṅcera vicāra

SYNONYMS

pūrve—in the beginning; *guru-ādi*—the spiritual master and others; *chaya*—six; *tattve*—in the subjects of; *kaila*—I have done; *namaskāra*—obeisances; *guru-tattva*—the truth in understanding the spiritual master; *kahiyāchi*—I have already described; *ebe*—now; *pāṅcera*—of the five; *vicāra*—consideration.

TRANSLATION

In the beginning I have discussed the truth about the spiritual master. Now I shall try to explain the Pañca-tattva.

PURPORT

In the First Chapter of *Caitanya-caritāmṛta, Ādi-līlā,* the author, Śrīla Kṛṣṇadāsa Kavirāja Gosvāmī, has described the initiator spiritual master and the instructor spiritual master in the verse beginning with the words *vande gurūn īśa-bhaktān īśam īśāvatārakān.* In that verse there are six transcendental subject matters, of which the truth regarding the spiritual master has already been described. Now the author will describe the other five *tattvas* (truths), namely, *īśa-tattva* (the Supreme Lord), His expansion *tattva,* His incarnation *tattva,* His energy *tattva* and His devotee *tattva.*

TEXT 4

পঞ্চতত্ত্ব অবতীর্ণ চৈতন্যের সঙ্গে ।
পঞ্চতত্ত্ব লঞা করেন সংকীর্তন রঙ্গে ॥ ৪ ॥

pañca-tattva avatīrṇa caitanyera saṅge
pañca-tattva lañā karena saṅkīrtana raṅge

SYNONYMS

pañca-tattva—these five *tattvas*; *avatīrṇa*—advented; *caitanyera*—with Caitanya Mahāprabhu; *saṅge*—in company with; *pañca-tattva*—the same five subjects; *lañā*—taking with Himself; *karena*—He does; *saṅkīrtana*—the *saṅkīrtana* movement; *raṅge*—in great pleasure.

TRANSLATION

These five tattvas incarnate with Lord Caitanya Mahāprabhu, and thus the Lord executes His saṅkīrtana movement with great pleasure.

PURPORT

In the *Śrīmad-Bhāgavatam* there is the following statement regarding Śrī Caitanya Mahāprabhu:

kṛṣṇa-varṇaṁ tviṣākṛṣṇaṁ sāṅgopāṅgāstra-pārṣadam
yajñaiḥ saṅkīrtana-prāyair yajanti hi sumedhasaḥ

"In the age of Kali, people who are endowed with sufficient intelligence will worship the Lord, who is accompanied by His associates, by performance of *saṅkīrtana yajña.*" (*Bhāg.* 11.5.32) Śrī Caitanya Mahāprabhu is always accompanied by His plenary expansion Śrī Nityānanda Prabhu, His incarnation Śrī Advaita Prabhu, His internal potency Śrī Gadādhara Prabhu and His marginal potency Śrīvāsa Prabhu. He is in the midst of them as the Supreme Personality of Godhead. One should know that Śrī Caitanya Mahāprabhu is always accompanied by these other *tattvas.* Therefore our obeisances to Śrī Caitanya Mahāprabhu are complete when we say, *śrī-kṛṣṇa-caitanya prabhu nityānanda śrī-advaita gadādhara śrīvāsādi-gaura-bhakta-vṛnda.* As preachers of the Kṛṣṇa consciousness movement, we first offer our obeisances to Śrī Caitanya Mahāprabhu by chanting this Pañca-tattva *mantra;* then we say, Hare Kṛṣṇa, Hare Kṛṣṇa, Kṛṣṇa Kṛṣṇa, Hare Hare/ Hare Rāma, Hare Rāma, Rāma Rāma, Hare Hare. There are ten offenses in the chanting of the Hare Kṛṣṇa *mahā-mantra,* but these are not considered in the chanting of the Pañca-tattva *mantra,* namely, *śrī-kṛṣṇa-caitanya prabhu nityānanda śrī-advaita gadādhara śrīvāsādi-gaura-bhakta-vṛnda.* Śrī Caitanya Mahāprabhu is known as *mahā-vadānyāvatāra,* the most magnanimous incarnation, for He does not consider the offenses of the fallen souls. Thus to derive the full benefit of the chanting of the *mahā-mantra* (Hare Kṛṣṇa, Hare Kṛṣṇa, Kṛṣṇa Kṛṣṇa, Hare Hare/ Hare Rāma, Hare Rāma, Rāma Rāma, Hare Hare), we must first take shelter of Śrī Caitanya Mahāprabhu, learn the Pañca-tattva *mahā-mantra,* and then chant the Hare Kṛṣṇa *mahā-mantra.* That will be very effective.

Taking advantage of Śrī Caitanya Mahāprabhu, there are many unscrupulous devotees who manufacture a *mahā-mantra* of their own. Sometimes they sing, *bhaja nitāi gaura rādhe śyāma hare kṛṣṇa hare rāma* or *śrī-kṛṣṇa-caitanya prabhu nityānanda hare kṛṣṇa hare rāma śrī rādhe govinda.* Actually, however, one should chant the names of the full Pañca-tattva *(śrī-kṛṣṇa-caitanya prabhu nityānanda śrī-advaita gadādhara śrīvāsādi-gaura-bhakta-vṛnda)* and then the sixteen words Hare Kṛṣṇa, Hare Kṛṣṇa, Kṛṣṇa Kṛṣṇa, Hare Hare/ Hare Rāma, Hare Rāma, Rāma Rāma, Hare Hare, but these unscrupulous, less intelligent men confuse the entire process. Of course, since they are also devotees they can express their feelings in that way, but the method prescribed by Śrī Caitanya Mahāprabhu's pure devotees is to chant first the full Pañca-tattva *mantra* and then chant the *mahā-mantra*—Hare Kṛṣṇa, Hare Kṛṣṇa, Kṛṣṇa Kṛṣṇa, Hare Hare/ Hare Rāma, Hare Rāma, Rāma Rāma, Hare Hare.

TEXT 5

পঞ্চতত্ত্ব—একবস্তু, নাহি কিছু ভেদ ।
রস আস্বাদিতে তবু বিবিধ বিভেদ ॥ ৫ ॥

pañca-tattva—eka-vastu, nāhi kichu bheda
rasa āsvādite tabu vividha vibheda

SYNONYMS

pañca-tattva—the five subjects; *eka-vastu*—they are one in five; *nāhi*—there is not; *kichu*—anything; *bheda*—difference; *rasa*—mellows; *āsvādite*—to taste; *tabu*—yet; *vividha*—varieties; *vibheda*—differences.

TRANSLATION

Spiritually there are no differences between these five tattvas, for on the transcendental platform everything is absolute. Yet there are also varieties in the spiritual world, and in order to taste these spiritual varieties one should distinguish between them.

PURPORT

In his *Anubhāṣya* commentary Śrī Bhaktisiddhānta Sarasvatī Ṭhākura describes the Pañca-tattva as follows. The supreme energetic, the Personality of Godhead, manifesting in five kinds of pastimes, appears as the Pañca-tattva. Actually there is no difference between them because they are situated on the absolute platform, but they manifest different spiritual varieties as a challenge to impersonalists to taste different kinds of spiritual humors *(rasas)*. In the *Vedas* it is said, *parāsya śaktir vividhaiva śrūyate:* "The varieties of energy of the Supreme Personality of Godhead are differently known." From this statement of the *Vedas* one can understand that there are eternal varieties of humors or tastes in the spiritual world. Śrī Gaurāṅga, Śrī Nityānanda, Śrī Advaita, Śrī Gadādhara and Śrīvāsa are all on the same platform, but in spiritually distinguishing between them one should understand that Śrī Caitanya Mahāprabhu is the form of a devotee, Nityānanda Prabhu appears in the form of a devotee's spiritual master, Advaita Prabhu is the form of a *bhakta* (devotee) incarnation, Gadādhara Prabhu is the energy of a *bhakta,* and Śrīvāsa is a pure devotee. Thus there are spiritual distinctions between them. The *bhakta-rūpa* (Śrī Caitanya Mahāprabhu), the *bhakta-svarūpa* (Śrī Nityānanda Prabhu) and the *bhakta-avatāra* (Śrī Advaita Prabhu) are described as the Supreme Personality of Godhead Himself, His immediate manifestation and His plenary expansion, and They all belong to the Viṣṇu category. Although the spiritual and marginal energies of the Supreme Personality of Godhead are nondifferent from the Supreme Personality of Godhead Viṣṇu, they are predominated subjects, whereas Lord Viṣṇu is the predominator. As such, although they are on the same platform, they have appeared differently in order to facilitate tasting of transcendental mellows. Actually, however, there is no possibility of one being different from the other, for the worshiper and the worshipable cannot be separated at any stage. On the absolute platform, one cannot be understood without the other.

TEXT 6

পঞ্চতত্ত্বাত্মকং কৃষ্ণং ভক্তরূপ-স্বরূপকম্ ।
ভক্তাবতারং ভক্তাখ্যং নমামি ভক্তশক্তিকম্ ॥ ৬ ॥

pañca-tattvātmakaṁ kṛṣṇaṁ
bhaktarūpa-svarūpakam
bhaktāvatāraṁ bhaktākhyaṁ
namāmi bhakta-śaktikam

SYNONYMS

pañca-tattva-ātmakam—comprehending the five transcendental subject matters; *kṛṣṇam*—unto Lord Kṛṣṇa; *bhakta-rūpa*—in the form of a devotee; *svarūpakam*—in the expansion of a devotee; *bhakta-avatāram*—in the incarnation of a devotee; *bhakta-ākhyam*—known as a devotee; *namāmi*—I offer my obeisances; *bhakta-śaktikam*—the energy of the Supreme Personality of Godhead.

TRANSLATION

Let me offer my obeisances unto Lord Śrī Kṛṣṇa, who has manifested Himself in five as a devotee, expansion of a devotee, incarnation of a devotee, pure devotee and devotional energy.

PURPORT

Śrī Nityānanda Prabhu is the immediate expansion of Śrī Caitanya Mahāprabhu as His brother. He is the personified spiritual bliss of *sac-cid-ānanda-vigraha.* His body is transcendental and full of ecstasy in devotional service. Śrī Caitanya Mahāprabhu is therefore called *bhakta-rūpa* (the form of a devotee), and Śrī Nityānanda Prabhu is called *bhakta-svarūpa* (the expansion of a devotee). Śrī Advaita Prabhu, the incarnation of a devotee, is *Viṣṇu-tattva* and belongs to the same category.There are also different types of *bhaktas* or devotees on the platforms of neutrality, servitude, friendship, paternity and conjugal love. Devotees like Śrī Dāmodara, Śrī Gadādhara and Śrī Rāmānanda are different energies. This confirms the Vedic *sūtra, parāsya śaktir vividhaiva śrūyate.* All these *bhakta* subjects taken together constitute Śrī Caitanya Mahāprabhu, who is Kṛṣṇa Himself.

TEXT 7

স্বয়ং ভগবান্ কৃষ্ণ একলে ঈশ্বর ।
অদ্বিতীয়, নন্দাত্মজ, রসিক-শেখর ॥ ৭ ॥

svayaṁ bhagavān kṛṣṇa ekale īśvara
advitīya, nandātmaja, rasika-śekhara

SYNONYMS

svayam—Himself; *bhagavān*—the Supreme Personality of Godhead; *kṛṣṇa*—Lord Kṛṣṇa; *ekale*—the only one; *īśvara*—the supreme controller; *advitīya*—without a second; *nanda-ātmaja*—appeared as the son of Mahārāja Nanda; *rasika*—the most mellow; *śekhara*—summit.

TRANSLATION

Kṛṣṇa, the reservoir of all pleasure, is the Supreme Personality of Godhead Himself, the supreme controller. No one is greater than or equal to Śrī Kṛṣṇa, yet He appears as the son of Mahārāja Nanda.

PURPORT

In this verse Kavirāja Gosvāmī gives an accurate description of Lord Kṛṣṇa, the Supreme Personality of Godhead, by stating that although no one is equal to or greater than Him, and He is the reservoir of all spiritual pleasure, He nevertheless appears as the son of Mahārāja Nanda and Yaśodāmayī.

TEXT 8

রাসাদি-বিলাসী, ব্রজললনা-নাগর ।
আর যত সব দেখ,—তাঁর পরিকর ॥ ৮ ॥

rāsādi-vilāsī, vrajalalanā-nāgara
āra yata saba dekha,—tāṅra parikara

SYNONYMS

rāsa-ādi—the *rāsa* dance; *vilāsī*—the enjoyer; *vraja-lalanā*—the damsels of Vṛndāvana; *nāgara*—the leader; *āra*—others; *yata*—all; *saba*—everyone; *dekha*—must know; *tāṅra*—His; *parikara*—associates.

TRANSLATION

Lord Śrī Kṛṣṇa, the Supreme Personality of Godhead, is the supreme enjoyer in the rāsa dance. He is the leader of the damsels of Vraja, and all others are simply His associates.

PURPORT

The word *rāsādi-vilāsī* ("the enjoyer of the *rāsa* dance") is very important. The *rāsa* dance can be enjoyed only by Śrī Kṛṣṇa because He is the supreme leader and chief of the damsels of Vṛndāvana. All other devotees are His associates. Although no one can compare with Śrī Kṛṣṇa, the Supreme Personality of Godhead, there are many unscrupulous rascals who imitate the *rāsa* dance of Śrī Kṛṣṇa. They are Māyāvādīs, and people should be wary of them. The *rāsa* dance can be performed only by Śrī Kṛṣṇa and no one else.

TEXT 9

সেই কৃষ্ণ অবতীর্ণ শ্রীকৃষ্ণচৈতন্য ।
সেই পরিকরগণ সঙ্গে সব ধন্য ॥ ৯ ॥

sei kṛṣṇa avatīrṇa śrī-kṛṣṇa-caitanya
sei parikara-gaṇa saṅge saba dhanya

SYNONYMS

sei kṛṣṇa—that very Lord Kṛṣṇa; *avatīrṇa*—has advented; *śrī-kṛṣṇa-caitanya*—in the form of Lord Caitanya Mahāprabhu; *sei*—those; *parikara-gaṇa*—associates; *saṅge*—with Him; *saba*—all; *dhanya*—glorious.

TRANSLATION

The selfsame Lord Kṛṣṇa advented Himself as Śrī Caitanya Mahāprabhu with all His eternal associates, who are also equally glorious.

TEXT 10

একলে ঈশ্বর-তত্ত্ব চৈতন্য-ঈশ্বর ।
ভক্তভাবময় তাঁর শুদ্ধ কলেবর ॥ ১০ ॥

ekale īśvara-tattva caitanya-īśvara
bhakta-bhāvamaya tāṅra śuddha kalevara

SYNONYMS

ekale—only one person; *īśvara-tattva*—the supreme controller; *caitanya*—the supreme living force; *īśvara*—controller; *bhakta-bhāvamaya*—in the ecstasy of a devotee; *tāṅra*—His; *śuddha*—transcendental; *kalevara*—body.

TRANSLATION

Śrī Caitanya Mahāprabhu, who is the supreme controller, the one Personality of Godhead, has ecstatically become a devotee, yet His body is transcendental and not materially tinged.

PURPORT

There are different *tattvas* or truths, including *īśa-tattva, jīva-tattva* and *śakti-tattva. Īśa-tattva* refers to the Supreme Personality of Godhead Viṣṇu, who is the supreme living force. In the *Kaṭha Upaniṣad* it is said, *nityo nityānāṁ cetanaś cetanānām:* the Supreme Personality of Godhead is the supreme eternal and the supreme living force. The living entities are also eternal and are also living forces, but they are very minute in quantity, whereas the Supreme Lord is the supreme living force and the supreme eternal. The supreme eternal never accepts a body of a temporary material nature, whereas the living entities who are part and parcel of the supreme eternal are prone to do so. Thus according to the Vedic *mantras* the Supreme Lord is the supreme master of innumerable living entities. The Māyāvādī philosophers, however, try to equate the minute living entities with the supreme living entity. Because they recognize no distinctions between them, their philosophy is called *advaita-vāda,* or monism. Factually, however, there is a distinction. This verse is especially meant to impart to the Māyāvādī philosopher the understanding that the Supreme Personality of Godhead is the supreme controller. The supreme controller, the Personality of Godhead, is Kṛṣṇa Himself, but as a transcendental pastime He has accepted the form of a devotee, Lord Caitanya Mahāprabhu.

As stated in *Bhagavad-gītā,* when the Supreme Personality of Godhead Kṛṣṇa comes to this planet exactly like a human being, some rascals consider Him to be one of the ordinary humans. One who thinks in that mistaken way is described as *mūḍha,* or foolish. Therefore one should not foolishly consider Caitanya Mahāprabhu to be an ordinary human being. He has accepted the ecstasy of a devotee, but He is the Supreme Personality of Godhead. Since Caitanya Mahāprabhu, there have been many imitation incarnations of Kṛṣṇa who cannot understand that Caitanya Mahāprabhu was Kṛṣṇa Himself and not an ordinary human being. Less intelligent men create their own Gods by advertising a human being as God. This is their mistake. Therefore here the words *tāṅra śuddha kalevara* warn that Caitanya Mahāprabhu's body is not material but purely spiritual. One should not, therefore, accept Caitanya Mahāprabhu as an ordinary devotee, although He has assumed the form of a devotee. Yet one must certainly know that although Caitanya Mahāprabhu is the Supreme Personality of Godhead, because He accepted the ecstasy of a devotee one should not misunderstand His pastimes and place Him in exactly the same position as Kṛṣṇa. It is for this reason only that when Śrī Kṛṣṇa Caitanya Mahāprabhu was addressed as Kṛṣṇa or Viṣṇu He blocked His ears, not wanting to hear Himself addressed as the Supreme Personality of Godhead. There is a class of devotees called *Gaurāṅga-nāgarī* who stage plays of Kṛṣṇa's pastimes using a *vigraha* or form of Caitanya Mahāprabhu. This is a mistake which is technically called *rasābhāsa.* While Caitanya Mahāprabhu is trying to enjoy as a devotee, one should not disturb Him by addressing Him as the Supreme Personality of Godhead.

TEXT 11

কৃষ্ণমাধুর্যের এক অদ্ভুত স্বভাব ।
আপনা আস্বাদিতে কৃষ্ণ করে ভক্তভাব ॥ ১১ ॥

kṛṣṇa-mādhuryera eka adbhuta svabhāva
āpanā āsvādite kṛṣṇa kare bhakta-bhāva

SYNONYMS

kṛṣṇa-mādhuryera—the supreme pleasure potency of Kṛṣṇa; *eka*—is one; *adbhuta*—wonderful; *svabhāva*—nature; *āpanā*—Himself; *āsvādite*—to taste; *kṛṣṇa*—the Supreme Personality of Godhead; *kare*—does; *bhakta-bhāva*—accept the form of a devotee.

TRANSLATION

The transcendental mellow of conjugal love of Kṛṣṇa is so wonderful that Kṛṣṇa Himself accepts the form of a devotee to relish and taste it fully.

PURPORT

Although Kṛṣṇa is the reservoir of all pleasure, He has a special intention to taste Himself by accepting the form of a devotee. It is to be concluded that although

Lord Caitanya is present in the form of a devotee, He is Kṛṣṇa Himself. Therefore Vaiṣṇavas sing, *śrī-kṛṣṇa-caitanya rādhā-kṛṣṇa nahe anya:* Rādhā and Kṛṣṇa combined together are Śrī Kṛṣṇa Caitanya Mahāprabhu. *Caitanyākhyaṁ prakaṭam adhunā tad-dvayaṁ caikyam āptam.* Śrī Svarūpa-dāmodara Gosvāmī has said that Rādhā and Kṛṣṇa assumed oneness in the form of Śrī Caitanya Mahāprabhu.

TEXT 12

ইথে ভক্তভাব ধরে চৈতন্য গোসাঞি ।
'ভক্তস্বরূপ' তাঁর নিত্যানন্দ-ভাই ॥ ১২ ॥

ithe bhakta-bhāva dhare caitanya gosāñi
'bhakta-svarūpa' tāṅra nityānanda-bhāi

SYNONYMS

ithe—for this reason; *bhakta-bhāva*—the ecstasy of a devotee; *dhare*—accepts; *caitanya*—Lord Caitanya Mahāprabhu; *gosāñi*—the transcendental teacher; *bhakta-svarūpa*—exactly like a pure devotee; *tāṅra*—His; *nityānanda*—Lord Nityānanda; *bhāi*—brother.

TRANSLATION

For this reason Śrī Caitanya Mahāprabhu, the supreme teacher, accepts the form of a devotee and accepts Lord Nityānanda as His elder brother.

TEXT 13

'ভক্ত-অবতার' তাঁর আচার্য-গোসাঞি ।
এই তিন তত্ত্ব সবে প্রভু করি' গাই ॥ ১৩ ॥

'bhakta-avatāra' tāṅra ācārya-gosāñi
ei tina tattva sabe prabhu kari' gāi

SYNONYMS

bhakta-avatāra—incarnation as a devotee; *tāṅra*—His; *ācārya-gosāñi*—the supreme teacher, Advaita Ācārya Prabhu; *ei*—all these; *tina*—three; *tattva*—truths; *sabe*—all; *prabhu*—the predominator; *kari'*—by such understanding; *gāi*—we sing.

TRANSLATION

Śrī Advaita Ācārya is Lord Caitanya's incarnation as a devotee. Therefore these three tattvas [Caitanya Mahāprabhu, Nityānanda Prabhu and Advaita Gosāñi] are the predominators or masters.

PURPORT

Gosāñi means *gosvāmī.* A person who has full control over the senses and mind is called a *gosvāmī* or *gosāñi.* One who does not have such control is called *godāsa,* or a servant of the senses, and cannot become a spiritual master. A spiritual master who actually has control over the mind and senses is called *gosvāmī.* Although the *gosvāmī* title has become a hereditary designation for unscrupulous men, actually the title *gosāñi* or *gosvāmī* began from Śrī Rūpa Gosvāmī, who presented himself as an ordinary *gṛhastha* and minister in government service but became *gosvāmī* when he was actually elevated by the instruction of Lord Caitanya Mahāprabhu. Therefore *gosvāmī* is not a hereditary title but refers to one's qualifications. When one is highly elevated in spiritual advancement, regardless of wherefrom he comes, he may be called *gosvāmī.* Śrī Caitanya Mahāprabhu, Śrī Nityānanda Prabhu and Śrī Advaita Gosāñi Prabhu are natural *gosvāmīs* because They belong to the *Viṣṇu-tattva* category. As such, all of Them are *prabhus* ("predominators" or "masters"), and They are sometimes called Caitanya Gosāñi, Nityānanda Gosāñi and Advaita Gosāñi. Unfortunately Their so-called descendants who do not have the qualifications of *gosvāmīs* have accepted this title as a hereditary designation or a professional degree. That is not in accord with the śāstric injunctions.

TEXT 14

এক মহাপ্রভু, আর প্রভু দুইজন ।
দুই প্রভু সেবে মহাপ্রভুর চরণ ॥ ১৪ ॥

eka mahāprabhu, āra prabhu duijana
dui prabhu sebe mahāprabhura caraṇa

SYNONYMS

eka mahāprabhu—one Mahāprabhu, or the supreme predominator; *āra prabhu duijana*—and the other two (Nityānanda and Advaita) are two *prabhus* (masters); *dui prabhu*—the two *prabhus* (Nityānanda and Advaita Gosāñi); *sebe*—serve; *mahāprabhura*—of the supreme predominator, Lord Caitanya Mahāprabhu; *caraṇa*—the lotus feet.

TRANSLATION

One of Them is Mahāprabhu, and the other two are prabhus. These two prabhus serve the lotus feet of Mahāprabhu.

PURPORT

Although Śrī Caitanya Mahāprabhu, Śrī Nityānanda Prabhu and Śrī Advaita Prabhu all belong to the same Viṣṇu category, Śrī Caitanya Mahāprabhu is nevertheless accepted as the Supreme, and the other two *prabhus* engage in His transcendental loving service to teach ordinary living entities that every one of us is subordinate to Śrī Caitanya Mahāprabhu. In another place in *Caitanya-caritāmṛta* (*Ādi.*5.142) it is said, *ekalā īśvara kṛṣṇa, āra saba bhṛtya:* the only supreme master is Kṛṣṇa, and all others, both *Viṣṇu-tattva* and *jīva-tattva,* engage in the service of the Lord. Both the *Viṣṇu-tattva* (as Nityānanda Prabhu and Advaita) and the *jīva-tattva (Śrīvāsādi-gaura-bhakta-vṛnda)* engage in the service of the Lord, but one must distinguish between the *Viṣṇu-tattva* servitors and the *jīva-tattva* servitors. The *jīva-tattva* servitor, the spiritual master, is actually the servitor God. As explained in previous verses, in the absolute world there are no such differences, yet one must observe these differences in order to distinguish the Supreme from His subordinates.

TEXT 15

এই তিন তত্ত্ব,—'সর্বারাধ্য' করি মানি ।
চতুর্থ যে ভক্ততত্ত্ব,—'আরাধক' জানি ॥ ১৫ ॥

ei tina tattva,—'sarvārādhya' kari māni
caturtha ye bhakta-tattva,—'ārādhaka' jāni

SYNONYMS

ei tina tattva—all three of these truths; *sarva-ārādhya*—worshipable by all living entities; *kari māni*—accepting such; *caturtha*—fourth; *ye*—who is; *bhakta-tattva*—in the category of devotees; *ārādhaka*—worshiper; *jāni*—I understand.

TRANSLATION

The three predominators [Caitanya Mahāprabhu, Nityānanda Prabhu and Advaita Prabhu] are worshipable by all living entities, and the fourth principle [Śrī Gadādhara Prabhu] is to be understood as Their worshiper.

PURPORT

In his *Anubhāṣya,* Śrī Bhaktisiddhānta Sarasvatī Ṭhākura, describing the truth about the Pañca-tattva, explains that we can understand that Lord Śrī Caitanya Mahāprabhu is the supreme predominator, and Nityānanda Prabhu and Advaita Prabhu are His subordinates but are also predominators. Lord Śrī Caitanya Mahāprabhu is the Supreme Lord, and Nityānanda Prabhu and Advaita Prabhu are manifestations of the Supreme Lord. All of Them are *Viṣṇu-tattva,* the Supreme, and are therefore worshipable by the living entities. Although the other two *tattvas* within the category of Pañca-tattva—namely, *śakti-tattva* and *jīva-tattva,* represented by Gadādhara and Śrīvāsa—are worshipers of the Supreme Lord, they are in the same category because they eternally engage in the transcendental loving service of the Lord.

TEXT 16

শ্রীবাসাদি যত কোটি কোটি ভক্তগণ ।
'শুদ্ধভক্ত'-তত্ত্বমধ্যে তাঁ-সবার গণন ॥ ১৬ ॥

śrīvāsādi yata koṭi koṭi bhakta-gaṇa
'śuddha-bhakta'-tattva-madhye tāṅ-sabāra gaṇana

SYNONYMS

śrīvāsa-ādi—devotees headed by Śrīvāsa Ṭhākura; *yata*—all others; *koṭi koṭi*—innumerable; *bhakta-gaṇa*—devotees; *śuddha-bhakta*—pure devotees; *tattva-madhye*—in the truth; *tāṅ-sabāra*—all of them; *gaṇana*—accounted.

TRANSLATION

There are innumerable pure devotees of the Lord, headed by Śrīvāsa Ṭhākura, who are known as unalloyed devotees.

TEXT 17

গদাধর-পণ্ডিতাদি প্রভুর 'শক্তি'-অবতার ।
'অন্তরঙ্গ-ভক্ত' করি' গণন যাঁহার ॥ ১৭ ॥

gadādhara-paṇḍitādi prabhura 'śakti'-avatāra
'antaraṅga-bhakta' kari' gaṇana yāṅhāra

SYNONYMS

gadādhara—of the name Gadādhara; *paṇḍita*—of the learned scholar; *ādi*—headed by; *prabhura*—of the Lord; *śakti*—potency; *avatāra*—incarnation; *antaraṅga*—very confidential; *bhakta*—devotee; *kari'*—accepting; *gaṇana*—counting; *yāṅhāra*—of whom.

TRANSLATION

The devotees headed by Gadādhara Paṇḍita are to be considered incarnations of the potency of the Lord. They are internal potential devotees engaged in the service of the Lord.

PURPORT

In connection with verses sixteen and seventeen, Śrī Bhaktisiddhānta Sarasvatī Ṭhākura explains in his *Anubhāṣya:* "There are specific symptoms by which the internal devotees and the unalloyed or pure devotees are to be known. All unalloyed devotees are *śakti-tattvas,* or potencies of the Lord. Some of them are situated in conjugal love and others in filial affection, fraternity and servitude. Certainly all of them are devotees, but by making a comparative study it is found that the devotees or potencies who are engaged in conjugal love are better situated than the others. Thus devotees who are in a relationship with the Supreme Personality of Godhead in conjugal love are considered to be the most confidential devotees of Lord Śrī Caitanya Mahāprabhu. Those who engage in the service of Lord Nityānanda Prabhu and Lord Advaita Prabhu generally have relationships of parental love, fraternity, servitude and neutrality. When such devotees develop great attachment for Śrī Caitanya Mahāprabhu, they too become situated within the intimate circle of devotees in conjugal love." This gradual development of devotional service is described by Śrī Narottama dāsa Ṭhākura as follows:

gaurāṅga balite habe pulaka śarīra
hari hari balite nayane ba'be nīra
āra kabe nitāicāṅda karuṇā karibe
saṁsāra-vāsanā mora kabe tuccha habe
viṣaya chāḍiyā kabe śuddha habe mana
kabe hāma heraba śrī-vṛndāvana
rūpa-raghunātha-pade ha-ibe ākuti
kabe hāma bujhaba śrī-yugala-pirīti

"When will there be eruptions on my body as soon as I chant the name of Lord Caitanya, and when will there be incessant torrents of tears as soon as I chant the holy names Hare Kṛṣṇa? When will Lord Nityānanda be merciful toward me and free me from all desires for material enjoyment? When will my mind be completely freed from all contamination of desires for material pleasure? Only at that time will it be possible for me to understand Vṛndāvana. Only if I become attached to the instructions given by the six Gosvāmīs headed by Rūpa Gosvāmī and Raghunātha dāsa Gosvāmī will it be possible for me to understand the conjugal love of Rādhā and Kṛṣṇa." By attachment to the devotional service of Lord Caitanya Mahāprabhu one immediately comes to the ecstatic position. When he develops his love for Nityānanda Prabhu he is freed from all attachment to the material world, and at that time he becomes eligible to understand the Lord's pastimes in Vṛndāvana. In that condition, when one develops his love for the six Gosvāmīs, he can understand the conjugal love between Rādhā and Kṛṣṇa. These are the different stages of a pure devotee's promotion to conjugal love in the service of Rādhā and Kṛṣṇa in an intimate relationship with Śrī Caitanya Mahāprabhu.

TEXTS 18-19

যাঁ-সবা লঞা প্রভুর নিত্য বিহার ।
যাঁ-সবা লঞা প্রভুর কীর্তন-প্রচার ॥ ১৮ ॥
যাঁ-সবা লঞা করেন প্রেম আস্বাদন ।
যাঁ-সবা লঞা দান করে প্রেমধন ॥ ১৯ ॥

yāṅ-sabā lañā prabhura nitya vihāra
yāṅ-sabā lañā prabhura kīrtana-pracāra

yāṅ-sabā lañā karena prema āsvādana
yāṅ-sabā lañā dāna kare prema-dhana

SYNONYMS

yāṅ-sabā—all; *lañā*—taking company; *prabhura*—of the Lord; *nitya*—eternal; *vihāra*—pastime; *yāṅ-sabā*—all those who are; *lañā*—taking company; *prabhura*—of the

Lord; *kīrtana—saṅkīrtana;pracāra—*movement;*yāṅ-sabā—*persons with whom; *lañā—*in accompaniment;*karena—*He does;*prema—*love of God;*āsvādana—*taste;*yāṅ-sabā—*those who are; *lañā—*in accompaniment; *dāna kare—*gives in charity;*prema-dhana—*love of Godhead.

TRANSLATION

The internal devotees or potencies are all eternal associates in the pastimes of the Lord. Only with them does the Lord advent to propound the saṅkīrtana movement, only with them does the Lord taste the mellow of conjugal love, and only with them does He distribute this love of God to people in general.

PURPORT

Distinguishing between pure devotees and internal or confidential devotees, Śrī Rūpa Gosvāmī, in his book *Upadeśāmṛta,* traces the following gradual process of development. Out of many thousands of *karmīs,* one is better when he is situated in perfect Vedic knowledge. Out of many such learned scholars and philosophers, one who is actually liberated from material bondage is better, and out of many such persons who are actually liberated, one who is a devotee of the Supreme Personality of Godhead is considered to be the best. Among the many such transcendental lovers of the Supreme Personality of Godhead, the *gopīs* are the best, and among the *gopīs* Śrīmatī Rādhikā is the best. Śrīmatī Rādhikā is very dear to Lord Kṛṣṇa, and similarly Her ponds, namely, Śyāmakuṇḍa and Rādhākuṇḍa, are also very much dear to the Supreme Personality of Godhead.

Śrīla Bhaktisiddhānta Sarasvatī Ṭhākura comments in his *Anubhāṣya* that among the five *tattvas,* two are energies *(śakti-tattva)* and the three others are energetic *(śaktimān tattva).* Unalloyed and internal devotees are both engaged in the favorable culture of Kṛṣṇa consciousness untinged by philosophical speculation or fruitive activities. They are all understood to be pure devotees, and those among them who simply engage in conjugal love are called *mādhurya-bhaktas* or internal devotees. The potential loving services in parental love, fraternity and servitude are included in conjugal love of God. In conclusion, therefore, every confidential devotee is a pure devotee of the Lord.

Śrī Caitanya Mahāprabhu enjoys His pastimes with His immediate expansion Nityānanda Prabhu. His pure devotees and His three *puruṣa* incarnations, namely, Kāraṇodakaśāyī Viṣṇu, Garbhodakaśāyī Viṣṇu and Kṣīrodakaśāyī Viṣṇu, always accompany the Supreme Lord to propound the *saṅkīrtana* movement.

TEXTS 20-21

সেই পঞ্চতত্ত্ব মিলি' পৃথিবী আসিয়া ।
পূর্ব-প্রেমভাণ্ডারের মুদ্রা উঘাড়িয়া ॥ ২০ ॥
পাঁচে মিলি' লুটে প্রেম, করে আস্বাদন ।
যত যত পিয়ে, তৃষ্ণা বাড়ে অনুক্ষণ ॥ ২১ ॥

sei pañca-tattva mili' pṛthivī āsiyā
pūrva-premabhāṇḍārera mudrā ughāḍiyā

pāṅce mili' luṭe prema, kare āsvādana
yata yata piye, tṛṣṇā bāḍhe anukṣaṇa

SYNONYMS

sei—those; *pañca-tattva*—five truths; *mili'*—combined together; *pṛthivī*—on this earth; *āsiyā*—descending; *pūrva*—original; *prema-bhāṇḍārera*—the store of transcendental love; *mudrā*—seal; *ughāḍiyā*—opening; *pāṅce mili'*—mixing together all these five; *luṭe*—plunder; *prema*—love of Godhead; *kare āsvādana*—taste; *yata yata*—as much as; *piye*—drink; *tṛṣṇā*—thirst; *bāḍhe*—increases; *anukṣaṇa*—again and again.

TRANSLATION

The characteristics of Kṛṣṇa are understood to be a storehouse of transcendental love. Although that storehouse of love certainly came with Kṛṣṇa when He was present, it was sealed. But when Śrī Caitanya Mahāprabhu came with His other associates of the Pañca-tattva, they broke the seal and plundered the storehouse to taste transcendental love of Kṛṣṇa. The more they tasted it, the more their thirst for it grew.

PURPORT

Śrī Caitanya Mahāprabhu is called *mahā-vadānyāvatāra* because although He is Śrī Kṛṣṇa Himself, He is even more favorably disposed to the poor fallen souls than Lord Śrī Kṛṣṇa. When Lord Śrī Kṛṣṇa Himself was personally present He demanded that everyone surrender unto Him and promised that He would then give one all protection, but when Śrī Caitanya Mahāprabhu came to this earth with His associates, He simply distributed transcendental love of God without discrimination. Śrī Rūpa Gosvāmī, therefore, could understand that Lord Caitanya was none other than Śrī Kṛṣṇa Himself, for no one but the Supreme Personality of Godhead can distribute confidential love of the Supreme Person.

TEXT 22

পুনঃ পুনঃ পিয়াইয়া হয় মহামত্ত ।
নাচে, কান্দে, হাসে, গায়, যৈছে মদমত্ত ॥ ২২ ॥

punaḥ punaḥ piyāiyā haya mahāmatta
nāce, kānde, hāse, gāya, yaiche mada-matta

SYNONYMS

punaḥ punaḥ—again and again; *piyāiyā*—causing to drink; *haya*—becomes; *mahā-matta*—highly ecstatic; *nāce*—dances; *kānde*—cries; *hāse*—laughs; *gāya*—chants; *yaiche*—as if; *mada-matta*—one is drunk.

TRANSLATION

Śrī Pañca-tattva themselves danced again and again and thus made it easier to drink nectarean love of Godhead. They danced, cried, laughed and chanted like madmen, and in this way they distributed love of Godhead.

PURPORT

People generally cannot understand the actual meaning of chanting and dancing. Describing the Gosvāmīs, Śrī Śrīnivāsa Ācārya stated, *kṛṣṇotkīrtana-gāna-nartana-parau:* not only did Lord Caitanya Mahāprabhu and His associates demonstrate this chanting and dancing, but the six Gosvāmīs also followed in the next generation. The present Kṛṣṇa consciousness movement follows the same principle, and therefore simply by chanting and dancing we have received good responses all over the world. It is to be understood, however, that this chanting and dancing do not belong to this material world. They are actually transcendental activities, for the more one engages in chanting and dancing, the more he can taste the nectar of transcendental love of Godhead.

TEXT 23

পাত্রাপাত্র-বিচার নাহি, নাহি স্থানাস্থান ।
যেই যাঁহা পায়, তাঁহা করে প্রেমদান ॥ ২৩ ॥

pātrāpātra-vicāra nāhi, nāhi sthānāsthāna
yei yāṅhā pāya, tāṅhā kare prema-dāna

SYNONYMS

pātra—recipient; *apātra*—not a recipient; *vicāra*—consideration; *nāhi*—there is none; *nāhi*—there is none; *sthāna*—favorable place; *asthāna*—unfavorable place; *yei*—anyone; *yāṅhā*—wherever; *pāya*—gets the opportunity; *tāṅhā*—there only; *kare*—does; *prema-dāna*—distribution of love of Godhead.

TRANSLATION

In distributing love of Godhead, Caitanya Mahāprabhu and His associates did not consider who was a fit candidate and who was not, nor where such distribution should or should not take place. They made no conditions. Wherever they got the opportunity the members of the Pañca-tattva distributed love of Godhead.

PURPORT

There are some rascals who dare to speak against the mission of Lord Caitanya by criticizing the Kṛṣṇa consciousness movement for accepting Europeans and Americans as *brāhmaṇas* and offering them *sannyāsa.* But here is an authoritative statement that in distributing love of Godhead one should not consider whether the recipients are Europeans, Americans, Hindus, Muslims, etc. The Kṛṣṇa consciousness movement should be spread wherever possible, and one should accept those who thus become Vaiṣṇavas as being greater than *brāhmaṇas,* Hindus or Indians. Śrī Caitanya Mahāprabhu desired that His name be spread in each and every town and village on the surface of the globe. Therefore, when the cult of Caitanya Mahāprabhu is spread all over the world, should those who embrace it not be accepted as Vaiṣṇavas, *brāhmaṇas* and *sannyāsīs?* These foolish arguments are sometimes raised by envious rascals, but Kṛṣṇa conscious devotees do not care about them. We strictly follow the principles set down by the Pañca-tattva.

TEXT 24

লুটিয়া, খাইয়া, দিয়া, ভাণ্ডার উজাড়ে ।
আশ্চর্য ভাণ্ডার, প্রেম শতগুণ বাড়ে ॥ ২৪ ॥

luṭiyā, khāiyā, diyā, bhāṇḍāra ujāḍe
āścarya bhāṇḍāra, prema śata-guṇa bāḍe

SYNONYMS

luṭiyā—plundering; *khāiyā*—eating; *diyā*—distributing; *bhāṇḍāra*—store; *ujāḍe*—emptied; *āścarya*—wonderful; *bhāṇḍāra*—store; *prema*—love of Godhead; *śata-guṇa*—one hundred times; *bāḍe*—increases.

TRANSLATION

Although the members of the Pañca-tattva plundered the storehouse of love of Godhead and ate and distributed its contents, there was no scarcity, for this wonderful storehouse is so complete that as the love is distributed, the supply increases hundreds of times.

PURPORT

A pseudo-incarnation of Kṛṣṇa once told his disciple that he had emptied himself by giving him all knowledge and was thus spiritually bankrupt. Such bluffers speak in this way to cheat the public, but actual spiritual consciousness is so perfect that the more it is distributed, the more it increases. Bankruptcy is a term which applies in the material world, but the storehouse of love of Godhead in the spiritual world can never be depleted. Kṛṣṇa is providing for millions and trillions of living entities by supplying all their necessities, and even if all the innumerable living entities wanted to become Kṛṣṇa conscious, there would be no scarcity of love of Godhead, nor would there be insufficiency in providing for their maintenance. Our Kṛṣṇa consciousness movement was started single-handedly, and no one provided for our livelihood, but at present we are spending hundreds and thousands of dollars all over the world, and the movement is increasing more and more. Thus there is no question of scarcity. Although jealous persons may be envious, if we stick to our principles and follow in the footsteps of the Pañca-tattva, this movement will go on unchecked by imitation *svāmīs, sannyāsīs,* religionists, philosophers or scientists, for it is transcendental to all material considerations. Therefore those who propagate the Kṛṣṇa consciousness movement should not be afraid of such rascals and fools.

TEXT 25

উছলিল প্রেমবন্যা চৌদিকে বেড়ায় ।
স্ত্রী, বৃদ্ধ, বালক, যুবা, সবারে ডুবায় ॥ ২৫ ॥

uchalila prema-vanyā caudike veḍāya
strī, vṛddha, bālaka, yuvā, sabāre ḍuvāya

SYNONYMS

uchalila—became agitated; *prema-vanyā*—the inundation of love of Godhead; *caudike*—in all directions; *veḍāya*—surrounding; *strī*—woman; *vṛddha*—old man; *bālaka*—child; *yuvā*—young man; *sabāre*—all of them; *ḍuvāya*—merged into.

TRANSLATION

The flood of love of Godhead swelled in all directions, and thus young men, old men, women and children were all immersed in that inundation.

PURPORT

When the contents of the storehouse of love of Godhead is thus distributed, there is a powerful inundation which covers the entire land. In Śrīdhāma Māyāpura there is sometimes a great flood after the rainy season. This is an indication that from the birthplace of Lord Caitanya the inundation of love of Godhead should be spread all over the world, for this will help everyone, including old men, young men, women and children. The Kṛṣṇa consciousness movement of Śrī Caitanya Mahāprabhu is so powerful that it can inundate the entire world and interest all classes of men in the subject of love of Godhead.

TEXT 26

সজ্জন, দুর্জন, পঙ্গু, জড়, অন্ধগণ ।
প্রেমবন্যায় ডুবাইল জগতের জন ॥ ২৬ ॥

saj-jana, dur-jana, paṅgu, jaḍa, andha-gaṇa
prema-vanyāya ḍuvāila jagatera jana

SYNONYMS

sat-jana—gentlemen; *dur-jana*—rogues; *paṅgu*—lame; *jaḍa*—invalid; *andha-gaṇa*—blind men; *prema-vanyāya*—in the inundation of love of Godhead; *ḍuvāila*—drowned; *jagatera*—all over the world; *jana*—people.

TRANSLATION

The Kṛṣṇa consciousness movement will inundate the entire world and drown everyone, whether one be a gentleman, a rogue or even lame, invalid or blind.

PURPORT

Here again it may be emphasized that although jealous rascals protest that Europeans and Americans cannot be given the sacred thread or *sannyāsa,* there is no need even to consider whether one is a gentleman or a rogue because this is a spiritual movement which is not concerned with the external body of skin and bones. Because it is being properly conducted under the guidance of the Pañca-tattva, strictly following the regulative principles, it has nothing to do with external impediments.

TEXT 27

জগৎ ডুবিল, জীবের হৈল বীজ নাশ ।
তাহা দেখি' পাঁচ জনের পরম উল্লাস ॥ ২৭ ॥

jagat ḍuvila, jīvera haila bīja nāśa
tāhā dekhi' pāṅca janera parama ullāsa

SYNONYMS

jagat—the whole world; *ḍuvila*—drowned; *jīvera*—of the living entities; *haila*—it so became; *bīja*—the seed; *nāśa*—completely finished; *tāhā*—then; *dekhi'*—by seeing; *pāṅca*—five; *janera*—of the persons; *parama*—highest; *ullāsa*—happiness.

TRANSLATION

When the five members of the Pañca-tattva saw the entire world drowned in love of Godhead and the seed of material enjoyment in the living entities completely destroyed, they all became exceedingly happy.

PURPORT

In this connection, Śrīla Bhaktisiddhānta Sarasvatī Ṭhākura writes in his *Anubhāṣya* that since the living entities all belong to the marginal potency of the Lord, each and every living entity has a natural tendency to become Kṛṣṇa conscious, although at the same time the seed of material enjoyment is undoubtedly within him. The seed of material enjoyment, watered by the course of material nature, fructifies to become a tree of material entanglement which endows the living entity with all kinds of material enjoyment. To enjoy such material facilities is to be afflicted with the three material miseries. However, when by nature's law there is a flood, the seeds within the earth become inactive. Similarly, as the inundation of love of Godhead spreads all over the world, the seeds of material enjoyment become impotent. Thus the more the Kṛṣṇa consciousness movement spreads, the more the desire for material enjoyment decreases. The seed of material enjoyment automatically becomes impotent with the increase of the Kṛṣṇa consciousness movement. Instead of being envious that Kṛṣṇa consciousness is spreading all over the world by the grace of Lord Caitanya, those who are jealous should be happy, as indicated here by the words *parama ullāsa.* But because they are *kaniṣṭha-adhikārīs* or *prākṛta-bhaktas* (materialistic devotees who are not advanced in spiritual knowledge), they are envious instead of happy, and they try to find faults in Kṛṣṇa consciousness. Yet Śrīmat Prabodhānanda Sarasvatī writes in his *Caitanya-candrāmṛta* that when influenced by Lord Caitanya's Kṛṣṇa consciousness movement, materialists become averse to talking about their wives and children, supposedly learned scholars give up their tedious studies of Vedic literature, *yogīs* give up their impractical practices of mystic *yoga,* ascetics give up their austere activities of penance and austerity, and *sannyāsīs* give up their study of *Sāṅkhya* philosophy. Thus they are all attracted by the *bhakti-yoga* practices of Lord Caitanya and cannot relish a mellow taste superior to that of Kṛṣṇa consciousness.

TEXT 28

যত যত প্রেমবৃষ্টি করে পঞ্চজনে ।
তত তত বাঢ়ে জল, ব্যাপে ত্রিভুবনে ॥ ২৮ ॥

yata yata prema-vṛṣṭi kare pañca-jane
tata tata bāḍhe jala, vyāpe tri-bhuvane

SYNONYMS

yata—as many; *yata*—so many; *prema-vṛṣṭi*—showers of love of Godhead; *kare*—causes; *pañca-jane*—the five members of the Pañca-tattva; *tata tata*—as much as; *bāḍhe*—increases; *jala*—water; *vyāpe*—spreads; *tri-bhuvane*—all over the three worlds.

TRANSLATION

The more the five members of the Pañca-tattva cause the rains of love of Godhead to fall, the more the inundation increases and spreads all over the world.

PURPORT

The Kṛṣṇa consciousness movement is not stereotyped or stagnant. It will spread all over the world in spite of all objections by fools and rascals that European and American *mlecchas* cannot be accepted as *brāhmaṇas* or *sannyāsīs.* Here it is indicated that this process will spread and inundate the entire world with Kṛṣṇa consciousness.

TEXTS 29-30

মায়াবাদী, কর্মনিষ্ঠ কুতার্কিকগণ ।
নিন্দক, পাষণ্ডী, যত পড়ুয়া অধম ॥ ২৯ ॥

সেই সব মহাদক্ষ ধাঞা পলাইল ।
সেই বন্যা তা-সবারে ছুঁইতে নারিল ॥ ৩০ ॥

māyāvādī, karma-niṣṭha kutārkika-gaṇa
nindaka, pāṣaṇḍī, yata paḍuyā adhama

sei saba mahādakṣa dhāñā palāila
sei vanyā tā-sabāre chuṅite nārila

SYNONYMS

māyāvādī—the impersonalist philosophers; *karma-niṣṭha*—the fruitive workers; *kutārkika-gaṇa*—the false logicians; *nindaka*—the blasphemers; *pāṣaṇḍī*—nondevotees; *yata*—all; *paḍuyā*—students; *adhama*—the lowest class; *sei saba*—all of them; *mahā-dakṣa*—they are very expert; *dhāñā*—running; *palāila*—went away; *sei vanyā*—that inundation; *tā-sabāre*—all of them; *chuṅite*—touching; *nārila*—could not.

TRANSLATION

The impersonalists, fruitive workers, false logicians, blasphemers, nondevotees and lowest among the student community are very expert in avoiding the Kṛṣṇa consciousness movement, and therefore the inundation of Kṛṣṇa consciousness cannot touch them.

PURPORT

Like Māyāvādī philosophers in the past such as Prakāśānanda Sarasvatī of Benares, modern impersonalists are not interested in Lord Caitanya's Kṛṣṇa consciousness movement. They do not know the value of this material world; they consider it false and cannot understand how the Kṛṣṇa consciousness movement can utilize it. They are so absorbed in impersonal thought that they take it for granted that all spiritual variety is material. Because they do not know anything beyond their misconception of the *brahmajyoti,* they cannot understand that Kṛṣṇa, the Supreme Personality of Godhead, is spiritual and therefore beyond the conception of material illusion. Whenever Kṛṣṇa incarnates personally or as a devotee, these Māyāvādī philosophers accept Him as an ordinary human being. This is condemned in *Bhagavad-gītā:*

avajānanti māṁ mūḍhā
mānuṣīṁ tanum āśritam
paraṁ bhāvam ajānanto
mama bhūta-maheśvaram

"Fools deride Me when I descend in the human form. They do not know My transcendental nature and My supreme dominion over all that be." (Bg. 9.11)

There are also other unscrupulous persons who exploit the Lord's appearance by posing as incarnations to cheat the innocent public. An incarnation of God should pass the tests of the statements of the *śāstras* and also perform uncommon activities. One should not accept a rascal as an incarnation of God but should test his ability to act as the Supreme Personality of Godhead. For example, Kṛṣṇa taught Arjuna in *Bhagavad-gītā,* and Arjuna also accepted Him as the Supreme Personality of Godhead, but for our understanding Arjuna requested the Lord to manifest His universal form, thus testing whether He was actually the Supreme Lord. Similarly, one must test a so-called incarnation of Godhead according to the standard criteria. To avoid being misled by an exhibition of mystic powers, it is best to examine a so-called incarnation of God in the light of the statements of *śāstras.* Caitanya Mahāprabhu is described in the *śāstras* as an incarnation of Kṛṣṇa; therefore if one wants to imitate Lord Caitanya and claim to be an incarnation, he must show evidence from the *śāstras* about his appearance to substantiate his claim.

TEXTS 31-32

তাহা দেখি' মহাপ্রভু করেন চিন্তন ।
জগৎ ডুবাইতে আমি করিলুঁ যতন ॥ ৩১ ॥
কেহ কেহ এড়াইল, প্রতিজ্ঞা হইল ভঙ্গ ।
তা-সবা ডুবাইতে পাতিব কিছু রঙ্গ ॥ ৩২ ॥

tāhā dekhi' mahāprabhu karena cintana
jagat ḍuvāite āmi kariluṅ yatana

keha keha eḍāila, pratijñā ha-ila bhaṅga
tā-sabā ḍuvāite pātiba kichu raṅga

SYNONYMS

tāhā dekhi'—observing this advancement; *mahāprabhu*—Lord Śrī Caitanya Mahāprabhu; *karena*—does; *cintana*—thinking; *jagat*—the whole world; *ḍuvāite*—to drown; *āmi*—I; *kariluṅ*—endeavored; *yatana*—attempts; *keha keha*—some of them; *eḍāila*—escaped; *pratijñā*—promise; *ha-ila*—became; *bhaṅga*—broken; *tā-sabā*—all of them; *ḍuvāite*—to make them drown; *pātiba*—shall devise; *kichu*—some; *raṅga*—trick.

TRANSLATION

Seeing that the Māyāvādīs and others were fleeing, Lord Caitanya thought: I wanted everyone to be immersed in this inundation of love of Godhead, but some of them have escaped. Therefore I shall devise a trick to drown them also.

PURPORT

Here is an important point. Lord Caitanya Mahāprabhu wanted to invent a way to capture the Māyāvādīs and others who did not take interest in the Kṛṣṇa consciousness movement. This is the symptom of an *ācārya.* An *ācārya* who comes for the service of the Lord cannot be expected to conform to a stereotype, for he must find the ways and means by which Kṛṣṇa consciousness may be spread. Sometimes jealous persons criticize the Kṛṣṇa consciousness movement because it engages equally both boys and girls in distributing love of Godhead. Not knowing that boys and girls in countries like Europe and America mix very freely, these fools and rascals criticize the boys and girls in Kṛṣṇa consciousness for intermingling. But these rascals should consider that one cannot suddenly change a community's social customs. However, since both the boys and girls are being trained to become preachers, those girls are not ordinary girls but are as good as their brothers who are preaching Kṛṣṇa consciousness. Therefore, to engage both boys and girls in fully transcendental activities is a policy intended to spread the Kṛṣṇa consciousness movement. These jealous fools who criticize the intermingling of boys and girls will simply have to be satisfied with their own foolishness because they cannot think of how to spread Kṛṣṇa consciousness by adopting ways and means which are favorable for this purpose. Their stereotyped methods will never help spread Kṛṣṇa consciousness. Therefore, what we are doing is perfect by the grace of Lord Caitanya Mahāprabhu, for it is He who proposed to invent a way to capture those who strayed from Kṛṣṇa consciousness.

TEXT 33

এত বলি' মনে কিছু করিয়া বিচার ।
সন্ন্যাস-আশ্রম প্রভু কৈলা অঙ্গীকার ॥ ৩৩ ॥

eta bali' mane kichu kariyā vicāra
sannyāsa-āśrama prabhu kailā aṅgīkāra

SYNONYMS

eta bali'—saying this; *mane*—within the mind; *kichu*—something; *kariyā*—doing; *vicāra*—consideration; *sannyāsa-āśrama*—the renounced order of life; *prabhu*—the Lord; *kailā*—did; *aṅgīkāra*—accept.

TRANSLATION

Thus the Lord accepted the sannyāsa order of life after full consideration.

PURPORT

There was no need for Lord Śrī Caitanya Mahāprabhu to accept *sannyāsa,* for He is God Himself and therefore has nothing to do with the material bodily concept of life. Śrī Caitanya Mahāprabhu did not identify Himself with any of the eight *varṇas* and *āśramas,* namely, *brāhmaṇa, kṣatriya, vaiśya, śūdra, brahmacārī, gṛhastha, vānaprastha* and *sannyāsa.* He identified Himself as the Supreme Spirit. Śrī Caitanya Mahāprabhu, or for that matter any pure devotee, never identifies with these social and spiritual divisions of life, for a devotee is always transcendental to these different gradations of society. Nevertheless, Lord Caitanya decided to accept *sannyāsa* on the grounds that when He became a *sannyāsī* everyone would show Him respect and in that way be favored. Although there was actually no need for Him to accept *sannyāsa,* He did so for the benefit of those who might think Him an ordinary human being. The main purpose of His accepting *sannyāsa* was to deliver the Māyāvādī *sannyāsīs.* This will be evident later in this chapter.

Śrīla Bhaktisiddhānta Sarasvatī Ṭhākura has explained the term "Māyāvādī" as follows: "The Supreme Personality of Godhead is transcendental to the material conception of life. A Māyāvādī is one who considers the body of the Supreme Personality of Godhead Kṛṣṇa to be made of *māyā* and who also considers the abode of the Lord and the process of approaching Him, devotional service, to be *māyā.* The Māyāvādī considers all the paraphernalia of devotional service to be *māyā.*" *Māyā* refers to material existence, which is characterized by the reactions of fruitive activities. Māyāvādīs consider devotional service to be among such fruitive activities. According to them, when *bhāgavatas* or devotees are purified by philosophical speculation, they will come to the real point of liberation. Those who speculate in this way regarding devotional service are called *kutārkikas* (false logicians), and those who consider devotional service to be fruitive activity are also called *karma-niṣṭhas.* Those who criticize devotional service are called *nindakas* (blasphemers). Similarly, nondevotees who consider devotional activities to be material are also called *pāṣaṇḍīs,* and scholars with a similar viewpoint are called *adhama paḍuyās.* The *kutārkikas, nindakas, pāṣaṇḍīs* and *adhama paḍuyās* all avoided the benefit of Śrī Caitanya Mahāprabhu's movement of developing love of Godhead. Śrī Caitanya Mahāprabhu felt compassion for them, and it is for this reason that He decided to accept the *sannyāsa* order, for by seeing Him as a *sannyāsī* they would offer Him respects. The *sannyāsa* order is still respected in India. Indeed, the very dress of a *sannyāsī* still commands respect from the Indian public. Therefore Śrī Caitanya Mahāprabhu accepted *sannyāsa* to facilitate preaching His devotional cult, although otherwise He had no need to accept the fourth order of spiritual life.

TEXT 34

চব্বিশ বৎসর ছিলা গৃহস্থ-আশ্রমে ।
পঞ্চবিংশতি বর্ষে কৈল যতিধর্মে ॥ ৩৪ ॥

cabbiśa vatsara chilā gṛhastha-āśrame
pañca-viṁśati varṣe kaila yati-dharme

SYNONYMS

cabbiśa—twenty-four; *vatsara*—years; *chilā*—He remained; *gṛhastha*—householder life; *āśrame*—the order of; *pañca*—five; *viṁśati*—twenty; *varṣe*—in the year; *kaila*—did; *yati-dharme*—accepted the *sannyāsa* order.

TRANSLATION

Śrī Caitanya Mahāprabhu remained in householder life for twenty-four years, and on the verge of His twenty-fifth year He accepted the sannyāsa order.

PURPORT

There are four orders of spiritual life, namely, *brahmacarya, gṛhastha, vānaprastha* and *sannyāsa,* and in each of these *āśramas* there are four divisions. The divisions of the *brahmacaryāśrama* are *sāvitrya, prājāpatya, brāhma* and *bṛhat,* and the divisions of the *gṛhasthāśrama* are *vārtā* (professionals), *sañcaya* (accumulators), *śālīna* (those who do not ask anything from anyone) and *śiloñchana* (those who collect grains from the paddy fields). Similarly, the divisions of the *vānaprasthāśrama* are *vaikhānasa, bālikhilya, auḍumbara* and *pheṇapa,* and the divisions of *sannyāsa* are *kuṭīcaka, bahūdaka, haṁsa* and *niṣkriya.* There are two kinds of *sannyāsīs,* who are called *dhīras* and *narottamas,* as stated in *Śrīmad-Bhāgavatam* (1.13.26-27). At the end of the month of January in the year 1432 *śakābda,* Śrī Caitanya Mahāprabhu accepted the *sannyāsa* order from Keśava Bhāratī, who belonged to the Śaṅkara-sampradāya.

TEXT 35

সন্ন্যাস করিয়া প্রভু কৈলা আকর্ষণ ।
যতেক পালাঞাছিল তার্কিকাদিগণ ॥ ৩৫ ॥

sannyāsa kariyā prabhu kailā ākarṣaṇa
yateka pālāñāchila tārkikādigaṇa

SYNONYMS

sannyāsa—the *sannyāsa* order; *kariyā*—accepting; *prabhu*—the Lord; *kailā*—did; *ākarṣaṇa*—attract; *yateka*—all; *pālāñāchila*—fled; *tārkika-ādi-gaṇa*—all persons, beginning with the logicians.

TRANSLATION

After accepting the sannyāsa order, Śrī Caitanya Mahāprabhu attracted the attention of all those who had evaded Him, beginning with the logicians.

TEXT 36

পড়ুয়া, পাষণ্ডী, কর্মী, নিন্দকাদি যত ।
তারা আসি' প্রভু-পায় হয় অবনত ॥ ৩৬ ॥

paḍuyā, pāṣaṇḍī, karmī, nindakādi yata
tārā āsi' prabhu-pāya haya avanata

SYNONYMS

paḍuyā—students; *pāṣaṇḍī*—material adjusters; *karmī*—fruitive actors; *nindaka-ādi*—critics; *yata*—all; *tārā*—they; *āsi'*—coming; *prabhu*—the Lord's; *pāya*—lotus feet; *haya*—became; *avanata*—surrendered.

TRANSLATION

Thus the students, infidels, fruitive workers and critics all came to surrender unto the lotus feet of the Lord.

TEXT 37

অপরাধ ক্ষমাইল, ডুবিল প্রেমজলে।
কেবা এড়াইবে প্রভুর প্রেম-মহাজালে ॥ ৩৭ ॥

aparādha kṣamāila, ḍubila prema-jale
kebā eḍāibe prabhura prema-mahājāle

SYNONYMS

aparādha—offense; *kṣamāila*—excused; *ḍubila*—merged into; *prema-jale*—in the ocean of love of Godhead; *kebā*—who else; *eḍāibe*—will go away; *prabhura*—the Lord's; *prema*—loving; *mahā-jāle*—network.

TRANSLATION

Lord Caitanya excused them all, and they merged into the ocean of devotional service, for no one can escape the unique loving network of Śrī Caitanya Mahāprabhu.

PURPORT

Śrī Caitanya Mahāprabhu was an ideal *ācārya.* An *ācārya* is an ideal teacher who knows the purpose of the revealed scriptures, behaves exactly according to their injunctions and teaches his students to adopt these principles also. As an ideal *ācārya,* Śrī Caitanya Mahāprabhu devised ways to capture all kinds of atheists and materialists. Every *ācārya* has a specific means of propagating his spiritual movement with the aim of bringing men to Kṛṣṇa consciousness. Therefore, the method of one *ācārya* may be different from that of another, but the ultimate goal is never neglected. Śrīla Rūpa Gosvāmī recommends:

yena tena prakāreṇa manaḥ kṛṣṇe niveśayet
sarve vidhi-niṣedhā syur etayor eva kiṅkarāḥ

An *ācārya* should devise a means by which people may somehow or other come to Kṛṣṇa consciousness. First they should become Kṛṣṇa conscious, and all the prescribed rules and regulations may later gradually be introduced. In our Kṛṣṇa consciousness movement we follow this policy of Lord Śrī Caitanya Mahāprabhu. For example, since boys and girls in the Western countries freely intermingle, special concessions regarding their customs and habits are necessary to bring them to Kṛṣṇa consciousness. The *ācārya* must devise a means to bring them to devotional service. Therefore, although I am a *sannyāsī* I sometimes take part in getting boys and girls married, although in the history of *sannyāsa* no *sannyāsī* has personally taken part in marrying his disciples.

TEXT 38

সবা নিস্তারিতে প্রভু কৃপা-অবতার।
সবা নিস্তারিতে করে চাতুরী অপার ॥ ৩৮ ॥

sabā nistārite prabhu kṛpā-avatāra
sabā nistārite kare cāturī apāra

SYNONYMS

sabā—all; *nistārite*—to deliver; *prabhu*—the Lord; *kṛpā*—mercy; *avatāra*—incarnation; *sabā*—all; *nistārite*—to deliver; *kare*—did; *cāturī*—devices; *apāra*—unlimited.

TRANSLATION

Śrī Caitanya Mahāprabhu appeared to deliver all the fallen souls. Therefore He devised many methods to liberate them from the clutches of māyā.

PURPORT

It is the concern of the *ācārya* to show mercy to the fallen souls. In this connection, *deśa-kāla-pātra* (the place, the time and the object) should be taken into consideration. Since the European and American boys and girls in our Kṛṣṇa consciousness movement preach together, less intelligent men criticize that they are mingling without restriction. In Europe and America boys and girls mingle unrestrictedly and have equal rights; therefore it is not possible to completely separate the men from the women. However, we are thoroughly instructing both men and women how to preach, and actually they are preaching wonderfully. Of course, we very strictly prohibit illicit sex. Boys and girls who are not married are not allowed to sleep together or live together, and there are separate arrangements for boys and girls in every temple. *Gṛhasthas* live outside the temple, for in the temple we do not allow even husband and wife to live together. The results of this are wonderful. Both men and women are preaching the gospel of Lord Caitanya Mahāprabhu and Lord Kṛṣṇa with redoubled strength. In this verse the words *sabā nistārite kare cāturī apāra* indicate that Śrī Caitanya Mahāprabhu wanted to deliver one and all. Therefore it is a principle that a preacher must strictly follow the rules and regulations laid down in the *śāstras* yet at the same time devise a means by which the preaching work to reclaim the fallen may go on with full force.

TEXT 39

তবে নিজ ভক্ত কৈল যত ম্লেচ্ছ আদি।
সবে এড়াইল মাত্র কাশীর মায়াবাদী ॥ ৩৯ ॥

tabe nija bhakta kaila yata mleccha ādi
sabe eḍāila mātra kāśīra māyāvādī

SYNONYMS

tabe—thereafter; *nija*—own; *bhakta*—devotee; *kaila*—converted; *yata*—all; *mleccha*—one who does not follow the Vedic principles; *ādi*—heading the list; *sabe*—all those; *eḍāila*—escaped; *mātra*—only; *kāśīra*—of Vārāṇasī; *māyāvādī*—impersonalists.

TRANSLATION

All were converted into devotees of Lord Caitanya, even the mlecchas and yavanas. Only the impersonalist followers of Śaṅkarācārya evaded Him.

PURPORT

In this verse it is clearly indicated that although Lord Caitanya Mahāprabhu converted Mohammedans and other *mlecchas* into devotees, the impersonalist followers of Śaṅkarācārya could not be converted. After accepting the renounced order of life, Caitanya Mahāprabhu converted many *karma-niṣṭhas* who were addicted to fruitive activities, many great logicians like Sārvabhauma Bhaṭṭācārya, *nindakas* (blasphemers) like Prakāśānanda Sarasvatī, *pāṣaṇḍīs* (nondevotees) like Jagāi and Mādhāi, and *adhama paḍuyās* (degraded students) like Mukunda and his friends. All of them gradually became devotees of the Lord, even the Pathans or Muslims, but the worst offenders, the impersonalists, were extremely difficult to convert, for they very tactfully escaped the devices of Lord Caitanya Mahāprabhu.

In describing the Kāśīra Māyāvādīs, Śrīla Bhaktisiddhānta Sarasvatī Ṭhākura has explained that persons who are bewildered by empiric knowledge or direct sensual perception, and who thus consider that even this limited material world can be gauged by their material estimations, conclude that anything that one can discern by direct sense perception is but *māyā* or illusion. They maintain that although the Absolute Truth is beyond the range of sense perception, it includes no spiritual variety or enjoyment. According to the Kāśīra Māyāvādīs, the spiritual world is simply void. They do not believe in the Personality of the Absolute Truth nor in His varieties of activities in the spiritual world. Although they have their own arguments which are not very strong, they have no conception of the variegated activities of the Absolute Truth. These impersonalists, who are followers of Śaṅkarācārya, are generally known as Kāśīra Māyāvādīs.

Near Vārāṇasī there is another group of impersonalists, who are known as Saranātha Māyāvādīs. Outside the city of Vārāṇasī is a place known as Saranātha where there is a big Buddhist *stūpa*. Many followers of Buddhist philosophy live there, and they are known as Saranātha Māyāvādīs. The impersonalists of Saranātha differ from those of Vārāṇasī, for the Vārāṇasī impersonalists propagate the idea that the impersonal Brahman is truth whereas material varieties are false, but the Saranātha impersonalists do not even believe that the Absolute Truth or Brahman can be understood as the opposite of *māyā* or illusion. According to their vision, materialism is the only manifestation of the Absolute Truth.

Factually both the Kāśīra and Saranātha Māyāvādīs, as well as any other philosophers who have no knowledge of the spirit soul, are advocates of utter materialism. None of them have clear knowledge regarding the Absolute or the spiritual world. Philosophers like the Saranātha Māyāvādīs who do not believe in the spiritual existence of the Absolute Truth but consider material varieties to be everything do not believe that there are two kinds of nature, inferior (material) and superior (spiritual), as described in *Bhagavad-gītā*. Actually, neither the Vārāṇasī nor Saranātha Māyāvādīs accept the principles of *Bhagavad-gītā,* due to a poor fund of knowledge.

Since these impersonalists who do not have perfect spiritual knowledge cannot understand the principles of *bhakti-yoga,* they must be classified among the nondevotees who are against the Kṛṣṇa consciousness movement. We sometimes feel inconvenienced by the hindrances offered by these impersonalists, but we do not care about their so-called philosophy, for we are propagating our own philosophy as presented in *Bhagavad-gītā As It Is* and getting successful results. Theorizing as if devotional service were subject to their mental speculation, both kinds of Māyāvādī impersonalists conclude that the subject matter of *bhakti-yoga* is a creation of *māyā* and that Kṛṣṇa, devotional service and the devotee are also *māyā.* Therefore, as stated by Śrī Caitanya Mahāprabhu, *māyāvādī kṛṣṇe aparādhī:* "All the Māyāvādīs are offenders to Lord Kṛṣṇa." (Cc. *Madhya* 17.129) It is not possible for them to understand the Kṛṣṇa consciousness movement; therefore we do not value their philosophical conclusions. However expert such quarrelsome impersonalists are in putting forward their so-called logic, we defeat them in every respect and go forward with our Kṛṣṇa consciousness movement. Their imaginative mental speculation cannot deter the progress of the Kṛṣṇa consciousness movement, which is completely spiritual and is never under the control of such Māyāvādīs.

TEXT 40

বৃন্দাবন যাইতে প্রভু রহিলা কাশীতে ।
মায়াবাদিগণ তাঁরে লাগিল নিন্দিতে ॥ ৪০ ॥

vṛndāvana yāite prabhu rahilā kāśīte
māyāvādi-gaṇa tāṅre lāgila nindite

SYNONYMS

vṛndāvana—the holy place called Vṛndāvana; *yāite*—while going there; *prabhu*—Lord Śrī Caitanya Mahāprabhu; *rahilā*—remained; *kāśīte*—at Vārāṇasī; *māyāvādi-gaṇa*—the Māyāvādī philosophers; *tāṅre*—unto Him; *lāgila*—began; *nindite*—to speak against Him.

TRANSLATION

While Lord Caitanya Mahāprabhu was passing through Vārāṇasī on His way to Vṛndāvana, the Māyāvādī sannyāsī philosophers blasphemed against Him in many ways.

PURPORT

While preaching Kṛṣṇa consciousness with full vigor, Śrī Caitanya Mahāprabhu faced many Māyāvādī philosophers. Similarly, we are also facing opposing *svāmīs, yogīs,* impersonalists, scientists, philosophers and other mental speculators, and by the grace of Lord Kṛṣṇa we successfully defeat all of them without difficulty.

TEXT 41

সন্ন্যাসী হইয়া করে গায়ন, নাচন ।
না করে বেদান্ত-পাঠ, করে সংকীর্তন ॥ ৪১ ॥

sannyāsī ha-iyā kare gāyana, nācana
nā kare vedānta-pāṭha, kare saṅkīrtana

SYNONYMS

sannyāsī—a person in the renounced order of life; *ha-iyā*—accepting such a position; *kare*—does; *gāyana*—singing; *nācana*—dancing; *nā kare*—does not practice; *vedānta-pāṭha*—study of the Vedānta philosophy; *kare saṅkīrtana*—but simply engages in *saṅkīrtana.*

TRANSLATION

"Although a sannyāsī, He does not take interest in the study of Vedānta but instead always engages in chanting and dancing in saṅkīrtana.

PURPORT

Fortunately or unfortunately, we also meet such Māyāvādīs who criticize our method of chanting and accuse us of not being interested in study. They do not know that we have translated volumes and volumes of books into English and that the students in our temples regularly study them in the morning, afternoon and evening. We are writing and printing books, and our students study them and distribute them all over the world. No Māyāvādī school can present as many books as we have; nevertheless, they accuse us of not being fond of study. Such accusations are completely false. But although we study, we do not study the nonsense of the Māyāvādīs.

Māyāvādī *sannyāsīs* neither chant nor dance. Their technical objection is that this method of chanting and dancing is called *tauryatrika,* which indicates that a *sannyāsī* should completely avoid such activities and engage his time in the study of Vedānta. Actually, such men do not understand what is meant by Vedānta. In *Bhagavad-gītā* it is said: *vedaiś ca sarvair aham eva vedyo vedānta-kṛd veda-vid eva cāham.* "By all the *Vedas* I am to be known; indeed I am the compiler of Vedānta, and I am the knower of the *Vedas.*" (Bg. 15.15) Lord Kṛṣṇa is the actual compiler of Vedānta, and whatever He speaks is Vedānta philosophy. Although they are lacking the knowledge of Vedānta presented by the Supreme Personality of Godhead in the transcendental form of *Śrīmad-Bhāgavatam,* the Māyāvādīs are very proud of their study. Foreseeing the bad effects of their presenting Vedānta philosophy in a perverted way, Śrīla Vyāsadeva compiled *Śrīmad-Bhāgavatam* as a commentary on *Vedānta-sūtra. Śrīmad-Bhāgavatam* is *bhāṣyaṁ brahma-sūtrāṇām;* in other words, all the Vedānta philosophy in the codes of the *Brahma-sūtras* is thoroughly described in the pages of *Śrīmad-Bhāgavatam.* Thus the factual propounder of Vedānta philosophy is a Kṛṣṇa conscious person who always engages in reading and understanding *Bhagavad-gītā* and *Śrīmad-Bhāgavatam* and teaching the purport of these books to the entire world. The Māyāvādīs are very proud of having monopolized the Vedānta philosophy, but devotees have their own commentaries on Vedānta such as *Śrīmad-Bhāgavatam* and others written by the *ācāryas.* The commentary of the Gauḍīya Vaiṣṇavas is the *Govinda-bhāṣya.*

The Māyāvādīs' accusation that devotees do not study Vedānta is false. They do not know that chanting, dancing and preaching the principles of *Śrīmad-Bhāgavatam,* called *Bhāgavata-dharma,* are the same as studying Vedānta. Since they think that reading Vedānta philosophy is the only function of a *sannyāsī* and they did not find Caitanya Mahāprabhu engaged in such direct study, they criticized the Lord. Śrīpāda Śaṅkarācārya has given special stress to the study of Vedānta philosophy. *Vedānta-vākyeṣu sadā ramantaḥ kaupīnavantaḥ khalu bhāgyavantaḥ.* "A *sannyāsī,* accepting the renounced order very strictly and wearing nothing more than a loincloth, should always enjoy the philosophical statements in the *Vedānta-sūtra.* Such a person in the renounced order is to be considered very fortunate." The Māyāvādīs in Vārāṇasī blasphemed Lord Caitanya because His behavior did not follow these principles. Lord Caitanya, however, bestowed His mercy upon these Māyāvādī *sannyāsīs* and delivered them by means of His Vedānta discourses with Prakāśānanda Sarasvatī and Sārvabhauma Bhaṭṭācārya.

TEXT 42

মূর্খ সন্ন্যাসী নিজ-ধর্ম নাহি জানে ।
ভাবুক হইয়া ফেরে ভাবুকের সনে ॥ ৪২ ॥

mūrkha sannyāsī nija-dharma nāhi jāne
bhāvuka ha-iyā phere bhāvukera sane

SYNONYMS

mūrkha—illiterate; *sannyāsī*—one in the renounced order of life; *nija-dharma*—own duty; *nāhi*—does not; *jāne*—know; *bhāvuka*—in ecstasy; *ha-iyā*—becoming; *phere*—wanders; *bhāvukera*—with another ecstatic person; *sane*—with.

TRANSLATION

"This Caitanya Mahāprabhu is an illiterate sannyāsī and therefore does not know His real function. Guided only by His sentiments, He wanders about in the company of other sentimentalists."

PURPORT

Foolish Māyāvādīs, not knowing that the Kṛṣṇa consciousness movement is based on a solid philosophy of transcendental science, superficially conclude that those who dance and chant do not have philosophical knowledge. Those who are Kṛṣṇa conscious actually have full knowledge of the essence of Vedānta philosophy, for they study the real commentary on the Vedānta philosophy, *Śrīmad-Bhāgavatam,* and follow the actual words of the Supreme Personality of Godhead as found in *Bhagavad-gītā As It Is.* After understanding the *Bhāgavata* philosophy or *Bhāgavata-dharma,* they become fully spiritually conscious or Kṛṣṇa conscious, and therefore their chanting and dancing is not material but is on the spiritual platform. Although everyone admires the ecstatic chanting and dancing of the devotees, who are therefore popularly known as the "Hare Kṛṣṇa people," Māyāvādīs cannot appreciate these activities because of their poor fund of knowledge.

TEXT 43

এ সব শুনিয়া প্রভু হাসে মনে মনে ।
উপেক্ষা করিয়া কারো না কৈল সম্ভাষণে ॥ ৪৩ ॥

e saba śuniyā prabhu hāse mane mane
upekṣā kariyā kāro nā kaila sambhāṣaṇe

SYNONYMS

e saba—all these; *śuniyā*—after hearing; *prabhu*—the Lord; *hāse*—smiled; *mane mane*—within His mind; *upekṣā*—rejection; *kariyā*—doing so; *kāro*—with anyone; *nā*—did not; *kaila*—make; *sambhāṣaṇe*—conversation.

TRANSLATION

Hearing all this blasphemy, Lord Caitanya Mahāprabhu merely smiled to Himself, rejected all these accusations and did not talk with the Māyāvādīs.

PURPORT

As Kṛṣṇa conscious devotees, we do not like to converse with Māyāvādī philosophers simply to waste valuable time, but whenever there is an opportunity we impress our philosophy upon them with great vigor and success.

TEXT 44

উপেক্ষা করিয়া কৈল মথুরা গমন ।
মথুরা দেখিয়া পুনঃ কৈল আগমন ॥ ৪৪ ॥

upekṣā kariyā kaila mathurā gamana
mathurā dekhiyā punaḥ kaila āgamana

SYNONYMS

upekṣā—neglecting them; *kariyā*—doing so; *kaila*—did; *mathurā*—the town named Mathurā; *gamana*—traveling; *mathurā*—Mathurā; *dekhiyā*—after seeing it; *punaḥ*—again; *kaila āgamana*—came back.

TRANSLATION

Thus neglecting the blasphemy of the Vārāṇasī Māyāvādīs, Lord Caitanya Mahāprabhu proceeded to Mathurā, and after visiting Mathurā He returned to meet the situation.

PURPORT

Lord Caitanya Mahāprabhu did not talk with the Māyāvādī philosophers when He first visited Vārāṇasī, but He returned there from Mathurā to convince them of the real purpose of Vedānta.

TEXT 45

কাশীতে লেখক শূদ্র-শ্রীচন্দ্রশেখর ।
তাঁর ঘরে রহিলা প্রভু স্বতন্ত্র ঈশ্বর ॥ ৪৫ ॥

kāśīte lekhaka śūdra-śrīcandraśekhara
tāṅra ghare rahilā prabhu svatantra īśvara

SYNONYMS

kāśīte—in Vārāṇasī; *lekhaka*—writer; *śūdra*—born of a *śūdra* family; *śrī-candra-śekhara*—of the name Candraśekhara; *tāṅra ghare*—in his house; *rahilā*—remained; *prabhu*—the Lord; *svatantra*—independent; *īśvara*—the supreme controller.

TRANSLATION

This time Lord Caitanya stayed at the house of Candraśekhara, although he was regarded as a śūdra or kāyastha, for the Lord, as the Supreme Personality of Godhead, is completely independent.

PURPORT

Lord Caitanya stayed at the house of Candraśekhara, a clerk, although a *sannyāsī* is not supposed to reside in a *śūdra's* house. Five hundred years ago, especially in Bengal, it was the system that persons who were born in the families of *brāhmaṇas* were accepted as *brāhmaṇas,* and all those who took birth in other families—even the higher castes, namely, the *kṣatriyas* and *vaiśyas*—were considered *śūdra* non-*brāhmaṇas.* Therefore although Śrī Candraśekhara was a clerk from a *kāyastha* family in upper India, he was considered a *śūdra.* Similarly, *vaiśyas,* especially those of the *suvarṇa-vaṇik* community, were accepted as *śūdras* in Bengal, and even the *vaidyas,* who were generally physicians, were also considered *śūdras.* Lord Caitanya

Mahāprabhu, however, did not accept this artificial principle, which was introduced in society by self-interested men, and later the *kāyasthas, vaidyas* and *vaṇiks* all began to accept the sacred thread, despite objections from the so-called *brāhmaṇas.*

Before the time of Caitanya Mahāprabhu, the *suvarṇa-vaṇik* class was condemned by Ballal Sen, who was then the King of Bengal, due to a personal grudge. In Bengal the *suvarṇa-vaṇik* class are always very rich, for they are bankers and dealers in gold and silver. Therefore, Ballal Sen used to borrow money from a *suvarṇa-vaṇik* banker. Ballal Sen's bankruptcy later obliged the *suvarṇa-vaṇik* banker to stop advancing money to him, and thus he became angry and condemned the entire *suvarṇa-vaṇik* society as belonging to the *śūdra* community. Ballal Sen tried to induce the *brāhmaṇas* not to accept the *suvarṇa-vaṇiks* as followers of the instructions of the *Vedas* under the brahminical directions, but although some *brāhmaṇas* approved of Ballal Sen's actions, others did not. Thus the *brāhmaṇas* also became divided amongst themselves, and those who supported the *suvarṇa-vaṇik* class were rejected from the *brāhmaṇa* community. At the present day the same biases are still being followed.

There are many Vaiṣṇava families in Bengal whose members, although not actually born *brāhmaṇas,* act as *ācāryas* by initiating disciples and offering the sacred thread as enjoined in the Vaiṣṇava *tantras.* For example, in the families of Ṭhākura Raghunanda, Ācārya Ṭhākura Kṛṣṇadāsa, Navanī Hoḍa and Rasikānanda-deva (a disciple of Śyāmānanda Prabhu), the sacred thread ceremony is performed, as it is for the caste Gosvāmīs, and this system has continued for the past three to four hundred years. Accepting disciples born in *brāhmaṇa* families, they are bona fide spiritual masters who have the facility to worship the Śālagrāma-śilā which is worshiped with the Deity. As of this writing, Śālagrāma-śilā worship has not yet been introduced in our Kṛṣṇa consciousness movement, but soon it will be introduced in all our temples as an essential function of *arcana-mārga* (Deity worship).

TEXT 46

তপন-মিশ্রের ঘরে ভিক্ষা-নির্বাহণ ।
সন্ন্যাসীর সঙ্গে নাহি মানে নিমন্ত্রণ ॥ ৪৬ ॥

tapana-miśrera ghare bhikṣā-nirvāhaṇa
sannyāsīra saṅge nāhi māne nimantraṇa

SYNONYMS

tapana-miśrera—of Tapana Miśra; *ghare*—in the house; *bhikṣā*—accepting food; *nirvāhaṇa*—regularly executed; *sannyāsīra*—with other Māyāvādī *sannyāsīs; saṅge*—in company with them; *nāhi*—never; *māne*—accepted; *nimantraṇa*—invitation.

TRANSLATION

As a matter of principle, Lord Caitanya regularly accepted His food at the house of Tapana Miśra. He never mixed with other sannyāsīs, nor did He accept invitations from them.

PURPORT

This exemplary behavior of Lord Caitanya definitely proves that a Vaiṣṇava *sannyāsī* cannot accept invitations from Māyāvādī *sannyāsīs* nor intimately mix with them.

TEXT 47

সনাতন গোসাঞি আসি' তাঁহাই মিলিলা ।
তাঁর শিক্ষা লাগি' প্রভু দু-মাস রহিলা ॥ ৪৭ ॥

sanātana gosāñi āsi' tāṅhāi mililā
tāṅra śikṣā lāgi' prabhu du-māsa rahilā

SYNONYMS

sanātana—of the name Sanātana; *gosāñi*—a great devotee; *āsi'*—coming there; *tāṅhāi*—there at Vārāṇasī; *mililā*—visited Him; *tāṅra*—His; *śikṣā*—instruction; *lāgi'*—for the matter of; *prabhu*—Lord Caitanya Mahāprabhu; *du-māsa*—two months; *rahilā*—remained there.

TRANSLATION

When Sanātana Gosvāmī came from Bengal, he met Lord Caitanya at the house of Tapana Miśra, where Lord Caitanya remained continuously for two months to teach him devotional service.

PURPORT

Lord Caitanya taught Sanātana Gosvāmī in the line of disciplic succession. Sanātana Gosvāmī was a very learned scholar in Sanskrit and other languages, but until instructed by Lord Caitanya Mahāprabhu he did not write anything about Vaiṣṇava behavior. His very famous book *Hari-bhakti-vilāsa,* which gives directions for Vaiṣṇava candidates, was written completely in compliance with the instructions of Śrī Caitanya Mahāprabhu. In this *Hari-bhakti-vilāsa* Śrī Sanātana Gosvāmī gives definite instructions that by proper initiation by a bona fide spiritual master one can immediately become a *brāhmaṇa.* In this connection he says:

yathā kāñcanatāṁ yāti kāṁsyaṁ rasa-vidhānataḥ
tathā dīkṣā-vidhānena dvijatvaṁ jāyate nṛṇām

"As bell metal is turned to gold when mixed with mercury in an alchemical process, so one who is properly trained and initiated by a bona fide spiritual master immediately becomes a *brāhmaṇa.*" Sometimes those born in *brāhmaṇa* families protest this, but they have no strong arguments against this principle. By the grace of Kṛṣṇa and His devotee, one's life can change. This is confirmed in the *Śrīmad-Bhāgavatam* by the words *jahāti bandham* and *śuddhanti. Jahāti bandham* indicates that a living entity is conditioned by a particular type of body. The body is certainly an impediment, but one who associates with a pure devotee and follows his instructions can avoid this impediment and become a regular *brāhmaṇa* by initiation under his strict guidance. Śrīla Jīva Gosvāmī states how a non-*brāhmaṇa* can be turned into a *brāhmaṇa* by the association of a pure devotee. *Prabha viṣṇave namaḥ:* Lord Viṣṇu is so powerful that He can do anything He likes. Therefore it is not difficult for Viṣṇu to change the body of a devotee who is under the guidance of a pure devotee of the Lord.

TEXT 48

তাঁরে শিখাইলা সব বৈষ্ণবের ধর্ম ।
ভাগবত-আদি শাস্ত্রের যত গূঢ় মর্ম ॥ ৪৮ ॥

tāṅre śikhāilā saba vaiṣṇavera dharma
bhāgavata-ādi śāstrera yata gūḍha marma

SYNONYMS

tāṅre—unto him (Sanātana Gosvāmī); *śikhāilā*—the Lord taught him; *saba*—all; *vaiṣṇavera*—of the devotees; *dharma*—regular activities; *bhāgavata*—*Śrīmad-Bhāgavatam*; *ādi*—beginning with; *śāstrera*— of the revealed scriptures; *yata*— all; *gūḍha*—confidential; *marma*—purpose.

TRANSLATION

On the basis of scriptures like Śrīmad-Bhāgavatam which reveal these confidential directions, Śrī Caitanya Mahāprabhu instructed Sanātana Gosvāmī regarding all the regular activities of a devotee.

PURPORT

In the *paramparā* system, the instructions taken from the bona fide spiritual master must also be based on revealed Vedic scriptures. One who is in the line of disciplic succession cannot manufacture his own way of behavior. There are many so-called followers of the Vaiṣṇava cult in the line of Caitanya Mahāprabhu who do not scrupulously follow the conclusions of the *śāstras,* and therefore they are considered to be *apa-sampradāya,* which means "outside of the *sampradāya.*" Some of these groups are known as *āula, bāula, karttābhajā, neḍā, daraveśa, sāṅi sahajiyā, sakhībhekī, smārta, jata-gosāñi, ativāḍī, cūḍādhārī* and *gaurāṅga-nāgarī.* In order to follow strictly the disciplic succession of Lord Caitanya Mahāprabhu, one should not associate with these *apa-sampradāya* communities.

One who is not taught by a bona fide spiritual master cannot understand the Vedic literature. To emphasize this point, Lord Kṛṣṇa, while instructing Arjuna, clearly said that it was because Arjuna was His devotee and confidential friend that he could understand the mystery of *Bhagavad-gītā.* It is to be concluded, therefore, that one who wants to understand the mystery of revealed scriptures must approach a bona fide spiritual master, hear from him very submissively and render service to him. Then the import of the scriptures will be revealed. It is stated in the *Vedas:*

yasya deve parā bhaktir yathā deve tathā gurau
tasyaite kathitā hy arthāḥ prakāśante mahātmanaḥ

"The real import of the scriptures is revealed to one who has unflinching faith in both the Supreme Personality of Godhead and the spiritual master." Śrīla Narottama dāsa Ṭhākura advises, *sādhu-śāstra-guru-vākya, hṛdaye kariyā aikya.* The meaning of this instruction is that one must consider the instructions of the *sādhu,* the revealed scriptures and the spiritual master in order to understand the real purpose of spiritual life. Neither a *sādhu* (saintly person or Vaiṣṇava) nor a bona fide spiritual master says anything that is beyond the scope of the sanction of the revealed scriptures. Thus the statements of the revealed scriptures correspond to those of the bona fide spiritual master and saintly persons. One must therefore act with reference to these three important sources of understanding.

TEXT 49

ইতিমধ্যে চন্দ্রশেখর, মিশ্র-তপন ।
দুঃখী হঞা প্রভু-পায় কৈল নিবেদন ॥ ৪৯ ॥

itimadhye candraśekhara, miśra-tapana
duḥkhī hañā prabhu-pāya kaila nivedana

SYNONYMS

iti-madhye—in the meantime; *candraśekhara*—the clerk of the name Candraśekhara; *miśra-tapana*—as well as Tapana Miśra; *duḥkhī hañā*—becoming very unhappy; *prabhu-pāya*—at the lotus feet of the Lord; *kaila*—made; *nivedana*—an appeal.

TRANSLATION

While Lord Caitanya Mahāprabhu was instructing Sanātana Gosvāmī, both Candraśekhara and Tapana Miśra became very unhappy. Therefore they submitted an appeal unto the lotus feet of the Lord.

TEXT 50

কতেক শুনিব প্রভু তোমার নিন্দন ।
না পারি সহিতে, এবে ছাড়িব জীবন ॥ ৫০ ॥

kateka śuniba prabhu tomāra nindana
nā pāri sahite, ebe chāḍiba jīvana

SYNONYMS

kateka—how much; *śuniba*—shall we hear; *prabhu*—O Lord; *tomāra*—Your; *nindana*—blasphemy; *nā pāri*—we are not able; *sahite*—to tolerate; *ebe*—now; *chāḍiba*—give up; *jīvana*—life.

TRANSLATION

"How long can we tolerate the blasphemy of Your critics against Your conduct? We should give up our lives rather than hear such blasphemy.

PURPORT

One of the most important instructions by Śrī Caitanya Mahāprabhu regarding regular Vaiṣṇava behavior is that a Vaiṣṇava should be tolerant like a tree and submissive like grass.

tṛṇād api sunīcena
taror api sahiṣṇunā
amāninā mānadena
kīrtanīyaḥ sadā hariḥ

"One should chant the holy name of the Lord in a humble state of mind, thinking oneself lower than the straw in the street; one should be more tolerant than a tree, devoid of all sense of false prestige and should be ready to offer all respect to others. In such a state of mind one can chant the holy name of the Lord constantly." Nevertheless, the author of these instructions, Lord Caitanya Mahāprabhu, did not tolerate the misbehavior of Jagāi and Mādhāi. When they harmed Lord Nityānanda Prabhu, He immediately became angry and wanted to kill them, and it was only by the mercy of Lord Nityānanda Prabhu that they were saved. One should be very meek and humble in his personal transactions, and if insulted a Vaiṣṇava should be tolerant and not angry. But if there is blasphemy against one's *guru* or another Vaiṣṇava, one should be as angry as fire. This was exhibited by Lord Caitanya Mahāprabhu. One should not tolerate blasphemy against a Vaiṣṇava but should immediately take one of three actions. If someone blasphemes a Vaiṣṇava, one should stop him with arguments and higher reason. If one is not expert enough to do this he should give up his life on the spot, and if he cannot do this, he must go away. While Caitanya Mahāprabhu was in Benares or Kāśī, the Māyāvādī *sannyāsīs* blasphemed Him in many ways because although He was a *sannyāsī* He was indulging in chanting and dancing. Tapana Miśra and Candraśekhara heard this criticism, and it was intolerable for them because they were great devotees of Lord Caitanya. They could not stop it, however, and therefore they appealed to Lord Caitanya Mahāprabhu because this blasphemy was so intolerable that they had decided to give up their lives.

TEXT 51

তোমারে নিন্দয়ে যত সন্ন্যাসীর গণ ।
শুনিতে না পারি, ফাটে হৃদয়-শ্রবণ ॥ ৫১ ॥

tomāre nindaye yata sannyāsīra gaṇa
śunite nā pāri, phāṭe hṛdaya-śravaṇa

SYNONYMS

tomāre—unto You; *nindaye*—blasphemes; *yata*—all; *sannyāsīra gaṇa*—the Māyāvādī *sannyāsīs*; *śunite*—to hear; *nā*—cannot; *pāri*—tolerate; *phāṭe*—it breaks; *hṛdaya*—our hearts; *śravaṇa*—while hearing such blasphemy.

TRANSLATION

"The Māyāvādī sannyāsīs are all criticizing Your Holiness. We cannot tolerate hearing such criticism, for this blasphemy breaks our hearts."

PURPORT

This is a manifestation of real love for Kṛṣṇa and Lord Caitanya Mahāprabhu. There are three categories of Vaiṣṇavas: *kaniṣṭha-adhikārīs, madhyama-adhikārīs* and *uttama-adhikārīs.* The *kaniṣṭha-adhikārī,* or the devotee in the lowest stage of Vaiṣṇava life, has firm faith but is not familiar with the conclusions of the *śāstras.* The devotee in the second stage, the *madhyama-adhikārī,* is completely aware of the śāstric conclusion and has firm faith in his *guru* and the Lord. He, therefore, avoiding non-devotees, preaches to the innocent. However, the *mahā-bhāgavata* or *uttama-adhikārī,* the devotee in the highest stage of devotional life, does not see anyone as being against the Vaiṣṇava principles, for he regards everyone as a Vaiṣṇava but himself. This is the essence of Caitanya Mahāprabhu's instruction that one be more tolerant than a tree and think oneself lower than the straw in the street *(tṛṇād api sunīcena taror api sahiṣṇunā).* However, even if a devotee is in the *uttama-bhāgavata* status he must come down to the second status of life, *madhyama-adhikārī,* to be a preacher, for a preacher should not tolerate blasphemy against another Vaiṣṇava. Although a *kaniṣṭha-adhikārī* also cannot tolerate such blasphemy, he is not competent to stop it by citing śāstric evidences. Therefore Tapana Miśra and Candraśekhara are understood to be *kaniṣṭha-adhikārīs* because they could not refute the arguments of the *sannyāsīs* in Benares. They appealed to Lord Caitanya Mahāprabhu to take action, for they felt that they could not tolerate such criticism although they also could not stop it.

TEXT 52

ইহা শুনি রহে প্রভু ঈষৎ হাসিয়া ।
সেই কালে এক বিপ্র মিলিল আসিয়া ॥ ৫২ ॥

ihā śuni rahe prabhu īṣat hāsiyā
sei kāle eka vipra milila āsiyā

SYNONYMS

ihā—this; *śuni*—hearing; *rahe*—remained; *prabhu*—Lord Caitanya Mahāprabhu; *īṣat*—slightly; *hāsiyā*—smiling; *sei kāle*—at that time; *eka*—one; *vipra*—*brāhmaṇa*; *milila*—met; *āsiyā*—coming there.

TRANSLATION

While Tapana Miśra and Candraśekhara were thus talking with Śrī Caitanya Mahāprabhu, He only smiled slightly and remained silent. At that time a brāhmaṇa came there to meet the Lord.

PURPORT

Because the blasphemy was cast against Śrī Caitanya Mahāprabhu Himself, He did not feel sorry, and therefore He was smiling. This is ideal Vaiṣṇava behavior. One should not become angry upon hearing criticism of himself, but if other Vaiṣṇavas are criticized one must be prepared to act as previously suggested. Śrī Caitanya Mahāprabhu was very compassionate for His pure devotees Tapana Miśra and Candraśekhara; therefore by His grace this *brāhmaṇa* immediately came to Him. By His omnipotency the Lord created this situation for the happiness of His devotees.

TEXT 53

আসি' নিবেদন করে চরণে ধরিয়া ।
এক বস্তু মাগোঁ, দেহ প্রসন্ন হইয়া ॥ ৫৩ ॥

āsi' nivedana kare caraṇe dhariyā
eka vastu māgoṅ, deha prasanna ha-iyā

SYNONYMS

āsi'—coming there; *nivedana*—submissive statement; *kare*—made; *caraṇe*—unto the lotus feet; *dhariyā*—capturing; *eka*—one; *vastu*—thing; *māgoṅ*—beg from You; *deha*—kindly give it to me; *prasanna*—being pleased; *ha-iyā*—becoming so.

TRANSLATION

The brāhmaṇa immediately fell at the lotus feet of Caitanya Mahāprabhu and requested Him to accept his proposal in a joyful mood.

PURPORT

The Vedic injunctions state, *tad viddhi praṇipātena paripraśnena sevayā:* one must approach a superior authority in humbleness (Bg. 4.34). One cannot challenge a superior authority, but with great submission one can submit his proposal for acceptance by the spiritual master or spiritual authorities. Śrī Caitanya Mahāprabhu is an ideal teacher by His personal behavior, and so also are all His disciples. Thus this *brāhmaṇa,* being purified in association with Caitanya Mahāprabhu, followed these principles in submitting his request to the higher authority. He fell down at the lotus feet of Śrī Caitanya Mahāprabhu and then spoke as follows.

TEXT 54

সকল সন্ন্যাসী মুঞি কৈনু নিমন্ত্রণ ।
তুমি যদি আইস, পূর্ণ হয় মোর মন ॥ ৫৪ ॥

sakala sannyāsī muñi kainu nimantraṇa
tumi yadi āisa, pūrṇa haya mora mana

SYNONYMS

sakala—all; *sannyāsī*—renouncers; *muñi*—I; *kainu*—made; *nimantraṇa*—invited; *tumi*—Your good self; *yadi*—if; *āisa*—come; *pūrṇa*—fulfillment; *haya*—becomes; *mora*—my; *mana*—mind.

TRANSLATION

"My dear Lord, I have invited all the sannyāsîs of Benares to my home. My desires will be fulfilled if You also accept my invitation.

PURPORT

This *brāhmaṇa* knew that Caitanya Mahāprabhu was the only Vaiṣṇava *sannyāsī* in Benares at that time and all the others were Māyāvādîs. It is the duty of a *gṛhastha* to sometimes invite *sannyāsīs* to take food at his home. This *gṛhastha-brāhmaṇa* wanted to invite all the *sannyāsīs* to his house, but he also knew that it would be very difficult to induce Lord Caitanya Mahāprabhu to accept such an invitation because the Māyāvādî *sannyāsīs* would be present. Therefore he fell down at His feet and fervently appealed to the Lord to be compassionate and grant his request. Thus he humbly submitted his desire.

TEXT 55

না যাহ সন্ন্যাসি-গোষ্ঠী, ইহা আমি জানি ।
মোরে অনুগ্রহ কর নিমন্ত্রণ মানি' ॥ ৫৫ ॥

nā yāha sannyāsi-goṣṭhī, ihā āmi jāni
more anugraha kara nimantraṇa māni'

SYNONYMS

nā—not; *yāha*—You go; *sannyāsi-goṣṭhī*—the association of Māyāvādî *sannyāsīs*; *ihā*—this; *āmi*—I; *jāni*—know; *more*—unto me; *anugraha*—merciful; *kara*—become; *nimantraṇa*—invitation; *māni'*—accepting.

TRANSLATION

"My dear Lord, I know that You never mix with other sannyāsīs, but please be merciful unto me and accept my invitation."

PURPORT

An *ācārya* or great personality of the Vaiṣṇava school is very strict in his principles, but although he is as hard as a thunderbolt, sometimes he is as soft as a rose. Thus actually he is independent. He follows all the rules and regulations strictly, but sometimes he slackens this policy. It was known that Lord Caitanya never mixed with the Māyāvādī *sannyāsīs,* yet He conceded to the request of the *brāhmaṇa,* as stated in the next verse.

TEXT 56

প্রভু হাসি' নিমন্ত্রণ কৈল অঙ্গীকার ।
সন্ন্যাসীরে কৃপা লাগি' এ ভঙ্গী তাঁহার ॥ ৫৬ ॥

prabhu hāsi' nimantraṇa kaila aṅgīkāra
sannyāsīre kṛpā lāgi' e bhaṅgī tāṅhāra

SYNONYMS

prabhu—the Lord; *hāsi'*—smiling; *nimantraṇa*—invitation; *kaila*—made; *aṅgīkāra*—acceptance; *sannyāsīre*—unto the Māyāvādī *sannyāsīs*; *kṛpā*—to show them mercy; *lāgi'*—for the matter of; *e*—this; *bhaṅgī*—gesture; *tāṅhāra*—His.

TRANSLATION

Lord Caitanya smiled and accepted the invitation of the brāhmaṇa. He made this gesture to show His mercy to the Māyāvādī sannyāsīs.

PURPORT

Tapana Miśra and Candraśekhara appealed to the lotus feet of the Lord regarding their grief at the criticism of Him by the *sannyāsīs* in Benares. Caitanya Mahāprabhu merely smiled, yet He wanted to fulfill the desires of His devotees, and the opportunity came when the *brāhmaṇa* came to request Him to accept his invitation to be present in the midst of the other *sannyāsīs.* This coincidence was made possible by the omnipotency of the Lord.

TEXT 57

সে বিপ্র জানেন প্রভু না যা'ন কা'র ঘরে ।
তাঁহার প্রেরণায় তাঁরে অত্যাগ্রহ করে ॥ ৫৭ ॥

se vipra jānena prabhu nā yā'na kā'ra ghare
tāṅhāra preraṇāya tāṅre atyāgraha kare

SYNONYMS

se—that; *vipra*—*brāhmaṇa*; *jānena*—knew it; *prabhu*—Lord Caitanya Mahāprabhu; *nā*—never; *yā'na*—goes; *kā'ra*—anyone's; *ghare*—house; *tāṅhāra*—His; *preraṇāya*—by inspiration; *tāṅre*—unto Him; *atyāgraha kare*—strongly urging to accept the invitation.

TRANSLATION

The brāhmaṇa knew that Lord Caitanya Mahāprabhu never went to anyone else's house, yet due to inspiration from the Lord he earnestly requested Him to accept this invitation.

TEXT 58

আর দিনে গেলা প্রভু সে বিপ্র-ভবনে।
দেখিলেন, বসিয়াছেন সন্ন্যাসীর গণে ॥ ৫৮ ॥

āra dine gelā prabhu se vipra-bhavane
dekhilena, vasiyāchena sannyāsīra gaṇe

SYNONYMS

āra—next; *dine*—day; *gelā*—went; *prabhu*—the Lord; *se*—that; *vipra*—*brāhmaṇa*; *bhavane*—in the house of; *dekhilena*—He saw; *vasiyāchena*—there were sitting; *sannyāsīra*—all the *sannyāsīs*; *gaṇe*—in a group.

TRANSLATION

The next day, when Lord Śrī Caitanya Mahāprabhu went to the house of that brāhmaṇa, he saw all the sannyāsīs of Benares sitting there.

TEXT 59

সবা নমস্করি' গেলা পাদ-প্রক্ষালনে।
পাদ প্রক্ষালন করি বসিলা সেই স্থানে ॥ ৫৯ ॥

sabā namaskari' gelā pāda-prakṣālane
pāda prakṣālana kari vasilā sei sthāne

SYNONYMS

sabā—to all; *namaskari'*—offering obeisances; *gelā*—went; *pāda*—foot; *prakṣālane*—for washing; *pāda*—foot; *prakṣālana*—washing; *kari*—finishing; *vasilā*—sat down; *sei*—in that; *sthāne*—place.

TRANSLATION

As soon as Śrī Caitanya Mahāprabhu saw the sannyāsīs He immediately offered obeisances, and then He went to wash His feet. After washing His feet, He sat down by the place where He had done so.

PURPORT

By offering His obeisances to the Māyāvādī *sannyāsīs* Śrī Caitanya Mahāprabhu very clearly exhibited His humbleness to everyone. Vaiṣṇavas must not be disrespectful to anyone, to say nothing of a *sannyāsī.* Śrī Caitanya Mahāprabhu teaches, *amāninā mānadena:* one should always be respectful to others but should not demand respect for himself. A *sannyāsī* should always walk barefoot, and therefore when he enters a temple or a society of devotees he should first wash his feet and then sit down in a proper place. In India it is still the prevalent custom that one put his shoes in a specified place and then enter the temple barefoot after washing his feet. Śrī Caitanya Mahāprabhu is an ideal *ācārya,* and those who follow in His footsteps should practice the methods of devotional life that He teaches us.

TEXT 60

বসিয়া করিলা কিছু ঐশ্বর্য প্রকাশ ।
মহাতেজোময় বপু কোটিসূর্যাভাস ॥ ৬০ ॥

vasiyā karilā kichu aiśvarya prakāśa
mahātejomaya vapu koṭi-sūryābhāsa

SYNONYMS

vasiyā—after sitting; *karilā*—exhibited; *kichu*—some; *aiśvarya*—mystic power; *prakāśa*—manifested; *mahātejomaya*—very brilliantly; *vapu*—body; *koṭi*—millions; *sūrya*—sun; *ābhāsa*—reflection.

TRANSLATION

After sitting on the ground, Caitanya Mahāprabhu exhibited His mystic power by manifesting an effulgence as brilliant as the illumination of millions of suns.

PURPORT

Śrī Caitanya Mahāprabhu, as the Supreme Personality of Godhead Kṛṣṇa, is full of all potencies. Therefore it is not remarkable for Him to manifest the illumination of millions of suns. Lord Śrī Kṛṣṇa is known as *Yogeśvara,* the master of all mystic powers. Śrī Kṛṣṇa Caitanya Mahāprabhu is Lord Kṛṣṇa Himself; therefore He can exhibit any mystic power.

TEXT 61

প্রভাবে আকর্ষিল সব সন্ন্যাসীর মন ।
উঠিল সন্ন্যাসী সব ছাড়িয়া আসন ॥ ৬১ ॥

prabhāve ākarṣila saba sannyāsīra mana
uṭhila sannyāsī saba chāḍiyā āsana

SYNONYMS

prabhāve—by such illumination; *ākarṣila*—He attracted; *saba*—all; *sannyāsīra*—the Māyāvādī *sannyāsīs*; *mana*—mind; *uṭhila*—stood up; *sannyāsī*—all the Māyāvādī *sannyāsīs*; *saba*—all; *chāḍiyā*—giving up; *āsana*—sitting places.

TRANSLATION

When the sannyāsīs saw the brilliant illumination of the body of Śrī Caitanya Mahāprabhu, their minds were attracted, and they all immediately gave up their sitting places and stood in respect.

PURPORT

To draw the attention of common men, sometimes saintly persons, *ācāryas* and teachers exhibit extraordinary opulences. This is necessary to attract the attention of fools, but a saintly person should not misuse such power for personal sense gratification like false saints who declare themselves to be God. Even a magician can exhibit extraordinary feats which are not understandable to common men, but this does not mean that the magician is God. It is a most sinful activity to attract attention by exhibiting mystic powers and utilizing this opportunity to declare oneself to be God. A real saintly person never declares himself to be God but always places himself in the position of a servant of God. For a servant of God there is no need to exhibit mystic powers, and he does not like to do so, but on behalf of the Supreme Personality of Godhead a humble servant of God performs his activities in such a wonderful way that no common man can dare try to act like him. Yet a saintly person never takes credit for such actions because he knows very well that when wonderful things are done on his behalf by the grace of the Supreme Lord, all credit goes to the master and not to the servant.

TEXT 62

প্রকাশানন্দ-নামে সর্ব সন্ন্যাসি-প্রধান ।
প্রভুকে কহিল কিছু করিয়া সম্মান ॥ ৬২ ॥

prakāśānanda-nāme sarva sannyāsi-pradhāna
prabhuke kahila kichu kariyā sammāna

SYNONYMS

prakāśānanda—Prakāśānanda; *nāme*—of the name; *sarva*—all; *sannyāsi-pradhāna*—chief of the Māyāvādī *sannyāsīs*; *prabhuke*—unto the Lord; *kahila*—said; *kichu*—something; *kariyā*—showing Him; *sammāna*—respect.

TRANSLATION

The leader of all the Māyāvādī sannyāsīs present was named Prakāśānanda Sarasvatī, and after standing up he addressed Lord Caitanya Mahāprabhu as follows with great respect.

PURPORT

As Lord Śrī Caitanya Mahāprabhu showed respect to all the Māyāvādī *sannyāsīs*, similarly the leader of the Māyāvādī *sannyāsīs*, Prakāśānanda, also showed his respects to the Lord.

TEXT 63

ইহাঁ আইস, ইহাঁ আইস, শুনহ শ্রীপাদ ।
অপবিত্র স্থানে বৈস, কিবা অবসাদ ॥ ৬৩ ॥

ihāṅ āisa, ihāṅ āisa, śunaha śrīpāda
apavitra sthāne vaisa, kibā avasāda

SYNONYMS

ihāṅ āisa—come here; *ihāṅ āisa*—come here; *śunaha*—kindly hear; *śrīpāda*—Your Holiness; *apavitra*—unholy; *sthāne*—place; *vaisa*—You are sitting; *kibā*—what is that; *avasāda*—lamentation.

TRANSLATION

"Please come here. Please come here, Your Holiness. Why do You sit in that unclean place? What has caused Your lamentation?"

PURPORT

Here is the distinction between Lord Caitanya Mahāprabhu and Prakāśānanda Sarasvatī. In the material world everyone wants to introduce himself as very important and great, but Caitanya Mahāprabhu introduced Himself very humbly and meekly. The Māyāvādīs were sitting in an exalted position, and Caitanya Mahāprabhu sat in a place which was not even clean. Therefore the Māyāvādī *sannyāsīs* thought that He must have been aggrieved for some reason, and Prakāśānanda Sarasvatī inquired about the cause for His lamentation.

TEXT 64

প্রভু কহে,—আমি হই হীন-সম্প্রদায়।
তোমা-সবার সভায় বসিতে না যুয়ায় ॥ ৬৪ ॥

prabhu kahe,—āmi ha-i hīna-sampradāya
tomā-sabāra sabhāya vasite nā yuyāya

SYNONYMS

prabhu kahe—the Lord replied; *āmi*—I; *ha-i*—am; *hīna-sampradāya*—belonging to a lower spiritual school; *tomā-sabāra*—of all of you; *sabhāya*—in the assembly; *vasite*—to sit down; *nā*—never; *yuyāya*—I can dare.

TRANSLATION

The Lord replied: "I belong to a lower order of sannyāsîs. Therefore I do not deserve to sit with you."

PURPORT

Māyāvādî *sannyāsīs* are always very puffed up because of their knowledge of Sanskrit and because they belong to the Śaṅkara-sampradāya. They are always under the impression that unless one is a *brāhmaṇa* and a very good Sanskrit scholar, especially in grammar, one cannot accept the renounced order of life nor become a preacher. Māyāvādî *sannyāsīs* always misinterpret all the *śāstras* with their word jugglery and grammatical compositions, yet Śrīpāda Śaṅkarācārya himself condemned such jugglery of words in the verse, *prāpte sannihite khalu maraṇe nahi nahi rakṣati ḍukṛñ-karaṇe. Ḍukṛn* refers to suffixes and prefixes in Sanskrit grammar. Śaṅkarācārya warned his disciples that if they concerned themselves only with the principles of grammar, not worshiping Govinda, they were fools who would never be saved. Yet in spite of Śrîpāda Śaṅkarācārya's instructions, foolish Māyāvādî *sannyāsīs* are always busy juggling words on the basis of strict Sanskrit grammar.

Māyāvādî *sannyāsīs* are very puffed up if they hold the elevated *sannyāsa* titles *tīrtha, āśrama,* and *sarasvatī.* Even among Māyāvādîs, those who belong to other *sampradāyas* and hold other titles such as Vana, Āraṇya, Bhāratī, etc., are considered to be lower-grade *sannyāsīs.* Śrî Caitanya Mahāprabhu accepted *sannyāsa* from the Bhāratî-sampradāya, and thus He considered Himself a lower *sannyāsī* than Prakāśānanda Sarasvatī. To remain distinct from Vaiṣṇava *sannyāsīs,* the *sannyāsīs* of the Māyāvādi-sampradāya always think themselves to be situated in a very elevated spiritual order, but Lord Śrî Caitanya Mahāprabhu, in order to teach them how to become humble and meek, accepted Himself as belonging to a lower *sampradāya* of *sannyāsīs.* Thus He wanted to point out clearly that a *sannyāsī* is one who is advanced in spiritual knowledge. One who is advanced in spiritual knowledge should be accepted as occupying a better position than those who lack such knowledge.

The Māyāvādi-sampradāya *sannyāsīs* are generally known as Vedāntīs, as if Vedānta were their monopoly. Actually, however, Vedāntī refers to a person who perfectly knows Kṛṣṇa. As confirmed in *Bhagavad-gītā, vedaiś ca sarvair aham eva vedyaḥ:* "By all the *Vedas* it is Kṛṣṇa who is to be known." (Bg. 15.15) The so-called Māyāvādī Vedāntīs do not know who Kṛṣṇa is; therefore their title of Vedāntī, or knower of Vedānta philosophy, is simply a pretension. Māyāvādī *sannyāsīs* always think of themselves as real *sannyāsīs* and consider *sannyāsīs* of the Vaiṣṇava order to be *brahmacārīs.* A *brahmacārī* is supposed to engage in the service of a *sannyāsī* and accept him as his *guru.* Māyāvādī *sannyāsīs* therefore declare themselves to be not only *gurus* but *jagad-gurus,* or the spiritual masters of the entire world, although, of course, they cannot see the entire world. Sometimes they dress gorgeously and travel on the backs of elephants in processions, and thus they are always puffed up, accepting themselves as *jagad-gurus.* Śrīla Rūpa Gosvāmī, however, has explained that *jagad-guru* properly refers to one who is the controller of his tongue, mind, words, belly, genitals and anger. *Pṛthivīṁ sa śiṣyāt:* such a *jagad-guru* is completely fit to make disciples all over the world. Due to false prestige, Māyāvādī *sannyāsīs* who do not have these qualifications sometimes harass and blaspheme a Vaiṣṇava *sannyāsī* who humbly engages in the service of the Lord.

TEXT 65

আপনে প্রকাশানন্দ হাতেতে ধরিয়া ।
বসাইলা সভামধ্যে সম্মান করিয়া ॥ ৬৫ ॥

āpane prakāśānanda hātete dhariyā
vasāilā sabhā-madhye sammāna kariyā

SYNONYMS

āpane—personally; *prakāśānanda*—Prakāśānanda; *hātete*—by His hand; *dhariyā*—capturing; *vasāilā*—made Him sit; *sabhā-madhye*—in the assembly of; *sammāna*—with great respect; *kariyā*—offering Him.

TRANSLATION

Prakāśānanda Sarasvatī, however, caught Śrī Caitanya Mahāprabhu personally by the hand and seated Him with great respect in the midst of the assembly.

PURPORT

The respectful behavior of Prakāśānanda Sarasvatī toward Śrī Caitanya Mahāprabhu is very much to be appreciated. Such behavior is calculated to be *ajñāta-sukṛti,* or pious activities that one executes without his knowledge. Thus Śrī Caitanya Mahāprabhu very tactfully gave Prakāśānanda Sarasvatī an opportunity to advance in *ajñāta-sukṛti* so that in the future he might actually become a Vaiṣṇava *sannyāsī.*

TEXT 66

পুছিল, তোমার নাম 'শ্রীকৃষ্ণচৈতন্য'।
কেশব-ভারতীর শিষ্য, তাতে তুমি ধন্য ॥ ৬৬ ॥

puchila, tomāra nāma 'śrī-kṛṣṇa-caitanya'
keśava-bhāratīra śiṣya, tāte tumi dhanya

SYNONYMS

puchila—inquired; *tomāra*—Your; *nāma*—name; *śrī-kṛṣṇa-caitanya*—the name Śrī Kṛṣṇa Caitanya; *keśava-bhāratīra śiṣya*—You are a disciple of Keśava Bhāratī; *tāte*—in that connection; *tumi*—You are; *dhanya*—glorious.

TRANSLATION

Prakāśānanda Sarasvatī then said: "I understand that Your name is Śrī Kṛṣṇa Caitanya. You are a disciple of Śrī Keśava Bhāratī, and therefore You are glorious.

TEXT 67

সাম্প্রদায়িক সন্ন্যাসী তুমি, রহ এই গ্রামে।
কি কারণে আমা-সবার না কর দর্শনে ॥ ৬৭ ॥

sāmpradāyika sannyāsī tumi, raha ei grāme
ki kāraṇe āmā-sabāra nā kara darśane

SYNONYMS

sāmpradāyika—of the community; *sannyāsī*—Māyāvādī *sannyāsī; tumi*—You are; *raha*—live; *ei*—this; *grāme*—in Vārāṇasī; *ki kāraṇe*—for what reason; *āmā-sabāra*—with us; *nā*—do not; *kara*—endeavor; *darśane*—to mix.

TRANSLATION

"You belong to our Śaṅkara-sampradāya and live in our village, Vārāṇasī. Why then do You not associate with us? Why is it that You avoid even seeing us?

PURPORT

A Vaiṣṇava *sannyāsī* or a Vaiṣṇava in the second stage of advancement in spiritual knowledge can understand four principles—namely, the Supreme Personality of Godhead, the devotees, the innocent and the jealous—and he behaves differently with each. He tries to increase his love for Godhead, make friendship with devotees and preach Kṛṣṇa consciousness among the innocent, but he avoids the jealous who are envious of the Kṛṣṇa consciousness movement. Lord Caitanya Mahāprabhu Himself exemplified such behavior, and this is why Prakāśānanda Sarasvatī inquired why He did not associate or even talk with them. Caitanya Mahāprabhu confirmed by example that a preacher of the Kṛṣṇa consciousness movement generally should not waste his time talking with Māyāvādī *sannyāsīs,* but when there are arguments on the basis of *śāstra,* a Vaiṣṇava must come forward to talk and defeat them in philosophy.

According to Māyāvādī *sannyāsīs,* only one who takes *sannyāsa* in the disciplic succession from Śaṅkarācārya is a Vedic *sannyāsī.* Sometimes it is challenged that the *sannyāsīs* who are preaching in the Kṛṣṇa consciousness movement are not genuine because they do not belong to *brāhmaṇa* families, for Māyāvādīs do not offer *sannyāsa* to one who does not belong to a *brāhmaṇa* family by birth. Unfortunately, however, they do not know that at present everyone is born a *śūdra (kalau śūdra sambhava).* It is to be understood that there are no *brāhmaṇas* in this age because those who claim to be *brāhmaṇas* simply on the basis of birthright do not have the brahminical qualifications. However, even if one is born in a non-*brāhmaṇa* family, if he has the brahminical qualifications he should be accepted as a *brāhmaṇa,* as confirmed by Śrīla Nārada Muni and the great saint Śrīdhara Svāmī. This is also stated in *Śrīmad-Bhāgavatam.* Both Nārada and Śrīdhara Svāmī completely agree that one cannot be a *brāhmaṇa* by birthright but must possess the qualities of a *brāhmaṇa.* Thus in our Kṛṣṇa consciousness movement we never offer the *sannyāsa* order to a person whom we do not find to be qualified in terms of the prescribed brahminical principles. Although it is a fact that unless one is a *brāhmaṇa* he cannot become a *sannyāsī,* it is not a valid principle that an unqualified man who is born in a *brāhmaṇa* family is a *brāhmaṇa* whereas a brahminically qualified person born in a non-*brāhmaṇa* family cannot be accepted. The Kṛṣṇa consciousness movement strictly follows the injunctions of *Śrīmad-Bhāgavatam,* avoiding misleading heresy and manufactured conclusions.

TEXT 68

সন্ন্যাসী হইয়া কর নর্তন-গায়ন ।
ভাবুক সব সঙ্গে লঞা কর সংকীর্তন ॥ ৬৮ ॥

sannyāsī ha-iyā kara nartana-gāyana
bhāvuka saba saṅge lañā kara saṅkīrtana

SYNONYMS

sannyāsī—the renounced order of life; *ha-iyā*—accepting; *kara*—You do; *nartana-gāyana*—dancing and chanting; *bhāvuka*—fanatics; *saba*—all; *saṅge*—in Your company; *lañā*—accepting them; *kara*—You do; *saṅkīrtana*—chanting of the holy name of the Lord.

TRANSLATION

"You are a sannyāsī. Why then do You indulge in chanting and dancing, engaging in Your saṅkīrtana movement in the company of fanatics?

PURPORT

This is a challenge by Prakāśānanda Sarasvatī to Śrī Caitanya Mahāprabhu. Śrīla Bhaktisiddhānta Sarasvatī Ṭhākura writes in his *Anubhāṣya* that Śrī Caitanya Mahāprabhu, who is the object of Vedānta philosophical research, has very kindly determined who is an appropriate candidate for study of Vedānta philosophy. The first qualification of such a candidate is expressed by Śrī Caitanya Mahāprabhu in His *Śikṣāṣṭaka:*

tṛṇād api sunīcena taror api sahiṣṇunā
amāninā mānadena kīrtanīyaḥ sadā hariḥ

This statement indicates that one can hear or speak about Vedānta philosophy through the disciplic succession. One must be very humble and meek, more tolerant than a tree and more humble than the grass. One should not claim respect for himself but should be prepared to give all respect to others. One must have these qualifications to be eligible to understand Vedic knowledge.

TEXT 69

বেদান্ত-পঠন, ধ্যান, —সন্ন্যাসীর ধর্ম ।
তাহা ছাড়ি' কর কেনে ভাবুকের কর্ম ॥ ৬৯ ॥

vedānta-paṭhana, dhyāna,—sannyāsīra dharma
tāhā chāḍi' kara kene bhāvukera karma

SYNONYMS

vedānta-paṭhana—studying Vedānta philosophy; *dhyāna*—meditation; *sannyāsīra*—of a *sannyāsī*; *dharma*—duties; *tāhā chāḍi'*—giving them up; *kara*—You do; *kene*—why; *bhāvukera*—of the fanatics; *karma*—activities.

TRANSLATION

"Meditation and the study of Vedānta are the sole duties of a sannyāsī. Why do You abandon these to dance with fanatics?

PURPORT

As explained in regard to verse 41, Māyāvādī *sannyāsīs* do not approve of chanting and dancing. Prakāśānanda Sarasvatī, like Sārvabhauma Bhaṭṭācārya, misunderstood Śrī Caitanya Mahāprabhu to be a misled young *sannyāsī,* and therefore he asked Him why He indulged in the association of fanatics instead of executing the duty of a *sannyāsī.*

TEXT 70

প্রভাবে দেখিয়ে তোমা সাক্ষাৎ নারায়ণ ।
হীনাচার কর কেনে, ইথে কি কারণ ॥ ৭০ ॥

prabhāve dekhiye tomā sākṣāt nārāyaṇa
hīnācāra kara kene, ithe ki kāraṇa

SYNONYMS

prabhāve—in Your opulence; *dekhiye*—I see; *tomā*—You; *sākṣāt*—directly; *nārāyaṇa*—the Supreme Personality of Godhead; *hīna-ācāra*—lower-class behavior; *kara*—You do; *kene*—why; *ithe*—in this; *ki*—what is; *kāraṇa*—reason.

TRANSLATION

"You look as brilliant as if You were Nārāyaṇa Himself. Will You kindly explain the reason that You have adopted the behavior of lower-class people?"

PURPORT

Due to renunciation, Vedānta study, meditation and the strict regulative principles of their daily routine, Māyāvādī *sannyāsīs* are certainly in a position to execute pious activities. Thus Prakāśānanda Sarasvatī, on account of his piety, could understand that Caitanya Mahāprabhu was not an ordinary person but the Supreme Personality of Godhead. *Sākṣāt nārāyaṇa:* he considered Him to be Nārāyaṇa Himself. Māyāvādī *sannyāsīs* address each other as Nārāyaṇa because they think that they are all going to be Nārāyaṇa or merge with Nārāyaṇa in the next life. Prakāśānanda Sarasvatī appreciated that Caitanya Mahāprabhu had already directly become Nārāyaṇa and did not need to wait until His next life. One difference between the Vaiṣṇava and Māyāvādī philosophies is that Māyāvādī philosophers think that after giving up their bodies they are going to become Nārāyaṇa by merging with His body, whereas Vaiṣṇava philosophers understand that after the body dies they are going to have a transcendental, spiritual body in which to associate with Nārāyaṇa.

TEXT 71

প্রভু কহে —শুন, শ্রীপাদ, ইহার কারণ ।
গুরু মোরে মূর্খ দেখি' করিল শাসন ॥ ৭১ ॥

prabhu kahe—śuna, śrīpāda, ihāra kāraṇa
guru more mūrkha dekhi' karila śāsana

SYNONYMS

prabhu kahe—the Lord replied; *śuna*—kindly hear; *śrīpāda*—Your Holiness; *ihāra*—of this; *kāraṇa*—reason; *guru*—My spiritual master; *more*—Me; *mūrkha*—fool; *dekhi'*—understanding; *karila*—he did; *śāsana*—chastisement.

TRANSLATION

Śrī Caitanya Mahāprabhu replied to Prakāśānanda Sarasvatī: "My dear sir, kindly hear the reason. My spiritual master considered Me a fool, and therefore he chastised Me.

PURPORT

When Prakāśānanda Sarasvatī inquired from Lord Caitanya Mahāprabhu why He neither studied Vedānta nor performed meditation, Lord Caitanya presented Himself as a number one fool in order to indicate that the present age, Kali-yuga, is an age of fools and rascals in which it is not possible to obtain perfection simply by reading Vedānta philosophy and meditating. The *śāstras* strongly recommend:

harer nāma harer nāma harer nāmaiva kevalam
kalau nāsty eva nāsty eva nāsty eva gatir anyathā

"In this age of quarrel and hypocrisy the only means of deliverance is the chanting of the holy names of the Lord. There is no other way. There is no other way. There is no other way." People in general in Kali-yuga are so fallen that it is not possible for them to obtain perfection simply by studying *Vedānta-sūtra*. One should therefore seriously take to the constant chanting of the holy name of the Lord.

TEXT 72

মূর্খ তুমি, তোমার নাহিক বেদান্তাধিকার ।
'কৃষ্ণমন্ত্র' জপ সদা, —এই মন্ত্রসার ॥ ৭২ ॥

mūrkha tumi, tomāra nāhika vedāntādhikāra
'kṛṣṇa-mantra' japa sadā,—ei mantra-sāra

SYNONYMS

mūrkha tumi—You are a fool; *tomāra*—Your; *nāhika*—there is not; *vedānta*—Vedānta philosophy; *adhikāra*—qualification to study; *kṛṣṇa-mantra*—the hymn of Kṛṣṇa (Hare Kṛṣṇa); *japa*—chant; *sadā*—always; *ei*—this; *mantra*—hymn; *sāra*—essence of all Vedic knowledge.

TRANSLATION

"'You are a fool,' he said. 'You are not qualified to study Vedānta philosophy, and therefore You must always chant the holy name of Kṛṣṇa. This is the essence of all mantras or Vedic hymns.

PURPORT

Śrī Bhaktisiddhānta Sarasvatī Gosvāmī Mahārāja comments in this connection, "One can become perfectly successful in the mission of his life if he acts exactly according to the words he hears from the mouth of his spiritual master." This acceptance of the words of the spiritual master is called *śrauta-vākya,* which indicates that the disciple must carry out the spiritual master's instructions without deviation. Śrīla Viśvanātha Cakravartī Ṭhākura remarks in this connection that a disciple must accept the words of his spiritual master as his life and soul. Śrī Caitanya Mahāprabhu here confirms this by saying that since His spiritual master ordered Him only to chant the holy name of Kṛṣṇa, He always chanted the Hare Kṛṣṇa *mahā-mantra* according to this direction *('kṛṣṇa-mantra' japa sadā,—ei mantra-sāra).*

Kṛṣṇa is the origin of everything. Therefore when a person is fully Kṛṣṇa conscious it is to be understood that his relationship with Kṛṣṇa has been fully confirmed. Lacking Kṛṣṇa consciousness, one is only partially related with Kṛṣṇa and is therefore not in his constitutional position. Although Śrī Caitanya Mahāprabhu is the Supreme Personality of Godhead Kṛṣṇa, the spiritual master of the entire universe, He nevertheless took the position of a disciple in order to teach by example how a devotee should strictly follow the orders of a spiritual master in executing the duty of always chanting the Hare Kṛṣṇa *mahā-mantra.* One who is very much attracted to the study of Vedānta philosophy must take lessons from Śrī Caitanya Mahāprabhu. In this age, no one is actually competent to study Vedānta, and therefore it is better that one chant the holy name of the Lord, which is the essence of all Vedic knowledge, as Kṛṣṇa Himself confirms in *Bhagavad-gītā:*

vedaiś ca sarvair aham eva vedyo
vedānta-kṛd veda-vid eva cāham

"By all the *Vedas* am I to be known; indeed I am the compiler of Vedānta, and I am the knower of the *Vedas.*" (Bg. 15.15)

Only fools give up the service of the spiritual master and think themselves advanced in spiritual knowledge. In order to check such fools, Caitanya Mahāprabhu Himself presented the perfect example of how to be a disciple. A spiritual master knows very well how to engage each disciple in a particular duty, but if a disciple, thinking himself more advanced than his spiritual master, gives up his orders and acts independently, he checks his own spiritual progress. Every disciple must consider himself completely unaware of the science of Kṛṣṇa and must always be ready to carry out the orders of the spiritual master to become competent in Kṛṣṇa consciousness. A disciple should always remain a fool before his spiritual master. Therefore sometimes pseudo-spiritualists accept a spiritual master who is not even fit to become a disciple because they want to keep him under their control. This is useless for spiritual realization.

One who imperfectly knows Kṛṣṇa consciousness cannot know Vedānta philosophy. A showy display of Vedānta study without Kṛṣṇa consciousness is a feature of the external energy, *māyā,* and as long as one is attracted by the inebrieties of this ever changing material energy, he deviates from devotion to the Supreme Personality of Godhead. An actual follower of Vedānta philosophy is a devotee of Lord Viṣṇu, who is the greatest of the great and the maintainer of the entire universe. Unless one surpasses the field of activities in service to the limited, one cannot reach the unlimited. Knowledge of the unlimited is actual *brahma jñāna,* or knowledge of the Supreme. Those who are addicted to fruitive activities and speculative knowledge cannot understand the value of the holy name of the Lord, Kṛṣṇa, who is always completely pure, eternally liberated and full of spiritual bliss. One who has taken shelter of the holy name of the Lord, which is identical with the Lord, does not have to study Vedānta philosophy, for he has already completed all such study.

One who is unfit to chant the holy name of Kṛṣṇa but thinks that the holy name is different from Kṛṣṇa and thus takes shelter of Vedānta study in order to understand Him must be considered a number one fool, as confirmed by Caitanya Mahāprabhu by His personal behavior, and philosophical speculators who want to make Vedānta philosophy an academic career are also considered to be within the material energy. A person who always chants the holy name of the Lord, however, is already beyond the ocean of nescience, and thus even a person born in a low family who engages in chanting the holy name of the Lord is considered to be beyond the study of Vedānta philosophy. In this connection the *Śrīmad-Bhāgavatam* states:

aho bata śvapaco'to garīyān
yaj jihvāgre vartate nāma tubhyam
tepus tapas te juhuvuḥ sasnur āryā
brahmān ūcur nāma gṛṇanti ye te

"If a person born in a family of dog-eaters takes to the chanting of the holy name of Kṛṣṇa, it is to be understood that in his previous life he must have executed all kinds of austerities and penances and performed all the Vedic *yajñas.*" (*Bhāg.* 3.33.7) Another quotation states:

ṛg-vedo 'tha yajur-vedaḥ sāma-vedo 'py atharvaṇaḥ
adhītās tena yenoktaṁ harir ity akṣara-dvayam

"A person who chants the two syllables *Ha-ri* has already studied the four *Vedas—Sāma, Ṛk, Yajuḥ* and *Atharva.*"

Taking advantage of these verses, there are some *sahajiyās* who, taking everything very cheaply, consider themselves elevated Vaiṣṇavas but do not care even to touch the *Vedānta-sūtras* or Vedānta philosophy. A real Vaiṣṇava should, however, study Vedānta philosophy, but if after studying Vedānta one does not adopt the chanting of the holy name of the Lord, he is no better than a Māyāvādī. Therefore, one should not be a Māyāvādī, yet one should not be unaware of the subject matter of Vedānta philosophy. Indeed, Caitanya Mahāprabhu exhibited His knowledge of Vedānta in His discourses with Prakāśānanda Sarasvatī. Thus it is to be understood that a Vaiṣṇava should be completely conversant with Vedānta philosophy, yet he should not think that studying Vedānta is all in all and therefore be unattached to the chanting of the holy name. A devotee must know the importance of simultaneously understanding Vedānta philosophy and chanting the holy names. If by studying Vedānta one becomes an impersonalist, he has not been able to understand Vedānta. This is confirmed in *Bhagavad-gītā* (Bg. 15.15). Vedānta means "the end of knowledge." The ultimate end of knowledge is knowledge of Kṛṣṇa, who is identical with His holy name. Cheap Vaiṣṇavas *(sahajiyās)* do not care to study the Vedānta philosophy as commented upon by the four *ācāryas.* In the Gauḍīya-sampradāya there is a Vedānta commentary called the *Govinda-bhāṣya,* but the *sahajiyās* consider such commentaries to be untouchable philosophical speculation, and they consider the *ācāryas* to be mixed devotees. Thus they clear their way to hell.

TEXT 73

কৃষ্ণমন্ত্র হৈতে হবে সংসার-মোচন ।
কৃষ্ণনাম হৈতে পাবে কৃষ্ণের চরণ ॥ ৭৩ ॥

kṛṣṇa-mantra haite habe saṁsāra-mocana
kṛṣṇa-nāma haite pābe kṛṣṇera caraṇa

SYNONYMS

kṛṣṇa-mantra—the chanting of the Hare Kṛṣṇa *mahā-mantra*; *haite*—from; *habe*—it will be; *saṁsāra*—material existence; *mocana*—deliverance; *kṛṣṇa-nāma*—the holy name of Lord Kṛṣṇa; *haite*—from; *pābe*—one will get; *kṛṣṇera*—of Lord Kṛṣṇa; *caraṇa*—lotus feet.

TRANSLATION

"'Simply by chanting the holy name of Kṛṣṇa one can obtain freedom from material existence. Indeed, simply by chanting the Hare Kṛṣṇa mantra one will be able to see the lotus feet of the Lord.

PURPORT

In the *Anubhāṣya,* Śrī Bhaktisiddhānta Sarasvatī Gosvāmī says that the actual effect that will be visible as soon as one achieves transcendental knowledge is that he will immediately become free from the clutches of *māyā* and fully engage in the service of the Lord. Unless one serves the Supreme Personality of Godhead Mukunda one cannot become free from fruitive activities under the external energy. However, when one chants the holy name of the Lord offenselessly, he can realize a transcendental position which is completely aloof from the material conception of life. Rendering service to the Lord, a devotee relates to the Supreme Personality of Godhead in one of five relationships—namely, *śānta, dāsya, sakhya, vātsalya* and *mādhurya*—and thus he relishes transcendental bliss in that relationship. Such a relationship certainly transcends the body and mind. When one realizes that the holy name of the Lord is identical with the Supreme Person, he becomes completely eligible to chant the holy name of the Lord. Such an ecstatic chanter and dancer must be considered to have a direct relationship with the Lord.

According to the Vedic principles, there are three stages of spiritual advancement, namely, *sambandha-jñāna, abhidheya* and *prayojana. Sambandha-jñāna* refers to establishing one's original relationship with the Supreme Personality of Godhead, *abhidheya* refers to acting according to that constitutional relationship, and *prayojana* is the ultimate goal of life, which is to develop love of Godhead *(premā pumartho mahān).* If one adheres to the regulative principles under the order of the spiritual master, he very easily achieves the ultimate goal of his life. A person who is addicted to the chanting of the Hare Kṛṣṇa *mantra* very easily gets the opportunity to serve the Supreme Personality of Godhead directly. There is no need for such a person to understand the grammatical jugglery in which Māyāvādī *sannyāsīs* generally indulge. Śrī Śaṅkarācārya also stressed this point. *Nahi nahi rakṣati ḍukṛñ-karaṇe:* "Simply by juggling grammatical suffixes and prefixes one cannot save himself from the clutches of death." The grammatical word jugglers cannot bewilder a devotee who engages in chanting the Hare Kṛṣṇa *mahā-mantra.* Simply addressing the energy of the Supreme Lord as Hare and the Lord Himself as Kṛṣṇa very soon situates the Lord within the heart of the devotee. By thus addressing Rādhā and Kṛṣṇa one directly engages in His Lordship's service. The essence of all revealed scriptures and all knowledge is present when one addresses the Lord and His energy by the Hare Kṛṣṇa *mantra,* for this transcendental vibration can completely liberate a conditioned soul and directly engage him in the service of the Lord.

Śrī Caitanya Mahāprabhu presented Himself as a grand fool, yet He maintained that all the words that He had heard from His spiritual master strictly followed the principles stated by Vyāsadeva in *Śrīmad-Bhāgavatam.*

anarthopaśamaṁ sākṣād
bhakti-yogam adhokṣaje
lokasyājānato vidvāṁś
cakre sātvata-saṁhitām

"The material miseries of a living entity, which are superfluous to him, can be directly mitigated by the linking process of devotional service. But the mass of people do not know this, and therefore the learned Vyāsadeva compiled this Vedic literature, which is in relation to the Supreme Truth." (*Bhāg.* 1.7.6) One can overcome all misconceptions and entanglement in the material world by practicing *bhakti-yoga,* and therefore Vyāsadeva, acting on the instruction of Śrī Nārada, has very kindly introduced *Śrīmad-Bhāgavatam* to relieve the conditioned souls from the clutches of *māyā.* Lord Caitanya's spiritual master instructed Him, therefore, that one must read *Śrīmad-Bhāgavatam* regularly and with scrutiny to gradually become attached to the chanting of the Hare Kṛṣṇa *mahā-mantra.*

The holy name and the Lord are identical. One who is completely free from the clutches of *māyā* can understand this fact. This knowledge, which is achieved by the mercy of the spiritual master, places one on the supreme transcendental platform. Śrī Caitanya Mahāprabhu presented Himself as a fool because prior to accepting the shelter of a spiritual master He could not understand that simply by chanting one can be relieved from all material conditions. But as soon as He became a faithful servant of His spiritual master and followed his instructions, He very easily saw the path of liberation. Śrī Caitanya Mahāprabhu's chanting of the Hare Kṛṣṇa *mantra* must be understood to be devoid of all offenses. The ten offenses against the holy name are as follows: (1) to blaspheme a devotee of the Lord, (2) to consider the Lord and the demigods to be on the same level or to think that there are many gods, (3) to neglect the orders of the spiritual master, (4) to minimize the authority of scriptures *(Vedas),* (5) to interpret the holy name of God, (6) to commit sins on the strength of chanting, (7) to instruct the glories of the Lord's name to the unfaithful, (8) to compare the chanting of the holy name with material piety, (9) to be inattentive while chanting the holy name, and (10) to be attached to material things in spite of chanting the holy name.

TEXT 74

নাম বিনু কলিকালে নাহি আর ধর্ম ।
সর্বমন্ত্রসার নাম, এই শাস্ত্রমর্ম ॥ ৭৪ ॥

nāma vinu kali-kāle nāhi āra dharma
sarva-mantra-sāra nāma, ei śāstra-marma

SYNONYMS

nāma—the holy name; *vinu*—without; *kali-kāle*—in this age of Kali; *nāhi*—there is none; *āra*—or any alternative; *dharma*—religious principle; *sarva*—all; *mantra*—hymns; *sāra*—essence; *nāma*—the holy name; *ei*—this is; *śāstra*—revealed scriptures; *marma*—purport.

TRANSLATION

"'In this age of Kali there is no other religious principle than the chanting of the holy name, which is the essence of all Vedic hymns. This is the purport of all scriptures.'

PURPORT

The principles of the *paramparā* system were strictly honored in the ages *Satya-yuga, Tretā-yuga* and *Dvāpara-yuga,* but in the present age, *Kali-yuga,* people neglect the importance of this system of *śrauta-paramparā,* or receiving knowledge by disciplic succession. In this age, people are prepared to argue that they can understand that which is beyond their limited knowledge and perception through so-called scientific observations and experiments, not knowing that actual truth comes down to man from authorities. This argumentative attitude is against the Vedic principles, and it is very difficult for one who adopts it to understand that the holy name of Kṛṣṇa is as good as Kṛṣṇa Himself. Since Kṛṣṇa and His holy name are identical, the holy name is eternally pure and beyond material contamination. It is the Supreme Personality of Godhead as a transcendental vibration. The holy name is completely different from material sound, as confirmed by Narottama dāsa Ṭhākura. *Golokera prema-dhana, hari-nāma-saṅkīrtana:* the transcendental vibration of *hari-nāma-saṅkīrtana* is imported from the spiritual world. Thus although materialists who are addicted to experimental knowledge and the so-called "scientific method" cannot place their faith in the chanting of the Hare Kṛṣṇa *mahā-mantra,* it is a fact that simply by chanting the Hare Kṛṣṇa *mantra* offenselessly one can be freed from all subtle and gross material conditions. The spiritual world is called *Vaikuṇṭha,* which means "without anxiety." In the material world everything is full of anxiety *(kuṇṭha),* whereas in the spiritual world *(Vaikuṇṭha)* everything is free from anxiety. Therefore those who are afflicted by a combination of anxieties cannot understand the Hare Kṛṣṇa *mantra,* which is free from all anxiety. In the present age the vibration of the Hare Kṛṣṇa *mahā-mantra* is the only process which is in a transcendental position beyond material contamination. Since the holy name can deliver a conditioned soul, it is explained here to be *sarva-mantra-sāra,* the essence of all Vedic hymns.

A name which represents an object of this material world may be subjected to arguments and experimental knowledge, but in the absolute world a name and its owner, fame and the famous, are identical, and similarly the qualities, pastimes and everything else pertaining to the Absolute are also absolute. Although Māyāvādīs profess monism, they differentiate between the holy name of the Supreme Lord and the Lord Himself. For this offense of *nāmāparādha* they gradually glide down from their exalted position of *brahma-jñāna,* as confirmed in the *Śrīmad-Bhāgavatam* (*Bhāg.* 10.2.32):

āruhya kṛcchreṇa paraṁ padaṁ tataḥ
patanty adho 'nādṛta-yuṣmad-aṅghrayaḥ

Although by severe austerities they rise to the exalted position of *brahma-jñāna,* they nevertheless fall down due to imperfect knowledge of the Absolute Truth. Although they profess to understand the Vedic *mantra, sarvaṁ khalv idaṁ brahma* ("everything is *brahman*"), they are unable to understand that the holy name is also *brahman.* If they regularly chant the *mahā-mantra,* however, they can be relieved from this misconception. Unless one properly takes shelter of the holy name, he cannot be relieved from the offensive stage in chanting the holy name.

TEXT 75

এত বলি' এক শ্লোক শিখাইল মোরে ।
কণ্ঠে করি' এই শ্লোক করিহ বিচারে ॥ ৭৫ ॥

eta bali' eka śloka śikhāila more
kaṇṭhe kari' ei śloka kariha vicāre

SYNONYMS

eta bali'—saying this; *eka śloka*—one verse; *śikhāila*—taught; *more*—Me; *kaṇṭhe*—in the throat; *kari'*—keeping; *ei*—this; *śloka*—verse; *kariha*—You should do; *vicāre*—in consideration.

TRANSLATION

"After describing the potency of the Hare Kṛṣṇa mahā-mantra, My spiritual master taught Me another verse, advising Me to always keep the name within My throat.

TEXT 76

হরের্নাম হরের্নাম হরের্নামৈব কেবলম্ ।
কলৌ নাস্ত্যেব নাস্ত্যেব নাস্ত্যেব গতিরন্যথা ॥ ৭৬ ॥

harer nāma harer nāma
harer nāmaiva kevalam
kalau nāsty eva nāsty eva
nāsty eva gatir anyathā

SYNONYMS

hareḥ nāma—the holy name of the Lord; *hareḥ nāma*—the holy name of the Lord; *hareḥ nāma*—the holy name of the Lord; *eva*—certainly; *kevalam*—only; *kalau*—in this age of Kali; *na asti*—there is none; *eva*—certainly; *na asti*—there is none; *eva*—certainly; *na asti*—there is none; *eva*—certainly; *gatiḥ*—progress; *anyathā*—otherwise.

TRANSLATION

"'In this age of Kali there is no alternative, there is no alternative, there is no alternative for spiritual progress than the holy name, the holy name, the holy name of the Lord.'

PURPORT

For progress in spiritual life, the *śāstras* recommend meditation in Satya-yuga, sacrifice for the satisfaction of Lord Viṣṇu in Tretā-yuga and gorgeous worship of the Lord in the temple in Dvāpara-yuga, but in the age of Kali one can achieve spiritual progress only by chanting the holy name of the Lord. This is confirmed in various scriptures. In the *Śrīmad-Bhāgavatam* there are many references to this fact. In the Twelfth Canto it is said, *kīrtanād eva kṛṣṇasya mukta-saṅgaḥ paraṁ vrajet:* In the age of Kali there are many faults, for people are subjected to many miserable conditions, yet in this age there is one great benediction—simply by chanting the Hare Kṛṣṇa *mantra* one can be freed from all material contamination and thus be elevated to the spiritual world. The *Nārada-pañcarātra* also praises the Hare Kṛṣṇa *mahā-mantra* as follows:

trayo vedāḥ ṣaḍ-aṅgāni
chandāṁsi vividhāḥ surāḥ
sarvam aṣṭākṣarāntaḥsthaṁ
yac cānyad api vāṅ-mayam
sarva-vedānta-sārārthaḥ
saṁsārārṇava-tāraṇaḥ

"The essence of all Vedic knowledge—comprehending the three kinds of Vedic activity [*karma-kāṇḍa, jñāna-kāṇḍa* and *upāsanā-kāṇḍa*], the *chandaḥ* or Vedic hymns, and the processes for satisfying the demigods—is included in the eight syllables Hare Kṛṣṇa, Hare Kṛṣṇa. This is the reality of all Vedānta. The chanting of the holy name is the only means to cross the ocean of nescience." Similarly, the *Kalisantaraṇa Upaniṣad* states, "Hare Kṛṣṇa, Hare Kṛṣṇa, Kṛṣṇa Kṛṣṇa, Hare Hare/ Hare Rāma, Hare Rāma, Rāma Rāma, Hare Hare—these sixteen names composed of thirty-two syllables are the only means to counteract the evil effects of Kali-yuga. In all the *Vedas* it is seen that to cross the ocean of nescience there is no alternative to the chanting of the holy name." Similarly, Śrī Madhvācārya, while commenting upon the *Muṇḍaka Upaniṣad,* has said:

dvāparīyair janair viṣṇuḥ
pañcarātraiś ca kevalam
kalau tu nāma-mātreṇa
pūjyate bhagavān hariḥ

"In the Dvāpara-yuga one could satisfy Kṛṣṇa or Viṣṇu only by worshiping Him gorgeously according to the *Pāñcarātrikī* system, but in the age of Kali one can satisfy and worship the Supreme Personality of Godhead Hari simply by chanting the holy name." In his *Bhakti-sandarbha* (verse 284), Śrīla Jīva Gosvāmī strongly emphasizes the chanting of the holy name of the Lord as follows:

nanu bhagavan-nāmātmakā eva mantrāḥ; tatra viśeṣeṇa namaḥ-śabdādy-alaṅkṛtāḥ śrī-bhagavatā śrīmad-ṛṣibhiś cāhita-śakti-viśeṣāḥ, śrī-bhagavatā samam ātma-sambandha-viśeṣa-pratipādakāś ca tatra kevalāni śrī-bhagavan-nāmāny api nirapekṣāṇy eva parama-puruṣārtha-phala-paryanta-dāna-samarthāni tato mantreṣu nāmato'py adhika-sāmarthye labdhe kathaṁ dīkṣādy-apekṣā? ucyate—yady api svarūpato nāsti, tathāpi prāyaḥ svabhāvato dehādi-sambandhena kadarya-śīlānāṁ vikṣipta-cittānāṁ janānāṁ tat-saṅkocīkaraṇāya śrīmad-ṛṣi-prabhṛtibhir atrārcana-mārge kvacit kvacit kācit kācin maryādā sthāpitāsti

Śrīla Jīva Gosvāmī states that the substance of all the Vedic *mantras* is the chanting of the holy name of the Lord. Every *mantra* begins with the prefix *nama oṁ* and eventually addresses by name the Supreme Personality of Godhead. By the supreme will of the Lord there is a specific potency in each and every *mantra* chanted by great sages like Nārada Muni and other *ṛṣis.* Chanting the holy name of the Lord immediately renovates the transcendental relationship of the living being with the Supreme Lord.

To chant the holy name of the Lord, one need not depend upon other paraphernalia, for one can immediately get all the desired results of connecting or linking with the Supreme Personality of Godhead. It may therefore be questioned why there is a necessity for initiation or further spiritual activities in devotional service for one who engages in the chanting of the holy name of the Lord. The answer is that although it is correct that one who fully engages in chanting the holy name need not depend upon the process of initiation, generally a devotee is addicted to many abominable material habits due to material contamination from his previous life. In order to get quick relief from all these contaminations, it is required that one engage in the worship of the Lord in the temple. The worship of the Deity in the temple is essential to reduce one's restlessness due to the contaminations of conditional life. Thus Nārada, in his *Pāñcarātrikī-vidhi,* and other great sages have sometimes stressed that since every conditioned soul has a bodily concept of life aimed at sense enjoyment, to restrict this sense enjoyment the rules and regulations for worshiping the Deity in the temple are essential. Śrīla Rūpa Gosvāmī has described that the holy name of the Lord can be chanted by liberated souls, but almost all the souls we have to initiate are conditioned. It is advised that one chant the holy name of the Lord without offenses and according to the regulative principles, yet due to their past bad habits they violate these rules and regulations. Thus the regulative principles for worship of the Deity are also simultaneously essential.

TEXT 77

এই আজ্ঞা পাঞা নাম লই অনুক্ষণ ।
নাম লৈতে লৈতে মোর ভ্রান্ত হৈল মন ॥ ৭৭ ॥

ei ājñā pāñā nāma la-i anukṣaṇa
nāma laite laite mora bhrānta haila mana

SYNONYMS

ei—this; *ājñā*—order; *pāñā*—receiving; *nāma*—the holy name; *la-i*—chant; *anukṣaṇa*—always; *nāma*—the holy name; *laite*—accepting; *laite*—accepting; *mora*—My; *bhrānta*—bewilderment; *haila*—taking place; *mana*—in the mind.

TRANSLATION

"Since I received this order from My spiritual master, I always chant the holy name, but I think that by chanting and chanting the holy name I have been bewildered.

TEXT 78

ধৈর্য ধরিতে নারি, হৈলাম উন্মত্ত ।
হাসি, কান্দি, নাচি, গাই, যৈছে মদমত্ত ॥ ৭৮ ॥

dhairya dharite nāri, hailāma unmatta
hāsi, kāndi, nāci, gāi, yaiche madamatta

SYNONYMS

dhairya—patience; *dharite*—capturing; *nāri*—unable to take; *hailāma*—I have become; *unmatta*—mad after it; *hāsi*—laugh; *kāndi*—cry; *nāci*—dance; *gāi*—sing; *yaiche*—as much as; *madamatta*—madman.

TRANSLATION

"While chanting the holy name of the Lord in pure ecstasy, I lose myself, and thus I laugh, cry, dance and sing just like a madman.

TEXT 79

তবে ধৈর্য ধরি' মনে করিলুঁ বিচার ।
কৃষ্ণনামে জ্ঞানাচ্ছন্ন হইল আমার ॥ ৭৯ ॥

tave dhairya dhari' mane kariluṅ vicāra
kṛṣṇa-nāme jñānācchana ha-ila āmāra

SYNONYMS

tave—thereafter; *dhairya*—patience; *dhari'*—accepting; *mane*—in the mind; *kariluṅ*—I did; *vicāra*—consideration; *kṛṣṇa-nāme*—in the holy name of Kṛṣṇa; *jñāna-ācchanna*—covering of My knowledge; *ha-ila*—has become; *āmāra*—of Me.

TRANSLATION

"Collecting My patience, therefore, I began to consider that chanting the holy name of Kṛṣṇa had covered all My spiritual knowledge.

PURPORT

Śrī Caitanya Mahāprabhu hints in this verse that to chant the holy name of Kṛṣṇa one does not need to speculate on the philosophical aspects of the science of God, for one automatically becomes ecstatic and without consideration immediately chants, dances, laughs, cries and sings just like a madman.

TEXT 80

পাগল হইলাঙ আমি, ধৈর্য নাহি মনে ।
এত চিন্তি' নিবেদিলুঁ গুরুর চরণে ॥ ৮০ ॥

pāgala ha-ilāṅ āmi, dhairya nāhi mane
eta cinti' nivediluṅ gurura caraṇe

SYNONYMS

pāgala—madman; *ha-ilāṅ*—I have become; *āmi*—I; *dhairya*—patience; *nāhi*—not; *mane*—in the mind; *eta*—thus; *cinti'*—considering; *nivediluṅ*—I submitted; *gurura*—of the spiritual master; *caraṇe*—on his lotus feet.

TRANSLATION

"I saw that I had become mad by chanting the holy name, and I immediately submitted this at the lotus feet of my spiritual master.

PURPORT

Śrī Caitanya Mahāprabhu, as an ideal teacher, shows us how a disciple should deal with his spiritual master. Whenever there is doubt regarding any point, he should refer the matter to his spiritual master for clarification. Śrī Caitanya Mahāprabhu said that while chanting and dancing He had developed the kind of mad ecstasy that is possible only for a liberated soul. Yet even in His liberated position, He referred everything to His spiritual master whenever there were doubts. Thus in any condition, even when liberated, we should never think ourselves independent of the spiritual master, but must refer to him as soon as there is some doubt regarding our progressive spiritual life.

TEXT 81

কিবা মন্ত্র দিলা, গোসাঞি, কিবা তার বল ।
জপিতে জপিতে মন্ত্র করিল পাগল ॥ ৮১ ॥

kibā mantra dilā, gosāñi, kibā tāra bala
japite japite mantra karila pāgala

SYNONYMS

kibā—what kind of; *mantra*—hymn; *dilā*—you have given; *gosāñi*—My lord; *kibā*—what is; *tāra*—its; *bala*—strength; *japite*—chanting; *japite*—chanting; *mantra*—the hymn; *karila*—has made Me; *pāgala*—madman.

TRANSLATION

"'My dear lord, what kind of mantra have you given Me? I have become mad simply by chanting this mahā-mantra!

PURPORT

Śrī Caitanya Mahāprabhu prays in His *Śikṣāṣṭaka:*

yugāyitaṁ nimeṣeṇa
cakṣuṣā prāvṛṣāyitam

śūnyāyitaṁ jagat sarvaṁ
govinda viraheṇa me

"O Govinda! Feeling Your separation, I am considering a moment to be like twelve years or more. Tears are flowing from my eyes like torrents of rain, and I am feeling all vacant in the world in Your absence." It is the aspiration of a devotee that while he chants the Hare Kṛṣṇa *mahā-mantra* his eyes will fill with tears, his voice falter and his heart throb. These are good signs in chanting the holy name of the Lord. In ecstasy, one should feel the entire world to be vacant without the presence of Govinda. This is a sign of separation from Govinda. In material life we are all separated from Govinda and are absorbed in material sense gratification. Therefore, when one comes to his senses on the spiritual platform he becomes so eager to meet Govinda that without Govinda the entire world becomes a vacant place.

TEXT 82

হাসায়, নাচায়, মোরে করায় ক্রন্দন ।
এত শুনি' গুরু হাসি বলিলা বচন ॥ ৮২ ॥

hāsāya, nācāya, more karāya krandana
eta śuni' guru hāsi balilā vacana

SYNONYMS

hāsāya—it causes Me to laugh; *nācāya*—it causes Me to dance; *more*—unto Me; *karāya*—it causes; *krandana*—crying; *eta*—thus; *śuni'*—hearing; *guru*—My spiritual master; *hāsi*—smiling; *balilā*—said; *vacana*—words.

TRANSLATION

"'Chanting the holy name in ecstasy causes one to dance, laugh and cry.' When My spiritual master heard all this, he smiled and then began to speak.

PURPORT

When a disciple very perfectly makes progress in spiritual life, this gladdens the spiritual master, who then also smiles in ecstasy, thinking, "How successful my disciple has become!" He feels so glad that he smiles as he enjoys the progress of the disciple, just as a smiling parent enjoys the activities of a child who is trying to stand up or crawl perfectly.

TEXT 83

কৃষ্ণনাম-মহামন্ত্রের এই ত' স্বভাব ।
যেই জপে, তার কৃষ্ণে উপজয়ে ভাব ॥ ৮৩ ॥

kṛṣṇa-nāma-mahā-mantrera ei ta' svabhāva
yei jape, tāra kṛṣṇe upajaye bhāva

SYNONYMS

kṛṣṇa-nāma—the holy name of Kṛṣṇa; *mahā-mantrera*—of the supreme hymn; *ei ta'*—this is its; *svabhāva*—nature; *yei*—anyone; *jape*—chants; *tāra*—his; *kṛṣṇe*—unto Kṛṣṇa; *upajaye*—develops; *bhāva*—ecstasy.

TRANSLATION

"'It is the nature of the Hare Kṛṣṇa mahā-mantra that anyone who chants it immediately develops his loving ecstasy for Kṛṣṇa.

PURPORT

In *Bhagavad-gītā* it is said:

ahaṁ sarvasya prabhavo
mattaḥ sarvaṁ pravartate
iti matvā bhajante māṁ
budhā bhāva-samanvitāḥ

"I am the source of all spiritual and material worlds. Everything emanates from Me. The wise who know this perfectly engage in My devotional service and worship Me with all their hearts." (Bg. 10.8) In this verse it is explained that one who chants the Hare Kṛṣṇa *mantra* develops *bhāva,* ecstasy, which is the point at which revelation begins. It is the preliminary stage in developing one's original love for God. A neophyte disciple begins by hearing and chanting, associating with devotees and practicing the regulative principles, and thus he vanquishes all of his unwanted bad habits. In this way he develops attachment for Kṛṣṇa and cannot forget Kṛṣṇa even for a moment. *Bhāva* is almost the successful stage of spiritual life. A sincere student aurally receives the holy name from the spiritual master, and after being initiated he follows the regulative principles given by the spiritual master. When the holy name is properly served in this way, automatically the spiritual nature of the holy name spreads; in other words, the devotee becomes qualified in offenselessly chanting the holy name. When one is completely fit to chant the holy name in this way, he is eligible to make disciples all over the world, and he actually becomes *jagad-guru.* Then the entire world, under his influence, begins to chant the holy names of the Hare Kṛṣṇa *mahā-mantra.* Thus all the disciples of such a spiritual master increase in attachment for Kṛṣṇa, and therefore he sometimes cries, sometimes laughs, sometimes dances and sometimes chants. These symptoms are very prominently manifest in the body of a pure devotee. Sometimes when our students of the Kṛṣṇa consciousness movement chant and dance, even in India people are astonished to see how these foreigners have learned to chant and dance in this ecstatic fashion. As explained by Caitanya Mahāprabhu, however, actually this is not due to practice, for without extra endeavor these symptoms become manifest in anyone who sincerely chants the Hare Kṛṣṇa *mahā-mantra.*

Many fools, not knowing the transcendental nature of the Hare Kṛṣṇa *mahā-mantra,* sometimes impede our loudly chanting this *mantra,* yet one who is actually advanced in the fulfillment of chanting the Hare Kṛṣṇa *mahā-mantra* induces others to chant also. Kṛṣṇadāsa Kavirāja Gosvāmī explains, *kṛṣṇa-śakti vinā nahe tāra pravartana:* unless one receives special power of attorney from the Supreme Personality of Godhead, he cannot preach the glories of the Hare Kṛṣṇa *mahā-mantra.* As devotees propagate the Hare Kṛṣṇa *mahā-mantra,* the general population of the entire world gets the opportunity to understand the glories of the holy name. While chanting and dancing or hearing the holy name of the Lord, one automatically remembers the Supreme Personality of Godhead, and because there is no difference between the holy name and Kṛṣṇa, the chanter is immediately linked with Kṛṣṇa. Thus connected, a devotee develops his original attitude of service to the Lord. In this attitude of constantly serving Kṛṣṇa, which is called *bhāva,* one always thinks of Kṛṣṇa in many different ways. One who has attained this *bhāva* stage is no longer under the clutches of the illusory energy. When other spiritual ingredients, such as trembling, perspiration, tears, etc., are added to this *bhāva* stage, the devotee gradually attains love of Kṛṣṇa.

The holy name of Kṛṣṇa is called the *mahā-mantra.* Other *mantras* mentioned in the *Nārada-pañcarātra* are known simply as *mantras,* but the chanting of the holy name of the Lord is called the *mahā-mantra.*

TEXT 84

কৃষ্ণবিষয়ক প্রেমা —পরম পুরুষার্থ।
যার আগে তৃণতুল্য চারি পুরুষার্থ ॥ ৮৪ ॥

kṛṣṇa-viṣayaka premā——parama puruṣārtha
yāra āge tṛṇa-tulya cāri puruṣārtha

SYNONYMS

kṛṣṇa-viṣayaka—in the subject of Kṛṣṇa; *premā*—love; *parama*—the highest; *puruṣa-artha*—achievement of the goal of life; *yāra*—whose; *āge*—before; *tṛṇa-tulya*—like the grass in the street; *cāri*—four; *puruṣa-artha*—achievements.

TRANSLATION

"'Religiosity, economic development, sense gratification and liberation are known as the four goals of life, but before love of Godhead, the fifth and highest goal, these appear as insignificant as straw in the street.

PURPORT

While chanting the holy name of the Lord, one should not desire the material advancements represented by economic development, religiosity, sense gratification and ultimately liberation from the material world. As stated by Caitanya Mahāprabhu, the highest perfection in life is to develop one's love for Kṛṣṇa (*premā pumartho mahān śrī-caitanya-mahāprabhor matam idam*). When we compare love of Godhead with religiosity, economic development, sense gratification and liberation, we can understand that these achievements may be desirable objectives for *bubhukṣus,* or those who desire to enjoy this material world, and *mumukṣus,* or those who desire liberation from it, but they are very insignificant in the eyes of a pure devotee who has developed *bhāva,* the preliminary stage of love of Godhead.

Dharma (religiosity), *artha* (economic development), *kāma* (sense gratification) and *mokṣa* (liberation) are the four principles of religion which pertain to the material world. Therefore in the beginning of *Śrīmad-Bhāgavatam* it is declared, *dharmaḥ projjhita-kaitavo'tra:* cheating religious systems in terms of these four material principles are completely discarded from *Śrīmad-Bhāgavatam,* for *Śrīmad-Bhāgavatam* teaches only how to develop one's dormant love of God. *Bhagavad-gītā* is the preliminary study of *Śrīmad-Bhāgavatam,* and therefore it ends with the words, *sarva-dharmān parityajya mām ekaṁ śaraṇaṁ vraja:* "Abandon all varieties of religion and just surrender unto Me." (Bg. 18.66) To adopt this means, one should reject all ideas of religiosity, economic development, sense gratification and liberation and fully engage in the service of the Lord, which is transcendental to these four principles. Love of Godhead is the original function of the spirit soul, and it is as eternal as the soul and the Supreme Personality of Godhead. This eternity is called *sanātana.* When one revives his loving service to the Supreme Personality of Godhead, it should be understood that he has been successful in achieving the desired goal of his life. At that time everything is automatically done by the mercy of the holy name, and the devotee automatically advances in his spiritual progress.

TEXT 85

পঞ্চম পুরুষার্থ–প্রেমানন্দামৃতসিন্ধু ।
মোক্ষাদি আনন্দ যার নহে এক বিন্দু ॥ ৮৫ ॥

pañcama puruṣārtha—premānandāmṛta-sindhu
mokṣādi ānanda yāra nahe eka bindu

SYNONYMS

pañcama—fifth; *puruṣa-artha*—goal of life; *prema-ānanda*—the spiritual bliss of love of Godhead; *amṛta*—eternal; *sindhu*—ocean; *mokṣa-ādi*—liberation and other principles of religiosity; *ānanda*—pleasures derived from them; *yāra*—whose; *nahe*—never comparable; *eka*—one; *bindu*—drop.

TRANSLATION

"'For a devotee who has actually developed bhāva, the pleasure derived from dharma, artha, kāma and mokṣa appears like a drop in the presence of the sea.

TEXT 86

কৃষ্ণনামের ফল—'প্রেমা', সর্বশাস্ত্রে কয়।
ভাগ্যে সেই প্রেমা তোমায় করিল উদয় ॥ ৮৬ ॥

kṛṣṇa-nāmera phala—'premā', sarva-śāstre kaya
bhāgye sei premā tomāya karila udaya

SYNONYMS

kṛṣṇa-nāmera—of the holy name of the Lord; *phala*—result; *premā*—love of Godhead; *sarva*—in all; *śāstre*—revealed scriptures; *kaya*—describe; *bhāgye*—fortunately; *sei*—that; *premā*—love of Godhead; *tomāya*—Your; *karila*—has done; *udaya*—arisen.

TRANSLATION

"'The conclusion of all revealed scriptures is that one should awaken his dormant love of Godhead. You are greatly fortunate to have already done so.

TEXT 87

প্রেমার স্বভাবে করে চিত্ত-তনু ক্ষোভ।
কৃষ্ণের চরণ-প্রাপ্ত্যে উপজায় লোভ ॥ ৮৭ ॥

premāra sva-bhāve kare citta-tanu kṣobha
kṛṣṇera caraṇa-prāptye upajāya lobha

SYNONYMS

premāra—out of love of Godhead; *sva-bhāve*—by nature; *kare*—it induces; *citta*—the consciousness; *tanu*—the body; *kṣobha*—agitated; *kṛṣṇera*—of Lord Kṛṣṇa; *caraṇa*—lotus feet; *prāptye*—having obtained; *upajāya*—it so becomes; *lobha*—aspiration.

TRANSLATION

"'It is a characteristic of love of Godhead that by nature it induces transcendental symptoms in one's body and makes one more and more greedy to achieve the shelter of the lotus feet of the Lord.

TEXT 88

প্রেমার স্বভাবে ভক্ত হাসে, কান্দে, গায়।
উন্মত্ত হইয়া নাচে, ইতি-উতি ধায় ॥ ৮৮ ॥

premāra sva-bhāve bhakta hāse, kānde, gāya
unmatta ha-iyā nāce, iti-uti dhāya

SYNONYMS

premāra—by such love of Godhead; *sva-bhāve*—by nature; *bhakta*—the devotee; *hāse*—laughs; *kānde*—cries; *gāya*—chants; *unmatta*—mad; *ha-iyā*—becoming; *nāce*—dances; *iti*—here; *uti*—there; *dhāya*—moves.

TRANSLATION

"'When one actually develops love of Godhead, he naturally sometimes cries, sometimes laughs, sometimes chants and sometimes runs here and there just like a madman.

PURPORT

In this connection Bhaktisiddhānta Sarasvatī Gosvāmī says that sometimes persons who have no love of Godhead at all display ecstatic bodily symptoms. Artificially they sometimes laugh, cry and dance just like madmen, but this cannot help one progress in Kṛṣṇa consciousness. Rather, such artificial agitation of the body is to be given up when one naturally develops the necessary bodily symptoms. Actual blissful life, manifested in genuine spiritual laughing, crying and dancing, is the symptom of real advancement in Kṛṣṇa consciousness, which can be achieved by a person who always voluntarily engages in the transcendental loving service of the Lord. If one who is not yet developed imitates such symptoms artificially, he creates chaos in the spiritual life of human society.

TEXTS 89-90

স্বেদ, কম্প, রোমাঞ্চাশ্রু, গদ্গদ, বৈবর্ণ্য ।
উন্মাদ, বিষাদ, ধৈর্য, গর্ব, হর্ষ, দৈন্য ॥ ৮৯ ॥
এত ভাবে প্রেমা ভক্তগণেরে নাচায় ।
কৃষ্ণের আনন্দামৃতসাগরে ভাসায় ॥ ৯০ ॥

sveda, kampa, romāñcāśru, gadgada, vaivarṇya
unmāda, viṣāda, dhairya, garva, harṣa, dainya

eta bhāve premā bhaktagaṇere nācāya
kṛṣṇera ānandāmṛta-sāgare bhāsāya

SYNONYMS

sveda—perspiration; *kampa*—trembling; *romāñca*—standing of the hairs on the body; *aśru*—tears; *gadgada*—faltering; *vaivarṇya*—changing of bodily color; *unmāda*—madness; *viṣāda*—melancholy; *dhairya*—patience; *garva*—pride; *harṣa*—joyfulness; *dainya*—humbleness; *eta*—in many ways; *bhāve*—in ecstasy; *premā*—love of Godhead; *bhakta-gaṇere*—unto the devotees; *nācāya*—causes to dance; *kṛṣṇera*—of Lord Kṛṣṇa; *ānanda*—transcendental bliss; *amṛta*—nectar; *sāgare*—in the ocean; *bhāsāya*—floats.

TRANSLATION

"'Perspiration, trembling, standing of one's bodily hairs, tears, faltering, fading, madness, melancholy, patience, pride, joy and humility—these are various natural symptoms of ecstatic love of Godhead, which causes a devotee to dance and float in an ocean of transcendental bliss while chanting the Hare Kṛṣṇa mantra.

PURPORT

Śrīla Jīva Gosvāmī, in his *Prīti-sandarbha* (verse 66), explains this stage of love of Godhead: *bhagavat-prīti-rūpā vṛttir māyādimayī na bhavati; kintu svarūpa-śaktyānanda-rūpā, yadānanda-parādhīnaḥ śrī-bhagavān apīti.* Similarly, in the 69th verse he offers further explanation: *tad evaṁ prīter lakṣaṇaṁ citta-dravas tasya ca romaharṣādikam. kathañcij jāte'pi citta-drave romaharṣādike vā na ced āśaya-śuddhis tadāpi na bhakteḥ samyag-āvirbhāva iti jñāpitam. āśaya-śuddhir nāma cānya-tātparya-parityāgaḥ prīti-tātparyaṁ ca. ataevānimittā svābhāvikī ceti tad viśeṣaṇam.* Transcendental love of Godhead is not under the jurisdiction of the material energy, for it is the transcendental bliss and pleasure potency of the Supreme Personality of Godhead. Since the Supreme Lord is also under the influence of transcendental bliss, when one comes in touch with such bliss in love of Godhead, one's heart melts, and the symptoms of this are standing of the hairs on end, etc. Sometimes a person thus melts and manifests these transcendental symptoms yet at the same time is not well behaved in his personal transactions. This indicates that he has not yet reached complete perfection in devotional life. In other words, a devotee who dances in ecstasy but after dancing and crying appears to be attracted to material affairs has not yet reached the perfection of devotional service, which is called *āśaya-śuddhi,* or the perfection of existence. One who attains the perfection of existence is completely averse to material enjoyment and engrossed in transcendental love of Godhead. It is therefore to be concluded that the ecstatic symptoms of *āśaya-śuddhi* are visible when a devotee's service has no material cause and is purely spiritual in nature. These are characteristics of transcendental love of Godhead, as stated in *Śrīmad-Bhāgavatam:*

sa vai puṁsāṁ paro dharmo
yato bhaktir adhokṣaje
ahaituky apratihatā
yayātmā suprasīdati

"That religion is best which causes its followers to become ecstatic in love of God which is unmotivated and free from material impediments, for this only can completely satisfy the self." (*Bhāg.* 1.2.6)

TEXT 91

ভাল হৈল, পাইলে তুমি পরমপুরুষার্থ।
তোমার প্রেমেতে আমি হৈলাঙ কৃতার্থ॥ ৯১ ॥

bhāla haila, pāile tumi parama-puruṣārtha
tomāra premete āmi hailāṅ kṛtārtha

SYNONYMS

bhāla haila—let it be good; *pāile*—You have gotten; *tumi*—You; *parama-puruṣārtha*—superexcellent goal of life; *tomāra*—Your; *premete*—by development in love of Godhead; *āmi*—I; *hailāṅ*—become; *kṛta-artha*—very much obliged.

TRANSLATION

"'It is very good, my dear child, that You have attained the supreme goal of life by developing love of Godhead. Thus You have pleased me very much, and I am very much obliged to You.

PURPORT

According to revealed scriptures, if a spiritual master can convert even one soul into a perfectly pure devotee, his mission in life is fulfilled. Śrīla Bhaktisiddhānta Sarasvatī Ṭhākura always used to say, "Even at the expense of all the properties, temples and *maṭhas* that I have, if I could convert even one person into a pure devotee, my mission would be fulfilled." It is very difficult, however, to understand the science of Kṛṣṇa, not to speak of developing love of Godhead. Therefore if by the grace of Lord Caitanya and the spiritual master a disciple attains the standard of pure devotional service, the spiritual master is very happy. The spiritual master is not actually happy if the disciple brings him money, but when he sees that a disciple is following the regulative principles and advancing in spiritual life, he is very glad and feels obliged to such an advanced disciple.

TEXT 92

নাচ, গাও, ভক্তসঙ্গে কর সংকীর্তন ।
কৃষ্ণনাম উপদেশি' তার' সর্বজন ॥ ৯২ ॥

nāca, gāo, bhakta-saṅge kara saṅkīrtana
kṛṣṇa-nāma upadeśi' tāra' sarva-jana

SYNONYMS

nāca—go on dancing; *gāo*—chant; *bhakta-saṅge*—in the society of devotees; *kara*—continue; *saṅkīrtana*—chanting of the holy name in assembly; *kṛṣṇa-nāma*—the holy name of Kṛṣṇa; *upadeśi'*—by instructing; *tāra'*—deliver; *sarva-jana*—all fallen souls.

TRANSLATION

"'My dear child, continue dancing, chanting and performing saṅkīrtana in association with devotees. Furthermore, go out and preach the value of

chanting Kṛṣṇa-nāma, for by this process You will be able to deliver all fallen souls.'

PURPORT

It is another ambition of the spiritual master to see his disciples not only chant, dance and follow the regulative principles but also preach the *saṅkīrtana* movement to others in order to deliver them, for the Kṛṣṇa consciousness movement is based on the principle that one should become as perfect as possible in devotional service oneself and also preach the cult for others' benefit. There are two classes of unalloyed devotees—namely, *goṣṭhy-ānandīs* and *bhajanānandīs. Bhajanānandī* refers to one who is satisfied to cultivate devotional service for himself, and *goṣṭhy-ānandī* is one who is not satisfied simply to become perfect himself but wants to see others also take advantage of the holy name of the Lord and advance in spiritual life. The outstanding example is Prahlāda Mahārāja. When he was offered a benediction by Lord Nṛsiṁhadeva, Prahlāda Mahārāja said:

naivodvije para duratyaya-vaitaraṇyās
tvad-vīrya-gāyana-mahāmṛta-magna-cittaḥ
śoce tato vimukha-cetasa indriyārtha-
māyā-sukhāya bharam udvahato vimūḍhān

"My dear Lord, I have no problems and want no benediction from You because I am quite satisfied to chant Your holy name. This is sufficient for me because whenever I chant I immediately merge in an ocean of transcendental bliss. I only lament to see others bereft of Your love. They are rotting in material activities for transient material pleasure and spoiling their lives toiling all day and night simply for sense gratification, with no attachment for love of Godhead. I am simply lamenting for them and devising various plans to deliver them from the clutches of *māyā.*" (*Bhāg.* 7.9.43)

Śrīla Bhaktisiddhānta Sarasvatī Ṭhākura explains in his *Anubhāṣya,* "A person who has attracted the attention of the spiritual master by his sincere service likes to dance and chant with similarly developed Kṛṣṇa conscious devotees. The spiritual master authorizes such a devotee to deliver fallen souls in all parts of the world. Those who are not advanced prefer to chant the Hare Kṛṣṇa *mantra* in a solitary place." Such activities constitute, in the language of Śrīla Bhaktisiddhānta Sarasvatī Ṭhākura, a type of cheating process in the sense that they imitate the activities of exalted personalities like Haridāsa Ṭhākura. One should not attempt to imitate such exalted devotees. Rather, everyone should endeavor to preach the cult of Śrī Caitanya Mahāprabhu in all parts of the world and thus become successful in spiritual life. One who is not very expert in preaching may chant in a secluded place, avoiding bad association, but for one who is actually advanced, preaching and meeting people who are not engaged in devotional service are not disadvantages. A devotee gives the nondevotees his association but is not affected by their misbehavior. Thus by the activities of a pure devotee even those who are bereft of love of Godhead get a chance to become devotees of the Lord one day. In this connection

Śrīla Bhaktisiddhānta Sarasvatī Ṭhākura advises that one discuss the verse in *Śrīmad-Bhāgavatam, naitat samācarej jātu manasāpi hy anīśvaraḥ* (10.33.31), and the following verse in *Bhakti-rasāmṛta-sindhu:*

anāsaktasya viṣayān yathārham upayuñjataḥ
nirbandhaḥ kṛṣṇa-sambandhe yuktaṁ vairāgyam ucyate
(B.r.s. 1.2.255)

One should not imitate the activities of great personalities. One should be detached from material enjoyment and should accept everything in connection with Kṛṣṇa's service.

TEXT 93

এত বলি' এক শ্লোক শিখাইল মোরে ।
ভাগবতের সার এই বলে বারে বারে ॥ ৯৩ ॥

eta bali' eka śloka śikhāila more
bhāgavatera sāra ei—bale vāre vāre

SYNONYMS

eta bali'—saying this; *eka*—one; *śloka*—verse; *śikhāila*—has taught; *more*—unto Me; *bhāgavatera*—of *Śrīmad-Bhāgavatam*; *sāra*—essence; *ei*—this is; *bale*—he said; *vāre vāre*—again and again.

TRANSLATION

"Saying this, My spiritual master taught Me one verse from Śrīmad-Bhāgavatam. It is the essence of all the Bhāgavatam's instructions; therefore he instructed Me this verse again and again.

PURPORT

This verse from *Śrīmad-Bhāgavatam* (11.2.40) was spoken by Śrī Nārada Muni to Vasudeva to teach him about *Bhāgavata-dharma.* Vasudeva had already achieved the result of *Bhāgavata-dharma* because Lord Kṛṣṇa appeared in his house as his son, yet in order to teach others, he desired to hear from Śrī Nārada Muni to be enlightened in the process of *Bhāgavata-dharma.* This is the humbleness of a great devotee.

TEXT 94

এবংব্রতঃ স্বপ্রিয়নামকীর্ত্যা
জাতানুরাগো দ্রুতচিত্ত উচ্চৈঃ ।
হসত্যথো রোদিতি রৌতি গায়-
ত্যুন্মাদবন্নৃত্যতি লোকবাহ্যঃ ॥ ৯৪ ॥

evaṁvrataḥ sva-priya-nāma-kīrtyā
jātānurāgo druta-citta uccaiḥ
hasaty atho roditi rauti gāyaty
unmādavan nṛtyati loka-bāhyaḥ

SYNONYMS

evaṁvrataḥ—when one thus engages in the vow to chant and dance; *sva*—own; *priya*—very dear; *nāma*—holy name; *kīrtyā*—by chanting; *jāta*—in this way develops; *anurāgaḥ*—attachment; *druta-cittaḥ*—very eagerly; *uccaiḥ*—loudly; *hasati*—laughs; *atho*—also; *roditi*—cries; *rauti*—becomes agitated; *gāyati*—chants; *unmādavat*—like a madman; *nṛtyati*—dancing; *loka-bāhyaḥ*—without caring for outsiders.

TRANSLATION

"'When a person is actually advanced and takes pleasure in chanting the holy name of the Lord, who is very dear to him, he is agitated and loudly chants the holy name. He also laughs, cries, becomes agitated and chants just like a madman, not caring for outsiders.'

TEXTS 95-96

এই তাঁর বাক্যে আমি দৃঢ় বিশ্বাস ধরি' ।
নিরন্তর কৃষ্ণনাম সংকীর্তন করি ॥ ৯৫ ॥
সেই কৃষ্ণনাম কভু গাওয়ায়, নাচায় ।
গাহি, নাচি নাহি আমি আপন-ইচ্ছায় ॥ ৯৬ ॥

ei tāṅra vākye āmi dṛḍha viśvāsa dhari'
nirantara kṛṣṇa-nāma saṅkīrtana kari

sei kṛṣṇa-nāma kabhu gāoyāya, nācāya
gāhi, nāci nāhi āmi āpana-icchāya

SYNONYMS

ei—this; *tāṅra*—his (My spiritual master's); *vākye*—in the words of; *āmi*—I; *dṛḍha*—firm; *viśvāsa*—faith; *dhari'*—depend; *nirantara*—always; *kṛṣṇa-nāma*—the holy name of Lord Kṛṣṇa; *saṅkīrtana*—chanting; *kari*—continue; *sei*—that; *kṛṣṇa-nāma*—the holy name of Lord Kṛṣṇa; *kabhu*—sometimes; *gāoyāya*—causes Me to chant; *nācāya*—causes Me to dance; *gāhi*—by chanting; *nāci*—dancing; *nāhi*—not; *āmi*—Myself; *āpana*—own; *icchāya*—will.

TRANSLATION

"I firmly believe in these words of My spiritual master, and therefore I always chant the holy name of the Lord, alone and in the association of devotees. That holy name of Lord Kṛṣṇa sometimes causes Me to chant and dance, and therefore I chant and dance. Please do not think that I intentionally do it. I do it automatically.

PURPORT

A person who cannot keep his faith in the words of his spiritual master but acts independently never receives the authority to chant the holy name of the Lord. It is said in the *Vedas:*

yasya deve parā bhaktir yathā deve tathā gurau
tasyaite kathitā hy arthāḥ prakāśante mahātmanaḥ

"Only unto those great souls who have implicit faith in both the Lord and the spiritual master are all the imports of Vedic knowledge automatically revealed." This Vedic injunction is very important, and Śrī Caitanya Mahāprabhu supported it by His personal behavior. Believing in the words of His spiritual master, He introduced the *saṅkīrtana* movement, just as the present Kṛṣṇa consciousness movement was started with belief in the words of our spiritual master. He wanted to preach, we believed in his words and tried somehow or other to fulfill them, and now this movement has become successful all over the world. Therefore faith in the words of the spiritual master and in the Supreme Personality of Godhead is the secret of success. Śrī Caitanya Mahāprabhu never disobeyed the orders of His spiritual master and stopped propagating the *saṅkīrtana* movement. Śrī Bhaktisiddhānta Sarasvatī Gosvami, at the time of his passing away, ordered all his disciples to work conjointly to preach the mission of Caitanya Mahāprabhu all over the world. Later, however, some self-interested, foolish disciples disobeyed his orders. Each one of them wanted to become head of the mission, and they fought in the courts, neglecting the order of the spiritual master, and the entire mission was defeated. We are not proud of this; however, the truth must be explained. We believed in the words of our spiritual master and started in a humble way—in a helpless way—but due to the spiritual force of the order of the supreme authority, this movement has become successful.

It is to be understood that when Śrī Caitanya Mahāprabhu chanted and danced, He did so by the influence of the pleasure potency of the spiritual world. Śrī Caitanya Mahāprabhu never considered the holy name of the Lord to be a material vibration, nor does any pure devotee mistake the chanting of the Hare Kṛṣṇa *mantra* to be a material musical manifestation. Lord Caitanya never tried to be the master of the holy name; rather He taught us how to be servants of the holy name. If one chants the holy name of the Lord just to make a show, not knowing the secret of success, he may increase his bile secretion, but he will never attain perfection in chanting the holy name. Śrī Caitanya Mahāprabhu presented himself in this way: "I am a great fool and do not have knowledge of right and wrong. In order to understand the real meaning of *Vedānta-sūtra*, I never followed the explanation of the Śaṅkara-sampradāya or Māyāvādī *sannyāsīs*. I'm very much afraid of the illogical arguments of the Māyāvādī philosophers. Therefore I think I have no authority regarding their explanations of *Vedānta-sūtra.* I firmly believe that simply chanting the holy name of the Lord can remove all misconceptions of the material world. I believe that simply by chanting the holy name of the Lord one can attain the shelter of the lotus feet of the Lord. In this age of quarrel and disagreement, the chanting of the holy names is the only way to liberation from the material clutches.

"By chanting the holy name," Lord Caitanya continued, "I became almost mad. However, after inquiring from My spiritual master I have come to the conclusion that instead of striving for achievement in the four principles of religiosity *(dharma),* economic development *(artha),* sense gratification *(kāma)* and liberation *(mokṣa),* it is better if somehow or other one develops transcendental love of Godhead. That is the greatest success in life. One who has attained love of Godhead chants and dances by his nature, not caring for the public." This stage of life is known as *bhāgavata-jīvana,* or the life of a devotee.

Śrī Caitanya Mahāprabhu continued, "I never chanted and danced to make an artificial show. I dance and chant because I firmly believe in the words of My spiritual master. Although the Māyāvādī philosophers do not like this chanting and dancing, I nevertheless perform it on the strength of his words. Therefore it is to be concluded that I deserve very little credit for these activities of chanting and dancing, for they are being done automatically by the grace of the Supreme Personality of Godhead."

TEXT 97

কৃষ্ণনামে যে আনন্দসিন্ধু-আস্বাদন ।
ব্রহ্মানন্দ তার আগে খাতোদক-সম ॥ ৯৭ ॥

kṛṣṇa-nāme ye ānanda-sindhu-āsvādana
brahmānanda tāra āge khātodaka-sama

SYNONYMS

kṛṣṇa-nāme—in the holy name of the Lord; *ye*—which; *ānanda*—transcendental bliss; *sindhu*—ocean; *āsvādana*—tasting; *brahmānanda*—the transcendental bliss of impersonal understanding; *tāra*—its; *āge*—in front; *khāta-udaka*—shallow water in the canals; *sama*—like.

TRANSLATION

"Compared to the ocean of transcendental bliss which is tasted by chanting the Hare Kṛṣṇa mantra, the pleasure derived from impersonal Brahman realization [brahmānanda] is like the shallow water in a canal.

PURPORT

In the *Bhakti-rasāmṛta-sindhu* it is stated:

brahmānando bhaved eṣa
cet parārddha-guṇīkṛtaḥ
naiti bhakti-sukhāmbhodheḥ
paramāṇu-tulām api

"If *brahmānanda,* the transcendental bliss derived from understanding impersonal Brahman, were multiplied a million times, such a quantity of *brahmānanda* could not compare with even an atomic portion of the pleasure relished in pure devotional service." (B.r.s. 1.1.38)

TEXT 98

ত্বৎসাক্ষাৎকরণাহ্লাদ-বিশুদ্ধাব্ধিস্থিতস্য মে ।
সুখানি গোষ্পদায়ন্তে ব্রাহ্মাণ্যপি জগদ্গুরো ॥ ৯৮ ॥

tvat-sākṣātkaraṇāhlāda-
viśuddhābdhi-sthitasya me
sukhāni goṣpadāyante
brāhmāṇy api jagad-guro

SYNONYMS

tvat—Your; *sākṣāt*—meeting; *karaṇa*—such action; *āhlāda*—pleasure; *viśuddha*—spiritually purified; *abdhi*—ocean; *sthitasya*—being situated; *me*—by me; *sukhāni*—happiness; *goṣpadāyante*—a small hole created by the hoof of a calf; *brāhmāṇi*—the pleasure derived from impersonal Brahman understanding; *api*—also; *jagat-guro*—O master of the universe.

TRANSLATION

"'My dear Lord, O master of the universe, since I have directly seen You, my transcendental bliss has taken the shape of a great ocean. Being situated in that ocean, I now realize all other so-called happiness to be like the water contained in the hoofprint of a calf.'"

PURPORT

The transcendental bliss enjoyed in pure devotional service is like an ocean, whereas material happiness and even the happiness to be derived from the realization of impersonal Brahman are just like the water in the hoofprint of a calf. This is a verse from the *Hari-bhakti-sudhodaya* (14.36).

TEXT 99

প্রভুর মিষ্টবাক্য শুনি' সন্ন্যাসীর গণ ।
চিত্ত ফিরি' গেল, কহে মধুর বচন ॥ ৯৯ ॥

prabhura miṣṭa-vākya śuni' sannyāsīra gaṇa
citta phiri' gela, kahe madhura vacana

SYNONYMS

prabhura—of the Lord; *miṣṭa-vākya*—sweet words; *śuni'*—after hearing; *sannyāsīra gaṇa*—all the groups of *sannyāsīs; citta*—consciousness; *phiri'*—moved; *gela*—went; *kahe*—said; *madhura*—pleasing; *vacana*—words.

TRANSLATION

After hearing Lord Śrī Caitanya Mahāprabhu, all the Māyāvādī sannyāsīs were moved. Their minds changed, and thus they spoke with pleasing words.

PURPORT

The Māyāvādī *sannyāsīs* met Caitanya Mahāprabhu at Vārāṇasī to criticize the Lord regarding His participation in the *saṅkīrtana* movement, which they did not like. This demonic nature of opposition to the *saṅkīrtana* movement perpetually exists. As it existed in the time of Śrī Caitanya Mahāprabhu, similarly it existed long before that, even in the time of Prahlāda Mahārāja. He used to chant in *saṅkīrtana* although his father did not like it, and that was the reason for misunderstanding between the father and son. In *Bhagavad-gītā* the Lord says:

na māṁ duṣkṛtino mūḍhāḥ
prapadyante narādhamāḥ
māyayāpahṛta-jñānā
āsuraṁ bhāvam āśritāḥ

"Those miscreants who are grossly foolish, lowest among mankind, whose knowledge is stolen by illusion, and who partake of the atheistic nature of demons, do not surrender unto Me." (Bg. 7.15) The Māyāvādī *sannyāsīs* are *āsuraṁ bhāvam āśritāḥ,* which means that they have taken the path of the *asuras* (demons) who do not believe in the existence of the form of the Lord. The Māyāvādīs say that the ultimate source of everything is impersonal, and in this way they deny the existence of God. Saying that there is no God is direct denial of God, and saying that God exists but has no head, legs and hands and cannot speak, hear or eat is a negative way of denying His existence. A person who cannot see is called blind, one who cannot walk can be called lame, one who has no hands can be called helpless, one who cannot speak can be called dumb, and one who cannot hear can be called deaf. The Māyāvādīs' proposition that God has no legs, no eyes, no ears and no hands is an indirect way of insulting Him by defining Him as blind, deaf, dumb, lame, helpless, etc. Therefore although they present themselves as great Vedāntists, they are factually *māyayāpahṛta-jñāna;* in other words, they seem to be very learned scholars, but the essence of their knowledge has been taken away.

Impersonalist Māyāvādīs always try to defy Vaiṣṇavas because Vaiṣṇavas accept the Supreme Personality as the supreme cause and want to serve Him, talk with Him and see Him, just as the Lord is also eager to see His devotees and talk, eat and dance with them. These personal exchanges of love do not appeal to the Māyāvādī *sannyāsīs.* Therefore the original purpose of the Māyāvādī *sannyāsīs* of Benares in meeting Caitanya Mahāprabhu was to defeat His personal conception of God. Śrī Caitanya Mahāprabhu, however, as a preacher, turned the minds of the Māyāvādī *sannyāsīs.* They were melted by the sweet words of Śrī Caitanya Mahāprabhu and thus became friendly and spoke to Him also in sweet words. Similarly, all preachers will have to meet opponents, but they should not make them more inimical. They are already enemies, and if we talk with them harshly or impolitely their enmity will merely increase. We should therefore follow in the footsteps of Lord Caitanya

Mahāprabhu as far as possible and try to convince the opposition by quoting from the *śāstras* and presenting the conclusion of the *ācāryas*. It is in this way that we should try to defeat all the enemies of the Lord.

TEXT 100

যে কিছু কহিলে তুমি, সব সত্য হয়।
কৃষ্ণপ্রেমা সেই পায়, যার ভাগ্যোদয় ॥ ১০০ ॥

ye kichu kahile tumi, saba satya haya
kṛṣṇa-premā sei pāya, yāra bhāgyodaya

SYNONYMS

ye—all; *kichu*—that; *kahile*—You spoke; *tumi*—You; *saba*—everything; *satya*—truth; *haya*—becomes; *kṛṣṇa-premā*—love of Godhead; *sei*—anyone; *pāya*—achieves; *yāra*—whose; *bhāgya-udaya*—fortune is now awakened.

TRANSLATION

"Dear Śrī Caitanya Mahāprabhu, what You have said is all true. Only one who is favored by fortune attains love of Godhead.

PURPORT

One who is actually very fortunate can begin Kṛṣṇa consciousness, as stated by Caitanya Mahāprabhu to Śrīla Rūpa Gosvāmī:

brahmāṇḍa bhramite kona bhāgyavān jīva
guru-kṛṣṇa-prasāde pāya bhakti-latā-bīja
(Cc. *Madhya* 19.151)

There are millions of living entities who have become conditioned by the laws of material nature, and they are wandering throughout the planetary systems of this universe in different bodily forms. Among them, one who is fortunate meets a bona fide spiritual master by the grace of Kṛṣṇa and comes to understand the meaning of devotional service. By discharging devotional service under the direction of the bona fide spiritual master or *ācārya,* he develops love of Godhead. One whose love of Godhead (*Kṛṣṇa-premā*) is awakened and who thus becomes a devotee of the inconceivable Supreme Personality of Godhead is to be considered extremely fortunate. The Māyāvādī *sannyāsīs* admitted this fact to Śrī Caitanya Mahāprabhu. It is not easy for one to become a Kṛṣṇa conscious person, but by the mercy of Śrī Caitanya Mahāprabhu it can be possible, as will be proven in the course of this narration.

TEXT 101

কৃষ্ণে ভক্তি কর ইহায় সবার সন্তোষ।
বেদান্ত না শুন কেনে, তার কিবা দোষ ॥ ১০১ ॥

kṛṣṇe bhakti kara——ihāya sabāra santoṣa
vedānta nā śuna kene, tāra kibā doṣa

SYNONYMS

kṛṣṇe—unto Kṛṣṇa; *bhakti*—devotional service; *kara*—do; *ihāya*—in this matter; *sabāra*—of everyone; *santoṣa*—there is satisfaction; *vedānta*—the philosophy of *Vedānta-sūtra; nā*—do not; *śuna*—hear; *kene*—why; *tāra*—of the philosophy; *kibā*—what is; *doṣa*—fault.

TRANSLATION

"Dear sir, there is no objection to Your being a great devotee of Lord Kṛṣṇa. Everyone is satisfied with this. But why do You avoid discussion on the Vedānta-sūtra? What is the fault in it?"

PURPORT

Śrīla Bhaktisiddhānta Sarasvatī Ṭhākura comments in this connection, "Māyāvādī *sannyāsīs* accept that the commentary by Śrī Śaṅkarācārya known as *Śārīraka-bhāṣya* gives the real meaning of *Vedānta-sūtra.* In other words, Māyāvādī *sannyāsīs* accept the meanings expressed in the explanations of *Vedānta-sūtra* by Śaṅkarācārya, which are based on monism. Thus they explain *Vedānta-sūtra*, the *Upaniṣads* and all such Vedic literatures in their own impersonal way." The great Māyāvādī *sannyāsī* Sadānanda Yogīndra has written a book known as *Vedānta-sāra* in which he writes:

vedānto nāma upaniṣat-pramāṇam
tad-upakārīṇi śārīraka-sūtrādīni ca

According to Sadānanda Yogīndra, the *Vedānta* and *Upaniṣads,* as presented by Śrī Śaṅkarācārya in his *Śārīraka-bhāṣya* commentary, are the only sources of Vedic evidence. Actually, however, *Vedānta* refers to the essence of Vedic knowledge, and it is not a fact that there is nothing more than Śaṅkarācārya's *Śārīraka-bhāṣya.* There are other *Vedānta* commentaries written by Vaiṣṇava *ācāryas*, none of whom follow Śrī Śaṅkarācārya or accept the imaginative commentary of his school. Their commentaries are based on the philosophy of duality. Monist philosophers like Śaṅkarācārya and his followers want to establish that God and the living entity are one, and instead of worshiping the Supreme Personality of Godhead they present themselves as God. They want to be worshiped as God by others. Such persons do not accept the philosophies of the Vaiṣṇava *ācāryas,* which are known as *śuddhādvaita* (purified monism), *śuddha-dvaita* (purified dualism), *viśiṣṭādvaita* (specific monism), *dvaitādvaita* (monism and dualism) and *acintya-bhedābheda* (inconceivable oneness and difference). Māyāvādīs do not discuss these philosophies, for they are firmly convinced of their own philosophy of *kevalādvaita,* exclusive monism. Accepting this system of philosophy as the pure understanding of *Vedānta-sūtra,* they believe that Kṛṣṇa has a body made of material elements and that the activities of loving service to Kṛṣṇa are sentimentality. They are known as Māyāvādīs because according to their opinion Kṛṣṇa has a body which is made of *māyā,* and the loving service of the

Lord executed by devotees is also *māyā.* They consider such devotional service to be an aspect of fruitive activities (*karma-kāṇḍa*). According to their view, *bhakti* consists of mental speculation or sometimes meditation. This is the difference between the Māyāvādī and Vaiṣṇava philosophies.

TEXT 102

এত শুনি' হাসি' প্রভু বলিলা বচন ।
দুঃখ না মানহ যদি, করি নিবেদন ॥ ১০২ ॥

eta śuni' hāsi' prabhu balilā vacana
duḥkha nā mānaha yadi, kari nivedana

SYNONYMS

eta—thus; *śuni'*—hearing; *hāsi'*—smiling; *prabhu*— Lord Caitanya Mahāprabhu; *balilā*—said; *vacana*—His words; *duḥkha*—unhappy; *nā*—do not; *mānaha*—take it; *yadi*—if; *kari*—I say; *nivedana*—something unto you.

TRANSLATION

After hearing the Māyāvādī sannyāsīs speak in that way, Lord Caitanya Mahāprabhu smiled slightly and said, "My dear sirs, if you don't mind I can say something to you regarding Vedānta philosophy."

PURPORT

The Māyāvādī *sannyāsīs,* appreciating Lord Caitanya Mahāprabhu, inquired from Him why He did not discuss Vedānta philosophy. Actually, however, the entire system of Vaiṣṇava activities is based on Vedānta philosophy. Vaiṣṇavas do not neglect Vedānta, but they do not care to understand Vedānta on the basis of the *Śārīraka-bhāṣya* commentary. Therefore, to clarify the situation, Lord Śrī Caitanya Mahāprabhu, with the permission of the Māyāvādī *sannyāsīs,* wanted to speak regarding Vedānta philosophy. The Vaiṣṇavas are by far the greatest philosophers in the world, and the greatest among them was Śrīla Jīva Gosvāmī Prabhu, whose philosophy was again presented less than four hundred years later by Śrīla Bhaktisiddhānta Sarasvatī Ṭhākura Mahārāja. Therefore one must know very well that Vaiṣṇava philosophers are not sentimentalists or cheap devotees like the *sahajiyās.* All the Vaiṣṇava *ācāryas* were vastly learned scholars who understood Vedānta philosophy fully, for unless one knows Vedānta philosophy he cannot be an *ācārya.* To be accepted as an *ācārya* among Indian transcendentalists who follow the Vedic principles, one must become a vastly learned scholar in Vedānta philosophy, either by studying it or hearing it.

Bhakti develops in pursuance of Vedānta philosophy. This is stated in *Śrīmad-Bhāgavatam* (1.2.12):

tac chraddadhānā munayo
jñāna-vairāgya-yuktayā

paśyanty ātmani cātmānaṁ
bhaktyā śruta-gṛhītayā

The words *bhaktyā śruta-gṛhītayā* in this verse are very important, for they indicate that *bhakti* must be based upon the philosophy of the *Upaniṣads* and *Vedānta-sūtra.* Śrīla Rūpa Gosvāmī said:

śruti-smṛti-purāṇādi-
pañcarātra-vidhiṁ vinā
aikāntikī harer bhaktir
utpātāyaiva kalpate

"Devotional service performed without reference to the *Vedas, Purāṇas, Pañcarātras,* etc., must be considered sentimentalism, and it causes nothing but disturbance to society." There are different grades of Vaiṣṇavas *(kaniṣṭha-adhikārī, madhyama-adhikārī, uttama-adhikārī),* but to be a *madhyama-adhikārī* preacher one must be a learned scholar in *Vedānta-sūtra* and other Vedic literature because when *bhakti-yoga* develops on the basis of Vedānta philosophy it is factual and steady. In this connection we may quote the translation and purport of the verse mentioned above (*Śrīmad-Bhāgavatam,* 1.2.12):

TRANSLATION

That Absolute Truth is realized by the seriously inquisitive student or sage who is well equipped with knowledge and who has become detached by rendering devotional service and hearing the *Vedānta-śruti.*

PURPORT

The Absolute Truth is realized in full by the process of devotional service to the Lord Vāsudeva or the Personality of Godhead who is the full-fledged Absolute Truth. Brahman is His transcendental bodily effulgence, and Paramātmā is His partial representation. As such, Brahman or Paramātmā realization of the Absolute Truth is but a partial realization. There are four different types of living beings, the *karmīs,* the *jñānīs,* the *yogīs* and the devotees. The *karmīs* are materialistic, whereas the other three are transcendental. The first-class transcendentalists are the devotees who have realized the Supreme Person. The second-class transcendentalists are those who have partially realized the plenary portion of the absolute person. And the third-class transcendentalists are those who have barely realized the spiritual focus of the absolute person. As stated in the *Bhagavad-gītā* and other Vedic literatures, the Supreme Person is realized by devotional service, which is backed by full knowledge and detachment from the material association. We have already discussed the point that devotional service is followed by knowledge and detachment from material association. As Brahman and Paramātmā realization are imperfect realizations of the Absolute Truth, so the means of realizing Brahman and Paramātmā, i.e., the paths of *jñāna* and *yoga,* are also imperfect means of realizing the Absolute Truth. Devotional service, which is based on the foreground of full knowledge combined with detachment from material association fixed up on the aural reception of the *Vedānta-śruti,* is the only perfect method of realizing the Absolute Truth by the seriously inquisitive student. Devotional service is not, therefore, meant for the less intelligent class of transcendentalist.

There are three classes of devotees, namely first, second and third class. The third-class devotees, or the neophytes, who have no knowledge nor are detached from the material association, but who are simply attracted by the preliminary processes of worshiping the Deity in the temple, are called material devotees. Material devotees are more attached to material benefit than transcendental profit. Therefore, one has to make definite progress from the position of material devotional service to the second-class devotional position. In the second-class position, the devotee can see four principles in the devotional line, namely the Personality of Godhead, His devotees, the ignorant and the envious. One has to raise himself at least to the stage of a second-class devotee and thus become eligible to know the Absolute Truth.

A third-class devotee, therefore, has to receive the instructions of devotional service from the authoritative sources of *Bhāgavatam.* The number one *Bhāgavatam* is the established personality of devotee, and the other *Bhāgavatam* is the message of Godhead. The third-class devotee has, therefore, to go to the personality of devotee in order to learn the instructions of devotional service. Such a personality of devotee is not a professional man who earns his livelihood by the business of *Bhāgavatam.* Such a devotee must be a representative of Śukadeva Gosvāmī, like Sūta Gosvāmī, and must preach the cult of devotional service for the all-around benefit of all people. A neophyte devotee has very little taste for hearing from the authorities. Such a neophyte devotee makes a show of hearing from the professional man to satisfy his senses. This sort of hearing and chanting has spoiled the whole thing, so one should be very careful about the faulty process. The holy messages of Godhead, as inculcated in the *Bhagavad-gītā* or in the *Śrīmad-Bhāgavatam,* are undoubtedly transcendental subjects, but even though they are so, such transcendental matters are not to be received from the professional man who spoils them like the serpent spoils the milk simply by the touch of his tongue.

A sincere devotee must, therefore, be prepared to hear the Vedic literature like the *Upaniṣads, Vedānta* and other literatures left by the previous authorities or Gosvāmīs, for the benefit of his progress. Without hearing such literatures, one cannot make actual progress. And without hearing and following the instructions, the show of devotional service becomes worthless and therefore a sort of disturbance in the path of devotional service. Unless, therefore, devotional service is established on the principles of *śruti, smṛti, purāṇa* or *pañcarātra* authorities, the make-show of devotional service should at once be rejected. An unauthorized devotee should never be recognized as a pure devotee. By assimilation of such messages from the Vedic literatures, one can see the all-pervading localized aspect of the Personality of Godhead within his own self constantly. This is called *samādhi.*

TEXT 103

ইহা শুনি' বলে সর্ব সন্ন্যাসীর গণ ।
তোমাকে দেখিয়ে যৈছে সাক্ষাৎ নারায়ণ ॥ ১০৩ ॥

ihā śuni' bale sarva sannyāsīra gaṇa
tomāke dekhiye yaiche sākṣāt nārāyaṇa

SYNONYMS

ihā—this; *śuni'*—hearing; *bale*—spoke; *sarva*—all; *sannyāsīra*—of the Māyāvādī *sannyāsīs*; *gaṇa*—group; *tomāke*—unto You; *dekhiye*—we see; *yaiche*—exactly like; *sākṣāt*—directly; *nārāyaṇa*—the Supreme Personality of Godhead.

TRANSLATION

Hearing this, the Māyāvādī sannyāsīs became somewhat humble and addressed Caitanya Mahāprabhu as Nārāyaṇa Himself, who they all agreed He was.

PURPORT

Māyāvādī *sannyāsīs* address each other as Nārāyaṇa. Whenever they see another *sannyāsī*, they offer him respect by calling, *namo nārāyaṇa* ("I offer my respect unto you, Nārāyaṇa"), although they know perfectly well what kind of Nārāyaṇa he is. Nārāyaṇa has four hands, but although they are puffed-up with the idea of being Nārāyaṇa, they cannot exhibit more than two. Since their philosophy declares that Nārāyaṇa and an ordinary human being are both on the same level, they sometimes use the term *daridrā-nārāyaṇa* ("poor Nārāyaṇa"), which was invented by a so-called *svāmī* who did not know anything about Vedānta philosophy. Therefore although all these Māyāvādī *sannyāsīs* who called themselves Nārāyaṇa were actually unaware of the position of Nārāyaṇa, due to their austerities Lord Caitanya Mahāprabhu enabled them to understand Him to be Nārāyaṇa Himself. Lord Caitanya is certainly the Supreme Personality of Godhead Nārāyaṇa appearing as a devotee of Nārāyaṇa, and thus the Māyāvādī *sannyāsīs*, understanding that He was directly Nārāyaṇa Himself whereas they were false puffed-up Nārāyaṇas, spoke to Him as follows.

TEXT 104

তোমার বচন শুনি' জুড়ায় শ্রবণ ।
তোমার মাধুরী দেখি' জুড়ায় নয়ন ॥ ১০৪ ॥

tomāra vacana śuni' juḍāya śravaṇa
tomāra mādhurī dekhi' juḍāya nayana

SYNONYMS

tomāra—Your; *vacana*—speeches; *śuni'*—hearing; *juḍāya*—very much satisfied; *śravaṇa*—aural reception; *tomāra*—Your; *mādhurī*—nectar; *dekhi'*—seeing; *juḍāya*—satisfies; *nayana*—our eyes.

TRANSLATION

"Dear Caitanya Mahāprabhu," they said, "to tell You the truth, we are greatly pleased to hear Your words, and furthermore Your bodily features are so pleasing that we feel extraordinary satisfaction in seeing You.

PURPORT

In the *śāstras* it is said:

ataḥ śrī-kṛṣṇa-nāmādi na bhaved grāhyam indriyaiḥ
sevonmukhe hi jihvādau svayam eva sphuraty adaḥ

"One cannot understand the Supreme Personality of Godhead or His name, form, qualities or paraphernalia, but if one renders service unto Him the Lord reveals Himself." (*Bhakti-rasāmṛta-sindhu* 1.2.234) Here one can see the effect of the Māyāvādī *sannyāsīs'* service toward Nārāyaṇa. Because they offered a little respect to Śrī Caitanya Mahāprabhu and because they were pious and actually followed the austere rules and regulations of *sannyāsa,* they had some understanding of Vedānta philosophy, and by the grace of Lord Caitanya Mahāprabhu they could appreciate that He was none other than the Supreme Personality of Godhead, who is endowed with all six opulences. One of these opulences is His beauty. By His extraordinarily beautiful bodily features the Māyāvādī *sannyāsīs* recognized Śrī Caitanya Mahāprabhu as Nārāyaṇa Himself. He was not a farcical Nārāyaṇa like the *daridrā-nārāyaṇas* invented by so-called *sannyāsīs.*

TEXT 105

তোমার প্রভাবে সবার আনন্দিত মন ।
কভু অসঙ্গত নহে তোমার বচন ॥ ১০৫ ॥

tomāra prabhāve sabāra ānandita mana
kabhu asaṅgata nahe tomāra vacana

SYNONYMS

tomāra—Your; *prabhāve*—by influence; *sabāra*—of everyone; *ānandita*—joyful; *mana*—mind; *kabhu*—at any time; *asaṅgata*—unreasonable; *nahe*—does not; *tomāra*—Your; *vacana*—speeches.

TRANSLATION

"Dear sir, by Your influence our minds are greatly satisfied, and we believe that Your words will never be unreasonable. Therefore You can speak on Vedānta-sūtra."

PURPORT

In this verse the words *tomāra prabhāve* ("Your influence") are very important. Unless one is spiritually advanced he cannot influence an audience. Bhaktivinoda Ṭhākura has sung, *śuddha-bhakata-caraṇa-reṇu, bhajana-anukūla:* "Unless one associates with a pure devotee he cannot be influenced to understand devotional service." These Māyāvādī *sannyāsīs* were fortunate enough to meet the Supreme Personality of Godhead in the form of a devotee, and certainly they were greatly influenced by the Lord. They knew that since a perfectly advanced spiritualist never says anything false, all his words are reasonable and agree with the Vedic version. A highly realized person never says anything that has no meaning. Māyāvādī philosophers claim to be the Supreme Personality of Godhead, and this has no meaning, but Śrī Caitanya Mahāprabhu never uttered such nonsense. The Māyāvādī *sannyāsīs* were convinced about His personality, and therefore they wanted to hear from Him the purport of Vedānta philosophy.

TEXT 106

প্রভু কহে, বেদান্ত-সূত্র ঈশ্বর-বচন।
ব্যাসরূপে কৈল যাহা শ্রীনারায়ণ ॥ ১০৬ ॥

prabhu kahe, vedānta-sūtra īśvara-vacana
vyāsa-rūpe kaila yāhā śrī-nārāyaṇa

SYNONYMS

prabhu kahe—the Lord began to speak; *vedānta-sūtra*—the philosophy of *Vedānta-sūtra*; *īśvara-vacana*—spoken by the Supreme Personality of Godhead; *vyāsa-rūpe*—in the form of Vyāsadeva; *kaila*—He has made; *yāhā*—whatever; *śrī-nārāyaṇa*—the Supreme Personality of Godhead.

TRANSLATION

The Lord said: "Vedānta philosophy consists of words spoken by the Supreme Personality of Godhead Nārāyaṇa in the form of Vyāsadeva.

PURPORT

Vedānta-sūtra, which consists of codes revealing the method of understanding Vedic knowledge, is the concise form of all Vedic knowledge. It begins with the words *athāto brahma-jijñāsā* ("now is the time to inquire about the Absolute Truth"). The human form of life is especially meant for this purpose, and therefore the *Vedānta-sūtra* very concisely explains the human mission. This is confirmed by the words of the *Vāyu* and *Skanda Purāṇas,* which define a *sūtra* as follows:

alpākṣaram asandigdhaṁ sāravat viśvatomukham
astobhamanavadyaṁ ca sūtraṁ sūtra-vido viduḥ

"A *sūtra* is a code that expresses the essence of all knowledge in a minimum of words. It must be universally applicable and faultless in its linguistic presentation." Anyone familiar with such *sūtras* must be aware of the *Vedānta-sūtra,* which is well known among scholars by the following different names: (1) *Brahma-sūtra,* (2) *Śārīraka,* (3) *Vyāsa-sūtra,* (4) *Bādarāyaṇa-sūtra,* (5) *Uttara-mīmāṁsā* and (6) *Vedānta-darśana.*

There are four chapters *(adhyāyas)* in the *Vedānta-sūtra,* and there are four divisions *(pādas)* in each chapter. Therefore the *Vedānta-sūtra* may be referred to as *ṣoḍaśa-pāda,* or sixteen divisions of codes. The theme of each and every division is fully described in terms of five different subject matters *(adhikaraṇas),* which are technically called *pratijñā, hetu, udāharaṇa, upanaya* and *nigamana.* Every theme must necessarily be explained with reference to *pratijñā,* or a solemn declaration of the purpose of the treatise. The solemn declaration given in the beginning of the *Vedānta-sūtra* is *athāto brahma-jijñāsā,* which indicates that this book was written with the solemn declaration to inquire about the Absolute Truth. Similarly, reasons must be expressed *(hetu),* examples must be given in terms of various facts *(udāharaṇa),* the theme must gradually be brought nearer for understanding *(upanaya),* and finally it must be supported by authoritative quotations from the Vedic *śāstras (nigamana).*

According to the great dictionary compiler Hemacandra, also known as Koṣakāra, Vedānta refers to the purport of the *Upaniṣads* and the *Brāhmaṇa* portion of the *Vedas.* Professor Apte, in his dictionary, describes the *Brāhmaṇa* portion of the *Vedas* as that portion which states the rules for employment of hymns at various sacrifices and gives detailed explanations of their origin, sometimes with lengthy illustrations in the form of legends and stories. It is distinct from the *mantra* portion of the *Vedas.* Hemacandra said that the supplement of the *Vedas* is called the *Vedānta-sūtra. Veda* means knowledge, and *anta* means the end. In other words, proper understanding of the ultimate purpose of the *Vedas* is called Vedānta knowledge. Such knowledge, as given in the codes of the *Vedānta-sūtra,* must be supported by the *Upaniṣads.*

According to learned scholars, there are three different sources of knowledge, which are called *prasthāna-traya.* According to these scholars, Vedānta is one of such sources, for it presents Vedic knowledge on the basis of logic and sound arguments. In *Bhagavad-gītā* (13.5) the Lord said, *brahma-sūtra-padaiś caiva hetumadbhir viniścitaiḥ:* "Understanding of the ultimate goal of life is ascertained in the *Brahma-sūtra* by legitimate logic and argument concerning cause and effect." Therefore the *Vedānta-sūtra* is known as *nyāya-prasthāna,* the *Upaniṣads* are known as *śruti-prasthāna,* and the *Gītā, Mahābhārata* and *Purāṇas* are known as *smṛti-prasthāna.* All scientific knowledge of transcendence must be supported by *śruti, smṛti* and a sound logical basis.

It is said that both the Vedic knowledge and the supplement of the *Vedas* called the *Sātvata-pañcarātra* emanated from the breathing of Nārāyaṇa, the Supreme Personality of Godhead. The *Vedānta-sūtra* codes were compiled by Śrīla Vyāsadeva, the powerful incarnation of Śrī Nārāyaṇa, although it is sometimes said that they were compiled by a great sage named Apāntaratamā. Both the *Pañcarātra* and *Vedānta-sūtra,* however, express the same opinions. Śrī Caitanya Mahāprabhu therefore confirms that there is no difference in opinion between the two, and He declares that because *Vedānta-sūtra* was compiled by Śrīla Vyāsadeva, it may be understood to have emanated from the breathing of Śrī Nārāyaṇa. Śrīla Bhaktisiddhānta Sarasvatī Ṭhākura comments that while Vyāsadeva was compiling the *Vedānta-sūtra,* seven of his great saintly contemporaries were also engaged in similar work. These saints were Ātreya Ṛṣi, Āśmarathya, Auḍulomi, Kārṣṇājini, Kāśakṛtsna, Jaimini and Bādarī. In addition, it is stated that Pārāśarī and Karmandībhikṣu also discussed the *Vedānta-sūtra* codes before Vyāsadeva.

The *Vedānta-sūtra* consists of four chapters. The first two chapters discuss the relationship of the living entity with the Supreme Personality of Godhead. This is known as *sambandha-jñāna,* or knowledge of the relationship. The third chapter describes how one can act in his relationship with the Supreme Personality of Godhead. This is called *abhidheya-jñāna.* The relationship of the living entity with the Supreme Lord is described by Śrī Caitanya Mahāprabhu. *Jīvera svarūpa haya kṛṣṇera 'nitya-dāsa':* the living entity is an eternal servant of the Supreme God. (Cc. *Madhya* 20.108) Therefore, to act in that relationship, one must perform *sādhana-bhakti,* or the prescribed duties of service to the Supreme Personality of Godhead. This is called *abhidheya-jñāna.* The fourth chapter describes the result of such devotional service *(prayojana-jñāna).* This ultimate goal of life is to go back home, back to Godhead. The words *anāvṛttiḥ śabdāt* in the *Vedānta-sūtra* indicate this ultimate goal.

Śrīla Vyāsadeva, the powerful incarnation of Nārāyaṇa, compiled *Vedānta-sūtra,* and in order to protect it from unauthorized commentaries, he personally composed *Śrīmad-Bhāgavatam* on the instruction of his spiritual master, Nārada Muni, as the original commentary on *Vedānta-sūtra.* Besides *Śrīmad-Bhāgavatam,* there are commentaries on the *Vedānta-sūtra* composed by all the major Vaiṣṇava *ācāryas,* and in each of them devotional service to the Lord is described very explicitly. Only those who follow Śaṅkara's commentary have described *Vedānta-sūtra* in an impersonal way, without reference to *Viṣṇu-bhakti,* or devotional service to the Lord, Viṣṇu. Generally people very much appreciate this *Śārīraka-bhāṣya* or impersonal description of the *Vedānta-sūtra,* but all commentaries which are devoid of devotional service to Lord Viṣṇu must be considered to differ in purpose from the original *Vedānta-sūtra.* In other words, Lord Caitanya definitely confirmed that the commentaries or *bhāṣyas* written by the Vaiṣṇava *ācāryas* on the basis of devotional service to Lord Viṣṇu, and not the *Śārīraka-bhāṣya* of Śaṅkarācārya, give the actual explanation of *Vedānta-sūtra.*

TEXT 107

ভ্রম, প্রমাদ, বিপ্রলিপ্সা, করণাপাটব ।
ঈশ্বরের বাক্যে নাহি দোষ এই সব ॥ ১০৭ ॥

bhrama, pramāda, vipralipsā, karaṇāpāṭava
īśvarera vākye nāhi doṣa ei saba

bhrama—mistake; *pramāda*—illusion; *vipralipsā*—cheating purposes; *karaṇāpāṭava*—inefficiency of the material senses; *īśvarera*—of the Lord; *vākye*—in the speech; *nāhi*—there is not; *doṣa*—fault; *ei saba*—all this.

TRANSLATION

"The material defects of mistakes, illusions, cheating and sensory inefficiency do not exist in the words of the Supreme Personality of Godhead.

PURPORT

A mistake is the acceptance of an object to be different than what it is or the acceptance of false knowledge. For example, one may see a rope in the dark and think it to be a serpent, or one may see a glittering oyster shell and think it to be gold. These are mistakes. Similarly, an illusion is a misunderstanding which arises from inattention while hearing, and cheating is the transmission of such defective knowledge to others. Materialistic scientists and philosophers generally use such words as "maybe" and "perhaps" because they do not have actual knowledge of complete facts. Therefore their instructing others is an example of cheating. The final defect of the materialistic person is his inefficient senses. Although our eyes, for example, have the power to see, they cannot see that which is situated at a distance, nor can they see the eyelid, which is the object nearest to the eye. To our untrained eyes the sun appears to be just like a plate, and to the eyes of one who is suffering from jaundice everything appears to be yellow. Therefore we cannot rely on the knowledge acquired through such imperfect eyes. The ears are equally imperfect. We cannot hear a sound vibrated a long distance away unless we put a telephone to our ear. Similarly, if we analyze all our senses in this way, we will find them all to be imperfect. Therefore it is useless to acquire knowledge through the senses. The Vedic process is to hear from authority. In *Bhagavad-gītā* the Lord says, *evaṁ paramparā-prāptam imaṁ rājarṣayo viduḥ:* "The supreme science was thus received through the chain of disciplic succession, and the saintly kings understood it in that way." (Bg. 4.2) We have to hear not from a telephone but from an authorized person, for it is he who has real knowledge.

TEXT 108

উপনিষৎ-সহিত সূত্র কহে যেই তত্ত্ব ।
মুখ্যবৃত্ত্যে সেই অর্থ পরম মহত্ত্ব ॥ ১০৮ ॥

upaniṣat-sahita sūtra kahe yei tattva
mukhya-vṛttye sei artha parama mahattva

SYNONYMS

upaniṣat—the authorized Vedic version; *sahita*—along with; *sūtra*—the *Vedānta-sūtra*; *kahe*—it is said; *yei*—the subject matter; *tattva*—in truth; *mukhya-vṛttye*—by direct understanding; *sei*—that truth; *artha*—meaning; *parama*—ultimate; *mahattva*—glory.

TRANSLATION

"The Absolute Truth is described by the Upaniṣads and Brahma-sūtra, but one must understand the verses as they are. That is the supreme glory in understanding.

PURPORT

It has become fashionable since the time of Śaṅkarācārya to explain everything regarding the *śāstras* in an indirect way. Scholars take pride in explaining everything in their own way, and they declare that one can understand the Vedic scriptures in any way he likes. This "any way you like" method is foolishness, and it has created havoc in the Vedic culture. One cannot accept scientific knowledge in his own whimsical way. In the science of mathematics, for example, two plus two equals four, and one cannot make it equal three or five. Yet although it is not possible to alter real knowledge, people have taken to the fashion of understanding Vedic knowledge in any way they like. It is for this reason that we have presented *Bhagavad-gītā As It Is.* We do not create meanings by concoction. Sometimes commentators say that the word *kurukṣetra* in the first verse of *Bhagavad-gītā* refers to one's body, but we do not accept this. We understand that Kurukṣetra is a place which still exists, and according to the Vedic version it is a *dharmakṣetra,* or place of pilgrimage. People still go there to perform Vedic sacrifices. Foolish commentators, however, say that Kurukṣetra means the body and that *Pañca Pāṇḍavas* refers to the five senses. In this way they distort the meaning, and people are misled. Here Śrī Caitanya Mahāprabhu confirms that all Vedic literatures, including the *Upaniṣads, Brahma-sūtras* and others, whether *śruti, smṛti* or *nyāya,* must be understood according to their original statements. To describe the direct meaning of the Vedic literatures is glorious, but to describe them in one's own way, using imperfect senses and imperfect knowledge, is a disastrous blunder. Śrī Caitanya Mahāprabhu fully deprecated the attempt to describe the *Vedas* in this way.

Regarding the *Upaniṣads,* the following eleven *Upaniṣads* are considered to be the topmost: *Īśa, Kena, Kaṭha, Praśna, Muṇḍaka, Māṇḍūkya, Taittirīya, Aitareya, Chāndogya, Bṛhad-āraṇyaka* and *Śvetāśvatara.* However, in the *Muktikopaniṣad,* verses 30-39, there is a description of 108 *Upaniṣads.* They are as follows: (1) *Īśopaniṣad,* (2) *Kenopaniṣad,* (3) *Kaṭhopaniṣad,* (4) *Praśnopaniṣad,* (5) *Muṇḍakopaniṣad,* (6) *Māṇḍūkyopaniṣad,* (7) *Taittirīyopaniṣad,* (8) *Aitareyopaniṣad,* (9) *Chāndogyopaniṣad,* (10) *Bṛhad-āraṇyakopaniṣad,* (11) *Brahmopaniṣad,* (12) *Kaivalyopaniṣad,* (13) *Jābālopaniṣad,* (14) *Śvetāśvataropaniṣad,* (15) *Haṁsopaniṣad,* (16) *Āruṇeyopaniṣad,* (17) *Garbhopaniṣad,* (18) *Nārāyaṇopaniṣad,* (19) *Paramahaṁsopaniṣad,* (20) *Amṛta-bindūpaniṣad,* (21) *Nāda-bindūpaniṣad,* (22) *Śira-upaniṣad,* (23) *Atharva-śikhopaniṣad,* (24) *Maitrāyaṇy-upaniṣad,* (25) *Kauṣītaky-upaniṣad,* (26) *Bṛhaj-jābālopaniṣad,* (27) *Nṛsiṁha-tāpanīyopaniṣad,* (28) *Kālāgni-rudropaniṣad,* (29) *Maitreyy-upaniṣad,* (30) *Subālopaniṣad,* (31) *Kṣurikopaniṣad,* (32) *Mantrikopaniṣad,* (33) *Sarva-sāropaniṣad,* (34) *Nirālambopaniṣad,* (35) *Śuka-rahasyopaniṣad,* (36) *Vajra-sūcikopaniṣad,* (37) *Tejo-bindūpaniṣad,* (38) *Nāda-bindūpaniṣad,* (39) *Dhyāna-bindūpaniṣad,* (40) *Brahma-vidyopaniṣad,* (41) *Yoga-tattvopaniṣad,* (42) *Ātma-bodhopaniṣad,* (43) *Nārada-parivrājakopaniṣad,* (44) *Triśikhy-upaniṣad,* (45) *Sītopaniṣad,* (46) *Yoga-cūḍāmaṇy-upaniṣad,* (47) *Nirvāṇopaniṣad,* (48) *Maṇḍala-brāhmaṇopaniṣad,* (49) *Dakṣiṇā-mūrty-upaniṣad,* (50) *Śarabhopaniṣad,* (51) *Skandopaniṣad,* (52) *Mahānārāyaṇopaniṣad,* (53) *Advaya-tārakopaniṣad,* (54) *Rāma-rahasyopaniṣad,* (55) *Rāma-tāpaṇy-upaniṣad,* (56) *Vāsudevopaniṣad,* (57) *Mudgalopaniṣad,* (58) *Śāṇḍilyopaniṣad,* (59) *Paiṅgalopaniṣad,* (60) *Bhikṣūpaniṣad,* (61) *Mahadupaniṣad,* (62) *Śārīrakopaniṣad,* (63) *Yoga-śikhopaniṣad,* (64) *Turīyātītopaniṣad,* (65) *Sannyāsopaniṣad,* (66) *Paramahaṁsa-parivrājakopaniṣad,* (67) *Mālikopaniṣad,* (68) *Avyaktopaniṣad,* (69) *Ekākṣaropaniṣad,* (70) *Pūrṇopaniṣad,* (71) *Sūryopaniṣad,* (72) *Akṣy-upaniṣad,* (73) *Adhyātmopaniṣad,* (74) *Kuṇḍikopaniṣad,* (75) *Sāvitry-upaniṣad,* (76) *Ātmopaniṣad,* (77) *Pāśupatopaniṣad,* (78) *Paraṁ Brahmopaniṣad,* (79) *Avadhūtopaniṣad,* (80) *Tripurātapanopaniṣad,* (81) *Devy-upaniṣad,* (82) *Tripuropaniṣad,* (83) *Kaṭha-rudropaniṣad,* (84) *Bhāvanopaniṣad,* (85) *Hṛdayo-*

paniṣad, (86) *Yoga-kuṇḍaliny-upaniṣad,* (87) *Bhasmopaniṣad,* (88) *Rudrākṣopaniṣad,* (89) *Gaṇopaniṣad,* (90) *Darśanopaniṣad,* (91) *Tārasāropaniṣad,* (92) *Mahāvākyopaniṣad,* (93) *Pañca-brahmopaniṣad,* (94) *Prāṇāgni-hotropaniṣad,* (95) *Gopāla-tapanopaniṣad,* (96) *Kṛṣṇopaniṣad,* (97) *Yājña-valkyopaniṣad,* (98) *Varāhopaniṣad,* (99) *Śāṭyāyany-upaniṣad,* (100) *Hayagrīvopaniṣad,* (101) *Dattātreyopaniṣad,* (102) *Gāruḍopaniṣad,* (103) *Kaly-upaniṣad,* (104) *Jābāly-upaniṣad,* (105) *Saubhāgyopaniṣad,* (106) *Sarasvatī-rahasyopaniṣad,* (107) *Bahvṛcopaniṣad* and (108) *Muktikopaniṣad.* Thus there are 108 generally accepted *Upaniṣads,* of which eleven are the most important, as previously stated.

TEXT 109

গৌণ-বৃত্ত্যে যেবা ভাষ্য করিল আচার্য ।
তাহার শ্রবণে নাশ হয় সর্ব কার্য ॥ ১০৯ ॥

gauṇa-vṛttye yebā bhāṣya karila ācārya
tāhāra śravaṇe nāśa haya sarva kārya

SYNONYMS

gauṇa-vṛttya—by indirect meanings; *yebā*—which; *bhāṣya*—commentary; *karila*—prepared; *ācārya*—Śaṅkarācārya; *tāhāra*—its; *śravaṇe*—hearing; *nāśa*—destruction; *haya*—becomes; *sarva*—all; *kārya*—business.

TRANSLATION

"Śrīpāda Śaṅkarācārya has described all the Vedic literatures in terms of indirect meanings. One who hears such explanations is ruined.

TEXT 110

তাঁহার নাহিক দোষ, ঈশ্বর-আজ্ঞা পাঞা ।
গৌণার্থ করিল মুখ্য অর্থ আচ্ছাদিয়া ॥ ১১০ ॥

tāṅhāra nāhika doṣa, īśvara-ājñā pāñā
gauṇārtha karila mukhya artha ācchādiyā

SYNONYMS

tāṅhāra—of Śrī Śaṅkarācārya; *nāhika*—there is none; *doṣa*—fault; *īśvara*—the Supreme Lord; *ājñā*—order; *pāñā*—receiving; *gauṇa-artha*—indirect meaning; *karila*—make; *mukhya*—direct; *artha*—meaning; *ācchādiyā*—covering.

TRANSLATION

"Śaṅkarācārya is not at fault, for he has thus covered the real purpose of the Vedas under the order of the Supreme Personality of Godhead.

PURPORT

The Vedic literature is to be considered a source of real knowledge, but if one does not take it as it is, one will be misled. For example, *Bhagavad-gītā* is an important Vedic literature which has been taught for many years, but because it was commented upon by unscrupulous rascals, people derived no benefit from it, and no one came to the conclusion of Kṛṣṇa consciousness. Since the purpose of *Bhagavad-gītā* is now being presented as it is, however, within four or five short years thousands of people all over the world have become Kṛṣṇa conscious. That is the difference between direct and indirect explanations of Vedic literature. Therefore Śrī Caitanya Mahāprabhu said, *mukhya-vṛttye sei artha parama mahattva:* to instruct Vedic literature according to its direct meaning, without false commentary, is glorious. Unfortunately, Śrī Śaṅkarācārya, by the order of the Supreme Personality of Godhead, compromised between atheism and theism in order to cheat the atheists and bring them to theism, and to do so he gave up the direct method of Vedic knowledge and tried to present a meaning which is indirect. It is with this purpose that he wrote his *Śārīraka-bhāṣya* commentary on the *Vedānta-sūtra.* One should not, therefore, attribute very much importance to the *Śārīraka-bhāṣya.* In order to understand Vedānta philosophy, one must study the *Śrīmad-Bhāgavatam,* which begins with the words, *oṁ namo bhagavate vāsudevāya, janmādy asya yato 'nvayād itarataś cārtheṣv abhijñaḥ sva-rāṭ:* "I offer my obeisances unto Lord Śrī Kṛṣṇa, son of Vasudeva, who is the Supreme All-pervading Personality of Godhead. I meditate upon Him, the transcendent reality, who is the primeval cause of all causes, from whom all manifested universes arise, in whom they dwell and by whom they are destroyed. I meditate upon that eternally effulgent Lord who is directly and indirectly conscious of all manifestations and yet is fully independent." (*Bhāg.* 1.1.1) *Śrīmad-Bhāgavatam* is the real commentary on the *Vedānta-sūtra.* Unfortunately, if one is attracted to Śrī Śaṅkarācārya's commentary, *Śārīraka-bhāṣya,* his spiritual life is doomed.

One may argue that since Śaṅkarācārya is an incarnation of Lord Śiva, how is it that he cheated people in this way? The answer is that he did so on the order of his master, the Supreme Personality of Godhead. This is confirmed in the *Padma Purāṇa* in the words of Lord Śiva himself:

māyāvādam asac-chāstraṁ
pracchannaṁ bauddham ucyate
mayaiva kalpitaṁ devi
kalau brāhmaṇa-rūpiṇā

brahmaṇaś cāparaṁ rūpaṁ
nirguṇaṁ vakṣyate mayā
sarvasvaṁ jagato'py asya
mohanārthaṁ kalau yuge

vedānte tu mahā-śāstre
māyāvādam avaidikam

mayaiva vakṣyate devi
jagatāṁ nāśa-kāraṇāt

"The Māyāvāda philosophy," Lord Śiva informed his wife Pārvatī, "is impious [*asac-chāstra*]. It is covered Buddhism. My dear Pārvatī, in the form of a *brāhmaṇa* in Kali-yuga I teach this imagined Māyāvāda philosophy. In order to cheat the atheists, I describe the Supreme Personality of Godhead to be without form and without qualities. Similarly, in explaining Vedānta I describe the same Māyāvāda philosophy in order to mislead the entire population toward atheism by denying the personal form of the Lord." In the *Śiva Purāṇa* the Supreme Personality of Godhead told Lord Śiva:

dvāparādau yuge bhūtvā
kalayā mānuṣādiṣu
svāgamaiḥ kalpitais tvaṁ ca
janān mad-vimukhān kuru

"In Kali-yuga, mislead the people in general by propounding imaginary meanings for the *Vedas* to bewilder them." These are the descriptions of the *Purāṇas.*

Śrīla Bhaktisiddhānta Sarasvatī Ṭhākura comments that *mukhya-vṛtti* ("the direct meaning") is *abhidhā-vṛtti,* or the meaning which one can understand immediately from the statements of dictionaries, whereas *gauṇa-vṛtti* ("the indirect meaning") is a meaning that one imagines without consulting the dictionary. For example, one politician has said that Kurukṣetra refers to the body, but in the dictionary there is no such definition. Therefore this imaginary meaning is *gauṇa-vṛtti,* whereas the direct meaning found in the dictionary is *mukhya-vṛtti* or *abhidhā-vṛtti.* This is the distinction between the two. Śrī Caitanya Mahāprabhu recommends that one understand the Vedic literature in terms of *abhidhā-vṛtti,* and the *gauṇa-vṛtti* He rejects. Sometimes, however, as a matter of necessity, Vedic literature is described in terms of the *lakṣaṇā-vṛtti* or *gauṇa-vṛtti,* but one should not accept such explanations as permanent truths.

The purpose of the discussions in the *Upaniṣads* and *Vedānta-sūtra* is to philosophically establish the personal feature of the Absolute Truth. The impersonalists, however, in order to establish their philosophy, accept these discussions in terms of *lakṣanā-vṛtti,* or indirect meanings. Thus instead of being *tattva-vāda,* or in search of the Absolute Truth, they become Māyāvāda, or illusioned by the material energy. When Śrī Viṣṇusvāmī, one of the four *ācāryas* of the Vaiṣṇava cult, presented his thesis on the subject matter of *śuddhādvaita-vāda,* immediately the Māyāvādīs took advantage of this philosophy and tried to establish their *advaita-vāda* or *kevalādvaita-vāda.* To defeat this *kevalādvaita-vāda,* Śrī Rāmānujācārya presented his philosophy as *viśiṣṭādvaita-vāda,* and Śrī Madhvācārya presented his philosophy of *tattva-vāda,* both of which are stumbling blocks to the Māyāvādīs because they defeat their philosophy in scrupulous detail. Students of Vedic philosophy know very well how strongly Śrī Rāmānujācārya's *viśiṣṭādvaita-vāda* and Śrī Madhvācārya's *tattva-vāda* contest the impersonal Māyāvāda philosophy. Śrī Caitanya Mahāprabhu, however, accepted the direct meaning of the Vedānta philosophy and thus defeated the Māyāvāda philosophy immediately. He opined in this connection that anyone who follows the principles of the *Śārīraka-bhāṣya* is doomed. This is confirmed in the *Padma Purāṇa* where Lord Śiva tells Pārvatī:

śṛṇu devi pravakṣyāmi
tāmasāni yathākramam
yeṣāṁ śravaṇa-mātreṇa
pātityaṁ jñāninām api

apārthaṁ śruti-vākyānāṁ
darśayal loka-garhitam
karma-svarūpa-tyājyatvam
atra ca pratipādyate

sarva-karma-paribhraṁśān
naiṣkarmyaṁ tatra cocyate
parātma-jīvayor aikyaṁ
mayātra pratipādyate

"My dear wife, hear my explanations of how I have spread ignorance through Māyāvāda philosophy. Simply by hearing it, even an advanced scholar will fall down. In this philosophy, which is certainly very inauspicious for people in general, I have misrepresented the real meaning of the *Vedas* and recommended that one give up all activities in order to achieve freedom from *karma.* In this Māyāvāda philosophy I have described the *jīvātmā* and Paramātmā to be one and the same." How the Māyāvāda philosophy was condemned by Śrī Caitanya Mahāprabhu and His followers is described in *Śrī-Caitanya-caritāmṛta, Antya-līlā,* Second Chapter, verses 94 through 99, where Svarūpa–dāmodara Gosvāmī says that anyone who is eager to understand the Māyāvāda philosophy must be considered insane. This especially applies to a Vaiṣṇava who reads the *Śārīraka-bhāṣya* and considers himself to be one with God. The Māyāvādī philosophers have presented their arguments in such attractive flowery language that hearing Māyāvāda philosophy may sometimes change the mind of even a *mahā-bhāgavata,* or very advanced devotee. An actual Vaiṣṇava cannot tolerate any philosophy that claims God and the living being to be one and the same.

TEXT 111

'ব্রহ্ম'-শব্দে মুখ্য অর্থে কহে —'ভগবান্' ।
চিদৈশ্বর্য-পরিপূর্ণ, অনূর্ধ্ব-সমান ॥ ১১১ ॥

'brahma'śabde mukhya arthe kahe—'bhagavān'
cid-aiśvarya-paripūrṇa, anūrdhva-samāna

SYNONYMS

brahma—the Absolute Truth; *śabde*—by this word; *mukhya*—direct; *arthe*—meaning; *kahe*—says; *bhagavān*—the Supreme Personality of Godhead; *cit-aiśvarya*—spiritual opulence; *paripūrṇa*—full of; *anūrdhva*—unsurpassed by anyone; *samāna*—not equalled by anyone.

TRANSLATION

"According to direct understanding, the Absolute Truth is the Supreme Personality of Godhead, who has all spiritual opulences. No one can be equal to or greater than Him.

PURPORT

This statement by Śrī Caitanya Mahāprabhu is confirmed in the *Śrīmad-Bhāgavatam:*

vadanti tat tattva-vidas
tattvaṁ yaj jñānam advayam
brahmeti paramātmeti
bhagavān iti śabdyate

"Learned transcendentalists who know the Absolute Truth call this nondual substance Brahman, Paramātmā or Bhagavān." (*Bhāg.* 1.2.11) The Absolute Truth is ultimately understood as Bhagavān, partially understood as Paramātmā and vaguely understood as the impersonal Brahman. Bhagavān, or the Supreme Personality of Godhead, is opulent in all excellence; no one can be equal to or greater than Him. This is also confirmed in *Bhagavad-gītā*, where the Lord says, *mattaḥ parataraṁ nānyat kiñcid asti dhanañjaya:* "O conqueror of wealth [Arjuna], there is no truth superior to Me." (Bg. 7.7) There are many other verses which prove that the Absolute Truth in the ultimate sense is understood to be the Supreme Personality of Godhead, Kṛṣṇa.

TEXT 112

তাঁহার বিভূতি, দেহ,—সব চিদাকার ।
চিদ্বিভূতি আচ্ছাদি' তাঁরে কহে 'নিরাকার' ॥ ১১২ ॥

tāṅhāra vibhūti, deha,—saba cid-ākāra
cid-vibhūti ācchādi' tāṅre kahe 'nirākāra'

SYNONYMS

tāṅhāra—His (the Supreme Personality of Godhead's); *vibhūti*—spiritual power; *deha*—body; *saba*—everything; *cit-ākāra*—spiritual form; *cit-vibhūti*—spiritual opulence; *ācchādi'*—covering; *tāṅre*—Him; *kahe*—said; *nirākāra*—without form.

TRANSLATION

"Everything about the Supreme Personality of Godhead is spiritual, including His body, opulence and paraphernalia. Māyāvāda philosophy, however, covering His spiritual opulence, advocates the theory of impersonalism.

PURPORT

It is stated in the *Brahma-saṁhitā, īśvaraḥ paramaḥ kṛṣṇaḥ sac-cid-ānanda-vigrahaḥ:* "The Supreme Personality of Godhead, Kṛṣṇa, has a spiritual body which is full of knowledge, eternity and bliss." In this material world everyone's body is just the opposite—temporary, full of ignorance and full of misery. Therefore when the Supreme Personality of Godhead is sometimes described as *nirākāra,* this is to indicate that He does not have a material body like us.

Māyāvādī philosophers do not know how it is that the Supreme Personality of Godhead is formless. The Supreme Lord does not have a form like ours but has a spiritual form. Not knowing this, Māyāvādī philosophers simply advocate the one-sided view that the Supreme Godhead, or Brahman, is formless *(nirākāra).* In this connection Śrīla Bhaktivinoda Ṭhākura offers many quotes from the Vedic literature. If one accepts the real or direct meaning of these Vedic statements, one can understand that the Supreme Personality of Godhead has a spiritual body *(sac-cid-ānanda-vigrahaḥ).*

In the *Bṛhad-āraṇyaka Upaniṣad* it is said, *pūrṇam adaḥ pūrṇam idaṁ pūrṇāt pūrṇam udacyate.* This indicates that the body of the Supreme Personality of Godhead is spiritual, for even though He expands in many ways, He remains the same. In *Bhagavad-gītā* the Lord says, *ahaṁ sarvasya prabhavo mattaḥ sarvaṁ pravartate:* "I am the origin of all. Everything emanates from Me." (Bg. 10.8) Māyāvādī philosophers materialistically think that if the Supreme Truth expands Himself in everything, He must lose His original form. Thus they think that there cannot be any form other than the expansive gigantic body of the Lord. But the *mantra* of the *Bṛhad-āraṇyaka Upaniṣad* confirms, *pūrṇam idaṁ pūrṇāt pūrṇam udacyate:* "Although He expands in many ways, He keeps His original personality. His original spiritual body remains as it is." Similarly, in the *Śvetāśvatara Upaniṣad* it is stated, *vicitra-śaktiḥ puruṣaḥ purāṇaḥ:* "The Supreme Personality of Godhead, the original person *[puruṣa],* has multifarious energies." *Sa vṛkṣa-kālākṛtibhiḥ paro 'nyo yasmāt prapañcaḥ parivartate 'yaṁ dharmāvahaṁ pāpanudaṁ bhageśam:* "He is the origin of material creation, and it is due to Him only that everything changes. He is the protector of religion and annihilator of all sinful activities. He is the master of all opulences." (6.6) *Vedāham etaṁ puruṣaṁ mahāntam āditya-varṇaṁ tamasaḥ parastāt:* "Now I understand the Supreme Personality of Godhead to be the greatest of the great. He is effulgent like the sun and is beyond this material world." (3.8) *Patiṁ patīnāṁ paramaṁ parastāt:* "He is the master of all masters, the superior of all superiors." (6.7) *Mahān prabhur vai puruṣaḥ:* "He is the supreme master and supreme person." (3.12) *Parāsya śaktir vividhaiva śrūyate:* "We can understand His opulences in different ways." (6.8) These are statements of the *Śvetāśvatara*

Upaniṣad. Similarly, in the *Ṛg-veda* it is stated, *tad viṣṇoḥ paramaṁ padaṁ sadā paśyanti sūrayaḥ:* "Viṣṇu is the Supreme, and those who are actually learned think only of His lotus feet." In the *Praśna Upaniṣad* it is said, *sa īkṣāñcakre:* "He glanced over the material creation." (6.3) In the *Aitareya Upaniṣad* it is said, *sa aikṣata—* "He glanced over the material creation"—and *sa imāl lokān asṛjata—*"He created this entire material world." (1.1.1-2)

Thus many verses can be quoted from the *Upaniṣads* and *Vedas* which prove that the Supreme Godhead is not impersonal. In the *Kaṭha Upaniṣad* (2.2.13) it is also said, *nityo nityānāṁ cetanaś cetanānām eko bahūnāṁ yo vidadhāti kāmān:* "He is the supreme eternally conscious person who maintains all other living entities." From all these Vedic references one can understand that the Absolute Truth is a person, although no one can equal or excel Him. Although there are many foolish Māyāvādī philosophers who think that they are even greater than Kṛṣṇa, Kṛṣṇa is *asamaurdhva;* no one is equal to or above Him.

As stated in the *Śvetāśvatara Upaniṣad* (3.19), *apāṇi-pādo javano grahītā.* This verse describes the Absolute Truth as having no legs or hands. Although this is an impersonal description, however, it does not mean that the Absolute Personality of Godhead has no form. He has a spiritual form which is distinct from the forms of matter. In this verse Caitanya Mahāprabhu clarifies this distinction.

TEXT 113

চিদানন্দ—তেঁহো, তাঁর স্থান, পরিবার ।
তাঁরে কহে—প্রাকৃত-সত্ত্বের বিকার ॥ ১১৩ ॥

cid-ānanda—teṅho, tāṅra sthāna, parivāra
tāṅre kahe—prākṛta-sattvera vikāra

SYNONYMS

cit-ānanda—spiritual bliss; *teṅho*—He is personally; *tāṅra*—His; *sthāna*—abode; *parivāra*—entourage; *tāṅre*—unto Him; *kahe*—someone says; *prākṛta*—material; *sattvera*—goodness; *vikāra*—transformation.

TRANSLATION

"The Supreme Personality of Godhead is full of spiritual potencies. Therefore His body, name, fame and entourage are all spiritual. The Māyāvādī philosopher, due to ignorance, says that these are all merely transformations of the material mode of goodness.

PURPORT

In the Seventh Chapter of *Bhagavad-gītā* the Supreme Personality of Godhead has classified His energies in two distinct divisions—namely, *prākṛta* and *aprākṛta*, or *parā-prakṛti and aparā-prakṛti.* In the *Viṣṇu Purāṇa* the same distinction is made. The Māyāvādī philosophers cannot understand these two *prakṛtis* or natures—material and spiritual—but one who is actually intelligent can understand them. Considering the many varieties and activities in material nature, why should the Māyāvādī philosophers deny the spiritual varieties of the spiritual world? The *Bhāgavatam* says:

ye 'nye 'ravindākṣa vimukta-māninas
tvayy asta-bhāvād aviśuddha-buddhayaḥ
(*Bhāg.* 10.2.32)

The intelligence of those who think themselves liberated but have no information of the spiritual world is not yet clear. In this verse the term *aviśuddha-buddhayaḥ* refers to unclean intelligence. Due to unclean intelligence or a poor fund of knowledge, the Māyāvādī philosophers cannot understand the distinction between material and spiritual varieties; therefore they cannot even think of spiritual varieties because they take it for granted that all variety is material.

Śrī Caitanya Mahāprabhu, therefore, explains in this verse that Kṛṣṇa, the Supreme Personality of Godhead or the Absolute Truth, has a spiritual body which is distinct from material bodies, and thus His name, abode, entourage and qualities are all spiritual. The material mode of goodness has nothing to do with spiritual varieties. Māyāvādī philosophers, however, cannot clearly understand spiritual varieties; therefore they imagine a negation of the material world to be the spiritual world. The material qualities of goodness, passion and ignorance cannot act in the spiritual world, which is therefore called *nirguṇa*, as clearly indicated in *Bhagavad-gītā (traiguṇya-viṣayā vedā nistraiguṇyo bhavārjuna).* The material world is a manifestation of the three modes of material nature, but one has to become free from these modes to come to the spiritual world where their influence is completely absent. Now Lord Śrī Caitanya Mahāprabhu will disassociate Lord Śiva from Māyāvāda philosophy in the following verse.

TEXT 114

তাঁর দোষ নাহি, তেঁহো আজ্ঞাকারী দাস ।
আর যেই শুনে তার হয় সর্বনাশ ॥ ১১৪ ॥

tāṅra doṣa nāhi, teṅho ājñā-kārī dāsa
āra yei śune tāra haya sarva-nāśa

SYNONYMS

tāṅra—his (Lord Śiva's); *doṣa*—fault; *nāhi*—there is none; *teṅho*—he; *ājñā-kārī*—obedient order carrier; *dāsa*—servant; *āra*—others; *yei*—anyone; *śune*—hears (the Māyāvāda philosophy); *tāra*—of him; *haya*—becomes; *sarva-nāśa*—everything lost.

TRANSLATION

"Śaṅkarācārya, who is an incarnation of Lord Śiva, is faultless because he is a servant carrying out the orders of the Lord. But those who follow his Māyāvādī philosophy are doomed. They will lose all their advancement in spiritual knowledge.

PURPORT

Māyāvādī philosophers are very proud of exhibiting their Vedānta knowledge through grammatical jugglery, but Lord Śrī Kṛṣṇa in *Bhagavad-gītā* certifies that they are *māyayāpahṛta-jñānāḥ*, bereft of real knowledge due to *māyā*. *Māyā* has two potencies with which to execute her two functions—*prakṣepātmikā-śakti*, the power to throw the living entity in the ocean of material existence, and *āvaraṇātmikā-śakti*, the power to cover the knowledge of the living entity. The function of the *āvaraṇātmikā-śakti* is explained in *Bhagavad-gītā* by the word *māyayāpahṛta-jñāna*.

Why the *daivī-māyā* or illusory energy of Kṛṣṇa takes away the knowledge of the Māyāvādī philosophers is also explained in *Bhagavad-gītā* by the use of the words *āsuraṁ bhāvam āśritāḥ*, which refer to a person who does not agree to the existence of the Lord. The Māyāvādīs who are not in agreement with the existence of the Lord can be classified in two groups, exemplified by the impersonalist Śaṅkarites of Vārāṇasī and the Buddhists of Saranātha. Both of them are Māyāvādīs, and Kṛṣṇa takes away their knowledge due to their atheistic philosophies. Neither of them agree to accept the existence of a personal God. The Buddhist philosophers clearly deny both the soul and God, and although the Śaṅkarites do not openly deny God, they say that the Absolute is *nirākāra*, or formless. Thus both of them are *aviśuddha-buddhayaḥ*, or imperfect and unclean in their knowledge and intelligence.

The most prominent Māyāvādī scholar, Sadānanda Yogīndra, has written a book called *Vedānta-sāra* in which he expounds the philosophy of Śaṅkarācārya, and all the followers of Śaṅkara's philosophy attribute great importance to his statements. In this *Vedānta-sāra* Sadānanda Yogīndra defines Brahman as *sac-cid-ānanda* combined with knowledge and without duality, and he defines ignorance *(jaḍa)* as knowledge distinct from that of *sat* and *asat*. This is almost inconceivable, but it is a product of the three material qualities. Thus he considers anything other than pure knowledge to be material. The center of ignorance is considered to be sometimes all-pervading and sometimes individual. Thus according to his opinion both the all-pervading Viṣṇu and the individual living entities are products of ignorance.

In simple language, it is the opinion of Sadānanda Yogīndra that since everything is *nirākāra* (formless), the conception of Viṣṇu and the conception of the individual soul are both products of ignorance. He also explains that the *viśuddha-sattva* conception of the Vaiṣṇavas is nothing but *pradhāna*, or the chief principle of creation. He maintains that when all-pervading knowledge is contaminated by the *viśuddha-sattva*, which consists of a transformation of the quality of goodness, there arises the conception of the Supreme Personality of Godhead who is the omnipotent, omniscient supreme ruler, the Supersoul, the cause of all causes, the supreme *Īśvara*, etc. According to Sadānanda Yogīndra, because *Īśvara*, the Supreme Lord, is the reservoir of all ignorance, He may be called *sarva-jña* or omniscient, but one who denies the existence of the omnipotent Supreme Personality of Godhead is more than *Īśvara*, or the Lord. His conclusion, therefore, is that the Supreme Personality of Godhead *(Īśvara)* is a transformation of material ignorance and that the living entity *(jīva)* is covered by ignorance. Thus he describes both collective and individual existence in darkness. According to Māyāvādī philosophers, the Vaiṣṇava conception of the Lord as the Supreme Personality of Godhead and of the *jīva* or individual soul as His eternal servant is a manifestation of ignorance. If we accept the judgment of Lord Kṛṣṇa in *Bhagavad-gītā,* however, the Māyāvādīs are to be considered *māyayā-pahṛta-jñāna,* or bereft of all knowledge, because they do not recognize the existence of the Supreme Personality of Godhead or they claim that His existence is a product of the material conception *(māyā).* These are characteristics of *asuras* or demons.

Lord Śrī Caitanya Mahāprabhu, in His discourses with Sārvabhauma Bhaṭṭācārya, said:

jīvera nistāra lāgi' sūtra kaila vyāsa
māyāvādi-bhāṣya śunile haya sarva-nāśa
(Cc. *Madhya* 6.169)

Vyāsadeva composed the *Vedānta-sūtra* to deliver the conditioned souls from this material world, but Śaṅkarācārya, by presenting the *Vedānta-sūtra* in his own way, has clearly done a great disservice to human society, for one who follows his Māyāvāda philosophy is doomed. In the *Vedānta-sūtra,* devotional service is clearly indicated, but the Māyāvādī philosophers refuse to accept the spiritual body of the Supreme Absolute Person and refuse to accept that the living entity has an individual existence separate from that of the Supreme Lord. Thus they have created atheistic havoc all over the world, for such a conclusion is against the very nature of the transcendental process of pure devotional service. The Māyāvādī philosophers' unrealizable ambition to become one with the Supreme through denying the existence of the Personality of Godhead results in a most calamitous misrepresentation of spiritual knowledge, and one who follows this philosophy is doomed to remain perpetually in this material world. Therefore they are called *aviśuddha-buddhayaḥ,* or unclean in knowledge. Because they are unclean in knowledge, all their austerities and penances end in frustration. Thus although they may be honored at first as very learned scholars, ultimately they descend to physical activities of politics, social work, etc. Instead of becoming one with the Supreme Lord, they again become one with these material activities. This is explained by *Śrīmad-Bhāgavatam:*

āruhya kṛcchreṇa paraṁ padaṁ tataḥ
patanty adho 'nādṛta-yuṣmad-aṅghrayaḥ
(*Bhāg.* 10.2.32)

In actuality the Māyāvādī philosophers very strictly follow the austerities and penances of spiritual life and in this way are elevated to the impersonal Brahman platform, but due to their negligence of the lotus feet of the Lord they again fall down to material existence.

TEXT 115

প্রাকৃত করিয়া মানে বিষ্ণু-কলেবর ।
বিষ্ণুনিন্দা আর নাহি ইহার উপর ॥ ১১৫ ॥

prākṛta kariyā māne viṣṇu-kalevara
viṣṇu-nindā āra nāhi ihāra upara

SYNONYMS

prākṛta—material; *kariyā*—taking it to be so; *māne*—accepts; *viṣṇu*—Lord Viṣṇu's; *kalevara*—body; *viṣṇu-nindā*—defaming or blaspheming Lord Viṣṇu; *āra*—beyond this; *nāhi*—none; *ihāra*—of this; *upara*—above.

TRANSLATION

"One who considers the transcendental body of Lord Viṣṇu to be made of material nature is the greatest offender at the lotus feet of the Lord. There is no greater blasphemy against the Supreme Personality of Godhead.

PURPORT

Śrī Bhaktisiddhānta Sarasvatī Gosvāmī explains that the variegated personal feature of the Absolute Truth is the *Viṣṇu-tattva,* and the material energy which creates this cosmic manifestation is the energy of Lord Viṣṇu. The creative force is merely the energy of the Lord, but the foolish conclude that the Lord has no separate existence because He has distributed Himself in an impersonal form. The impersonal Brahman, however, cannot possess energies, nor do the Vedic literatures state that *māyā* (the illusory energy) is covered by another *māyā.* There are hundreds and thousands of references, however, to *Viṣṇu-māyā (parāsya śaktiḥ),* or the energy of Lord Viṣṇu. In *Bhagavad-gītā* (7.14) Kṛṣṇa refers to *mama māyā* ("My energy"). *Māyā* is controlled by the Supreme Personality of Godhead; it is not that He is covered by *māyā.* Therefore Lord Viṣṇu cannot be a product of the material energy. In the beginning of the *Vedānta-sūtra* it is said, *janmādy asya yataḥ,* indicating that the material energy is also an emanation of the Supreme Brahman. How then could He be covered by the material energy? If that were possible, material energy would be greater than the Supreme Brahman. Even these simple arguments, however, cannot be understood by the Māyāvādī philosophers, and therefore the term *māyayāpahṛta-jñāna* which is applied to them in *Bhagavad-gītā* is extremely appropriate. Anyone who thinks that Lord Viṣṇu is a product of the material energy, as explained by Sadānanda Yogīndra, should immediately be understood to be insane, for his knowledge has been stolen by the illusory energy.

Lord Viṣṇu cannot be placed within the category of the demigods. Those who are actually bewildered by the Māyāvāda philosophy and are still in the darkness of ignorance consider Lord Viṣṇu to be a demigod, in defiance of the Ṛg-vedic *mantra, oṁ tad viṣṇoḥ paramaṁ padam* ("Viṣṇu is always in a superior position"). This *mantra* is also confirmed in *Bhagavad-gītā. Mattaḥ parataraṁ nānyat:* there is no truth superior to Lord Kṛṣṇa or Viṣṇu. Thus only those whose knowledge has been bewildered consider Lord Viṣṇu to be a demigod and therefore suggest that one may either worship Lord Viṣṇu, the goddess Kālī or Durgā or whomever he likes and achieve the same result. This is an ignorant conclusion that is not accepted in

Bhagavad-gītā, which distinctly says, *yānti deva-vratā devān. . .yānti mad-yājino'pi mām:* "The worshipers of the demigods will be promoted to the respective planets of the demigods, but devotees of the Supreme Lord will go back home, back to Godhead." (Bg. 9.25) Lord Kṛṣṇa explains very clearly in *Bhagavad-gītā* that His material energy is very difficult to overcome *(daivī hy eṣā guṇamayī mama māyā duratyayā). Māyā's* influence is so strong that even learned scholars and spiritualists are also covered by *māyā* and think themselves to be as good as the Supreme Personality of Godhead. Actually, however, to free oneself from the influence of *māyā* one must surrender to the Supreme Personality of Godhead, as Kṛṣṇa also states in *Bhagavad-gītā (mām eva ye prapadyante māyām etāṁ taranti te).* It is to be concluded, therefore, that Lord Viṣṇu does not belong to this material creation but to the spiritual world. To misconceive Lord Viṣṇu to have a material body or to equate Him with the demigods is the most offensive blasphemy against Lord Viṣṇu, and offenders against the lotus feet of Lord Viṣṇu cannot advance in spiritual knowledge. They are called *māyayāpahṛta-jñāna,* or those whose knowledge has been stolen by the influence of illusion.

One who thinks that there is a difference between Lord Viṣṇu's body and His soul dwells in the darkest region of ignorance. There is no difference between Lord Viṣṇu's body and Viṣṇu's soul, for they are *advaya-jñāna,* one knowledge. In this world there is a difference between the material body and spiritual soul, but in the spiritual world everything is spiritual, and there are no such differences. The greatest offense of the Māyāvādī philosophers is to consider Lord Viṣṇu and the living entities to be one and the same. In this connection the *Padma Purāṇa* states:

arcye viṣṇau śilādhīr guruṣu
nara-matir vaiṣṇave jāti-buddhiḥ

"One who considers the *arcā-mūrti* or worshipable Deity of Lord Viṣṇu to be stone, the spiritual master to be an ordinary human being, and a Vaiṣṇava to belong to a particular caste or creed, is possessed of hellish intelligence." One who follows such conclusions is doomed.

TEXT 116

ঈশ্বরের তত্ত্ব – যেন জ্বলিত জ্বলন ।
জীবের স্বরূপ – যৈছে স্ফুলিঙ্গের কণ ॥ ১১৬ ॥

īśvarera tattva—yena jvalita jvalana
jīvera svarūpa—yaiche sphuliṅgera kaṇa

SYNONYMS

īśvarera tattva—the truth of the Supreme Personality of Godhead; *yena*—is like; *jvalita*—blazing; *jvalana*—fire; *jīvera*—of the living entities; *svarūpa*—identity; *yaiche*—is like; *sphuliṅgera*—of the spark; *kaṇa*—particle.

TRANSLATION

"The Lord is like a great blazing fire, and the living entities are like small sparks of that fire.

PURPORT

Although sparks and a big fire are both fire and both have the power to burn, the burning power of the fire and that of the spark are not the same. Why should one artificially try to become like a big fire although by constitution he is like a small spark? It is due to ignorance. One should therefore understand that neither the Supreme Personality of Godhead nor the small sparklike living entities have anything to do with matter, but when the spiritual spark comes in contact with the material world his fiery quality is extinguished. That is the position of the conditioned souls. Because they are in touch with the material world, their spiritual quality is almost dead, but because these spiritual sparks are all Kṛṣṇa's parts and parcels, as the Lord states in *Bhagavad-gītā (mamaivāṁśaḥ),* they can revive their original position by getting free from material contact. This is pure philosophical understanding. In *Bhagavad-gītā* the spiritual sparks are declared to be *sanātana* (eternal); therefore the material energy, *māyā,* cannot affect their constitutional position.

Someone may argue, "Why is there a need to create the spiritual sparks?" The answer can be given in this way. Since the Absolute Personality of Godhead is omnipotent, He has both unlimited and limited potencies. This is the meaning of omnipotent. To be omnipotent, He must have not only unlimited potencies but limited potencies also. Thus to exhibit His omnipotency He displays both. The living entities are endowed with limited potency although they are part of the Lord. The Lord displays the spiritual world by His unlimited potencies, whereas by His limited potencies the material world is displayed. In *Bhagavad-gītā* the Lord says:

apareyam itas tv anyāṁ
prakṛtiṁ viddhi me parām
jīva-bhūtāṁ mahā-bāho
yayedaṁ dhāryate jagat

"Besides the inferior nature, O mighty-armed Arjuna, there is a superior energy of Mine, which is all living entities who are struggling with material nature and are sustaining the universe." (Bg. 7.5) The *jīva-bhūta,* living entities, control this material world with their limited potencies. Generally, people are bewildered by the activities of scientists and technologists. Due to *māyā* they think that there is no need of God and that they can do everything and anything, but actually they cannot. Since this cosmic manifestation is limited, their existence is also limited. Everything in this material world is limited, and for this reason there is creation, sustenance and dissolution. However, in the world of unlimited energy, the spiritual world, there is neither creation nor destruction.

If the Personality of Godhead did not possess both limited and unlimited energies, He could not be called omnipotent. *Mahato mahīyān aṇuto 'ṇīyān:* He is greater than the greatest and smaller than the smallest. He is smaller than the smallest in the form of the living entities and greater than the greatest in His form of Kṛṣṇa. If there were no one to control, there would be no meaning to the conception of the supreme controller *(īśvara),* just as there is no meaning to a king without his subjects. If all the subjects became king, there would be no distinction between the king and an ordinary citizen. Thus for the Lord to be the supreme controller there must be a creation to control. The basic principle for the existence of the living entities is called *cid-vilāsa,* or spiritual pleasure. The omnipotent Lord displays His pleasure potency as the living entities. The Lord is described in *Vedānta-sūtra* as *ānandamayo 'bhyāsāt.* He is by nature the reservoir of all pleasures, and because He wants to enjoy pleasure, there must be energies to give Him pleasure or supply Him the impetus for pleasure. This is the perfect philosophical understanding of the Absolute Truth.

TEXT 117

জীবতত্ত্ব—শক্তি, কৃষ্ণতত্ত্ব—শক্তিমান্ ।
গীতা-বিষ্ণুপুরাণাদি তাহাতে প্রমাণ ॥ ১১৭ ॥

jīva-tattva—śakti, kṛṣṇa-tattva—śaktimān
gītā-viṣṇupurāṇādi tāhāte pramāṇa

SYNONYMS

jīva-tattva—the truth of the living entities; *śakti*—energy; *kṛṣṇa-tattva*—the truth of the Supreme Personality of Godhead; *śaktimān*—the possessor of the energies; *gītā*—*Bhagavad-gītā*; *viṣṇu-purāṇa-ādi*—*Viṣṇu Purāṇa* and other *Purāṇas*; *tāhāte*—in them; *pramāṇa*—there are evidences.

TRANSLATION

"The living entities are energies, not the energetic. The energetic is Kṛṣṇa. This is very vividly described in Bhagavad-gītā, the Viṣṇu Purāṇa and other Vedic literatures.

PURPORT

As already explained, there are three *prasthānas* on the path of advancement in spiritual knowledge—namely, *nyāya-prasthāna* (Vedānta philosophy), *śruti-prasthāna* (the *Upaniṣads* and Vedic *mantras*) and *smṛti-prasthāna* (the *Bhagavad-gītā, Mahābhārata, Purāṇas,* etc.). Unfortunately, Māyāvādī philosophers do not accept the *smṛti-prasthāna. Smṛti* refers to the conclusions drawn from the Vedic evidence. Sometimes Māyāvādī philosophers do not accept the authority of *Bhagavad-gītā* and the *Purāṇas,* and this is called *ardha-kukkuṭī-nyāya.* If one believes in the Vedic literatures, one must accept all the Vedic literatures recognized by the great *ācāryas,* but these Māyāvādī philosophers accept only the *nyāya-prasthāna* and *śruti-prasthāna,* rejecting the *smṛti-prasthāna.* Here, however, Śrī Caitanya Mahāprabhu cites evidence from the *Gītā, Viṣṇu Purāṇa,* etc., which are *smṛti-prasthāna.* No one can avoid the Personality of Godhead in the statements of *Bhagavad-gītā* and other Vedic literatures such as the *Mahābhārata* and the *Purāṇas.* Lord Caitanya therefore quotes a passage from *Bhagavad-gītā* (Bg. 7.5).

TEXT 118

অপরেয়মিতস্ত্বন্যাং প্রকৃতিং বিদ্ধি মে পরাম্ ।
জীবভূতাং মহাবাহো যয়েদং ধার্যতে জগৎ ॥ ১১৮ ॥

apareyam itas tv anyāṁ
prakṛtiṁ viddhi me parām
jīva-bhūtāṁ mahā-bāho
yayedaṁ dhāryate jagat

SYNONYMS

aparā—inferior energy; *iyam*—this material world; *itaḥ*—beyond this; *tu*—but; *anyām*—another; *prakṛtim*—energy; *viddhi*—you must know; *me*—of Me; *parām*—which is superior energy; *jīva-bhūtām*—they are the living entities; *mahā-bāho*—O mighty-armed; *yayā*—by which; *idam*—this material world; *dhāryate*—is being conducted; *jagat*—the cosmic manifestation.

TRANSLATION

"'Besides the inferior nature, O mighty-armed Arjuna, there is a superior energy of Mine, which is all living entities who are struggling with material nature and are sustaining the universe.'

PURPORT

In *Bhagavad-gītā* it is explained that the five elements earth, water, fire, air and ether constitute the gross energy of the Absolute Truth and that there are also three subtle energies, namely, the mind, intelligence and false ego, or identification with the phenomenal world. Thus the entire cosmic manifestation is divided into eight energies, all of which are inferior. As explained in *Bhagavad-gītā (mama māyā duratyayā),* the inferior energy known as *māyā* is so strong that although the living entity does not belong to this energy, due to the superior strength of the inferior energy the living entity *(jīva-bhūta)* forgets his real position and identifies with it. Kṛṣṇa says distinctly that beyond the material energy there is a superior energy which is known as the *jīva-bhūta* or living entities. When in contact with the material energy, this superior energy conducts all the activities of the entire material phenomenal world.

The supreme cause is Kṛṣṇa *(janmādy asya yataḥ),* who is the origin of all energies, which work variously. The Supreme Personality of Godhead has both inferior and superior energies, and the difference between them is that the superior energy is factual whereas the inferior energy is a reflection of the superior. A reflection of the sun in a mirror or on water appears to be the sun but is not. Similarly, the material world is but a reflection of the spiritual world. Although it appears to be factual, it is not; it is only a temporary reflection, whereas the spiritual world is a factual reality. The material world, with its gross and subtle forms, is merely a reflection of the spiritual world.

The living entity is not a product of the material energy; he is spiritual energy, but in contact with matter he forgets his identity. Thus the living entity identifies himself with matter and enthusiastically engages in material activities in the guises of a technologist, scientist, philosopher, etc. He does not know that he is not at all a material product but is spiritual. His real identity thus being lost, he struggles very hard in the material world, and the Hare Kṛṣṇa movement or Kṛṣṇa consciousness movement tries to revive his original consciousness. His activities in manufacturing big skyscrapers are evidence of intelligence, but this kind of intelligence is not at all advanced. One should know that his only real concern is how to get free from material contact, for by absorbing his mind in material activities he takes material bodies again and again, and although he falsely claims to be very intelligent, in material consciousness he is not at all intelligent. When we speak about the Kṛṣṇa consciousness movement, which is meant to make people intelligent, the conditioned living entity therefore misunderstands it. He is so engrossed in the material concept of life that he does not think that there can be any activities which are actually based on intelligence beyond the construction of skyscrapers and big roads and the manufacturing of cars. This is proof of *māyayāpahṛta-jñāna,* or loss of all intelligence due to the influence of *māyā.* When a living entity is freed from such misconceptions, he is called liberated. When one is actually liberated he no longer identifies with the material world. The symptom of *mukti* (liberation) is that one engages in spiritual activities instead of falsely engaging in material activities.

Transcendental loving devotional service is the spiritual activity of the spirit soul. Māyāvādī philosophers confuse such spiritual activity with material activity, but *Bhagavad-gītā* confirms:

māṁ ca yo'vyabhicāreṇa bhakti-yogena sevate
sa guṇān samatītyaitān brahma-bhūyāya kalpate
(Bg. 14.26)

One who engages in the spiritual activities of unalloyed devotional service *(avyabhicāriṇī-bhakti)* is immediately elevated to the transcendental platform, and he is to be considered *brahma-bhūta,* which indicates that he is no longer in the material world but in the spiritual world. Devotional service is enlightenment or awakening. When the living entity perfectly performs spiritual activities under the direction of the spiritual master, he becomes perfect in knowledge and understands that he is not God but a servant of God. As explained by Caitanya Mahāprabhu, *jīvera 'svarūpa' haya—kṛṣṇera 'nitya-dāsa':* the real identity of the living entity is that he is an eternal servant of the Supreme (Cc. *Madhya* 20.108). As long as one does not come to this conclusion, he must be in ignorance. This is also confirmed by the Lord in *Bhagavad-gītā* (Bg.7.19). *Bahūnāṁ janmanām ante jñānavān māṁ prapadyate:* "After many births of struggling for existence and cultivating knowledge, when one comes to the point of real knowledge he surrenders unto Me." Such an advanced *mahātmā* or great soul is very rarely to be seen. Thus although the Māyāvādī philosophers appear to be very advanced in knowledge, they are not yet perfect. To come to the point of perfection they must voluntarily surrender to Kṛṣṇa.

TEXT 119

বিষ্ণুশক্তিঃ পরা প্রোক্তা ক্ষেত্রজ্ঞাখ্যা তথাপরা ।
অবিদ্যাকর্মসংজ্ঞান্যা তৃতীয়া শক্তিরিষ্যতে ॥ ১১৯ ॥

viṣṇu-śaktiḥ parā proktā
kṣetrajñākhyā tathā parā
avidyā-karma-saṁjñānyā
tṛtīyā śaktir iṣyate

SYNONYMS

viṣṇu-śaktiḥ—the potency of Lord Viṣṇu; *parā*—spiritual; *proktā*—it is said; *kṣetrajña-ākhyā*—the potency known as *kṣetrajña*; *tathā*—as well as; *parā*—spiritual; *avidyā*—ignorance; *karma*—fruitive activities; *saṁjña*—known as; *anyā*—other; *tṛtīyā*—third; *śaktiḥ*—potency; *iṣyate*—known thus.

TRANSLATION

"'The potency of Lord Viṣṇu is summarized in three categories—namely, the spiritual potency, the living entities and ignorance. The spiritual potency is full of knowledge; the living entities, although belonging to the spiritual potency, are subject to bewilderment; and the third energy, which is full of ignorance, is always visible in fruitive activities.'

PURPORT

In the previous verse, quoted from *Bhagavad-gītā,* it has been established that the living entities are to be categorized among the Lord's potencies. The Lord is potent, and there are varieties of potencies *(parāsya śaktir vividhaiva śrūyate).* Now, in this quotation from the *Viṣṇu Purāṇa,* this is further confirmed. There are varieties of potencies, and they have been divided into three categories—namely, spiritual, marginal and external.

The spiritual potency is manifested in the spiritual world. Kṛṣṇa's form, qualities, activities and entourage are all spiritual. This is also confirmed in *Bhagavad-gītā:*

ajo 'pi sann avyayātmā
bhūtānām īśvaro 'pi san
prakṛtiṁ svām adhiṣṭhāya
sambhavāmy ātma-māyayā

"Although I am unborn and My transcendental body never deteriorates, and although I am the Lord of all sentient beings, I still appear in every millennium in My original transcendental form." (Bg. 4.6) *Ātma-māyā* refers to the spiritual potency. When Kṛṣṇa comes to this or any other universe, He does so with His spiritual potency. We take birth by the force of the material potency, but as stated here with reference to the *Viṣṇu Purāṇa,* the *kṣetrajña,* or living entity, belongs to the spiritual potency; thus when we free ourselves from the clutches of the material potency we can also enter the spiritual world.

The material potency is the energy of darkness, or complete ignorance of spiritual activities. In the material potency, the living entity engages himself in fruitive activities, thinking that he can be happy through expansion in terms of material energy. This fact is prominently manifest in this age of Kali because human society, not understanding the spiritual nature, is busily expanding in material activities. The men of the present day are almost unaware of their spiritual identity. They think that they are products of the elements of the material world and that everything will end with the annihilation of the body. Therefore they conclude that as long as one has a material body consisting of material senses, one should enjoy the senses as much as possible. Since they are atheists, they do not care whether there is a next life. Such activities are described in this verse as *avidyā-karma-saṁjñānyā.*

The material energy is separated from the spiritual energy of the Supreme Personality of Godhead. Thus although it is originally created by the Supreme Lord, He is not actually present within it. The Lord also confirms in *Bhagavad-gītā, mat-sthāni sarva-bhūtāni:* "Everything is resting on Me." (Bg. 9.4) This indicates that everything is resting on His own energy. For example, the planets are resting within outer space, which is the separated energy of Kṛṣṇa. The Lord explains in *Bhagavad-gītā:*

bhūmir āpo 'nalo vāyuḥ
khaṁ mano buddhir eva ca
ahaṅkāra itīyaṁ me
bhinnā prakṛtir aṣṭadhā

"Earth, water, fire, air, ether, mind, intelligence and false ego—all together these eight comprise My separated energies." (Bg. 7.4) The separated energy acts as if it were independent, but here it is said that although such energies are certainly factual, they are not independent but merely separated.

The separated energy can be understood from a practical example. I compose books by speaking into a dictaphone, and when the dictaphone is replayed, it appears that I am speaking personally, but actually I am not. I spoke personally, but then the dictaphone tape, which is separate from me, acts exactly like me. Similarly, the material energy originally emanates from the Supreme Personality of Godhead, but it acts separately, although the energy is supplied by the Lord. This is also explained in *Bhagavad-gītā. Mayādhyakṣeṇa prakṛtiḥ sūyate sa-carācaram:* "This material nature is working under My direction, O son of Kuntī, and it is producing all moving and unmoving beings." (Bg. 9.10) Under the guidance or superintendence of the Supreme Personality of Godhead, the material energy works as if independent, although it is not actually independent.

In this verse from the *Viṣṇu Purāṇa* the total energy of the Supreme Personality of Godhead is classified in three divisions—namely, the spiritual or internal potency of the Lord, the marginal potency or *kṣetrajña* (the living entity), and the material potency, which is separated from the Supreme Personality of Godhead and appears to act independently. When Śrīla Vyāsadeva, by meditation and self-realization, saw the Supreme Personality of Godhead, he also saw the separated energy of the Lord standing behind Him (*apaśyat puruṣaṁ pūrṇaṁ māyāṁ ca tad-apāśrayam*). Vyāsadeva also realized that it is this separated energy of the Lord, the material energy, that covers the knowledge of the living entities (*yayā sammohito jīva ātmānaṁ tri-guṇātmakam*). The separated, material energy bewilders the living entities (*jīvas*), and thus they work very hard under its influence, not knowing that they are not fulfilling their mission in life. Unfortunately, most of them think that they are the body and should therefore enjoy the material senses irresponsibly, since when death comes everything will be finished. This atheistic philosophy also flourished in India, where it was sometimes propagated by Cārvāka Muni, who said:

ṛṇaṁ kṛtvā ghṛtaṁ pibet
yāvaj jīvet sukhaṁ jīvet
bhasmī-bhūtasya dehasya kutaḥ
punar āgamano bhavet

His theory was that as long as one lives one should eat as much ghee as possible. In India, ghee (clarified butter) is a basic ingredient in preparing many varieties of foodstuffs. Since everyone wants to enjoy nice food, Cārvāka Muni advised that one eat as much ghee as possible. One may say, "I have no money. How shall I purchase ghee?" Cārvāka Muni, however, says, "If you have no money, then beg, borrow or steal, but in some way secure ghee and enjoy life." For one who further objects that he will be held accountable for such unauthorized activities as begging, borrowing and stealing, Cārvāka Muni replies, "You will not be held responsible. As soon as your body is burned to ashes after death, everything is finished." This is called ignorance. From *Bhagavad-gītā* it is understood that one does not die with the annihilation of his body (*na hanyate hanyamāne śarīre*). The annihilation of one body involves changing to another (*tathā dehāntara-prāptiḥ*). Therefore, to perform irresponsible activities in the material world is very dangerous. Without knowledge of the spirit soul and its transmigration, people are allured by the material energy to engage in many such activities, as if one could become happy simply by dint of material knowledge, without reference to spiritual existence. Therefore the entire material world and its activities are referred to as *avidyā-karma-saṁjñānyā.*

In order to dissipate the ignorance of the human beings who work under the material energy, which is separated from the Supreme Personality of Godhead, the Lord comes down to revive their original nature of spiritual activities (*yadā yadā hi dharmasya glānir bhavati bhārata*). As soon as they deviate from their original nature, the Lord comes to teach them, *sarva-dharmān parityajya mām ekaṁ śaraṇaṁ vraja:* "My dear living entities, give up all material activities and simply surrender unto Me for protection." (Bg. 18.66)

It is the statement of Cārvāka Muni that one should beg, borrow or steal money to purchase ghee and enjoy life (*ṛṇaṁ kṛtvā ghṛtaṁ pibet*). Thus even the greatest atheist of India recommends that one eat ghee, not meat. No one could conceive of human beings' eating meat like tigers and dogs, but men have become so degraded that they are just like animals and can no longer claim to have a human civilization.

TEXT 120

হেন জীবতত্ত্ব লঞা লিখি' পরতত্ত্ব ।
আচ্ছন্ন করিল শ্রেষ্ঠ ঈশ্বর-মহত্ত্ব ॥ ১২০ ॥

hena jīva-tattva lañā likhi' para-tattva
ācchanna karila śreṣṭha īśvara-mahattva

SYNONYMS

hena—such degraded; *jīva-tattva*—the living entities; *lañā*—taking them; *likhi'*—having written; *para-tattva*—as the Supreme; *ācchanna*—covering; *karila*—did; *śreṣṭha*—the Supreme Personality of Godhead; *īśvara*—the Lord's; *mahattva*—glories.

TRANSLATION

"The Māyāvāda philosophy is so degraded that it has taken the insignificant living entities to be the Lord, the Supreme Truth, thus covering the glory and supremacy of the Absolute Truth with monism.

PURPORT

Śrīla Bhaktivinoda Ṭhākura comments in this connection that in all Vedic scriptures the *jīva-tattva,* the truth of the living entities, is mentioned to be one of the energies of the Lord. If one does not accept the living entity to be a minute, infinitesimal spark of the Supreme but equates the *jīva-tattva* with the Supreme Brahman or Supreme Personality of Godhead, it must be understood that his entire philosophy is based on a misunderstanding. Unfortunately, Śrīpāda Śaṅkarācārya purposely claimed the *jīva-tattva,* or living entities, to be equal to the Supreme God. Therefore his entire philosophy is based on a misunderstanding, and it misguides people to become atheists whose mission in life is unfulfilled. The mission of human life, as described in *Bhagavad-gītā,* is to surrender unto the Supreme Lord and become His devotee, but the Māyāvāda philosophy misleads one to defy the existence of the Supreme Personality of Godhead and pose oneself as the Supreme Lord. Thus it has misguided hundreds and thousands of innocent men.

In the *Vedānta-sūtra,* Vyāsadeva has described that the Supreme Personality of Godhead is potent and that everything, material or spiritual, is but an emanation of His energy. The Lord, the Supreme Brahman, is the origin or source of everything (*janmādy asya yataḥ*), and all other manifestations are emanations of different energies of the Lord. This is also confirmed in the *Viṣṇu-Purāṇa:*

ekadeśa-sthitasyāgner
jyotsnā vistāriṇī yathā
parasya brahmaṇaḥ śaktis
tathedam akhilaṁ jagat

"Whatever we see in this world is simply an expansion of different energies of the Supreme Personality of Godhead, who is exactly like a fire which spreads illumination for a long distance although it is situated in one place." This is a very vivid example. Similarly, it is stated that just as everything in the material world exists in the sunshine, which is the energy of the sun, so everything exists on the basis of the spiritual and material energies of the Supreme Personality of Godhead. Thus although Kṛṣṇa is situated in His own abode (*goloka eva nivasaty akhilātma-bhūto*) where He enjoys His transcendental pastimes with the cowherd boys and *gopīs,* He is nevertheless present everywhere, even within the atoms of this universe (*aṇḍāntarastha-paramāṇu-cayāntarastham*). This is the verdict of the Vedic literature.

Unfortunately, the Māyāvāda philosophy, misguiding people by claiming the living entity to be the Lord, has created havoc throughout the entire world and led almost everyone to godlessness. By thus covering the glories of the Supreme Lord, the Māyāvādī philosophers have done the greatest disservice to human society. It is to counteract these most abominable activities of the Māyāvādī philosophers that Lord Caitanya has introduced the Hare Kṛṣṇa *mahā-mantra.*

harer nāma harer nāma harer nāmaiva kevalam
kalau nāsty eva nāsty eva nāsty eva gatir anyathā

"In this age of quarrel and hypocrisy the only means of deliverance is chanting the holy name of the Lord. There is no other way. There is no other way. There is no other way." People should simply engage in the chanting of the Hare Kṛṣṇa *mahā-mantra,* for thus they will gradually come to understand that they are not the Supreme Personality of Godhead, as they have been taught by the Māyāvādī philosophers, but are eternal servants of the Lord. As soon as one engages himself in the transcendental service of the Lord, he becomes free.

māṁ ca yo 'vyabhicāreṇa
bhakti-yogena sevate
sa guṇān samatītyaitān
brahma-bhūyāya kalpate

"One who engages in full devotional service, who does not fall down in any circumstances, at once transcends the modes of material nature and thus comes to the level of Brahman." (Bg. 14.26) Therefore the Hare Kṛṣṇa movement or Kṛṣṇa consciousness movement is the only light for the foolish living entities who think either that there is no God or that if God exists He is formless and they themselves are also God. These misconceptions are very dangerous, and the only way to counteract them is to spread the Hare Kṛṣṇa movement.

TEXT 121

ব্যাসের সূত্রেতে কহে 'পরিণাম'-বাদ।
'ব্যাস ভ্রান্ত'— বলি' তার উঠাইল বিবাদ ॥ ১২১ ॥

vyāsera sūtrete kahe 'pariṇāma'-vāda
'vyāsa bhrānta'—bali' tāra uṭhāila vivāda

SYNONYMS

vyāsera—of Śrīla Vyāsadeva; *sūtrete*—in the codes; *kahe*—describes; *pariṇāma*—transformation; *vāda*—philosophy; *vyāsa*—Śrīla Vyāsadeva; *bhrānta*—mistaken; *bali'*—accusing him; *tāra*—his; *uṭhāila*—raised; *vivāda*—opposition.

TRANSLATION

"In his Vedānta-sūtra Śrīla Vyāsadeva has described that everything is but a transformation of the energy of the Lord. Śaṅkarācārya, however, has misled the world by commenting that Vyāsadeva was mistaken. Thus he has raised great opposition to theism throughout the entire world.

PURPORT

Śrīla Bhaktivinoda Ṭhākura explains, "In the *Vedānta-sūtra* of Śrīla Vyāsadeva it is definitely stated that all cosmic manifestations result from transformations of various energies of the Lord. Śaṅkarācārya, however, not accepting the energy of the Lord, thinks that it is the Lord who is transformed. He has taken many clear statements from the Vedic literature and twisted them to try to prove that if the Lord, or the Absolute Truth, were transformed, His oneness would be disturbed. Thus he has accused Śrīla Vyāsadeva of being mistaken. In developing his philosophy of monism, therefore, he has established *vivarta-vāda,* or the Māyāvāda theory of illusion."

In the *Brahma-sūtra,* Second Chapter, the first quote is as follows: *tad ananyatvam ārambhaṇa-śabdādibhyaḥ.* Commenting on this *sūtra* in his *Śārīraka-bhāṣya,* Śaṅkarācārya has introduced the statement *vācārambhaṇaṁ vikāro nāmadheyam* from the *Chāndogya Upaniṣad* to try to prove that acceptance of the transformation of the energy of the Supreme Lord is faulty. He has tried to defy this transformation of energy in a misguided way, which will be explained later. Since his conception of God is impersonal, he does not believe that the entire cosmic manifestation is a transformation of the energies of the Lord, for as soon as one accepts the various energies of the Absolute Truth, one must immediately accept the Absolute Truth to be personal, not impersonal. A person can create many things by the transformation of his energy. For example, a businessman transforms his energy by establishing many big factories or business organizations, yet he remains a person although his energy has been transformed into these many factories or business concerns. The Māyāvādī philosophers do not understand this simple fact. Their tiny brains and poor fund of knowledge cannot afford them sufficient enlightenment to realize that when a man's energy is transformed, the man himself is not transformed but remains the same person.

Not believing in the fact that the energy of the Absolute Truth is transformed, Śaṅkarācārya has propounded his theory of illusion. This theory states that although the Absolute Truth is never transformed, we think that it is transformed, which is an illusion. Śaṅkarācārya does not believe in the transformation of the energy of the Absolute Truth, for he claims that everything is one and that the living entity is therefore also one with the Supreme. This is the Māyāvāda theory.

Śrīla Vyāsadeva has explained that the Absolute Truth is a person who has different potencies. Merely by His desire that there be creation and by His glance *(sa aikṣata),* He created this material world *(sa asṛjata).* After creation, He remains the same person; He is not transformed into everything. One should accept that the Lord has inconceivable energies and that it is by His order and will that varieties of manifestation have come into existence. In the *Vedānta-sūtra* it is said, *sa-tattvato 'nyathā-buddhir vikāra ity udāhṛtaḥ.* This *mantra* indicates that from one fact another fact is generated. For example, a father is one fact, and a son generated from the father is a second fact. Thus both of them are truths, although one is generated from the other. This generation of a second, independent truth from a first truth is called *vikāra,* or transformation resulting in a by-product. The Supreme Brahman is the Absolute Truth, and the other energies that have emanated from Him and are existing separately, such as the living entities and the cosmic manifestation, are also truths. This is an example of transformation, which is called *vikāra* or *pariṇāma.* To give another example of *vikāra,* milk is a truth, but the same milk may be transformed into yogurt. Thus yogurt is a transformation of milk, although the ingredients of yogurt and milk are the same.

In the *Chāndogya Upaniṣad* there is the following *mantra: aitad ātmyam idaṁ sarvam.* This *mantra* indicates without a doubt that the entire world is Brahman. The Absolute Truth has inconceivable energies, as confirmed in the *Śvetāśvatara Upaniṣad (parāsya śaktir vividhaiva śrūyate),* and the entire cosmic manifestation is evidence of these different energies of the Supreme Lord. The Supreme Lord is a fact, and therefore whatever is created by the Supreme Lord is also factual. Everything is true and complete *(pūrṇam),* but the original *pūrṇam,* the complete Absolute Truth, always remains the same. *Pūrṇāt pūrṇam udacyate pūrṇasya pūrṇam ādāya.* The Absolute Truth is so perfect that although innumerable energies emanate from Him and manifest creations which appear to be different from Him, He nevertheless maintains His personality. He never deteriorates under any circumstances.

It is to be concluded that the entire cosmic manifestation is a transformation of the energy of the Supreme Lord, not of the Supreme Lord or Absolute Truth Himself, who always remains the same. The material world and the living entities are transformations of the energy of the Lord, the Absolute Truth or Brahman, who is the original source. In other words, the Absolute Truth, Brahman, is the original ingredient, and the other manifestations are transformations of this ingredient. This is also confirmed in the *Taittirīya Upaniṣad. Yato vā imāni bhūtāni jāyante:* "This entire cosmic manifestation is made possible by the Absolute

Truth, the Supreme Personality of Godhead." In this verse it is indicated that Brahman, the Absolute Truth, is the original cause, and the living entities *(jīvas)* and cosmic manifestation are effects of this cause. The cause being a fact, the effects are also factual. They are not illusion. Śaṅkarācārya has inconsistently tried to prove that acceptance of the material world and the *jīvas* to be by-products of the Supreme Lord is an illusion because in this conception the existence of the material world and the *jīvas* is different and separate from that of the Absolute Truth. With this jugglery of understanding, Māyāvādī philosophers have propagated the slogan *brahma satyaṁ jagan-mithyā,* which declares that the Absolute Truth is fact but the cosmic manifestation and the living entities are simply illusions, or that all of them are in fact the Absolute Truth and that the material world and living entities do not separately exist.

It is therefore to be concluded that Śaṅkarācārya, in order to present the Supreme Lord, the living entities and the material nature as indivisible and ignorant, tries to cover the glories of the Supreme Personality of Godhead. He maintains that the material cosmic manifestation is *mithyā,* or false, but this is a great blunder. If the Supreme Personality of Godhead is a fact, how can His creation be false? Even in ordinary dealings, one cannot think the material cosmic manifestation to be false. Therefore Vaiṣṇava philosophers say that the cosmic creation is not false but temporary. It is separated from the Supreme Personality of Godhead, but since it is wonderfully created by the energy of the Lord, to say that it is false is blasphemous.

Nondevotees factually appreciate the wonderful creation of material nature, but they cannot appreciate the intelligence and energy of the Supreme Personality of Godhead who is behind this material creation. Śrīpāda Rāmānujācārya, however, refers to a Vedic *sūtra, ātmā vā idam agra āsīt,* which points out that the supreme *ātmā,* the Absolute Truth, existed before the creation. One may argue, "If the Supreme Personality of Godhead is completely spiritual, how is it possible for Him to be the origin of creation and have within Himself both material and spiritual energies?" To answer this challenge, Śrīpāda Rāmānujācārya quotes a *mantra* from the *Taittirīya Upaniṣad* which states:

yato vā imāni bhūtāni jāyante
yena jātāni jīvanti
yat prayanty abhisaṁviśanti.

This *mantra* confirms that the entire cosmic manifestation emanates from the Absolute Truth, rests upon the Absolute Truth and after annihilation again reenters the body of the Absolute Truth, the Supreme Personality of Godhead. The living entity is originally spiritual, and when he enters the spiritual world or the body of the Supreme Lord, he still retains his identity as an individual soul. In this connection Śrīpāda Rāmānujācārya gives the example that when a green bird enters a green tree it does not become one with the tree; it retains its identity as a bird, although it appears to merge in the greenness of the tree. To give another example, an animal that enters a forest keeps its individuality, although apparently the beast merges in the forest. Similarly, in material existence, both the material energy and the living entities of the marginal potency maintain their individuality. Thus although the energies of the Supreme Personality of Godhead interact within the cosmic manifestation, each keeps its separate individual existence. Merging in the material or spiritual energies, therefore, does not involve loss of individuality. According to Śrī Rāmānujapāda's theory of *viśiṣṭādvaita,* although all the energies of the Lord are one, each keeps its individuality *(vaiśiṣṭya).*

Śrīpāda Śaṅkarācārya has tried to mislead the readers of *Vedānta-sūtra* by misinterpreting the words *ānandamayo 'bhyāsāt,* and he has even tried to find fault with Vyāsadeva. All the codes of the *Vedānta-sūtra* need not be examined here, however, since we intend to present the *Vedānta-sūtra* in a separate volume.

TEXT 122

পরিণাম-বাদে ঈশ্বর হয়েন বিকারী ।
এত কহি' 'বিবর্ত'-বাদ স্থাপনা যে করি ॥ ১২২ ॥

pariṇāma-vāde īśvara hayena vikārī
eta kahi' 'vivarta'-vāda sthāpanā ye kari

SYNONYMS

pariṇāma-vāde—by accepting the theory of transformation of energy; *īśvara*—the Supreme Lord; *hayena*—becomes; *vikārī*—transformed; *eta kahi'*—saying this; *vivarta*—illusion; *vāda*—theory; *sthāpanā*—establishing; *ye*—what; *kari*—do.

TRANSLATION

"According to Śaṅkarācārya, by accepting the theory of the transformation of the energy of the Lord, one creates an illusion by indirectly accepting that the Absolute Truth is transformed.

PURPORT

Śrīla Bhaktivinoda Ṭhākura comments that if one does not clearly understand the meaning of *pariṇāma-vāda,* or transformation of energy, one is sure to misunderstand the truth regarding this material cosmic manifestation and the living entities. In the *Chāndogya Upaniṣad* it is said, *san-mūlāḥ saumyemāḥ prajāḥ sadāyatanāḥ sat-pratiṣṭhāḥ* (*Chā. U.* 6.8.4). The material world and the living entities are separate beings, and they are eternally true, not false. Śaṅkarācārya, however, unnecessarily fearing that by *pariṇāma-vāda* (transformation of energy) Brahman would be transformed *(vikārī),* has imagined both the material world and the living entities to be false and to have no individuality. By word jugglery he has tried to prove that the individual identities of the living entities and the material world are illusory, and he has cited the examples of mistaking a rope for a snake or an oyster shell for gold. Thus he has most abominably cheated people in general.

The example of misunderstanding a rope to be a snake is mentioned in the *Māṇḍūkya Upaniṣad,* but it is meant to explain the error of identifying the body with the soul. Since the soul is actually a spiritual particle, as confirmed in *Bhagavad-gītā (mamaivāṁśo jīva-loke),* it is due to illusion *(vivarta-vāda)* that a human being, like an animal, identifies the body with the self. This is a proper example of *vivarta,* or illusion. The verse *atattvato 'nyathā-buddhir vivarta ity udāhṛtaḥ* describes such an illusion. To not know actual facts and thus to mistake one thing for another (as, for example, to accept the body as oneself) is called *vivarta-vāda.* Every conditioned living entity who considers the body to be the soul is deluded by this *vivarta-vāda.* One can be attacked by this *vivarta-vāda* philosophy when he forgets the inconceivable power of the omnipotent Personality of Godhead.

How the Supreme Personality of Godhead remains as He is, never changing, is explained in the *Īśopaniṣad: pūrṇasya pūrṇam ādāya pūrṇam evāvaśiṣyate.* God is complete. Even if a complete manifestation is taken away from Him, He continues to be complete. The material creation is manifested by the energy of the Lord, but He is still the same person. His form, entourage, qualities and so on never deteriorate. Śrīla Jīva Gosvāmī, in his *Paramātma-sandarbha,* comments regarding the *vivarta-vāda* as follows: "Under the spell of *vivarta-vāda* one imagines the separate entities, namely, the cosmic manifestation and the living entities, to be one with Brahman. This is due to complete ignorance regarding the actual fact. The Absolute Truth, or Parabrahman, is always one and always the same. He is completely free from all other conceptions of existence. He is completely free from false ego, for He is the full spiritual identity. It is absolutely impossible for Him to be subjected to ignorance and fall under the spell of a misconception (*vivarta-vāda*). The Absolute Truth is beyond our conception. One must admit that He has unblemished qualities that He does not share with every living entity. He is never tainted in the slightest degree by the flaws of ordinary living beings. Everyone must therefore understand the Absolute Truth to possess inconceivable potencies."

TEXT 123

বস্তুতঃ পরিণাম-বাদ— সেই সে প্রমাণ ।
দেহে আত্মবুদ্ধি—এই বিবর্তের স্থান ॥ ১২৩ ॥

vastutaḥ pariṇāma-vāda—sei se pramāṇa
dehe ātma-buddhi—ei vivartera sthāna

SYNONYMS

vastutaḥ—factually; *pariṇāma-vāda*—transformation of the energy; *sei*—that; *se*—only; *pramāṇa*—proof; *dehe*—in the body; *ātma-buddhi*—concept of self; *ei*—this; *vivartera*—of illusion; *sthāna*—place.

TRANSLATION

"Transformation of energy is a proven fact. It is the false bodily conception of the self that is an illusion.

PURPORT

The *jīva,* or living entity, is a spiritual spark who is part of the Supreme Personality of Godhead. Unfortunately, he thinks the body to be the self, and that misunderstanding is called *vivarta,* or acceptance of untruth to be truth. The body is not the self, but animals and foolish people think that it is. *Vivarta* (illusion) does not, however, denote a change in the identity of the spirit soul; it is the misconception that the body is the self that is an illusion. Similarly, the Supreme Personality of Godhead does not change when His external energy, consisting of the eight gross and subtle material elements listed in *Bhagavad-gītā (bhūmir āpo 'nalo vāyuḥ,* etc.), acts and reacts in different phases.

TEXT 124

অবিচিন্ত্য-শক্তিযুক্ত শ্রীভগবান্ ।
ইচ্ছায় জগদ্রূপে পায় পরিণাম ॥ ১২৪ ॥

avicintya-śakti-yūkta śrī-bhagavān
icchāya jagad-rūpe pāya pariṇāma

SYNONYMS

avicintya—inconceivable; *śakti*—potency; *yūkta*—possessed of; *śrī*—the affluent; *bhagavān*—Personality of Godhead; *icchāya*—by His wish; *jagat-rūpe*—in the form of the cosmic manifestation; *pāya*—becomes; *pariṇāma*—transformed by His energy.

TRANSLATION

"The Supreme Personality of Godhead is opulent in all respects. Therefore by His inconceivable energies He has transformed the material cosmic manifestation.

TEXT 125

তথাপি অচিন্ত্যশক্ত্যে হয় অবিকারী ।
প্রাকৃত চিন্তামণি তাহে দৃষ্টান্ত যে ধরি ॥ ১২৫ ॥

tathāpi acintya-śaktye haya avikārī
prākṛta cintāmaṇi tāhe dṛṣṭānta ye dhari

SYNONYMS

tathāpi—yet; *acintya-śaktye*—by inconceivable potency; *haya*—remains; *avikārī*—without change; *prākṛta*—material; *cintāmaṇi*—touchstone; *tāhe*—in that respect; *dṛṣṭānta*—example; *ye*—which; *dhari*—we accept.

TRANSLATION

"Using the example of a touchstone, which by its energy turns iron to gold and yet remains the same, we can understand that although the Supreme Personality of Godhead transforms His innumerable energies, He remains unchanged.

TEXT 126

নানা রত্নরাশি হয় চিন্তামণি হৈতে ।
তথাপিহ মণি রহে স্বরূপে অবিকৃতে ॥ ১২৬ ॥

nānā ratna-rāśi haya cintāmaṇi haite
tathāpiha maṇi rahe svarūpe avikṛte

SYNONYMS

nānā—varieties; *ratna-rāśi*—valuable jewels; *haya*—become possible; *cintāmaṇi*—the touchstone; *haite*—from; *tathāpiha*—still, certainly; *maṇi*—the touchstone; *rahe*—remains; *svarūpe*—in its original form; *avikṛte*—without change.

TRANSLATION

"Although touchstone produces many varieties of valuable jewels, it nevertheless remains the same. It does not change its original form.

TEXT 127

প্রাকৃত-বস্তুতে যদি অচিন্ত্যশক্তি হয় ।
ঈশ্বরের অচিন্ত্যশক্তি,—ইথে কি বিস্ময় ॥ ১২৭ ॥

prākṛta-vastute yadi acintya-śakti haya
īśvarera acintya-śakti,—ithe ki vismaya

SYNONYMS

prākṛta-vastute—in material things; *yadi*—if; *acintya*—inconceivable; *śakti*—potency; *haya*—becomes possible; *īśvarera*—of the Supreme Lord; *acintya*—inconceivable; *śakti*—potency; *ithe*—in this; *ki*—what; *vismaya*—wonderful.

TRANSLATION

"If there is such inconceivable potency in material objects, why should we not believe in the inconceivable potency of the Supreme Personality of Godhead?

PURPORT

The argument of Śrī Caitanya Mahāprabhu described in this verse can be very easily understood even by a common man if he simply thinks of the activities of the sun, which has been giving off unlimited amounts of heat and light since time immemorial and yet has not even slightly decreased in power. Modern science believes that it is by sunshine that the entire cosmic manifestation is maintained, and actually one can see how the actions and reactions of sunshine maintain order throughout the universe. The growth of vegetables and even the rotation of the planets take place due to the heat and light of the sun. Sometimes, therefore, modern scientists consider the sun to be the original cause of creation, not knowing that the sun is only a medium, for it is also created by the supreme energy of the Supreme Personality of Godhead. Aside from the sun and touchstone, there are many other material things which transform their energy in different ways and yet remain as they are. It is not necessary, therefore, for the original cause, the Supreme Personality of Godhead, to change due to the changes or transformations of His different energies.

The falsity of Śrīpāda Śaṅkarācārya's explanation of *vivarta-vāda* and *pariṇāma-vāda* has been detected by the Vaiṣṇava *ācāryas,* especially Jīva Gosvāmī, whose opinion is that actually Śaṅkara did not understand the *Vedānta-sūtra.* In Śaṅkara's explanation of one *sūtra, ānandamayo 'bhyāsāt,* he has interpreted the affix *mayaṭ* with such word jugglery that this very explanation proves that he had little knowledge of the *Vedānta-sūtra* but simply wanted to support his impersonalism through the codes of the Vedānta philosophy. Actually, however, he failed to do so because he could not put forward strong arguments. In this connection, Śrīla Jīva Gosvāmī cites the code *brahma-puccham pratiṣṭhā,* which gives Vedic evidence that Brahman is the origin of everything. In explaining this verse, Śrīpāda Śaṅkarācārya interpreted various Sanskrit words in such a way that he implied, according to Jīva Gosvāmī, that Vyāsadeva had very little knowledge of higher logic. Such unscrupulous deviation from the real meaning of the *Vedānta-sūtra* has created a class of men who by word jugglery try to derive various indirect meanings from the Vedic literatures, especially *Bhagavad-gītā.* One of them has even explained that the word *kurukṣetra* refers to the body. Such interpretations imply, however, that neither Lord Kṛṣṇa nor Vyāsadeva had a proper sense of word usage or etymological adjustment. They lead one to assume that since Lord Kṛṣṇa could not personally sense the meaning of what He was speaking and Vyāsadeva did not know the meaning of what he was writing, Lord Kṛṣṇa left His book to be explained later by the Māyāvādīs. Such interpretations merely prove, however, that their proponents have very little philosophical sense.

Instead of wasting one's time falsely deriving such indirect meanings from *Vedānta-sūtra* and other Vedic literatures, one should accept the words of these books as they are. In presenting *Bhagavad-gītā As It Is,* therefore, we have not changed the meaning of the original words. Similarly, if one studies *Vedānta-sūtra* as it is, without whimsical and capricious adulteration, one can understand the *Vedānta-sūtra* very easily. Śrīla Vyāsadeva therefore explains *Vedānta-sūtra,* beginning from the first *sūtra, janmādy asya yataḥ,* in his *Śrīmad-Bhāgavatam:*

janmādy asya yato 'nvayād itarataś cārtheṣv abhijñaḥ sva-rāṭ

"I meditate upon Him [Lord Śrī Kṛṣṇa], the transcendent reality, who is the primeval cause of all causes, from whom all manifested universes arise, in whom they dwell and by whom they are destroyed. I meditate upon that eternally effulgent Lord who is directly and indirectly conscious of all manifestations and yet is fully independent." The Supreme Personality of Godhead knows very well how to do everything perfectly. He is *abhijñaḥ,* always fully conscious. The Lord therefore says in *Bhagavad-gītā* (Bg. 7.26) that He knows everything, past, present and future, but no one but a devotee knows Him as He is. Therefore, the Absolute Truth, the Personality of Godhead, is at least partially understood by devotees of the Lord, but the Māyāvādī philosophers who unnecessarily speculate to understand the Absolute Truth simply waste their time.

TEXT 128

'প্রণব' সে মহাবাক্য—বেদের নিদান ।
ঈশ্বরস্বরূপ প্রণব সর্ববিশ্ব-ধাম ॥ ১২৮ ॥

'praṇava' se mahāvākya—vedera nidāna
īśvara-svarūpa praṇava sarva-viśva-dhāma

SYNONYMS

praṇava—the *oṁkāra; se*—that; *mahā-vākya*—transcendental sound vibration; *vedera*—of the *Vedas*; *nidāna*—basic principle; *īśvara-svarūpa*—direct representation of the Supreme Personality of Godhead; *praṇava—oṁkāra; sarva-viśva*—of all universes; *dhāma*—is the reservoir.

TRANSLATION

"The Vedic sound vibration oṁkāra, the principle word in the Vedic literatures, is the basis of all Vedic vibrations. Therefore one should accept oṁkāra as the sound representation of the Supreme Personality of Godhead and the reservoir of the cosmic manifestation.

PURPORT

In *Bhagavad-gītā* (Bg. 8.13) the glories of *oṁkāra* are described as follows:

oṁ ity ekākṣaraṁ brahma
vyāharan mām anusmaran
yaḥ prayāti tyajan dehaṁ
sa yāti paramāṁ gatim

This verse indicates that *oṁkāra,* or *praṇava,* is a direct representation of the Supreme Personality of Godhead. Therefore if at the time of death one simply remembers *oṁkāra,* he remembers the Supreme Personality of Godhead and is therefore immediately transferred to the spiritual world. *Oṁkāra* is the basic principle of all

Vedic *mantras,* for it is a representation of Lord Kṛṣṇa, understanding of whom is the ultimate goal of the *Vedas,* as stated in *Bhagavad-gītā (vedaiś ca sarvair aham eva vedyaḥ).* Māyāvādī philosophers cannot understand these simple facts explained in *Bhagavad-gītā,* and yet they are very proud of being Vedāntīs. Sometimes, therefore, we refer to the Vedāntī philosophers as having no teeth (*danta* means "teeth," and *ve* means "without"). The statements of the Śaṅkara philosophy, which are the teeth of the Māyāvādī philosopher, are always broken by the strong arguments of Vaiṣṇava philosophers such as the great *ācāryas,* especially Rāmānujācārya. Śrīpāda Rāmānujācārya and Madhvācārya break the teeth of the Māyāvādī philosophers, who can therefore be called Vedāntīs in the sense of "toothless."

The transcendental vibration *oṁkāra* is explained in *Bhagavad-gītā,* Chapter Eight, verse thirteen:

om ity ekākṣaraṁ brahma
vyāharan mām anusmaran
yaḥ prayāti tyajan dehaṁ
sa yāti paramāṁ gatim

"After being situated in the *yoga* practice and vibrating the sacred syllable *om,* the supreme combination of letters, if one thinks of the Supreme Personality of Godhead and quits his body, he will certainly reach the spiritual planets." If one actually understands that *oṁkāra* is the sound representation of the Supreme Personality of Godhead, whether he chants *oṁkāra* or the Hare Kṛṣṇa *mantra,* the result is certainly the same.

The transcendental vibration of *oṁkāra* is further explained in *Bhagavad-gītā,* Chapter Nine, verse seventeen:

pitāham asya jagato
mātā dhātā pitāmahaḥ
vedyaṁ pavitram oṁkāra
ṛk sāma yajur eva ca

"I am the father of this universe, the mother, the support, and the grandsire. I am the object of knowledge, the purifier and the syllable *om.* I am also the *Ṛg-veda, Sāma-veda* and *Yajur-veda.*"

Similarly, the transcendental sound *om* is further explained in *Bhagavad-gītā,* Chapter Seventeen, verse twenty-three:

oṁ-tat-sad iti nirdeśo
brahmaṇas tri-vidhaḥ smṛtaḥ
brāhmaṇās tena vedāś ca
yajñāś ca vihitāḥ purā

"From the beginning of creation, the three syllables *om tat sat* have been used to indicate the Supreme Absolute Truth [Brahman]. They were uttered by *brāhmaṇas* while chanting Vedic hymns and during sacrifices for the satisfaction of the Supreme."

Throughout all the Vedic literatures the glories of *oṁkāra* are specifically mentioned. Śrīla Jīva Gosvāmī, in his thesis *Bhagavat-sandarbha,* says that in the Vedic literature *oṁkāra* is considered to be the sound vibration of the holy name of the Supreme Personality of Godhead. Only this vibration of transcendental sound can deliver a conditioned soul from the clutches of *māyā*. Sometimes *oṁkāra* is also called the deliverer *(tāra). Śrīmad-Bhāgavatam* begins with the *oṁkāra* vibration: *oṁ namo bhagavate vāsudevāya.* Therefore *oṁkāra* has been described by the great commentator Śrīdhara Svāmī as *tārāṅkura,* the seed of deliverance from the material world. Since the Supreme Godhead is absolute, His holy name and His sound vibration *oṁkāra* are as good as He Himself. Caitanya Mahāprabhu says that the holy name, or *oṁkāra,* the transcendental representation of the Supreme Personality of Godhead, has all the potencies of the Personality of Godhead.

nāmnām akāri bahudhā nija-sarva-śaktis
tatrārpitā niyamitaḥ smaraṇe na kālaḥ

All potencies are invested in the holy vibration of the holy name of the Lord. There is no doubt that the holy name of the Lord, or *oṁkāra,* is the Supreme Personality of Godhead Himself. In other words, anyone who chants *oṁkāra* and the holy name of the Lord, Hare Kṛṣṇa, immediately meets the Supreme Lord directly in His sound form. In the *Nārada-pañcarātra* it is clearly said that the Supreme Personality of Godhead Nārāyaṇa personally appears before the chanter who engages in chanting the *aṣṭākṣara,* or eight-syllable *mantra, oṁ namo nārāyaṇāya.* A similar statement in the *Māṇḍūkya Upaniṣad* declares that whatever one sees in the spiritual world is all an expansion of the spiritual potency of *oṁkāra.*

On the basis of all the *Upaniṣads,* Śrīla Jīva Gosvāmī says that *oṁkāra* is the Supreme Absolute Truth and is accepted as such by all the *ācāryas* and authorities. *Oṁkāra* is beginningless, changeless, supreme and free from deterioration and external contamination. *Oṁkāra* is the origin, middle and end of everything, and any living entity who thus understands *oṁkāra* attains the perfection of spiritual identity in *oṁkāra. Oṁkāra,* being situated in everyone's heart, is *Īśvara,* the Supreme Personality of Godhead, as confirmed in *Bhagavad-gītā (īśvaraḥ sarva-bhūtānāṁ hṛd-deśe 'rjuna tiṣṭhati). Oṁkāra* is as good as Viṣṇu because *oṁkāra* is as all-pervasive as Viṣṇu. One who knows *oṁkāra* and Lord Viṣṇu to be identical no longer has to lament or hanker. One who chants *oṁkāra* no longer remains a *śūdra,* but immediately comes to the position of a *brāhmaṇa.* Simply by chanting *oṁkāra* one can understand the whole creation to be one unit, or an expansion of the energy of the Supreme Lord. *Idaṁ hi viśvaṁ bhagavān ivetaro, yato jagat-sthāna-nirodha-sambhavāḥ:* "The Supreme Lord Personality of Godhead is Himself this cosmos, and still He is aloof from it. From Him only this cosmic manifestation has emanated, in Him it rests, and unto Him it enters after annihilation." (*Bhāg.* 1.5.20) Although one who does not understand concludes otherwise, *Śrīmad-Bhāgavatam* states that the entire cosmic manifestation is but an expansion of the energy of the Supreme Lord. Realization of this is possible simply by chanting the holy name of the Lord, *oṁkāra.*

One should not, however, foolishly conclude that because the Supreme Personality of Godhead is omnipotent, we have manufactured a combination of letters—*a, u* and *m*—to represent Him. Factually the transcendental sound *oṁkāra*, although a combination of the three letters *a, u* and *m,* has transcendental potency, and one who chants *oṁkāra* will very soon realize *oṁkāra* and Lord Viṣṇu to be nondifferent. Kṛṣṇa declares, *praṇavaḥ sarva-vedeṣu:* "I am the syllable *oṁ* in the Vedic *mantras.*" (Bg. 7.8) One should therefore conclude that among the many incarnations of the Supreme Personality of Godhead, *oṁkāra* is the sound incarnation. All the *Vedas* accept this thesis. One should always remember that the holy name of the Lord and the Lord Himself are always identical *(abhinnatvān nāma-nāminoḥ).* Since *oṁkāra* is the basic principle of all Vedic knowledge, it is uttered before one begins to chant any Vedic hymn. Without *oṁkāra,* no Vedic *mantra* is successful. The Gosvāmīs therefore declare that *praṇava (oṁkāra)* is the complete representation of the Supreme Personality of Godhead, and they have analyzed *oṁkāra* in terms of its alphabetical constituents as follows:

a-kāreṇocyate kṛṣṇaḥ
sarva-lokaika-nāyakaḥ
u-kāreṇocyate rādhā
ma-kāro jīva-vācakaḥ

Oṁkāra is a combination of the letters *a, u* and *m. A-kāreṇocyate kṛṣṇaḥ:* the letter *a (a-kāra)* refers to Kṛṣṇa, who is *sarva-lokaika-nāyakaḥ,* the master of all living entities and planets, material and spiritual. *Nāyaka* means "leader." He is the supreme leader *(nityo nityānāṁ cetanaś cetanānām).* The letter *u (u-kāra)* indicates Śrīmatī Rādhārāṇī, the pleasure potency of Kṛṣṇa, and *m (ma-kāra)* indicates the living entities *(jīvas).* Thus *oṁ* is the complete combination of Kṛṣṇa, His potency and His eternal servitors. In other words, *oṁkāra* represents Kṛṣṇa, His name, fame, pastimes, entourage, expansions, devotees, potencies and everything else pertaining to Him. *Sarva-viśva-dhāma: oṁkāra* is the resting place of everything, just as Kṛṣṇa is the resting place of everything *(brahmaṇo hi pratiṣṭhāham).*

The Māyāvādī philosophers consider many Vedic *mantras* to be the *mahā-vākya,* or principal Vedic *mantra,* such as *tattvamasi* (*Chāndogya Upaniṣad,* 6.8.7), *idaṁ sarvaṁ yad ayam ātmā* and *brahmedaṁ sarvam* (*Bṛhad-āraṇyaka Upaniṣad,* 2.5.1), *ātmaivedaṁ sarvam* (*Chāndogya Upaniṣad,* 7.25.2) and *neha nānāsti kiñcana* (*Kaṭha Upaniṣad,* 2.1.11). That is a great mistake. Only *oṁkāra* is the *mahā-vākya.* All these other *mantras* which the Māyāvādīs accept as the *mahā-vākya* are only incidental. They cannot be taken as the *mahā-vākya,* or *mahā-mantra.* The *mantra tattvamasi* indicates only a partial understanding of the *Vedas,* unlike *oṁkāra,* which represents the full understanding of the *Vedas.* Therefore the transcendental sound which includes all Vedic knowledge is *oṁkāra (praṇava).*

Aside from *oṁkāra,* none of the words uttered by the followers of Śaṅkarācārya can be considered the *mahā-vākya.* They are merely passing remarks. Śaṅkarācārya, however, has never stressed chanting of the *mahā-vākya oṁkāra;* he has accepted only *tattvamasi* as the *mahā-vākya.* Imagining the living entity to be God, he has misrepresented all the *mantras* of the *Vedānta-sūtra* with the motive of proving that there is no separate existence of the living entities and the Supreme Absolute Truth. This is similar to the politician's attempt to prove nonviolence from *Bhagavad-gītā*. Kṛṣṇa is violent to demons, and to attempt to prove that Kṛṣṇa is not violent is ultimately to deny Kṛṣṇa. As such explanations of *Bhagavad-gītā* are absurd, so also is Śaṅkarācārya's explanation of *Vedānta-sūtra,* and no sane and reasonable man will accept it. At present, however, *Vedānta-sūtra* is misrepresented not only by the so-called Vedāntīs but also by other unscrupulous persons who are so degraded that they even recommend that *sannyāsīs* eat meat, fish and eggs. In this way, the so-called followers of Śaṅkara, the impersonalist Māyāvādīs, are sinking lower and lower. How can these degraded men explain *Vedānta-sūtra,* which is the essence of all Vedic literature?

Lord Śrī Caitanya Mahāprabhu has declared, *māyāvādi-bhāṣya śunile haya sarva-nāśa:* anyone who hears commentary on the *Vedānta-sūtra* from the Māyāvāda school is completely doomed. As explained in *Bhagavad-gītā, vedaiś ca sarvair aham eva vedyaḥ:* all Vedic literature aims to understand Kṛṣṇa (Bg. 15.15). Māyāvāda philosophy, however, has deviated everyone from Kṛṣṇa. Therefore there is a great need for the Kṛṣṇa consciousness movement all over the world to save the world from degradation. Every intelligent and sane man must abandon the philosophical explanation of the Māyāvādīs and accept the explanation of Vaiṣṇava *ācāryas*. One should read *Bhagavad-gītā As It Is* to try to understand the real purpose of the *Vedas.*

TEXT 129

সর্বাশ্রয় ঈশ্বরের প্রণব উদ্দেশ।
'তত্ত্বমসি'-বাক্য হয় বেদের একদেশ ॥ ১২৯ ॥

sarvāśraya īśvarera praṇava uddeśa
'tattvamasi'—vākya haya vedera ekadeśa

SYNONYMS

sarva-āśraya—the reservoir of everything; *īśvarera*—of the Supreme Personality of Godhead; *praṇava—oṁkāra; uddeśa*—purpose; *tattvamasi*—the Vedic *mantra tattvamasi* ("you are the same"); *vākya*—statement; *haya*—becomes; *vedera*—of the Vedic literature; *eka-deśa*—partial understanding.

TRANSLATION

"It is the purpose of the Supreme Personality of Godhead to present praṇava [oṁkāra] as the reservoir of all Vedic knowledge. The words tat tvam asi are only a partial explanation of the Vedic knowledge.

PURPORT

Tat tvam asi means "you are the same spiritual identity."

TEXT 130

'প্রণব, মহাবাক্য—তাহা করি' আচ্ছাদন।
মহাবাক্যে করি 'তত্ত্বমসি'র স্থাপন ॥ ১৩০ ॥

'praṇava, mahā-vākya—tāhā kari' ācchādana
mahāvākye kari 'tattvamasi'ra sthāpana

SYNONYMS

praṇava—*oṁkāra; mahā-vākya*—principal *mantra; tāhā*—that; *kari'*—making; *ācchādana*—covered; *mahā-vākye*—in place of the principal *mantra; kari*—I do; *tattvam-asira sthāpana*—establishment of the statement *tat tvam asi.*

TRANSLATION

"Praṇava [oṁkāra] is the mahā-vākya [mahā-mantra] in the Vedas. Śaṅkarācārya's followers cover this to stress without authority the mantra tat tvam asi.

PURPORT

The Māyāvādī philosophers stress the statements *tat tvam asi, so'ham,* etc., but they do not stress the real *mahā-mantra, praṇava (oṁkāra).* Therefore, because they misrepresent Vedic knowledge, they are the greatest offenders to the lotus feet of the Lord. Caitanya Mahāprabhu says clearly, *māyāvādī kṛṣṇe aparādhī:* Māyāvādī philosophers are the greatest offenders to Lord Kṛṣṇa. Lord Kṛṣṇa declares:

tān ahaṁ dviṣataḥ krūrān
saṁsāreṣu narādhamān
kṣipāmy ajasram aśubhān
āsurīṣv eva yoniṣu

"Those who are envious and mischievous, who are the lowest among mankind, are cast by Me into the ocean of material existence, into various demoniac species of life." (Bg. 16.19) Life in demoniac species awaits the Māyāvādī philosophers after death because they are envious of Kṛṣṇa. When Kṛṣṇa says in *Bhagavad-gītā* (9.34), *man-manā bhava mad-bhakto mad-yājī māṁ namaskuru* ("Engage your mind always in thinking of Me, offer obeisances and worship Me"), one demoniac scholar says that it is not Kṛṣṇa to whom one must surrender. This scholar is already suffering in this life, and he will have to suffer again in the next if in this life he does not complete his prescribed suffering. One should be very careful not to be envious of the Supreme Personality of Godhead. In the next verse, therefore, Śrī Caitanya Mahāprabhu clearly states the purpose of the *Vedas.*

TEXT 131

সর্ববেদসূত্রে করে কৃষ্ণের অভিধান।
মুখ্যবৃত্তি ছাড়ি' কৈল লক্ষণা-ব্যাখ্যান ॥ ১৩১ ॥

sarva-veda-sūtre kare kṛṣṇera abhidhāna
mukhya-vṛtti chāḍi' kaila lakṣaṇā-vyākhyāna

SYNONYMS

sarva-veda-sūtre—in all the codes of *Vedānta-sūtra*; *kare*—establishes; *kṛṣṇera*—of Lord Kṛṣṇa; *abhidhāna*—explanation; *mukhya-vṛtti*—direct interpretation; *chāḍi'*—giving up; *kaila*—made; *lakṣaṇā*—indirect; *vyākhyāna*—explanation.

TRANSLATION

"In all the Vedic sūtras and literatures, it is Lord Kṛṣṇa who is to be understood, but the followers of Śaṅkarācārya have covered the real meaning of the Vedas with indirect explanations.

PURPORT

It is said:

vede rāmāyaṇe caiva purāṇe bhārate tathā
ādāv ante ca madhye ca hariḥ sarvatra gīyate

In the Vedic literature, including the *Rāmāyaṇa, Purāṇas* and *Mahābhārata,* from the very beginning *(ādau)* to the end *(ante ca),* as well as within the middle *(madhye ca),* only Hari, the Supreme Personality of Godhead, is explained.

TEXT 132

স্বতঃপ্রমাণ বেদ প্রমাণ-শিরোমণি ।
লক্ষণা করিলে স্বতঃপ্রমাণতা-হানি ॥ ১৩২ ॥

svataḥ-pramāṇa veda—pramāṇa-śiromaṇi
lakṣaṇā karile svataḥ-pramāṇatā-hāni

SYNONYMS

svataḥ-pramāṇa—self-evident; *veda*—the Vedic literature; *pramāṇa*—evidence; *śiromaṇi*—topmost; *lakṣaṇā*—interpretation; *karile*—doing; *svataḥ-pramāṇatā*—self-evidence; *hāni*—lost.

TRANSLATION

"The self-evident Vedic literatures are the highest evidence of all, but if these literatures are interpreted, their self-evident nature is lost.

PURPORT

We quote Vedic evidence to support our statements, but if we interpret it according to our own judgment, the authority of the Vedic literature is rendered imperfect or useless. In other words, by interpreting the Vedic version one minimizes the value of Vedic evidence. When one quotes from Vedic literature, it is understood that the quotations are authoritative. How can one bring the authority under his own control? That is a case of *principiis obsta.*

TEXT 133

এই মত প্রতিসূত্রে সহজার্থ ছাড়িয়া।
গৌণার্থ ব্যাখ্যা করে কল্পনা করিয়া ॥ ১৩৩ ॥

ei mata pratisūtre sahajārtha chāḍiyā
gauṇārtha vyākhyā kare kalpanā kariyā

SYNONYMS

ei mata—like this; *pratisūtre*—in every *sūtra* or code of the *Vedānta; sahaja-artha*—the clear, simple meaning; *chāḍiyā*—giving up; *gauṇa-artha*—indirect meaning; *vyākhyā*—explanation; *kare*—he makes; *kalpanā kariyā*—by imagination.

TRANSLATION

"The Māyāvāda school, giving up the real, easily understood meaning of Vedic literature, has introduced indirect meanings, based on their imaginative powers, to prove their philosophy."

PURPORT

Unfortunately, the Śaṅkarite interpretation has covered almost the entire world. Therefore there is a great need to present the original, easily understood natural import of the Vedic literature. We have therefore begun by presenting *Bhagavad-gītā As It Is,* and we propose to present all the Vedic literature in terms of the direct meaning of its words.

TEXT 134

এই মতে প্রতিসূত্রে করেন দূষণ।
শুনি' চমৎকার হৈল সন্ন্যাসীর গণ ॥ ১৩৪ ॥

ei mate pratisūtre karena dūṣaṇa
śuni' camatkāra haila sannyāsīra gaṇa

SYNONYMS

ei mate—in this way; *pratisūtre*—in each and every code; *karena*—shows; *dūṣaṇa*—defects; *śuniyā*—hearing; *camatkāra*—struck with wonder; *haila*—they became; *sannyāsīra*—of all the Māyāvādīs; *gaṇa*—the group.

TRANSLATION

When Śrī Caitanya Mahāprabhu thus showed for each and every sūtra the defects in Śaṅkarācārya's explanations, all the assembled Māyāvādī sannyāsīs were struck with wonder.

TEXT 135

সকল সন্ন্যাসী কহে,—'শুনহ শ্রীপাদ ।
তুমি যে খণ্ডিলে অর্থ, এ নহে বিবাদ ॥ ১৩৫ ॥

sakala sannyāsī kahe,—'śunaha śrīpāda
tumi ye khaṇḍile artha, e nahe vivāda

SYNONYMS

sakala—all; *sannyāsī*—the Māyāvādī *sannyāsīs; kahe*—say; *śunaha*—please hear; *śrīpāda*—Your Holiness; *tumi*—You; *ye*—that; *khaṇḍile*—refuted; *artha*—meaning; *e*—this; *nahe*—not; *vivāda*—quarrel.

TRANSLATION

All the Māyāvādī sannyāsīs said: "Your Holiness, kindly know from us that we actually have no quarrel with Your refutation of these meanings, for You have given a clear understanding of the sūtras.

TEXT 136

আচার্য-কল্পিত অর্থ,—ইহা সভে জানি ।
সম্প্রদায়-অনুরোধে তবু তাহা মানি ॥ ১৩৬ ॥

ācārya-kalpita artha,—ihā sabhe jāni
sampradāya-anurodhe tabu tāhā māni

SYNONYMS

ācārya—Śaṅkarācārya; *kalpita*—imaginative; *artha*—meaning; *ihā*—this; *sabhe*—all of us; *jāni*—know; *sampradāya-anurodhe*—but for the sake of our party; *tabu*—still; *tāhā*—that; *māni*—we accept.

TRANSLATION

"We know that all this word jugglery springs from the imagination of Śaṅkarācārya, and yet because we belong to his sect, we accept it although it does not satisfy us.

TEXT 137

মুখ্যার্থ ব্যাখ্যা কর, দেখি তোমার বল ।'
মুখ্যার্থে লাগাল প্রভু সূত্রসকল ॥ ১৩৭ ॥

mukhyārtha vyākhyā kara, dekhi tomāra bala'
mukhyārthe lāgāla prabhu sūtra-sakala

SYNONYMS

mukhya-artha—direct meaning; *vyākhyā*—explanation; *kara*—You do; *dekhi*—let us see; *tomāra*—Your; *bala*—strength; *mukhya-arthe*—direct meaning; *lāgāla*—began; *prabhu*—the Lord; *sūtra-sakala*—all the *sūtras* of *Vedānta.*

TRANSLATION

"Now let us see," the Māyāvādī sannyāsīs continued, "how well You can describe the sūtras in terms of their direct meaning." Hearing this, Lord Caitanya Mahāprabhu began His direct explanation of the Vedānta-sūtra.

TEXT 138

বৃহদ্বস্তু 'ব্রহ্ম' কহি—'শ্রীভগবান্' ।
ষড়্‌বিধৈশ্বর্যপূর্ণ, পরতত্ত্বধাম ॥ ১৩৮ ॥

bṛhad-vastu 'brahma' kahi—'śrī-bhagavān'
ṣaḍ-vidhaiśvarya-pūrṇa, para-tattva-dhāma

SYNONYMS

bṛhat-vastu—the substance, which is greater than the greatest; *brahma*—called by the name Brahman; *kahi*—we call; *śrī-bhagavān*—the Supreme Personality of Godhead; *ṣaṭ*—six; *vidha*—varieties; *aiśvarya*—opulences; *pūrṇa*—full; *para-tattva*—Absolute Truth; *dhāma*—reservoir.

TRANSLATION

"Brahman, who is greater than the greatest, is the Supreme Personality of Godhead. He is full of six opulences, and therefore He is the reservoir of ultimate truth and absolute knowledge.

PURPORT

In the *Śrīmad-Bhāgavatam* it is said that the Absolute Truth is understood in three phases of realization: the impersonal Brahman, the localized Paramātmā and ultimately the Supreme Personality of Godhead. The impersonal Brahman and localized Paramātmā are expansions of the potency of the Supreme Personality of Godhead, who is complete in six opulences, namely, wealth, fame, strength, beauty, knowledge and renunciation. Since He possesses His six opulences, the Personality of Godhead is the ultimate truth in absolute knowledge.

TEXT 139

স্বরূপ-ঐশ্বর্যে তাঁর নাহি মায়াগন্ধ ।
সকল বেদের হয় ভগবান্ সে 'সম্বন্ধ' ॥ ১৩৯ ॥

svarūpa-aiśvarye tāṅra nāhi māyā-gandha
sakala vedera haya bhagavān se 'sambandha'

SYNONYMS

svarūpa—in His original form; *aiśvarye*—opulence; *tāṅra*—His; *nāhi*—there is none; *māyā-gandha*—contamination of the material world; *sakala*—in all; *vedera*—*Vedas;* *haya*—it is so; *bhagavān*—the Supreme Personality of Godhead; *se*—that; *sambandha*—relationship.

TRANSLATION

"In His original form the Supreme Personality of Godhead is full of transcendental opulences which are free from the contamination of the material world. It is to be understood that in all Vedic literature the Supreme Personality of Godhead is the ultimate goal.

TEXT 140

তাঁরে 'নির্বিশেষ' কহি, চিচ্ছক্তি না মানি।
অর্ধস্বরূপ না মানিলে পূর্ণতা হয় হানি ॥ ১৪০ ॥

tāṅre 'nirviśeṣa' kahi, cic-chakti nā māni
ardha-svarūpa nā mānile pūrṇatā haya hāni

SYNONYMS

tāṅre—unto Him; *nirviśeṣa*—impersonal; *kahi*—we say; *cit-śakti*—spiritual energy; *nā*—do not; *māni*—accept; *ardha*—half; *svarūpa*—form; *nā*—not; *mānile*—accepting; *pūrṇatā*—fullness; *haya*—becomes; *hāni*—defective.

TRANSLATION

"When we speak of the Supreme as impersonal, we deny His spiritual potencies. Logically, if you accept half of the truth, you cannot understand the whole.

PURPORT

In the *Upaniṣads* it is said:

oṁ pūrṇam adaḥ pūrṇam idaṁ
pūrṇāt pūrṇam udacyate
pūrṇasya pūrṇam ādāya
pūrṇam evāvaśiṣyate

This verse, which is mentioned in the *Īśopaniṣad, Bṛhad-āraṇyaka Upaniṣad* and many other *Upaniṣads,* indicates that the Supreme Personality of Godhead is full in six opulences. His position is unique, for He possesses all riches, strength, influence, beauty, knowledge and renunciation. Brahman means the greatest, but the Supreme Personality of Godhead is greater than the greatest, just as the sun globe is greater than the sunshine which is all-pervading in the universe. Although the sunshine that spreads all over the universes appears very great to the less knowledgeable, greater than the sunshine is the sun itself, and greater than the sun is the sun-god. Similarly, impersonal Brahman is not the greatest, although it appears to be so. Impersonal Brahman is only the bodily effulgence of the Supreme Personality of Godhead, but the transcendental form of the Lord is greater than both the impersonal Brahman and localized Paramātmā. Therefore whenever the word Brahman is used in Vedic literature, it is understood to refer to the Supreme Personality of Godhead.

In *Bhagavad-gītā* the Lord is also addressed as Parabrahman. Māyāvādīs and others sometimes misunderstand Brahman because every living entity is also Brahman. Therefore Kṛṣṇa is referred to as Parabrahman (the Supreme Brahman). In the Vedic literature, whenever the words Brahman or Parabrahman are used, they are to be understood to refer to the Supreme Personality of Godhead, Kṛṣṇa. This is their real meaning. Since the entire Vedic literature deals with the subject of Brahman, Kṛṣṇa is therefore the ultimate goal of Vedic understanding. The impersonal *brahmajyoti* rests on the personal form of the Lord. Therefore although the impersonal effulgence, the *brahmajyoti,* is the first realization, one must enter into it, as mentioned in the *Īśopaniṣad,* to find the Supreme Person, and then one's knowledge is perfect. *Bhagavad-gītā* (7.19) also confirms this. *Bahūnāṁ janmanām ante jñānavān māṁ prapadyate:* one's search for the Absolute Truth by dint of speculative knowledge is complete when one comes to the point of understanding Kṛṣṇa and surrenders unto Him. That is the real point of perfectional knowledge.

Partial realization of the Absolute Truth as impersonal Brahman denies the complete opulences of the Lord. This is a hazardous understanding of the Absolute Truth. Unless one accepts all the features of the Absolute Truth—namely, impersonal Brahman, localized Paramātmā and ultimately the Supreme Personality of Godhead—his knowledge is imperfect. Śrīpāda Rāmānujācārya, in his *Vedārtha-saṅgraha,* says:

jñānena dharmeṇa svarūpam api nirūpitam,
na tu jñāna-mātraṁ brahmeti katham idam
avagamyate iti cet?

He thus indicates that the real absolute identity must be understood in terms of both His knowledge and characteristics. Simply to understand the Absolute Truth to be full of knowledge is not sufficient. In the Vedic literature we find the statement *yaḥ sarva-jñaḥ sarva-vit*, which means that the Absolute Truth knows everything perfectly, but we also learn from the Vedic description *parāsya śaktir vividhaiva śrūyate* that not only does He know everything, but He also acts accordingly by utilizing His different energies. Thus to understand that Brahman, the Supreme, is conscious is not sufficient. One must know how He consciously acts through His different energies. Māyāvāda philosophy simply informs us of the consciousness of the Absolute Truth but does not give us information of how He acts with His consciousness. That is the defect of that philosophy.

TEXT 141

ভগবান্-প্রাপ্তিহেতু যে করি উপায়।
শ্রবণাদি ভক্তি—কৃষ্ণ-প্রাপ্তির সহায় ॥ ১৪১ ॥

bhagavān-prāptihetu ye kari upāya
śravaṇādi bhakti— kṛṣṇa-prāptira sahāya

SYNONYMS

bhagavān—the Supreme Personality of Godhead; *prāpti-hetu*—the means by which He can be approached; *ye*—what; *kari*—I do; *upāya*—means; *śravaṇa-ādi*—devotional service, beginning with hearing; *bhakti*—devotional service; *kṛṣṇa*—the Supreme Lord; *prāptira*—to approach Him; *sahāya*—means.

TRANSLATION

"It is only by devotional service, beginning with hearing, that one can approach the Supreme Personality of Godhead. That is the only means to approach Him.

PURPORT

Māyāvādī philosophers are satisfied simply to understand Brahman to be the sum total of knowledge, but Vaiṣṇava philosophers not only know in detail about the Supreme Personality of Godhead but also know how to approach Him directly. The method for this is described by Śrī Caitanya Mahāprabhu as nine kinds of devotional service, beginning with hearing.

śravaṇaṁ kīrtanaṁ viṣṇoḥ smaraṇaṁ pāda-sevanam
arcanaṁ vandanaṁ dāsyaṁ sakhyam ātma-nivedanam
(*Bhāg.* 7.5.23)

One can directly approach the Supreme Personality of Godhead simply by executing the nine kinds of devotional service, of which hearing about the Lord is the most important (*śravaṇādi*). Śrī Caitanya Mahāprabhu has very favorably stressed the importance of this process of hearing. According to His method, if people are simply given a chance to hear about Kṛṣṇa, certainly they will gradually develop their dormant awareness or love of Godhead. *Śravaṇādi-śuddha-citte karaye udaya* (Cc. *Madhya* 22.107). Love of God is dormant in everyone, but if one is given a chance to hear about the Lord, certainly that love develops. Our Kṛṣṇa consciousness movement acts on this principle. We simply give people the chance to hear about the Supreme Personality of Godhead and give them *prasāda* to eat, and the actual result is that all over the world people are responding to this process and becoming pure devotees of Lord Kṛṣṇa. We open hundreds of centers all over the world just to give people in general a chance to hear about Kṛṣṇa and accept Kṛṣṇa's *prasāda.* These two processes can be accepted by anyone, even a child. It doesn't matter whether one is poor or rich, learned or foolish, black or white, old or still a child—anyone who simply hears about the Supreme Personality of Godhead and takes *prasāda* is certainly elevated to the transcendental position of devotional service.

TEXT 142

সেই সর্ববেদের 'অভিধেয়' নাম ।
সাধনভক্তি হৈতে হয় প্রেমের উদ্গম ॥ ১৪২ ॥

sei sarva-vedera 'abhidheya' nāma
sādhana-bhakti haite haya premera udgama

SYNONYMS

sei sarva-vedera—that is the essence of all Vedic literature; *abhidheya nāma*—the process called *abhidheya,* or devotional activities; *sādhana-bhakti*—another name of this process, "devotional service in practice"; *haite*—from this; *haya*—there is; *premera*—of love of Godhead; *udgama*—awakening.

TRANSLATION

"By practicing this regulated devotional service under the direction of the spiritual master, certainly one awakens his dormant love of Godhead. This process is called abhidheya.

PURPORT

By the practice of devotional service, beginning with hearing and chanting, the impure heart of a conditioned soul is purified, and thus he can understand his eternal relationship with the Supreme Personality of Godhead. That eternal relationship is described by Śrī Caitanya Mahāprabhu. *Jīvera 'svarūpa' haya kṛṣṇera nitya-dāsa:* the living entity is an eternal servitor of the Supreme Personality of Godhead. When one is convinced about this relationship, which is called *sambandha,* he then acts accordingly. That is called *abhidheya.* The next step is *prayojana-siddhi,* or fulfillment of the ultimate goal of one's life. If one can understand his relationship with the Supreme Personality of Godhead and act accordingly, automatically his mission in life is fulfilled. The Māyāvādī philosophers miss even the first stage in self-realization because they have no conception of God's being personal. He is the master of all, and He is the only person who can accept the service of all living entities, but since this knowledge is lacking in Māyāvāda philosophy, Māyāvādīs do not have knowledge even of their relationship with God. They wrongly think that everyone is God or that everyone is equal to God. Therefore, since the real position of the living entity is not clear to them, how can they advance further? Although they are very puffed-up at being liberated, Māyāvādī philosophers very shortly fall down again to material activities due to their neglecting the lotus feet of the Lord. That is called *patanty adhaḥ.*

āruhya kṛcchreṇa paraṁ padaṁ tataḥ
patanty adho 'nādṛta-yuṣmad-aṅghrayaḥ
(*Bhāg.* 10.2.32)

It is the statement of Prahlāda Mahārāja that persons who think themselves liberated but do not execute devotional service, not knowing their relationship with the Lord, are certainly misled. One must know his relationship with the Lord and act accordingly. Then the fulfillment of his life's mission will be possible.

TEXT 143

কৃষ্ণের চরণে হয় যদি অনুরাগ ।
কৃষ্ণ বিনু অন্যত্র তার নাহি রহে রাগ ॥ ১৪৩ ॥

kṛṣṇera caraṇe haya yadi anurāga
kṛṣṇa binu anyatra tāra nāhi rahe rāga

SYNONYMS

kṛṣṇera—of Kṛṣṇa; *caraṇe*—at the lotus feet; *haya*—becomes; *yadi*—if; *anurāga*—attachment; *kṛṣṇa*—the Supreme Personality of Godhead; *binu*—without; *anyatra*—anywhere else; *tāra*—his; *nāhi*—there does not; *rahe*—remain; *rāga*—attachment.

TRANSLATION

"If one develops his love of Godhead and becomes attached to the lotus feet of Kṛṣṇa, gradually he loses his attachment to everything else.

PURPORT

This is a test of advancement in devotional service. *Bhaktir parasyānubhavo viraktir anyatra syāt:* in *bhakti,* a devotee's only attachment is Kṛṣṇa; he no longer wants to maintain his attachments to many other things. Although Māyāvādī philosophers are supposed to be very advanced on the path of liberation, we see that after some time they descend to politics and philanthropic activities. Many big *sannyāsīs* who were supposedly liberated and very advanced have come down again to materialistic activities, although they left this world as *mithyā* (false). When a devotee develops in devotional service, however, he no longer has attachments to such philanthropic activities. He is simply inspired to serve the Lord, and he engages his entire life in such service. This is the difference between Vaiṣṇava and Māyāvādī philosophers. Devotional service, therefore, is practical, whereas Māyāvāda philosophy is merely mental speculation.

TEXT 144

পঞ্চম পুরুষার্থ সেই প্রেম-মহাধন ।
কৃষ্ণের মাধুর্য-রস করায় আস্বাদন ॥ ১৪৪ ॥

pañcama puruṣārtha sei prema-mahādhana
kṛṣṇera mādhurya-rasa karāya āsvādana

SYNONYMS

pañcama—fifth; *puruṣa-artha*—goal of life; *sei*—that; *prema*—love of God; *mahā-dhana*—foremost wealth; *kṛṣṇera*—of Lord Kṛṣṇa; *mādhurya*—conjugal love; *rasa*—mellow; *karāya*—causes; *āsvādana*—taste.

TRANSLATION

"Love of Godhead is so exalted that it is considered to be the fifth goal of human life. By awakening one's love of Godhead, one can attain the platform of conjugal love, tasting it even during the present span of life.

PURPORT

The Māyāvādī philosophers consider the highest goal of perfection to be liberation (*mukti*), which is the fourth perfectional platform. Generally people are aware of four principal goals of life—religiosity (*dharma*), economic development (*artha*), sense gratification (*kāma*) and ultimately liberation (*mokṣa*)—but devotional service is situated on the platform above liberation. In other words, when one is actually liberated (*mukta*) he can understand the meaning of love of Godhead (*kṛṣṇa-prema*). While teaching Rūpa Gosvāmī, Śrī Caitanya Mahāprabhu stated, *koṭimukta-madhye 'durlabha' eka kṛṣṇa-bhakta:* "Out of millions of liberated persons, one may become a devotee of Lord Kṛṣṇa."

The most elevated Māyāvādī philosopher can rise to the platform of liberation, but *Kṛṣṇa-bhakti,* devotional service to Kṛṣṇa, is transcendental to such liberation. Śrīla Vyāsadeva explains this fact in *Śrīmad-Bhāgavatam* (*Bhāg.* 1.1.2):

dharmaḥ projjhita-kaitavo 'tra paramo nirmatsarāṇāṁ satāṁ
vedyaṁ vāstavam atra vastu śivadaṁ tāpa-trayonmūlanam

"Completely rejecting all religions which are materially motivated, the *Bhāgavata Purāṇa* propounds the highest truth, which is understandable by those devotees who are pure in heart. The highest truth is reality, distinguished from illusion for the welfare of all. Such truth uproots the threefold miseries." *Śrīmad-Bhāgavatam,* the explanation of *Vedānta-sūtra,* is meant for *paramo nirmatsarāṇām,* those who are completely aloof from jealousy. Māyāvādī philosophers are jealous of the existence of the Personality of Godhead. Therefore *Vedānta-sūtra* is not actually meant for them. They unnecessarily poke their noses in the *Vedānta-sūtra,* but they have no ability to understand it because the author of *Vedānta-sūtra* writes in his commentary, *Śrīmad-Bhāgavatam,* that it is meant for those who are pure in heart (*paramo nirmatsarāṇām*). If one is envious of Kṛṣṇa, how can he understand *Vedānta-sūtra* or *Śrīmad-Bhāgavatam?* The Māyāvādīs' primary occupation is to offend the Supreme Personality of Godhead Kṛṣṇa. For example, although Kṛṣṇa demands our surrender in *Bhagavad-gītā,* the greatest scholar and so-called philosopher in India has protested that it is "not to Kṛṣṇa" that we have to surrender. Therefore, he is envious. Since Māyāvādīs of all different descriptions are envious of Kṛṣṇa, they have no scope to understand the meaning of *Vedānta-sūtra.* Even if they were on the liberated platform as they falsely claim, here Kṛṣṇadāsa Kavirāja Gosvāmī repeats the statement of Śrī Caitanya Mahāprabhu that love of Kṛṣṇa is beyond the state of liberation.

TEXT 145

প্রেমা হৈতে কৃষ্ণ হয় নিজ ভক্তবশ ।
প্রেমা হৈতে পায় কৃষ্ণের সেবা-সুখরস ॥ ১৪৫ ॥

premā haite kṛṣṇa haya nija bhakta-vaśa
premā haite pāya kṛṣṇera sevā-sukha-rasa

SYNONYMS

premā—love of Kṛṣṇa; *haite*—from; *kṛṣṇa*—the Supreme Personality of Godhead; *haya*—becomes; *nija*—His own; *bhakta-vaśa*—submissive to devotees; *premā*—love of God; *haite*—from; *pāya*—he gets; *kṛṣṇera*—of Lord Kṛṣṇa; *sevā-sukha-rasa*—the mellow of devotional service.

TRANSLATION

"The Supreme Lord, who is greater than the greatest, becomes submissive to even a very insignificant devotee because of his devotional service. It is the beautiful and exalted nature of devotional service that the infinite Lord becomes submissive to the infinitesimal living entity because of it. In reciprocal devotional activities with the Lord, the devotee actually enjoys the transcendental mellow quality of devotional service.

PURPORT

Becoming one with the Supreme Personality of Godhead is not very important for a devotee. *Muktiḥ svayaṁ mukulitāñjali sevate 'smān* (*Kṛṣṇa-karṇāmṛta* 107). Speaking from his actual experience, Śrīla Bilvamaṅgala Ṭhākura says that if one develops love of Godhead, *mukti* (liberation) becomes subservient and unimportant to him. *Mukti* stands before the devotee and is prepared to render all kinds of services. The Māyāvādī philosophers' standard of *mukti* is very insignificant for a devotee, for by devotional service even the Supreme Personality of Godhead becomes subordinate to him. An actual example is that the Supreme Lord Kṛṣṇa became the chariot driver of Arjuna, and when Arjuna asked Him to draw his chariot between the two armies (*senayor ubhayor madhye rathaṁ sthāpaya me 'cyuta*), Kṛṣṇa executed his order. Such is the relationship between the Supreme Lord and a devotee that although the Lord is greater than the greatest, He is prepared to render service to the insignificant devotee by dint of his sincere and unalloyed devotional service.

TEXT 146

সম্বন্ধ, অভিধেয়, প্রয়োজন নাম ।
এই তিন অর্থ সর্বসূত্রে পর্যবসান ॥ ১৪৬ ॥

sambandha, abhidheya, prayojana nāma
ei tina artha sarva-sūtre paryavasāna

SYNONYMS

sambandha—relationship; *abhidheya*—functional duties; *prayojana*—the goal of life; *nāma*—name; *ei*—there; *tina*—three; *artha*—purport; *sarva*—all; *sūtre*—in the codes of Vedānta; *paryavasāna*—culmination.

TRANSLATION

"One's relationship with the Supreme Personality of Godhead, activities in terms of that relationship, and the ultimate goal of life [to develop love of God]—these three subjects are explained in every code of the Vedānta-sūtra, for they form the culmination of the entire Vedānta philosophy."

PURPORT

In the *Śrīmad-Bhāgavatam* (5.5.5) it is said:

parābhavas tāvad abodha-jāto
yāvan na jijñāsata ātma-tattvam

A human being is defeated in all his activities as long as he does not know the goal of life, which can be understood when one is inquisitive about Brahman. It is such inquiry that begins *Vedānta-sūtra: athāto brahma-jijñāsā.* A human being should be inquisitive to know who he is, what the universe is, what God is and what the relationship is between himself, God and the material world. Such questions cannot be asked by cats and dogs, but they must arise in the heart of a real human being. Knowledge of these four items—namely, oneself, the universe, God, and their internal relationship—is called *sambandha-jñāna,* or the knowledge of one's relationship. When one's relationship with the Supreme Lord is established, the next program is to act in that relationship. This is called *abhidheya,* or activity in relationship with the Lord. After executing such prescribed duties, when one attains the highest goal of life, love of Godhead, he achieves *prayojana-siddhi,* or the fulfillment of his human mission. In the *Brahma-sūtra,* or *Vedānta-sūtra,* these subjects are very carefully explained. Therefore one who does not understand the *Vedānta-sūtra* in terms of these principles is simply wasting his time. This is the version of *Śrīmad-Bhāgavatam* (1.2.8):

dharmaḥ svanuṣṭhitaḥ puṁsāṁ
viṣvaksena-kathāsu yaḥ
notpādayed yadi ratiṁ
śrama eva hi kevalam

One may be a very learned scholar and execute his prescribed duty very nicely, but if he does not ultimately become inquisitive about the Supreme Personality of Godhead and is indifferent to *śravaṇaṁ kīrtanam* (hearing and chanting), all that he has done is but a waste of time. Māyāvādī philosophers who do not understand the relationship between themselves, the cosmic manifestation and the Supreme Personality of Godhead are simply wasting their time, and their philosophical speculation has no value.

TEXT 147

এইমত সর্বসূত্রের ব্যাখ্যান শুনিয়া ।
সকল সন্ন্যাসী কহে বিনয় করিয়া ॥ ১৪৭ ॥

eimata sarva-sūtrera vyākhyāna śuniyā
sakala sannyāsī kahe vinaya kariyā

SYNONYMS

ei-mata—in this way; *sarva-sūtrera*—of all the codes of *Vedānta-sūtra; vyākhyāna*—explanation; *śuniyā*—by hearing; *sakala*—all; *sannyāsī*—the groups of Māyāvādī *sannyāsīs; kahe*—said; *vinaya*—humbly; *kariyā*—doing so.

TRANSLATION

When all the Māyāvādī sannyāsīs thus heard the explanation of Caitanya Mahāprabhu on the basis of sambandha, abhidheya and prayojana, they spoke very humbly.

PURPORT

Everyone who actually desires to understand Vedānta philosophy must certainly accept the explanation of Lord Caitanya Mahāprabhu or the Vaiṣṇava *ācāryas* who have also commented on the *Vedānta-sūtra* according to the principles of *bhakti-yoga.* After hearing the explanation of *Vedānta-sūtra* from Śrī Caitanya Mahāprabhu, all the *sannyāsīs,* headed by Prakāśānanda Sarasvatī, became very humble and obedient to the Lord, and they spoke as follows.

TEXT 148

বেদময়-মূর্তি তুমি,—সাক্ষাৎ নারায়ণ ।
ক্ষম অপরাধ,—পূর্বে যে কৈলুঁ নিন্দন ॥ ১৪৮ ॥

vedamaya-mūrti tumi,—sākṣāt nārāyaṇa
kṣama aparādha,—pūrve ye kailuṅ nindana

SYNONYMS

vedamaya—transformation of the Vedic knowledge; *mūrti*—form; *tumi*—You; *sākṣāt*—directly; *nārāyaṇa*—the Supreme Personality of Godhead; *kṣama*—excuse; *aparādha*—offense; *pūrve*—before; *ye*—that; *kailuṅ*—we have done; *nindana*—criticism.

TRANSLATION

"Dear sir, You are Vedic knowledge personified and are directly Nārāyaṇa Himself. Kindly excuse us for the offenses we previously committed by criticizing You."

PURPORT

The complete path of *bhakti-yoga* is based upon the process of becoming humble and submissive. By the grace of Lord Caitanya Mahāprabhu, all the Māyāvādī *sannyāsīs* were very humble and submissive after hearing His explanation of *Vedānta-sūtra,* and they begged to be pardoned for the offenses that they had committed by criticizing the Lord for simply chanting and dancing, not taking part in the study of *Vedānta-sūtra*. We are propagating the Kṛṣṇa consciousness movement simply by following in the footsteps of Lord Caitanya Mahāprabhu. We may not be very well versed in the *Vedānta-sūtra* codes and may not understand their meaning, but we follow in the footsteps of the *ācāryas,* and because of our strictly and obediently following in the footsteps of Lord Caitanya Mahāprabhu, it is to be understood that we know everything regarding *Vedānta-sūtra.*

TEXT 149

সেই হৈতে সন্ন্যাসীর ফিরি গেল মন ।
'কৃষ্ণ' 'কৃষ্ণ' নাম সদা করয়ে গ্রহণ ॥ ১৪৯ ॥

sei haite sannyāsīra phiri gela mana
'kṛṣṇa' 'kṛṣṇa' nāma sadā karaye grahaṇa

SYNONYMS

sei haite—from that time; *sannyāsīra*—all the Māyāvādī *sannyāsīs*; *phiri*—turn; *gela*—became; *mana*—mind; *kṛṣṇa, kṛṣṇa*—the holy name of the Supreme Personality of Godhead, Kṛṣṇa; *nāma*—name; *sadā*—always; *karaye*—do; *grahaṇa*—accept.

TRANSLATION

From that moment when the Māyāvādī sannyāsīs heard the explanation of Vedānta-sūtra from the Lord, their minds changed, and on the instruction of Caitanya Mahāprabhu, they too chanted, "Kṛṣṇa! Kṛṣṇa!" always.

PURPORT

In this connection it may be mentioned that sometimes the *sahajiyā* class of devotees opine that Prakāśānanda Sarasvatī and Prabodhānanda Sarasvatī are the same man. Prabodhānanda Sarasvatī was a great Vaiṣṇava devotee of Lord Caitanya Mahāprabhu, but Prakāśānanda Sarasvatī, the head of the Māyāvādī *sannyāsīs* in Benares, was a different person. Prabodhānanda Sarasvatī belonged to the Rāmānuja-sampradāya, whereas Prakāśānanda Sarasvatī belonged to the Śaṅkarācārya-sampradāya. Prabodhānanda Sarasvatī wrote a number of books, among which are *Caitanya-candrāmṛta, Rādhā-rasa-sudhā-nidhi, Saṅgīta-mādhava, Vṛndāvana-śataka* and *Navadvīpa-śataka.* While traveling in Southern India, Caitanya Mahāprabhu met Prabodhānanda Sarasvatī, who had two brothers, Vyeṅkaṭa Bhaṭṭa and Tirumalaya Bhaṭṭa, who were Vaiṣṇavas of the Rāmānuja-sampradāya. Gopāla Bhaṭṭa Gosvāmī was the nephew of Prabodhānanda Sarasvatī. From historical records it is found that Śrī Caitanya Mahāprabhu traveled in South India in the year 1433 *śakābda* during the Cāturmāsya period, and it was at that time that He met Prabodhānanda, who belonged to the Rāmānuja-sampradāya. How then could the same person meet Him as a member of the Śaṅkara-sampradāya in 1435 *śakābda,* two years later? It is to be concluded that the guess of the *sahijiyā-sampradāya* that Prabodhānanda Sarasvatī and Prakāśānanda Sarasvatī were the same man is a mistaken idea.

TEXT 150

এইমতে তাঁ-সবার ক্ষমি' অপরাধ ।
সবাকারে কৃষ্ণনাম করিলা প্রসাদ ॥ ১৫০ ॥

eimate tāṅ-sabāra kṣami' aparādha
sabākāre kṛṣṇa-nāma karilā prasāda

SYNONYMS

ei-mate—in this way; *tāṅ-sabāra*—of all the *sannyāsīs*; *kṣami'*—excusing; *aparādha*—offense; *sabākāre*—all of them; *kṛṣṇa-nāma*—the holy name of Kṛṣṇa; *karilā*—gave; *prasāda*—as mercy.

TRANSLATION

Thus Lord Caitanya excused all the offenses of the Māyāvādī sannyāsīs and very mercifully blessed them with Kṛṣṇa-nāma.

PURPORT

Śrī Caitanya Mahāprabhu is the mercy incarnation of the Supreme Personality of Godhead. He is addressed by Śrīla Rūpa Gosvāmī as *mahā-vadānyāvatāra,* or the most magnanimous incarnation. Śrīla Rūpa Gosvāmī also says, *karuṇayāvatīrṇaḥ kalau:* it is only by His mercy that He has descended in this age of Kali. Here this is exemplified. Śrī Caitanya Mahāprabhu did not like to see Māyāvādī *sannyāsīs* because He thought of them as offenders to the lotus feet of Kṛṣṇa, but here He excuses them *(tāṅ-sabāra kṣami' aparādha).* This is an example in preaching. *Āpani ācari' bhakti-śikhāimu sabāre.* Śrī Caitanya Mahāprabhu teaches us that those whom preachers meet are almost all offenders who are opposed to Kṛṣṇa consciousness, but it is a preacher's duty to convince them of the Kṛṣṇa consciousness movement and then induce them to chant the Hare Kṛṣṇa *mahā-mantra.* Our propagation of the *saṅkīrtana* movement is continuing, despite many opponents, and people are taking this chanting process even in remote parts of the world like Africa. By inducing the offenders to chant the Hare Kṛṣṇa *mantra,* Lord Caitanya Mahāprabhu exemplified the success of the Kṛṣṇa consciousness movement. We should follow very respectfully in the footsteps of Lord Caitanya, and there is no doubt that we shall be successful in our attempts.

TEXT 151

তবে সব সন্ন্যাসী মহাপ্রভুকে লৈয়া ।
ভিক্ষা করিলেন সভে, মধ্যে বসাইয়া ॥ ১৫১ ॥

tabe saba sannyāsī mahāprabhuke laiyā
bhikṣā karilena sabhe, madhye vasāiyā

SYNONYMS

tabe—after this; *saba*—all; *sannyāsī*—the Māyāvādī *sannyāsīs; mahāprabhuke*—Caitanya Mahāprabhu; *laiyā*—taking Him; *bhikṣā karilena*—took *prasāda* or took lunch; *sabhe*—all together; *madhye*—in the middle; *vasāiyā*—seating Him.

TRANSLATION

After this, all the sannyāsīs took the Lord in their midst, and thus they all took their meal together.

PURPORT

Previously Śrī Caitanya Mahāprabhu neither mixed nor talked with the Māyāvādī *sannyāsīs,* but now He is taking lunch with them. It is to be concluded that when Lord Caitanya induced them to chant Hare Kṛṣṇa and excused them for their offenses, they were purified, and therefore there was no objection to taking lunch or *Bhagavat-prasāda* with them, although Śrī Caitanya Mahāprabhu knew that the foodstuffs were not offered to the Deity. Māyāvādī *sannyāsīs* do not worship the Deity, or if they do so they generally worship the deity of Lord Śiva or the *pañcopāsanā* (Lord Viṣṇu, Lord Śiva, Durgādevī, Gaṇeśa and Sūrya). Here we do not find any mention of the demigods or Viṣṇu, and yet Caitanya Mahāprabhu accepted food in the midst of the *sannyāsīs* on the basis that they had chanted the Hare Kṛṣṇa *mahā-mantra* and that He had excused their offenses.

TEXT 152

ভিক্ষা করি' মহাপ্রভু আইলা বাসাঘর।
হেন চিত্র-লীলা করে গৌরাঙ্গ-সুন্দর ॥ ১৫২ ॥

bhikṣā kari' mahāprabhu āilā vāsāghara
hena citra-līlā kare gaurāṅga-sundara

SYNONYMS

bhikṣā—accepting foodstuff from others; *kari'*—accepting; *mahāprabhu*—Lord Caitanya; *āilā*—returned; *vāsāghara*—to His residence; *hena*—thus; *citra-līlā*—wonderful pastimes; *kare*—does; *gaurāṅga*—Lord Śrī Caitanya Mahāprabhu; *sundara*—very beautiful.

TRANSLATION

After taking lunch among the Māyāvādī sannyāsīs, Śrī Caitanya Mahāprabhu, who is known as Gaurasundara, returned to His residence. Thus the Lord performs His wonderful pastimes.

TEXT 153

চন্দ্রশেখর, তপন মিশ্র, আর সনাতন।
শুনি' দেখি' আনন্দিত সবাকার মন ॥ ১৫৩ ॥

candraśekhara, tapana miśra, āra sanātana
śuni' dekhi' ānandita sabākāra mana

SYNONYMS

candraśekhara—of the name Candraśekhara; *tapana miśra*—of the name Tapana Miśra; *āra*—and; *sanātana*—of the name Sanātana; *śuni'*—hearing; *dekhi'*—seeing; *ānandita*—very pleased; *sabākāra*—all of them; *mana*—minds.

TRANSLATION

Hearing the arguments of Śrī Caitanya Mahāprabhu and seeing His victory, Candraśekhara, Tapana Miśra and Sanātana were all extremely pleased.

PURPORT

Here is an example of how a *sannyāsī* should preach. When Śrī Caitanya Mahāprabhu went to Vārāṇasī, He went there alone, not with a big party. Locally, however, He made friendships with Candraśekhara and Tapana Miśra, and Sanātana Gosvāmī also came to see Him. Therefore, although He did not have many friends there, due to His sound preaching and His victory in arguing with the local *sannyāsīs* on Vedānta philosophy, He became greatly famous in that part of the country, as explained in the next verse.

TEXT 154

প্রভুকে দেখিতে আইসে সকল সন্ন্যাসী ।
প্রভুর প্রশংসা করে সব বারাণসী ॥ ১৫৪ ॥

prabhuke dekhite āise sakala sannyāsī
prabhura praśaṁsā kare saba vārāṇasī

SYNONYMS

prabhuke—unto Lord Caitanya Mahāprabhu; *dekhite*—to see; *āise*—they came; *sakala*—all; *sannyāsī*—the Māyāvādī *sannyāsīs*; *prabhura*—of Lord Caitanya Mahāprabhu; *praśaṁsā*—praise; *kare*—they do; *saba*—all; *vārāṇasī*—the city of Vārāṇasī.

TRANSLATION

Many Māyāvādī sannyāsīs of Vārāṇasī came to see the Lord after this incident, and the entire city praised Him.

TEXT 155

বারাণসীপুরী আইলা শ্রীকৃষ্ণচৈতন্য ।
পুরীসহ সর্বলোক হৈল মহাধন্য ॥ ১৫৫ ॥

vārāṇasī-purī āilā śrī-kṛṣṇa-caitanya
purī-saha sarva-loka haila mahā-dhanya

SYNONYMS

vārāṇasī—of the name Vārāṇasī; *purī*—city; *āilā*—came; *śrī-kṛṣṇa-caitanya*—Lord Śrī Caitanya Mahāprabhu; *purī*—city; *saha*—with; *sarva-loka*—all the people; *haila*—became; *mahā-dhanya*—thankful.

TRANSLATION

Śrī Caitanya Mahāprabhu visited the city of Vārāṇasī, and all of its people were very thankful.

TEXT 156

লক্ষ লক্ষ লোক আইসে প্রভুকে দেখিতে ।
মহাভিড় হৈল দ্বারে, নারে প্রবেশিতে ॥ ১৫৬ ॥

lakṣa lakṣa loka āise prabhuke dekhite
mahā-bhiḍa haila dvāre, nāre praveśite

SYNONYMS

lakṣa lakṣa—hundreds and thousands; *loka*—people; *āise*—came; *prabhuke*—unto the Lord; *dekhite*—to see; *mahā-bhiḍa*—a great crowd; *haila*—there happened; *dvāre*—at the door; *nāre*—may not; *praveśite*—to enter.

TRANSLATION

The crowd at the door of His residence was so great that it numbered hundreds and thousands.

TEXT 157

প্রভু যবে যা'ন বিশ্বেশ্বর-দরশনে ।
লক্ষ লক্ষ লোক আসি' মিলে সেই স্থানে ॥ ১৫৭ ॥

prabhu yabe yā'na viśveśvara-daraśane
lakṣa lakṣa loka āsi' mile sei sthāne

SYNONYMS

prabhu—Lord Caitanya Mahāprabhu; *yabe*—when; *yā'na*—goes; *viśveśvara*—the deity of Vārāṇasī; *daraśane*—to visit; *lakṣa lakṣa*—hundreds and thousands; *loka*—people; *āsi'*—come; *mile*—meet; *sei*—that; *sthāne*—on the place.

TRANSLATION

When the Lord went to visit the temple of Viśveśvara, hundreds and thousands of people assembled to see Him.

PURPORT

The important point in this verse is that Śrī Caitanya Mahāprabhu regularly visited the temple of Viśveśvara (Lord Śiva) at Vārāṇasī. Vaiṣṇavas generally do not visit a demigod's temple, but here we see that Śrī Caitanya Mahāprabhu regularly visited the temple of Viśveśvara, who was the predominating deity of Vārāṇasī. Generally Māyāvādī *sannyāsīs* and worshipers of Lord Śiva live in Vārāṇasī, but how is it that Caitanya Mahāprabhu, who took the part of a Vaiṣṇava *sannyāsī,* also visited the Viśveśvara temple? The answer is that a Vaiṣṇava does not behave impudently toward the demigods. A Vaiṣṇava gives proper respect to all, although he never accepts a demigod to be as good as the Supreme Personality of Godhead.

In the *Brahma-saṁhitā* there are *mantras* offering obeisances to Lord Śiva, Lord Brahmā, the sun-god and Lord Gaṇeśa, as well as Lord Viṣṇu, all of whom are worshiped by the impersonalists as *pañcopāsanā.* In their temples impersonalists also install deities of Lord Viṣṇu, Lord Śiva, the sun-god, goddess Durgā and sometimes Lord Brahmā also, and this system is continuing at present in India under the guise of the Hindu religion. Vaiṣṇavas can also worship all these demigods, but only on the principles of *Brahma-saṁhitā,* which is recommended by Śrī Caitanya Mahāprabhu. We may note in this connection the *mantras* for worshiping Lord Śiva, Lord Brahmā, goddess Durgā, the sun-god and Gaṇeśa, as described in the *Brahma-saṁhitā:*

sṛṣṭi-sthiti-pralaya-sādhana-śaktir ekā
chāyeva yasya bhuvanāni bibharti durgā
icchānurūpam api yasya ca ceṣṭate sā
govindam ādi-puruṣaṁ tam ahaṁ bhajāmi

"The external potency, *māyā,* who is of the nature of the shadow of the *cit* [spiritual] potency, is worshiped by all people as Durgā, the creating, preserving and destroying agency of this mundane world. I adore the primeval Lord Govinda, in accordance with whose will Durgā conducts herself." (Bs. 5.44)

kṣīraṁ yathā dadhi vikāra-viśeṣa-yogāt
sañjāyate na hi tataḥ pṛthag asti hetoḥ
yaḥ śambhutām api tathā samupaiti kāryād
govindam ādi-puruṣaṁ tam ahaṁ bhajāmi

"Milk is transformed into curd by the actions of acids, yet the effect 'curd' is neither the same as nor different from its cause, viz., milk. I adore the primeval Lord Govinda, of whom the state of Śambu is a similar transformation for the performance of the work of destruction." (Bs. 5.45)

bhāsvān yathāśma-śakaleṣu nijeṣu tejaḥ
svīyaṁ kiyat prakaṭayaty api tad-vadatra
brahmā ya eṣa jagadaṇḍa-vidhāna-kartā
govindam ādi-puruṣaṁ tam ahaṁ bhajāmi

"I adore the primeval Lord Govinda, from whom the separated subjective portion Brahmā receives his power for the regulation of the mundane world, just as the sun manifests a portion of his own light in all the effulgent gems that bear such names as *sūrya-kānta.*" (Bs. 5.49)

yat-pāda-pallava-yugaṁ vinidhāya kumbha-
dvandve praṇāma-samaye sa gaṇādhirājaḥ
vighnān vihantum alam asya jagat-trayasya
govindam ādi-puruṣaṁ tam ahaṁ bhajāmi

"I worship the primeval Lord Govinda. Gaṇeśa always holds His lotus feet upon the pair of tumuli protruding from his elephant head in order to obtain power for his function of destroying all obstacles on the path of progress in the three worlds." (Bs. 5.50)

yac cakṣur eṣa savitā sakala-grahāṇāṁ
rājā samasta-sura-mūrtir aśeṣa-tejāḥ
yasyājñayā bhramati sambhṛta-kāla-cakro
govindam ādi-puruṣaṁ tam ahaṁ bhajāmi

"The sun, full of infinite effulgence, who is the king of all the planets and the image of the good soul, is like the eye of this world. I adore the primeval Lord Govinda, in pursuance of whose order the sun performs his journey, mounting the wheel of time." (Bs. 5.52)

All the demigods are servants of Kṛṣṇa; they are not equal with Kṛṣṇa. Therefore even if one goes to a temple of the *pañcopāsanā,* as mentioned above, one should not accept the deities as they are accepted by the impersonalists. All of them are to be accepted as personal demigods, but they all serve the order of the Supreme Personality of Godhead. Śaṅkarācārya, for example, is understood to be an incarnation of Lord Śiva, as described in the *Padma Purāṇa.* He propagated the Māyāvāda philosophy under the order of the Supreme Lord. We have already discussed this point in text 114 of this chapter:

tāṅra doṣa nāhi, teṅho ājñākārī dāsa
āra yei śune tāra haya sarva-nāśa

"Śaṅkarācārya is not at fault, for he has thus covered the real purpose of the *Vedas* under the order of the Supreme Personality of Godhead." Although Lord Śiva, in the form of a *brāhmaṇa* (Śaṅkarācārya), preached the false philosophy of Māyāvāda, Śrī Caitanya Mahāprabhu nevertheless said that since he did it on the order of the Supreme Personality of Godhead, there was no fault on his part *(tāṅra doṣa nāhi).*

We must offer proper respects to all the demigods. If one can offer respects even to an ant, why not to the demigods? One must always know, however, that no demigod is equal to or above the Supreme Lord. *Ekalā īśvara kṛṣṇa, āra saba bhṛtya.* "Only Kṛṣṇa is the Supreme Personality of Godhead, and all others, including the demigods such as Lord Śiva, Lord Brahmā, goddess Durgā and Gaṇeśa, are His servants." Everyone serves the purpose of the Supreme Godhead, and what to speak of such small and insignificant living entities as ourselves? We are surely eternal servants of the Lord. The Māyāvāda philosophy maintains that the demigods, living entities and Supreme Personality of Godhead are all equal. It is therefore a most foolish misrepresentation of Vedic knowledge.

TEXT 158

স্নান করিতে যবে যা'ন গঙ্গাতীরে ।
তাহাঞি সকল লোক হয় মহাভিড়ে ॥ ১৫৮ ॥

snāna karite yabe yā'na gaṅgā-tīre
tāhāñi sakala loka haya mahā-bhiḍe

SYNONYMS

snāna—bath; *karite*—taking; *yabe*—when; *yā'na*—goes; *gaṅgā*—Ganges; *tīre*—bank; *tāhāñi*—then and there; *sakala*—all; *loka*—people; *haya*—assembled; *mahā-bhiḍe*—in great crowds.

TRANSLATION

Whenever Lord Caitanya went to the banks of the Ganges to take bath, big crowds of many hundreds and thousands of people also assembled there.

TEXT 159

বাহু তুলি' প্রভু বলে,—বল হরি হরি ।
হরিধ্বনি করে লোক স্বর্গমর্ত্য ভরি' ॥ ১৫৯ ॥

bāhu tuli' prabhu bale,—bala hari hari
hari-dhvani kare loka svarga-martya bhari'

SYNONYMS

bāhu tuli'—raising the arms; *prabhu*—Lord Śrī Caitanya Mahāprabhu; *bale*—speaks; *bala*—all of you chant; *hari hari*—the holy name of Lord Kṛṣṇa (Hari); *hari-dhvani*—the sound vibration of Hari; *kare*—does; *loka*—all people; *svarga-martya*—in heaven, the sky and the land; *bhari'*—completely filling.

TRANSLATION

Whenever the crowds were too great, Śrī Caitanya Mahāprabhu stood up, raised His hands and chanted, "Hari! Hari!" to which all the people again responded, filling both the land and sky with the vibration.

TEXT 160

লোক নিস্তারিয়া প্রভুর চলিতে হৈল মন ।
বৃন্দাবনে পাঠাইলা শ্রীসনাতন ॥ ১৬০ ॥

loka nistāriyā prabhura calite haila mana
vṛndāvane pāṭhāilā śrī-sanātana

SYNONYMS

loka—people; *nistāriyā*—delivering; *prabhura*—of the Lord; *calite*—to leave; *haila*—became; *mana*—mind; *vṛndāvane*—toward Vṛndāvana; *pāṭhāilā*—sent; *śrī-sanātana*—Sanātana Gosvāmī.

TRANSLATION

After thus delivering the people in general, the Lord desired to leave Vārāṇasī. After instructing Śrī Sanātana Gosvāmī, He sent him toward Vṛndāvana.

PURPORT

The actual purpose of Lord Caitanya's stay at Vārāṇasī after coming back from Vṛndāvana was to meet Sanātana Gosvāmī and teach him. Sanātana Gosvāmī met Śrī Caitanya Mahāprabhu after the Lord's return to Vārāṇasī, where the Lord taught him for two months about the implications of Vaiṣṇava philosophy and Vaiṣṇava activities. After completely instructing him, He sent him to Vṛndāvana to execute His orders. When Sanātana Gosvāmī went to Vṛndāvana, there were no temples. The city was lying vacant like an open field. Sanātana Gosvāmī sat down on the bank of the Yamunā, and after some time he gradually constructed the first temple; then other temples were constructed, and now the city is full of temples, numbering about 5,000.

TEXT 161

রাত্রি-দিবসে লোকের শুনি' কোলাহল ।
বারাণসী ছাড়ি' প্রভু আইলা নীলাচল ॥ ১৬১ ॥

rātri-divase lokera śuni' kolāhala
vārāṇasī chāḍi' prabhu āilā nīlācala

SYNONYMS

rātri—night; *divase*—day; *lokera*—of the people in general; *śuni'*—hearing; *kolāhala*—tumult; *vārāṇasī*—the city of Benares; *chāḍi'*—leaving; *prabhu*—the Lord; *āilā*—returned; *nīlācala*—to Purī.

TRANSLATION

Because the city of Vārāṇasī was always full of tumultuous crowds, Śrī Caitanya Mahāprabhu, after sending Sanātana to Vṛndāvana, returned to Jagannātha Purī.

TEXT 162

এই লীলা কহিব আগে বিস্তার করিয়া ।
সংক্ষেপে কহিলাঙ ইহাঁ প্রসঙ্গ পাইয়া ॥ ১৬২ ॥

ei līlā kahiba āge vistāra kariyā
saṅkṣepe kahilāṅ ihāṅ prasaṅga pāiyā

SYNONYMS

ei—these; *līlā*—pastimes; *kahiba*—I shall speak; *āge*—later on; *vistāra*—vivid description; *kariyā*—making; *saṅkṣepe*—in short; *kahilāṅ*—I have spoken; *ihāṅ*—in this place; *prasaṅga*—topics; *pāiyā*—taking advantage of.

TRANSLATION

I have here given a brief account of these pastimes of Lord Caitanya, but later I shall describe them in an extensive way.

TEXT 163

এই পঞ্চতত্ত্বরূপে শ্রীকৃষ্ণচৈতন্য ।
কৃষ্ণ-নাম-প্রেম দিয়া বিশ্ব কৈলা ধন্য ॥ ১৬৩ ॥

ei pañcatattva-rūpe śrī-kṛṣṇa-caitanya
kṛṣṇa-nāma-prema diyā viśva kailā dhanya

SYNONYMS

ei—this; *pañcatattva-rūpe*—the Lord in His five forms; *śrī-kṛṣṇa-caitanya*—Lord Śrī Caitanya Mahāprabhu; *kṛṣṇa-nāma*—the holy name of Lord Kṛṣṇa; *prema*—love of Kṛṣṇa; *diyā*—delivering; *viśva*—the whole world; *kailā*—made; *dhanya*—thankful.

TRANSLATION

Śrī Kṛṣṇa Caitanya Mahāprabhu and His associates of the Pañca-tattva distributed the holy name of the Lord to invoke love of Godhead throughout the universe, and thus the entire universe was thankful.

PURPORT

Here it is said that Lord Caitanya made the entire universe thankful to Him for propagating the *saṅkīrtana* movement with His associates. Lord Caitanya Mahāprabhu has already sanctified the entire universe by His presence 500 years ago, and therefore anyone who attempts to serve Śrī Caitanya Mahāprabhu sincerely by following in His footsteps and following the instructions of the *ācāryas* will successfully be able to preach the holy names of the Hare Kṛṣṇa *mahā-mantra* all over the universe. There are some foolish critics who say that Europeans and Americans cannot be offered *sannyāsa,* but here we find that Śrī Caitanya Mahāprabhu wanted to preach the *saṅkīrtana* movement all over the universe. For preaching work, *sannyāsīs* are essential. These critics think that only Indians or Hindus should be offered *sannyāsa* to preach, but their knowledge is practically nil. Without *sannyāsīs,* the preaching work will be impeded. Therefore, under the instruction of Lord Caitanya and with the blessings of His associates, there should be no discrimination in this matter, but people in all parts of the world should be trained to preach and given *sannyāsa* so that the cult of Śrī Caitanya Mahāprabhu's *saṅkīrtana* movement will expand boundlessly. We do not care about the criticism of fools. We shall go on with our work and simply depend on the blessings of Lord Caitanya Mahāprabhu and His associates, the Pañca-tattva.

TEXT 164

মথুরাতে পাঠাইল রূপ-সনাতন ।
দুই সেনাপতি কৈল ভক্তি প্রচারণ ॥ ১৬৪ ॥

mathurāte pāṭhāila rūpa-sanātana
dui senā-pati kaila bhakti pracāraṇa

SYNONYMS

mathurāte—toward Mathurā; *pāṭhāila*—sent; *rūpa-sanātana;* the two brothers Rūpa Gosvāmī and Sanātana Gosvāmī; *dui*—both of them; *senā-pati*—as commanders in chief; *kaila*—He made them; *bhakti*—devotional service; *pracāraṇa*—to broadcast.

TRANSLATION

Lord Caitanya dispatched the two generals Rūpa Gosvāmī and Sanātana Gosvāmī to Vṛndāvana to preach the bhakti cult.

PURPORT

When Rūpa Gosvāmī and Sanātana Gosvāmī went to Vṛndāvana, there was not a single temple, but by their preaching they were gradually able to construct various temples. Sanātana Gosvāmī constructed the Madana-mohana temple, and Rūpa Gosvāmī constructed the Govindajī temple. Similarly, their nephew Jīva Gosvāmī constructed the Rādhā-Dāmodara temple, Śrī Gopāla Bhaṭṭa Gosvāmī constructed the Rādhā-ramaṇa temple, Śrī Lokanātha Gosvāmī constructed the Gokulānanda temple, and Śyāmānanda Gosvāmī constructed the Śyāmasundara temple. In this way, many temples were gradually constructed. For preaching, construction of temples is also necessary. The Gosvāmīs not only engaged in writing books but also constructed temples because both are needed for preaching work. Śrī Caitanya Mahāprabhu wanted the cult of His *saṅkīrtana* movement to spread all over the world. Now that the International Society for Krishna Consciousness has taken up this task of preaching the cult of Lord Caitanya, its members should not only construct temples in every town and village of the globe but also distribute books which have already been written and further increase the number of books. Both distribution of books and construction of temples must continue side by side in parallel lines.

TEXT 165

নিত্যানন্দ-গোসাঞে পাঠাইলা গৌড়দেশে ।
তেঁহো ভক্তি প্রচারিলা অশেষ-বিশেষে ॥ ১৬৫ ॥

nityānanda-gosāñe pāṭhāilā gauḍa-deśe
teṅho bhakti pracārilā aśeṣa-viśeṣe

SYNONYMS

nityānanda—Lord Nityānanda; *gosāñe*—the *ācārya*; *pāṭhāilā*—was sent; *gauḍa-deśe*—in Bengal; *teṅho*—He; *bhakti*—devotional cult; *pracārilā*—preached; *aśeṣa-viśeṣe*—in a very extensive way.

TRANSLATION

As Rūpa Gosvāmī and Sanātana Gosvāmī were sent toward Mathurā, so Nityānanda Prabhu was sent to Bengal to preach extensively the cult of Caitanya Mahāprabhu.

PURPORT

The name of Lord Nityānanda is very famous in Bengal. Of course, anyone who knows Lord Nityānanda knows Śrī Caitanya Mahāprabhu also, but there are some misguided devotees who stress the importance of Lord Nityānanda more than that of Śrī Caitanya Mahāprabhu. This is not good. Nor should Śrī Caitanya Mahāprabhu be stressed more than Lord Nityānanda. The author of *Caitanya-caritāmṛta,* Kṛṣṇa-dāsa Kavirāja Gosvāmī, left his home because of his brother's stressing the importance of Śrī Caitanya Mahāprabhu over that of Nityānanda Prabhu. Actually, one should offer respect to the Pañca-tattva without such foolish discrimination, not considering Nityānanda Prabhu to be greater, Caitanya Mahāprabhu to be greater or Advaita Prabhu to be greater. The respect should be offered equally: *śrī-kṛṣṇa-caitanya prabhu nityānanda śrī-advaita gadādhara śrīvāsādi-gaura-bhakta-vṛnda.* All devotees of Lord Caitanya or Nityānanda are worshipable persons.

TEXT 166

আপনে দক্ষিণ দেশ করিলা গমন ।
গ্রামে গ্রামে কৈলা কৃষ্ণনাম প্রচারণ ॥ ১৬৬ ॥

āpane dakṣiṇa deśa karilā gamana
grāme grāme kailā kṛṣṇa-nāma pracāraṇa

SYNONYMS

āpane—personally; *dakṣiṇa deśa*—South India; *karilā*—went; *gamana*—traveling; *grāme grāme*—in each and every village; *kailā*—He did; *kṛṣṇa-nāma*—the holy name of Lord Kṛṣṇa; *pracāraṇa*—broadcasting.

TRANSLATION

Śrī Caitanya Mahāprabhu personally went to South India, and He broadcast the holy name of Lord Kṛṣṇa in every village and town.

TEXT 167

সেতুবন্ধ পর্যন্ত কৈলা ভক্তির প্রচার ।
কৃষ্ণপ্রেম দিয়া কৈলা সবার নিস্তার ॥ ১৬৭ ॥

setubandha paryanta kailā bhaktira pracāra
kṛṣṇa-prema diyā kailā sabāra nistāra

SYNONYMS

setubandha—the place where Lord Rāmacandra constructed His bridge; *paryanta*—up to that place; *kailā*—did; *bhaktira*—of the cult of devotional service; *pracāra*—broadcast; *kṛṣṇa-prema*—love of Kṛṣṇa; *diyā*—delivering; *kailā*—did; *sabāra*—everyone; *nistāra*—deliverance.

TRANSLATION

Thus the Lord went to the southernmost tip of the Indian peninsula, known as Setubandha [Cape Comorin]. Everywhere He distributed the bhakti cult and love of Kṛṣṇa, and in this way He delivered everyone.

TEXT 168

এই ত' কহিল পঞ্চতত্ত্বের ব্যাখ্যান ।
ইহার শ্রবণে হয় চৈতন্যতত্ত্ব-জ্ঞান ॥ ১৬৮ ॥

ei ta' kahila pañca-tattvera vyākhyāna
ihāra śravaṇe haya caitanya-tattva-jñāna

SYNONYMS

ei ta'—this; *kahila*—described; *pañca-tattvera*—of the Pañca-tattva; *vyākhyāna*—explanation; *ihāra*—of this; *śravaṇe*—hearing; *haya*—becomes; *caitanya-tattva*—the truth of Śrī Caitanya Mahāprabhu; *jñāna*—knowledge.

TRANSLATION

I thus explain the truth of the Pañca-tattva. One who hears this explanation increases in knowledge of Śrī Caitanya Mahāprabhu.

PURPORT

The Pañca-tattva is a very important factor in understanding Śrī Caitanya Mahāprabhu. There are *sahajiyās* who, not knowing the importance of the Pañca-tattva, concoct their own slogans such as *bhaja nitāi gaura, rādhe śyāma, japa hare kṛṣṇa hare rāma* or *śrī kṛṣṇa caitanya prabhu nityānanda hare kṛṣṇa hare rāma śrī rādhe govinda.* Such chants may be good poetry, but they cannot help us to go forward in devotional service. In such chants there are also many discrepancies, which need not be discussed here. Strictly speaking, when chanting the names of the Pañca-tattva, one should fully offer his obeisances: *śrī-kṛṣṇa-caitanya prabhu nityānanda śrī-advaita gadādhara śrīvāsādi-gaura-bhakta-vṛnda.* By such chanting one is blessed with the competency to chant the Hare Kṛṣṇa *mahā-mantra* without offense. When chanting the Hare Kṛṣṇa *mahā-mantra,* one should also chant it fully: Hare Kṛṣṇa, Hare Kṛṣṇa, Kṛṣṇa Kṛṣṇa, Hare Hare/ Hare Rāma, Hare Rāma, Rāma Rāma, Hare Hare. One should not foolishly adopt any of the slogans concocted by imaginative devotees. If one actually wants to derive the effects of chanting, one must strictly follow the great *ācāryas*. This is confirmed in the *Mahābhārata. Mahā-jano yena gataḥ sa panthāḥ:* "The real path of progress is that which is traversed by great *ācāryas* and authorities."

TEXT 169

শ্রীচৈতন্য, নিত্যানন্দ, অদ্বৈত,—তিন জন ।
শ্রীবাস-গদাধর-আদি যত ভক্তগণ ॥ ১৬৯ ॥

śrī-caitanya, nityānanda, advaita,—tina jana
śrīvāsa-gadādhara-ādi yata bhakta-gaṇa

SYNONYMS

śrī-caitanya, nityānanda, advaita—Śrī Caitanya Mahāprabhu, Nityānanda Prabhu and Advaita Prabhu; *tina*—these three; *jana*—personalities; *śrīvāsa-gadādhara*—Śrīvāsa and Gadādhara; *ādi*—etc.; *yata*—all; *bhakta-gaṇa*—the devotees.

TRANSLATION

While chanting the Pañca-tattva mahā-mantra, one must chant the names of Śrī Caitanya, Nityānanda, Advaita, Gadādhara and Śrīvāsa with their many devotees. This is the process.

TEXT 170

সবাকার পাদপদ্মে কোটি নমস্কার ।
যৈছে তৈছে কহি কিছু চৈতন্য-বিহার ॥ ১৭০ ॥

sabākāra pādapadme koṭi namaskāra
yaiche taiche kahi kichu caitanya-vihāra

SYNONYMS

sabākāra—all of them; *pāda-padme*—on the lotus feet; *koṭi*—countless; *namaskāra*—obeisances; *yaiche taiche*—somehow or other; *kahi*—I speak; *kichu*—something; *caitanya-vihāra*—about the pastimes of Lord Caitanya Mahāprabhu.

TRANSLATION

I again and again offer obeisances unto the Pañca-tattva. Thus I think that I will be able to describe something about the pastimes of Lord Caitanya Mahāprabhu.

TEXT 171

শ্রীরূপ-রঘুনাথ-পদে যার আশ ।
চৈতন্যচরিতামৃত কহে কৃষ্ণদাস ॥ ১৭১ ॥

śrī-rūpa-raghunātha-pade yāra āśa
caitanya-caritāmṛta kahe kṛṣṇadāsa

SYNONYMS

śrī-rūpa—Śrīla Rūpa Gosvāmī; *raghunātha*—Śrīla Raghunātha dāsa Gosvāmī; *pade*—at the lotus feet; *yāra*—whose; *āśa*—expectation; *caitanya-caritāmṛta*—the book named *Caitanya-caritāmṛta; kahe*—describes; *kṛṣṇa-dāsa*—Śrīla Kṛṣṇadāsa Kavirāja Gosvāmī.

TRANSLATION

Praying at the lotus feet of Śrī Rūpa and Śrī Raghunātha, always desiring their mercy, I, Kṛṣṇadāsa, narrate Śrī-Caitanya-caritāmṛta, following in their footsteps.

PURPORT

Śrī Caitanya Mahāprabhu wanted to preach the *saṅkīrtana* movement of love of Kṛṣṇa throughout the entire world, and therefore during His presence He inspired the *saṅkīrtana* movement. Specifically, He sent Rūpa Gosvāmī to Vṛndāvana and Nityānanda to Bengal and personally went to South India. In this way He kindly left the task of preaching His cult in the rest of the world to the International Society for Krishna Consciousness. The members of this Society must always remember that if they stick to the regulative principles and preach sincerely according to the instructions of the *ācāryas,* surely they will have the profound blessings of Lord Caitanya Mahāprabhu, and their preaching work will be successful everywhere throughout the world.

Thus end the Bhaktivedanta purports to the Śrī Caitanya-caritāmṛta, Ādi-līlā, *Seventh Chapter, describing Lord Caitanya in five features.*

Ādi-Līlā

CHAPTER 8

The Eighth Chapter of *Śrī-Caitanya-caritāmṛta* is summarized by Śrīla Bhaktivinoda Ṭhākura in his *Amṛta-pravāha-bhāṣya.* In this Eighth Chapter, the glories of Śrī Caitanya Mahāprabhu and Nityānanda are described, and it also stated that if one commits offenses in chanting the Hare Kṛṣṇa *mantra,* he does not achieve love of Godhead even after chanting for many years. In this connection, Śrīla Bhaktivinoda Ṭhākura warns against artificial displays of the bodily symptoms called *aṣṭa-sāttvika-vikāra.* That is also another offense. One should seriously and sincerely continue to chant the Pañca-tattva names *śrī-kṛṣṇa-caitanya prabhu nityānanda śrī-advaita gadādhara śrīvāsādi-gaura-bhakta-vṛnda.* All these *ācāryas* will bestow their causeless mercy upon a devotee and gradually purify his heart. When he is actually purified, automatically he will experience ecstasy in chanting the Hare Kṛṣṇa *mahā-mantra.* Previous to the composition of *Caitanya-caritāmṛta,* Śrīla Vṛndāvana dāsa Ṭhākura wrote a book called *Śrī-Caitanya-bhāgavata.* Only those subjects which were not discussed by Śrīla Vṛndāvana dāsa Ṭhākura in his *Caitanya-bhāgavata* have been taken up by Kṛṣṇadāsa Kavirāja Gosvāmī to be depicted in *Śrī-Caitanya-caritāmṛta.* In his very old age, Kṛṣṇadāsa Kavirāja Gosvāmī went to Vṛndāvana, and by the order of Śrī Madana-mohanajī he wrote *Śrī-Caitanya-caritāmṛta.* Thus we are now able to relish its transcendental bliss.

TEXT 1

বন্দে চৈতন্যদেবং তং ভগবন্তং যদিচ্ছয়া।
প্রসভং নর্ত্যতে চিত্রং লেখরঙ্গে জড়োঽপ্যয়ম্॥ ১ ॥

vande caitanya-devaṁ taṁ bhagavantaṁ yad-icchayā
prasabhaṁ nartyate citraṁ lekharaṅge jaḍo 'py ayam

SYNONYMS

vande—I offer my respectful obeisances; *caitanya-devam*—unto Lord Śrī Caitanya Mahāprabhu; *tam*—Him; *bhagavantam*—the Personality of Godhead; *yat-icchayā*—by whose desires; *prasabham*—all of a sudden; *nartyate*—dancing; *citram*—wonderfully; *lekharaṅge*—in the matter of writing; *jaḍaḥ*—dull fool; *api*—although; *ayam*—this.

TRANSLATION

I offer my respects to the Supreme Personality of Godhead, Śrī Caitanya Mahāprabhu, by whose desire I have become like a dancing dog and, although I am a fool, I have suddenly taken to the writing of Śrī-Caitanya-caritāmṛta.

TEXT 2

জয় জয় শ্রীকৃষ্ণচৈতন্য গৌরচন্দ্র ।
জয় জয় পরমানন্দ জয় নিত্যানন্দ ॥ ২ ॥

jaya jaya śrī-kṛṣṇa-caitanya gauracandra
jaya jaya paramānanda jaya nityānanda

SYNONYMS

jaya jaya—all glories; *śrī-kṛṣṇa-caitanya*—Śrī Kṛṣṇa Caitanya Mahāprabhu; *gaura-candra*—whose name is Lord Gaurāṅga; *jaya jaya*—all glories; *paramānanda*—most joyful; *jaya*—all glories; *nityānanda*—unto Nityānanda Prabhu.

TRANSLATION

Let me offer my respectful obeisances unto Śrī Kṛṣṇa Caitanya Mahāprabhu, who is known as Gaurasundara. I also offer my respectful obeisances unto Nityānanda Prabhu, who is always very joyful.

TEXT 3

জয় জয়াদ্বৈত আচার্য কৃপাময় ।
জয় জয় গদাধর পণ্ডিত মহাশয় ॥ ৩ ॥

jaya jayādvaita ācārya kṛpāmaya
jaya jaya gadādhara paṇḍita mahāśaya

SYNONYMS

jaya jaya—all glories; *advaita*—unto Advaita Prabhu; *ācārya*—teacher; *kṛpāmaya*—very merciful; *jaya jaya*—all glories to; *gadādhara*—of the name Gadādhara; *paṇḍita*—learned scholar; *mahāśaya*—great personality.

TRANSLATION

Let me offer my respectful obeisances unto Advaita Ācārya, who is very merciful, and also to that great personality Gadādhara Paṇḍita, the learned scholar.

TEXT 4

জয় জয় শ্রীবাসাদি যত ভক্তগণ ।
প্রণত হইয়া বন্দোঁ সবার চরণ ॥ ৪ ॥

jaya jaya śrīvāsādi yata bhakta-gaṇa
praṇata ha-iyā vandoṅ sabāra caraṇa

SYNONYMS

jaya jaya—all glories; *śrīvāsa-ādi*—unto Śrīvāsa Ṭhākura, etc.; *yata*—all; *bhakta-gaṇa*—devotees; *praṇata*—offering obeisances; *ha-iyā*—doing so; *vandoṅ*—I pray; *sabāra*—all; *caraṇa*—lotus feet.

TRANSLATION

Let me offer my respectful obeisances unto Śrīvāsa Ṭhākura and all other devotees of the Lord. I fall down to offer them respect. I worship their lotus feet.

PURPORT

Kṛṣṇadāsa Kavirāja Gosvāmī teaches us first to offer respect to the Pañca-tattva—Śrī Kṛṣṇa Caitanya Mahāprabhu, Nityānanda Prabhu, Advaita Prabhu, Gadādhara Prabhu and Śrīvāsa and other devotees. We must strictly follow the principle of offering our respects to the Pañca-tattva, as summarized in the *mantra—śrī-kṛṣṇa-caitanya prabhu nityānanda śrī-advaita gadādhara śrīvāsādi-gaura-bhakta-vṛnda.* At the beginning of every function in preaching, especially before chanting the Hare Kṛṣṇa *mahā-mantra*—Hare Kṛṣṇa, Hare Kṛṣṇa, Kṛṣṇa Kṛṣṇa, Hare Hare/ Hare Rāma, Hare Rāma, Rāma Rāma, Hare Hare—we must chant the Pañca-tattva's names and offer our respects to them.

TEXT 5

মূক কবিত্ব করে যাঁ-সবার স্মরণে ।
পঙ্গু গিরি লঙ্ঘে, অন্ধ দেখে তারাগণে ॥ ৫ ॥

mūka kavitva kare yāṅ-sabāra smaraṇe
paṅgu giri laṅghe, andha dekhe tārā-gaṇe

SYNONYMS

mūka—dumb; *kavitva*—poet; *kare*—becomes; *yāṅ*—whose; *sabāra*—all; *smaraṇe*—by remembering; *paṅgu*—the lame; *giri*—mountains; *laṅghe*—crosses; *andha*—blind; *dekhe*—sees; *tārā-gaṇe*—the stars.

TRANSLATION

By remembering the lotus feet of the Pañca-tattva, a dumb man can become a poet, a lame man can cross mountains, and a blind man can see the stars in the sky.

PURPORT

In Vaiṣṇava philosophy there are three ways for perfection—namely, *sādhana-siddha,* perfection attained by executing devotional service according to the rules and regulations, *nitya-siddha,* eternal perfection attained by never forgetting Kṛṣṇa at any time, and *kṛpā-siddha,* perfection attained by the mercy of the spiritual master or a Vaiṣṇava. Kavirāja Gosvāmī here stresses *kṛpā-siddha,* perfection by the mercy of superior authorities. This mercy does not depend on the qualifications of a devotee. By such mercy, even if a devotee is dumb he can speak or write to glorify the Lord splendidly, even if lame he can cross mountains, and even if blind he can see the stars in the sky.

TEXT 6

এ-সব না মানে যেই পণ্ডিত সকল ।
তা-সবার বিদ্যাপাঠ ভেক-কোলাহল ॥ ৬ ॥

e-saba nā māne yei paṇḍita sakala
tā-sabāra vidyā-pāṭha bheka-kolāhala

SYNONYMS

e-saba—all these; *nā*—does not; *māne*—accept; *yei*—anyone; *paṇḍita*—so-called learned; *sakala*—all; *tā-sabāra*—of all of them; *vidyā-pāṭha*—the educational cultivation; *bheka*—of frogs; *kolāhala*—tumultuous sound.

TRANSLATION

The education cultivated by so-called learned scholars who do not believe these statements of Caitanya-caritāmṛta is like the tumultuous croaking of frogs.

PURPORT

The croaking of the frogs in the rainy season resounds very loudly in the forest, with the result that snakes, hearing the croaking in the darkness, approach the frogs and swallow them. Similarly, the so-called educational vibrations of the tongues of university professors who do not have spiritual knowledge is like the croaking of frogs.

TEXT 7

এই সব না মানে যেবা করে কৃষ্ণভক্তি ।
কৃষ্ণ-কৃপা নাহি তারে, নাহি তার গতি ॥ ৭ ॥

ei saba nā māne yebā kare kṛṣṇa-bhakti
kṛṣṇa-kṛpā nāhi tāre, nāhi tāra gati

SYNONYMS

ei—these; *saba*—all; *nā māne*—does not accept; *yebā*—anyone who; *kare*—executes; *kṛṣṇa-bhakti*—devotional service; *kṛṣṇa-kṛpā*—mercy of Kṛṣṇa; *nāhi*—is not; *tāre*—unto him; *nāhi*—there is not; *tāra*—his; *gati*—advancement.

TRANSLATION

One who does not accept the glories of the Pañca-tattva but still makes a show of devotional service to Kṛṣṇa can never achieve the mercy of Kṛṣṇa nor advance to the ultimate goal.

PURPORT

If one is seriously interested in Kṛṣṇa conscious activities, he must be ready to follow the rules and regulations laid down by the *ācāryas,* and he must understand their conclusions. The *śāstra* says: *dharmasya tattvaṁ nihitaṁ guhāyāṁ mahā-jano yena gataḥ sa panthāḥ* (*Mahābhārata, Vana Parva* 313.117). It is very difficult to understand the secret of Kṛṣṇa consciousness, but one who advances by the instruction of the previous *ācāryas* and follows in the footsteps of his predecessors in the line of disciplic succession will have success. Others will not. Śrīla Narottama dāsa Ṭhākura says in this connection, *chāḍiyā vaiṣṇava-sevā nistāra pāyeche kebā:* "Unless one serves the spiritual master and *ācāryas,* one cannot be liberated." Elsewhere he says:

ei chaya gosāñi yāṅra—mui tāṅra dāsa
tāṅ-sabāra pada-reṇu mora pañca-grāsa

"I simply accept a person who follows in the footsteps of the six Gosvāmīs, and the dust of such a person's lotus feet is my foodstuff."

TEXT 8

পূর্বে যৈছে জরাসন্ধ-আদি রাজগণ ।
বেদ-ধর্ম করি' করে বিষ্ণুর পূজন ॥ ৮ ॥

pūrve yaiche jarāsandha-ādi rāja-gaṇa
veda-dharma kari' kare viṣṇura pūjana

SYNONYMS

pūrve—formerly; *yaiche*—as it was; *jarāsandha*—King Jarāsandha; *ādi*—heading; *rāja-gaṇa*—kings; *veda-dharma*—performance of Vedic rituals; *kari'*—doing; *kare*—does; *viṣṇura*—of Lord Viṣṇu; *pūjana*—worship.

TRANSLATION

Formerly kings like Jarāsandha [the father-in-law of Kaṁsa] strictly followed the Vedic rituals, thus worshiping Lord Viṣṇu.

PURPORT

In these verses the author of *Caitanya-caritāmṛta,* Kṛṣṇadāsa Kavirāja Gosvāmī, is very seriously stressing the importance of worship of the Pañca-tattva. If one becomes a devotee of Gaurasundara or Kṛṣṇa but does not give importance to the Pañca-tattva (*śrī-kṛṣṇa-caitanya prabhu nityānanda śrī-advaita gadādhara śrīvāsādi-gaura-bhakta-vṛnda*), his activities are considered to be offenses, or, in the words of Śrīla Rūpa Gosvāmī, *utpāta* (disturbances). One must therefore be ready to offer due respects to the Pañca-tattva before becoming a devotee of Lord Gaurasundara or of Śrī Kṛṣṇa, the Supreme Personality of Godhead.

TEXT 9

কৃষ্ণ নাহি মানে, তাতে দৈত্য করি' মানি ।
চৈতন্য না মানিলে তৈছে দৈত্য তারে জানি ॥ ৯ ॥

kṛṣṇa nāhi māne, tāte daitya kari' māni
caitanya nā mānile taiche daitya tāre jāni

SYNONYMS

kṛṣṇa—Lord Kṛṣṇa; *nāhi*—does not; *māne*—accept; *tāte*—therefore; *daitya*—demon; *kari' māni*—we accept; *caitanya*—Lord Śrī Caitanya Mahāprabhu; *nā*—without; *mānile*—accepting; *taiche*—similarly; *daitya*—demon; *tāre*—to him; *jāni*—we know.

TRANSLATION

One who does not accept Kṛṣṇa as the Supreme Personality of Godhead is certainly a demon. Similarly, anyone who does not accept Śrī Caitanya Mahāprabhu as Kṛṣṇa, the same Supreme Lord, is also to be considered a demon.

PURPORT

Formerly there were kings like Jarāsandha who strictly followed the Vedic rituals, acted as charitable, competent *kṣatriyas,* possessed all *kṣatriya* qualities and were even obedient to the brahminical culture but who did not accept Kṛṣṇa as the Supreme Personality of Godhead. Jarāsandha attacked Kṛṣṇa many times, and each time, of course, he was defeated. Like Jarāsandha, any man who performs Vedic rituals but does not accept Kṛṣṇa as the Supreme Personality of Godhead must be considered an *asura* or demon. Similarly, one who does not accept Śrī Caitanya Mahāprabhu as Kṛṣṇa Himself is also a demon. This is the conclusion of authoritative scriptures. Therefore, both so-called devotion to Gaurasundara without devotional service to Kṛṣṇa and so-called *Kṛṣṇa-bhakti* without devotional service to

Gaurasundara are nondevotional activities. If one wants to be successful on the path of Kṛṣṇa consciousness, he must be thoroughly conscious of the personality of Gaurasundara as well as the personality of Kṛṣṇa. Knowing the personality of Gaurasundara means knowing the personalities of *śrī-kṛṣṇa-caitanya prabhu nityānanda śrī-advaita gadādhara śrīvāsādi-gaura-bhakta-vṛnda.* The author of *Caitanya-caritāmṛta,* pursuant to the authorities, stresses this principle for perfection in Kṛṣṇa consciousness.

TEXT 10

মোরে না মানিলে সব লোক হবে নাশ ।
ইথি লাগি' কৃপার্দ্র প্রভু করিল সন্ন্যাস ॥ ১০ ॥

more nā mānile saba loka habe nāśa
ithi lāgi' kṛpārdra prabhu karila sannyāsa

SYNONYMS

more—unto Me; *nā*—without; *mānile*—accepting; *saba*—all; *loka*—people in general; *habe*—will go to; *nāśa*—destruction; *ithi*—for this; *lāgi'*—for the reason of; *kṛpā-ārdra*—all merciful; *prabhu*—Lord Caitanya; *karila*—accepted; *sannyāsa*—the *sannyāsa* order.

TRANSLATION

Lord Śrī Caitanya Mahāprabhu thought that unless people accepted Him they would all be destroyed. Thus the merciful Lord accepted the sannyāsa order.

PURPORT

In the *Śrīmad-Bhāgavatam* it is said, *kīrtanād eva kṛṣṇasya mukta-saṅgaḥ paraṁ vrajet:* "Simply by chanting the Hare Kṛṣṇa *mantra,* or Lord Kṛṣṇa's name, one is liberated and goes back home, back to Godhead." (*Bhāg.* 12.3.51) This Kṛṣṇa consciousness must be achieved through the mercy of Lord Caitanya Mahāprabhu. One cannot be complete in Kṛṣṇa consciousness unless he accepts Śrī Caitanya Mahāprabhu and His associates as the only means for success. It is because of these considerations that the Lord accepted *sannyāsa,* for thus people would offer Him respect and very quickly come to the platform of Kṛṣṇa consciousness. Since Lord Caitanya Mahāprabhu, who is Kṛṣṇa Himself, inaugurated the Kṛṣṇa consciousness movement, without His mercy one cannot be elevated to the transcendental platform of Kṛṣṇa consciousness.

TEXT 11

সন্ন্যাসি-বুদ্ধ্যে মোরে করিবে নমস্কার ।
তথাপি খণ্ডিবে দুঃখ, পাইবে নিস্তার ॥ ১১ ॥

sannyāsi-buddhye more karibe namaskāra
tathāpi khaṇḍibe duḥkha, pāibe nistāra

SYNONYMS

sannyāsi-buddhye—by consideration of a *sannyāsī; more*—unto Me; *karibe*—they will; *namaskāra*—offer obeisances; *tathāpi*—therefore; *khaṇḍibe*—will diminish; *duḥkha*—distress; *pāibe*—will get; *nistāra*—liberation.

TRANSLATION

If a person offers obeisances to Lord Caitanya, even due to accepting Him only as an ordinary sannyāsī, his material distresses will diminish, and he will ultimately get liberation.

PURPORT

Kṛṣṇa is so merciful that He always thinks of how to liberate the conditioned souls from the material platform. It is for this reason that Kṛṣṇa incarnates, as clearly indicated in *Bhagavad-gītā:*

yadā yadā hi dharmasya
glānir bhavati bhārata
abhyutthānam adharmasya
tadātmānaṁ sṛjāmy aham

"Whenever and wherever there is a decline in religious practice, O descendant of Bharata, and a predominant rise of irreligion—at that time I descend Myself." (Bg. 4.7) Kṛṣṇa always protects the living entities in many ways. He comes Himself, He sends His own confidential devotees, and He leaves behind Him *śāstras* like *Bhagavad-gītā.* Why? It is so that people may take advantage of the benediction to be liberated from the clutches of *māyā.* Śrī Caitanya Mahāprabhu accepted *sannyāsa* so that even a foolish person who accepted Him as an ordinary *sannyāsī* would offer Him respect, for this would help diminish his material distresses and ultimately liberate him from the material clutches. Śrīla Bhaktisiddhānta Sarasvatī points out in this connection that Śrī Kṛṣṇa Caitanya Mahāprabhu is the combined form of Śrī Rādhā and Kṛṣṇa *(mahāprabhu śrī-caitanya, rādhā-kṛṣṇa—nahe anya).* Therefore when fools considered Caitanya Mahāprabhu to be an ordinary human being and thus treated Him disrespectfully, the merciful Lord, in order to deliver these offenders, accepted *sannyāsa* so that they would offer Him obeisances, accepting Him as a *sannyāsī.* Śrī Caitanya Mahāprabhu accepted *sannyāsa* to bestow His great mercy on people in general who cannot appreciate Him as Rādhā and Kṛṣṇa Themselves.

TEXT 12

হেন কৃপাময় চৈতন্য না ভজে যেই জন ।
সর্বোত্তম হইলেও তারে অসুরে গণন ॥ ১২ ॥

hena kṛpāmaya caitanya nā bhaje yei jana
sarvottama ha-ileo tāre asure gaṇana

SYNONYMS

hena—such; *kṛpāmaya*—merciful; *caitanya*—Lord Śrī Caitanya; *nā*—does not; *bhaje*—worship; *yei*—one; *jana*—person; *sarvottama*—supreme; *ha-ileo*—in spite of his being; *tāre*—unto him; *asure*—among the demons; *gaṇana*—the calculation.

TRANSLATION

One who does not show respect unto this merciful Lord, Caitanya Mahāprabhu, or does not worship Him should be considered a demon, even if he is very exalted in human society.

PURPORT

Śrīla Bhaktisiddhānta Sarasvatī Mahārāja says in this connection: "O living entities, simply engage yourselves in Kṛṣṇa consciousness. This is the message of Śrī Caitanya Mahāprabhu." Lord Caitanya preached this cult, instructing the philosophy of Kṛṣṇa consciousness in His eight verses, or *Śikṣāṣṭaka,* and He said, *ihā haite sarva-siddhi haibe tomāra:* "By chanting the Hare Kṛṣṇa *mantra,* one will get all perfection in life." Therefore one who does not show Him respect or cannot appreciate His mercy despite all these merciful gestures is still an *asura,* or opponent of bona fide devotional service to Lord Viṣṇu, even though he is very exalted in human society. *Asura* refers to one who is against devotional service to the Supreme Personality of Godhead, Viṣṇu. It should be noted that unless one worships Śrī Caitanya Mahāprabhu it is useless to become a devotee of Kṛṣṇa, and unless one worships Kṛṣṇa it is also useless to become a devotee of Śrī Caitanya Mahāprabhu. Such devotional service is to be understood to be a product of Kali-yuga. Śrīla Bhaktisiddhānta Sarasvatī Ṭhākura remarks in this connection that atheist *smārtas,* or worshipers of the five kinds of demigods, worship Lord Viṣṇu for a little satisfaction in material success but have no respect for Śrī Caitanya Mahāprabhu. Thinking Him to be one of the ordinary living entities, they discriminate between Gaurasundara and Śrī Kṛṣṇa. Such understanding is also demoniac and is against the conclusion of the *ācāryas.* Such a conclusion is a product of Kali-yuga.

TEXT 13

অতএব পুনঃ কহোঁ ঊর্ধ্ববাহু হঞা ।
চৈতন্য-নিত্যানন্দ ভজ কুতর্ক ছাড়িয়া ॥ ১৩ ॥

ataeva punaḥ kahoṅ ūrdhva-bāhu hañā
caitanya-nityānanda bhaja kutarka chāḍiyā

SYNONYMS

ataeva—therefore; *punaḥ*—again; *kahoṅ*—I speak; *ūrdhva*—lifting; *bāhu*—arms; *hañā*—so doing; *caitanya*—Śrī Caitanya Mahāprabhu; *nityānanda*—Lord Nityānanda; *bhaja*—worship; *kutarka*—useless arguments; *chāḍiyā*—giving up.

TRANSLATION

Therefore I say again, lifting my arms: O fellow human beings, please worship Śrī Caitanya and Nityānanda without false arguments!

PURPORT

Because a person who performs *Kṛṣṇa-bhakti* but does not understand Śrī Kṛṣṇa Caitanya and Prabhu Nityānanda will simply waste his time, the author, Kṛṣṇadāsa Kavirāja Gosvāmī, requests everyone take to the worship of Śrī Caitanya and Nityānanda Prabhu and the Pañca-tattva. He assures everyone that any person who does so will be successful in Kṛṣṇa consciousness.

TEXT 14

যদি বা তার্কিক কহে,—তর্ক সে প্রমাণ ।
তর্কশাস্ত্রে সিদ্ধ যেই, সেই সেব্যমান ॥ ১৪ ॥

yadi vā tārkika kahe,—tarka se pramāṇa
tarka-śāstre siddha yei, sei sevyamāna

SYNONYMS

yadi—if; *vā*—or; *tārkika*—logician; *kahe*—says; *tarka*—logic; *se*—that; *pramāṇa*—evidence; *tarka-śāstre*—in the logic; *siddha*—accepted; *yei*—whatever; *sei*—that; *sevyamāna*—is worshipable.

TRANSLATION

Logicians say, "Unless one gains understanding through logic and argument, how can one decide upon a worshipable Deity?"

TEXT 15

শ্রীকৃষ্ণচৈতন্য-দয়া করহ বিচার ।
বিচার করিলে চিত্তে পাবে চমৎকার ॥ ১৫ ॥

śrī-kṛṣṇa-caitanya-dayā karaha vicāra
vicāra karile citte pābe camatkāra

SYNONYMS

śrī-kṛṣṇa-caitanya—Lord Śrī Caitanya Mahāprabhu; *dayā*—His mercy; *karaha*—just put into; *vicāra*—consideration; *vicāra*—when such consideration; *karile*—will be done by you; *citte*—in your heart; *pābe*—you will get; *camatkāra*—striking wonder.

TRANSLATION

If you are indeed interested in logic and argument, kindly apply it to the mercy of Śrī Caitanya Mahāprabhu. If you do so, you will find it to be strikingly wonderful.

PURPORT

Śrīla Bhaktisiddhānta Sarasvatī Ṭhākura comments in this connection that people in general, in their narrow-minded conception of life, create many different types of humanitarian activities, but the humanitarian activities inaugurated by Śrī Caitanya Mahāprabhu are different. For logicians who want to accept only that which is proven through logic and argument, it is a fact that without logic and reason there can be no question of accepting the Absolute Truth. Unfortunately, when such logicians take to this path without the mercy of Śrī Caitanya Mahāprabhu, they remain on the platform of logic and argument and do not advance in spiritual life. However, if one is intelligent enough to apply his arguments and logic to the subtle understanding of the fundamental spiritual substance, he will be able to know that a poor fund of knowledge established on the basis of material logic cannot help one understand the Absolute Truth, which is beyond the reach of imperfect senses. The *Mahābhārata* therefore says: *acintyāḥ khalu ye bhāvā na tāṁs tarkeṇa yojayet* (*Mahābhārata, Bhīṣma Parva.* 5.22). How can that which is beyond the imagination or sensory speculation of mundane creatures be approached simply by logic? Logic and argument are very poor in spiritual strength and always imperfect when applied to spiritual understanding. By putting forward mundane logic one frequently comes to the wrong conclusion regarding the Absolute Truth, and as a result of such a conclusion one may fall down to accept a body like that of a jackal.

Despite all this, those who are actually inquisitive to understand the philosophy of Śrī Caitanya Mahāprabhu through logic and argument are welcome. Kṛṣṇadāsa Kavirāja Gosvāmī addresses them, "Please put Śrī Caitanya Mahāprabhu's mercy to your crucial test, and if you are actually a logician you will come to the right conclusion that there is no personality more merciful than Lord Caitanya." Let the logicians compare all the results of other humanitarian work with the merciful activities of Lord Caitanya. If their judgment is impartial, they will understand that no other humanitarian activities can surpass those of Śrī Caitanya Mahāprabhu.

Everyone is engaged in humanitarian activities on the basis of the body, but from *Bhagavad-gītā* (2.18) we understand, *antavanta ime dehā nityasyoktāḥ śarīriṇaḥ:* The material body is ultimately subject to destruction, whereas the spiritual soul is eternal. Śrī Caitanya Mahāprabhu's philanthropic activities are performed in connection with the eternal soul. However one tries to benefit the body, it will be destroyed, and one will have to accept another body according to his present activities. If one does not, therefore, understand this science of transmigration but considers the body to be all in all, his intelligence is not very advanced. Śrī Caitanya Mahāprabhu, without neglecting the necessities of the body, imparted spiritual advancement to purify the existential condition of humanity. Therefore if a logician makes his judgment impartially, he will surely find that Śrī Caitanya Mahāprabhu is the *mahā-vadānyāvatāra,* the most magnanimous incarnation. He is even more magnanimous than Lord Kṛṣṇa Himself. Lord Kṛṣṇa demanded that one surrender unto Him, but He did not distribute love of Godhead as magnanimously as Śrī Caitanya Mahāprabhu. Therefore Śrīla Rūpa Gosvāmī offers Lord Caitanya his respectful obeisances with the words *namo mahā-vadānyāya kṛṣṇa-prema-pradāya te kṛṣṇāya kṛṣṇa-caitanya-nāmne gaura-tviṣe namaḥ.* Lord Kṛṣṇa simply gave *Bhagavad-gītā,* by which one can understand Lord Kṛṣṇa as He is, but Śrī Caitanya Mahāprabhu, who is also Kṛṣṇa Himself, gave people love of Kṛṣṇa without discrimination.

TEXT 16

বহু জন্ম করে যদি শ্রবণ, কীর্তন ।
তবু ত' না পায় কৃষ্ণপদে প্রেমধন ॥ ১৬ ॥

bahu janma kare yadi śravaṇa, kīrtana
tabu ta' nā pāya kṛṣṇa-pade prema-dhana

SYNONYMS

bahu—many; *janma*—births; *kare*—does; *yadi*—if; *śravaṇa*—hearing; *kīrtana*—chanting; *tabu*—still; *ta'*—in spite of; *nā*—does not; *pāya*—get; *kṛṣṇa-pade*—unto the lotus feet of Kṛṣṇa; *prema-dhana*—love of Godhead.

TRANSLATION

If one is infested with the ten offenses in the chanting of the Hare Kṛṣṇa mahā-mantra, despite his endeavor to chant the holy name for many births, he will not get the love of Godhead which is the ultimate goal of this chanting.

PURPORT

Śrīla Bhaktisiddhānta Sarasvatī Ṭhākura says in this connection that unless one accepts Śrī Caitanya Mahāprabhu, although one goes on chanting the Hare Kṛṣṇa *mantra* for many, many years, there is no possibility of his attaining the platform of devotional service. One must follow strictly the instruction of Śrī Caitanya Mahāprabhu given in the *Śikṣāṣṭaka:*

tṛṇād api sunīcena taror api sahiṣṇunā
amāninā mānadena kīrtanīyaḥ sadā hariḥ

"One should chant the holy name of the Lord in a humble state of mind, thinking oneself lower than the straw in the street; one should be more tolerant than a tree, devoid of all sense of false prestige, and should be ready to offer all respect to others. In such a state of mind one can chant the holy name of the Lord constantly." (*Śikṣāṣṭaka,* 3) One who follows this direction, being freed from the ten kinds of offenses, becomes successful in Kṛṣṇa consciousness and ultimately reaches the platform of loving service to the Personality of Godhead.

One must come to the understanding that the holy name of the Lord and the Supreme Personality of Godhead Himself are identical. One cannot reach this conclusion unless one is offenseless in chanting the holy name. By our material calculation we see a difference between the name and the substance, but in the spiritual world the Absolute is always absolute; the name, form, quality and pastimes of the Absolute are all as good as the Absolute Himself. As such, one is understood to be an eternal servant of the Supreme Personality of Godhead if he considers himself an eternal servant of the holy name and in this spirit distributes the holy name to the world. One who chants in that spirit, without offenses, is certainly elevated to the platform of understanding that the holy name and the Personality of Godhead are identical. To associate with the holy name and chant the holy name is to associate with the Personality of Godhead directly. In *Bhakti-rasāmṛta-sindhu* it is clearly said: *sevonmukhe hi jihvādau svayam eva sphuraty adaḥ.* The holy name becomes manifest when one engages in the service of the holy name. This service in a submissive attitude begins with one's tongue. *Sevonmukhe hi jihvādau:* One must engage his tongue in the service of the holy name. Our Kṛṣṇa consciousness movement is based on this principle. We try to engage all the members of the Kṛṣṇa consciousness movement in the service of the holy name. Since the holy name and Kṛṣṇa are nondifferent, the members of the Kṛṣṇa consciousness movement not only chant the holy name of the Lord offenselessly, but also do not allow their tongues to eat anything which is not first offered to the Supreme Personality of Godhead. The Supreme Lord declares:

patraṁ puṣpaṁ phalaṁ toyaṁ
yo me bhaktyā prayacchati
tad ahaṁ bhakty-upahṛtam
aśnāmi prayatātmanaḥ

"If one offers Me with love and devotion a leaf, a flower, a fruit or water, I will accept it." (Bg. 9.26) Therefore the International Society for Krishna Consciousness has many temples all over the world, and in each and every temple the Lord is offered these foodstuffs. On the basis of His demands, the devotees chant the holy name of the Lord offenselessly and never eat anything that is not first offered to the Lord. The functions of the tongue in devotional service are to chant the Hare Kṛṣṇa *mahā-mantra* and eat *prasāda* that is offered to the Lord.

TEXT 17

জ্ঞানতঃ সুলভা মুক্তির্ভুক্তির্যজ্ঞাদিপুণ্যতঃ ।
সেয়ং সাধনসাহস্রৈর্হরিভক্তিঃ সুদুর্লভা ॥ ১৭ ॥

jñānataḥ sulabhā muktir
bhuktir yajñādi-puṇyataḥ
seyaṁ sādhana-sāhasrair
hari-bhaktiḥ sudurlabhā

SYNONYMS

jñānataḥ—by cultivation of knowledge; *su-labhā*—easily obtainable; *muktiḥ*—liberation; *bhuktiḥ*—sense enjoyment; *yajña-ādi*—performance of sacrifices, etc.; *puṇyataḥ*—and by performing pious activities; *sā*—that; *iyam*—this; *sādhana-sāhasraiḥ*—execution of thousands of sacrifices; *hari-bhaktiḥ*—devotional service; *sudurlabhā*—is very rare.

TRANSLATION

"By cultivating philosophical knowledge one can understand his spiritual position and thus be liberated, and by performing sacrifices and pious activities one can achieve sense gratification in a higher planetary system, but the devotional service of the Lord is so rare that even by executing hundreds and thousands of such sacrifices one cannot obtain it."

PURPORT

Prahlāda Mahārāja instructs:

matir na kṛṣṇe parataḥ svato vā
mitho 'bhipadyeta gṛha-vratānām
(*Bhāg.* 7.5.30)

naiṣāṁ matis tāvad urukramāṅghriṁ
spṛśaty anarthāpagamo yad arthaḥ
mahīyasāṁ pāda-rajo 'bhiṣekaṁ
niṣkiñcanānāṁ na vṛṇīta yāvat
(*Bhāg.* 7.5.32)

These *ślokas* are to be discussed. Their purport is that one cannot obtain *Kṛṣṇa-bhakti,* or the devotional service of the Lord, by official execution of the Vedic rituals. One has to approach a pure devotee. Narottama dāsa Ṭhākura sings, *chāḍiyā vaiṣṇava-sevā nistāra pāyeche kebā:* "Who has been elevated without rendering service to a pure Vaiṣṇava?" It is the statement of Prahlāda Mahārāja that unless one is able to accept the dust from the lotus feet of a pure Vaiṣṇava there is no possibility of his achieving the platform of devotional service. That is the secret. The above-mentioned *Tantra-vacana,* quoted from the *Bhakti-rasāmṛta-sindhu,* is our perfect guidance in this connection.

TEXT 18

কৃষ্ণ যদি ছুটে ভক্তে ভুক্তি মুক্তি দিয়া ।
কভু প্রেমভক্তি না দেন রাখেন লুকাইয়া ॥ ১৮ ॥

kṛṣṇa yadi chuṭe bhakte bhukti mukti diyā
kabhu prema-bhakti nā dena rākhena lukāiyā

SYNONYMS

kṛṣṇa—Lord Kṛṣṇa; *yadi*—of course; *chuṭe*—goes away; *bhakte*—unto the devotee; *bhukti*—material enjoyment; *mukti*—liberation; *diyā*—offering; *kabhu*—at any time; *prema-bhakti*—love of Godhead; *nā*—does not; *dena*—give; *rākhena*—keeps; *lukāiyā*—hiding.

TRANSLATION

If a devotee wants material sense gratification or liberation from the Lord, Kṛṣṇa immediately delivers it, but pure devotional service He keeps hidden.

TEXT 19

রাজন্ পতির্গুরুরলং ভবতাং যদূনাং
দৈবং প্রিয়ঃ কুলপতিঃ ক্ব চ কিঙ্করো বঃ ।
অস্ত্বেবমঙ্গ ভগবান্ ভজতাং মুকুন্দো
মুক্তিং দদাতি কর্হিচিৎ স্ম ন ভক্তিযোগম্ ॥ ১৯ ॥

rājan patir gurur alaṁ bhavatāṁ yadūnāṁ
daivaṁ priyaḥ kula-patiḥ kva ca kiṅkaro vaḥ
astv evam aṅga bhagavān bhajatāṁ mukundo
muktiṁ dadāti karhicit sma na bhakti-yogam

SYNONYMS

rājan—O King; *patiḥ*—master; *guruḥ*—spiritual master; *alam*—certainly; *bhavatām*—of your; *yadūnām*—of the Yadus; *daivam*—God; *priyaḥ*—very dear; *kula-patiḥ*—head of the family; *kva*—even sometimes; *ca*—also; *kiṅkaraḥ*—order carrier; *vaḥ*—you; *astu*—there is; *evam*—thus; *aṅga*—however; *bhagavān*—the Supreme Personality of Godhead; *bhajatām*—those who are in devotional service; *mukundaḥ*—Lord Kṛṣṇa; *muktim*—liberation; *dadāti*—gives; *karhicit*—sometimes; *sma*—certainly; *na*—not; *bhakti-yogam*—devotional service.

TRANSLATION

"The great sage Nārada said: 'My dear Mahārāja Yudhiṣṭhira, the Supreme Personality of Godhead Kṛṣṇa is always ready to help you. He is your master, guru, God, very dear friend and head of your family. Yet sometimes He agrees to act as your servant or order carrier. You are greatly fortunate because this relationship is only possible by bhakti-yoga. The Lord can give liberation [mukti] very easily, but He does not give one bhakti-yoga because by that process He is bound to the devotee.'"

PURPORT

This passage is a quotation from *Śrīmad-Bhāgavatam* (5.6.18). While Śukadeva Gosvāmī was describing the character of Ṛṣabhadeva, he distinguished between *bhakti-yoga* and liberation by reciting this verse. In relationship with the Yadus and Pāṇḍavas, the Lord acted sometimes as their master, sometimes as their advisor, sometimes as their friend, sometimes as the head of their family and sometimes even as their servant. Kṛṣṇa once had to carry out an order of Yudhiṣṭhira's by carrying a letter he had written to Duryodhana regarding peace negotiations. Similarly, He also became the chariot driver of Arjuna. This illustrates that in *bhakti-yoga* there is a relationship established between the Supreme Personality of Godhead and the devotee. Such a relationship is established in the transcendental mellows known as *dāsya, sakhya, vātsalya* and *mādhurya.* If a devotee wants simple liberation, he gets it very easily from the Supreme Personality of Godhead, as confirmed by Bilvamaṅgala Ṭhākura. *Muktiḥ svayaṁ mukulitāñjali sevate 'smān:* for a devotee, *mukti* is not very important because *mukti* is always standing on his doorstep waiting to serve him in some way. A devotee, therefore, must be attracted by the behavior of the inhabitants of Vṛndāvana who live in a relationship with Kṛṣṇa. The land, water, cows, trees and flowers serve Kṛṣṇa in *śānta-rasa,* Kṛṣṇa's servants serve Kṛṣṇa in *dāsya-rasa,* and Kṛṣṇa's cowherd friends serve Him in *sakhya-rasa.* Similarly, the elderly *gopīs* and *gopas* serve Kṛṣṇa as father and mother, uncle and other relatives, and the *gopīs,* the young girls, serve Kṛṣṇa in conjugal love.

While executing devotional service, one must be naturally inclined to serve Kṛṣṇa in one of these transcendental relationships. That is the actual success of life. For a devotee, to get liberation is not very difficult. Even one who is unable to establish a relationship with Kṛṣṇa can achieve liberation by merging in the Brahman effulgence. This is called *sāyujya-mukti.* Vaiṣṇavas never accept *sāyujya-mukti,* although sometimes they accept the other forms of liberation, namely, *sārūpya, sālokya, sāmīpya* and *sārṣṭi.* A pure devotee, however, does not accept any kind of *mukti.* He wants only to serve Kṛṣṇa in a transcendental relationship. This is the perfectional stage of spiritual life. Māyāvādī philosophers desire to merge in the existence of the Brahman effulgence, although this aspect of liberation is always neglected by devotees. Śrīla Prabodhānanda Sarasvatī Ṭhākura, describing this kind of *mukti,* which is called *kaivalya,* or becoming one with the Supreme, has said, *kaivalyaṁ narakāyate:* "Becoming one with the Supreme is as good as going to hell." Therefore the ideal of Māyāvāda philosophy, becoming one with the Supreme, is hellish for a devotee; he never accepts it. Māyāvādī philosophers do not know that even if they merge in the effulgence of the Supreme, this will not give them ultimate rest. An individual soul cannot live in the Brahman effulgence in a state of inactivity; after some time, he must desire to be active. However, since he is not related with the Supreme Personality of Godhead and therefore has no spiritual activity, he must come down for further activities in this material world. This is confirmed in *Śrīmad-Bhāgavatam:*

āruhya kṛcchreṇa paraṁ padaṁ tataḥ
patanty adho 'nādṛta-yuṣmad-aṅghrayaḥ
(*Bhāg.* 10.2.32)

Because Māyāvādī philosophers have no information regarding the transcendental service of the Lord, even after attaining liberation from material activities and merging in the Brahman effulgence, they must come down again to this material world to open hospitals or schools or perform similar philanthropic activities.

TEXT 20

হেন প্রেম শ্রীচৈতন্য দিলা যথা তথা ।
জগাই মাধাই পর্যন্ত—অন্যের কা কথা ॥ ২০ ॥

hena prema śrī-caitanya dilā yathā tathā
jagāi mādhāi paryanta—anyera kā kathā

SYNONYMS

hena—such; *prema*—love of Godhead; *śrī-caitanya*—Lord Śrī Caitanya Mahāprabhu; *dilā*—has given; *yathā*—anywhere; *tathā*—everywhere; *jagāi*—of the name Jagāi; *mādhāi*—of the name Mādhāi; *paryanta*—up to them; *anyera*—of others; *kā*—what to speak; *kathā*—words.

TRANSLATION

Lord Śrī Caitanya Mahāprabhu has freely given this love of Kṛṣṇa everywhere and anywhere, even to the most fallen, such as Jagāi and Mādhāi. What then to speak of those who are already pious and elevated?

PURPORT

The distinction between Śrī Caitanya Mahāprabhu's gift to human society and the gifts of others is that whereas so-called philanthropic and humanitarian workers have given some relief to human society as far as the body is concerned, Śrī Caitanya Mahāprabhu offers the best facilities for going back home, back to Godhead, with love of Godhead. If one seriously makes a comparative study of the two gifts, certainly if he is at all sober he will give the greatest credit to Śrī Caitanya Mahāprabhu. It was with this purpose that Kavirāja Gosvāmī said:

śrī-kṛṣṇa-caitanya-dayā karaha vicāra
vicāra karile citte pābe camatkāra

"If you are indeed interested in logic and argument, kindly apply it to the mercy of Śrī Caitanya Mahāprabhu. If you do so, you will find it to be strikingly wonderful." (Cc. *Ādi* 8.15)

Śrīla Narottama dāsa Ṭhākura says:

dīna-hīna yata chila,
hari-nāme uddhārila,
tāra sākṣī jagāi mādhāi

The two brothers Jagāi and Mādhāi epitomize the sinful population of this age of Kali. They were most disturbing elements in society because they were meat eaters, drunkards, women hunters, rogues and thieves. Yet Śrī Caitanya Mahāprabhu delivered them, to say nothing of others who were sober, pious, devoted and conscientious. *Bhagavad-gītā* also confirms *(kiṁ punar brāhmaṇāḥ puṇyā bhaktā rājarṣayas tathā)* that to say nothing of the brahminically qualified devotees and *rājarṣis*, anyone who by the association of a pure devotee comes to Kṛṣṇa consciousness becomes eligible to go back home, back to Godhead. In *Bhagavad-gītā* the Lord declares:

māṁ hi pārtha vyapāśritya
ye 'pi syuḥ pāpa-yonayaḥ
striyo vaiśyās tathā śūdrās
te 'pi yānti parāṁ gatim

"O son of Pṛthā, those who take shelter in Me, though they be of lower birth—women, *vaiśyas* [merchants], as well as *śūdras* [workers]—can approach the supreme destination." (Bg. 9.32)

Lord Caitanya Mahāprabhu delivered the two fallen brothers Jagāi and Mādhāi, but the entire world is presently full of Jagāis and Mādhāis, or, in other words, women hunters, meat eaters, gamblers, thieves and other rogues, who create all kinds of disturbance in society. The activities of such persons have now become common practices. It is no longer considered abominable to be a drunkard, woman hunter, meat eater, thief or rogue, for these elements have been assimilated by human society. That does not mean, however, that the abominable qualities of such persons will help free human society from the clutches of *māyā*. Rather, they will entangle humanity more and more in the reactions of the stringent laws of material nature. One's activities are all performed under the influence of the modes of material nature *(prakṛteḥ kriyamāṇāni guṇaiḥ karmāṇi sarvaśaḥ)*. Because people are now associating with the modes of ignorance *(tamo-guṇa)* and, to some extent, passion *(rajo-guṇa)*, with no trace of goodness *(sattva-guṇa)*, they are becoming increasingly greedy and lusty, for that is the effect of associating with these modes. *Tadā rajas-tamo-bhāvāḥ kāma-lobhādayaś ca ye:* "By associating with the two lower qualities of material nature, one becomes lusty and greedy." (*Bhāg.* 1.2.19) Actually, in modern human society, everyone is greedy and lusty, and therefore the only means for deliverance is Śrī Caitanya Mahāprabhu's *saṅkīrtana* movement, which can promote all the Jagāis and Mādhāis to the topmost position of *sattva-guṇa*, or brahminical culture.

Śrīmad-Bhāgavatam states:

naṣṭa-prāyeṣv abhadreṣu
nityaṁ bhāgavata-sevayā
bhagavaty uttama-śloke
bhaktir bhavati naiṣṭhikī

tadā rajas-tamo-bhāvāḥ
kāma-lobhādayaś ca ye
(*Bhāg.* 1.2.18-19)

Considering the chaotic condition of human society, if one actually wants peace and tranquility, one must take to the Kṛṣṇa consciousness movement and engage always in *bhagavata-dharma.* Engagement in *bhagavata-dharma* dissipates all ignorance and passion, and when ignorance and passion are dissipated one is freed from greed and lust. When freed from greed and lust, one becomes brahminically qualified, and when a brahminically qualified person makes further advancement, he becomes situated on the Vaiṣṇava platform. It is only on this Vaiṣṇava platform that it is possible to awaken one's dormant love of Godhead, and as soon as one does so, his life is successful.

At present, human society is specifically cultivating the mode of ignorance *(tamo-guṇa),* although there may also be some symptoms of passion *(rajo-guṇa).* Full of *kāma* and *lobha,* lust and greed, the entire population of the world consists mostly of *śūdras* and a few *vaiśyas,* and gradually it is coming about that there are *śūdras* only. Communism is a movement of *śūdras,* and capitalism is meant for *vaiśyas.* In the fighting between these two factions, the *śūdras* and *vaiśyas,* gradually, due to the abominable condition of society, the communists will emerge triumphant, and as soon as this takes place, whatever is left of society will be ruined. The only possible remedy that can counteract the tendency toward communism is the Kṛṣṇa consciousness movement, which can give even communists the real idea of communist society. According to the doctrine of communism, the state should be the proprietor of everything. But the Kṛṣṇa consciousness movement, expanding this same idea, accepts God as the proprietor of everything. People can't understand this because they have no sense of God, but the Kṛṣṇa consciousness movement can help them to understand God and to understand that everything belongs to God. Since everything is the property of God, and all living entities—not only human beings but even animals, birds, plants and so on—are children of God, everyone has the right to live at the cost of God with God consciousness. This is the sum and substance of the Kṛṣṇa consciousness movement.

TEXT 21

স্বতন্ত্র ঈশ্বর প্রেম-নিগূঢ়ভাণ্ডার ।
বিলাইল যারে তারে, না কৈল বিচার ॥ ২১ ॥

svatantra īśvara prema-nigūḍha-bhāṇḍāra
bilāila yāre tāre, nā kaila vicāra

SYNONYMS

svatantra—fully independent; *īśvara*—the Supreme Personality of Godhead; *prema*—love of God; *nigūḍha*—very confidential; *bhāṇḍāra*—stock; *bilāila*—distributed; *yāre*—to anyone; *tāre*—to everyone; *nā*—not; *kaila*—did; *vicāra*—consideration.

TRANSLATION

Śrī Caitanya Mahāprabhu, as the Supreme Personality of Godhead Himself, is fully independent. Therefore, although it is the most confidentially stored benediction, He can distribute love of Godhead to anyone and everyone without consideration.

PURPORT

This is the benefit of Lord Caitanya's movement. If one somehow or other comes in contact with the Hare Kṛṣṇa movement, without consideration of his being a *śūdra, vaiśya,* Jagāi, Mādhāi or even lower, he becomes advanced in spiritual consciousness and immediately develops love of Godhead. We now have actual experience that throughout the entire world this movement is making many such persons lovers of God simply by the chanting of the Hare Kṛṣṇa *mahā-mantra.* Actually, Śrī Caitanya Mahāprabhu has appeared as the spiritual master of the entire world. He does not discriminate between offenders and the innocent. *Kṛṣṇa-prema-pradāya te:* He liberally gives love of Godhead to anyone and everyone. This can be actually experienced, as stated in the next verse.

TEXT 22

অদ্যাপিহ দেখ চৈতন্য-নাম যেই লয় ।
কৃষ্ণ-প্রেমে পুলকাশ্রু-বিহ্বল সে হয় ॥ ২২ ॥

adyāpiha dekha caitanya-nāma yei laya
kṛṣṇa-preme pulakāśru-vihvala se haya

SYNONYMS

adyāpiha—even up to date; *dekha*—you see; *caitanya-nāma*—Lord Śrī Caitanya Mahāprabhu's name; *yei*—anyone; *laya*—who takes; *kṛṣṇa-preme*—love of Kṛṣṇa; *pulaka-aśru*—tears in ecstasy; *vihvala*—overwhelmed; *se*—he; *haya*—becomes.

TRANSLATION

Whether he is offensive or inoffensive, anyone who even now chants śrī-kṛṣṇa-caitanya prabhu nityānanda is immediately overwhelmed with ecstasy, and tears fill his eyes.

PURPORT

The *prākṛta sahajiyās* who chant *nitāi gaura rādhe śyāma* have very little knowledge of the *Bhāgavata* conclusion, and they hardly follow the Vaiṣṇava rules and regulations, and yet because they chant *bhaja nitāi gaura,* their chanting immediately invokes tears and other signs of ecstasy. Although they do not know the principles of Vaiṣṇava philosophy and are not very advanced in education, by these symptoms they attract many men to become their followers. Their ecstatic tears will of course help them in the long run, for as soon as they come in contact with a pure devotee their lives will become successful. Even in the beginning, however, because they are chanting the holy names of *nitāi-gaura,* their swift advancement on the path of love of Godhead is very prominently visible.

TEXT 23

'নিত্যানন্দ বলিতে হয় কৃষ্ণপ্রেমোদয় ।
আউলায় সকল অঙ্গ, অশ্রু-গঙ্গা বয় ॥ ২৩ ॥

'nityānanda' balite haya kṛṣṇa-premodaya
āulāya sakala aṅga, aśru-gaṅgā vaya

SYNONYMS

nityānanda balite—while talking of Nityānanda Prabhu; *haya*—it so becomes; *kṛṣṇa-prema-udaya*—awakening of love of Kṛṣṇa; *āulāya*—agitated; *sakala*—all; *aṅga*—limbs of the body; *aśru-gaṅgā*—tears like the Ganges waters; *vaya*—flow down.

TRANSLATION

Simply by talking of Nityānanda Prabhu one awakens his love for Kṛṣṇa. Thus all his bodily limbs are agitated by ecstasy, and tears flow from his eyes like the waters of the Ganges.

TEXT 24

'কৃষ্ণনাম' করে অপরাধের বিচার ।
কৃষ্ণ বলিলে অপরাধীর না হয় বিকার ॥ ২৪ ॥

'kṛṣṇa-nāma' kare aparādhera vicāra
kṛṣṇa balile aparādhīra nā haya vikāra

SYNONYMS

kṛṣṇa-nāma—the holy name of Lord Kṛṣṇa; *kare*—takes; *aparādhera*—of offenses; *vicāra*—consideration; *kṛṣṇa*—Lord Kṛṣṇa; *balile*—if one chants; *aparādhīra*—of the offenders; *nā*—never; *haya*—becomes; *vikāra*—changed.

TRANSLATION

There are offenses to be considered while chanting the Hare Kṛṣṇa mantra. Therefore simply by chanting Hare Kṛṣṇa one does not become ecstatic.

PURPORT

It is very beneficial to chant the names *śrī-kṛṣṇa-caitanya prabhu nityānanda* before chanting the Hare Kṛṣṇa *mahā-mantra* because by chanting these two holy names *śrī-kṛṣṇa-caitanya prabhu nityānanda* one immediately becomes ecstatic, and if he then chants the Hare Kṛṣṇa *mahā-mantra* he becomes free of offenses.

There are ten offenses to avoid in chanting the Hare Kṛṣṇa *mahā-mantra.* The first offense is to blaspheme great personalities who are engaged in distributing the holy name of the Lord. It is said in the *śāstra* (Cc. *Antya.* 7.11), *kṛṣṇa-śakti vinā nahe tāra pravartana:* one cannot distribute the holy names of the Hare Kṛṣṇa *mahā-mantra* unless he is empowered by the Supreme Personality of Godhead. Therefore one should not criticize or blaspheme a devotee who is thus engaged.

Śrī Padma Purāṇa states:

satāṁ nindā nāmnaḥ paramam aparādhaṁ vitanute
yataḥ khyātiṁ yātaṁ katham u sahate tad-vigarhām

To blaspheme the great saintly persons who are engaged in preaching the glories of the Hare Kṛṣṇa *mahā-mantra* is the worst offense at the lotus feet of the holy name. One should not criticize a preacher of the glories of the Hare Kṛṣṇa *mahā-mantra.* If one does so, he is an offender. The Nāma-prabhu, who is identical with Kṛṣṇa, will never tolerate such blasphemous activities, even from one who passes as a great devotee.

The second *nāmāparādha* is described as follows:

śivasya śrī-viṣṇor ya iha guṇa-nāmādi-sakalaṁ
dhiyā bhinnaṁ paśyet sa khalu hari-nāmāhita-karaḥ

In this material world, the holy name of Viṣṇu is all-auspicious. Viṣṇu's name, form, qualities and pastimes are all transcendental absolute knowledge. Therefore, if one tries to separate the Absolute Personality of Godhead from His holy name or His transcendental form, qualities and pastimes, thinking them to be material, that is offensive. Similarly, to think the names of demigods such as Lord Śiva to be as good as the name of Lord Viṣṇu—or, in other words, to think Lord Śiva and the other demigods to be other forms of God and therefore equal to Viṣṇu—is also blasphemous. This is the second offense at the lotus feet of the Lord.

The third offense at the lotus feet of the holy name, which is called *guror avajñā,* is to consider the spiritual master to be material and therefore envy his exalted position. The fourth offense *(śruti-śāstra-nindanam)* is to blaspheme Vedic literatures such as the four *Vedas* and the *Purāṇas.* The fifth offense *(tathārtha-vādaḥ)* is to consider the glories of the holy name to be exaggerations. Similarly, the sixth offense *(hari-nāmni kalpanam)* is to consider the holy name of the Lord to be imaginary.

The seventh offense is described as follows:

nāmno balād yasya hi pāpa-buddhir
na vidyate tasya yamair hi śuddhiḥ

To think that since the Hare Kṛṣṇa *mantra* can counteract all sinful reactions one may therefore go on with his sinful activities and at the same time chant the Hare Kṛṣṇa *mantra* to neutralize them is the greatest offense at the lotus feet of *hari-nāma.*

The eighth offense is stated thus: *dharma-vrata-tyāga-hutādi-sarva-śubha-kriyā-sāmyam api pramādaḥ.* It is offensive to consider the chanting of the Hare Kṛṣṇa *mantra* to be a religious ritualistic ceremony. Performing religious ceremonies, following vows and practicing renunciation and sacrifice are all materialistic auspicious activities. The chanting of the Hare Kṛṣṇa *mahā-mantra* must not be compared to such materialistic religiosity. This is an offense at the lotus feet of the Lord.

The ninth offense is described as follows:

aśraddadhāne vimukhe 'py aśṛṇvati
yaś copadeśaḥ śiva-nāmāparādhaḥ

It is an offense to preach the glories of the holy name among persons who have no intelligence or no faith in the subject matter. Such people should be given the chance to hear the chanting of the Hare Kṛṣṇa *mantra,* but in the beginning they should not be instructed about the glories of the spiritual significance of the holy name. By constant hearing of the holy name, their hearts will be purified, and then they will be able to understand the transcendental position of the holy name.

The tenth offense is as follows:

śrute 'pi nāma-māhātmye yaḥ prīti-rahito naraḥ
aham-mamādi-paramo nāmni so 'py aparādha-kṛt

If one has heard the glories of the transcendental holy name of the Lord but nevertheless continues in a materialistic concept of life, thinking, "I am this body and everything belonging to this body is mine *[ahaṁ mameti],*" and does not show respect and love for the chanting of the Hare Kṛṣṇa *mahā-mantra,* that is an offense.

TEXT 25

তদশ্মসারং হৃদয়ং বতেদং, যদ্গৃহ্যমাণৈর্হরিনামধেয়ৈঃ ।
ন বিক্রিয়েতাথ যদা বিকারো,নেত্রে জলং গাত্ররুহেষু হর্ষঃ ॥

tad aśma-sāraṁ hṛdayaṁ batedaṁ
yad gṛhyamāṇair hari-nāma-dheyaiḥ
na vikriyetātha yadā vikāro
netre jalaṁ gātra-ruheṣu harṣaḥ

SYNONYMS

tat—that; *aśma-sāram*—as hard as iron; *hṛdayam*—heart; *bata*—O; *idam*—this; *yat*—which; *gṛhyamāṇaiḥ*—in spite of taking the chanting; *hari-nāma-dheyaiḥ*—meditating on the holy name of the Lord; *na*—does not; *vikriyeta*—change; *atha*—thus; *yadā*—

when; *vikāraḥ*—transformation; *netre*—in the eyes; *jalam*—tears; *gātra-ruheṣu*—in the pores of the body; *harṣaḥ*—ecstasy.

TRANSLATION

"If one's heart does not change, tears do not flow from his eyes, his body does not shiver, nor his hairs stand on end as he chants the Hare Kṛṣṇa mahā-mantra, it should be understood that his heart is as hard as iron. This is due to his offenses at the lotus feet of the Lord's holy name."

PURPORT

Śrīla Bhaktisiddhānta Sarasvatī Ṭhākura, commenting on this verse, which is a quotation from *Śrīmad-Bhāgavatam* (2.3.24), remarks that sometimes a *mahā-bhāgavata,* or very advanced devotee, does not manifest such transcendental symptoms as tears in the eyes, although sometimes a *kaniṣṭha-adhikārī,* neophyte devotee, displays them artificially. This does not mean, however, that the neophyte is more advanced than the *mahā-bhāgavata* devotee. The test of the real change of heart that takes place when one chants the Hare Kṛṣṇa *mahā-mantra* is that one becomes detached from material enjoyment. This is the real change. *Bhaktir parasyānubhavo viraktir anyatra syāt.* If one is actually advancing in spiritual life, he must become very much detached from material enjoyment. If it is sometimes found that a *kaniṣṭha-adhikārī* (neophyte devotee) shows artificial tears in his eyes while chanting the Hare Kṛṣṇa *mantra* but is still completely attached to material things, his heart has not really changed. The change must be manifested in terms of one's real activities.

TEXT 26

'এক' কৃষ্ণনামে করে সর্বপাপ নাশ ।
প্রেমের কারণ ভক্তি করেন প্রকাশ ॥ ২৬ ॥

'eka' kṛṣṇa-nāme kare sarva-pāpa nāśa
premera kāraṇa bhakti karena prakāśa

SYNONYMS

eka—one; *kṛṣṇa-nāme*—by chanting the holy name of Lord Kṛṣṇa; *kare*—makes; *sarva*—all; *pāpa*—sinful life; *nāśa*—exhausted; *premera*—of love of Godhead; *kāraṇa*—cause; *bhakti*—devotional service; *karena*—becomes; *prakāśa*—manifest.

TRANSLATION

Simply chanting the Hare Kṛṣṇa mahā-mantra without offenses vanquishes all sinful activities. Thus pure devotional service, which is the cause of love of Godhead, becomes manifest.

PURPORT

One cannot be situated in the devotional service of the Lord unless one is free from sinful life. This is confirmed in *Bhagavad-gītā:*

yeṣāṁ tv anta-gataṁ pāpaṁ
janānāṁ puṇya-karmaṇām
te dvandva-moha-nirmuktā
bhajante māṁ dṛḍha-vratāḥ

"Persons who have acted piously in previous lives and in this life, whose sinful actions are completely eradicated and who are freed from the duality of delusion, engage themselves in My service with determination." (Bg. 7.28) A person who is already cleansed of all tinges of sinful life engages without deviation or duality of purpose in the transcendental loving service of the Lord. In this age, although people are greatly sinful, simply chanting the Hare Kṛṣṇa *mahā-mantra* can relieve them from the reactions of their sins. *Eka kṛṣṇa-nāme:* only by chanting Kṛṣṇa's name is this possible. This is also confirmed in *Śrīmad-Bhāgavatam (kīrtanād eva kṛṣṇasya).* Caitanya Mahāprabhu has also taught us this. While passing on the road, He used to chant:

kṛṣṇa kṛṣṇa kṛṣṇa kṛṣṇa kṛṣṇa kṛṣṇa kṛṣṇa he
kṛṣṇa kṛṣṇa kṛṣṇa kṛṣṇa kṛṣṇa kṛṣṇa kṛṣṇa he
kṛṣṇa kṛṣṇa kṛṣṇa kṛṣṇa kṛṣṇa kṛṣṇa rakṣa mām
kṛṣṇa kṛṣṇa kṛṣṇa kṛṣṇa kṛṣṇa kṛṣṇa pāhi mām
rāma rāghava rāma rāghava rāma rāghava rakṣa mām
kṛṣṇa keśava kṛṣṇa keśava kṛṣṇa keśava pāhi mām

If one always chants the holy name Kṛṣṇa, gradually one is freed from all reactions of sinful life, provided he chants offenselessly and does not commit more sinful activities on the strength of chanting the Hare Kṛṣṇa *mantra.* In this way one is purified, and his devotional service causes the arousal of his dormant love of God. Simply by chanting the Hare Kṛṣṇa *mantra* and not committing sinful activities and offenses, one's life is purified, and thus one comes to the fifth stage of perfection, or engagement in the loving service of the Lord (*premā pumartho mahān*).

TEXT 27

প্রেমের উদয়ে হয় প্রেমের বিকার।
স্বেদ-কম্প-পুলকাদি গদ্গদাশ্রুধার ॥ ২৭ ॥

premera udaye haya premera vikāra
sveda-kampa-pulakādi gadgadāśrudhāra

SYNONYMS

premera—of love of Godhead; *udaye*—when there is awakening; *haya*—it becomes so; *premera*—of love of Godhead; *vikāra*—transformation; *sveda*—perspiration; *kam-*

pa—trembling; *pulaka-ādi*—throbbing of the heart; *gadgada*—faltering; *aśru-dhāra*—tears in the eyes.

TRANSLATION

When one's transcendental loving service to the Lord is actually awakened, it generates transformations in the body such as perspiration, trembling, throbbing of the heart, faltering of the voice and tears in the eyes.

PURPORT

These bodily transformations are automatically manifested when one is actually situated in love of Godhead. One should not artificially imitate them. Our disease is desire for that which is material; even while advancing in spiritual life, we want material acclaim. One must be freed from this disease. Pure devotion must be *anyābhilāṣitā-śūnyam,* without desire for anything material. Advanced devotees manifest many bodily transformations which are symptoms of ecstasy, but one should not imitate them to achieve cheap adoration from the public. When one actually attains the advanced stage, the ecstatic symptoms will appear automatically; one does not need to imitate them.

TEXT 28

অনায়াসে ভবক্ষয়, কৃষ্ণের সেবন ।
এক কৃষ্ণনামের ফলে পাই এত ধন ॥ ২৮ ॥

anāyāse bhava-kṣaya, kṛṣṇera sevana
eka kṛṣṇa-nāmera phale pāi eta dhana

SYNONYMS

anāyāse—without hard labor; *bhava-kṣaya*—stoppage of repetition of birth and death; *kṛṣṇera*—of Lord Kṛṣṇa; *sevana*—service; *eka*—one; *kṛṣṇa-nāmera*—chanting the name of Kṛṣṇa; *phale*—as a result of; *pāi*—we achieve; *eta*—so much; *dhana*—wealth.

TRANSLATION

As a result of chanting the Hare Kṛṣṇa mahā-mantra, one makes such great advancement in spiritual life that simultaneously his material existence terminates and he receives love of Godhead. The holy name of Kṛṣṇa is so powerful that by chanting even one name, one very easily achieves these transcendental riches.

TEXTS 29-30

হেন কৃষ্ণনাম যদি লয় বহুবার ।
তবু যদি প্রেম নহে, নহে অশ্রুধার ॥ ২৯ ॥

তবে জানি, অপরাধ তাহাতে প্রচুর ।
কৃষ্ণনাম-বীজ তাহে না করে অঙ্কুর ॥ ৩০ ॥

hena kṛṣṇa-nāma yadi laya bahu-bāra
tabu yadi prema nahe, nahe aśrudhāra

tabe jāni, aparādha tāhāte pracura
kṛṣṇa-nāma-bīja tāhe nā kare aṅkura

SYNONYMS

hena—such; *kṛṣṇa-nāma*—holy name of the Lord; *yadi*—if; *laya*—one takes; *bahu-bāra*—again and again; *tabu*—still; *yadi*—if; *prema*—love of Godhead; *nahe*—is not visible; *nahe aśru-dhāra*—there are no tears in the eyes; *tabe*—then; *jāni*—I understand; *aparādha*—offense; *tāhāte*—there (in that process); *pracura*—enough; *kṛṣṇa-nāma*—the holy name of Kṛṣṇa; *bīja*—seed; *tāhe*—in those activities; *nā*—does not; *kare*—do; *aṅkura*—sprout.

TRANSLATION

If one chants the exalted holy name of the Lord again and again and yet his love for the Supreme Lord does not develop and tears do not appear in his eyes, it is evident that because of his offenses in chanting, the seed of the holy name of Kṛṣṇa does not sprout.

PURPORT

If one chants the Hare Kṛṣṇa *mantra* offensively, one does not achieve the desired result. Therefore one should carefully avoid the offenses which have already been described in connection with verse 24.

TEXT 31

চৈতন্য-নিত্যানন্দে নাহি এসব বিচার ।
নাম লৈতে প্রেম দেন, বহে অশ্রুধার ॥ ৩১ ॥

caitanya-nityānande nāhi esaba vicāra
nāma laite prema dena, bahe aśrudhāra

SYNONYMS

caitanya-nityānande—when chanting the holy names of Lord Caitanya and Nityānanda; *nāhi*—there are not; *esaba*—all these; *vicāra*—considerations; *nāma*—the holy name; *laite*—simply by chanting; *prema*—love of Godhead; *dena*—they give; *bahe*—there is a flow; *aśru-dhāra*—tears in the eyes.

TRANSLATION

But if one only chants, with some slight faith, the holy names of Lord Caitanya and Nityānanda, very quickly he is cleansed of all offenses. Thus as soon as he chants the Hare Kṛṣṇa mahā-mantra, he feels the ecstasy of love for God.

PURPORT

Śrīla Bhaktisiddhānta Sarasvatī Ṭhākura remarks in this connection that if one takes shelter of Lord Śrī Caitanya Mahāprabhu and Nityānanda, follows Their instructions to become more tolerant than the tree and humbler than the grass, and in this way chants the holy name of the Lord, very soon he achieves the platform of transcendental loving service to the Lord, and tears appear in his eyes. There are offenses to be considered in chanting the Hare Kṛṣṇa *mahā-mantra,* but there are no such considerations in chanting the names of Gaura-Nityānanda. Therefore, if one chants the Hare Kṛṣṇa *mahā-mantra* but his life is still full of sinful activities, it will be very difficult for him to achieve the platform of loving service to the Lord. But if in spite of being an offender one chants the holy names of Gaura-Nityānanda, he is very quickly freed from the interactions of his offenses. Therefore, one should first approach Lord Caitanya and Nityānanda, or worship Guru-Gaurāṅga, and then come to the stage of worshiping Rādhā-Kṛṣṇa. In our Kṛṣṇa consciousness movement, our students are first advised to worship Guru-Gaurāṅga, and then, when they are somewhat advanced, the Rādhā-Kṛṣṇa Deity is installed, and they are engaged in the worship of the Lord.

One should first take shelter of Gaura-Nityānanda in order to reach, ultimately, Rādhā-Kṛṣṇa. Śrīla Narottama dāsa Ṭhākura sings in this connection:

gaurāṅga balite ha'be pulaka śarīra
hari hari balite nayane ba'be nīra
āra kabe nitāicāṅdera karuṇā ha-ibe
saṁsāra-vāsanā mora kabe tuccha habe
viṣaya chāḍiyā kabe śuddha habe mana
kabe hāma heraba śrī-vṛndāvana

In the beginning one should very regularly chant Śrī Gaurasundara's holy name and then chant the holy name of Lord Nityānanda. Thus one's heart will be cleansed of impure desires for material enjoyment. Then one can approach Vṛndāvana-dhāma to worship Lord Kṛṣṇa. Unless one is favored by Lord Caitanya and Nityānanda, there is no need to go to Vṛndāvana, for unless one's mind is purified, he cannot see Vṛndāvana, even if he goes there. Actually going to Vṛndāvana involves taking shelter of the six Gosvāmīs by reading *Bhakti-rasāmṛta-sindhu, Vidagdha-mādhava, Lalita-mādhava* and the other books that they have given. In this way one can understand the transcendental loving affairs between Rādhā and Kṛṣṇa. *Kabe hāma bujhaba se yugala-pirīti.* The conjugal love between Rādhā and Kṛṣṇa is not an ordinary human affair; it is fully transcendental. In order to understand Rādhā and Kṛṣṇa, worship Them and engage in Their loving service, one must be guided by Śrī Caitanya Mahāprabhu, Nityānanda Prabhu and the six Gosvāmīs, Lord Caitanya's direct disciples.

For an ordinary man, worship of Śrī Caitanya and Nityānanda Prabhu or the Pañca-tattva is easier than worship of Rādhā and Kṛṣṇa. Unless one is very fortunate, he should not be induced to worship Rādhā-Kṛṣṇa directly. A neophyte student who is not sufficiently educated or enlightened should not indulge in the worship of Śrī Rādhā and Kṛṣṇa or the chanting of the Hare Kṛṣṇa *mantra.* Even if he does so, he cannot get the desired result. One should therefore chant the names of Nitāi-Gaura and worship Them without false prestige. Since everyone within this material world is more or less influenced by sinful activities, in the beginning it is essential that one take to the worship of Guru-Gaurāṅga and ask their favor, for thus despite all his disqualifications one will very soon become qualified to worship the Rādhā-Kṛṣṇa *vigraha.*

It should be noted in this connection that the holy names of Lord Kṛṣṇa and Gaurasundara are both identical with the Supreme Personality of Godhead. Therefore one should not consider one name to be more potent than the other. Considering the position of the people of this age, however, the chanting of Śrī Caitanya Mahāprabhu's name is more essential than the chanting of the Hare Kṛṣṇa *mahā-mantra* because Śrī Caitanya Mahāprabhu is the most magnanimous incarnation and His mercy is very easily achieved. Therefore one must first take shelter of Śrī Caitanya Mahāprabhu by chanting *śrī-kṛṣṇa-caitanya prabhu nityānanda śrī-advaita gadādhara śrīvāsādi-gaura-bhakta-vṛnda.* By serving Gaura-Nityānanda one is freed from the entanglements of material existence and thus becomes qualified to worship the Rādhā-Kṛṣṇa Deity.

TEXT 32

স্বতন্ত্র ঈশ্বর প্রভু অত্যন্ত উদার ।
তাঁরে না ভজিলে কভু না হয় নিস্তার ॥ ৩২ ॥

svatantra īśvara prabhu atyanta udāra
tāṅre nā bhajile kabhu nā haya nistāra

SYNONYMS

svatantra īśvara—the fully independent Supreme Lord; *prabhu*—the Lord; *atyanta*—very much; *udāra*—magnanimous; *tāṅre*—unto Him; *nā*—without; *bhajile*—worshiping; *kabhu nā*—never at any time; *haya*—becomes so; *nistāra*—liberation.

TRANSLATION

Śrī Caitanya Mahāprabhu, the independent Supreme Personality of Godhead, is greatly magnanimous. Unless one worships Him, one can never be liberated.

PURPORT

Śrī Bhaktisiddhānta Sarasvatī Ṭhākura here remarks that one should not give up the worship of Rādhā-Kṛṣṇa to worship Śrī Caitanya Mahāprabhu. By worshiping either Rādhā-Kṛṣṇa or Lord Caitanya alone, one cannot become advanced. One should not try to supersede the instructions of the six Gosvāmīs, for they are *ācāryas* and very dear to Lord Caitanya. Therefore Narottama dāsa Ṭhākura sings:

rūpa-raghunātha-pade haibe ākuti
kabe hāma bujhaba se yugala-pirīti

One must be a submissive student of the six Gosvāmīs, from Śrīla Rūpa Gosvāmī to Raghunātha dāsa Gosvāmī. Not following their instructions but imagining how to worship Gaurasundara and Rādhā-Kṛṣṇa is a great offense, as a result of which one clears a path to hell. If one neglects the instructions of the six Gosvāmīs and yet becomes a so-called devotee of Rādhā-Kṛṣṇa, he merely criticizes the real devotees of Rādhā-Kṛṣṇa. As a result of speculation, he considers Gaurasundara to be an ordinary devotee and therefore cannot make progress in serving the Supreme Personality of Godhead, Rādhā-Kṛṣṇa.

TEXT 33

ওরে মূঢ় লোক, শুন চৈতন্যমঙ্গল ।
চৈতন্য-মহিমা যাতে জানিবে সকল ॥ ৩৩ ॥

ore mūḍha loka, śuna caitanya-maṅgala
caitanya-mahimā yāte jānibe sakala

SYNONYMS

ore—O all of you; *mūḍha*—foolish; *loka*—people; *śuna*—just hear; *caitanya-maṅgala*—the book of this name; *caitanya*—Lord Caitanya's; *mahimā*—glories; *yāte*—in which; *jānibe*—you will know; *sakala*—all.

TRANSLATION

O fools, just read Caitanya-maṅgala! By reading this book you can understand all the glories of Śrī Caitanya Mahāprabhu.

PURPORT

Śrī Vṛndāvana dāsa Ṭhākura's *Caitanya-bhāgavata* was originally entitled *Caitanya-maṅgala,* but when Śrīla Locana dāsa Ṭhākura later wrote another book named *Caitanya-maṅgala,* Śrīla Vṛndāvana dāsa Ṭhākura changed the name of his own book, which is now therefore known as *Caitanya-bhāgavata.* The life of Śrī Caitanya Mahāprabhu is very elaborately described in *Caitanya-bhāgavata,* and Kṛṣṇadāsa Kavirāja Gosvāmī has already informed us that in his *Śrī-Caitanya-caritāmṛta* he has described whatever Vṛndāvana dāsa Ṭhākura has not mentioned. This acceptance of *Śrī-Caitanya-bhāgavata* by Kṛṣṇadāsa Kavirāja Gosvāmī indicates his acceptance of the disciplic succession. A writer of transcendental literature never tries to surpass the previous *ācāryas.*

TEXT 34

কৃষ্ণলীলা ভাগবতে কহে বেদব্যাস ।
চৈতন্য-লীলার ব্যাস—বৃন্দাবন-দাস ॥ ৩৪ ॥

kṛṣṇa-līlā bhāgavate kahe veda-vyāsa
caitanya-līlāra vyāsa—vṛndāvana-dāsa

SYNONYMS

kṛṣṇa-līlā—the pastimes of Lord Kṛṣṇa; *bhāgavate*—in the book *Śrīmad-Bhāgavatam; kahe*—tells; *veda-vyāsa*—Vyāsadeva, the editor of the Vedic literatures; *caitanya-līlāra*—of the pastimes of Lord Caitanya; *vyāsa*—compiler; *vṛndāvana-dāsa*—is Vṛndāvana dāsa.

TRANSLATION

As Vyāsadeva has compiled all the pastimes of Lord Kṛṣṇa in the Śrīmad-Bhāgavatam, Ṭhākura Vṛndāvana dāsa has depicted the pastimes of Lord Caitanya.

TEXT 35

বৃন্দাবন-দাস কৈল 'চৈতন্যমঙ্গল' ।
যাঁহার শ্রবণে নাশে সর্ব অমঙ্গল ॥ ৩৫ ॥

vṛndāvana-dāsa kaila 'caitanya-maṅgala'
yāṅhāra śravaṇe nāśe sarva amaṅgala

SYNONYMS

vṛndāvana-dāsa—of the name Vṛndāvana dāsa; *kaila*—compiled; *caitanya-maṅgala*—the book named *Caitanya-maṅgala*; *yāṅhāra*—of which; *śravaṇe*—by hearing; *nāśe*—annihilated; *sarva*—all; *amaṅgala*—inauspiciousness.

TRANSLATION

Ṭhākura Vṛndāvana dāsa has composed Caitanya-maṅgala. Hearing this book will annihilate all misfortune.

TEXT 36

চৈতন্য-নিতাইর যাতে জানিয়ে মহিমা ।
যাতে জানি কৃষ্ণভক্তিসিদ্ধান্তের সীমা ॥ ৩৬ ॥

caitanya-nitāira yāte jāniye mahimā
yāte jāni kṛṣṇa-bhakti-siddhāntera sīmā

SYNONYMS

caitanya-nitāira—of Lord Śrī Caitanya Mahāprabhu and Nityānanda Prabhu; *yāte*—in which; *jāniye*—one can know; *mahimā*—all glories; *yāte*—in which; *jāni*—I can understand; *kṛṣṇa-bhakti*—of devotion to Lord Kṛṣṇa; *siddhāntera*—of the conclusion; *sīmā*—limit.

TRANSLATION

By reading Caitanya-maṅgala one can understand all the glories or truths of Lord Caitanya and Nityānanda and come to the ultimate conclusion of devotional service to Lord Kṛṣṇa.

PURPORT

Śrīmad-Bhāgavatam is the authoritative reference book from which to understand devotional service, but because it is very elaborate, few men can understand its purpose. *Śrīmad-Bhāgavatam* is the original commentary on *Vedānta-sūtra,* which is called *nyāya-prasthāna.* It was written to enable one to understand the Absolute Truth through infallible logic and argument, and therefore its natural commentary, *Śrīmad-Bhāgavatam,* is extremely elaborate. Professional reciters have created the impression that *Śrīmad-Bhāgavatam* deals only with Kṛṣṇa's *rāsa-līlā,* although Kṛṣṇa's *rāsa-līlā* is only described in the Tenth Canto (Chapters 29-35). They have in this way presented Kṛṣṇa to the Western world as a great woman hunter, and therefore we sometimes have to deal with such misconceptions in preaching. Another difficulty in understanding *Śrīmad-Bhāgavatam* is that the professional reciters have introduced *Bhāgavata-saptāha,* or seven-day readings of the *Bhāgavatam.* They want to finish *Śrīmad-Bhāgavatam* in a week, although it is so sublime that even one verse of *Śrīmad-Bhāgavatam,* if properly explained, cannot be completed in three months. Under these circumstances, it is a great aid for the common man to read Śrīla Vṛndāvana dāsa Ṭhākura's *Caitanya-bhāgavata,* for thus he can actually understand devotional service, Kṛṣṇa, Lord Caitanya and Nityānanda. Śrīla Rūpa Gosvāmī has said:

śruti-smṛti-purāṇādi-pañcarātra-vidhiṁ vinā
aikāntikī harer bhaktir utpātāyaiva kalpate

"Devotional service of the Lord that ignores the authorized Vedic literatures like the *Upaniṣads, Purāṇas, Nārada-pañcarātra,* etc., is simply an unnecessary disturbance in society." Due to misunderstanding *Śrīmad-Bhāgavatam,* people are misled regarding the science of Kṛṣṇa. However, by reading Śrīla Vṛndāvana dāsa Ṭhākura's book one can very easily understand this science.

TEXT 37

ভাগবতে যত ভক্তিসিদ্ধান্তের সার ।
লিখিয়াছেন ইঁহা জানি' করিয়া উদ্ধার ॥ ৩৭ ॥

bhāgavate yata bhakti-siddhāntera sāra
likhiyāchena iṅhā jāni' kariyā uddhāra

SYNONYMS

bhāgavate—in the *Śrīmad-Bhāgavatam*; *yata*—all; *bhakti-siddhāntera*—in understanding devotional service; *sāra*—essence; *likhiyāchena*—has written; *iṅhā*—this; *jāni'*—I know; *kariyā*—making; *uddhāra*—quotation.

TRANSLATION

In Caitanya-maṅgala [later known as Śrī-Caitanya-bhāgavata] Śrīla Vṛndāvana dāsa Ṭhākura has given the conclusion and essence of devotional service by quoting the authoritative statements of Śrīmad-Bhāgavatam.

TEXT 38

চৈতন্যমঙ্গল' শুনে যদি পাষণ্ডী, যবন ।
সেহ মহাবৈষ্ণব হয় ততক্ষণ ॥ ৩৮ ॥

'caitanya-maṅgala' śune yadi pāṣaṇḍī, yavana
seha mahā-vaiṣṇava haya tatakṣaṇa

SYNONYMS

caitanya-maṅgala—the book named *Caitanya-maṅgala*; *śune*—anyone hears; *yadi*—if; *pāṣaṇḍī*—great atheist; *yavana*—a disbeliever in the Vedic culture; *seha*—he also; *mahā-vaiṣṇava*—great devotee; *haya*—becomes; *tatakṣaṇa*—immediately.

TRANSLATION

If even a great atheist hears Caitanya-maṅgala, he immediately becomes a great devotee.

TEXT 39

মনুষ্যে রচিতে নারে ঐছে গ্রন্থ ধন্য ।
বৃন্দাবনদাস-মুখে বক্তা শ্রীচৈতন্য ॥ ৩৯ ॥

manuṣye racite nāre aiche grantha dhanya
vṛndāvana-dāsa-mukhe vaktā śrī-caitanya

SYNONYMS

manuṣye—a human being; *racite*—compiled; *nāre*—cannot; *aiche*—such; *grantha*—book; *dhanya*—so glorious; *vṛndāvana-dāsa*—the author, Śrīla Vṛndāvana dāsa Ṭhākura; *mukhe*—from his mouth; *vaktā*—speaker; *śrī-caitanya*—Lord Śrī Caitanya Mahāprabhu.

TRANSLATION

The subject matter of this book is so sublime that it appears that Śrī Caitanya Mahāprabhu has personally spoken through the writings of Śrī Vṛndāvana dāsa Ṭhākura.

PURPORT

Śrīla Sanātana Gosvāmī has written in his *Hari-bhakti-vilāsa:*

avaiṣṇava-mukhodgīrṇaṁ pūtaṁ hari-kathāmṛtam
śravaṇaṁ naiva kartavyaṁ sarpocchiṣṭaṁ yathā payaḥ

Transcendental literature that strictly follows the Vedic principles and the conclusion of the *Purāṇas* and *Pāñcarātrika-vidhi* can be written only by a pure devotee.

It is not possible for a common man to write books on *bhakti,* for his writings will not be effective. He may be a very great scholar and expert in presenting literature in flowery language, but this is not at all helpful in understanding transcendental literature. Even if transcendental literature is written in faulty language, it is acceptable if it is written by a devotee, whereas so-called transcendental literature written by a mundane scholar, even if it is a very highly polished literary presentation, cannot be accepted. The secret in a devotee's writing is that when he writes about the pastimes of the Lord, the Lord helps him; he does not write himself. As stated in *Bhagavad-gītā, dadāmi buddhi-yogaṁ taṁ yena mām upayānti te* (Bg. 10. 10). Since a devotee writes in service to the Lord, the Lord from within gives him so much intelligence that he sits down near the Lord and goes on writing books. Kṛṣṇadāsa Kavirāja Gosvāmī confirms that what Vṛndāvana dāsa Ṭhākura wrote was actually spoken by Lord Caitanya Mahāprabhu, and he simply repeated it. The same holds true for *Caitanya-caritāmṛta.* Kṛṣṇadāsa Kavirāja Gosvāmī wrote *Caitanya-caritāmṛta* in his old age in an invalid condition, but it is such a sublime literature that Śrīla Bhaktisiddhānta Sarasvatī Gosvāmī Mahārāja used to say, "The time will come when the people of the world will learn Bengali to read *Śrī-Caitanya-caritāmṛta.*" We are trying to present *Śrī-Caitanya-caritāmṛta* in English and do not know how successful it will be, but if one reads the original *Caitanya-caritāmṛta* in Bengali he will relish increasing ecstasy in devotional service.

TEXT 40

বৃন্দাবনদাস-পদে কোটি নমস্কার ।
ঐছে গ্রন্থ করি' তেঁহো তারিলা সংসার ॥ ৪০ ॥

vṛndāvana-dāsa-pade koṭi namaskāra
aiche grantha kari' teṅho tārilā saṁsāra

SYNONYMS

vṛndāvana-dāsa-pade—on the lotus feet of Śrīla Vṛndāvana dāsa Ṭhākura; *koṭi*—millions; *namaskāra*—obeisances; *aiche*—such; *grantha*—book; *kari'*—compiling; *teṅho*—he; *tārilā*—delivered; *saṁsāra*—all the world.

TRANSLATION

I offer millions of obeisances unto the lotus feet of Vṛndāvana dāsa Ṭhākura. No one else could write such a wonderful book for the deliverance of all fallen souls.

TEXT 41

নারায়ণী—চৈতন্যের উচ্ছিষ্ট-ভাজন ।
তাঁর গর্ভে জন্মিলা শ্রীদাস-বৃন্দাবন ॥ ৪১ ॥

nārāyaṇī—caitanyera ucchiṣṭa-bhājana
tāṅra garbhe janmilā śrī-dāsa-vṛndāvana

SYNONYMS

nārāyaṇī—of the name Nārāyaṇī; *caitanyera*—of Lord Caitanya Mahāprabhu; *ucchiṣṭa-bhājana*—eater of the remnants of foodstuff; *tāṅra*—of her; *garbhe*—in the womb; *janmilā*—took birth; *śrī-dāsa-vṛndāvana*—Śrīla Vṛndāvana dāsa Ṭhākura.

TRANSLATION

Nārāyaṇī eternally eats the remnants of the foodstuffs of Caitanya Mahāprabhu. Śrīla Vṛndāvana dāsa Ṭhākura was born of her womb.

PURPORT

In *Gaura-gaṇoddeśa-dīpikā,* a book written by Kavikarṇapūra that describes all the associates of Śrī Caitanya Mahāprabhu and who they previously were, there is the following statement regarding Nārāyaṇī:

ambikāyāḥ svasā yāsīn nāmnā śrīla-kilimbikā
kṛṣṇocchiṣṭaṁ prabhuñjānā seyaṁ nārāyaṇī matā

When Lord Kṛṣṇa was a child, He was nursed by a woman named Ambikā who had a younger sister named Kilimbikā. During the time of Lord Caitanya's incarnation, the same Kilimbikā used to eat the remnants of foodstuffs left by Lord Śrī Caitanya Mahāprabhu. That Kilimbikā was Nārāyaṇī, who was a niece of Śrīvāsa Ṭhākura's. Later on, when she grew up and married, Śrīla Vṛndāvana dāsa Ṭhākura was born from her womb. A devotee of Lord Śrī Kṛṣṇa is celebrated in terms of devotional service rendered to the Lord; thus we know Śrīla Vṛndāvana dāsa Ṭhākura as the son of Nārāyaṇī. Śrīla Bhaktisiddhānta Sarasvatī Ṭhākura notes in this connection that there is no reference to his paternal ancestry because there is no need to understand it.

TEXT 42

তাঁর কি অদ্ভুত চৈতন্যচরিত-বর্ণন ।
যাহার শ্রবণে শুদ্ধ কৈল ত্রিভুবন ॥ ৪২ ॥

tāṅra ki adbhuta caitanya-carita-varṇana
yāhāra śravaṇe śuddha kaila tri-bhuvana

SYNONYMS

tāṅra—Śrīla Vṛndāvana dāsa Ṭhākura's; *ki*—what; *adbhuta*—wonderful; *caitanya-carita*—of the pastimes of Lord Caitanya Mahāprabhu; *varṇana*—description; *yāhāra*—

of which; *śravaṇe*—by hearing; *śuddha*—purified; *kaila*—made; *tri-bhuvana*—the three worlds.

TRANSLATION

What a wonderful description he has given of the pastimes of Lord Caitanya! Anyone in the three worlds who hears it is purified.

TEXT 43

অতএব ভজ, লোক, চৈতন্য-নিত্যানন্দ ।
খণ্ডিবে সংসার-দুঃখ, পাবে প্রেমানন্দ ॥ ৪৩ ॥

ataeva bhaja, loka, caitanya-nityānanda
khaṇḍibe saṁsāra-duḥkha, pābe premānanda

SYNONYMS

ataeva—therefore; *bhaja*—worship; *loka*—O people in general; *caitanya*—Lord Śrī Caitanya Mahāprabhu; *nityānanda*—Nityānanda Prabhu; *khaṇḍibe*—will vanquish; *saṁsāra-duḥkha*—miserable condition of material existence; *pābe*—he will get; *premānanda*—the transcendental bliss of devotional service.

TRANSLATION

I fervently appeal to everyone to adopt the method of devotional service given by Lord Caitanya and Nityānanda and thus be freed from the miseries of material existence and ultimately achieve the loving service of the Lord.

TEXT 44

বৃন্দাবন-দাস কৈল 'চৈতন্য-মঙ্গল' ।
তাহাতে চৈতন্য-লীলা বর্ণিল সকল ॥ ৪৪ ॥

vṛndāvana-dāsa kaila 'caitanya-maṅgala'
tāhāte caitanya-līlā varṇila sakala

SYNONYMS

vṛndāvana-dāsa—Śrīla Vṛndāvana dāsa Ṭhākura; *kaila*—did; *caitanya-maṅgala*—the book of the name *Caitanya-maṅgala*; *tāhāte*—in that book; *caitanya-līlā*—the pastimes of Lord Caitanya; *varṇila*—described; *sakala*—everything.

TRANSLATION

Śrīla Vṛndāvana dāsa Ṭhākura has written Caitanya-maṅgala and therein described in all respects the pastimes of Lord Caitanya.

TEXT 45

সূত্র করি' সব লীলা করিল গ্রন্থন ।
পাছে বিস্তারিয়া তাহার কৈল বিবরণ ॥ ৪৫ ॥

sūtra kari' saba līlā karila granthana
pāche vistāriyā tāhāra kaila vivaraṇa

SYNONYMS

sūtra kari'—making a synopsis; *saba*—all; *līlā*—pastimes; *karila*—did; *granthana*—writing in the book; *pāche*—later; *vistāriyā*—vividly describing; *tāhāra*—all of them; *kaila*—did; *vivaraṇa*—description.

TRANSLATION

He first summarized all the pastimes of the Lord and later described them vividly in detail.

TEXT 46

চৈতন্যচন্দ্রের লীলা অনন্ত অপার ।
বর্ণিতে বর্ণিতে গ্রন্থ হইল বিস্তার ॥ ৪৬ ॥

caitanya-candrera līlā ananta apāra
varṇite varṇite grantha ha-ila vistāra

SYNONYMS

caitanya-candrera—of Lord Caitanya Mahāprabhu; *līlā*—pastimes; *ananta*—unlimited; *apāra*—unfathomable; *varṇite*—describing; *varṇite*—describing; *grantha*—the book; *ha-ila*—became; *vistāra*—expansive.

TRANSLATION

The pastimes of Lord Caitanya are unlimited and unfathomable. Therefore, in describing all those pastimes, the book became voluminous.

TEXT 47

বিস্তার দেখিয়া কিছু সঙ্কোচ হৈল মন ।
সূত্রধৃত কোন লীলা না কৈল বর্ণন ॥ ৪৭ ॥

vistāra dekhiyā kichu saṅkoca haila mana
sūtra-dhṛta kona līlā nā kaila varṇana

SYNONYMS

vistāra—expansive; *dekhiyā*—seeing; *kichu*—some; *saṅkoca*—with hesitation; *haila*—became; *mana*—mind; *sūtra-dhṛta*—taking the codes; *kona*—some; *līlā*—pastimes; *nā*—did not; *kaila*—make; *varṇana*—description.

TRANSLATION

He saw them to be so extensive that he later felt that some had not been properly described.

TEXT 48

নিত্যানন্দ-লীলা-বর্ণনে হইল আবেশ ।
চৈতন্যের শেষ-লীলা রহিল অবশেষ ॥ ৪৮ ॥

nityānanda-līlā-varṇane ha-ila āveśa
caitanyera śeṣa-līlā rahila avaśeṣa

SYNONYMS

nityānanda—Lord Nityānanda; *līlā*—pastime; *varṇane*—in the matter of description; *ha-ila*—there was; *āveśa*—ecstasy; *caitanyera*—of Lord Caitanya Mahāprabhu; *śeṣa-līlā*—pastimes in the last portion of His life; *rahila*—remained; *avaśeṣa*—supplement.

TRANSLATION

He ecstatically described the pastimes of Lord Nityānanda, but the later pastimes of Caitanya Mahāprabhu remained untold.

TEXT 49

সেই সব লীলার শুনিতে বিবরণ ।
বৃন্দাবনবাসী ভক্তের উৎকণ্ঠিত মন ॥ ৪৯ ॥

sei saba līlāra śunite vivaraṇa
vṛndāvana-vāsī bhaktera utkaṇṭhita mana

SYNONYMS

sei—those; *saba*—all; *līlāra*—of the pastimes; *śunite*—to hear; *vivaraṇa*—description; *vṛndāvana-vāsī*—the inhabitants of Vṛndāvana; *bhaktera*—of devotees; *utkaṇṭhita*—in anxiety; *mana*—minds.

TRANSLATION

The devotees of Vṛndāvana were all very anxious to hear those pastimes.

TEXT 50

বৃন্দাবনে কল্পদ্রুমে সুবর্ণ-সদন ।
মহা-যোগপীঠ তাহাঁ, রত্ন-সিংহাসন ॥ ৫০ ॥

vṛndāvane kalpa-drume suvarṇa-sadana
mahā-yogapīṭha tāhāṅ, ratna-siṁhāsana

SYNONYMS

vṛndāvane—in Vṛndāvana; *kalpa-drume*—under the desire trees; *suvarṇa-sadana*—golden throne; *mahā*—great; *yoga-pīṭha*—pious temple; *tāhāṅ*—there; *ratna*—bedecked with jewels; *siṁhāsana*—throne.

TRANSLATION

In Vṛndāvana, in a great place of pilgrimage underneath the desire trees, is a golden throne bedecked with jewels.

TEXT 51

তাতে বসি' আছে সদা ব্রজেন্দ্রনন্দন ।
'শ্রীগোবিন্দ-দেব' নাম সাক্ষাৎ মদন ॥ ৫১ ॥

tāte vasi' āche sadā vrajendra-nandana
'śrī-govinda-deva' nāma sākṣāt madana

SYNONYMS

tāte—on that throne; *vasi'*—sitting; *āche*—there is; *sadā*—always; *vrajendra-nandana*—the son of Mahārāja Nanda; *śrī-govinda-deva*—whose name is Govinda; *nāma*—name; *sākṣāt*—direct; *madana*—transcendental cupid.

TRANSLATION

On that throne sits the son of Nanda Mahārāja, Śrī Govindadeva, the transcendental cupid.

TEXT 52

রাজ-সেবা হয় তাঁহা বিচিত্র প্রকার ।
দিব্য সামগ্রী, দিব্য বস্ত্র, অলঙ্কার ॥ ৫২ ॥

rāja-sevā haya tāṅhā vicitra prakāra
divya sāmagrī, divya vastra, alaṅkāra

SYNONYMS

rāja-sevā—majestic service; *haya*—render; *tāṅhā*—there; *vicitra*—varieties; *prakāra*—all kinds of; *divya*—spiritual; *sāmagrī*—ingredients; *divya*—spiritual; *vastra*—garments; *alaṅkāra*—ornaments.

TRANSLATION

Varieties of majestic service are rendered to Govinda there. His garments, ornaments and paraphernalia are all transcendental.

TEXT 53

সহস্র সেবক সেবা করে অনুক্ষণ ।
সহস্র-বদনে সেবা না যায় বর্ণন ॥ ৫৩ ॥

sahasra sevaka sevā kare anukṣaṇa
sahasra-vadane sevā nā yāya varṇana

SYNONYMS

sahasra—many thousands; *sevaka*—servitors; *sevā*—service; *kare*—render; *anukṣaṇa*—always; *sahasra*—thousands; *vadane*—mouths; *sevā*—process of service; *nā*—not possible; *yāya*—goes on; *varṇana*—description.

TRANSLATION

In that temple of Govindajī, thousands of servitors always render service to the Lord in devotion. Even with thousands of mouths, one could not describe this service.

TEXT 54

সেবার অধ্যক্ষ—শ্রীপণ্ডিত হরিদাস ।
তাঁর যশঃ-গুণ সর্বজগতে প্রকাশ ॥ ৫৪ ॥

sevāra adhyakṣa—śrī-paṇḍita haridāsa
tāṅra yaśaḥ-guṇa sarva-jagate prakāśa

SYNONYMS

sevāra—of the service; *adhyakṣa*—commander; *śrī-paṇḍita haridāsa*—Haridāsa Paṇḍita; *tāṅra*—of his; *yaśaḥ*—fame; *guṇa*—quality; *sarva-jagate*—all over the world; *prakāśa*—known.

TRANSLATION

In that temple the chief servitor was Śrī Haridāsa Paṇḍita. His qualities and fame are known all over the world.

PURPORT

Śrī Haridāsa Paṇḍita was a disciple of Śrī Ananta Ācārya, who was a disciple of Gadādhara Paṇḍita.

TEXT 55

সুশীল, সহিষ্ণু, শান্ত, বদান্য, গম্ভীর ।
মধুর-বচন, মধুর-চেষ্টা, মহাধীর ॥ ৫৫ ॥

suśīla, sahiṣṇu, śānta, vadānya, gambhīra
madhura-vacana, madhura-ceṣṭā, mahā-dhīra

SYNONYMS

suśīla—well behaved; *sahiṣṇu*—tolerant; *śānta*—peaceful; *vadānya*—magnanimous; *gambhīra*—grave; *madhura-vacana*—sweet words; *madhura-ceṣṭā*—sweet endeavor; *mahā-dhīra*—completely sober.

TRANSLATION

He was gentle, tolerant, peaceful, magnanimous, grave, sweet in his words and very sober in his endeavors.

TEXT 56

সবার সম্মান-কর্তা, করেন সবার হিত ।
কৌটিল্য-মাৎসর্য-হিংসা না জানে তাঁর চিত ॥ ৫৬ ॥

sabāra sammāna-kartā, karena sabāra hita
kauṭilya-mātsarya-hiṁsā nā jāne tāṅra cita

SYNONYMS

sabāra—of all; *sammāna-kartā*—respectful; *karena*—does; *sabāra*—everyone's; *hita*—benefit; *kauṭilya*—diplomatic; *mātsarya*—jealousy; *hiṁsā*—envy; *nā jāne*—does not know; *tāṅra*—his; *cita*—heart.

TRANSLATION

He was respectful to everyone and worked for the benefit of all. Diplomacy, envy and jealousy were unknown to his heart.

TEXT 57

কৃষ্ণের যে সাধারণ সদ্‌গুণ পঞ্চাশ ।
সে সব গুণের তাঁর শরীরে নিবাস ॥ ৫৭ ॥

kṛṣṇera ye sādhāraṇa sad-guṇa pañcāśa
se saba guṇera tāṅra śarīre nivāsa

SYNONYMS

kṛṣṇera—of Lord Kṛṣṇa; *ye*—that; *sādhāraṇa*—general; *sat-guṇa*—good qualities; *pañcāśa*—fifty; *se*—those; *saba*—all; *guṇera*—qualities; *tāṅra*—his; *śarīre*—in the body; *nivāsa*—were always present.

TRANSLATION

The fifty qualities of Lord Kṛṣṇa were all present in his body.

PURPORT

In *Bhakti-rasāmṛta-sindhu,* the transcendental qualities of Śrī Kṛṣṇa are mentioned. Among these, fifty are primary *(ayaṁ netā suramyāṅgaḥ,* etc.*),* and in minute quantity they were all present in the body of Śrī Haridāsa Paṇḍita. Since every living entity is a part of the Supreme Personality of Godhead, all fifty of these good qualities of Śrī Kṛṣṇa are originally minutely present in every living being. Due to his contact with material nature, these qualities are not visible in the conditioned soul, but when one becomes a purified devotee, they all automatically manifest themselves. This is stated in *Śrīmad-Bhāgavatam* (5.18.12), as mentioned in the text below.

TEXT 58

যস্যাস্তি ভক্তির্ভগবত্যকিঞ্চনা
সর্বৈর্গুণৈস্তত্র সমাসতে সুরাঃ ।
হরাবভক্তস্য কুতো মহদ্‌গুণা
মনোরথেনাসতি ধাবতো বহিঃ ॥ ৫৮ ॥

yasyāsti bhaktir bhagavaty akiñcanā
sarvair guṇais tatra samāsate surāḥ
harāv abhaktasya kuto mahad-guṇā
mano-rathenāsati dhāvato bahiḥ

SYNONYMS

yasya—one who; *asti*—has; *bhaktiḥ*—devotional service; *bhagavati*—unto the Supreme Personality of Godhead; *akiñcanā*—without motive; *sarvaiḥ*—all; *guṇaiḥ*—qualities; *tatra*—there; *samāsate*—become manifested; *surāḥ*—with all the demigods; *harau*—unto the Supreme Personality; *abhaktasya*—one who is not a devotee; *kutaḥ*—where; *mahat-guṇāḥ*—high qualities; *manaḥ-rathena*—concoction; *asati*—the material existence; *dhāvataḥ*—run on; *bahiḥ*—externally.

TRANSLATION

"In one who has unflinching devotional faith in Kṛṣṇa, all the good qualities of Kṛṣṇa and the demigods are consistently manifested. However, one who has no devotion to the Supreme Personality of Godhead has no good qualifications because he is engaged by mental concoction in material existence, which is the external feature of the Lord."

TEXT 59

পণ্ডিত-গোসাঞির শিষ্য—অনন্ত আচার্য।
কৃষ্ণপ্রেমময়-তনু, উদার, সর্ব-আর্য॥ ৫৯॥

paṇḍita-gosāñira śiṣya—ananta ācārya
kṛṣṇa-premamaya-tanu, udāra, sarva-ārya

SYNONYMS

paṇḍita-gosāñira—of Gadādhara Paṇḍita; *śiṣya*—disciple; *ananta ācārya*—of the name Ananta Ācārya; *kṛṣṇa-premamaya*—always overwhelmed by love of God; *tanu*—body; *udāra*—magnanimous; *sarva*—in all respects; *ārya*—advanced.

TRANSLATION

Ananta Ācārya was a disciple of Gadādhara Paṇḍita. His body was always absorbed in love of Godhead. He was magnanimous and advanced in all respects.

TEXT 60

তাঁহার অনন্ত গুণ কে করু প্রকাশ।
তাঁর প্রিয় শিষ্য ইঁহ—পণ্ডিত হরিদাস॥ ৬০॥

tāṅhāra ananta guṇa ke karu prakāśa
tāṅra priya śiṣya iṅha—paṇḍita haridāsa

SYNONYMS

tāṅhāra—his; *ananta*—unlimited; *guṇa*—qualities; *ke*—who; *karu*—can; *prakāśa*—display; *tāṅra*—his; *priya*—dear; *śiṣya*—disciple; *iṅha*—this person; *paṇḍita haridāsa*—of the name Haridāsa Paṇḍita.

TRANSLATION

Ananta Ācārya was a reservoir of all good qualities. No one can estimate how great he was. Paṇḍita Haridāsa was his beloved disciple.

PURPORT

Śrī Ananta Ācārya is one of the eternal associates of Śrī Caitanya Mahāprabhu. Previously, during the advent of Lord Śrī Kṛṣṇa, Ananta Ācārya was Sudevī, one of the eight *gopīs.* This is stated in the *Gaura-gaṇoddeśa-dīpikā,* verse 165, as follows: *anantācārya-gosvāmī yā sudevī purā vraje.* "Ananta Ācārya Gosvāmī was formerly Sudevī-gopī in Vraja [Vṛndāvana]." In Jagannātha Purī, or Puruṣottama-kṣetra, there is a monastery known as Gaṅgā-mātā Maṭha that was established by Ananta Ācārya. In the disciplic succession of the Gaṅgā-mātā Maṭha, he is known as Vinoda-mañjarī. One of his disciples was Haridāsa Paṇḍita Gosvāmī, who is also known as Śrī Raghu Gopāla and as Śrī Rāsa-mañjarī. His disciple Lakṣmīpriyā was the maternal aunt of Gaṅgā-mātā, a princess who was the daughter of the King of Puṭiyā. Gaṅgā-mātā brought a Deity of the name Śrī Rasika Rāya from Kṛṣṇa Miśra of Jaipur and installed Him in the house of Sārvabhauma in Jagannātha Purī. The disciple in the fifth generation after Śrī Ananta Ācārya was Śrī Vanamālī; in the sixth generation, Śrī Bhagavān dāsa, who was a Bengali; in the seventh generation, Madhusūdana dāsa, who was an Oriyā; in the eighth generation, Nīlāmbara dāsa; in the ninth generation, Śrī Narottama dāsa; in the tenth generation, Pītāmbara dāsa; and in the eleventh generation, Śrī Mādhava dāsa. The disciple in the twelfth generation is presently in charge of the Gaṅgā-mātā monastery.

TEXT 61

চৈতন্য-নিত্যানন্দে তাঁর পরম বিশ্বাস।
চৈতন্য-চরিতে তাঁর পরম উল্লাস ॥ ৬১ ॥

caitanya-nityānande tāṅra parama viśvāsa
caitanya-carite tāṅra parama ullāsa

SYNONYMS

caitanya—Śrī Caitanya Mahāprabhu; *nityānande*—in Lord Nityānanda; *tāṅra*—his; *parama*—very great; *viśvāsa*—faith; *caitanya-carite*—in the pastimes of Lord Caitanya; *tāṅra*—his; *parama*—great; *ullāsa*—satisfaction.

TRANSLATION

Paṇḍita Haridāsa had great faith in Lord Caitanya and Nityānanda. Therefore he took great satisfaction in knowing about Their pastimes and qualities.

TEXT 62

বৈষ্ণবের গুণগ্রাহী, না দেখয়ে দোষ।
কায়মনোবাক্যে করে বৈষ্ণব-সন্তোষ ॥ ৬২ ॥

vaiṣṇavera guṇa-grāhī, nā dekhaye doṣa
kāya-mano-vākye kare vaiṣṇava-santoṣa

SYNONYMS

vaiṣṇavera—of devotees; *guṇa-grāhī*—accepting good qualities; *nā*—never; *dekhaye*—sees; *doṣa*—any fault; *kāya-manaḥ-vākye*—with heart and soul; *kare*—does; *vaiṣṇava*—devotee; *santoṣa*—pacification.

TRANSLATION

He always accepted the good qualities of Vaiṣṇavas and never found fault in them. He engaged his heart and soul only to satisfy the Vaiṣṇavas.

PURPORT

It is a qualification of a Vaiṣṇava that he is *adoṣa-darśī;* he never sees others' faults. Of course, every human being has both good qualities and faults. Therefore it is said, *sajjanā guṇam icchanti doṣam icchanti pāmarāḥ:* everyone has a combination of faults and glories. But a Vaiṣṇava, a sober man, accepts only a man's glories and not his faults, for flies seek sores whereas honeybees seek honey. Haridāsa Paṇḍita never found fault with a Vaiṣṇava but considered only his good qualities.

TEXT 63

নিরন্তর শুনে তেঁহো 'চৈতন্যমঙ্গল' ।
তাঁহার প্রসাদে শুনেন বৈষ্ণবসকল ॥ ৬৩ ॥

nirantara śune teṅho 'caitanya-maṅgala'
tāṅhāra prasāde śunena vaiṣṇava-sakala

SYNONYMS

nirantara—always; *śune*—hears; *teṅho*—he; *caitanya-maṅgala*—the book *Caitanya-maṅgala*; *tāṅhāra*—by his; *prasāde*—mercy; *śunena*—hear; *vaiṣṇava-sakala*—all other Vaiṣṇavas.

TRANSLATION

He always heard the reading of Śrī Caitanya-maṅgala, and all the other Vaiṣṇavas used to hear it by his grace.

TEXT 64

কথায় সভা উজ্জ্বল করে যেন পূর্ণচন্দ্র ।
নিজ-গুণামৃতে বাড়ায় বৈষ্ণব-আনন্দ ॥ ৬৪ ॥

kathāya sabhā ujjvala kare yena pūrṇa-candra
nija-guṇāmṛte bāḍāya vaiṣṇava-ānanda

SYNONYMS

kathāya—by words; *sabhā*—assembly; *ujjvala*—illuminated; *kare*—does; *yena*—as; *pūrṇa-candra*—full moon; *nija*—own; *guṇa-amṛte*—nectar of qualities; *bāḍāya*—increases; *vaiṣṇava*—of the devotees; *ānanda*—pleasure.

TRANSLATION

Like the full moon, he illuminated the entire assembly of the Vaiṣṇavas by speaking Caitanya-maṅgala, and by the nectar of his qualities he increased their transcendental bliss.

TEXT 65

তেঁহো অতি কৃপা করি' আজ্ঞা কৈলা মোরে।
গৌরাঙ্গের শেষলীলা বর্ণিবার তরে ॥ ৬৫ ॥

teṅho ati kṛpā kari' ājñā kailā more
gaurāṅgera śeṣa-līlā varṇibāra tare

SYNONYMS

teṅho—he; *ati*—very much; *kṛpā*—mercy; *kari'*—showing; *ājñā*—order; *kailā*—made it; *more*—unto me; *gaurāṅgera*—of Lord Caitanya; *śeṣa-līlā*—last portion of the pastimes; *varṇibāra*—describing; *tare*—for the matter of.

TRANSLATION

By his causeless mercy he ordered me to write about the last pastimes of Śrī Caitanya Mahāprabhu.

TEXT 66

কাশীশ্বর গোসাঞির শিষ্য—গোবিন্দ গোসাঞি।
গোবিন্দের প্রিয়সেবক তাঁর সম নাঞি ॥ ৬৬ ॥

kāśīśvara gosāñira śiṣya—govinda gosāñi
govindera priya-sevaka tāṅra sama nāñi

SYNONYMS

kāśīśvara gosāñira—of Kāśīśvara Gosvāmī; *śiṣya*—disciple; *govinda*—of the name Govinda; *gosāñi*—spiritual master; *govindera*—of Govinda; *priya-sevaka*—most confidential servitor; *tāṅra*—his; *sama*—equal; *nāñi*—is none.

TRANSLATION

Govinda Gosāñi, the priest engaged in the service of Lord Govinda in Vṛndāvana, was a disciple of Kāśīśvara Gosāñi. There was no servant more dear to the Govinda Deity.

PURPORT

Kāśīśvara Gosāñi, also known as Kāśīśvara Paṇḍita, was a disciple of Īśvara Purī and son of Vāsudeva Bhaṭṭācārya, who belonged to the dynasty of Kāñjilāla Kānu. His surname was Caudhurī. His nephew, his sister's son, who was named Rudra Paṇḍita, was the original priest of Vallabhapura, which is situated about one mile from the Śrīrāmapura railway station in the village of Cātarā. Installed there are the Deities of Rādhā-Govinda and Lord Śrī Caitanya Mahāprabhu. Kāśīśvara Gosāñi was a very strong man, and therefore when Lord Caitanya visited the temple of Jagannātha, he used to protect the Lord from the crowds. Another of his duties was to distribute *prasāda* to the devotees after *kīrtana.* He was also one of the contemporaries of Śrī Caitanya Mahāprabhu who was with the Lord in Jagannātha Purī.

Śrīla Bhaktisiddhānta Sarasvatī Ṭhākura also visited this temple at Vallabhapura. At that time the person in charge was a Śaivite, Śrī Śivacandra Caudhurī, who was a descendant of Kāśīśvara Gosāñi's brother. In Vallabhapura there was a permanent arrangement to cook nine kilos of rice, vegetables and other foodstuffs, and near the village there is sufficient land, which belongs to the Deity, on which this rice was grown. Unfortunately, the descendants of Kāśīśvara Gosāñi's brother have sold a major portion of this land, and therefore the Deity worship has now been hampered.

It is said in the *Gaura-gaṇoddeśa-dīpikā* that the servant of Kṛṣṇa in Vṛndāvana named Bhṛṅgāra descended as Kāśīśvara Gosāñi during the pastimes of Lord Caitanya Mahāprabhu. In our householder life we also sometimes visited this temple of Vallabhapura and took *prasāda* there at noon. The Deities of this temple, Śrī Śrī Rādhā-Govinda and the Gaurāṅga *vigraha,* are extremely beautiful. Near Vallabhapura is another beautiful temple of Jagannātha. We sometimes used to take *prasāda* in this Jagannātha Temple also. These two temples are situated within a one-mile radius of the Śrīrāmapura railway station near Calcutta.

TEXT 67

যাদবাচার্য গোসাঞি শ্রীরূপের সঙ্গী ।
চৈতন্যচরিতে তেঁহো অতি বড় রঙ্গী ॥ ৬৭ ॥

yādavācārya gosāñi śrī-rūpera saṅgī
caitanya-carite teṅho ati baḍa raṅgī

SYNONYMS

yādavācārya—of the name Yādavācārya; *gosāñi*—spiritual master; *śrī-rūpera*—of Śrīla Rūpa Gosvāmī; *saṅgī*—associate; *caitanya-carite*—in the pastimes of Lord Caitanya; *teṅho*—he; *ati*—very much; *baḍa*—great; *raṅgī*—enthusiastic.

TRANSLATION

Śrī Yādavācārya Gosāñi, a constant associate of Śrīla Rūpa Gosvāmī, was also very enthusiastic in hearing and chanting about Lord Caitanya's pastimes.

TEXT 68

পণ্ডিত-গোসাঞির শিষ্য— ভুগর্ভ গোসাঞি ।
গৌরকথা বিনা আর মুখে অন্য নাই ॥ ৬৮ ॥

paṇḍita-gosāñira śiṣya—bhugarbha gosāñi
gaura-kathā vinā āra mukhe anya nāi

SYNONYMS

paṇḍita-gosāñira—of Paṇḍita Gosāñi (Paṇḍita Haridāsa); *śiṣya*—disciple; *bhugarbha gosāñi*—of the name Bhugarbha Gosāñi; *gaura-kathā*—topics of Lord Caitanya; *vinā*—without; *āra*—else; *mukhe*—in his mouth; *anya nāi*—nothing else.

TRANSLATION

Bhugarbha Gosāñi, a disciple of Paṇḍita Gosāñi, was always engaged in topics regarding Lord Caitanya, knowing nothing else.

TEXT 69

তাঁর শিষ্য - গোবিন্দ পূজক চৈতন্যদাস ।
মুকুন্দানন্দ চক্রবর্তী, প্রেমী কৃষ্ণদাস ॥ ৬৯ ॥

tāṅra śiṣya—govinda pūjaka caitanya-dāsa
mukundānanda cakravartī, premī kṛṣṇa-dāsa

SYNONYMS

tāṅra śiṣya—his disciple; *govinda*—the Govinda Deity; *pūjaka*—priest; *caitanya-dāsa*—of the name Caitanya dāsa; *mukundānanda cakravartī*—of the name Mukundānanda Cakravartī; *premī*—a great lover; *kṛṣṇa-dāsa*—of the name Kṛṣṇadāsa.

TRANSLATION

Among his disciples were Caitanya dāsa, who was a priest of the Govinda Deity, as well as Mukundānanda Cakravartī and the great devotee Kṛṣṇadāsa.

TEXT 70

আচার্যগোসাঞির শিষ্য - চক্রবর্তী শিবানন্দ ।
নিরবধি তাঁর চিত্তে চৈতন্য-নিত্যানন্দ ॥ ৭০ ॥

ācārya-gosāñira śiṣya—cakravartī śivānanda
niravadhi tāṅra citte caitanya-nityānanda

SYNONYMS

ācārya-gosāñira—of Ācārya Gosāñi; *śiṣya*—the disciple; *cakravartī śivānanda*—of the name Śivānanda Cakravartī; *niravadhi*—always; *tāṅra*—his; *citte*—in the heart; *caitanya-nityānanda*—Lord Caitanya and Nityānanda are situated.

TRANSLATION

Among the disciples of Ananta Ācārya was Śivānanda Cakravartī, in whose heart dwelled constantly Lord Caitanya and Nityānanda.

TEXT 71

আর যত বৃন্দাবনে বৈসে ভক্তগণ ।
শেষ-লীলা শুনিতে সবার হৈল মন ॥ ৭১ ॥

āra yata vṛndāvane baise bhakta-gaṇa
śeṣa-līlā śunite sabāra haila mana

SYNONYMS

āra yata—there are many others; *vṛndāvane*—in Vṛndāvana; *baise*—residents; *bhakta-gaṇa*—great devotees; *śeṣa-līlā*—the last portions of Caitanya Mahāprabhu's pastimes; *śunite*—to hear; *sabāra*—of everyone; *haila*—became; *mana*—the mind.

TRANSLATION

In Vṛndāvana there were also many other great devotees, all of whom desired to hear the last pastimes of Lord Caitanya.

TEXT 72

মোরে আজ্ঞা করিলা সবে করুণা করিয়া ।
তাঁ-সবার বোলে লিখি নির্লজ্জ হইয়া ॥ ৭২ ॥

more ājñā karilā sabe karuṇā kariyā
tāṅ-sabāra bole likhi nirlajja ha-iyā

SYNONYMS

more—unto me; *ājñā*—order; *karilā*—gave; *sabe*—all; *karuṇā*—merciful; *kariyā*—doing so; *tāṅ-sabāra*—of all of them; *bole*—by the order; *likhi*—I write; *nirlajja*—without shame; *ha-iyā*—becoming.

TRANSLATION

By their mercy, all these devotees ordered me to write of the last pastimes of Śrī Caitanya Mahāprabhu. Because of their order only, although I am shameless, I have attempted to write this Caitanya-caritāmṛta.

PURPORT

To write about the transcendental pastimes of the Supreme Personality of Godhead is not an ordinary endeavor. Unless one is empowered by the higher authorities, or advanced devotees, one cannot write transcendental literature, for all such literature must be above suspicion, or, in other words, it must have none of the defects of conditioned souls, namely, mistakes, illusions, cheating and imperfect sense perceptions. The words of Kṛṣṇa and the disciplic succession that carries the orders of Kṛṣṇa are actually authoritative. To be empowered to write transcendental literature is a privilege in which a writer can take great pride. As a humble Vaiṣṇava, Kṛṣṇadāsa Kavirāja Gosvāmī, being thus empowered, felt very much ashamed that it was he who was to narrate the pastimes of Lord Caitanya Mahāprabhu.

TEXT 73

বৈষ্ণবের আজ্ঞা পাঞা চিন্তিত-অন্তরে ।
মদনগোপালে গেলাঙ আজ্ঞা মাগিবারে ॥ ৭৩ ॥

vaiṣṇavera ājñā pāñā cintita-antare
madana-gopāle gelāṅ ājñā māgibāre

SYNONYMS

vaiṣṇavera—of all the Vaiṣṇava devotees; *ājñā*—order; *pāñā*—receiving; *cintita-antare*—anxiety within myself; *madana-gopāle*—to the temple of Śrī Madana-mohana; *gelāṅ*—I went; *ājñā*—order; *māgibāre*—to receive.

TRANSLATION

Having received the order of the Vaiṣṇavas but being anxious within my heart, I went to the temple of Madana-mohana in Vṛndāvana to ask His permission also.

PURPORT

A Vaiṣṇava always follows the order of *guru* and Kṛṣṇa. *Śrī-Caitanya-caritāmṛta* was written by Kṛṣṇadāsa Kavirāja Gosvāmī by their mercy. Kṛṣṇadāsa Kavirāja Gosvāmī considered all the devotees that have been mentioned to be his preceptor *gurus* or spiritual masters, and Madana-gopāla (Śrī Madana-mohana *vigraha*) is Kṛṣṇa Himself. Thus he took permission from both of them, and when he received the mercy of both *guru* and Kṛṣṇa, he was able to write this great literature, *Śrī-Caitanya-caritāmṛta.* This example should be followed. Anyone who attempts to write about

Kṛṣṇa must first take permission from the spiritual master and Kṛṣṇa. Kṛṣṇa is situated in everyone's heart, and the spiritual master is His direct external representative. Thus Kṛṣṇa is situated *antar-bahiḥ,* within and without. One must first become a pure devotee by following the strict regulative principles and chanting sixteen rounds daily, and when one thinks that he is actually on the Vaiṣṇava platform, he must then take permission from the spiritual master, and that permission must also be confirmed by Kṛṣṇa from within his heart. Then, if one is very sincere and pure, he can write transcendental literature, either prose or poetry.

TEXT 74

দরশন করি কৈলুঁ চরণ বন্দন ।
গোসাঞিদাস পূজারী করে চরণ-সেবন ॥ ৭৪ ॥

daraśana kari kailuṅ caraṇa vandana
gosāñi-dāsa pūjārī kare caraṇa-sevana

SYNONYMS

daraśana—by visiting; *kari*—doing; *kailuṅ*—made; *caraṇa*—lotus feet; *vandana*—worship; *gosāñi-dāsa*—of the name Gosāñi dāsa; *pūjārī*—priest; *kare*—does; *caraṇa*—lotus feet; *sevana*—service.

TRANSLATION

When I visited the temple of Madana-mohana, the priest Gosāñi dāsa was serving the feet of the Lord, and I also prayed at the Lord's lotus feet.

TEXT 75

প্রভুর চরণে যদি আজ্ঞা মাগিল ।
প্রভুকণ্ঠ হৈতে মালা খসিয়া পড়িল ॥ ৭৫ ॥

prabhura caraṇe yadi ājñā māgila
prabhu-kaṇṭha haite mālā khasiyā paḍila

SYNONYMS

prabhura—of the Lord; *caraṇe*—lotus feet; *yadi*—when; *ājñā*—order; *māgila*—requested; *prabhu-kaṇṭha*—the neck of the Lord; *haite*—from; *mālā*—garland; *khasiyā*—slipped; *paḍila*—fell down.

TRANSLATION

When I prayed to the Lord for permission, a garland from His neck immediately slipped down.

TEXT 76

সব বৈষ্ণবগণ হরিধ্বনি দিল ।
গোসাঞিদাস আনি' মালা মোর গলে দিল ॥ ৭৬ ॥

saba vaiṣṇava-gaṇa hari-dhvani dila
gosāñi-dāsa āni' mālā mora gale dila

SYNONYMS

saba—all; *vaiṣṇava*—devotees; *gaṇa*—group; *hari-dhvani*—chanting Hare Kṛṣṇa; *dila*—made; *gosāñi-dāsa*—of the name Gosāñi dāsa; *āni'*—bringing; *mālā*—garland; *mora*—my; *gale*—on the neck; *dila*—gave it.

TRANSLATION

As soon as this happened, the Vaiṣṇavas standing there all loudly chanted, "Haribol!" and the priest, Gosāñi dāsa, brought me the garland and put it around my neck.

TEXT 77

আজ্ঞামালা পাঞা আমার হইল আনন্দ ।
তাহাঁই করিনু এই গ্রন্থের আরম্ভ ॥ ৭৭ ॥

ājñā-mālā pāñā āmāra ha-ila ānanda
tāhāṅi karinu ei granthera ārambha

SYNONYMS

ājñā-mālā—the garland of order; *pāñā*—receiving; *āmāra*—my; *ha-ila*—became; *ānanda*—great pleasure; *tāhāṅi*—then and there; *karinu*—attempted; *ei*—this; *granthera*—of *Caitanya-caritāmṛta*; *ārambha*—beginning.

TRANSLATION

I was greatly pleased to have the garland signifying the order of the Lord, and then and there I commenced to write this book.

TEXT 78

এই গ্রন্থ লেখায় মোরে 'মদনমোহন' ।
আমার লিখন যেন শুকের পঠন ॥ ৭৮ ॥

ei grantha lekhāya more 'madana-mohana'
āmāra likhana yena śukera paṭhana

SYNONYMS

ei—this; *grantha*—great literature; *lekhāya*—causes me to write; *more*—unto me; *madana-mohana*—the Deity; *āmāra*—my; *likhana*—writing; *yena*—like; *śukera*—of the parrot; *paṭhana*—responding.

TRANSLATION

Actually Śrī-Caitanya-caritāmṛta is not my writing but the dictation of Śrī Madana-mohana. My writing is like the repetition of a parrot.

PURPORT

This should be the attitude of all devotees. When the Supreme Personality of Godhead recognizes a devotee, He gives him intelligence and dictates how he may go back home, back to Godhead. This is confirmed in *Śrīmad-Bhagavad-gītā:*

teṣāṁ satata-yuktānāṁ
bhajatāṁ prīti-pūrvakam
dadāmi buddhi-yogaṁ taṁ
yena mām upayānti te

"To those who are constantly devoted and worship Me with love, I give the understanding by which they can come to Me." (Bg. 10.10) The opportunity to engage in the transcendental loving service of the Lord is open to everyone because every living entity is constitutionally a servant of the Lord. To engage in the service of the Lord is the natural function of the living entity, but because he is covered by the influence of *māyā,* material energy, he thinks it to be a very difficult task. But if he places himself under the guidance of a spiritual master and does everything sincerely, immediately the Lord, who is situated within everyone's heart, dictates how to serve Him *(dadāmi buddhi-yogaṁ tam).* The Lord gives this direction, and thus the devotee's life becomes perfect. Whatever a pure devotee does is done by the dictation of the Supreme Lord. Thus it is confirmed by the author of *Caitanya-caritāmṛta* that whatever he wrote was written under the direction of the Śrī Madana-mohana Deity.

TEXT 79

সেই লিখি, মদনগোপাল যে লিখায়।
কাষ্ঠের পুত্তলী যেন কুহকে নাচায় ॥ ৭৯ ॥

sei likhi, madana-gopāla ye likhāya
kāṣṭhera puttalī yena kuhake nācāya

SYNONYMS

sei likhi—I write that; *madana-gopāla*—the Deity Madana-gopāla; *ye*—whatever; *likhāya*—dictates to me; *kāṣṭhera*—wooden; *puttalī*—a doll; *yena*—like; *kuhake*—the enchanter; *nācāya*—causes to dance.

TRANSLATION

As a wooden doll is made to dance by a magician, I write as Madana-gopāla orders me to do so.

PURPORT

This is the position of a pure devotee. One should not take any responsibility on his own but should be a soul surrendered to the Supreme Personality of Godhead, who will then give him dictation as *caitya-guru,* or the spiritual master within. The Supreme Personality of Godhead is pleased to guide a devotee from within and without. From within He guides him as the Supersoul, and from without He guides him as the spiritual master.

TEXT 80

কুলাধিদেবতা মোর—মদনমোহন।
যাঁর সেবক—রঘুনাথ, রূপ, সনাতন ॥ ৮০ ॥

kulādhidevatā mora—madana-mohana
yāṅra sevaka—raghunātha, rūpa, sanātana

SYNONYMS

kula-ādhidevatā—the family Deity; *mora*—mine; *madana-mohana*—Lord Madana-mohana; *yāṅra*—whose; *sevaka*—servitor; *raghunātha*—Raghunātha dāsa Gosvāmī; *rūpa*—Rūpa Gosvāmī; *sanātana*—Sanātana Gosvāmī.

TRANSLATION

I accept as my family Deity Madana-mohana, whose worshipers are Raghunātha dāsa, Śrī Rūpa and Sanātana Gosvāmī.

TEXT 81

বৃন্দাবন-দাসের পাদপদ্ম করি' ধ্যান।
তাঁর আজ্ঞা লঞা লিখি যাহাতে কল্যাণ ॥ ৮১ ॥

vṛndāvana-dāsera pāda-padma kari' dhyāna
tāṅra ājñā lañā likhi yāhāte kalyāṇa

SYNONYMS

vṛndāvana-dāsera—of Śrīla Vṛndāvana dāsa Ṭhākura; *pāda-padma*—lotus feet; *kari'*—doing; *dhyāna*—meditation; *tāṅra*—his; *ājñā*—order; *lañā*—receiving; *likhi*—I write; *yāhāte*—in which permission; *kalyāṇa*—all auspiciousness.

TRANSLATION

I took permission from Śrīla Vṛndāvana dāsa Ṭhākura by praying at his lotus feet, and upon receiving his order I have attempted to write this auspicious literature.

PURPORT

Śrīla Kṛṣṇadāsa Kavirāja Gosvāmī took permission not only from the Vaiṣṇavas and Madana-mohana but also from Vṛndāvana dāsa Ṭhākura, who is understood to be the Vyāsa of the pastimes of Śrī Caitanya Mahāprabhu.

TEXT 82

চৈতন্যলীলাতে 'ব্যাস'– বৃন্দাবন-দাস ।
তাঁর কৃপা বিনা অন্যে না হয় প্রকাশ ॥ ৮২ ॥

caitanya-līlāte 'vyāsa'—vṛndāvana-dāsa
tāṅra kṛpā vinā anye nā haya prakāśa

SYNONYMS

caitanya-līlāte—in describing the pastimes of Lord Caitanya; *vyāsa*—Vyāsadeva; *vṛndāvana-dāsa*—is Śrīla Vṛndāvana dāsa Ṭhākura; *tāṅra*—his; *kṛpā*—mercy; *vinā*—without; *anye*—other; *nā*—never; *haya*—becomes; *prakāśa*—manifest.

TRANSLATION

Śrīla Vṛndāvana dāsa Ṭhākura is the authorized writer on the pastimes of Lord Caitanya. Without his mercy, therefore, one cannot describe these pastimes.

TEXT 83

মূর্খ, নীচ, ক্ষুদ্র মুঞি বিষয়-লালস ।
বৈষ্ণবাজ্ঞা-বলে করি এতেক সাহস ॥ ৮৩ ॥

mūrkha, nīca, kṣudra muñi viṣaya-lālasa
vaiṣṇavājñā-bale kari eteka sāhasa

SYNONYMS

mūrkha—foolish; *nīca*—lowborn; *kṣudra*—very insignificant; *muñi*—I; *viṣaya*—material; *lālasa*—desires; *vaiṣṇava*—of the Vaiṣṇavas; *ājñā*—order; *bale*—on the strength of; *kari*—I do; *eteka*—so much; *sāhasa*—energy.

TRANSLATION

I am foolish, lowborn and insignificant, and I always desire material enjoyment; yet by the order of the Vaiṣṇavas I am greatly enthusiastic to write this transcendental literature.

TEXT 84

শ্রীরূপ-রঘুনাথ-চরণের এই বল ।
যাঁর স্মৃতে সিদ্ধ হয় বাঞ্ছিতসকল ॥ ৮৪ ॥

śrī-rūpa-raghunātha-caraṇera ei bala
yāṅra smṛte siddha haya vāñchita-sakala

SYNONYMS

śrī-rūpa—Rūpa Gosvāmī; *raghunātha*—Raghunātha dāsa Gosvāmī; *caraṇera*—of the lotus feet; *ei*—this; *bala*—strength; *yāṅra*—whose; *smṛte*—by remembrance; *siddha*—successful; *haya*—becomes; *vāñchita-sakala*—all desires.

TRANSLATION

The lotus feet of Śrī Rūpa Gosvāmī and Raghunātha dāsa Gosvāmī are my source of strength. Remembering their lotus feet can fulfill all one's desires.

TEXT 85

শ্রীরূপ-রঘুনাথ-পদে যার আশ ।
চৈতন্যচরিতামৃত কহে কৃষ্ণদাস ॥ ৮৫ ॥

śrī-rūpa-raghunātha-pade yāra āśa
caitanya-caritāmṛta kahe kṛṣṇadāsa

SYNONYMS

śrī-rūpa—Śrīla Rūpa Gosvāmī; *raghunātha*—Śrīla Raghunātha dāsa Gosvāmī; *pade*—at the lotus feet; *yāra*—whose; *āśa*—expectation; *caitanya-caritāmṛta*—the book named *Caitanya-caritāmṛta; kahe*—describes; *kṛṣṇa-dāsa*—Śrīla Kṛṣṇadāsa Kavirāja Gosvāmī.

TRANSLATION

Praying at the lotus feet of Śrī Rūpa and Śrī Raghunātha, always desiring their mercy, I, Kṛṣṇadāsa, narrate Śrī-Caitanya-caritāmṛta, following in their footsteps.

Thus end the Bhaktivedanta purports to the Śrī Caitanya-caritāmṛta, Ādi-līlā, *Eighth Chapter, in the matter of the author's receiving the orders of the authorities, Kṛṣṇa and* guru.

Ādi-Līlā

CHAPTER 9

A summary of Chapter Nine has been given as follows by Śrīla Bhaktivinoda Ṭhākura in his *Amṛta-pravāha-bhāṣya.* In the Ninth Chapter the author of *Caitanya-caritāmṛta* has devised a figurative example by describing the "plant of *bhakti.*" He considers Lord Caitanya Mahāprabhu, who is known as Viśvambhara, to be the gardener of this plant because He is the main personality who has taken charge of it. As the supreme enjoyer, He enjoyed the flowers Himself and distributed them as well. The seed of the plant was first sown in Navadvīpa, the birthsite of Lord Caitanya Mahāprabhu, and then the plant was brought to Puruṣottama-kṣetra (Jagannātha Purī) and then to Vṛndāvana. The seed fructified first in Śrīla Mādhavendra Purī and then his disciple Śrī Īśvara Purī. It is figuratively described that both the tree itself and the trunk of the tree are Śrī Caitanya Mahāprabhu. The devotees, headed by Paramānanda Purī and eight other great *sannyāsīs,* are like the spreading roots of the tree. From the main trunk there extend two special branches, Advaita Prabhu and Śrī Nityānanda Prabhu, and from those branches grow other branches and twigs. The tree surrounds the entire world, and the flowers of the tree are to be distributed to everyone. In this way the tree of Lord Caitanya Mahāprabhu intoxicates the entire world. It should be noted that this is a figurative example meant to explain the mission of Lord Caitanya Mahāprabhu.

TEXT 1

তং শ্রীমৎকৃষ্ণচৈতন্যদেবং বন্দে জগদ্গুরুম্ ।
যস্যানুকম্পয়া শ্বাপি মহাব্ধিং সন্তরেৎ সুখম্ ॥ ১ ॥

taṁ śrīmat-kṛṣṇa-caitanya-devaṁ vande jagad-gurum
yasyānukampayā śvāpi mahābdhiṁ santaret sukham

SYNONYMS

tam—unto Him; *śrīmat*—with all opulence; *kṛṣṇa-caitanya-devam*—unto Lord Kṛṣṇa Caitanyadeva; *vande*—I offer obeisances; *jagat-gurum*—spiritual master of the world; *yasya*—whose; *anukampayā*—by the mercy of; *śvā api*—even a dog; *mahā-abdhim*—great ocean; *santaret*—can swim; *sukham*—without difficulty.

TRANSLATION

Let me offer my respectful obeisances unto the spiritual master of the entire world, Lord Śrī Kṛṣṇa Caitanya Mahāprabhu, by whose mercy even a dog can swim across a great ocean.

PURPORT

Sometimes it is to be seen that a dog can swim in the water for a few yards and then come back to the shore. Here, however, it is stated that if a dog is blessed by Śrī Caitanya Mahāprabhu, he can swim across an ocean. Similarly, the author of *Caitanya-caritāmṛta,* Kṛṣṇadāsa Kavirāja Gosvāmī, placing himself in a helpless condition, states that he has no personal power, but by the desire of Lord Caitanya, expressed through the Vaiṣṇavas and Madana-mohana *vigraha,* it is possible for him to cross a transcendental ocean to present *Śrī-Caitanya-caritāmṛta.*

TEXT 2

জয় জয় শ্রীকৃষ্ণচৈতন্য গৌরচন্দ্র ।
জয় জয়াদ্বৈত জয় জয় নিত্যানন্দ ॥ ২ ॥

jaya jaya śrī-kṛṣṇa-caitanya gauracandra
jaya jayādvaita jaya jaya nityānanda

SYNONYMS

jaya jaya—all glories; *śrī-kṛṣṇa-caitanya*—to Lord Śrī Caitanya Mahāprabhu; *gauracandra*—whose name is Gaurahari; *jaya jaya*—all glories; *advaita*—to Advaita Gosāñi; *jaya jaya*—all glories; *nityānanda*—to Nityānanda.

TRANSLATION

All glories to Śrī Kṛṣṇa Caitanya, who is known as Gaurahari! All glories to Advaita and Nityānanda Prabhu!

TEXT 3

জয় জয় শ্রীবাসাদি গৌরভক্তগণ ।
সর্বাভীষ্ট-পূর্তি-হেতু যাঁহার স্মরণ ॥ ৩ ॥

jaya jaya śrīvāsādi gaura-bhakta-gaṇa
sarvābhīṣṭa-pūrti-hetu yāṅhāra smaraṇa

SYNONYMS

jaya jaya—all glories; *śrīvāsa-ādi*—to Śrīvāsa and others; *gaura-bhakta-gaṇa*—all devotees of Lord Caitanya; *sarva-abhīṣṭa*—all ambition; *pūrti*—satisfaction; *hetu*—for the matter of; *yāṅhāra*—whose; *smaraṇa*—remembrance.

TRANSLATION

All glories to the devotees of Lord Caitanya, headed by Śrīvāsa Ṭhākura! In order to fulfill all my desires, I remember their lotus feet.

PURPORT

The author here continues to follow the same principles of worship of the Pañca-tattva that were described in the Seventh Chapter of *Ādi-līlā.*

TEXT 4

শ্রীরূপ, সনাতন, ভট্ট রঘুনাথ ।
শ্রীজীব, গোপালভট্ট, দাস-রঘুনাথ ॥ ৪ ॥

śrīrūpa, sanātana, bhaṭṭa raghunātha
śrījīva, gopāla-bhaṭṭa, dāsa-raghunātha

SYNONYMS

śrī-rūpa—Śrīla Rūpa Gosvāmī; *sanātana*—Śrīla Sanātana Gosvāmī; *bhaṭṭa raghunātha*—Raghunātha Bhaṭṭa Gosvāmī; *śrī-jīva*—Śrī Jīva Gosvāmī; *gopāla-bhaṭṭa*—Śrī Gopāla Bhaṭṭa Gosvāmī; *dāsa-raghunātha*—Raghunātha dāsa Gosvāmī.

TRANSLATION

I also remember the six Gosvāmīs—Rūpa, Sanātana, Bhaṭṭa Raghunātha, Śrī Jīva, Gopāla Bhaṭṭa and Dāsa Raghunātha.

PURPORT

This is the process for writing transcendental literature. A sentimentalist who has no Vaiṣṇava qualifications cannot produce transcendental writings. There are many fools who consider *Kṛṣṇa-līlā* to be a subject of art and write or paint pictures about the pastimes of Lord Kṛṣṇa with the *gopīs,* sometimes depicting them in a manner practically obscene. These fools take pleasure in material sense gratification, but one who wants to make advancement in spiritual life must scrupulously avoid their literature. Unless one is a servant of Kṛṣṇa and the Vaiṣṇavas, as Kṛṣṇadāsa Kavirāja Gosvāmī presents himself to be in offering respects to Lord Caitanya, His associates and His disciples, one should not attempt to write transcendental literature.

TEXT 5

এসব-প্রসাদে লিখি চৈতন্য-লীলাগুণ ।
জানি বা না জানি, করি আপন-শোধন ॥ ৫ ॥

esaba-prasāde likhi caitanya-līlā-guṇa
jāni vā nā jāni, kari āpana-śodhana

SYNONYMS

esaba—all these; *prasāde*—by the mercy of; *likhi*—I write; *caitanya*—of Lord Caitanya; *līlā-guṇa*—pastimes and quality; *jāni*—know; *vā*—or; *nā*—not; *jāni*—know; *kari*—do; *āpana*—self; *śodhana*—purification.

TRANSLATION

It is by the mercy of all these Vaiṣṇavas and gurus that I attempt to write about the pastimes and qualities of Lord Caitanya Mahāprabhu. Whether I know or know not, it is for self-purification that I write this book.

PURPORT

This is the sum and substance of transcendental writing. One must be an authorized Vaiṣṇava, humble and pure. One should write transcendental literature to purify oneself, not for credit. By writing about the pastimes of the Lord, one associates with the Lord directly. One should not ambitiously think, "I shall become a great author. I shall be celebrated as a writer." These are material desires. One should attempt to write for self-purification. It may be published, or it may not be published, but that does not matter. If one is actually sincere in writing, all his ambitions will be fulfilled. Whether one is known as a great author is incidental. One should not attempt to write transcendental literature for material name and fame.

TEXT 6

মালাকারঃ স্বয়ং কৃষ্ণপ্রেমামরতরুঃ স্বয়ম্ ।
দাতা ভোক্তা তৎফলানাং যস্তং চৈতন্যমাশ্রয়ে ॥ ৬ ॥

mālākāraḥ svayaṁ kṛṣṇa-premāmara-taruḥ svayam
dātā bhoktā tat-phalānāṁ yas taṁ caitanyam āśraye

SYNONYMS

mālākāraḥ—gardener; *svayam*—Himself; *kṛṣṇa*—Lord Kṛṣṇa; *prema*—love; *amara*—transcendental; *taruḥ*—tree; *svayam*—Himself; *dātā*—giver; *bhoktā*—enjoyer; *tat-phalānām*—of all the fruits of that tree; *yaḥ*—one who; *tam*—unto Him; *caitanyam*—Lord Caitanya Mahāprabhu; *āśraye*—I take shelter.

TRANSLATION

I take shelter of the Supreme Personality of Godhead Śrī Caitanya Mahāprabhu, who Himself is the tree of transcendental love of Kṛṣṇa, its gardener and also the bestower and enjoyer of its fruits.

TEXT 7

প্রভু কহে, আমি 'বিশ্বম্ভর' নাম ধরি।
নাম সার্থক হয়, যদি প্রেমে বিশ্ব ভরি ॥ ৭ ॥

prabhu kahe, āmi 'viśvambhara' nāma dhari
nāma sārthaka haya, yadi preme viśva bhari

SYNONYMS

prabhu kahe—the Lord said; *āmi*—I; *viśvambhara*—Viśvambhara; *nāma*—named; *dhari*—accept; *nāma*—the name; *sārthaka*—complete; *haya*—becomes; *yadi*—if; *preme*—in love of God; *viśva*—the whole universe; *bhari*—fulfilled.

TRANSLATION

Lord Caitanya thought: "My name is Viśvambhara, 'one who maintains the entire universe.' Its meaning will be actualized if I can fill the whole universe with love of Godhead."

TEXT 8

এত চিন্তি' লৈলা প্রভু মালাকার-ধর্ম।
নবদ্বীপে আরম্ভিলা ফলোদ্যান-কর্ম ॥ ৮ ॥

eta cinti' lailā prabhu mālākāra-dharma
navadvīpe ārambhilā phalodyāna-karma

SYNONYMS

eta cinti'—thinking like this; *lailā*—took; *prabhu*—the Lord; *mālākāra-dharma*—the business of a gardener; *navadvīpe*—in Navadvīpa; *ārambhilā*—began; *phala-udyāna*—garden; *karma*—activities.

TRANSLATION

Thinking in this way, He accepted the duty of a planter and began to grow a garden in Navadvīpa.

TEXT 9

শ্রীচৈতন্য মালাকার পৃথিবীতে আনি'।
ভক্তি-কল্পতরু রোপিলা সিঞ্চি' ইচ্ছা-পানি ॥ ৯ ॥

śrī-caitanya mālākāra pṛthivīte āni'
bhakti-kalpataru ropilā siñci' icchā-pāni

SYNONYMS

śrī-caitanya—Lord Śrī Caitanya Mahāprabhu; *mālākāra*—gardener; *pṛthivīte*—on this planet; *āni'*—bringing; *bhakti-kalpataru*—the desire tree of devotional service; *ropilā*—sowed; *siñci'*—watering; *icchā*—will; *pāni*—water.

TRANSLATION

Thus the Lord brought the desire tree of devotional service to this earth and became its gardener. He sowed the seed and sprinkled upon it the water of His will.

PURPORT

In many places devotional service has been compared to a creeper. One has to sow the seed of the devotional creeper, *bhakti-latā,* within his heart. As he regularly hears and chants, the seed will fructify and gradually grow into a mature plant and then produce the fruit of devotional service, namely, love of Godhead, which the gardener *(mālākāra)* can then enjoy without impediments.

TEXT 10

জয় শ্রীমাধবপুরী কৃষ্ণপ্রেমপূর ।
ভক্তিকল্পতরুর তেঁহো প্রথম অঙ্কুর ॥ ১০ ॥

jaya śrī mādhavapurī kṛṣṇa-prema-pūra
bhakti-kalpatarura teṅho prathama aṅkura

SYNONYMS

jaya—all glories; *śrī mādhavapurī*—unto Mādhavendra Purī; *kṛṣṇa-prema-pūra*—a storehouse of all love of Godhead; *bhakti-kalpatarura*—of the desire tree of devotional service; *teṅho*—he is; *prathama*—first; *aṅkura*—fructification.

TRANSLATION

All glories to Śrī Mādhavendra Purī, the storehouse of all devotional service unto Kṛṣṇa! He is a desire tree of devotional service, and it is in him that the seed of devotional service first fructified.

PURPORT

Śrī Mādhavendra Purī, also known as Śrī Mādhava Purī, belonged to the disciplic succession from Madhvācārya and was a greatly celebrated *sannyāsī.* Śrī Caitanya Mahāprabhu was the third disciplic descendant from Śrī Mādhavendra Purī. The process of worship in the disciplic succession of Madhvācārya was full of ritualistic ceremonies, with hardly a sign of love of Godhead; Śrī Mādhavendra Purī was the first person in that disciplic succession to exhibit the symptoms of love of Godhead and the first to write a poem beginning with the words *ayi dīna-dayārdra-nātha,* "O supremely merciful Personality of Godhead." In that poetry is the seed of Caitanya Mahāprabhu's cultivation of love of Godhead.

TEXT 11

শ্রীঈশ্বরপুরী-রূপে অঙ্কুর পুষ্ট হৈল ।
আপনে চৈতন্যমালী স্কন্ধ উপজিল ॥ ১১ ॥

śrī-īśvarapurī-rūpe aṅkura puṣṭa haila
āpane caitanya-mālī skandha upajila

SYNONYMS

śrī-īśvara-purī—by the name Śrī Īśvara Purī; *rūpe*—in the form of; *aṅkura*—the seed; *puṣṭa*—cultivated; *haila*—became; *āpane*—Himself; *caitanya-mālī*—the gardener of the name Śrī Caitanya Mahāprabhu; *skandha*—trunk; *upajila*—expanded.

TRANSLATION

The seed of devotional service next fructified in the form of Śrī Īśvara Purī, and then the gardener Himself, Caitanya Mahāprabhu, became the main trunk of the tree of devotional service.

PURPORT

Śrī Īśvara Purī was a resident of Kumāra-haṭṭa, where there is now a railroad station known as Kāmarhaṭṭy. Nearby there is also another station named Hālisahara, which belongs to the eastern railway that runs from the eastern section of Calcutta. Īśvara Purī appeared in a *brāhmaṇa* family and was the most beloved disciple of Śrīla Mādhavendra Purī. In the last portion of *Caitanya-caritāmṛta*, Chapter Eight, verses 26-29, it is stated:

īśvara-purī kare śrī-pada sevana
sva-haste karena mala-mūtrādi mārjana
nirantara kṛṣṇa-nāma karāya smaraṇa
kṛṣṇa-nāma kṛṣṇa-līlā śunāya anukṣaṇa
tuṣṭa hañā purī tāṅre kaila āliṅgana
vara dila kṛṣṇe tomāra ha-uk prema-dhana
sei haite īśvara-purī premera sāgara

"At the last stage of his life Śrī Mādhavendra Purī became an invalid and was completely unable to move, and Īśvara Purī so completely engaged himself in his service that he personally cleaned up his stool and urine. Always chanting the Hare Kṛṣṇa *mahā-mantra* and reminding Śrī Mādhavendra Purī about the pastimes of Lord Kṛṣṇa in the last stage of his life, Īśvara Purī gave the best service among his disciples. Thus Mādhavendra Purī, being very pleased with him, blessed him, saying, 'My dear boy,

I can only pray to Kṛṣṇa that He will be pleased with you.' Thus Īśvara Purī, by the grace of his spiritual master, Śrī Mādhavendra Purī, became a great devotee in the ocean of love of Godhead." Śrīla Viśvanātha Cakravartī states in his *Gurvaṣṭaka* prayer, *yasya prasādād bhagavat-prasādo yasyāprasādān na gatiḥ kuto'pi:* "By the mercy of the spiritual master one is benedicted by the mercy of Kṛṣṇa. Without the grace of the spiritual master one cannot make any advancement." It is by the mercy of the spiritual master that one becomes perfect, as vividly exemplified here. A Vaiṣṇava is always protected by the Supreme Personality of Godhead, but if he appears to be an invalid, this gives a chance to his disciples to serve him. Īśvara Purī pleased his spiritual master by service, and by the blessings of his spiritual master he became such a great personality that Lord Caitanya Mahāprabhu accepted him as His spiritual master.

Śrīla Īśvara Purī was the spiritual master of Śrī Caitanya Mahāprabhu, but before initiating Lord Caitanya he went to Navadvīpa and lived for a few months in the house of Gopīnātha Ācārya. At that time Lord Caitanya became acquainted with him, and it is understood that he served Śrī Caitanya Mahāprabhu by reciting his book, *Kṛṣṇa-līlāmṛta.* This is explained in *Caitanya-bhāgavata, Ādi-līlā,* Seventh Chapter.

To teach others by example how to be a faithful disciple of one's spiritual master, Śrī Caitanya Mahāprabhu, the Supreme Personality of Godhead, visited the birthplace of Īśvara Purī at Kāmarhaṭṭy and collected some earth from his birthsite. This He kept very carefully, and He used to eat a small portion of it daily. This is stated in the *Caitanya-bhāgavata,* Chapter Twelve. It has now become customary for devotees, following the example of Śrī Caitanya Mahāprabhu, to go there and collect some earth from that place.

TEXT 12

নিজাচিন্ত্যশক্ত্যে মালী হঞা স্কন্ধ হয় ।
সকল শাখার সেই স্কন্ধ মূলাশ্রয় ॥ ১২ ॥

nijācintya-śaktye mālī hañā skandha haya
sakala śākhāra sei skandha mūlāśraya

SYNONYMS

nija—His own; *acintya*—inconceivable; *śaktye*—by potency; *mālī*—gardener; *hañā*—becoming; *skandha*—trunk; *haya*—became; *sakala*—all; *śākhāra*—of other branches; *sei*—that; *skandha*—trunk; *mūla-āśraya*—original support.

TRANSLATION

By His inconceivable powers, the Lord became the gardener, the trunk and the branches simultaneously.

TEXTS 13-15

পরমানন্দ পুরী, আর কেশব ভারতী ।
ব্রহ্মানন্দ পুরী, আর ব্রহ্মানন্দ ভারতী ॥ ১৩ ॥

বিষ্ণুপুরী, কেশবপুরী, পুরী কৃষ্ণানন্দ ।
শ্রীনৃসিংহতীর্থ, আর পুরী সুখানন্দ ॥ ১৪ ॥

এই নব মূল নিকসিল বৃক্ষমূলে ।
এই নব মূলে বৃক্ষ করিল নিশ্চলে ॥ ১৫ ॥

paramānanda purī, āra keśava bhāratī
brahmānanda purī, āra brahmānanda bhāratī

viṣṇu-purī, keśava-purī, purī kṛṣṇānanda
śrī-nṛsiṁhatīrtha, āra purī sukhānanda

ei nava mūla nikasila vṛkṣa-mūle
ei nava mūle vṛkṣa karila niścale

SYNONYMS

paramānanda purī—of the name Paramānanda Purī; *āra*—and; *keśava bhāratī*—of the name Keśava Bhāratī; *brahmānanda purī*—of the name Brahmānanda Purī; *āra*—and; *brahmānanda bhāratī*—of the name Brahmānanda Bhāratī; *viṣṇu-purī*—of the name Viṣṇu Purī; *keśava-purī*—of the name Keśava Purī; *purī kṛṣṇānanda*—of the name Kṛṣṇānanda Purī; *śrī-nṛsiṁhatīrtha*—of the name Śrī Nṛsiṁhatīrtha; *āra*—and; *purī sukhānanda*—of the name Sukhānanda Purī; *ei nava*—of these nine; *mūla*—roots; *nikasila*—fructified; *vṛkṣa-mūle*—in the trunk of the tree; *ei nava mūle*—in these nine roots; *vṛkṣa*—the tree; *karila niścale*—became very steadfast.

TRANSLATION

Paramānanda Purī, Keśava Bhāratī, Brahmānanda Purī and Brahmānanda Bhāratī, Śrī Viṣṇu Purī, Keśava Purī, Kṛṣṇānanda Purī, Śrī Nṛsiṁhatīrtha and Sukhānanda Purī—these nine sannyāsī roots all sprouted from the trunk of the tree. Thus the tree stood steadfastly on the strength of these nine roots.

PURPORT

Paramānanda Purī. Paramānanda Purī belonged to a *brāhmaṇa* family of the Trihut district in Uttara Pradesh. Mādhavendra Purī was his spiritual master. In relationship with Mādhavendra Purī, Paramānanda Purī was very dear to Śrī Caitanya Mahāprabhu. In the *Caitanya-bhāgavata, Antya-līlā,* Chapter Eleven, there is the following statement:

sannyāsīra madhye īśvarera priya-pātra
āra nāhi eka purī gosāñi se mātra
dāmodara-svarūpa paramānanda-purī
sannyāsi-pārṣade ei dui adhikārī
niravadhi nikaṭe thākena dui-jana
prabhura sannyāse kare daṇḍera grahaṇa
purī dhyāna-para dāmodarera kīrtana

yata-prīti īśvarera purī-gosāñire
dāmodara-svarūpere-o tata prīti kare

"Among his *sannyāsī* disciples, Īśvara Purī and Paramānanda Purī were very dear to Mādhavendra Purī. Thus Paramānanda Purī, like Svarūpa Dāmodara, who was also a *sannyāsī,* was very dear to Śrī Caitanya Mahāprabhu and was His constant associate. When Lord Caitanya accepted the renounced order, Paramānanda Purī offered Him the *daṇḍa.* Paramānanda Purī was always engaged in meditation, and Śrī Svarūpa was always engaged in chanting the Hare Kṛṣṇa *mahā-mantra.* As Śrī Caitanya Mahāprabhu offered full respect to His spiritual master, Īśvara Purī, He similarly respected Paramānanda Purī and Svarūpa Dāmodara." It is described in *Caitanya-bhāgavata, Antya-līlā,* Chapter Three, that when Śrī Caitanya Mahāprabhu first saw Paramānanda Purī He made the following statement:

āji dhanya locana, saphala āji janma
saphala āmāra āji haila sarva-dharma
prabhu bale āji mora saphala sannyāsa
āji mādhavendra more ha-ilā prakāśa

"My eyes, My mind, My religious activities and My acceptance of the *sannyāsa* order have now all become perfect because today Mādhavendra Purī is manifest before Me in the form of Paramānanda Purī." *Caitanya-bhāgavata* further states:

kathokṣaṇe anyo 'nye karena praṇāma
paramānanda-purī caitanyera priya-dhāma

"Thus Śrī Caitanya Mahāprabhu exchanged respectful obeisances with Paramānanda Purī, who was very dear to Him." Paramānanda Purī established a small monastery behind the western side of the Jagannātha Temple, where he had a well dug to supply water. The water, however, was bitter, and therefore Śrī Caitanya Mahāprabhu prayed to Lord Jagannātha to allow Ganges water to come into the well to make it sweet. When Lord Jagannātha granted the request, Lord Caitanya told all the devotees that from that day hence, the water of Paramānanda Purī's well should be celebrated as Ganges water, for any devotee who would drink it or bathe in it would certainly get the same benefit as that derived from drinking or bathing in the waters of the Ganges. Such a person would certainly develop pure love of Godhead. It is stated in the *Caitanya-bhāgavata:*

prabhu bale āmi ye āchiye pṛthivīte
niścayai jāniha purī-gosāñira prīte

"Śrī Caitanya Mahāprabhu used to say: 'I am living in this world only on account of the excellent behavior of Śrī Paramānanda Purī.'" The *Gaura-gaṇoddeśa-dīpikā,* verse 118, states, *purī śrī-paramānando ya āsīd uddhavaḥ purā:* "Paramānanda Purī is none other than Uddhava." Uddhava was Lord Kṛṣṇa's friend and uncle, and in the *Caitanya-līlā* the same Uddhava became the friend of Śrī Caitanya Mahāprabhu and His uncle in terms of their relationship in the disciplic succession.

Keśava Bhāratī. The Sarasvatī, Bhāratī and Purī *sampradāyas* belong to the Śṛṅgerī Maṭha in South India, and Śrī Keśava Bhāratī, who at that time was situated in a monastery in Katwa, belonged to the Bhāratī-sampradāya. According to some authoritative opinions, although Keśava Bhāratī belonged to the Śaṅkara-sampradāya, he was formerly initiated by a Vaiṣṇava. He is supposed to have been a Vaiṣṇava on account of having been initiated by Mādhavendra Purī, for some say that he took *sannyāsa* from Mādhavendra Purī. The temple and Deity worship started by Keśava Bhāratī are still existing in the village known as Khāṭundi, which is under the postal jurisdiction of Kāndarā in the district of Burdwan. According to the managers of that *maṭha,* the priests are descendants of Keśava Bhāratī, and some say that the worshipers of the Deity are descendants of the sons of Keśava Bhāratī. In his householder life he had two sons, Niśāpati and Ūṣāpati, and a *brāhmaṇa* of the name Śrī Nakaḍicandra Vidyāratna, who was a member of the family of Niśāpati, was the priest in charge at the time that Śrī Bhaktisiddhānta Sarasvatī visited this temple. According to some, the priests of the temple belong to the family of Keśava Bhāratī's brother. Still another opinion is that they descend from Mādhava Bhāratī, who was another disciple of Keśava Bhāratī. Mādhava Bhāratī's disciple Balabhadra, who also later became a *sannyāsī* of the Bhāratī-sampradāya, had two sons in his family life named Madana and Gopāla. Madana, whose family's surname was Bhāratī, lived in the village of Āuriyā, and Gopāla, whose family's surname was Brahmacārī, lived in the village of Denduḍa. There are still many living descendants of both families.

In the *Gaura-gaṇoddeśa-dīpikā,* verse 52, it is said:

mathurāyāṁ yajña-sūtraṁ purā kṛṣṇāya yo muniḥ
dadau sāndīpaniḥ so 'bhūd adya keśava-bhāratī

"Sāndīpani Muni, who formerly offered the sacred thread to Kṛṣṇa and Balarāma, later became Keśava Bhāratī." It is he who offered *sannyāsa* to Śrī Caitanya Mahāprabhu. There is another statement from the *Gaura-gaṇoddeśa-dīpikā,* verse 117. *Iti kecit prabhāṣante 'krūraḥ keśava-bhāratī:* "According to some authoritative opinions, Keśava Bhāratī is an incarnation of Akrūra." Keśava Bhāratī offered the *sannyāsa* order to Śrī Caitanya Mahāprabhu in the year 1432 *śakābda* (1510 A.D.) in Katwa. This is stated in the *Vaiṣṇava-mañjuṣā,* Part Two.

Brahmānanda Purī. Śrī Brahmānanda Purī was one of the associates of Śrī Caitanya Mahāprabhu while He was performing *kīrtana* in Navadvīpa, and he also joined Lord Caitanya in Jagannātha Purī. We may note in this connection that the name Brahmānanda is accepted not only by Māyāvādī *sannyāsīs* but Vaiṣṇava *sannyāsīs* also. One of our foolish Godbrothers criticized our *sannyāsī* Brahmānanda Svāmī, saying that this was a Māyāvādī name. The foolish man did not know that Brahmānanda does not always refer to the impersonal. Parabrahman, the Supreme Brahman, is Kṛṣṇa. A devotee of Kṛṣṇa can therefore also be called Brahmānanda; this is evident from the fact that Brahmānanda Purī was one of the chief *sannyāsī* associates of Lord Caitanya Mahāprabhu.

Brahmānanda Bhāratī. Brahmānanda Bhāratī went to see Śrī Kṛṣṇa Caitanya Mahāprabhu at Jagannātha-dhāma. At that time he used to wear only a deerskin to cover himself, and Śrī Caitanya Mahāprabhu indirectly indicated that He did not like this deerskin covering. Brahmānanda Bhāratī therefore gave it up and accepted a loincloth of saffron color as used by Vaiṣṇava *sannyāsīs.* For some time he lived with Śrī Caitanya Mahāprabhu at Jagannātha Purī.

TEXT 16

মধ্যমূল পরমানন্দ পুরী মহাধীর।
অষ্ট দিকে অষ্ট মূল বৃক্ষ কৈল স্থির ॥ ১৬ ॥

madhya-mūla paramānanda purī mahā-dhīra
aṣṭa dike aṣṭa mūla vṛkṣa kaila sthira

SYNONYMS

madhya-mūla—the middle root; *paramānanda purī*—of the name Paramānanda Purī; *mahā-dhīra*—most sober; *aṣṭa dike*—in the eight directions; *aṣṭa mūla*—eight roots; *vṛkṣa*—the tree; *kaila sthira*—fixed.

TRANSLATION

With the sober and grave Paramānanda Purī as the central root and the other eight roots in the eight directions, the tree of Caitanya Mahāprabhu stood firmly.

TEXT 17

স্কন্ধের উপরে বহু শাখা উপজিল।
উপরি উপরি শাখা অসংখ্য হইল ॥ ১৭ ॥

skandhera upare bahu śākhā upajila
upari upari śākhā asaṅkhya ha-ila

SYNONYMS

skandhera upare—upon the trunk; *bahu śākhā*—many branches; *upajila*—grew; *upari upari*—over and above them; *śākhā*—other branches; *asaṅkhya*—innumerable; *ha-ila*—fructified.

TRANSLATION

From the trunk grew many branches and above them innumerable others.

TEXT 18

বিশ বিশ শাখা করি' এক এক মণ্ডল ।
মহা-মহা-শাখা ছাইল ব্রহ্মাণ্ড সকল ॥ ১৮ ॥

viśa viśa śākhā kari' eka eka maṇḍala
mahā-mahā-śākhā chāila brahmāṇḍa sakala

SYNONYMS

viśa viśa—twenty, twenty; *śākhā*—branches; *kari'*—making a group; *eka eka maṇḍala*—form a society; *mahā-mahā-śākhā*—big branches; *chāila*—covered; *brahmāṇḍa*—the whole universe; *sakala*—all.

TRANSLATION

Thus the branches of the Caitanya tree formed a cluster or society, with great branches covering all the universe.

PURPORT

Our International Society for Krishna Consciousness is one of the branches of the Caitanya tree.

TEXT 19

একৈক শাখাতে উপশাখা শত শত ।
যত উপজিল শাখা কে গণিবে কত ॥ ১৯ ॥

ekaika śākhāte upaśākhā śata śata
yata upajila śākhā ke gaṇibe kata

SYNONYMS

ekaika—each branch; *śākhāte*—in the branch; *upaśākhā*—sub-branches; *śata śata*—hundreds and hundreds; *yata*—all; *upajila*—grew; *śākhā*—branches; *ke*—who; *gaṇibe*—can count; *kata*—how much.

TRANSLATION

From each branch grew many hundreds of sub-branches. No one can count how many branches thus grew.

TEXT 20

মুখ্য মুখ্য শাখাগণের নাম অগণন ।
আগে ত' করিব, শুন বৃক্ষের বর্ণন ॥ ২০ ॥

mukhya mukhya śākhā-gaṇera nāma agaṇana
āge ta' kariba, śuna vṛkṣera varṇana

SYNONYMS

mukhya mukhya—the foremost of them all; *śākhā-gaṇera*—of the branches; *nāma*—name; *agaṇana*—uncountable; *āge*—subsequently; *ta' kariba*—I shall do; *śuna*—please hear; *vṛkṣera varṇana*—the description of the Caitanya tree.

TRANSLATION

I shall try to name the foremost of the innumerable branches. Please hear the description of the Caitanya tree.

TEXT 21

বৃক্ষের উপরে শাখা হৈল দুই স্কন্ধ ।
এক 'অদ্বৈত' নাম, আর 'নিত্যানন্দ' ॥ ২১ ॥

vṛkṣera upare śākhā haila dui skandha
eka 'advaita' nāma, āra 'nityānanda'

SYNONYMS

vṛkṣera—of the tree; *upare*—on the top; *śākhā*—branch; *haila*—became; *dui*—two; *skandha*—trunks; *eka*—one; *advaita*—Śrī Advaita Prabhu; *nāma*—of the name; *āra*—and; *nityānanda*—of the name Nityānanda Prabhu.

TRANSLATION

At the top of the tree the trunk branched into two. One trunk was named Śrī Advaita Prabhu and the other Śrī Nityānanda Prabhu.

TEXT 22

সেই দুইস্কন্ধে বহু শাখা উপজিল ।
তার উপশাখাগণে জগৎ ছাইল ॥ ২২ ॥

sei dui-skandhe bahu śākhā upajila
tāra upaśākhā-gaṇe jagat chāila

SYNONYMS

sei—that; *dui-skandhe*—in two trunks; *bahu*—many; *śākhā*—branches; *upajila*—grew; *tāra*—of them; *upaśākhā-gaṇe*—sub-branches; *jagat*—the whole world; *chāila*—covered.

TRANSLATION

From these two trunks grew many branches and sub-branches that covered the entire world.

TEXT 23

**বড় শাখা, উপশাখা, তার উপশাখা ।
যত উপজিল তার কে করিবে লেখা ॥ ২৩ ॥**

baḍa śākhā, upaśākhā, tāra upaśākhā
yata upajila tāra ke karibe lekhā

SYNONYMS

baḍa śākhā—the big branches; *upaśākhā*—sub-branches; *tāra*—their; *upaśākhā*—sub-branches; *yata*—all that; *upajila*—grew; *tāra*—of them; *ke*—who; *karibe*—can count; *lekhā*—or write.

TRANSLATION

These branches and sub-branches and their sub-branches became so numerous that no one can actually write about them.

TEXT 24

**শিষ্য, প্রশিষ্য, আর উপশিষ্যগণ ।
জগৎ ব্যাপিল তার নাহিক গণন ॥ ২৪ ॥**

śiṣya, praśiṣya, āra upaśiṣya-gaṇa
jagat vyāpila tāra nāhika gaṇana

SYNONYMS

śiṣya—disciples; *praśiṣya*—grand-disciples; *āra*—and; *upaśiṣya-gaṇa*—admirers; *jagat*—the whole world; *vyāpila*—spread; *tāra*—of that; *nāhika*—there is none; *gaṇana*—enumeration.

TRANSLATION

Thus the disciples and the grand-disciples and their admirers spread throughout the entire world, and it is not possible to enumerate them all.

TEXT 25

**উড়ুম্বর-বৃক্ষ যেন ফলে সর্ব অঙ্গে ।
এই মত ভক্তিবৃক্ষে সর্বত্র ফল লাগে ॥ ২৫ ॥**

uḍumbara-vṛkṣa yena phale sarva aṅge
ei mata bhakti-vṛkṣe sarvatra phala lāge

SYNONYMS

uḍumbara-vṛkṣa—a big fig tree; *yena*—as if; *phale*—grew fruits; *sarva*—all; *aṅge*—parts of the body; *ei*—this; *mata*—like; *bhakti-vṛkṣe*—in the tree of devotional service; *sarvatra*—all over; *phala*—fruit; *lāge*—appears.

TRANSLATION

As a big fig tree bears fruits all over its body, each part of the tree of devotional service bore fruit.

PURPORT

This tree of devotional service is not of this material world. It grows in the spiritual world, where there is no distinction between one part of the body and another. It is something like a tree of sugar, for whichever part of such a tree one tastes, it is always sweet. The tree of *bhakti* has varieties of branches, leaves and fruits, but they are all meant for the service of the Supreme Personality of Godhead. There are nine different processes of devotional service *(śravaṇaṁ kīrtanaṁ viṣṇoḥ smaraṇaṁ pāda-sevanam arcanaṁ vandanaṁ dāsyaṁ sakhyam ātma-nivedanam),* but all of them are meant only for the service of the Supreme Lord. Therefore whether one hears, chants, remembers or worships, his activities will yield the same result. Which one of these processes will be the most suitable for a particular devotee depends upon his taste.

TEXT 26

মূলস্কন্ধের শাখা আর উপশাখাগণে ।
লাগিলা যে প্রেমফল,— অমৃতকে জিনে ॥ ২৬ ॥

mūla-skandhera śākhā āra upaśākhā-gaṇe
lāgilā ye prema-phala,—amṛtake jine

SYNONYMS

mūla-skandhera—of the chief trunk; *śākhā*—branches; *āra*—and; *upaśākhā-gaṇe*—sub-branches; *lāgilā*—as it grew; *ye*—that; *prema-phala*—the fruit of love; *amṛtake jine*—such a fruit conquers nectar.

TRANSLATION

Since Śrī Kṛṣṇa Caitanya Mahāprabhu was the original trunk, the taste of the fruits that grew on the branches and sub-branches surpassed the taste of nectar.

TEXT 27

পাকিল যে প্রেমফল অমৃত-মধুর ।
বিলায় চৈতন্যমালী, নাহি লয় মূল ॥ ২৭ ॥

pākila ye prema-phala amṛta-madhura
vilāya caitanya-mālī, nāhi laya mūla

SYNONYMS

pākila—ripened; *ye*—that; *prema-phala*—the fruit of love of Godhead; *amṛta*—nectarean; *madhura*—sweet; *vilāya*—distributes; *caitanya-mālī*—the gardener, Lord Caitanya; *nāhi*—does not; *laya*—take; *mūla*—price.

TRANSLATION

The fruits ripened and became sweet and nectarean. The gardener, Śrī Caitanya Mahāprabhu, distributed them without asking any price.

TEXT 28

ত্রিজগতে যত আছে ধন-রত্নমণি ।
একফলের মূল্য করি' তাহা নাহি গণি ॥ ২৮ ॥

tri-jagate yata āche dhana-ratnamaṇi
eka-phalera mūlya kari' tāhā nāhi gaṇi

SYNONYMS

tri-jagate—in the three worlds; *yata*—as much as; *āche*—there is; *dhana-ratnamaṇi*—wealth and riches; *eka-phalera*—one fruit's; *mūlya*—price; *kari'*—calculated; *tāhā*—that; *nāhi*—do not; *gaṇi*—count.

TRANSLATION

All the wealth in the three worlds cannot equal the value of one such nectarean fruit of devotional service.

TEXT 29

মাগে বা না মাগে কেহ, পাত্র বা অপাত্র ।
ইহার বিচার নাহি জানে, দেয় মাত্র ॥ ২৯ ॥

māge vā nā māge keha, pātra vā apātra
ihāra vicāra nāhi jāne, deya mātra

SYNONYMS

māge—begs; *vā*—or; *nā*—not; *māge*—begs; *keha*—anyone; *pātra*—candidate; *vā*—or; *apātra*—not a candidate; *ihāra*—of this; *vicāra*—consideration; *nāhi*—does not; *jāne*—know; *deya*—gives; *mātra*—only.

TRANSLATION

Not considering who asked for it and who did not, nor who was fit and who unfit to receive it, Caitanya Mahāprabhu distributed the fruit of devotional service.

PURPORT

This is the sum and substance of Lord Caitanya's *saṅkīrtana* movement. There is no distinction made between those who are fit and those who are not fit to hear or take part in the *saṅkīrtana* movement. It should therefore be preached without discrimination. The only purpose of the preachers of the *saṅkīrtana* movement must be to go on preaching without restriction. That is the way in which Śrī Caitanya Mahāprabhu introduced this *saṅkīrtana* movement to the world.

TEXT 30

অঞ্জলি অঞ্জলি ভরি' ফেলে চতুর্দিশে ।
দরিদ্র কুড়াঞা খায়, মালাকার হাসে ॥ ৩০ ॥

añjali añjali bhari' phele caturdiśe
daridra kuḍāñā khāya, mālākāra hāse

SYNONYMS

añjali—handful; *añjali*—handful; *bhari'*—filling; *phele*—distributes; *caturdiśe*—in all directions; *daridra*—poor; *kuḍāñā*—picking up; *khāya*—eats; *mālākāra*—the gardener; *hāse*—smiles.

TRANSLATION

The transcendental gardener, Śrī Caitanya Mahāprabhu, distributed handful after handful of fruit in all directions, and when the poor hungry people ate the fruit, the gardener smiled with great pleasure.

TEXT 31

মালাকার কহে,—শুন, বৃক্ষ-পরিবার ।
মূলশাখা-উপশাখা যতেক প্রকার ॥ ৩১ ॥

mālākāra kahe,—śuna, vṛkṣa-parivāra
mūlaśākhā-upaśākhā yateka prakāra

SYNONYMS

mālākāra—the gardener; *kahe*—said; *śuna*—hear; *vṛkṣa-parivāra*—the family of this transcendental tree of devotional service; *mūla-śākhā*—chief branches; *upaśākhā*—sub-branches; *yateka*—as many; *prakāra*—varieties.

TRANSLATION

Lord Caitanya thus addressed the multifarious varieties of branches and sub-branches of the tree of devotional service:

TEXT 32

অলৌকিক বৃক্ষ করে সর্বেন্দ্রিয়-কর্ম ।
স্থাবর হইয়া ধরে জঙ্গমের ধর্ম ॥ ৩২ ॥

alaukika vṛkṣa kare sarvendriya-karma
sthāvara ha-iyā dhare jaṅgamera dharma

SYNONYMS

alaukika—transcendental; *vṛkṣa*—tree; *kare*—does; *sarva-indriya*—all senses; *karma*—activities; *sthāvara*—immovable; *ha-iyā*—becoming; *dhare*—accepts; *jaṅgamera*—of the movable; *dharma*—activities.

TRANSLATION

"Since the tree of devotional service is transcendental, every one of its parts can perform the action of all the others. Although a tree is supposed to be immovable, this tree nevertheless moves.

PURPORT

It is our experience in the material world that trees stand in one place, but in the spiritual world a tree can go from one place to another. Therefore everything in the spiritual world is called *alaukika,* uncommon or transcendental. Another feature of such a tree is that it can act universally. In the material world the roots of a tree go deep within the earth to gather food, but in the spiritual world the twigs, branches and leaves of the upper portion of the tree can act as well as the roots.

TEXT 33

এ বৃক্ষের অঙ্গ হয় সব সচেতন ।
বাড়িয়া ব্যাপিল সবে সকল ভুবন ॥ ৩৩ ॥

e vṛkṣera aṅga haya saba sa-cetana
bāḍiyā vyāpila sabe sakala bhuvana

SYNONYMS

e—this; *vṛkṣera*—of the Caitanya tree; *aṅga*—parts; *haya*—are; *saba*—all; *sa-cetana*—spiritually cognizant; *bāḍiyā*—increasing; *vyāpila*—overflooded; *sabe*—all the parts; *sakala*—all; *bhuvana*—the world.

TRANSLATION

"All the parts of this tree are spiritually cognizant, and thus as they grow up they spread all over the world.

TEXT 34

একলা মালাকার আমি কাহাঁ কাহাঁ যাব।
একলা বা কত ফল পাড়িয়া বিলাব ॥ ৩৪ ॥

ekalā mālākāra āmi kāhāṅ kāhāṅ yāba
ekalā vā kata phala pāḍiyā vilāba

SYNONYMS

ekalā—alone; *mālākāra*—gardener; *āmi*—I am; *kāhāṅ*—where; *kāhāṅ*—where; *yāba*—shall I go; *ekalā*—alone; *vā*—or; *kata*—how many; *phala*—fruits; *pāḍiyā*—picking; *vilāba*—shall distribute.

TRANSLATION

"I am the only gardener. How many places can I go? How many fruits can I pick and distribute?

PURPORT

Here Śrī Caitanya Mahāprabhu indicates that the distribution of the Hare Kṛṣṇa *mahā-mantra* should be performed by combined forces. Although He is the Supreme Personality of Godhead, He laments, "How can I act alone? How can I alone pick the fruit and distribute it all over the world?" This indicates that all classes of devotees should combine to distribute the Hare Kṛṣṇa *mahā-mantra* without consideration of the time, place or situation.

TEXT 35

একলা উঠাঞা দিতে হয় পরিশ্রম।
কেহ পায়, কেহ না পায়, রহে মনে ভ্রম ॥ ৩৫ ॥

ekalā uṭhāñā dite haya pariśrama
keha pāya, keha nā pāya, rahe mane bhrama

SYNONYMS

ekalā—alone; *uṭhāñā*—picking up; *dite*—to give; *haya*—it becomes; *pariśrama*—too laborious; *keha*—someone; *pāya*—does get; *keha*—someone; *nā*—not; *pāya*—does get; *rahe*—remains; *mane*—in the mind; *bhrama*—suspicion.

TRANSLATION

"It would certainly be a very laborious task to pick the fruits and distribute them alone, and still I suspect that some would receive them and others would not.

TEXT 36

অতএব আমি আজ্ঞা দিলুঁ সবাকারে।
যাহাঁ তাহাঁ প্রেমফল দেহ' যারে তারে ॥ ৩৬ ॥

ataeva āmi ājñā diluṅ sabākāre
yāhāṅ tāhāṅ prema-phala deha' yāre tāre

SYNONYMS

ataeva—therefore; *āmi*—I; *ājñā*—order; *diluṅ*—give; *sabākāre*—to everyone; *yāhāṅ*—wherever; *tāhāṅ*—everywhere; *prema-phala*—the fruit of love of Godhead; *deha'*—distribute; *yāre*—anyone; *tāre*—everyone.

TRANSLATION

"Therefore I order every man within this universe to accept this Kṛṣṇa consciousness movement and distribute it everywhere.

PURPORT

In this connection there is a song sung by Śrīla Bhaktivinoda Ṭhākura:

enechi auṣadhi māyā nāśibāra lāgi'
harināma-mahāmantra lao tumi māgi'
bhakativinoda prabhu-caraṇe paḍiyā
sei harināma-mantra la-ila māgiyā

The *saṅkīrtana* movement has been introduced by Lord Caitanya Mahāprabhu just to dispell the illusion of *māyā,* by which everyone in this material world thinks himself to be a product of matter and therefore to have many duties pertaining to the body. Actually, the living entity is not his material body; he is a spirit soul. He has a spiritual need to be eternally blissful and full of knowledge, but unfortunately he identifies himself with the body, sometimes as a human being, sometimes as an animal, sometimes a tree, sometimes an aquatic, sometimes a demigod, and so on. Thus with each change of body he develops a different type of consciousness with different types of activities and thus becomes increasingly entangled in material existence, transmigrating perpetually from one body to another. Under the spell of *māyā,* or illusion, he does not consider the past or future but is simply satisfied with the short life span that he has gotten for the present. To eradicate this illusion, Śrī Caitanya Mahāprabhu has brought the *saṅkīrtana* movement, and He requests everyone to accept and distribute it. A person who is actually a follower of Śrī Bhaktivinoda Ṭhākura must immediately accept the request of Lord Caitanya Mahāprabhu by offering respectful obeisances unto His lotus feet and thus beg from Him the Hare Kṛṣṇa *mahā-mantra.* If one is fortunate enough to beg from the Lord this Hare Kṛṣṇa *mahā-mantra,* his life is successful.

TEXT 37

একলা মালাকার আমি কত ফল খাব ।
না দিয়া বা এই ফল আর কি করিব ॥ ৩৭ ॥

ekalā mālākāra āmi kata phala khāba
nā diyā vā ei phala āra ki kariba

SYNONYMS

ekalā—alone; *mālākāra*—gardener; *āmi*—I; *kata*—how many; *phala*—fruits; *khāba*—eat; *nā*—without; *diyā*—giving; *vā*—or; *ei*—this; *phala*—fruits; *āra*—else; *ki*—what; *kariba*—shall I do.

TRANSLATION

"I am the only gardener. If I do not distribute these fruits, what shall I do with them? How many fruits can I alone eat?

PURPORT

Lord Caitanya Mahāprabhu produced so many fruits of devotional service that they must be distributed all over the world; otherwise, how could He alone relish and taste each and every fruit? The original reason that Lord Śrī Kṛṣṇa descended as Śrī Caitanya Mahāprabhu was to understand Śrīmatī Rādhārāṇī's love for Kṛṣṇa and to taste that love. The fruits of the tree of devotional service were innumerable, and therefore He wanted to distribute them unrestrictedly to everyone. Śrīla Rūpa Gosvāmī therefore writes:

anarpita-carīṁ cirāt karuṇayāvatīrṇaḥ kalau
samarpayitum unnatojjvala-rasāṁ sva-bhakti-śriyam
hariḥ puraṭa-sundara-dyuti-kadamba-sandīpitaḥ
sadā hṛdaya-kandare sphuratu vaḥ śacī-nandanaḥ

There were many precious incarnations of the Supreme Personality of Godhead, but none were so generous, kind and magnanimous as Śrī Caitanya Mahāprabhu, for He distributed the most confidential aspect of devotional service, namely, the conjugal love of Rādhā and Kṛṣṇa. Therefore Śrī Rūpa Gosvāmī Prabhupāda desires that Śrī Caitanya Mahāprabhu live perpetually in the hearts of all devotees, for thus they can understand and relish the loving affairs of Śrīmatī Rādhārāṇī and Kṛṣṇa.

TEXT 38

আত্ম-ইচ্ছামৃতে বৃক্ষ সিঞ্চি নিরন্তর ।
তাহাতে অসংখ্য ফল বৃক্ষের উপর ॥ ৩৮ ॥

ātma-icchāmṛte vṛkṣa siñci nirantara
tāhāte asaṅkhya phala vṛkṣera upara

SYNONYMS

ātma—self; *icchā-amṛte*—by the nectar of the will; *vṛkṣa*—the tree; *siñci*—sprinkle; *nirantara*—constantly; *tāhāte*—there; *asaṅkhya*—unlimited; *phala*—fruits; *vṛkṣera*—on the tree; *upara*—upper.

TRANSLATION

"By the transcendental desire of the Supreme Personality of Godhead, water has been sprinkled all over the tree, and thus there are innumerable fruits of love of Godhead.

PURPORT

God is unlimited, and His desires are also unlimited. This example of unlimited fruits is factually appropriate even within the material context, for with the good will of the Supreme Personality of Godhead there can be enough fruits, grains and other foodstuffs produced so that all the people in the world could not finish them, even if they ate ten times their capacity. In this material world there is actually no scarcity of anything but Kṛṣṇa consciousness. If people become Kṛṣṇa conscious, by the transcendental will of the Supreme Personality of Godhead there will be enough foodstuffs produced so that people will have no economic problems at all. One can very easily understand this fact. The production of fruits and flowers depends not upon our will but the supreme will of the Personality of Godhead. If He is pleased, He can supply enough fruits, flowers, etc., but if people are atheistic and godless, nature, by His will, restricts the supply of food. For example, in several provinces in India, especially Mahārāṣṭra, Uttara Pradesh and other adjoining states, there is sometimes a great scarcity of foodstuffs due to lack of rainfall. So-called scientists and economists cannot do anything about this. Therefore, to solve all problems, one must seek the good will of the Supreme Personality of Godhead by becoming Kṛṣṇa conscious and worshiping Him regularly in devotional service.

TEXT 39

অতএব সব ফল দেহ' যারে তারে ।
খাইয়া হউক্ লোক অজর অমরে ॥ ৩৯ ॥

ataeva saba phala deha' yāre tāre
khāiyā ha-uk loka ajara amare

SYNONYMS

ataeva—therefore; *saba*—all; *phala*—fruits; *deha'*—distribute; *yāre tāre*—to everyone and anyone; *khāiyā*—eating; *ha-uk*—let them become; *loka*—all people; *ajara*—without old age; *amare*—without death.

TRANSLATION

"Distribute this Kṛṣṇa consciousness movement all over the world. Let people eat these fruits and ultimately become free from old age and death.

PURPORT

The Kṛṣṇa consciousness movement introduced by Lord Caitanya is extremely important because one who takes to it becomes eternal, being freed from birth, death and old age. People do not recognize that the real distresses in life are the four principles of birth, death, old age and disease. They are so foolish that they resign themselves to these four miseries, not knowing the transcendental remedy of the Hare Kṛṣṇa *mahā-mantra.* Simply by chanting the Hare Kṛṣṇa *mahā-mantra* one can become free from all misery, but because they are enchanted by the illusory energy, people do not take this movement seriously. Therefore those who are actually servants of Śrī Caitanya Mahāprabhu must seriously distribute this movement all over the world to render the greatest benefit to human society. Of course, animals and other lower species are not capable of understanding this movement, but if even a small number of living beings take it seriously, by their chanting loudly, all living entities, including even trees, animals and other lower species, will be benefited. When Śrī Caitanya Mahāprabhu inquired from Haridāsa Ṭhākura how he was to benefit living entities other than humans, Śrīla Haridāsa Ṭhākura replied that the Hare Kṛṣṇa *mahā-mantra* is so potent that if it is chanted loudly, everyone will benefit, including the lower species of life.

TEXT 40

জগৎ ব্যাপিয়া মোর হবে পুণ্য খ্যাতি ।
সুখী হইয়া লোক মোর গাহিবেক কীর্তি ॥ ৪০ ॥

jagat vyāpiyā mora habe puṇya khyāti
sukhī ha-iyā loka mora gāhibeka kīrti

SYNONYMS

jagat vyāpiyā—spreading all over the world; *mora*—My; *habe*—there will be; *puṇya*—pious; *khyāti*—reputation; *sukhī*—happy; *ha-iyā*—becoming; *loka*—all the people; *mora*—My; *gāhibeka*—glorify; *kīrti*—reputation.

TRANSLATION

"If the fruits are distributed all over the world, My reputation as a pious man will be known everywhere, and thus all people will glorify My name with great pleasure.

PURPORT

This prediction of Lord Caitanya Mahāprabhu is now actually coming to pass. The Kṛṣṇa consciousness movement is being distributed all over the world through the chanting of the holy name of the Lord, the Hare Kṛṣṇa *mahā-mantra,* and people who were leading confused, chaotic lives are now feeling transcendental happiness. They are finding peace in *saṅkīrtana,* and therefore they are acknowledging the supreme benefit of this movement. This is the blessing of Lord Caitanya Mahāprabhu. His prediction is now factually being fulfilled, and those who are sober and conscientious are appreciating the value of this great movement.

TEXT 41

ভারত-ভূমিতে হৈল মনুষ্য-জন্ম যার ।
জন্ম সার্থক করি' কর পর-উপকার ॥ ৪১ ॥

bhārata-bhūmite haila manuṣya-janma yāra
janma sārthaka kari' kara para-upakāra

SYNONYMS

bhārata—of India; *bhūmite*—in the land; *haila*—has become; *manuṣya*—human being; *janma*—birth; *yāra*—anyone; *janma*—such a birth; *sārthaka*—fulfillment; *kari'*—doing so; *kara*—do; *para*—others; *upakāra*—benefit.

TRANSLATION

"One who has taken his birth as a human being in the land of India [Bhārata-varṣa] should make his life successful and work for the benefit of all other people.

PURPORT

The magnanimity of Lord Caitanya Mahāprabhu is expressed in this very important verse. Although He was born in Bengal and Bengalis therefore have a special duty toward Him, Śrī Caitanya Mahāprabhu is addressing not only Bengalis but all the inhabitants of India. It is in the land of India that actual human civilization can be developed.

Human life is especially meant for God realization, as stated in the *Vedānta-sūtra (athāto brahma-jijñāsā).* Anyone who takes birth in the land of India (Bhārata-varṣa) has the special privilege of being able to take advantage of the instruction and guidance of the Vedic civilization. He automatically receives the basic principles of spiritual life, for 99.9% of the Indian people, even simple village farmers and others who are neither educated nor sophisticated, believe in the transmigration of the soul, believe in past and future lives, believe in God and naturally want to worship the Supreme Personality of Godhead or His representative. These ideas are the natural inheritance of a person born in India. India has many holy places of pilgrimage such as Gayā, Benares, Mathurā, Prayāg, Vṛndāvana, Haridvār, Rāmeśvaram and Jagannātha Purī, and still people go there by the hundreds and thousands. Although the present leaders of India are influencing the people not to believe in God, not to believe in a next life and not to believe in a distinction between pious and impious life, and they are teaching them how to drink wine, eat meat and become supposedly civilized, people are nevertheless afraid of the four activities of sinful life—namely, illicit sex, meat eating, intoxication and gambling—and whenever there is a religious festival, they gather together by the thousands. We have actual experience of this. Whenever the Kṛṣṇa consciousness movement holds a *saṅkīrtana* festival in a big city like Calcutta, Bombay, Madras, Ahmedabad or Hyderabad, thousands of people come to hear. Sometimes we speak in English, but even though most people do not understand English, they nevertheless come to hear us. Even when imitation incarnations of Godhead speak, people gather in thousands, for everyone who is born in the land of India has a natural spiritual inclination and is taught the basic principles of spiritual life; they merely need to be a little more educated in the Vedic principles. Therefore Śrī Caitanya Mahāprabhu said, *janma sārthaka kari' kara para-upakāra:* if an Indian is educated in the Vedic principles, he is able to perform the most beneficial welfare activity for the entire world.

At present, for want of Kṛṣṇa consciousness or God consciousness, the entire world is in darkness, having been covered by the four principles of sinful life—meat eating, illicit sex, gambling and intoxication. Therefore there is a need for vigorous propaganda to educate people to refrain from sinful activities. This will bring peace and prosperity; the rogues, thieves and debauchees will naturally decrease in number, and all of human society will be God conscious.

The practical effect of our spreading the Kṛṣṇa consciousness movement all over the world is that now the most degraded debauchees are becoming the most elevated saints. This is only one Indian's humble service to the world. If all Indians had taken to this path, as advised by Lord Caitanya Mahāprabhu, India would have given a unique gift to the world, and thus India would have been glorified. Now, however, India is known as a poverty-stricken country, and whenever anyone from America or another opulent country goes to India, he sees many people lying by the foot paths for whom there are not even provisions for two meals a day. There are also institutions collecting money from all parts of the world in the name of welfare activities for poverty-stricken people, but they are spending it for their own sense gratification. Now, on the order of Śrī Caitanya Mahāprabhu, the Kṛṣṇa consciousness movement has been started, and people are benefiting from this movement. Therefore it is now the duty of the leading men of India to consider the importance of this movement and train many Indians to go outside of India to preach this cult. People will accept it, there will be cooperation among the Indian people and among the other people of the world, and the mission of Śrī Caitanya Mahāprabhu will then be fulfilled. Śrī Caitanya Mahāprabhu will then be glorified all over the world, and people will naturally be happy, peaceful and prosperous, not only in this life but also in the next, for as stated in *Bhagavad-gītā,* anyone who understands Kṛṣṇa, the Supreme Personality of Godhead, will very easily get salvation, or freedom from the repetition of birth and death, and go back home, back to Godhead. Śrī Caitanya Mahāprabhu therefore requests every Indian to become a preacher of His cult to save the world from disastrous confusion.

This is not only the duty of Indians but the duty of everyone, and we are very happy that American and European boys and girls are seriously cooperating with this movement. One should know definitely that the best welfare activity for all of human society is to awaken man's God consciousness, or Kṛṣṇa consciousness. Therefore everyone should help this great movement. This is confirmed in the *Śrīmad-Bhāgavatam,* Tenth Canto, Twenty-second Chapter, verse 35, which is next quoted in *Caitanya-caritāmṛta.*

TEXT 42

এতাবজ্জন্মসাফল্যং দেহিনামিহ দেহিষু ।
প্রাণৈরর্থৈর্ধিয়া বাচা শ্রেয়আচরণং সদা ॥ ৪২ ॥

etāvaj janma-sāphalyaṁ dehinām iha dehiṣu
prāṇair arthair dhiyā vācā śreya-ācaraṇaṁ sadā

SYNONYMS

etāvat—up to this; *janma*—of birth; *sāphalyam*—perfection; *dehinām*—of every living being; *iha*—in this world; *dehiṣu*—toward those who are embodied; *prāṇaiḥ*—by life; *arthaiḥ*—by wealth; *dhiyā*—by intelligence; *vācā*—by words; *śreyaḥ*—eternal good fortune; *ācaraṇam*—acting practically; *sadā*—always.

TRANSLATION

"'It is the duty of every living being to perform welfare activities for the benefit of others with his life, wealth, intelligence and words.'

PURPORT

There are two kinds of general activities—*śreyas,* or activities which are ultimately beneficial and auspicious, and *preyas,* or those which are immediately beneficial and auspicious. For example, children are very fond of playing. They don't want to go to school to receive an education, and they think that to play all day and night and enjoy with their friends is the aim of life. Even in the transcendental life of Lord Kṛṣṇa, we find that when He was a child He was very fond of playing with His friends of the same age, the cowherd boys. He would not even go home to take His dinner. Mother Yaśodā would have to come out to induce Him to come home. Thus it is a child's nature to engage all day and night in playing, not caring even for his health and other important concerns. This is an example of *preyas,* or immediately beneficial activities, but there are also *śreyas,* or activities which are ultimately auspicious. According to Vedic civilization, a human being must be God conscious. He should understand what God is, what this material world is, who he is and what their interrelationships are. This is called *śreyas,* or ultimately auspicious activity.

In this verse of *Śrīmad-Bhāgavatam* it is said that one should be interested in *śreyas.* To achieve the ultimate goal of *śreyas,* or good fortune, one should engage everything, including his life, wealth and words, not only for himself but for others also. However, unless one is interested in *śreyas* in his own life, he cannot preach of *śreyas* for the benefit of others.

This verse cited by Śrī Caitanya Mahāprabhu applies to human beings, not to animals. As indicated in the previous verse by the words *manuṣya-janma,* these injunctions are for human beings. Unfortunately, human beings, although they have the bodies of men, are becoming less than animals in their behavior. This is the fault of modern education. Modern educators do not know the aim of human life; they are simply concerned with how to develop the economic condition of their countries or of human society. This is also necessary; the Vedic civilization considers all aspects of human life, including *dharma* (religion), *artha* (economic development), *kāma* (sense gratification) and *mokṣa* (liberation). But humanity's first concern should be religion. To be religious, one must abide by the orders of God, but unfortunately people in this age have rejected religion, and they are busy in economic development. Therefore they will adopt any means to get money. For economic development one does not need to get money by hook or by crook; one needs only sufficient money to maintain his body and soul. However, because modern economic development is going on with no religious background, people have become lusty, greedy and mad after money. They are simply developing the qualities of *rajas* (passion) and *tamas* (ignorance), neglecting the other quality of nature, *sattva* (goodness), and the brahminical qualifications. Therefore the entire society is in chaos.

The *Bhāgavatam* says that it is the duty of an advanced human being to act in such a way as to facilitate human society's attainment of the ultimate goal of life. There is a similar verse in the *Viṣṇu Purāṇa,* Part Three, Chapter Twelve, verse 45, which is quoted in this chapter of *Caitanya-caritāmṛta* as verse 43.

TEXT 43

প্রাণিনামুপকারায় যদেবেহ পরত্র চ ।
কর্মণা মনসা বাচা তদেব মতিমান্ ভজেৎ ॥ ৪৩ ॥

prāṇinām upakārāya yad eveha paratra ca
karmaṇā manasā vācā tad eva matimān bhajet

SYNONYMS

prāṇinām—of all living entities; *upakārāya*—for the benefit; *yat*—whichever; *eva*—certainly; *iha*—in this world or in this life; *paratra*—in the next life; *ca*—and; *karmaṇā*—by work; *manasā*—by the mind; *vācā*—by words; *tat*—that; *eva*—certainly; *matimān*—an intelligent man; *bhajet*—must act.

TRANSLATION

"'By his work, thoughts and words, an intelligent man must perform actions which will be beneficial for all living entities in this life and in the next.'

PURPORT

Unfortunately, people in general do not know what is to take place in the next life. To prepare oneself for his next life is common sense, and it is a principle of the Vedic civilization, but presently people throughout the world do not believe in a next life. Even influential professors and other educators say that as soon as the body is finished, everything is finished. This atheistic philosophy is killing human civilization. People are irresponsibly performing all sorts of sinful activities, and thus the privilege of the human life is being taken away by the educational propaganda of the so-called leaders. Actually it is a fact that this life is meant for preparation for the next life; by evolution one has come through many species or forms, and this human form of life is an opportunity to promote oneself to a better life. This is explained in *Bhagavad-gītā:*

yānti deva-vratā devān
pitṝn yānti pitṛ-vratāḥ
bhūtāni yānti bhūtejyā
yānti mad-yājino'pi mām

"Those who worship the demigods will take birth among the demigods; those who worship ghosts and spirits will take birth among such beings; those who worship ancestors go to the ancestors; and those who worship Me will live with Me." (Bg. 9.25) Therefore, one may promote himself to the higher planetary systems which are the residence of the demigods, one can promote himself to the Pitṛloka, one can remain on earth, or one can also go back home, back to Godhead. This is further confirmed by *Bhagavad-gītā* (4.9): *tyaktvā dehaṁ punar janma naiti mām eti so 'rjuna.* After giving up the body, one who knows Kṛṣṇa in truth does not come back again to this world to accept a material body, but he goes back home, back to Godhead. This knowledge is in the *śāstras,* and people should be given the opportunity to understand it. Even if one is not able to go back to Godhead in one life, the Vedic civilization at least gives one the opportunity to be promoted to the higher planetary systems where the demigods live and not glide down again to animal life. At present, people do not understand this knowledge, although it constitutes a great science, for they are uneducated and trained not to accept it. This is the horrible condition of modern human society. As such, the Kṛṣṇa consciousness movement is the only hope to direct the attention of intelligent men to a greater benefit in life.

TEXT 44

মালী মনুষ্য আমার নাহি রাজ্য-ধন ।
ফল-ফুল দিয়া করি' পুণ্য উপার্জন ॥ ৪৪ ॥

mālī manuṣya āmāra nāhi rājya-dhana
phala-phula diyā kari' puṇya upārjana

SYNONYMS

mālī—gardener; *manuṣya*—man; *āmāra*—My; *nāhi*—there is none; *rājya*—kingdom; *dhana*—wealth; *phala*—fruit; *phula*—flowers; *diyā*—giving; *kari'*—do; *puṇya*—piety; *upārjana*—achievement.

TRANSLATION

"I am merely a gardener. I have neither a kingdom nor very great riches. I simply have some fruits and flowers that I wish to utilize to achieve piety in My life.

PURPORT

In performing welfare activities for human society, Śrī Caitanya Mahāprabhu presents Himself as being not very rich, thus indicating that a man need not be rich or opulent to act for the welfare of humanity. Sometimes rich men are very proud that they can perform beneficial activities for human society whereas others cannot. A practical example is that when there is a scarcity of food in India on account of meager rainfall, some members of the richer class very proudly distribute foodstuffs, making huge arrangements with the help of the government, as if merely by such activities people will be benefited. Suppose there were no food grains. How would the rich men distribute food? Production of grains is completely in the hands of God. If there were no rain, there would be no grains, and these so-called rich men would be unable to distribute grains to the people.

The real purpose of life, therefore, is to satisfy the Supreme Personality of Godhead. Śrīla Rūpa Gosvāmī describes in his *Bhakti-rasāmṛta-sindhu* that devotional service is so exalted that it is beneficial and auspicious for every man. Śrī Caitanya Mahāprabhu also declared that to propagate the *bhakti* cult of devotional service in human society, one does not need to be very rich. Anyone can do it and thus render the highest benefit to humanity if he knows the art. Lord Caitanya Mahāprabhu takes the part of a gardener because although a gardener is naturally not a very rich man, he has some fruits and flowers. Any man can collect some fruits and flowers and satisfy the Supreme Personality of Godhead in devotional service, as recommended in *Bhagavad-gītā:*

patraṁ puṣpaṁ phalaṁ toyaṁ
yo me bhaktyā prayacchati
tad ahaṁ bhakty-upahṛtam
aśnāmi prayatātmanaḥ
(Bg. 9.26)

One cannot satisfy the Supreme Lord by his riches, wealth or opulent position, but anyone can collect a little fruit or flower and offer it to the Lord. The Lord says that if one brings such an offering in devotion, He will accept it and eat it. When

Kṛṣṇa eats, the entire world becomes satisfied. There is the story in the *Mahābhārata* illustrating how by Kṛṣṇa's eating, the 60,000 disciples of Durvāsā Muni were all satisfied. Therefore it is a fact that if by our life *(prāṇaiḥ)*, by our wealth *(arthaiḥ)*, by our intelligence *(dhiyā)* or by our words *(vācā)* we can satisfy the Supreme Personality of Godhead, naturally the entire world will become happy. Therefore our main duty is to satisfy the Supreme Godhead by our actions, our money and our words. This is very simple. Even if one does not have money, he can preach the Hare Kṛṣṇa *mantra* to everyone. One can go everywhere, to every home, and request everyone to chant the Hare Kṛṣṇa *mantra.* Thus the entire world situation will become very happy and peaceful.

TEXT 45

মালী হঞা বৃক্ষ হইলাঙ এই ত' ইচ্ছাতে।
সর্বপ্রাণীর উপকার হয় বৃক্ষ হৈতে ॥ ৪৫ ॥

mālī hañā vṛkṣa ha-ilāṅ ei ta' icchāte
sarva-prāṇīra upakāra haya vṛkṣa haite

SYNONYMS

mālī hañā—although I am the gardener; *vṛkṣa ha-ilāṅ*—I am also the tree; *ei ta'*—this is; *icchāte*—by My will; *sarva-prāṇīra*—of all living entities; *upakāra*—welfare; *haya*—there is; *vṛkṣa*—the tree; *haite*—from.

TRANSLATION

"Although I am acting as a gardener, I also want to be the tree, for thus I can bestow benefit upon all.

PURPORT

Śrī Caitanya Mahāprabhu is the most benevolent personality in human society because His only desire is to make people happy. His *saṅkīrtana* movement is especially meant for the purpose of making people happy. He wanted to become the tree Himself because a tree is supposed to be the most benevolent living entity. In the following verse, which is from *Śrīmad-Bhāgavatam* (10.22.33), Kṛṣṇa Himself highly praised the existence of a tree.

TEXT 46

অহো এষাং বরং জন্ম সর্বপ্রাণ্যুপজীবিনাম্।
সুজনস্যেব যেষাং বৈ বিমুখা যান্তি নার্থিনঃ ॥ ৪৬ ॥

aho eṣāṁ varaṁ janma sarva-prāṇy-upajīvinām
sujanasyeva yeṣāṁ vai vimukhā yānti nārthinaḥ

SYNONYMS

aho—oh, just see; *eṣām*—of these trees; *varam*—superior; *janma*—birth; *sarva*—all; *prāṇi*—living entities; *upajīvinām*—one who provides maintenance; *sujanasya iva*—like the great personalities; *yeṣām*—from whose; *vai*—certainly; *vimukhāḥ*—disappointed; *yānti*—goes away; *na*—never; *arthinaḥ*—one who is asking for something.

TRANSLATION

"'Just see how these trees are maintaining every living entity! Their birth is successful. Their behavior is just like that of great personalities, for anyone who asks anything from a tree never goes away disappointed.'"

PURPORT

According to Vedic civilization, *kṣatriyas* are considered to be great personalities because if anyone goes to a *kṣatriya* king to ask for charity, the king will never refuse. The trees are compared to those noble *kṣatriyas* because everyone derives all kinds of benefits from them—some people take fruit, others take flowers, others take leaves, others take twigs, and others even cut the tree, and yet the tree gives to everyone without hesitation.

Unnecessarily cutting trees without consideration is another example of human debauchery. The paper industry cuts many hundreds and thousands of trees for its mills, and with the paper so much rubbish literature is published for the whimsical satisfaction of human society. Unfortunately, although these industrialists are now happy in this life by dint of their industrial development, they do not know that they will incur the responsibility for killing these living entities who are in the forms of trees.

This verse, quoted from *Śrīmad-Bhāgavatam,* was spoken by Lord Kṛṣṇa to His friends when He was taking rest underneath a tree after His pastime of stealing the clothes of the *gopīs (vastra-haraṇa-līlā).* By quoting this verse, Caitanya Mahāprabhu teaches us that we should be tolerant like trees and also beneficial like trees, which give everything to the needy persons who come underneath them. A needy person may derive many advantages from trees and also from many animals, but in modern civilization people have become so ungrateful that they exploit the trees and animals and kill them. These are some of the sinful activities of modern civilization.

TEXT 47

এই আজ্ঞা কৈল যদি চৈতন্য-মালাকার ।
পরম আনন্দ পাইল বৃক্ষ-পরিবার ॥ ৪৭ ॥

ei ājñā kaila yadi caitanya-mālākāra
parama ānanda pāila vṛkṣa-parivāra

SYNONYMS

ei—this; *ājñā*—order; *kaila*—gave; *yadi*—when; *caitanya*—Śrī Caitanya Mahāprabhu; *mālākāra*—as a gardener; *parama*—the greatest; *ānanda*—pleasure; *pāila*—got; *vṛkṣa*—of the tree; *parivāra*—descendants.

TRANSLATION

The descendants of the tree [the devotees of Śrī Caitanya Mahāprabhu] were very glad to receive this order directly from the Lord.

PURPORT

It is the desire of Lord Caitanya Mahāprabhu that the benevolent activities of the *saṅkīrtana* movement which was inaugurated 500 years ago in Navadvīpa be spread all over the world for the benefit of all human beings. Unfortunately, there are many so-called followers of Caitanya Mahāprabhu who are satisfied simply to construct a temple, make a show of the Deities, collect some funds and utilize them for eating and sleeping. There is no question of their preaching the cult of Śrī Caitanya Mahāprabhu all over the world, but even though they are unable to do so, if anyone else does it they become envious. This is the condition of the modern followers of Caitanya Mahāprabhu. The age of Kali is so strong that it affects even the so-called followers of Lord Caitanya. At least the followers of Caitanya Mahāprabhu must come out of India to preach His cult all over the world, for this is the mission of Lord Caitanya. The followers of Lord Caitanya must execute His will with heart and soul, being more tolerant than the trees and humbler than the straw in the street.

TEXT 48

যেই যাহাঁ তাহাঁ দান করে প্রেমফল ।
ফলাস্বাদে মত্ত লোক হইল সকল ॥ ৪৮ ॥

yei yāhāṅ tāhāṅ dāna kare prema-phala
phalāsvāde matta loka ha-ila sakala

SYNONYMS

yei—anyone; *yāhāṅ*—wherever; *tāhāṅ*—anywhere; *dāna*—charity; *kare*—gives in; *prema-phala*—the fruit of love of Godhead; *phala*—fruit; *āsvāde*—by tasting; *matta*—intoxicated; *loka*—people; *ha-ila*—become; *sakala*—all.

TRANSLATION

The fruit of love of God is so tasteful that wherever a devotee distributes it, those who relish the fruit, anywhere in the world, immediately become intoxicated.

PURPORT

Here the wonderful fruit of love of Godhead distributed by Lord Caitanya Mahāprabhu is described. We have practical experience that anyone who accepts this fruit and sincerely tastes it immediately becomes mad after it and gives up all his bad habits, being intoxicated by Caitanya Mahāprabhu's gift, the Hare Kṛṣṇa *mahā-mantra.* The statements of *Caitanya-caritāmṛta* are so practical that anyone can test them. As far as we are concerned, we are most confident of the success of the distribution of the great fruit of love of Godhead through the medium of chanting of the *mahā-mantra*—Hare Kṛṣṇa, Hare Kṛṣṇa, Kṛṣṇa Kṛṣṇa, Hare Hare/ Hare Rāma, Hare Rāma, Rāma Rāma, Hare Hare.

TEXT 49

মহা-মাদক প্রেমফল পেট ভরি' খায় ।
মাতিল সকল লোক—হাসে, নাচে, গায় ॥ ৪৯ ॥

mahā-mādaka prema-phala peṭa bhari' khāya
mātila sakala loka—hāse, nāce, gāya

SYNONYMS

mahā-mādaka—great intoxicant; *prema-phala*—this fruit of love of God; *peṭa*—belly; *bhari'*—filling; *khāya*—let them eat; *mātila*—became mad; *sakala loka*—all the people in general; *hāse*—laugh; *nāce*—dance; *gāya*—chant.

TRANSLATION

The fruit of love of Godhead distributed by Caitanya Mahāprabhu is such a great intoxicant that anyone who eats it, filling his belly, immediately becomes maddened by it, and automatically he chants, dances, laughs and enjoys.

TEXT 50

কেহ গড়াগড়ি যায়, কেহ ত' হুঙ্কার ।
দেখি' আনন্দিত হঞা হাসে মালাকার ॥ ৫০ ॥

keha gaḍāgaḍi yāya, keha ta' huṅkāra
dekhi' ānandita hañā hāse mālākāra

SYNONYMS

keha—some of them; *gaḍāgaḍi yāya*—roll on the floor; *keha*—some of them; *ta'*—certainly; *huṅkāra*—hum very loudly; *dekhi'*—seeing this; *ānandita*—gladdened; *hañā*—becoming so; *hāse*—smiles; *mālākāra*—the great gardener.

TRANSLATION

When Śrī Caitanya Mahāprabhu, the great gardener, sees that people are chanting, dancing and laughing and that some of them are rolling on the floor and some are making loud humming sounds, He smiles with great pleasure.

PURPORT

This attitude of Śrī Caitanya Mahāprabhu is very important for persons engaged in the Hare Kṛṣṇa movement of Kṛṣṇa consciousness. In every center of our institution, ISKCON, we have arranged for a love feast every Sunday, and when we actually see people come to our center, chant, dance, take *prasāda,* become jubilant and purchase books, we know that certainly Śrī Caitanya Mahāprabhu is always present in such transcendental activities, and He is very pleased and satisfied. Therefore the members of ISKCON must increase this movement more and more, according to the principles that we are presently trying to execute. Śrī Caitanya Mahāprabhu, thus being pleased, will smilingly glance upon them, bestowing His favor, and the movement will be successful.

TEXT 51

এই মালাকার খায় এই প্রেমফল ।
নিরবধি মত্ত রহে, বিবশ-বিহ্বল ॥ ৫১ ॥

ei mālākāra khāya ei prema-phala
niravadhi matta rahe, vivaśa-vihvala

SYNONYMS

ei—this; *mālākāra*—great gardener; *khāya*—eats; *ei*—this; *prema-phala*—fruit of love of Godhead; *niravadhi*—always; *matta*—maddened; *rahe*—remains; *vivaśa*—as if helpless; *vihvala*—as if bewildered.

TRANSLATION

The great gardener, Lord Caitanya, personally eats this fruit, and as a result He constantly remains mad, as if helpless and bewildered.

PURPORT

It is the mission of Śrī Caitanya Mahāprabhu to act Himself and teach the people. He says, *āpani ācari' bhakti karila pracāra* (Cc. *Ādi.* 4.41). One must first act himself and then teach. This is the function of a real teacher. Unless one is able to understand the philosophy that he speaks, it will not be effective. Therefore one should not only understand the philosophy of the Caitanya cult but also implement it practically in one's life.

While chanting the Hare Kṛṣṇa *mahā-mantra,* Śrī Caitanya Mahāprabhu sometimes fainted and remained unconscious for many hours. He prays in His *Śikṣāṣṭaka:*

yugāyitaṁ nimeṣeṇa cakṣuṣā prāvṛṣāyitam
śūnyāyitaṁ jagat sarvaṁ govinda-viraheṇa me

"O Govinda! Feeling Your separation, I am considering a moment to be like twelve years or more. Tears are flowing from My eyes like torrents of rain, and I am feeling all vacant in the world in Your absence." (*Śikṣāṣṭaka* 7) This is the perfectional stage of chanting the Hare Kṛṣṇa *mantra* and eating the fruit of love of Godhead, as exhibited by Śrī Caitanya Mahāprabhu. One should not artificially imitate this stage, but if one is serious and sincerely follows the regulative principles and chants the Hare Kṛṣṇa *mantra,* the time will come when these symptoms will appear. Tears will fill his eyes, he will be unable to chant distinctly the *mahā-mantra,* and his heart will throb in ecstasy. Śrī Caitanya Mahāprabhu says that one should not imitate this, but a devotee should long for the day to come when such symptoms of trance will automatically appear in his body.

TEXT 52

সর্বলোকে মত্ত কৈলা আপন-সমান।
প্রেমে মত্ত লোক বিনা নাহি দেখি আন ॥ ৫২ ॥

sarva-loke matta kailā āpana-samāna
preme matta loka vinā nāhi dekhi āna

SYNONYMS

sarva-loke—all people; *matta*—maddened; *kailā*—He made; *āpana*—Himself; *samāna*—like; *preme*—in love of God; *matta*—maddened; *loka*—people in general; *vinā*—without; *nāhi*—do not; *dekhi*—we see; *āna*—anything else.

TRANSLATION

With His saṅkīrtana movement the Lord made everyone mad like Himself. We do not find anyone who was not intoxicated by His saṅkīrtana movement.

TEXT 53

যে যে পূর্বে নিন্দা কৈল, বলি' মাতোয়াল।
সেহো ফল খায়, নাচে, বলে—ভাল, ভাল ॥ ৫৩ ॥

ye ye pūrve nindā kaila, bali' mātoyāla
seho phala khāya, nāce, bale—bhāla bhāla

SYNONYMS

ye ye—persons who; *pūrve*—before; *nindā*—blasphemy; *kaila*—made; *bali'*—saying; *mātoyāla*—drunkard; *seho*—such persons; *phala*—fruit; *khāya*—takes; *nāce*—dance; *bale*—say; *bhāla bhāla*—very good, very good.

TRANSLATION

Persons who had formerly criticized Lord Caitanya Mahāprabhu, calling Him a drunkard, also ate the fruit and began to dance, saying, "Very good! Very good!"

PURPORT

When Lord Caitanya Mahāprabhu started the *saṅkīrtana* movement, even He was unnecessarily criticized by Māyāvādīs, atheists and fools. Naturally we are also criticized by such men. They will always remain and will always criticize anything that is actually good for human society, but the preachers of the *saṅkīrtana* movement should not be deterred by such criticism. Our method should be to convert such fools gradually by asking them to come and take *prasāda* and chant and dance with us. This should be our policy. Anyone who comes to join us, of course, must be sincere and serious regarding spiritual advancement in life; then such a person, simply by joining us, chanting with us, dancing with us and taking *prasāda* with us, will gradually also come to say that this movement is very good. But one who joins with an ulterior purpose, to get material benefit or personal gratification, will never be able to grasp the philosophy of this movement.

TEXT 54

এই ত' কহিলুঁ প্রেমফল-বিতরণ ।
এবে শুন, ফলদাতা যে যে শাখাগণ ॥ ৫৪ ॥

ei ta' kahiluṅ prema-phala-vitaraṇa
ebe śuna, phala-dātā ye ye śākhā-gaṇa

SYNONYMS

ei—this; *ta'*—however; *kahiluṅ*—I have explained; *prema-phala*—the fruit of love of Godhead; *vitaraṇa*—distribution; *ebe*—now; *śuna*—hear; *phala-dātā*—the giver of the fruit; *ye ye*—who and who; *śākhā-gaṇa*—branches.

TRANSLATION

After describing the Lord's distribution of the fruit of love of Godhead, I now wish to describe the different branches of the tree of Lord Caitanya Mahāprabhu.

TEXT 55

শ্রীরূপ-রঘুনাথ-পদে যার আশ ।
চৈতন্যচরিতামৃত কহে কৃষ্ণদাস ॥ ৫৫ ॥

śrī-rūpa-raghunātha-pade yāra āśa
caitanya-caritāmṛta kahe kṛṣṇadāsa

SYNONYMS

śrī-rūpa—Śrīla Rūpa Gosvāmī; *raghunātha*—Śrīla Raghunātha dāsa Gosvāmī; *pade*—at the lotus feet; *yāra*—whose; *āśa*—expectation; *caitanya-caritāmṛta*—the book named *Caitanya-caritāmṛta; kahe*—describes; *kṛṣṇa-dāsa*—Śrīla Kṛṣṇadāsa Kavirāja Gosvāmī.

TRANSLATION

Praying at the lotus feet of Śrī Rūpa and Śrī Raghunātha, always desiring their mercy, I, Kṛṣṇadāsa, narrate Śrī-Caitanya-caritāmṛta, following in their footsteps.

Thus end the Bhaktivedanta purports to the Śrī Caitanya-caritāmṛta, Ādi-līlā, *Ninth Chapter, describing the tree of devotional service.*

Ādi-Līlā

CHAPTER 10

This chapter describes the branches of the tree named Śrī Caitanya Mahāprabhu.

TEXT 1

শ্রীচৈতন্যপদাম্ভোজ-মধুপেভ্যো নমো নমঃ।
কথঞ্চিদাশ্রয়াদ্ যেষাং শ্বাপি তদ্গন্ধভাগ্ভবেৎ ॥১॥

śrīcaitanya-padāmbhoja-madhupebhyo namo namaḥ
kathañcid āśrayād yeṣāṁ śvāpi tad-gandha-bhāg bhavet

SYNONYMS

śrī-caitanya—Lord Śrī Caitanya Mahāprabhu; *padāmbhoja*—the lotus feet; *madhu*—honey; *pebhyaḥ*—unto those who drink; *namaḥ*—respectful obeisances; *namaḥ*—respectful obeisances; *kathañcit*—a little of it; *āśrayāt*—taking shelter of; *yeṣām*—of whom; *śvā*—dog; *api*—also; *tat-gandha*—the aroma of the lotus flower; *bhāk*—shareholder; *bhavet*—may become.

TRANSLATION

Let me repeatedly offer my respectful obeisances unto the beelike devotees who always taste the honey of the lotus feet of Lord Caitanya Mahāprabhu. If even a doggish nondevotee somehow takes shelter of such devotees, he enjoys the aroma of the lotus flower.

PURPORT

The example of a dog is very significant in this connection. A dog naturally does not become a devotee at any time, but still it is sometimes found that a dog of a devotee gradually becomes a devotee also. We have actually seen that a dog has no respect even for the *tulasī* plant. Indeed, a dog is especially inclined to pass urine on the *tulasī* plant. Therefore the dog is the number one nondevotee. But Śrī Caitanya Mahāprabhu's *saṅkīrtana* movement is so strong that even a doglike nondevotee can gradually become a devotee by the association of a devotee of Lord Caitanya. Śrīla Śivānanda Sena, a great householder devotee of Lord Caitanya Mahāprabhu, attracted a dog on the street while going to Jagannātha Purī. The dog began to follow him and ultimately went to see Caitanya Mahāprabhu and was liberated. Similarly, cats and dogs in the household of Śrīvāsa Ṭhākura were also liberated. Cats and dogs and other animals are not expected to become devotees, but in the association of a pure devotee they are also delivered.

TEXT 2

জয় জয় শ্রীকৃষ্ণচৈতন্য-নিত্যানন্দ।
জয়াদ্বৈতচন্দ্র জয় গৌরভক্তবৃন্দ ॥ ২ ॥

jaya jaya śrī-kṛṣṇa-caitanya-nityānanda
jayādvaitacandra jaya gaura-bhakta-vṛnda

SYNONYMS

jaya jaya—all glories; *śrī-kṛṣṇa-caitanya*—to Lord Śrī Kṛṣṇa Caitanya Mahāprabhu; *nityānanda*—Lord Nityānanda; *jaya advaitacandra*—all glories to Advaita Prabhu; *jaya*—all glories; *gaura-bhakta-vṛnda*—to the devotees of Lord Caitanya, headed by Śrīvāsa.

TRANSLATION

All glories to Lord Caitanya Mahāprabhu and Lord Nityānanda! All glories to Advaita Prabhu and all glories to the devotees of Lord Caitanya, headed by Śrīvāsa!

TEXT 3

এই মালীর — এই বৃক্ষের অকথ্য কথন।
এবে শুন মুখ্যশাখার নাম-বিবরণ ॥ ৩ ॥

ei mālīra—ei vṛkṣera akathya kathana
ebe śuna mukhya-śākhāra nāma-vivaraṇa

SYNONYMS

ei mālīra—of this gardener; *ei vṛkṣera*—of this tree; *akathya kathana*—inconceivable description; *ebe*—now; *śuna*—hear; *mukhya*—chief; *śākhāra*—branches; *nāma*—of the names; *vivaraṇa*—description.

TRANSLATION

The description of Lord Caitanya as the gardener and the tree is inconceivable. Now hear with attention about the branches of this tree.

TEXT 4

চৈতন্য-গোসাঞির যত পারিষদচয়।
গুরু-লঘু-ভাব তাঁর না হয় নিশ্চয় ॥ ৪ ॥

caitanya-gosāñira yata pāriṣada-caya
guru-laghu-bhāva tāṅra nā haya niścaya

SYNONYMS

caitanya—Lord Caitanya Mahāprabhu; *gosāñira*—of the supreme spiritual master; *yata*—all; *pāriṣada-caya*—groups of associates; *guru-laghu-bhāva*—conceptions of high and low; *tāṅra*—of them; *nā*—never; *haya*—become; *niścaya*—ascertained.

TRANSLATION

The associates of Śrī Caitanya Mahāprabhu were many, but none of them should be considered lower or higher. This cannot be ascertained.

TEXT 5

যত যত মহান্ত কৈলা তাঁ-সবার গণন।
কেহ করিবারে নারে জ্যেষ্ঠ-লঘু-ক্রম ॥ ৫ ॥

yata yata mahānta kailā tāṅ-sabāra gaṇana
keha karibāre nāre jyeṣṭha-laghu-krama

SYNONYMS

yata yata—as many as there are; *mahānta*—great devotees; *kailā*—made; *tāṅ-sabāra*—of all of them; *gaṇana*—counting; *keha*—all of them; *karibāre nāre*—cannot do; *jyeṣṭha*—elder; *laghu*—younger; *krama*—chronology.

TRANSLATION

All the great personalities in the line of Lord Caitanya enumerated these devotees, but they could not distinguish between the greater and the lesser.

TEXT 6

অতএব তাঁ-সবারে করি' নমস্কার।
নাম-মাত্র করি, দোষ না লবে আমার ॥ ৬ ॥

ataeva tāṅ-sabāre kari' namaskāra
nāma-mātra kari, doṣa nā labe āmāra

SYNONYMS

ataeva—therefore; *tāṅ-sabāre*—to all of them; *kari'*—doing; *namaskāra*—offer my obeisances; *nāma-mātra*—that is also a token; *kari*—I do; *doṣa*—fault; *nā*—do not; *labe*—take; *āmāra*—of me.

TRANSLATION

I offer my obeisances unto them as a token of respect. I request them not to consider my offenses.

TEXT 7

বন্দে শ্রীকৃষ্ণচৈতন্য-প্রেমামরতরোঃ প্রিয়ান্ ।
শাখারূপান্ ভক্তগণান্ কৃষ্ণপ্রেমফলপ্রদান্ ॥ ৭ ॥

vande śrīkṛṣṇacaitanya-premāmarataroḥ priyān
śākhā-rūpān bhakta-gaṇān kṛṣṇa-prema-phala-pradān

SYNONYMS

vande—I offer my obeisances; *śrī-kṛṣṇa-caitanya*—to Lord Śrī Caitanya Mahāprabhu; *prema-amara-taroḥ*—of the eternal tree full of love of Godhead; *priyān*—those who are devotees; *śākhā-rūpān*—represented as branches; *bhakta-gaṇān*—all the devotees; *kṛṣṇa-prema*—of love of Kṛṣṇa; *phala*—of the fruit; *pradān*—the givers.

TRANSLATION

I offer my obeisances to all the dear devotees of Śrī Caitanya Mahāprabhu, the eternal tree of love of Godhead. I offer my respects to all the branches of the tree, the devotees of the Lord who distribute the fruit of love of Kṛṣṇa.

PURPORT

Śrī Kṛṣṇadāsa Kavirāja Gosvāmī sets the example of offering obeisances to all the preacher devotees of Lord Caitanya, without distinction as to higher and lower. Unfortunately, at present there are many foolish so-called devotees of Lord Caitanya who make such distinctions. For example, the title *"Prabhupāda"* is offered to a spiritual master, especially to a distinguished spiritual master such as Śrīla Rūpa Gosvāmī Prabhupāda, Śrīla Jīva Gosvāmī Prabhupāda or Śrīla Bhaktisiddhānta Sarasvatī Gosvāmī Prabhupāda. When our disciples similarly wanted to address their spiritual master as Prabhupāda, some foolish people became envious. Not considering the propaganda work of the Hare Kṛṣṇa movement, simply because these disciples addressed their spiritual master as Prabhupāda they became so envious that they formed a faction along with other such envious persons just to minimize the value of the Kṛṣṇa consciousness movement. To chastise such fools, Kṛṣṇadāsa Kavirāja Gosvāmī very frankly says, *keha karibāre nāre jyeṣṭha-laghu-krama.* Anyone who is a bona fide preacher of the cult of Śrī Caitanya Mahāprabhu must be respectful to the real devotees of Lord Caitanya; one should not be envious, considering one preacher to be very great and another to be very lowly. This is a material distinction and has no place on the platform of spiritual activities. Kṛṣṇadāsa Kavirāja Gosvāmī therefore offers equal respect to all the preachers of the cult of Śrī Caitanya Mahāprabhu, who are compared to the branches of the tree. ISKCON is one of these branches, and it should therefore be respected by all sincere devotees of Lord Caitanya Mahāprabhu.

TEXT 8

শ্রীবাস পণ্ডিত, আর শ্রীরাম পণ্ডিত।
দুই ভাই – দুই শাখা, জগতে বিদিত ॥ ৮ ॥

śrīvāsa paṇḍita, āra śrī-rāma paṇḍita
dui bhāi—dui śākhā, jagate vidita

SYNONYMS

śrīvāsa paṇḍita—of the name Śrīvāsa Paṇḍita; *āra*—and; *śrī-rāma paṇḍita*—of the name Śrī Rāma Paṇḍita; *dui bhāi*—two brothers; *dui śākhā*—two branches; *jagate*—in the world; *vidita*—well known.

TRANSLATION

The two brothers Śrīvāsa Paṇḍita and Śrī Rāma Paṇḍita started two branches that are well known in the world.

PURPORT

In the *Gaura-gaṇoddeśa-dīpikā,* verse 90, Śrīvāsa Paṇḍita is described to be an incarnation of Nārada Muni, and Śrī Rāma Paṇḍita, his younger brother, is said to be an incarnation of Parvata Muni, a great friend of Nārada's. Śrīvāsa Paṇḍita's wife, Mālinī, is celebrated as an incarnation of the nurse Ambikā, who fed Lord Kṛṣṇa with her breast milk, and as already noted, his niece Nārāyaṇī, the mother of Ṭhākura Vṛndāvana dāsa, the author of *Caitanya-bhāgavata,* was the sister of Ambikā in *kṛṣṇa-līlā.* We also understand from the description of *Caitanya-bhāgavata* that after Lord Caitanya Mahāprabhu's acceptance of the *sannyāsa* order, Śrīvāsa Paṇḍita left Navadvīpa, possibly because of feelings of separation, and domiciled at Kumārahaṭṭa.

TEXT 9

শ্রীপতি, শ্রীনিধি—তাঁর দুই সহোদর।
চারি ভাইর দাস-দাসী, গৃহ-পরিকর ॥ ৯ ॥

śrīpati, śrīnidhi—tāṅra dui sahodara
cāri bhāira dāsa-dāsī, gṛha-parikara

SYNONYMS

śrīpati—of the name Śrīpati; *śrīnidhi*—of the name Śrīnidhi; *tāṅra*—their; *dui*—two; *sahodara*—own brothers; *cāri*—four; *bhāira*—brothers; *dāsa-dāsī*—family members, manservants and maidservants; *gṛha-parikara*—all counted in one family.

TRANSLATION

Their two brothers were named Śrīpati and Śrīnidhi. These four brothers and their servants and maidservants are considered one big branch.

TEXT 10

দুই শাখার উপশাখায় তাঁ-সবার গণন ।
যাঁর গৃহে মহাপ্রভুর সদা সংকীর্তন ॥ ১০ ॥

dui śākhāra upaśākhāya tāṅ-sabāra gaṇana
yāṅra gṛhe mahāprabhura sadā saṅkīrtana

SYNONYMS

dui śākhāra—of the two branches; *upaśākhāya*—on the sub-branches; *tāṅ-sabāra*—of all of them; *gaṇana*—counting; *yāṅra gṛhe*—in whose house; *mahāprabhura*—of Lord Caitanya Mahāprabhu; *sadā*—always; *saṅkīrtana*—congregational chanting.

TRANSLATION

There is no counting the sub-branches of these two branches. Śrī Caitanya Mahāprabhu held congregational chanting daily at the house of Śrīvāsa Paṇḍita.

TEXT 11

চারি ভাই সবংশে করে চৈতন্যের সেবা ।
গৌরচন্দ্র বিনা নাহি জানে দেবী-দেবা ॥ ১১ ॥

cāri bhāi sa-vaṁśe kare caitanyera sevā
gauracandra vinā nāhi jāne devī-devā

SYNONYMS

cāri bhāi—four brothers; *sa-vaṁśe*—with all family members; *kare*—do; *caitanyera*—of Lord Śrī Caitanya Mahāprabhu; *sevā*—service; *gauracandra*—Gaurasundara (Lord Caitanya Mahāprabhu); *vinā*—except; *nāhi jāne*—they do not know; *devī*—goddess; *devā*—or god.

TRANSLATION

These four brothers and their family members fully engaged in the service of Lord Caitanya. They knew no other god or goddess.

PURPORT

Śrīla Narottama dāsa Ṭhākura has said, *anya-devāśraya nāi, tomāre kahinu bhāi, ei bhakti parama-kāraṇa:* if one wants to become a pure, staunch devotee, one should not take shelter of any of the demigods or goddesses. Foolish Māyāvādīs say that worshiping demigods is as good as worshiping the Supreme Personality of Godhead, but that is not a fact. This philosophy misleads people to atheism. One who has no idea what God actually is thinks that any form he imagines or any rascal he accepts can be God. This acceptance of cheap gods or incarnations of God is actually atheism. It is to be concluded, therefore, that those who worship demigods or self-proclaimed incarnations of God are all atheists. They have lost their knowledge, as confirmed in *Bhagavad-gītā. Kāmais tais tair hṛta-jñānāḥ prapadyante 'nya-devatāḥ:* "Those whose minds are distorted by material desires surrender unto demigods." (Bg. 7.20) Unfortunately, those who do not cultivate Kṛṣṇa consciousness and do not properly understand the Vedic knowledge accept any rascal to be an incarnation of God, and they are of the opinion that one can become an incarnation simply by worshiping a demigod. This philosophical hodge-podge exists under the name of the Hindu religion, but the Kṛṣṇa consciousness movement does not approve of it. Indeed, we strongly condemn it. Such worship of demigods and so-called incarnations of God should never be confused with the pure Kṛṣṇa consciousness movement.

TEXT 12

'আচার্যরত্ন' নাম ধরে বড় এক শাখা।
তাঁর পরিকর, তাঁর শাখা-উপশাখা ॥ ১২ ॥

'ācāryaratna' nāma dhare baḍa eka śākhā
tāṅra parikara, tāṅra śākhā-upaśākhā

SYNONYMS

ācāryaratna—of the name Ācāryaratna; *nāma*—name; *dhare*—he accepts; *baḍa*—big; *eka*—one; *śākhā*—branch; *tāṅra*—his; *parikara*—associates; *tāṅra*—his; *śākhā*—branch; *upaśākhā*—sub-branches.

TRANSLATION

Another big branch was Ācāryaratna, and his associates were sub-branches.

TEXT 13

আচার্যরত্নের নাম 'শ্রীচন্দ্রশেখর'।
যাঁর ঘরে দেবী-ভাবে নাচিলা ঈশ্বর ॥ ১৩ ॥

ācāryaratnera nāma 'śrī-candraśekhara'—
yāṅra ghare devī-bhāve nācilā īśvara

SYNONYMS

ācāryaratnera—of Ācāryaratna; *nāma*—name; *śrī-candraśekhara*—of the name Śrī Candraśekhara; *yāṅra*—of whom; *ghare*—in the home; *devī-bhāve*—as the goddess; *nācilā*—danced; *īśvara*—Śrī Caitanya Mahāprabhu.

TRANSLATION

Ācāryaratna was also named Śrī Candraśekhara Ācārya. In a drama in his house, Lord Caitanya played the goddess of fortune.

PURPORT

Dramatic performances were also enacted during the presence of Śrī Caitanya Mahāprabhu, but the players who took part in such dramas were all pure devotees; no outsiders were allowed. The members of ISKCON should follow this example. Whenever they stage dramatic performances about the lives of Śrī Caitanya Mahāprabhu or Lord Kṛṣṇa, the players must be pure devotees. Professional players and dramatic actors have no sense of devotional service, and therefore although they can perform very artistically, there is no life in such performances. Śrīla Bhaktisiddhānta Sarasvatī Ṭhākura used to refer to such an actor as *yātrā-dale nārada,* which means "farcical Nārada." Sometimes an actor in a drama plays the part of Nārada Muni, although in his private life he is not at all like Nārada Muni because he is not a devotee. Such actors are not needed in dramatic performances about the lives of Śrī Caitanya Mahāprabhu and Lord Kṛṣṇa.

Śrī Caitanya Mahāprabhu used to perform dramas with Advaita Prabhu, Śrīvāsa Ṭhākura and other devotees in the house of Candraśekhara. The place where Candraśekhara's house was situated is now known as Vrajapattana. Śrīla Bhaktisiddhānta Sarasvatī Ṭhākura established a branch of his Śrī Caitanya Maṭha at this place. When Śrī Caitanya Mahāprabhu decided to accept the renounced order of life, Candraśekhara Ācārya was informed of this by Śrī Nityānanda Prabhu, and therefore he was also present when Lord Caitanya accepted *sannyāsa* from Keśava Bhāratī in Katwa. It is he who first spread word in Navadvīpa of Lord Caitanya's accepting *sannyāsa.* Śrī Candraśekhara Ācārya was present during many important incidents in the pastimes of Lord Caitanya Mahāprabhu. He therefore forms the second branch of the tree of Lord Caitanya.

TEXT 14

পুণ্ডরীক বিদ্যানিধি – বড়শাখা জানি ।
যাঁর নাম লঞা প্রভু কান্দিলা আপনি ॥ ১৪ ॥

puṇḍarīka vidyānidhi—baḍa-śākhā jāni
yāṅra nāma lañā prabhu kāndilā āpani

SYNONYMS

puṇḍarīka vidyānidhi—of the name Puṇḍarīka Vidyānidhi; *baḍa-śākhā*—another big branch; *jāni*—I know; *yāṅra nāma*—whose name; *lañā*—taking; *prabhu*—the Lord; *kāndilā*—cried; *āpani*—Himself.

TRANSLATION

Puṇḍarīka Vidyānidhi, the third big branch, was so dear to Lord Caitanya Mahāprabhu that in his absence Lord Caitanya Himself would sometimes cry.

PURPORT

In the *Gaura-gaṇoddeśa-dīpikā* Śrīla Puṇḍarīka Vidyānidhi is described to be the father of Śrīmatī Rādhārāṇī in *kṛṣṇa-līlā.* Caitanya Mahāprabhu therefore treated him as His father. Puṇḍarīka Vidyānidhi's father was known as Bāṇeśvara or, according to another opinion, Śuklāmbara Brahmacārī, and his mother's name was Gaṅgādevī. According to one opinion, Bāṇeśvara was a descendent of Śrī Śivarāma Gaṅgopādhyāya. The original home of Puṇḍarīka Vidyānidhi was in East Bengal in a village near Dacca named Bāghiyā which belonged to the Vārendra group of *brāhmaṇa* families. Sometimes these Vārendra *brāhmaṇas* were at odds with another group known as Rāḍhīya *brāhmaṇas,* and therefore Puṇḍarīka Vidyānidhi's family was ostracized and at that time was not living as a respectable family. Bhaktisiddhānta Sarasvatī informs us that one of the members of this family is living in Vṛndāvana and is named Sarojānanda Gosvāmī. One special characteristic of this family is that each of its members had only one son or no son at all, and therefore the family was not very expansive. There is a place in the district of Caṭṭagrāma in East Bengal that is known as Hāṭahājāri, and a short distance from this place is a village known as Mekhalā-grāma in which Puṇḍarīka Vidyānidhi's forefathers lived. One can approach Mekhalā-grāma from Caṭṭagrāma either on horseback, by bullock cart or by steamer. The steamer station is known as Annapūrṇāra-ghāṭa. The birthplace of Puṇḍarīka Vidyānidhi is about two miles southwest of Annapūrṇāra-ghāṭa. The temple constructed there by Puṇḍarīka Vidyānidhi is now very old and much in need of repair. Without repair, the temple may soon crumble. There are two inscriptions on the bricks of that temple, but they are so old that one cannot read them. There is another temple, however, about 200 yards south of this one, and some people say that this is the old temple constructed by Puṇḍarīka Vidyānidhi.

Śrī Caitanya Mahāprabhu called Puṇḍarīka Vidyānidhi "father," and He gave him the title Premanidhi. Puṇḍarīka Vidyānidhi later became the spiritual master of Gadādhara Paṇḍita and an intimate friend of Svarūpa Dāmodara. Gadādhara Paṇḍita at first misunderstood Puṇḍarīka Vidyānidhi to be an ordinary pounds and shillings man, but later, upon being corrected by Śrī Caitanya Mahāprabhu, he became his disciple. Another incident in the life of Puṇḍarīka Vidyānidhi involves his criticizing the priest of the Jagannātha temple, for which Jagannātha Prabhu chastised him personally by slapping his cheeks. This is described in *Caitanya-bhāgavata, Antya-līlā,* Chapter Seven. Śrī Bhaktisiddhānta Sarasvatī Ṭhākura informs us that there are still two living descendants of the family of Puṇḍarīka Vidyānidhi, who are named Śrī Harakumāra Smṛtitīrtha and Śrī Kṛṣṇakiṅkara Vidyālaṅkāra. For further information one should refer to the dictionary known as *Vaiṣṇava-mañjuṣā.*

TEXT 15

**বড় শাখা,—গদাধর পণ্ডিত-গোসাঞি ।
তেঁহো লক্ষ্মীরূপা, তাঁর সম কেহ নাই ॥ ১৫ ॥**

*baḍa śākhā,—gadādhara paṇḍita-gosāñi
teṅho lakṣmī-rūpā, tāṅra sama keha nāi*

SYNONYMS

baḍa śākhā—big branch; *gadādhara paṇḍita-gosāñi*—the descendants or disciplic succession of Gadādhara Paṇḍita; *teṅho*—Gadādhara Paṇḍita; *lakṣmī-rūpā*—incarnation of the pleasure potency of Lord Kṛṣṇa; *tāṅra*—his; *sama*—equal; *keha*—anyone; *nāi*—there is none.

TRANSLATION

Gadādhara Paṇḍita, the fourth branch, is described as an incarnation of the pleasure potency of Śrī Kṛṣṇa. No one, therefore, can equal him.

PURPORT

In the *Gaura-gaṇoddeśa-dīpikā*, verses 147 through 153, it is stated: "The pleasure potency of Śrī Kṛṣṇa formerly known as Vṛndāvaneśvarī is now personified in the form of Śrī Gadādhara Paṇḍita in the pastimes of Lord Caitanya Mahāprabhu. Śrī Svarūpa Dāmodara Gosvāmī has pointed out that in the shape of Lakṣmī, the pleasure potency of Kṛṣṇa, she was formerly very dear to the Lord as Śyāmasundara-vallabhā. The same Śyāmasundara-vallabhā is now present as Gadādhara Paṇḍita. Formerly, as Lalitā-sakhī, she was always devoted to Śrīmatī Rādhārāṇī. In the Twelfth Chapter of this part of *Caitanya-caritāmṛta* there is a description of the descendants or disciplic succession of Gadādhara Paṇḍita.

TEXT 16

**তাঁর শিষ্য-উপশিষ্য,—তাঁর উপশাখা ।
এইমত সব শাখা-উপশাখার লেখা ॥ ১৬ ॥**

*tāṅra śiṣya-upaśiṣya,—tāṅra upaśākhā
eimata saba śākhā-upaśākhāra lekhā*

SYNONYMS

tāṅra—his; *śiṣya*—disciples; *upaśiṣya*—grand-disciples and admirers; *tāṅra*—his; *upaśākhā*—sub-branches; *eimata*—in this way; *saba*—all; *śākhā*—branches; *upaśākhāra*—sub-branches; *lekhā*—to describe by writing.

TRANSLATION

His disciples and grand-disciples are his sub-branches. To describe them all would be difficult.

TEXT 17

বক্রেশ্বর পণ্ডিত—প্রভুর বড় প্রিয় ভৃত্য ।
এক-ভাবে চব্বিশ প্রহর যাঁর নৃত্য ॥ ১৭ ॥

vakreśvara paṇḍita—prabhura baḍa priya bhṛtya
eka-bhāve cabbiśa prahara yāṅra nṛtya

SYNONYMS

vakreśvara paṇḍita—of the name Vakreśvara Paṇḍita; *prabhura*—of the Lord; *baḍa*—very much; *priya*—dear; *bhṛtya*—servant; *eka-bhāve*—continuously in the same ecstasy; *cabbiśa*—twenty-four; *prahara*—a duration of time comprising three hours; *yāṅra*—whose; *nṛtya*—dancing.

TRANSLATION

Vakreśvara Paṇḍita, the fifth branch of the tree, was a very dear servant of Lord Caitanya's. He could dance with constant ecstasy for seventy-two hours.

PURPORT

In the *Gaura-gaṇoddeśa-dīpikā,* verse 71, it is stated that Vakreśvara Paṇḍita was an incarnation of Aniruddha, one of the quadruple expansions of Viṣṇu (Vāsudeva, Saṅkarṣaṇa, Aniruddha and Pradyumna). He could dance wonderfully for seventy-two continuous hours. When Lord Caitanya Mahāprabhu played in dramatic performances in the house of Śrīvāsa Paṇḍita, Vakreśvara Paṇḍita was one of the chief dancers, and he danced continually for that length of time. Śrī Govinda dāsa, an Oriyā devotee of Lord Caitanya Mahāprabhu, has described the life of Vakreśvara Paṇḍita in his book *Gaura-kṛṣṇodaya.* There are many disciples of Vakreśvara Paṇḍita in Orissa, and they are known as Gauḍīya Vaiṣṇavas although they are Oriyās. Among these disciples are Śrī Gopālaguru and his disciple Śrī Dhyānacandra Gosvāmī.

TEXT 18

আপনে মহাপ্রভু গায় যাঁর নৃত্যকালে ।
প্রভুর চরণ ধরি' বক্রেশ্বর বলে ॥ ১৮ ॥

āpane mahāprabhu gāya yāṅra nṛtya-kāle
prabhura caraṇa dhari' vakreśvara bale

SYNONYMS

āpane—personally; *mahāprabhu*—Śrī Caitanya Mahāprabhu; *gāya*—sang; *yāṅra*—whose; *nṛtya-kāle*—at the time of dancing; *prabhura*—of the Lord; *caraṇa*—lotus feet; *dhari'*—embracing; *vakreśvara*—Vakreśvara Paṇḍita; *bale*—said.

TRANSLATION

Śrī Caitanya Mahāprabhu personally sang while Vakreśvara Paṇḍita danced, and thus Vakreśvara Paṇḍita fell at the lotus feet of the Lord and spoke as follows.

TEXT 19

"দশসহস্র গন্ধর্ব মোরে দেহ' চন্দ্রমুখ ।
তারা গায়, মুঞি নাচোঁ—তবে মোর সুখ ॥" ১৯ ॥

daśa-sahasra gandharva more deha' candramukha
tārā gāya, muñi nācoṅ—tabe mora sukha

SYNONYMS

daśa-sahasra—ten thousand; *gandharva*—residents of Gandharvaloka; *more*—unto me; *deha'*—please deliver; *candramukha*—O moon-faced one; *tārā gāyā*—let them sing; *muñi nācoṅ*—let me dance; *tabe*—then; *mora*—my; *sukha*—happiness.

TRANSLATION

"O Candramukha! Please give me 10,000 Gandharvas. Let them sing as I dance, and then I will be greatly happy."

PURPORT

The Gandharvas, who are residents of Gandharvaloka, are celebrated as celestial singers. Whenever singing is needed in the celestial planets, the Gandharvas are invited to sing. The Gandharvas can sing continuously for days, and therefore Vakreśvara Paṇḍita wanted to dance as they sang.

TEXT 20

প্রভু বলে—তুমি মোর পক্ষ এক শাখা ।
আকাশে উড়িতাম যদি পাঙ আর পাখা ॥ ২০ ॥

prabhu bale—tumi mora pakṣa eka śākhā
ākāśe uḍitāma yadi pāṅ āra pākhā

SYNONYMS

prabhu bale—Lord Śrī Caitanya Mahāprabhu replied; *tumi*—you; *mora*—My; *pakṣa*—wing; *eka*—one; *śākhā*—one-sided; *ākāśe*—in the sky; *uḍitāma*—I could fly; *yadi*—if; *pāṅ*—I could get; *āra*—another; *pākhā*—wing.

TRANSLATION

Lord Caitanya replied: "I have only one wing like you, but if I had another, certainly I would fly in the sky!"

TEXT 21

পণ্ডিত জগদানন্দ প্রভুর প্রাণরূপ ।
লোকে খ্যাত যেঁহো সত্যভামার স্বরূপ ॥ ২১ ॥

paṇḍita jagadānanda prabhura prāṇa-rūpa
loke khyāta yeṅho satyabhāmāra svarūpa

SYNONYMS

paṇḍita jagadānanda—of the name Paṇḍita Jagadānanda; *prabhura*—of the Lord; *praṇa-rūpa*—life and soul; *loke*—in the world; *khyāta*—celebrated; *yeṅho*—who; *satyabhāmāra*—of Satyabhāmā; *svarūpa*—personification.

TRANSLATION

Paṇḍita Jagadānanda, the sixth branch of the Caitanya tree, was celebrated as the life and soul of the Lord. He is known to have been an incarnation of Satyabhāmā [one of the chief queens of Lord Kṛṣṇa].

PURPORT

There are many dealings of Jagadānanda Paṇḍita with Lord Śrī Caitanya Mahāprabhu. Most importantly, he was the Lord's constant companion and especially took part in all the pastimes of the Lord in the houses of Śrīvāsa Paṇḍita and Candraśekhara Ācārya.

TEXT 22

প্রীত্যে করিতে চাহে প্রভুর লালন-পালন ।
বৈরাগ্য-লোক-ভয়ে প্রভু না মানে কখন ॥ ২২ ॥

prītye karite cāhe prabhura lālana-pālana
vairāgya-loka-bhaye prabhu nā māne kakhana

SYNONYMS

prītye—in intimacy or affection; *karite*—to do; *cāhe*—wanted; *prabhura*—the Lord's; *lālana-pālana*—maintenance; *vairāgya*—renouncement; *loka-bhaye*—fearing the public; *prabhu*—the Lord; *nā*—did not; *māne*—accept; *kakhana*—any time.

TRANSLATION

Jagadānanda Paṇḍita [as an incarnation of Satyabhāmā] always wanted to see to the comfort of Lord Caitanya, but since the Lord was a sannyāsī He did not accept the luxuries that Jagadānanda Paṇḍita offered.

TEXT 23

দুইজনে খট্‌মটি লাগায় কোন্দল।
তাঁর প্রীত্যের কথা আগে কহিব সকল ॥ ২৩ ॥

dui-jane khaṭmaṭi lāgāya kondala
tāṅra prītyera kathā āge kahiba sakala

SYNONYMS

dui-jane—two persons; *khaṭmaṭi*—fighting over trifles; *lāgāya*—continued; *kondala*—quarrel; *tāṅra*—his; *prītyera*—affection; *kathā*—narration; *āge*—ahead; *kahiba*—I shall speak; *sakala*—all.

TRANSLATION

They sometimes appeared to fight over trifles, but these quarrels were based on their affection, of which I shall speak later.

TEXT 24

রাঘব-পণ্ডিত—প্রভুর আদ্য-অনুচর।
তাঁর এক শাখা মুখ্য,—মকরধ্বজ কর ॥ ২৪ ॥

rāghava-paṇḍita—prabhura ādya-anucara
tāṅra eka śākhā mukhya—makaradhvaja kara

SYNONYMS

rāghava paṇḍita—of the name Rāghava Paṇḍita; *prabhura*—of the Lord; *ādya*—original; *anucara*—follower; *tāṅra*—his; *eka*—one; *śākhā*—branch; *mukhya*—chief; *makaradhvaja*—of the name Makaradhvaja; *kara*—surname.

TRANSLATION

Rāghava Paṇḍita, Lord Śrī Caitanya Mahāprabhu's original follower, is understood to have been the seventh branch. From him proceeded another sub-branch, headed by Makaradhvaja Kara.

PURPORT

Kara was the surname of Makaradhvaja. At present this surname is generally found in the Kāyastha community. The *Gaura-gaṇoddeśa-dīpikā,* verse 166 states:

dhaniṣṭhā bhakṣya-sāmagrīṁ kṛṣṇāyādād vraje 'mitām
saiva sāmprataṁ gaurāṅga-priyo rāghava-paṇḍitaḥ

Rāghava Paṇḍita was formerly a confidential *gopī* in Vraja during the time of Lord Kṛṣṇa's pastimes, and his former name was Dhaniṣṭhā. This *gopī,* Dhaniṣṭhā, always engaged in preparing foodstuffs for Kṛṣṇa.

TEXT 25

তাঁহার ভগিনী দময়ন্তী প্রভুর প্রিয় দাসী ।
প্রভুর ভোগসামগ্রী যে করে বারমাসি ॥ ২৫ ॥

tāṅhāra bhaginī damayantī prabhura priya dāsī
prabhura bhoga-sāmagrī ye kare vāra-māsi

SYNONYMS

tāṅhāra—his; *bhaginī*—sister; *damayantī*—of the name Damayantī; *prabhura*—of the Lord; *priya*—dear; *dāsī*—maidservant; *prabhura*—of the Lord; *bhoga-sāmagrī*—cooking materials; *ye*—who; *kare*—does; *vāra-māsi*—throughout the whole year.

TRANSLATION

Rāghava Paṇḍita's sister Damayantī was the dear maidservant of the Lord. She always collected various ingredients with which to cook for Lord Caitanya.

PURPORT

In the *Gaura-gaṇoddeśa-dīpikā,* verse 167, it is mentioned, *guṇamālā vraje yāsīd damayantī tu tat-svasā:* "The *gopī* named Guṇamālā has now appeared as his sister Damayantī." On the East Bengal railway line beginning from the Sealdah station in Calcutta, there is a station named Sodapura which is not very far from Calcutta. Within one mile of this station, toward the western side of the Ganges, is a village known as Pāṇihāṭī in which the residential quarters of Rāghava Paṇḍita still exist. On Rāghava Paṇḍita's tomb is a creeper on a concrete platform. There is also a Madana-mohana Deity in a broken-down temple nearby. This temple is managed by a local Zamindar of the name Śrī Śivacandra Rāya Caudhurī. Makaradhvaja Kara was also an inhabitant of Pāṇihāṭī.

TEXT 26

সে সব সামগ্রী যত ঝালিতে ভরিয়া ।
রাঘব লইয়া যা'ন গুপত করিয়া ॥ ২৬ ॥

se saba sāmagrī yata jhālite bhariyā
rāghava la-iyā yā'na gupata kariyā

SYNONYMS

se saba—all those; *sāmagrī*—ingredients; *yata*—all of them; *jhālite bhariyā*—packing in a bag; *rāghava*—Rāghava Paṇḍita; *la-iyā*—carried; *yā'na*—goes; *gupata kariyā*—very confidentially.

TRANSLATION

The foodstuffs Damayantī cooked for Lord Caitanya when He was at Purī were carried in a bag by her brother Rāghava without the knowledge of others.

TEXT 27

বারমাস তাহা প্রভু করেন অঙ্গীকার ।
'রাঘবের ঝালি' বলি' প্রসিদ্ধি যাহার ॥ ২৭ ॥

vāra-māsa tāhā prabhu karena aṅgīkāra
'rāghavera jhāli' bali' prasiddhi yāhāra

SYNONYMS

vāra-māsa—the whole year; *tāhā*—all those foodstuffs; *prabhu*—Lord Śrī Caitanya Mahāprabhu; *karena*—did; *aṅgīkāra*—accept; *rāghavera jhāli* —the bag of Rāghava Paṇḍita; *bali'*—so called; *prasiddhi*—celebrated; *yāhāra*—of which.

TRANSLATION

The Lord accepted these foodstuffs throughout the entire year. That bag is still celebrated as Rāghavera jhāli ["the bag of Rāghava Paṇḍita"].

TEXT 28

সে-সব সামগ্রী আগে করিব বিস্তার ।
যাহার শ্রবণে ভক্তের বহে অশ্রুধার ॥ ২৮ ॥

se-saba sāmagrī āge kariba vistāra
yāhāra śravaṇe bhaktera vahe aśrudhāra

SYNONYMS

se-saba—all these things; *sāmagrī*—ingredients of the foodstuffs; *āge*—further on; *kariba*—I shall describe; *vistāra*—vividly; *yāhāra*—of which; *śravaṇe*—by the hearing; *bhaktera*—of a devotee; *vahe*—flowing; *aśrudhāra*—tears.

TRANSLATION

I shall describe the contents of the bag of Rāghava Paṇḍita later in this book. Hearing this narration, devotees generally cry, and tears glide down from their eyes.

PURPORT

A vivid description of this Rāghavera jhāli is to be found in Chapter Ten of the *Antya-līlā* portion of *Śrī Caitanya-caritāmṛta.*

TEXT 29

প্রভুর অত্যন্ত প্রিয়—পণ্ডিত গঙ্গাদাস ।
যাঁহার স্মরণে হয় সর্ববন্ধ-নাশ ॥ ২৯ ॥

prabhura atyanta priya—paṇḍita gaṅgādāsa
yāṅhāra smaraṇe haya sarva-bandha-nāśa

SYNONYMS

prabhura—of the Lord; *atyanta*—very much; *priya*—dear; *paṇḍita gaṅgādāsa*—of the name Paṇḍita Gaṅgādāsa; *yāṅhāra*—who; *smaraṇe*—by remembering; *haya*—it becomes; *sarva-bandha-nāśa*—freedom from all kinds of bondage.

TRANSLATION

Paṇḍita Gaṅgādāsa was the eighth dear branch of Śrī Caitanya Mahāprabhu. One who remembers his activities attains freedom from all bondage.

TEXT 30

চৈতন্য-পার্ষদ —শ্রীআচার্য পুরন্দর ।
পিতা করি' যাঁরে বলে গৌরাঙ্গসুন্দর ॥ ৩০ ॥

caitanya-pārṣada—śrī-ācārya purandara
pitā kari' yāṅre bale gaurāṅga-sundara

SYNONYMS

caitanya-pārṣada—associate of Lord Caitanya; *śrī-ācārya purandara*—of the name Śrī Ācārya Purandara; *pitā*—father; *kari'*—taking him; *yāṅre*—whom; *bale*—says; *gaurāṅga-sundara*—Lord Caitanya Mahāprabhu.

TRANSLATION

Śrī Ācārya Purandara, the ninth branch, was a constant associate of Lord Caitanya. The Lord accepted him as His father.

PURPORT

It is described in the *Caitanya-bhāgavata* that whenever Lord Caitanya Mahāprabhu visited the house of Rāghava Paṇḍita, He also visited Purandara Ācārya immediately upon receiving an invitation. Purandara Ācārya is to be considered most fortunate because the Lord used to greet him by addressing him as His father and embracing him in great love.

TEXT 31

দামোদরপণ্ডিত শাখা প্রেমেতে প্রচণ্ড ।
প্রভুর উপরে যেঁহো কৈল বাক্যদণ্ড ॥ ৩১ ॥

dāmodara-paṇḍita śākhā premete pracaṇḍa
prabhura upare yeṅho kaila vākya-daṇḍa

SYNONYMS

dāmodara-paṇḍita—of the name Dāmodara Paṇḍita; *śākhā*—another branch (the tenth branch); *premete*—in affection; *pracaṇḍa*—very much advanced; *prabhura*—the Lord; *upare*—upon; *yeṅho*—he who; *kaila*—did; *vākya-daṇḍa*—chastisement by speaking.

TRANSLATION

Dāmodara Paṇḍita, the tenth branch of the Caitanya tree, was so elevated in love of Lord Caitanya that he once unhesitatingly chastised the Lord with strong words.

TEXT 32

দণ্ড-কথা কহিব আগে বিস্তার করিয়া ।
দণ্ডে তুষ্ট প্রভু তাঁরে পাঠাইলা নদীয়া ॥ ৩২ ॥

daṇḍa-kathā kahiba āge vistāra kariyā
daṇḍe tuṣṭa prabhu tāṅre pāṭhāilā nadīyā

SYNONYMS

daṇḍa-kathā—the narration of such chastisement; *kahiba*—I shall speak; *āge*—ahead; *vistāra*—detailed description; *kariyā*—making; *daṇḍe*—in the matter of chastisement; *tuṣṭa prabhu*—the Lord is very much satisfied; *tāṅre*—him; *pāṭhāilā*—sent back; *nadīyā*—Nadia (a district in Bengal).

TRANSLATION

I shall describe in detail this incident of chastisement later in Caitanya-caritāmṛta. The Lord, being very much satisfied by this chastisement, sent Dāmodara Paṇḍita to Navadvīpa.

PURPORT

Dāmodara Paṇḍita, who was formerly known as Śaibyā in Vrajadhāma, used to carry messages from Lord Caitanya to Śacīmātā, and during the Rathayātrā festival he carried messages from Śacīmātā to Lord Caitanya Mahāprabhu.

TEXT 33

তাঁহার অনুজ শাখা - শঙ্করপণ্ডিত ।
'প্রভু-পাদোপাধান' যাঁর নাম বিদিত ॥ ৩৩ ॥

tāṅhāra anuja śākhā—śaṅkara-paṇḍita
'prabhu-pādopādhāna' yāṅra nāma vidita

SYNONYMS

tāṅhāra—his (Dāmodara Paṇḍita's); *anuja*—younger brother; *śākhā*—the eleventh branch; *śaṅkara-paṇḍita*—of the name Śaṅkara Paṇḍita; *prabhu*—the Lord's; *pāda-upādhāna*—shoes; *yāṅra*—whose; *nāma*—name; *vidita*—celebrated.

TRANSLATION

The eleventh branch, the younger brother of Dāmodara Paṇḍita, was known as Śaṅkara Paṇḍita. He was celebrated as the shoes of the Lord.

TEXT 34

সদাশিবপণ্ডিত যাঁর প্রভুপদে আশ ।
প্রথমেই নিত্যানন্দের যাঁর ঘরে বাস ॥ ৩৪ ॥

sadāśiva-paṇḍita yāṅra prabhu-pade āśa
prathamei nityānandera yāṅra ghare vāsa

SYNONYMS

sadāśiva-paṇḍita—of the name Sadāśiva Paṇḍita; *yāṅra*—whose; *prabhu-pade*—unto the lotus feet of the Lord; *āśa*—constant desire; *prathamei*—in the beginning; *nityānandera*—of Lord Nityānanda; *yāṅra*—of whom; *ghare*—in the home; *vāsa*—residence.

TRANSLATION

Sadāśiva Paṇḍita, the twelfth branch, was always anxious to serve the lotus feet of the Lord. It was his good fortune that when Lord Nityānanda came to Navadvīpa He resided at his house.

PURPORT

It is mentioned in the *Caitanya-bhāgavata, Antya-līlā,* Chapter Nine, that Sadāśiva Paṇḍita was a pure devotee and that Nityānanda Prabhu resided at his house.

TEXT 35

শ্রীনৃসিংহ-উপাসক – প্রদ্যুম্ন ব্রহ্মচারী ।
প্রভু তাঁর নাম কৈলা 'নৃসিংহানন্দ' করি' ॥ ৩৫ ॥

śrī-nṛsiṁha-upāsaka—pradyumna brahmacārī
prabhu tāṅra nāma kailā 'nṛsiṁhānanda' kari'

SYNONYMS

śrī-nṛsiṁha-upāsaka—the worshiper of Lord Nṛsiṁhadeva; *pradyumna brahmacārī*—of the name Pradyumna Brahmacārī; *prabhu*—the Lord; *tāṅra*—his; *nāma*—name; *kailā*—turned into; *nṛsiṁhānanda*—of the name Nṛsiṁhānanda; *kari'*—by such a name.

TRANSLATION

The thirteenth branch was Pradyumna Brahmacārī. Since he was a worshiper of Lord Nṛsiṁhadeva, Śrī Caitanya Mahāprabhu changed his name to Nṛsiṁhānanda Brahmacārī.

PURPORT

Pradyumna Brahmacārī is described in the *Antya-līlā,* Second Chapter, of *Śrī Caitanya-caritāmṛta.* He was a great devotee of Lord Caitanya, who changed his name to Nṛsiṁhānanda. While coming from the house of Rāghava Paṇḍita at Pāṇihāṭī to the house of Śivānanda, Lord Caitanya Mahāprabhu appeared in the heart of Nṛsiṁhānanda Brahmacārī. To acknowledge this, Nṛsiṁhānanda Brahmacārī used to accept as eatables the foodstuffs of three Deities, namely, Jagannātha, Nṛsiṁhadeva and Lord Caitanya Mahāprabhu. This is stated in the *Caitanya-caritāmṛta, Antya-līlā,* Second Chapter, verses 48 through 78. Upon receiving information that Lord Caitanya Mahāprabhu was proceeding toward Vṛndāvana from Kuliā, Nṛsiṁhānanda absorbed himself in meditation and by his mental activities constructed a very nice road from Kuliā to Vṛndāvana. All of a sudden, however, he broke his meditation and told the other devotees that this time Lord Caitanya Mahāprabhu would not go to Vṛndāvana but only as far as the place known as Kānāi's Nāṭaśālā. This is described in the *Madhya-līlā,* Chapter One, verses 55 through 62. The *Gaura-gaṇoddeśa-dīpikā,* verse 74, says, *āveśaś ca tathā jñeyo miśre pradyumna-saṁjñake:* Śrī Caitanya Mahāprabhu changed the name of Pradyumna Miśra, or Pradyumna Brahmacārī, to Nṛsiṁhānanda Brahmacārī, for in his heart Lord Nṛsiṁhadeva was manifest. It is said that Lord Nṛsiṁhadeva used to talk with him directly.

TEXT 36

নারায়ণ-পণ্ডিত এক বড়ই উদার ।
চৈতন্যচরণ বিনু নাহি জানে আর ॥ ৩৬ ॥

nārāyaṇa-paṇḍita eka baḍai udāra
caitanya-caraṇa vinu nāhi jāne āra

SYNONYMS

nārāyaṇa-paṇḍita—of the name Nārāyaṇa Paṇḍita; *eka*—one; *baḍai*—very much; *udāra*—liberal; *caitanya-caraṇa*—the lotus feet of Lord Caitanya; *vinu*—except; *nāhi*—not; *jāne*—know; *āra*—anything else.

TRANSLATION

Nārāyaṇa Paṇḍita, the fourteenth branch, a great and liberal devotee, did not know any shelter but Lord Caitanya's lotus feet.

PURPORT

Nārāyaṇa Paṇḍita was one of the associates of Śrīvāsa Ṭhākura. It is mentioned in *Caitanya-bhāgavata,* Ninth Chapter, verse 93, that he went to see Śrī Caitanya Mahāprabhu at Jagannātha Purī with Śrīvāsa Ṭhākura's brother Śrī Rāma Paṇḍita.

TEXT 37

শ্রীমান্‌পণ্ডিত শাখা—প্রভুর নিজ ভৃত্য ।
দেউটি ধরেন, যবে প্রভু করেন নৃত্য ॥ ৩৭ ॥

śrīmān-paṇḍita śākhā—prabhura nija bhṛtya
deuṭi dharena, yabe prabhu karena nṛtya

SYNONYMS

śrīmān-paṇḍita—of the name Śrīmān Paṇḍita; *śākhā*—branch; *prabhura*—of the Lord; *nija*—own; *bhṛtya*—servant; *deuṭi*—torchlight; *dharena*—carries; *yabe*—while; *prabhu*—Lord Caitanya; *karena*—does; *nṛtya*—dance.

TRANSLATION

The fifteenth branch was Śrīmān Paṇḍita, who was a constant servitor of Lord Caitanya Mahāprabhu. He used to carry a torch while the Lord danced.

PURPORT

Śrīmān Paṇḍita was among the companions of Lord Caitanya Mahāprabhu when the Lord performed *saṅkīrtana.* When Lord Caitanya dressed Himself in the form of the goddess Lakṣmī and danced in the streets of Navadvīpa, Śrīmān Paṇḍita carried a torch to light the way.

TEXT 38

শুক্লাম্বর-ব্রহ্মচারী বড় ভাগ্যবান্ ।
যাঁর অন্ন মাগি' কাড়ি' খাইলা ভগবান্ ॥ ৩৮ ॥

śuklāmbara-brahmacārī baḍa bhāgyavān
yāṅra anna māgi' kāḍi' khāilā bhagavān

SYNONYMS

śuklāmbara-brahmacārī—of the name Śuklāmbara Brahmacārī; *baḍa*—very much; *bhāgyavān*—fortunate; *yāṅra*—whose; *anna*—foodstuff; *māgi'*—begging; *kāḍi'*—snatching; *khāilā*—ate; *bhagavān*—the Supreme Personality of Godhead.

TRANSLATION

The sixteenth branch, Śuklāmbara Brahmacārī, was very fortunate because Lord Caitanya Mahāprabhu jokingly or seriously begged food from him or sometimes snatched it from him forcibly and ate it.

PURPORT

It is stated that Śuklāmbara Brahmacārī, an inhabitant of Navadvīpa, was Lord Caitanya Mahāprabhu's first companion in the *saṅkīrtana* movement. When Lord Caitanya returned from Gayā after initiation, He stayed with Śuklāmbara Brahmacārī because He wanted to hear from this devotee about the pastimes of Lord Kṛṣṇa. Śuklāmbara Brahmacārī collected alms of rice from the inhabitants of Navadvīpa, and Śrī Caitanya Mahāprabhu took pleasure in eating the rice that he cooked. It is said that Śuklāmbara Brahmacārī was one of the wives of the yajñic *brāhmaṇas* during the time of Lord Kṛṣṇa's pastimes in Vṛndāvana. Lord Kṛṣṇa begged foodstuffs from the wives of the yajñic *brāhmaṇas,* and Lord Caitanya Mahāprabhu performed a similar pastime by begging rice from Śuklāmbara Brahmacārī.

TEXT 39

নন্দন-আচার্য-শাখা জগতে বিদিত ।
লুকাইয়া দুই প্রভুর যাঁর ঘরে স্থিত ॥ ৩৯ ॥

nandana-ācārya-śākhā jagate vidita
lukāiyā dui prabhura yāṅra ghare sthita

SYNONYMS

nandana-ācārya—of the name Nandana Ācārya; *śākhā*—the seventeenth branch; *jagate*—in the world; *vidita*—celebrated; *lukāiyā*—hiding; *dui*—two; *prabhura*—of the Lords; *yāṅra*—of whom; *ghare*—in the house; *sthita*—situated.

TRANSLATION

Nandana Ācārya, the seventeenth branch of the Caitanya tree, is celebrated within the world because the two Prabhus [Lord Caitanya and Nityānanda] sometimes hid in his house.

PURPORT

Nandana Ācārya was another companion of Lord Caitanya Mahāprabhu during His *kīrtana* pastimes in Navadvīpa. Śrīla Nityānanda Prabhu, as Avadhūta, traveled on many pilgrimages, and when He first came to Śrī Navadvīpa-dhāma He remained hidden in the house of Nandana Ācārya. It is there that He first met all the devotees of Lord Caitanya Mahāprabhu. When Caitanya Mahāprabhu exhibited His *mahā-prakāśa,* He asked Rāmāi Paṇḍita to call Advaita Prabhu, who was hiding in the home of Nandana Ācārya, for Śrī Caitanya Mahāprabhu could understand that He was hiding. Similarly, Lord Caitanya also sometimes hid in the home of Nandana Ācārya. In this connection one may refer to *Caitanya-bhāgavata, Madhya-līlā,* Chapters Six and Seventeen.

TEXT 40

শ্রীমুকুন্দ-দত্ত শাখা - প্রভুর সমাধ্যায়ী ।
যাঁহার কীর্তনে নাচে চৈতন্য-গোসাঞি ॥ ৪০ ॥

śrī-mukunda-datta śākhā—prabhura samādhyāyī
yāṅhāra kīrtane nāce caitanya-gosāñi

SYNONYMS

śrī-mukunda-datta—of the name Śrī Mukunda Datta; *śākhā*—another branch; *prabhura*—of Lord Śrī Caitanya Mahāprabhu; *samādhyāyī*—class friend; *yāṅhāra*—whose; *kīrtane*—in *saṅkīrtana; nāce*—dances; *caitanya-gosāñi*—Śrī Caitanya Mahāprabhu.

TRANSLATION

Mukunda Datta, a class friend of Lord Caitanya's, was another branch of the Caitanya tree. Lord Caitanya danced while he sang.

PURPORT

Śrī Mukunda Datta was born in the Caṭṭagrāma district in the village of Chanhorā, which is under the jurisdiction of the police station named Paṭiyā. This village is situated ten *krośas,* or about twenty miles, from the home of Puṇḍarīka Vidyānidhi. In the *Gaura-gaṇoddeśa-dīpikā* (140) it is said:

vraje sthitau gāyakau yau madhukaṇṭha-madhuvratau
mukunda-vāsudevau tau dattau gaurāṅga-gāyakau

"In Vraja there were two very nice singers named Madhukaṇṭha and Madhuvrata. They appeared in *caitanya-līlā* as Mukunda and Vāsudeva Datta, who were singers in the society of Lord Caitanya Mahāprabhu." When Lord Caitanya was a student, Mukunda Datta was His class friend, and they frequently engaged in logical arguments. Sometimes Lord Caitanya Mahāprabhu would fight with Mukunda Datta, using tricks of logic. This is described in *Caitanya-bhāgavata, Ādi-līlā,* Chapters Seven and Eight. When Lord Caitanya Mahāprabhu returned from Gayā, Mukunda Datta gave Him pleasure by reciting verses from *Śrīmad-Bhāgavatam* about *kṛṣṇa-līlā.* It was by his endeavor that Gadādhara Paṇḍita Gosvāmī became a disciple of Puṇḍarīka Vidyānidhi, as stated in *Madhya-līlā,* Chapter Seven. When Mukunda Datta sang in the courtyard of Śrīvāsa Prabhu, Mahāprabhu danced with His singing, and when Lord Caitanya for twenty-one hours exhibited an ecstatic manifestation known as *sāta-prahariyā,* Mukunda Datta inaugurated the function by singing.

Sometimes Lord Caitanya Mahāprabhu chastised Mukunda Datta by calling him *kharjhatia beta* because he attended many functions held by different classes of non-devotees. This is stated in *Caitanya-bhāgavata, Madhya-līlā,* Chapter Ten. When Lord Caitanya Mahāprabhu dressed Himself as the goddess of fortune to dance in the house of Candraśekhara, Mukunda Datta began the first song.

Before disclosing His desire to take the renounced order of life, Lord Caitanya first went to the house of Mukunda Datta, but at that time Mukunda Datta requested Lord Caitanya Mahāprabhu to continue His *saṅkīrtana* movement for a few days more before taking *sannyāsa.* This is stated in *Caitanya-bhāgavata, Madhya-līlā,* Chapter Twenty-five. The information of Lord Caitanya's accepting the renounced order was made known to Gadādhara Paṇḍita, Candraśekhara Ācārya and Mukunda Datta by Nityānanda Prabhu, and therefore all of them went to Katwa and arranged for *kīrtana* and all the paraphernalia for Lord Caitanya's acceptance of *sannyāsa.* After the Lord took *sannyāsa,* they all followed Him, especially Śrī Nityānanda Prabhu, Gadādhara Prabhu and Govinda, who followed Him all the way to Puruṣottama-kṣetra. In this connection one may refer to *Antya-līlā,* Chapter Two. In the place known as Jaleśvara, Nityānanda Prabhu broke the *sannyāsa* rod of Caitanya Mahāprabhu. Mukunda Datta was also present at that time. He went every year from Bengal to see Lord Caitanya at Jagannātha Purī.

TEXT 41

বাসুদেব দত্ত—প্রভুর ভৃত্য মহাশয় ।
সহস্র-মুখে যাঁর গুণ কহিলে না হয় ॥ ৪১ ॥

vāsudeva datta—prabhura bhṛtya mahāśaya
sahasra-mukhe yāṅra guṇa kahile nā haya

SYNONYMS

vāsudeva datta—of the name Vāsudeva Datta; *prabhura*—of Lord Śrī Caitanya Mahāprabhu; *bhṛtya*—servant; *mahāśaya*—great personality; *sahasra-mukhe*—with thousands of mouths; *yāṅra*—whose; *guṇa*—qualities; *kahile*—describing; *nā*—never; *haya*—becomes fulfilled.

TRANSLATION

Vāsudeva Datta, the nineteenth branch of the Śrī Caitanya tree, was a great personality and a most confidential devotee of the Lord. One could not describe his qualities even with thousands of mouths.

PURPORT

Vāsudeva Datta, the brother of Mukunda Datta, was also a resident of Caṭṭagrāma. In the *Caitanya-bhāgavata* it is said, *yāṅra sthāne kṛṣṇa haya āpane vikraya:* Vāsudeva Datta was such a powerful devotee that Kṛṣṇa was purchased by him. Vāsudeva Datta stayed at Śrīvāsa Paṇḍita's house, and in *Caitanya-bhāgavata* it is described that Lord Caitanya Mahāprabhu was so pleased with Vāsudeva Datta and so affectionate toward him that He used to say, "I am only Vāsudeva Datta's man. My body is only meant to please Vāsudeva Datta, and he can sell Me anywhere." Thrice He vowed that this was a fact and that no one should disbelieve these statements. "All My dear devotees," He said, "I tell you the truth. My body is especially meant for Vāsudeva Datta." Vāsudeva Datta initiated Śrī Yadunandana Ācārya, the spiritual master of Raghunātha dāsa, who later became Raghunātha dāsa Gosvāmī. This will be found in the *Antya-līlā,* Sixth Chapter, verse 161. Vāsudeva Datta spent money very liberally; therefore Lord Caitanya Mahāprabhu asked Śivānanda Sen to become his *sarakhela,* or secretary, in order to control his extravagant expenses. Vāsudeva Datta was so kind to the living entities that he wanted to take all their sinful reactions so that they might be delivered by Śrī Caitanya Mahāprabhu. This is described in the Fifteenth Chapter of *Ādi-līlā,* verses 159 through 180.

There is a railway station named Pūrvasthalī near the Navadvīpa railway station, and about one mile away, in a village known as Māmagāchi, which is the birthplace of Vṛndāvana dāsa Ṭhākura, there is presently a temple of Madana-gopāla that was established by Vāsudeva Datta. The Gauḍīya Maṭha devotees have now taken charge of this temple, and the *sevā-pūjā* is going on very nicely. Every year all the pilgrims on the *navadvīpa-parikramā* visit Māmagāchi. Since Śrī Bhaktisiddhānta Sarasvatī Ṭhākura inaugurated the *navadvīpa-parikramā* function, the temple has been very well managed.

TEXT 42

জগতে যতেক জীব, তার পাপ লঞা ।
নরক ভুঞ্জিতে চাহে জীব ছাড়াইয়া ॥ ৪২ ॥

jagate yateka jīva, tāra pāpa lañā
naraka bhuñjite cāhe jīva chāḍāiyā

SYNONYMS

jagate—in the world; *yateka*—all; *jīva*—living entities; *tāra*—their; *pāpa*—sinful activities; *lañā*—taking; *naraka*—hell; *bhuñjite*—to suffer; *cāhe*—wanted; *jīva*—the living entities; *chāḍāiyā*—liberating them.

TRANSLATION

Śrīla Vāsudeva Datta Ṭhākura wanted to suffer for the sinful activities of all the people of the world so that Lord Caitanya Mahāprabhu might deliver them.

TEXT 43

হরিদাসঠাকুর শাখার অদ্ভুত চরিত ।
তিন লক্ষ নাম তেঁহো লয়েন অপতিত ॥ ৪৩ ॥

haridāsa-ṭhākura śākhāra adbhuta carita
tina lakṣa nāma teṅho layena apatita

SYNONYMS

haridāsa-ṭhākura—of the name Haridāsa Ṭhākura; *śākhāra*—of the branch; *adbhuta*—wonderful; *carita*—characteristics; *tina*—three; *lakṣa*—hundred thousand; *nāma*—names; *teṅho*—he; *layena*—chanted; *apatita*—without fail.

TRANSLATION

The twentieth branch of the Caitanya tree was Haridāsa Ṭhākura. His character was wonderful. He used to chant the holy name of Kṛṣṇa 300,000 times a day without fail.

PURPORT

Certainly the chanting of 300,000 holy names of the Lord is wonderful. No ordinary person can chant so many names, nor should one artificially imitate Haridāsa Ṭhākura's behavior. It is essential, however, that everyone fulfill a specific vow to chant the Hare Kṛṣṇa *mantra.* Therefore we have prescribed in our society that all our students must chant at least sixteen rounds daily. Such chanting must be offenseless in order to be of high quality. Mechanical chanting is not as powerful as chanting of the holy name without offenses. It is stated in the *Caitanya-bhāgavata, Ādi-līlā,* Chapter Two, that Haridāsa Ṭhākura was born in a village known as Buḍhana but after some time came to live on the bank of the Ganges at Fuliā near Śāntipura. From the description of his chastisement by a Muslim magistrate, which is found in the Eleventh Chapter of the *Ādi-līlā* of *Caitanya-bhāgavata,* we can understand how humble and meek Haridāsa Ṭhākura was and how he achieved the causeless mercy of the Lord. In the dramas performed by Lord Caitanya Mahāprabhu, Haridāsa Ṭhākura played the part of a police chief. While chanting the Hare Kṛṣṇa *mahā-mantra* in Benāpola, he was personally tested by Māyādevī herself. Haridāsa Ṭhākura's passing away is described in the *Antya-līlā* of *Caitanya-caritāmṛta,* Eleventh Chapter. It is not definitely certain whether Śrī Haridāsa Ṭhākura appeared in the village named Buḍhana that is in the district of Khulanā. Formerly this village was within a district of twenty-four *pargaṇas* within the Sātakṣīrā division.

TEXT 44

তাঁহার অনন্ত গুণ,—কহি দিঙ্মাত্র।
আচার্য গোসাঞি যাঁরে ভুঞ্জায় শ্রাদ্ধপাত্র ॥ ৪৪ ॥

tāṅhāra ananta guṇa—kahi diṅmātra
ācārya gosāñi yāṅre bhuñjāya śrāddha-pātra

SYNONYMS

tāṅhāra—Haridāsa Ṭhākura's; *ananta*—unlimited; *guṇa*—qualities; *kahi*—I speak; *diṅmātra*—only a small part; *ācārya gosāñi*—Śrī Advaita Ācārya Prabhu; *yāṅre*—to whom; *bhuñjāya*—offered to eat; *śrāddha-pātra*—*prasāda* offered to Lord Viṣṇu.

TRANSLATION

There was no end to the transcendental qualities of Haridāsa Ṭhākura. Here I mention but a fraction of his qualities. He was so exalted that Advaita Gosvāmī, when performing the śrāddha ceremony of his father, offered him the first plate.

TEXT 45

প্রহ্লাদ-সমান তাঁর গুণের তরঙ্গ ।
যবন-তাড়নেও যাঁর নাহিক ভ্রূভঙ্গ ॥ ৪৫ ॥

prahlāda-samāna tāṅra guṇera taraṅga
yavana-tāḍaneo yāṅra nāhika bhrū-bhaṅga

SYNONYMS

prahlāda-samāna—exactly like Prahlāda Mahārāja; *tāṅra*—his; *guṇera*—qualities; *taraṅga*—waves; *yavana*—of the Mohammedans; *tāḍaneo*—even by the persecution; *yāṅra*—whose; *nāhika*—there was none; *bhrū-bhaṅga*—even the slightest agitation of an eyebrow.

TRANSLATION

The waves of his good qualities were like those of Prahlāda Mahārāja. He did not even slightly raise an eyebrow when persecuted by the Mohammedan ruler.

TEXT 46

তেঁহো সিদ্ধি পাইলে তাঁর দেহ লঞা কোলে ।
নাচিল চৈতন্যপ্রভু মহাকুতূহলে ॥ ৪৬ ॥

teṅho siddhi pāile tāṅra deha lañā kole
nācila caitanya-prabhu mahā-kutūhale

SYNONYMS

teṅho—he; *siddhi*—perfection; *pāile*—after achieving; *tāṅra*—his; *deha*—body; *lañā*—taking; *kole*—on the lap; *nācila*—danced; *caitanya-prabhu*—Lord Śrī Caitanya Mahāprabhu; *mahā-kutūhale*—in great ecstasy.

TRANSLATION

After the passing away of Haridāsa Ṭhākura, the Lord Himself took his body on His lap, and He danced with it in great ecstasy.

TEXT 47

তাঁর লীলা বর্ণিয়াছেন বৃন্দাবনদাস ।
যেবা অবশিষ্ট, আগে করিব প্রকাশ ॥ ৪৭ ॥

tāṅra līlā varṇiyāchena vṛndāvana-dāsa
yebā avaśiṣṭa, āge kariba prakāśa

SYNONYMS

tāṅra—his; *līlā*—pastimes; *varṇiyāchena*—described; *vṛndāvana-dāsa*—Śrīla Vṛndāvana dāsa Ṭhākura; *yebā*—whatever; *avaśiṣṭa*—remained undescribed; *āge*—later in the book; *kariba*—I shall make; *prakāśa*—manifest.

TRANSLATION

Srīla Vṛndāvana dāsa Ṭhākura vividly described the pastimes of Haridāsa Ṭhākura in his Caitanya-bhāgavata. Whatever has remained undescribed I shall try to explain later in this book.

TEXT 48

তাঁর উপশাখা,— যত কুলীনগ্রামী জন ।
সত্যরাজ-আদি – তাঁর কৃপার ভাজন ॥ ৪৮ ॥

tāṅra upaśākhā—yata kulīna-grāmī jana
satyarāja-ādi—tāṅra kṛpāra bhājana

SYNONYMS

tāṅra upaśākhā—his sub-branch; *yata*—all; *kulīna-grāmī jana*—the inhabitants of Kulīna-grāma; *satyarāja*—of the name Satyarāja; *ādi*—heading the list; *tāṅra*—his; *kṛpāra*—of mercy; *bhājana*—recipient.

TRANSLATION

One sub-branch of Haridāsa Ṭhākura consisted of the residents of Kulīna-grāma. The most important among them was Satyarāja Khāna, or Satyarāja Vasu, who was a recipient of all the mercy of Haridāsa Ṭhākura.

PURPORT

Satyarāja Khāna was the son of Guṇarāja Khāna and father of Rāmānanda Vasu. Haridāsa Ṭhākura lived for some time during the Cāturmāsya period in the village named Kulīna-grāma, where he chanted the holy name, the Hare Kṛṣṇa *mahā-mantra,* and distributed his mercy to the descendants of the Vasu family. Satyarāja Khāna was allotted the service of supplying silk ropes for the Jagannātha Deity during the

Rathayātrā festival. The answers to his inquiries from Śrī Caitanya Mahāprabhu about the duty of householder devotees are vividly described in the *Madhya-līlā,* Chapters Fifteen and Sixteen. The village of Kulīna-grāma is situated two miles from the railway station named Jaugrāma on the Newcord line from Howrah to Burdwan. Lord Caitanya Mahāprabhu very highly praised the people of Kulīna-grāma, and He stated that even a dog of Kulīna-grāma was very dear to Him.

TEXT 49

শ্রীমুরারি গুপ্ত শাখা -প্রেমের ভাণ্ডার ।
প্রভুর হৃদয় দ্রবে শুনি' দৈন্য যাঁর ॥ ৪৯ ॥

śrī-murāri gupta śākhā—premera bhāṇḍāra
prabhura hṛdaya drave śuni' dainya yāṅra

SYNONYMS

śrī-murāri gupta—of the name Śrī Murāri Gupta; *śākhā*—branch; *premera*—of love of Godhead; *bhāṇḍāra*—store; *prabhura*—of the Lord; *hṛdaya*—the heart; *drave*—melts; *śuni'*—hearing; *dainya*—humility; *yāṅra*—of whom.

TRANSLATION

Murāri Gupta, the twenty-first branch of the tree of Śrī Caitanya Mahāprabhu, was a storehouse of love of Godhead. His great humility and meekness melted the heart of Lord Caitanya.

PURPORT

Śrī Murāri Gupta wrote a book called *Śrī Caitanya-carita.* He belonged to a *vaidya* physician family of Śrīhaṭṭa, the paternal home of Lord Caitanya, and later became a resident of Navadvīpa. He was among the elders of Śrī Caitanya Mahāprabhu. Lord Caitanya exhibited His Varāha form in the house of Murāri Gupta, as described in the *Caitanya-bhāgavata, Madhya-līlā,* Third Chapter. When Śrī Caitanya Mahāprabhu exhibited His *mahāprakāśa* form, He appeared before Murāri Gupta as Lord Rāmacandra. When Śrī Caitanya Mahāprabhu and Nityānanda Prabhu were sitting together in the house of Śrīvāsa Ṭhākura, Murāri Gupta first offered his respects to Lord Caitanya and then to Śrī Nityānanda Prabhu. Nityānanda Prabhu, however, was older than Caitanya Mahāprabhu, and therefore Lord Caitanya remarked that Murāri Gupta had violated social etiquette, for he should have first shown respect to Nityānanda Prabhu and then to Him. In this way, by the grace of Śrī Caitanya Mahāprabhu, Murāri Gupta was informed about the position of Śrī Nityānanda Prabhu, and the next day he offered obeisances first to Lord Nityānanda and then to Lord Caitanya. Śrī Caitanya Mahāprabhu gave chewed pan or betel nut to Murāri Gupta. Once Murāri Gupta offered foodstuffs to Lord Caitanya that were cooked with excessive ghee, and the next day the Lord became sick and went to Murāri Gupta for treatment. Lord Caitanya accepted some water from the water pot of

Murāri Gupta, and thus He was cured. The natural remedy for indigestion is to drink a little water, and since Murāri Gupta was a physician, he gave the Lord some drinking water and cured Him. When Caitanya Mahāprabhu appeared in the house of Śrīvāsa Ṭhākura in His Caturbhuja *mūrti*, Murāri Gupta became His carrier in the form of Garuḍa, and in these pastimes of ecstasy the Lord then got up on his back. It was the desire of Murāri Gupta to leave his body before the disappearance of Caitanya Mahāprabhu, but the Lord forbade him to do so. This is described in *Caitanya-bhāgavata, Madhya-līlā,* Chapter Twenty. When Śrī Caitanya Mahāprabhu one day appeared in ecstasy as the Varāha *mūrti*, Murāri Gupta offered Him prayers. He was a great devotee of Lord Rāmacandra, and his staunch devotion is vividly described in the *Madhya-līlā,* Fifteenth Chapter, verses 137 through 157.

TEXT 50

প্রতিগ্রহ নাহি করে, না লয় কার ধন ।
আত্মবৃত্তি করি' করে কুটুম্ব ভরণ ॥ ৫০ ॥

pratigraha nāhi kare, nā laya kāra dhana
ātma-vṛtti kari' kare kuṭumba bharaṇa

SYNONYMS

pratigraha nāhi kare—he did not accept charity from anyone; *nā*—not; *laya*—take; *kāra*—anyone's; *dhana*—wealth; *ātma-vṛtti*—own profession; *kari'*—executing; *kare*—maintained; *kuṭumba*—family; *bharaṇa*—provision.

TRANSLATION

Śrīla Murāri Gupta never accepted charity from friends, nor did he accept money from anyone. He practiced as a physician and maintained his family with his earnings.

PURPORT

It should be noted that a *gṛhastha* (householder) must not make his livelihood by begging from anyone. Every householder of the higher castes should engage himself in his own occupational duty as a *brāhmaṇa, kṣatriya* or *vaiśya,* but he should not engage in the service of others, for this is the duty of a *śūdra.* One should simply accept whatever he earns by his own profession. The engagements of a *brāhmaṇa* are *yajana, yājana, paṭhana, pāṭhana, dāna* and *pratigraha.* A *brāhmaṇa* should be a worshiper of Viṣṇu, and he should also instruct others how to worship Him. A *kṣatriya* can become a landholder and earn his livelihood by levying taxes or collecting rent from tenants. A *vaiśya* can accept agriculture or general trade as an occupational duty. Since Murāri Gupta was born in a physician's family *(vaidya-vaṁśa),* he practiced as a physician, and with whatever income he earned he maintained his family. As stated in *Śrīmad-Bhāgavatam,* everyone should execute his occupational duty, and thus he should satisfy the Supreme Personality of Godhead. That is the perfection of life. This system is called *daiva-varṇāśrama.* Murāri Gupta was an ideal *gṛhastha,* for he was a great devotee of Lord Rāmacandra and Caitanya Mahāprabhu. By practicing as a physician he maintained his family and at the same time satisfied Lord Caitanya to the best of his ability. This is the ideal of householder life.

TEXT 51

চিকিৎসা করেন যারে হইয়া সদয় ।
দেহরোগ ভবরোগ,—দুই তার ক্ষয় ॥ ৫১ ॥

cikitsā karena yāre ha-iyā sadaya
deha-roga bhava-roga,—dui tāra kṣaya

SYNONYMS

cikitsā—medical treatment; *karena*—did; *yāre*—upon whom; *ha-iyā*—becoming; *sadaya*—merciful; *deha-roga*—the disease of the body; *bhava-roga*—the disease of material existence; *dui*—both; *tāra*—his; *kṣaya*—diminished.

TRANSLATION

As Murāri Gupta treated his patients, by his mercy both their bodily and spiritual diseases subsided.

PURPORT

Murāri Gupta could treat both bodily and spiritual disease because he was a physician by profession and a great devotee of the Lord in terms of spiritual advancement. This is an example of service to humanity. Everyone should know that there are two kinds of diseases in human society. One disease, which is called *adhyātmika,* or material disease, pertains to the body, but the main disease is spiritual. The living entity is eternal, but somehow or other, when in contact with the material energy, he is subjected to the repetition of birth, death, old age and disease. The physicians of the modern day should learn from Murāri Gupta. Although modern philanthropic physicians open gigantic hospitals, there are no hospitals to cure the material disease of the spirit soul. The Kṛṣṇa consciousness movement has taken up the mission of curing this disease, but people are not very appreciative because they do not know what this disease is. A diseased person needs both proper medicine and a proper diet, and therefore the Kṛṣṇa consciousness movement supplies materially stricken people with the medicine of the chanting of the holy name, or the Hare Kṛṣṇa *mahā-mantra,* and the diet of *prasāda.* There are many hospitals and medical clinics to cure bodily diseases, but there are no such hospitals to cure the material disease of the spirit soul. The centers of the Kṛṣṇa consciousness movement are the only established hospitals that can cure man of birth, death, old age and disease.

TEXT 52

শ্রীমান্ সেন প্রভুর সেবক প্রধান ।
চৈতন্য-চরণ বিনু নাহি জানে আন ॥ ৫২ ॥

śrīmān sena prabhura sevaka pradhāna
caitanya-caraṇa vinu nāhi jāne āna

SYNONYMS

śrīmān sena—of the name Śrīmān Sena; *prabhura*—of the Lord; *sevaka*—servant; *pradhāna*—chief; *caitanya-caraṇa*—the lotus feet of Lord Caitanya Mahāprabhu; *vinu*—except; *nāhi*—does not; *jāne*—know; *āna*—anything else.

TRANSLATION

Śrīmān Sena, the twenty-second branch of the Caitanya tree, was a very faithful servant of Lord Caitanya. He knew nothing else but the lotus feet of Śrī Caitanya Mahāprabhu.

PURPORT

Śrīmān Sena was one of the inhabitants of Navadvīpa and was a constant companion of Lord Caitanya Mahāprabhu.

TEXT 53

শ্রীগদাধর দাস শাখা সর্বোপরি ।
কাজীগণের মুখে যেঁহ বোলাইল হরি ॥ ৫৩ ॥

śrī-gadādhara dāsa śākhā sarvopari
kājī-gaṇera mukhe yeṅha bolāila hari

SYNONYMS

śrī-gadādhara dāsa—of the name Śrī Gadādhara dāsa; *śākhā*—another branch; *sarva-upari*—above all; *kājī-gaṇera*—of the Kāzīs (Mohammedan magistrates); *mukhe*—in the mouth; *yeṅha*—one who; *bolāila*—caused to speak; *hari*—the holy name of Hari.

TRANSLATION

Śrī Gadādhara dāsa, the twenty-third branch, was understood to be the topmost, for he induced all the Mohammedan Kāzīs to chant the holy name of Lord Hari.

PURPORT

About eight or ten miles from Calcutta on the banks of the Ganges is a village known as Eṅḍiyādaha-grāma. Śrīla Gadādhara dāsa was known as an inhabitant of this village *(eṅḍiyādaha-vāsī gadādhara dāsa).* The *Bhakti-ratnākara,* Seventh Chapter, informs us that after the disappearance of Lord Caitanya Mahāprabhu, Gadādhara dāsa came from Navadvīpa to Katwa. Thereafter he came to Eṅḍiyādaha and resided there. He is stated to be the luster of the body of Śrīmatī Rādhārāṇī, just as Śrīla Gadādhara Paṇḍita Gosvāmī is an incarnation of Śrīmatī Rādhārāṇī

Herself. Caitanya Mahāprabhu is sometimes explained to be *rādhābhāva-dyuti-subalita,* or characterized by the emotions and bodily luster of Śrīmatī Rādhārāṇī. Gadādhara dāsa is this *dyuti,* or luster. In the *Gaura-gaṇoddeśa-dīpikā* he is described to be the expansion potency of Śrīmatī Rādhārāṇī. He counts among the associates of both Śrīla Gaurahari and Nityānanda Prabhu; as a devotee of Śrī Caitanya Mahāprabhu he was one of the associates of Lord Kṛṣṇa in conjugal love, and as a devotee of Lord Nityānanda he is considered to have been one of the friends of Kṛṣṇa in pure devotional service. Even though he was an associate of Lord Nityānanda Prabhu, he was not among the cowherd boys but was situated in the transcendental mellow of conjugal love. He established a temple of Śrī Gaurasundara in Katwa.

In 1434 *śakābda* (1534 A.D.) when Lord Nityānanda Prabhu was empowered by Lord Caitanya to preach the *saṅkīrtana* movement in Bengal, Śrī Gadādhara dāsa was one of Lord Nityānanda's chief assistants. He preached the *saṅkīrtana* movement by requesting everyone to chant the Hare Kṛṣṇa *mahā-mantra.* This simple preaching method of Śrīla Gadādhara dāsa can be followed by anyone and everyone in any position of society. One must simply be a sincere and serious servant of Nityānanda Prabhu and preach this cult door to door.

When Śrīla Gadādhara dāsa Prabhu was preaching the cult of *hari-kīrtana,* there was a magistrate who was very much against his *saṅkīrtana* movement. Following in the footsteps of Lord Caitanya Mahāprabhu, Śrīla Gadādhara dāsa one night went to the house of the Kāzī and requested him to chant the Hare Kṛṣṇa *mahā-mantra.* The Kāzī replied, "All right, I shall chant Hare Kṛṣṇa tomorrow." On hearing this, Śrīla Gadādhara dāsa Prabhu began to dance, and he said, "Why tomorrow? You have already chanted the Hare Kṛṣṇa *mantra,* so simply continue."

In the *Gaura-gaṇoddeśa-dīpikā* (Verses 154, 155) it is said:

rādhā-vibhūti-rūpā yā candrakāntiḥ purā vraje
sa śrī-gaurāṅga-nikaṭe dāsa-vaṁśyo gadādharaḥ
pūrṇānandā vraje yāsīd baladeva-priyāgraṇī
sāpi kārya-vaśād eva prāviśat taṁ gadādharam

Śrīla Gadādhara dāsa is considered to be a united form of Candrakānti, who is the effulgence of Śrīmatī Rādhārāṇī, and Pūrṇānandā, who is an expansion of Lord Balarāma's very dear girl friend. Thus Śrīla Gadādhara dāsa Prabhu was one of the associates of both Caitanya Mahāprabhu and Nityānanda Prabhu. Once while Śrīla Gadādhara dāsa Prabhu was returning to Bengal from Jagannātha Purī with Nityānanda Prabhu, he forgot himself and began talking very loudly as if he were a girl of Vrajabhūmi selling yogurt, and Śrīla Nityānanda Prabhu noted this. Another time, while absorbed in the ecstasy of the *gopīs,* he carried a jug filled with Ganges water on his head as if he were selling milk. When Lord Caitanya Mahāprabhu appeared in the house of Rāghava Paṇḍita while going to Vṛndāvana, Gadādhara dāsa went to see Him, and Śrī Caitanya Mahāprabhu was so glad that He put His foot on his head. When Gadādhara dāsa Prabhu was present in Eṅḍiyādaha he established a Bālagopāla *mūrti* for worship there. Śrī Mādhava Ghosh performed a drama known as *"Dāna-khaṇḍa"* with the help of Śrī Nityānanda Prabhu and Śrī Gadādhara dāsa.

This is explained in *Caitanya-bhāgavata, Antya-khaṇḍa,* Fifth Chapter.

The tomb of Gadādhara dāsa Prabhu, which is in the village of Eṅḍiyādaha, was under the control of the Saṁyogi Vaiṣṇavas and later under the direction of Siddha Bhagavān dāsa Bābājī of Kālnā. By his order, Śrī Madhusūdana Mullik, one of the members of the aristocratic Mullik family of the Nārikelaḍāṅgā in Calcutta, established a *pāṭavāṭī* (monastery) there in the Bengali year 1256. He also arranged for the worship of a Deity named Śrī Rādhākānta. His son Balāicāṇḍa Mullik, established Gaura-Nitāi Deities there in the Bengali year 1312. Thus on the throne of the temple are both Gaura-Nityānanda Deities and Rādhā-Kṛṣṇa Deities. Below the throne is a tablet with an inscription written in Sanskrit. In that temple there is also a small Deity of Lord Śiva as Gopeśvara. This is all described on a stone by the side of the entrance door.

TEXT 54

শিবানন্দ সেন—প্রভুর ভৃত্য অন্তরঙ্গ ।
প্রভুস্থানে যাইতে সবে লয়েন যাঁর সঙ্গ ॥ ৫৪ ॥

śivānanda sena—prabhura bhṛtya antaraṅga
prabhu-sthāne yāite sabe layena yāṅra saṅga

SYNONYMS

śivānanda sena—of the name Śivānanda Sena; *prabhura*—of the Lord; *bhṛtya*—servant; *antaraṅga*—very confidential; *prabhu-sthāne*—in Jagannātha Purī, where the Lord was staying; *yāite*—while going; *sabe*—all; *layena*—took; *yāṅra*—whose; *saṅga*—shelter.

TRANSLATION

Śivānanda Sena, the twenty-fourth branch of the tree, was an extremely confidential servant of Lord Caitanya Mahāprabhu. Everyone who went to Jagannātha Purī to visit Lord Caitanya took shelter and guidance from Śrī Śivānanda Sena.

TEXT 55

প্রতিবর্ষে প্রভুগণ সঙ্গেতে লইয়া ।
নীলাচলে চলেন পথে পালন করিয়া ॥ ৫৫ ॥

prativarṣe prabhugaṇa saṅgete la-iyā
nīlācale calena pathe pālana kariyā

SYNONYMS

prativarṣe—every year; *prabhu-gaṇa*—the devotees of Lord Caitanya; *saṅgete*—along with; *la-iyā*—taking; *nīlācale*—to Jagannātha Purī; *calena*—goes; *pathe*—on the road; *pālana*—maintenance; *kariyā*—providing.

TRANSLATION

Every year he took a party of devotees from Bengal to Jagannātha Purī to visit Lord Caitanya. He maintained the entire party as they journeyed on the road.

TEXT 56

ভক্তে কৃপা করেন প্রভু এ-তিন স্বরূপে ।
'সাক্ষাৎ', 'আবেশ' আর 'আবির্ভাব'-রূপে ॥ ৫৬ ॥

bhakte kṛpā karena prabhu e-tina svarūpe
'sākṣāt,' 'āveśa' āra 'āvirbhāva'—rūpe

SYNONYMS

bhakte—unto devotees; *kṛpā*—mercy; *karena*—bestows; *prabhu*—Lord Caitanya; *e*—these; *tina*—three; *svarūpe*—features; *sākṣāt*—directly; *āveśa*—empowered by the Lord; *āra*—and; *āvirbhāva*—appearance; *rūpe*—in the features.

TRANSLATION

Lord Śrī Caitanya Mahāprabhu bestows His causeless mercy upon His devotees in three features: His own direct appearance [sākṣāt], His prowess within someone He empowers [āveśa], and His manifestation [āvirbhāva].

PURPORT

The *sākṣāt* feature of Śrī Caitanya Mahāprabhu is His personal presence. *Āveśa* refers to invested power, like that invested in Nakula Brahmacārī. *Āvirbhāva* is a manifestation of the Lord that appears even though He is personally not present. For example, Śrī Śacīmātā offered foodstuffs at home to Śrī Caitanya Mahāprabhu although He was far away in Jagannātha Purī, and when she opened her eyes after offering the foodstuffs she saw that they had actually been eaten by Śrī Caitanya Mahāprabhu. Similarly, Śrīvāsa Ṭhākura performed *saṅkīrtana,* and everyone felt the presence of Śrī Caitanya Mahāprabhu even in His absence. This is another example of *āvirbhāva.*

TEXT 57

'সাক্ষাতে' সকল ভক্ত দেখে নির্বিশেষ ।
নকুল ব্রহ্মচারি-দেহে প্রভুর 'আবেশ' ॥ ৫৭ ॥

'sākṣāte' sakala bhakta dekhe nirviśeṣa
nakula brahmacāri-dehe prabhura 'āveśa'

SYNONYMS

sākṣāte—directly; *sakala*—all; *bhakta*—devotees; *dekhe*—see; *nirviśeṣa*—nothing peculiar but as He is; *nakula brahmacārī*—of the name Nakula Brahmacārī; *dehe*—in the body; *prabhura*—the Lord's; *āveśa*—symptoms of power.

TRANSLATION

The appearance of Lord Śrī Caitanya Mahāprabhu in every devotee's presence is called sākṣāt. His appearance in Nakula Brahmacārī as a symptom of special prowess is an example of āveśa.

TEXT 58

'প্রদ্যুম্ন ব্রহ্মচারী' তাঁর আগে নাম ছিল ।
'নৃসিংহানন্দ' নাম প্রভু পাছে ত' রাখিল ॥ ৫৮ ॥

'pradyumna brahmacārī' tāṅra āge nāma chila
'nṛsiṁhānanda' nāma prabhu pāche ta' rākhila

SYNONYMS

pradyumna brahmacārī—of the name Pradyumna Brahmacārī; *tāṅra*—his; *āge*—previously; *nāma*—name; *chila*—was; *nṛsiṁhānanda*—of the name Nṛsiṁhānanda; *nāma*—the name; *prabhu*—the Lord; *pāche*—afterward; *ta'*—certainly; *rākhila*—kept it.

TRANSLATION

The former Pradyumna Brahmacārī was given the name Nṛsiṁhānanda Brahmacārī by Śrī Caitanya Mahāprabhu.

TEXT 59

তাঁহাতে হইল চৈতন্যের 'আবির্ভাব' ।
অলৌকিক ঐছে প্রভুর অনেক স্বভাব ॥ ৫৯ ॥

tāṅhāte ha-ila caitanyera 'āvirbhāva'
alaukika aiche prabhura aneka svabhāva

SYNONYMS

tāṅhāte—in him; *ha-ila*—there was; *caitanyera*—of Lord Śrī Caitanya Mahāprabhu; *āvirbhāva*—appearance; *alaukika*—uncommon; *aiche*—like that; *prabhura*—of Lord Caitanya Mahāprabhu; *aneka*—various; *svabhāva*—features.

TRANSLATION

In his body there were symptoms of āvirbhāva. Such appearances are uncommon, but Lord Caitanya Mahāprabhu displayed many such pastimes through His different features.

PURPORT

In the *Gaura-gaṇoddeśa-dīpikā* (74) it is said that Nakula Brahmacārī displayed the prowess *(āveśa)* and Pradyumna Brahmacārī the appearance *(āvirbhāva)* of Śrī Caitanya Mahāprabhu. There are many hundreds and thousands of devotees of Lord Caitanya among whom there are no special symptoms, but when a devotee of Lord Śrī Caitanya Mahāprabhu functions with specific prowess, he displays the feature called *āveśa.* Śrī Caitanya Mahāprabhu personally spread the *saṅkīrtana* movement, and He advised all the inhabitants of Bhārata-varṣa to take up His cult and preach it all over the world. The visible bodily symptoms of devotees who follow such instructions are called *āveśa.* Śrīla Śivānanda Sena observed such *āveśa* symptoms in Nakula Brahmacārī, who displayed symptoms exactly like those of Śrī Caitanya Mahāprabhu. The *Caitanya-caritāmṛta* states that in this age of Kali the only spiritual function is to broadcast the holy name of the Lord, but this function can be performed only by one who is actually empowered by Lord Kṛṣṇa. The process by which a devotee is thus empowered is called *āveśa,* or sometimes it is called *śaktyāveśa.*

Pradyumna Brahmacārī was formerly a resident of a village known as Piyārīgañja in Kālnā. There is a description of him in the *Antya-līlā* of *Caitanya-caritāmṛta,* Second Chapter, and in the *Antya-līlā* of *Caitanya-bhāgavata,* Chapters Three and Nine.

TEXT 60

আস্বাদিল এ সব রস সেন শিবানন্দ ।
বিস্তারি' কহিব আগে এসব আনন্দ ॥ ৬০ ॥

āsvādila e saba rasa sena śivānanda
vistāri' kahiba āge esaba ānanda

SYNONYMS

āsvādila—tasted; *e*—these; *saba*—all; *rasa*—mellows; *sena śivānanda*—Śivānanda Sena; *vistāri'*—describing vividly; *kahiba*—I shall speak; *āge*—later on; *esaba*—all this; *ānanda*—transcendental bliss.

TRANSLATION

Śrīla Śivānanda Sena experienced the three features sākṣāt, āveśa and āvirbhāva. Later I shall vividly describe this transcendentally blissful subject.

PURPORT

Śrīla Śivānanda Sena has been described by Śrīla Bhaktisiddhānta Sarasvatī Mahārāja as follows. He was a resident of Kumārahaṭṭa, which is also known as Hālisahara, and was a great devotee of the Lord. About one and a half miles from Kumārahaṭṭa is another village, known as Kāñcaḍāpāḍā, in which there are Gaura-Gopāla Deities installed by Śivānanda Sena, who also established a temple of Kṛṣṇarāya that is still existing. Śivānanda Sena was the father of Paramānanda Sena, who was also known as Purīdāsa or Karṇapūra. Paramānanda Sena wrote in his *Gaura-gaṇoddeśa-dīpikā* (176) that two of the *gopīs* of Vṛndāvana, whose former names were Vīrā and Dūtī, combined to become his father. Śrīla Śivānanda Sena guided all the devotees of Lord Caitanya who went from Bengal to Jagannātha Purī, and he personally bore all the expenses for their journey. This is described in the *Madhya-līlā,* Chapter Sixteen, verses 19 through 26. Śrīla Śivānanda Sena had three sons, named Caitanya dāsa, Rāmadāsa and Paramānanda. This last son later became Kavikarṇapūra, and he is the author of *Gaura-gaṇoddeśa-dīpikā.* His spiritual master was Śrīnātha Paṇḍita, who was Śivānanda Sena's priest. Due to Vāsudeva Datta's lavish spending, Śivānanda Sena was engaged to supervise his expenditures.

Śrī Śivānanda Sena actually experienced Śrī Caitanya Mahāprabhu's features of *sākṣāt, āveśa* and *āvirbhāva.* He once picked up a dog while on his way to Jagannātha Purī, and it is described in the *Antya-līlā,* First Chapter, that this dog later attained salvation by his association. When Śrīla Raghunātha dāsa, who later became Raghunātha dāsa Gosvāmī, fled his paternal home to join Śrī Caitanya Mahāprabhu, his father wrote a letter to Śivānanda Sena to get information about him. Śivānanda Sena supplied him the details for which he asked, and later Raghunātha dāsa Gosvāmī's father sent some servants and money to Śivānanda Sena to take care of Raghunātha dāsa Gosvāmī. Once Śrī Śivānanda Sena invited Lord Caitanya Mahāprabhu to his home and fed Him so sumptuously that the Lord felt indigestion and was somewhat sick. This became known to his son, who gave the Lord some medicine for His digestion, and thus Lord Caitanya Mahāprabhu was very pleased. This is described in the *Antya-līlā,* Tenth Chapter, verses 124 through 151.

Once while going to Jagannātha Purī all the devotees had to stay underneath a tree, without the shelter of a house or even a shed, and Nityānanda Prabhu became very angry, as if He were greatly disturbed by hunger. Thus He cursed Śivānanda's sons to die. Śivānanda's wife was very much aggrieved at this, and she began to cry. She very seriously thought that since her sons had been cursed by Nityānanda Prabhu, certainly they would die. When Śivānanda later returned and saw his wife crying, he said, "Why are you crying? Let us all die if Śrī Nityānanda Prabhu desires." When Śivānanda Sena returned and Śrīla Nityānanda Prabhu saw him, the Lord kicked him severely, complaining that He was very hungry, and asked why he did not arrange for His food. Such is the behavior of the Lord with His devotees. Śrīla Nityānanda Prabhu behaved like an ordinary hungry man, as if completely dependent on the arrangements of Śivānanda Sena.

There was a nephew of Śivānanda Sena's named Śrīkānta who left the company in protest of Nityānanda Prabhu's curse and went directly to Śrī Caitanya Mahāprabhu at Jagannātha Purī, where the Lord pacified him. On that occasion, Lord Caitanya Mahāprabhu allowed His toe to be sucked by Purīdāsa, who was then a child. It is by the order of Caitanya Mahāprabhu that he could immediately compose Sanskrit verses. During the misunderstanding with Śivānanda's family, Śrī Caitanya Mahāprabhu ordered His personal attendant Govinda to give them all the remnants of His foodstuffs. This is described in the *Antya-khaṇḍa,* Chapter Twelve, verse 53.

TEXT 61

শিবানন্দের উপশাখা, তাঁর পরিকর ।
পুত্র-ভৃত্য-আদি করি' চৈতন্য-কিঙ্কর ॥ ৬১ ॥

śivānandera upaśākhā, tāṅra parikara
putra-bhṛtya-ādi kari' caitanya-kiṅkara

SYNONYMS

śivānandera—of Śivānanda Sena; *upaśākhā*—sub-branch; *tāṅra*—his; *parikara*—associates; *putra*—sons; *bhṛtya*—servants; *ādi*—all these; *kari'*—taking together; *caitanya-kiṅkara*—servants of Caitanya Mahāprabhu.

TRANSLATION

The sons, servants and family members of Śivānanda Sena constituted a sub-branch. They were all sincere servants of Lord Śrī Caitanya Mahāprabhu.

TEXT 62

চৈতন্যদাস, রামদাস, আর কর্ণপূর ।
তিন পুত্র শিবানন্দের প্রভুর ভক্তশূর ॥ ৬২ ॥

caitanya-dāsa, rāmadāsa, āra karṇapūra
tina putra śivānandera prabhura bhakta-śūra

SYNONYMS

caitanya-dāsa—of the name Caitanya dāsa; *rāmadāsa*—of the name Rāmadāsa; *āra*—and; *karṇapūra*—of the name Karṇapūra; *tina putra*—three sons; *śivānandera*—of Śivānanda Sena; *prabhura*—of the Lord; *bhakta-śūra*—of the heroic devotees.

TRANSLATION

The three sons of Śivānanda Sena, named Caitanya dāsa, Rāmadāsa and Karṇapūra, were all heroic devotees of Lord Caitanya.

PURPORT

Caitanya dāsa, the eldest son of Śivānanda Sena, wrote a commentary on *Kṛṣṇa-karṇāmṛta* which was later translated by Śrīla Bhaktivinoda Ṭhākura in his paper *Sajjana-toṣaṇī.* According to expert opinion, Caitanya dāsa was the author of the book *Caitanya-carita,* which was written in Sanskrit. The author was not Kavikarṇapūra, as generally supposed. This is the opinion of Śrīla Bhaktisiddhānta Sarasvatī Ṭhākura. Śrī Rāmadāsa was the second son of Śivānanda Sena. It is stated in the *Gaura-gaṇoddeśa-dīpikā* (145) that two experienced servants of Lord Kṛṣṇa named

Śuka and Dakṣa in *kṛṣṇa-līlā* became the elder brothers of Kavikarṇapūra, namely, Caitanya dāsa and Rāmadāsa. Karṇapūra, the third son, who was also known as Paramānanda dāsa or Purīdāsa, was initiated by Śrīnātha Paṇḍita, who was a disciple of Śrī Advaita Prabhu. Karṇapūra wrote many books that are important in Vaiṣṇava literature, such as *Ānanda-vṛndāvana-campū, Alaṅkāra-kaustubha, Gaura-gaṇoddeśa-dīpikā* and the great epic *Caitanya-candrodaya-nāṭaka.* He was born in the year *śakābda* 1448. He continually wrote books for ten years, from 1488 until 1498.

TEXT 63

শ্রীবল্লভসেন, আর সেন শ্রীকান্ত ।
শিবানন্দ-সম্বন্ধে প্রভুর ভক্ত একান্ত ॥ ৬৩ ॥

śrī-vallabhasena, āra sena śrīkānta
śivānanda-sambandhe prabhura bhakta ekānta

SYNONYMS

śrī-vallabha-sena—of the name Śrīvallabha Sena; *āra*—and; *sena śrīkānta*—of the name Śrīkānta Sena; *śivānanda*—Śivānanda Sena; *sambandhe*—in relationship; *prabhura*—the Lord's; *bhakta*—devotees; *ekānta*—unflinching.

TRANSLATION

Śrīvallabha Sena and Śrīkānta Sena were also sub-branches of Śivānanda Sena, for they were not only his nephews but also unalloyed devotees of Śrī Caitanya Mahāprabhu.

PURPORT

When Lord Nityānanda Prabhu rebuked Śivānanda Sena on the way to Purī, these two nephews of Śivānanda left the company as a protest and went to see Śrī Caitanya Mahāprabhu at Jagannātha Purī. The Lord could understand the feelings of the boys, and He asked His personal assistant Govinda to supply them *prasāda* until the party of Śivānanda arrived. During the Rathayātrā *saṅkīrtana* festival these two brothers were members of the party led by Mukunda. In the *Gaura-gaṇoddeśa-dīpikā* it is said that the *gopī* whose name was Kātyāyanī appeared as Śrīkānta Sena.

TEXT 64

প্রভুপ্রিয় গোবিন্দানন্দ মহাভাগবত ।
প্রভুর কীর্তনীয়া আদি শ্রীগোবিন্দ দত্ত ॥ ৬৪ ॥

prabhu-priya govindānanda mahābhāgavata
prabhura kīrtanīyā ādi śrī-govinda datta

SYNONYMS

prabhu-priya—the most dear to the Lord; *govindānanda*—of the name Govindānanda; *mahā-bhāgavata*—great devotee; *prabhura*—of the Lord; *kīrtanīyā*—performer of *kīrtana; ādi*—originally; *śrī-govinda datta*—of the name of Śrī Govinda Datta.

TRANSLATION

Govindānanda and Govinda Datta, the twenty-fifth and twenty-sixth branches of the tree, were performers of kīrtana in the company of Śrī Caitanya Mahāprabhu. Govinda Datta was the principal singer in Lord Caitanya's kīrtana party.

PURPORT

Govinda Datta appeared in the village of Sukhacara near Khaḍadaha.

TEXT 65

শ্রীবিজয়দাস-নাম প্রভুর আখরিয়া ।
প্রভুরে অনেক পুঁথি দিয়াছে লিখিয়া ॥ ৬৫ ॥

śri-vijaya-dāsa-nāma prabhura ākhariyā
prabhure aneka puṅthi diyāche likhiyā

SYNONYMS

śrī-vijaya-dāsa—of the name Śrī Vijaya dāsa; *nāma*—name; *prabhura*—of the Lord; *ākhariyā*—chief singer; *prabhure*—unto the Lord; *aneka*—many; *puṅthi*—literatures; *diyāche*—has given; *likhiyā*—by writing.

TRANSLATION

Śrī Vijaya dāsa, the twenty-seventh branch, another of the Lord's chief singers, gave the Lord many books written by hand.

PURPORT

Formerly there were no printing presses nor printed books. All books were handwritten. Precious books were kept in manuscript form in temples or important places, and anyone who was interested in a book had to copy it by hand. Vijaya dāsa was a professional writer who copied many manuscripts and gave them to Śrī Caitanya Mahāprabhu.

TEXT 66

'রত্নবাহু' বলি' প্রভু থুইল তাঁর নাম ।
অকিঞ্চন প্রভুর প্রিয় কৃষ্ণদাস-নাম ॥ ৬৬ ॥

'ratnabāhu' bali' prabhu thuila tāṅra nāma
akiñcana prabhura priya kṛṣṇadāsa-nāma

SYNONYMS

ratnabāhu—the title Ratnabāhu; *bali'*—calling him; *prabhu*—the Lord; *thuila*—kept; *tāṅra*—his; *nāma*—name; *akiñcana*—unalloyed; *prabhura*—of the Lord; *priya*—dear; *kṛṣṇadāsa*—of the name Kṛṣṇadāsa; *nāma*—name.

TRANSLATION

Śrī Caitanya Mahāprabhu gave Vijaya dāsa the name Ratnabāhu ["jewel-handed"] because he copied for Him many manuscripts. The twenty-eighth branch was Kṛṣṇadāsa, who was very dear to the Lord. He was known as Akiñcana Kṛṣṇadāsa.

PURPORT

Akiñcana means "one who possesses nothing in this world."

TEXT 67

খোলা-বেচা শ্রীধর প্রভুর প্রিয়দাস ।
যাঁহা-সনে প্রভু করে নিত্য পরিহাস ॥ ৬৭ ॥

kholā-vecā śrīdhara prabhura priyadāsa
yāṅhā-sane prabhu kare nitya parihāsa

SYNONYMS

kholā-vecā—a person who sells the bark of banana trees; *śrīdhara*—Śrīdhara Prabhu; *prabhura*—of the Lord; *priya-dāsa*—very dear servant; *yāṅhā-sane*—with whom; *prabhu*—the Lord; *kare*—does; *nitya*—daily; *parihāsa*—joking.

TRANSLATION

The twenty-ninth branch was Śrīdhara, a trader in banana tree bark. He was a very dear servant of the Lord. On many occasions, the Lord played jokes on him.

PURPORT

Śrīdhara was a poor *brāhmaṇa* who made a living by selling banana tree bark to be made into cups. Most probably he had a banana tree garden and collected the leaves, skin and pulp of the banana trees to sell daily in the market. He spent fifty percent of his income to worship the Ganges, and the balance he used for his subsistence. When Śrī Caitanya Mahāprabhu started His civil disobedience movement in defiance of the Kāzī, Śrīdhara danced in jublilation. The Lord used to drink water from his water jug. Śrīdhara presented a squash to Śacīdevī to cook before Lord Caitanya took *sannyāsa*. Every year he went to see Lord Caitanya Mahāprabhu at Jagannātha Purī. According to Kavikarṇapūra, Śrīdhara was a cowherd boy of Vṛndāvana whose name was Kusumāsava. In his *Gaura-gaṇoddeśa-dīpikā,* verse 133, it is stated:

kholāvecātayā khyātaḥ paṇḍitaḥ śrīdharo dvijaḥ
āsīd vraje hāsya-karo yo nāmnā kusumāsavaḥ

"The cowherd boy known as Kusumāsava in *kṛṣṇa-līlā* later became Kholāvecā Śrīdhara during Caitanya Mahāprabhu's *līlā* at Navadvīpa."

TEXT 68

প্রভু যাঁর নিত্য লয় থোড়-মোচা-ফল ।
যাঁর ফুটা-লৌহপাত্রে প্রভু পিলা জল ॥ ৬৮ ॥

prabhu yāṅra nitya laya thoḍa-mocā-phala
yāṅra phuṭā-lauhapātre prabhu pilā jala

SYNONYMS

prabhu—the Lord; *yāṅra*—whose; *nitya*—daily; *laya*—takes; *thoḍa*—the pulp of the banana tree; *mocā*—the flowers of the banana tree; *phala*—the fruits of the banana tree; *yāṅra*—whose; *phuṭā*—broken; *lauha-pātre*—in the iron pot; *prabhu*—the Lord; *pilā*—drank; *jala*—water.

TRANSLATION

Every day Lord Caitanya Mahāprabhu jokingly snatched fruits, flowers and pulp from Śrīdhara and drank from his broken iron pot.

TEXT 69

প্রভুর অতিপ্রিয় দাস ভগবান্ পণ্ডিত ।
যাঁর দেহে কৃষ্ণ পূর্বে হৈলা অধিষ্ঠিত ॥ ৬৯ ॥

prabhura atipriya dāsa bhagavān paṇḍita
yāṅra dehe kṛṣṇa pūrve hailā adhiṣṭhita

SYNONYMS

prabhura—of the Lord; *atipriya*—very dear; *dāsa*—servant; *bhagavān paṇḍita*—of the name Bhagavān Paṇḍita; *yāṅra*—whose; *dehe*—in the body; *kṛṣṇa*—Lord Kṛṣṇa; *pūrve*—previously; *hailā*—became; *adhiṣṭhita*—established.

TRANSLATION

The thirtieth branch was Bhagavān Paṇḍita. He was an extremely dear servant of the Lord, but even previously he was a great devotee of Lord Kṛṣṇa who always kept the Lord within his heart.

TEXT 70

জগদীশ পণ্ডিত, আর হিরণ্য মহাশয়।
যারে কৃপা কৈল বাল্যে প্রভু দয়াময় ॥ ৭০ ॥

jagadīśa paṇḍita, āra hiraṇya mahāśaya
yāre kṛpā kaila bālye prabhu dayāmaya

SYNONYMS

jagadīśa paṇḍita—of the name Jagadīśa Paṇḍita; *āra*—and; *hiraṇya*—of the name Hiraṇya; *mahāśaya*—great personality; *yāre*—unto whom; *kṛpā*—mercy; *kaila*—showed; *bālye*—in childhood; *prabhu*—the Lord; *dayāmaya*—merciful.

TRANSLATION

The thirty-first branch was Jagadīśa Paṇḍita, and the thirty-second was Hiraṇya Mahāśaya, unto whom Lord Caitanya in His childhood showed His causeless mercy.

PURPORT

Jagadīśa Paṇḍita was formerly a great dancer in *kṛṣṇa-līlā* and was known as Candrahāsa. Regarding Hiraṇya Paṇḍita, it is said that once Lord Nityānanda, decorated with valuable jewels, stayed at his home, and a great thief attempted all night long to plunder these jewels but was unsuccessful. Later he came to Nityānanda Prabhu and surrendered unto Him.

TEXT 71

এই দুই-ঘরে প্রভু একাদশী দিনে।
বিষ্ণুর নৈবেদ্য মাগি' খাইল আপনে ॥ ৭১ ॥

ei dui-ghare prabhu ekādaśī dine
viṣṇura naivedya māgi' khāila āpane

SYNONYMS

ei dui-ghare—in these two houses; *prabhu*—the Lord; *ekādaśī dine*—on the Ekādaśī day; *viṣṇura*—of Lord Viṣṇu; *naivedya*—foodstuffs offered to Lord Viṣṇu; *māgi'*—begging; *khāila*—ate; *āpane*—personally.

TRANSLATION

In their two houses Lord Caitanya Mahāprabhu begged foodstuffs on the Ekādaśī day and ate them personally.

PURPORT

The injunction to fast on Ekādaśī is especially meant for devotees; on Ekādaśī there are no restrictions regarding foodstuffs that may be offered to the Lord. Lord

Śrī Caitanya Mahāprabhu took the foodstuffs of Lord Viṣṇu in His ecstasy as *viṣṇu-tattva.*

TEXT 72

প্রভুর পড়ুয়া দুই,—পুরুষোত্তম, সঞ্জয়।
ব্যাকরণে দুই শিষ্য—দুই মহাশয় ॥ ৭২ ॥

prabhura paḍuyā dui,—puruṣottama, sañjaya
vyākaraṇe dui śiṣya—dui mahāśaya

SYNONYMS

prabhura paḍuyā dui—the Lord's two students; *puruṣottama*—of the name Puruṣottama; *sañjaya*—of the name Sañjaya; *vyākaraṇe*—studying grammar; *dui śiṣya*—two disciples; *dui mahāśaya*—very great personalities.

TRANSLATION

The thirty-third and thirty-fourth branches were the two students of Caitanya Mahāprabhu named Puruṣottama and Sañjaya, who were stalwart students in grammar. They were very great personalities.

PURPORT

These two students were inhabitants of Navadvīpa and were the Lord's first companions in the *saṅkīrtana* movement. According to *Caitanya-bhāgavata,* Puruṣottama Sañjaya was the son of Mukunda Sañjaya, but the author of *Śrī Caitanya-caritāmṛta* has clarified that Puruṣottama and Sañjaya were two people, not one.

TEXT 73

বনমালী পণ্ডিত শাখা বিখ্যাত জগতে।
সোণার মুষল হল দেখিল প্রভুর হাতে ॥ ৭৩ ॥

vanamālī paṇḍita śākhā vikhyāta jagate
soṇāra muṣala hala dekhila prabhura hāte

SYNONYMS

vanamālī paṇḍita—of the name Vanamālī Paṇḍita; *śākhā*—the next branch; *vikhyāta*—celebrated; *jagate*—in the world; *soṇāra*—made of gold; *muṣala*—club; *hala*—plow; *dekhila*—saw; *prabhura*—of the Lord; *hāte*—in the hand.

TRANSLATION

Vanamālī Paṇḍita, the thirty-fifth branch of the tree, was very celebrated in this world. He saw in the hands of the Lord a golden club and plow.

PURPORT

Vanamālī Paṇḍita saw Lord Caitanya in the ecstasy of Balarāma. This is described vividly in *Caitanya-bhāgavata, Antya-līlā,* Chapter Nine.

TEXT 74

শ্রীচৈতন্যের অতি প্রিয় বুদ্ধিমন্ত খান্।
আজন্ম আজ্ঞাকারী তেঁহো সেবক-প্রধান ॥ ৭৪ ॥

śrī-caitanyera ati priya buddhimanta khān
ājanma ājñākārī teṅho sevaka-pradhāna

SYNONYMS

śrī-caitanyera—of Lord Śrī Caitanya Mahāprabhu; *ati priya*—very dear; *buddhimanta khān*—of the name Buddhimanta Khān; *ājanma*—from the very beginning of his life; *ājñākārī*—follower of the orders; *teṅho*—he; *sevaka*—servant; *pradhāna*—chief.

TRANSLATION

The thirty-sixth branch, Buddhimanta Khān, was extremely dear to Lord Caitanya Mahāprabhu. He was always prepared to carry out the Lord's orders, and therefore he was considered to be a chief servant of the Lord.

PURPORT

Śrī Buddhimanta Khān was one of the inhabitants of Navadvīpa. He was very rich, and it is he who arranged for the marriage of Lord Caitanya with Viṣṇupriyā, the daughter of Sanātana Miśra, who was the priest of the local Zamindar. He personally defrayed all the expenditures for the marriage ceremony. When Lord Caitanya Mahāprabhu was attacked by *vāyu-vyādhi* (derangement of the air within the body) Buddhimanta Khān paid for all requisite medicines and treatments to cure the Lord. He was the Lord's constant companion in the *kīrtana* movement. He collected ornaments for the Lord when He played the part of the goddess of fortune in the house of Candraśekhara Ācārya. He also went to see Lord Caitanya Mahāprabhu when He was staying at Jagannātha Purī.

TEXT 75

গরুড় পণ্ডিত লয় শ্রীনাম-মঙ্গল।
নাম-বলে বিষ যাঁরে না করিল বল ॥ ৭৫ ॥

garuḍa paṇḍita laya śrīnāma-maṅgala
nāma-bale viṣa yāṅre nā karila bala

SYNONYMS

garuḍa paṇḍita—of the name Garuḍa Paṇḍita; *laya*—takes; *śrīnāma-maṅgala*—the auspicious Hare Kṛṣṇa *mahā-mantra; nāma-bale*—by the strength of this chanting; *viṣa*—poison; *yāṅre*—whom; *nā*—did not; *karila*—affect; *bala*—strength.

TRANSLATION

Garuḍa Paṇḍita, the thirty-seventh branch of the tree, always engaged in chanting the auspicious name of the Lord. Because of the strength of this chanting, even the effects of poison could not touch him.

PURPORT

Garuḍa Paṇḍita was once bitten by a poisonous snake, but the snake's poison could not affect him because of his chanting the Hare Kṛṣṇa *mahā-mantra.*

TEXT 76

গোপীনাথ সিংহ — এক চৈতন্যের দাস ।
অক্রূর বলি' প্রভু যাঁরে কৈলা পরিহাস ॥ ৭৬ ॥

gopīnātha siṁha—eka caitanyera dāsa
akrūra bali' prabhu yāṅre kailā parihāsa

SYNONYMS

gopīnātha siṁha—of the name of Gopīnātha Siṁha; *eka*—one: *caitanyera dāsa*—servant of Lord Caitanya; *akrūra bali'*—famous as Akrūra; *prabhu*—the Lord; *yāṅre*—whom; *kailā*—did; *parihāsa*—joking.

TRANSLATION

Gopīnātha Siṁha, the thirty-eighth branch of the tree, was a faithful servant of Lord Caitanya Mahāprabhu. The Lord jokingly addressed him as Akrūra.

PURPORT

Actually he was Akrūra, as stated in *Gaura-gaṇoddeśa-dīpikā.*

TEXT 77

ভাগবতী দেবানন্দ বক্রেশ্বর-কৃপাতে ।
ভাগবতের ভক্তি-অর্থ পাইল প্রভু হৈতে ॥ ৭৭ ॥

bhāgavatī devānanda vakreśvara-kṛpāte
bhāgavatera bhakti-artha pāila prabhu haite

SYNONYMS

bhāgavatī devānanda—Devānanda, who used to recite *Śrīmad-Bhāgavatam; vakreśvara-kṛpāte*—by the mercy of Vakreśvara; *bhāgavatera*—of *Śrīmad-Bhāgavatam; bhakti-artha*—the *bhakti* interpretation; *pāila*—got; *prabhu haite*—from the Lord.

TRANSLATION

Devānanda Paṇḍita was a professional reciter of Śrīmad-Bhāgavatam, but by the mercy of Vakreśvara Paṇḍita and the grace of the Lord he understood the devotional interpretation of the Bhāgavatam.

PURPORT

In the *Caitanya-bhāgavata, Madhya-līlā,* Chapter Twenty-one, it is stated that Devānanda Paṇḍita was an inhabitant of the same village in which the father of Sārvabhauma Bhaṭṭācārya, Viśārada, lived. He was a professional reciter of *Śrīmad-Bhāgavatam,* but Lord Caitanya Mahāprabhu did not like his interpretation of it. In the present town of Navadvīpa, which was formerly known as Kuliyā, Lord Caitanya showed such mercy to him that he gave up the Māyāvādī interpretation of *Śrīmad-Bhāgavatam* and learned how to explain *Śrīmad-Bhāgavatam* in terms of *bhakti.* Formerly, when Devānanda was expounding the Māyāvādī interpretation, Śrīvāsa Ṭhākura was once present in his meeting, and when he began to cry, Devānanda's students drove him away. Some days later, Caitanya Mahāprabhu passed that way, and when He met Devānanda He chastised him severely because of his Māyāvāda interpretation of *Śrīmad-Bhāgavatam.* At that time Devānanda had little faith in Śrī Caitanya Mahāprabhu as an incarnation of Lord Kṛṣṇa, but one night some time later Vakreśvara Paṇḍita was a guest in his house, and when he explained the science of Kṛṣṇa, Devānanda was convinced about the identity of Lord Caitanya Mahāprabhu. Thus he was induced to explain *Śrīmad-Bhāgavatam* according to the Vaiṣṇava understanding. In the *Gaura-gaṇoddeśa-dīpikā* it is described that he was formerly Bhāguri Muni, who was the *sabhā-paṇḍita* who recited Vedic literatures in the house of Nanda Mahārāja.

TEXTS 78-79

খণ্ডবাসী মুকুন্দদাস, শ্রীরঘুনন্দন ।
নরহরিদাস, চিরঞ্জীব, সুলোচন ॥ ৭৮ ॥
এই সব মহাশাখা – চৈতন্য-কৃপাধাম ।
প্রেম-ফল-ফুল করে যাহাঁ তাহাঁ দান ॥ ৭৯ ॥

khaṇḍavāsī mukunda-dāsa, śrī-raghunandana
narahari-dāsa, cirañjīva, sulocana

ei saba mahāśākhā—caitanya-kṛpādhāma
prema-phala-phula kare yāhāṅ tāhāṅ dāna

SYNONYMS

khaṇḍavāsī mukunda-dāsa—of the name Mukunda dāsa; *śrī-raghunandana*—of the name Raghunandana; *narahari-dāsa*—of the name Narahari dāsa; *ciranjīva*—of the name Cirañjīva; *sulocana*—of the name Sulocana; *ei saba*—all of them; *mahāśākhā*—great branches; *caitanya-kṛpādhāma*—of Lord Śrī Caitanya Mahāprabhu, the reservoir of mercy; *prema*—love of God; *phala*—fruit; *phula*—flower; *kare*—does; *yāhāṅ*—anywhere; *tāhāṅ*—everywhere; *dāna*—distribution.

TRANSLATION

Śrī Khaṇḍavāsī Mukunda and his son Raghunandana were the thirty-ninth branch of the tree, Narahari was the fortieth, Cirañjīva the forty-first and Sulocana the forty-second. They were all big branches of the all-merciful tree of Caitanya Mahāprabhu. They distributed the fruits and flowers of love of Godhead anywhere and everywhere.

PURPORT

Śrī Mukunda dāsa was the son of Nārāyaṇa dāsa and eldest brother of Narahari Sarakāra. His second brother's name was Mādhava dāsa, and his son was named Raghunandana dāsa. Descendants of Raghunandana dāsa still live four miles west of Katwa in the village named Śrīkhaṇḍa, where Raghunandana dāsa used to live. Raghunandana had one son named Kānāi, who had two sons—Madana Rāya, who was a disciple of Narahari Ṭhākura, and Vaṁśīvadana. It is estimated that at least four hundred men descended in this dynasty. All their names are recorded in the village known as Śrīkhaṇḍa. In the *Gaura-gaṇoddeśa-dīpikā* it is stated that the *gopī* whose name was Vṛndādevī became Mukunda dāsa, lived in Śrīkhaṇḍa village and was very dear to Śrī Caitanya Mahāprabhu. His wonderful devotion and love for Kṛṣṇa are described in the *Madhya-līlā*, Chapter Fifteen. It is stated in the *Bhakti-ratnākara,* Chapter Eight, that Raghunandana used to serve a Deity of Lord Caitanya Mahāprabhu.

Narahari dāsa Sarakāra was a very famous devotee. Locana dāsa Ṭhākura, the celebrated author of *Caitanya-maṅgala,* was his disciple. In *Caitanya-maṅgala* it is stated that Śrī Gadādhara dāsa and Narahari Sarakāra were extremely dear to Śrī Caitanya Mahāprabhu, but there is no specific statement regarding the inhabitants of the village of Śrīkhaṇḍa.

Cirañjīva and Sulocana were both residents of Śrīkhaṇḍa, where their descendants are still living. Of Cirañjīva's two sons, the elder, Rāmacandra Kavirāja, was a disciple of Śrīnivāsācārya and an intimate associate of Narottama dāsa Ṭhākura. The younger son was Govinda dāsa Kavirāja, the famous Vaiṣṇava poet. Cirañjīva's wife was Sunandā, and his father-in-law was Dāmodara Sena Kavirāja. Cirañjīva previously lived on the bank of the Ganges River in the village of Kumāranagara. The *Gaura-gaṇoddeśa-dīpikā* (verse 207) states that he was formerly Candrikā in Vṛndāvana.

TEXT 80

কুলীনগ্রামবাসী সত্যরাজ, রামানন্দ ।
যদুনাথ, পুরুষোত্তম, শঙ্কর, বিদ্যানন্দ ॥ ৮০ ॥

kulīnagrāma-vāsī satyarāja, rāmānanda
yadunātha, puruṣottama, śaṅkara, vidyānanda

SYNONYMS

kulīnagrāma-vāsī—the inhabitants of Kulīna-grāma; *satyarāja*—of the name Satyarāja;. *rāmānanda*—of the name Rāmānanda; *yadunātha*—of the name Yadunātha; *puruṣottama*—of the name Puruṣottama; *śaṅkara*—of the name Śaṅkara; *vidyānanda*—of the name Vidyānanda.

TRANSLATION

Satyarāja, Rāmānanda, Yadunātha, Puruṣottama, Śaṅkara and Vidyānanda all belonged to the twentieth branch. They were inhabitants of the village known as Kulīna-grāma.

TEXT 81

বাণীনাথ বসু আদি যত গ্রামী জন ।
সবেই চৈতন্যভৃত্য, — চৈতন্য-প্রাণধন ॥ ৮১ ॥

vāṇīnātha vasu ādi yata grāmī jana
sabei caitanya-bhṛtya,—caitanya-prāṇadhana

SYNONYMS

vāṇīnātha vasu—of the name Vāṇīnātha Vasu; *ādi*—heading the list; *yata*—all; *grāmī*—of the village; *jana*—inhabitants; *sabei*—all of them; *caitanya-bhṛtya*—servants of Lord Caitanya Mahāprabhu; *caitanya-prāṇadhana*—their life and soul was Lord Caitanya Mahāprabhu.

TRANSLATION

All the inhabitants of Kulīna-grāma village, headed by Vāṇīnātha Vasu, were servants of Lord Caitanya, who was their only life and wealth.

TEXT 82

প্রভু কহে, কুলীনগ্রামের যে হয় কুক্কুর ।
সেই মোর প্রিয়, অন্য জন রহু দূর ॥ ৮২ ॥

prabhu kahe, kulīnagrāmera ye haya kukkura
sei mora priya, anya jana rahu dūra

SYNONYMS

prabhu—the Lord; *kahe*—says; *kulīnagrāmera*—of the village of Kulīnagrāma; *ye*—anyone who; *haya*—becomes; *kukkura*—even a dog; *sei*—he; *mora*—My; *priya*—dear; *anya*—others; *jana*—persons; *rahu*—let them remain; *dūra*—away.

TRANSLATION

The Lord said: "Not to speak of others, even a dog in the village of Kulīna-grāma is My dear friend.

TEXT 83

কুলীনগ্রামীর ভাগ্য কহনে না যায়।
শূকর চরায় ডোম, সেহ কৃষ্ণ গায় ॥ ৮৩ ॥

kulīnagrāmīra bhāgya kahane nā yāya
śūkara carāya ḍoma, seha kṛṣṇa gāya

SYNONYMS

kulīnagrāmīra—the residents of Kulīna-grāma; *bhāgya*—fortune; *kahane*—to speak; *nā*—not; *yāya*—is possible; *śūkara*—hogs; *carāya*—tending; *ḍoma*—sweeper; *seha*—he also; *kṛṣṇa*—Lord Kṛṣṇa; *gāya*—chants.

TRANSLATION

"No one can speak about the fortunate position of Kulīna-grāma. It is so sublime that even sweepers who tend their hogs there also chant the Hare Kṛṣṇa mahā-mantra."

TEXT 84

অনুপম-বল্লভ, শ্রীরূপ, সনাতন।
এই তিন শাখা বৃক্ষের পশ্চিমে সর্বোত্তম ॥ ৮৪ ॥

anupama-vallabha, śrī-rūpa, sanātana
ei tina śākhā vṛkṣera paścime sarvottama

SYNONYMS

anupama—of the name Anupama; *vallabha*—of the name Vallabha; *śrī-rūpa*—of the name Śrī Rūpa; *sanātana*—of the name Sanātana; *ei*—these; *tina*—three; *śākhā*—branches; *vṛkṣera*—of the tree; *paścime*—on the western side; *sarvottama*—very great.

TRANSLATION

On the western side were the forty-third, forty-fourth and forty-fifth branches—Śrī Sanātana, Śrī Rūpa and Anupama. They were the best of all.

PURPORT

Śrī Anupama was the father of Śrīla Jīva Gosvāmī and youngest brother of Śrī Sanātana Gosvāmī and Śrī Rūpa Gosvāmī. His former name was Vallabha, but after Lord Caitanya met him He gave him the name Anupama. Because of working in the Mohammedan government, these three brothers were given the title Mullik. Our personal family is connected with the Mulliks of Mahātmā Gandhi Road in Calcutta, and we often used to visit their Rādhā-Govinda temple. They belong to the same family as we do. Our family *gotra,* or original genealogical line, is the *gautama-gotra,* or line of disciples of Gautama Muni, and our surname is De. But due to their accepting the posts of Zamindars in the Mohammedan government, they received the title Mullik. Similarly, Rūpa, Sanātana and Vallabha were also given the title Mullik. Mullik means "lord." Just as the English government gives rich and respectable persons the title "lord," so the Mohammedans give the title Mullik to rich, respectable families that have intimate connections with the government. The title Mullik is found not only among the Hindu aristocracy but also among Mohammedans. This title is not restricted to a particular family but is given to different families and castes. The qualifications for receiving it are wealth and respectability.

Sanātana Gosvāmī and Rūpa Gosvāmī belonged to the *bharadvāja-gotra,* which indicates that they belonged either to the family or disciplic succession of Bharadvāja Muni. As members of the Kṛṣṇa consciousness movement, we belong to the family or disciplic succession of Sarasvatī Gosvāmī, and thus we are known as Sārasvatas. Obeisances are therefore offered to the spiritual master as *sārasvata-deva,* or a member of the Sārasvata family *(namas te sārasvate devam),* whose mission is to broadcast the cult of Śrī Caitanya Mahāprabhu *(gaura-vāṇi-pracāriṇe)* and to fight with impersonalists and voidists *(nirviśeṣa-śūnyavādi-pāścātya-deśa-tāriṇe).* This was also the occupational duty of Sanātana Gosvāmī, Rūpa Gosvāmī and Anupama Gosvāmī.

The genealogical table of Sanātana Gosvāmī, Rūpa Gosvāmī and Vallabha Gosvāmī can be traced back to the Twelfth Century *śakābda,* when a gentleman of the name Sarvajña appeared in a very rich and opulent *brāhmaṇa* family in the province of Karṇāṭa. He had two sons named Aniruddhera Rūpeśvara and Harihara, who were both bereft of their kingdoms and thus obliged to reside in the highlands. The son of Rūpeśvara, who was named Padmanābha, moved to a place in Bengal known as Naihāṭī on the bank of the Ganges. There he had five sons, of whom the youngest, Mukunda, had a well-behaved son named Kumāradeva, who was the father of Rūpa, Sanātana and Vallabha. Kumāradeva lived in Bāklācandradvīpa, which was in the district of Yaśohara and is now known as Phateyābād. Of his many sons, three took to the path of Vaiṣṇavism. Later, Śrī Vallabha and his elder brothers Śrī Rūpa and Sanātana came from Candradvīpa to the village in the Maldah district of Bengal known as Rāmakeli. It is in this village that Śrīla Jīva Gosvāmī took birth, accepting Vallabha as his father. Because of engaging in the service of the Mohammedan government, the three brothers received the title Mullik. When Lord Caitanya Mahāprabhu visited the village of Rāmakeli, He met Vallabha there. Later, Śrī Rūpa

Gosvāmī, after meeting Śrī Caitanya Mahāprabhu, resigned from government service, and when he went to Vṛndāvana to meet Lord Caitanya, Vallabha accompanied him. The meeting of Rūpa Gosvāmī and Vallabha with Caitanya Mahāprabhu at Allahabad is described in the *Madhya-līlā,* Chapter Nineteen.

Actually, it is to be understood from the statement of Sanātana Gosvāmī that Śrī Rūpa Gosvāmī and Vallabha went to Vṛndāvana under the instructions of Śrī Caitanya Mahāprabhu. First they went to Mathurā, where they met a gentleman named Subuddhi Rāya who maintained himself by selling dry fuel wood. He was very pleased to meet Śrī Rūpa Gosvāmī and Anupama, and he showed them the twelve forests of Vṛndāvana. Thus they lived in Vṛndāvana for one month and then again went to search for Sanātana Gosvāmī. Following the course of the Ganges, they reached Allahabad, or Prayāga-tīrtha, but because Sanātana Gosvāmī had come there by a different road, they did not meet him there, and when Sanātana Gosvāmī came to Mathurā he was informed of the visit of Rūpa Gosvāmī and Anupama by Subuddhi Rāya. When Rūpa Gosvāmī and Anupama met Caitanya Mahāprabhu at Benares, they heard about Sanātana Gosvāmī's travels from Him, and thus they returned to Bengal, adjusted their affairs with the state and, on the order of Śrī Caitanya Mahāprabhu, went to see the Lord at Jagannātha Purī.

In the year 1436 *śakābda,* the youngest brother, Anupama, died and went back home, back to Godhead. He went to the abode in the spiritual sky where Śrī Rāmacandra is situated. At Jagannātha Purī, Śrī Rūpa Gosvāmī informed Śrī Caitanya Mahāprabhu of this incident. Vallabha was a great devotee of Śrī Rāmacandra; therefore he could not seriously consider the worship of Rādhā-Govinda according to the instructions of Śrī Caitanya Mahāprabhu. Yet he directly accepted Śrī Caitanya Mahāprabhu as an incarnation of the Supreme Personality of Godhead Rāmacandra. In the *Bhakti-ratnākara* there is the following statement: "Vallabha was given the name Anupama by Śrī Gaurasundara, but he was always absorbed in the devotional service of Lord Rāmacandra. He did not know anyone but Śrī Rāmacandra, but he knew that Caitanya Gosāñi was the same Lord Rāmacandra."

In the *Gaura-gaṇoddeśa-dīpikā* (180) Śrī Rūpa Gosvāmī is described to be the *gopī* named Śrī Rūpa-mañjarī. In the *Bhakti-ratnākara* there is a list of the books Śrī Rūpa Gosvāmī compiled. Of all his books, the following sixteen are very popular among Vaiṣṇavas: (1) *Haṁsadūta,* (2) *Uddhava-sandeśa,* (3) *Kṛṣṇa-janma-tithi-vidhi,* (4 and 5) *Gaṇoddeśa-dīpikā, Bṛhat* (major) and *Laghu* (minor), (6) *Stavamālā,* (7) *Vidagdha-mādhava,* (8) *Lalita-mādhava,* (9) *Dāna-keli-kaumudī,* (10) *Bhakti-rasāmṛta-sindhu* (this is the most celebrated book by Śrī Rūpa Gosvāmī), (11) *Ujjvala-nīlamaṇi,* (12) *Ākhyāta-candrikā,* (13) *Mathurā-mahimā,* (14) *Padyāvalī,* (15) *Nāṭaka-candrikā* and (16) *Laghu-bhāgavatāmṛta.* Śrī Rūpa Gosvāmī gave up all family connections, joined the renounced order of life and divided his money, giving fifty percent to the *brāhmaṇas* and Vaiṣṇavas and twenty-five percent to his *kuṭumbas* (family members) and keeping twenty-five percent for personal emergencies. He met Haridāsa Ṭhākura in Jagannātha Purī, where he also met Lord Caitanya and His other associates. Śrī Caitanya Mahāprabhu used to praise the handwriting of Rūpa Gosvāmī. Śrīla Rūpa Gosvāmī could compose verses according to the desires of Śrī Caitanya Mahāprabhu, and by His direction he wrote two books named *Lalita-mādhava* and *Vidagdha-mādhava.* Lord Caitanya desired the two brothers, Sanātana Gosvāmī and Rūpa Gosvāmī, to publish many books in support of the Vaiṣṇava religion. When Sanātana Gosvāmī met Śrī Caitanya Mahāprabhu, the Lord advised him also to go to Vṛndāvana.

Śrī Sanātana Gosvāmī is described in the *Gaura-gaṇoddeśa-dīpikā* (181). He was formerly known as Rati-mañjarī or sometimes Labaṅga-mañjarī. In the *Bhakti-ratnākara* it is stated that his spiritual master, Vidyāvācaspati, sometimes stayed in the village of Rāmakeli, and Sanātana Gosvāmī studied all the Vedic literature from him. He was so devoted to his spiritual master that this cannot be described. According to the Vedic system, if someone sees a Mohammedan he must perform rituals to atone for the meeting. Sanātana Gosvāmī always associated with Mohammedan kings. Not giving much attention to the Vedic injunctions, he used to visit the houses of Mohammedan kings, and thus he considered himself to have been converted into a Mohammedan. He was therefore always very humble and meek. When Sanātana Gosvāmī presented himself before Lord Caitanya Mahāprabhu, he admitted, "I am always in association with lower class people, and my behavior is therefore very abominable." He actually belonged to a respectable *brāhmaṇa* family, but because he considered his behavior to be abominable, he did not try to place himself among the *brāhmaṇas* but always remained among people of the lower castes. He wrote *Hari-bhakti-vilāsa* and *Vaiṣṇava-toṣaṇī,* which is a commentary on the Tenth Canto of *Śrīmad-Bhāgavatam.* In the year 1476 *śakābda* he completed the *Bṛhad-vaiṣṇava-toṣaṇī* commentary on *Śrīmad-Bhāgavatam.* In the year 1504 *śakābda* he finished the *Laghu-toṣaṇī.*

Śrī Caitanya Mahāprabhu taught his principles through four chief followers. Among them, Rāmānanda Rāya is exceptional, for through him the Lord taught how a devotee can completely vanquish the power of Cupid. By Cupid's power, as soon as one sees a beautiful woman he is conquered by her beauty. Śrī Rāmānanda Rāya vanquished Cupid's pride because in the *Jagannātha-vallabha-nāṭaka* he personally directed extremely beautiful young girls in dancing, but he was never affected by their youthful beauty. Śrī Rāmānanda Rāya personally bathed these girls, touching them and washing them with his own hands, yet he remained calm and passionless, as a great devotee should be. Lord Caitanya Mahāprabhu certified that this was possible only for Rāmānanda Rāya. Similarly, Dāmodara Paṇḍita was notable for his objectivity as a critic. He did not even spare Caitanya Mahāprabhu from his criticism. This also cannot be imitated by anyone else. Haridāsa Ṭhākura is exceptional for his forbearance because although he was beaten with canes in twenty-two marketplaces, nevertheless he was tolerant. Similarly, Śrī Sanātana Gosvāmī, although he belonged to a most respectable *brāhmaṇa* family, was exceptional for his humility and meekness.

In the *Madhya-līlā,* Chapter Nineteen, the device adopted by Sanātana Gosvāmī to get free from the government service is described. He served a notice of sickness to the Nawab, the Moslem governer, but actually he was studying *Śrīmad-Bhāgavatam* with *brāhmaṇas* at home. The Nawab received information of this through a royal physician, and he immediately went to see Sanātana Gosvāmī to uncover his intentions. The Nawab requested Sanātana to accompany him on an expedition to Orissa, but when Sanātana Gosvāmī refused, the Nawab ordered that he be imprisoned. When Rūpa Gosvāmī left home, he wrote a note for Sanātana Gosvāmī informing him of some money that he had entrusted to a local grocer. Sanātana Gosvāmī took advantage of this money to bribe the jail keeper and get free from detention. Then he left for Benares to meet Caitanya Mahāprabhu, bringing with him only one servant, whose name was Īśāna. On the way they stopped at a *sarāi,* or hotel, and when the hotel keeper found out that Īśāna had some golden coins with him, he planned to kill both Sanātana Gosvāmī and Īśāna to take away the coins. Later Sanātana Gosvāmī saw that although the hotel keeper did not know them, he was being especially attentive to their comfort. Therefore he concluded that Īśāna was secretly carrying some money and that the hotel keeper was aware of this and therefore planned to kill them for it. Upon being questioned by Sanātana Gosvāmi, Īśāna admitted that he indeed had money with him, and immediately Sanātana Gosvāmī took the money and gave it to the hotel keeper, requesting him to help them get though the jungle. Thus with the help of the hotel keeper, who was also the chief of the thieves of that territory, he crossed over the Hazipur mountains, which are presently known as the Hazaribags. He then met his brother-in-law Śrīkānta, who requested that he stay with him. Sanātana Gosvāmī refused, but before they parted, Śrīkānta gave him a valuable blanket.

Somehow or other Sanātana Gosvāmī reached Vārāṇasī and met Lord Caitanya Mahāprabhu at the house of Candraśekhara. By the order of the Lord, Sanātana Gosvāmī was cleanly shaved and his dress changed to that of a mendicant, or *bābājī.* He put on old garments of Tapana Miśra and took *prasāda* at the house of a Mahārāṣṭra *brāhmaṇa.* Then, in discourses with Lord Caitanya Mahāprabhu, the Lord Himself explained everything about devotional service to Sanātana Gosvāmī. He advised Sanātana Gosvāmī to write books on devotional service, including a book of directions for Vaiṣṇava activities, and to excavate the lost places of pilgrimage in Vṛndāvana. Lord Caitanya Mahāprabhu gave him His blessings to do all this work and also explained to Sanātana Gosvāmī the import of the *ātmārāma* verse from sixty-one different angles of vision.

Sanātana Gosvāmī went to Vṛndāvana by the main road, and when he reached Mathurā he met Subuddhi Rāya. Then he returned to Jagannātha Purī through Jhārikhaṇḍa, the Uttara Pradesh jungle. At Jagannātha Purī he decided to give up his body by falling down beneath a wheel of the Jagannātha *ratha,* but Caitanya Mahāprabhu saved him. Then Sanātana Gosvāmī met Haridāsa Ṭhākura and heard about the disappearance of Anupama. Sanātana Gosvāmī later described the glories of Haridāsa Ṭhākura. Sanātana observed the etiquette of Jagannātha's temple by going through the beach to visit Lord Caitanya, although it was extremely hot due to the sun. He requested Jagadānanda Paṇḍita to give him permission to return to Vṛndāvana. Lord Caitanya Mahāprabhu praised the character of Sanātana Gosvāmī, and He embraced Sanātana, accepting his body as spiritual. Sanātana Gosvāmī was ordered by Śrī Caitanya Mahāprabhu to live at Jagannātha Purī for one year. When he returned to Vṛndāvana after many years, he again met Rūpa Gosvāmī, and both brothers remained in Vṛndāvana to execute the orders of Śrī Caitanya Mahāprabhu.

The place where Śrī Rūpa Gosvāmī and Sanātana Gosvāmī formerly lived has now become a place of pilgrimage. It is generally known as Gupta Vṛndāvana, or hidden Vṛndāvana, and is situated about eight miles south of Iṁrejabājāra. There the following places are still visited: (1) the temple of Śrī Madana-mohana Deity, (2) the Keli-kadamba tree under which Śrī Caitanya Mahāprabhu met Sanātana Gosvāmī at night and (3) Rūpasāgara, a large pond excavated by Śrī Rūpa Gosvāmī. A society named Rāmakeli-saṁskāra-samiti was established in 1924 to repair the temple and renovate the pond.

TEXT 85

তাঁর মধ্যে রূপ-সনাতন— বড় শাখা।
অনুপম, জীব, রাজেন্দ্রাদি উপশাখা ॥ ৮৫ ॥

tāṅra madhye rūpa-sanātana—baḍa śākhā
anupama, jīva, rājendrādi upaśākhā

SYNONYMS

tāṅra—within that; *madhye*—in the midst of; *rūpa-sanātana*—the branch known as Rūpa-Sanātana; *baḍa śākhā*—the big branch; *anupama*—of the name Anupama; *jīva*—of the name Jīva; *rājendra-ādi*—and Rājendra and others; *upaśākhā*—their sub-branches.

TRANSLATION

Among these branches, Rūpa and Sanātana were principal. Anupama, Jīva Gosvāmī and others, headed by Rājendra, were their sub-branches.

PURPORT

In the *Gaura-gaṇoddeśa-dīpikā* it is said that Śrīla Jīva Gosvāmī was formerly Vilāsa-mañjarī *gopī.* From his very childhood Jīva Gosvāmī was greatly fond of *Śrīmad-Bhāgavatam.* He later came to Navadvīpa to study Sanskrit, and, following in the footsteps of Śrī Nityānanda Prabhu, he circumambulated the entire Navadvīpa-dhāma. After visiting Navadvīpa-dhāma he went to Benares to study Sanskrit under Madhusūdana Vācaspati, and after finishing his studies in Benares, he went to Vṛndāvana and took shelter of his uncles, Śrī Rūpa and Sanātana. This is described in the *Bhakti-ratnākara.* As far as our information goes, Śrīla Jīva Gosvāmī composed and edited at least twenty-five books. They are all very celebrated, and they are listed as follows: (1) *Hari-nāmāmṛta-vyākaraṇa,* (2) *Sūtra-mālikā,* (3) *Dhātu-saṅgraha,* (4) *Kṛṣṇārcā-dīpikā,* (5) *Gopāla-virudāvalī,* (6) *Rasāmṛta-śeṣa,* (7) *Śrī Mādhava-mahotsava,* (8) *Śrī Saṅkalpa-kalpavṛkṣa,* (9) *Bhāvārtha-sūcaka-campū,* (10) *Gopāla-tāpanī-ṭīkā,* (11) a commentary on *Brahma-saṁhitā,* (12) a commentary on *Bhakti-rasāmṛta-sindhu,* (13) a commentary on *Ujjvala-nīlamaṇi,* (14) a commentary on *Yogasāra-stava,* (15) a commentary on the *Gāyatrī-mantra* as described in the *Agni Purāṇa,* (16) a description derived from the *Padma Purāṇa* of the lotus feet of the Lord, (17) a description of the lotus feet of Śrīmatī Rādhārāṇī, (18) *Gopāla-campū* (in two parts) and (19-25) seven *sandarbhas:* the *Krama, Tattva, Bhagavat, Paramātma, Kṛṣṇa, Bhakti* and *Prīti Sandarbhas.* After the disappearance of Śrīla Rūpa Gosvāmī and Sanātana Gosvāmī in Vṛndāvana, Śrīla Jīva Gosvāmī became the *ācārya* of all the Vaiṣṇavas in Bengal, Orissa and the rest of the world, and it is he who used to guide them in their devotional service. In Vṛndāvana he established the Rādhā-Dāmodara temple, where we had the opportunity to live and retire until the age of 65, when we decided to come to the United States of America. When Jīva Gosvāmī was still present, Śrīla Kṛṣṇadāsa Kavirāja Gosvāmī compiled his famous *Caitanya-caritāmṛta.* Later, Śrīla Jīva Gosvāmī inspired Śrīnivāsa Ācārya, Narottama dāsa Ṭhākura and Duḥkhī Kṛṣṇadāsa to preach Kṛṣṇa consciousness in Bengal. Jīva Gosvāmī was informed that all the manuscripts that were collected from Vṛndāvana and sent to Bengal for preaching purposes were plundered near Viṣṇupura in Bengal, but later he received the information that the books had been recovered. Śrī Jīva Gosvāmī awarded the designation Kavirāja to Rāmacandra Sena, a disciple of Śrīnivāsa Ācārya, and his younger brother Govinda. While Jīva Gosvāmī was alive, Śrīmatī Jāhnavī-devī, the pleasure potency of Śrī Nityānanda Prabhu, went to Vṛndāvana with a few devotees. Jīva Gosvāmī was very kind to the Gauḍīya Vaiṣṇavas, the Vaiṣṇavas from Bengal. Whoever went to Vṛndāvana he provided with a residence and *prasāda.* His disciple Kṛṣṇadāsa Adhikārī listed all the books of the Gosvāmīs in his diary.

The *sahajiyās* level three accusations against Śrīla Jīva Gosvāmī. This is certainly not congenial with the execution of devotional service. The first accusation concerns a materialist who was very proud of his reputation as a great Sanskrit scholar and approached Śrī Rūpa and Sanātana to argue with them about the revealed scriptures. Śrīla Rūpa Gosvāmī and Sanātana Gosvāmī, not wanting to waste their time, gave him a written statement that he had defeated them in a debate on the revealed scriptures. Taking this paper, the scholar approached Jīva Gosvāmī for a similar certificate of defeat, but Jīva Gosvāmī did not agree to give him one. On the contrary, he argued with him regarding the scriptures and defeated him. Certainly it was right for Jīva Gosvāmī to stop such a dishonest scholar from advertising that he had defeated Śrīla Rūpa Gosvāmī and Sanātana Gosvāmī, but due to their illiteracy the *sahajiyā* class refer to this incident to accuse Śrīla Jīva Gosvāmī of deviating from the principle of humility. They do not know, however, that humility and meekness are appropriate when one's own honor is insulted. But when Lord Viṣṇu or the *ācāryas* are blasphemed, one should not be humble and meek but must act. One should follow the example given by Śrī Caitanya Mahāprabhu. Lord Caitanya says in His prayer:

tṛṇād api sunīcena
taror api sahiṣṇunā
amāninā mānadena
kīrtanīyaḥ sadā hariḥ

"One can chant the holy name of the Lord in a humble state of mind, thinking himself lower than the straw in the street; one should be more tolerant than a tree, devoid of all sense of false prestige, and should be ready to offer all respect to others. In such a state of mind one can chant the holy name of the Lord constantly." Nevertheless, when the Lord was informed that Nityānanda Prabhu was injured by Jagāi and Mādhāi, He immediately went to the spot, angry like fire, wanting to kill them. Thus Lord Caitanya has explained His verse by the example of His own behavior. One should tolerate insults against oneself, but when there is blasphemy committed against superiors such as other Vaiṣṇavas, one should be neither humble nor meek; one must take proper steps to counteract such blasphemy. This is the duty of a servant of a *guru* and Vaiṣṇavas. Anyone who understands the principle of eternal servitude to the *guru* and Vaiṣṇavas will appreciate the action of Śrī Jīva Gosvāmī in connection with the so-called scholar's victory over his *gurus,* Śrīla Rūpa and Śrīla Sanātana Gosvāmī.

Another story fabricated to defame Śrīla Jīva Gosvāmī states that after compiling *Śrī Caitanya-caritāmṛta,* Śrīla Kṛṣṇadāsa Kavirāja Gosvāmī showed the manuscript to Jīva Gosvāmī, who thought that it would hamper his reputation as a big scholar and therefore threw it in a well. Śrīla Kṛṣṇadāsa Kavirāja Gosvāmī was greatly shocked, and he died immediately. Fortunately a copy of the manuscript of *Caitanya-caritāmṛta* had been kept by a person named Mukunda, and therefore later it was possible to publish the book. This story is another ignominious example of blasphemy against a *guru* and Vaiṣṇava. Such a story should never be accepted as authoritative.

According to another accusation, Śrīla Jīva Gosvāmī did not approve of the principles of the *pārakīya-rasa* of Vrajadhāma and therefore supported *svakīya-rasa,* showing that Rādhā and Kṛṣṇa are eternally married. Actually, when Jīva Gosvāmī was alive, some of his followers disliked the *pārakīya-rasa* of the *gopīs.* Therefore Śrīla Jīva Gosvāmī, for their spiritual benefit, supported *svakīya-rasa,* for he could understand that *sahajiyās* would otherwise exploit the *pārakīya-rasa,* as they are actually doing at the present. Unfortunately, in Vṛndāvana and Navadvīpa it has become fashionable among *sahajiyās,* in their debauchery, to find an unmarried sexual partner to live with to execute devotional service in *pārakīya-rasa.* Foreseeing this, Śrīla Jīva Gosvāmī supported *svakīya-rasa,* and later all the Vaiṣṇava *ācāryas* also approved of it. Śrīla Jīva Gosvāmī was never opposed to the transcendental *pārakīya-rasa,* nor has any other Vaiṣṇava disapproved of it. Śrīla Jīva Gosvāmī strictly followed his predecessor *gurus* and Vaiṣṇavas, Śrīla Rūpa and Sanātana Gosvāmī, and Śrīla Kṛṣṇadāsa Kavirāja Gosvāmī accepted him as one of his instructor *gurus.*

TEXT 86

মালীর ইচ্ছায় শাখা বহুত বাড়িল ।
বাড়িয়া পশ্চিম দেশ সব আচ্ছাদিল ॥ ৮৬ ॥

mālīra icchāya śākhā bahuta bāḍila
bāḍiyā paścima deśa saba ācchādila

SYNONYMS

mālīra icchāya—on the desire of the gardener; *śākhā*—branches; *bahuta*—many; *bāḍila*—expanded; *bāḍiyā*—so expanding; *paścima*—western; *deśa*—countries; *saba*—all; *ācchādila*—covered.

TRANSLATION

By the will of the supreme gardener, the branches of Śrīla Rūpa Gosvāmī and Sanātana Gosvāmī grew many times over, expanding throughout the western countries and covering the entire region.

TEXT 87

আ-সিন্ধুনদী-তীর আর হিমালয় ।
বৃন্দাবন-মথুরাদি যত তীর্থ হয় ॥ ৮৭ ॥

ā-sindhunadī-tīra āra himālaya
vṛndāvana-mathurādi yata tīrtha haya

SYNONYMS

ā-sindhu-nadī—to the border of the River Sindhu; *tīra*—border; *āra*—and; *himālaya*—the Himalayan Mountains; *vṛndāvana*—of the name Vṛndāvana; *mathurā*—of the name Mathurā; *ādi*—heading the list; *yata*—all; *tīrtha*—places of pilgrimage; *haya*—there are.

TRANSLATION

Extending to the borders of the River Sindhu and the Himalayan Mountain valleys, they expanded throughout India, including all the places of pilgrimage such as Vṛndāvana, Mathurā and Haridvāra.

TEXT 88

দুই শাখার প্রেমফলে সকল ভাসিল ।
প্রেমফলাস্বাদে লোক উন্মত্ত হইল ॥ ৮৮ ॥

dui śākhāra prema-phale sakala bhāsila
prema-phalāsvāde loka unmatta ha-ila

SYNONYMS

dui śākhāra—of the two branches; *prema-phale*—by the fruit of love of Godhead; *sakala*—all; *bhāsila*—became overflooded; *prema-phala*—the fruit of love of Godhead; *āsvāde*—by tasting; *loka*—all people; *unmatta*—maddened; *ha-ila*—became.

TRANSLATION

The fruits of love of Godhead which fructified on these two branches were distributed in abundance. Tasting these fruits, everyone became mad after them.

TEXT 89

পশ্চিমের লোক সব মূঢ় অনাচার ।
তাহাঁ প্রচারিল দোঁহে ভক্তি-সদাচার ॥ ৮৯ ॥

paścimera loka saba mūḍha anācāra
tāhāṅ pracārila doṅhe bhakti-sadācāra

SYNONYMS

paścimera—on the western side; *loka*—people in general; *saba*—all; *mūḍha*—less intelligent; *anācāra*—not well behaved; *tāhāṅ*—there; *pracārila*—preached; *doṅhe*—Śrīla Rūpa and Sanātana Gosvāmī; *bhakti*—devotional service; *sadācāra*—good behavior.

TRANSLATION

The people in general on the western side of India were neither intelligent nor well behaved, but by the influence of Śrīla Rūpa Gosvāmī and Sanātana Gosvāmī they were trained in devotional service and good behavior.

PURPORT

Although it is not only in western India that people were contaminated by association with Mohammedans, it is a fact that the farther west one goes in India the more he will find the people to be fallen from the Vedic culture. Even until 5,000 years ago, when the entire planet was under the control of Mahārāja Parīkṣit, the Vedic culture was current everywhere. Gradually, however, people were influenced by non-Vedic culture, and they lost sight of how to behave in connection with devotional service. Śrīla Rūpa Gosvāmī and Sanātana Gosvāmī very kindly preached the *bhakti* cult in western India, and following in their footsteps the propagators of the Caitanya cult in the western countries are spreading the *saṅkīrtana* movement and inculcating the principles of Vaiṣṇava behavior, thus purifying and reforming many persons who were previously accustomed to the culture of *mlecchas* and *yavanas.* All of our devotees in the western countries give up their old habits of illicit sex, intoxication, meat-eating and gambling. Of course, 500 years ago these practices were unknown at least in eastern India, but unfortunately at present all of India has been victimized by these non-Vedic principles, which are sometimes even supported by the government.

TEXT 90

শাস্ত্রদৃষ্ট্যে কৈল লুপ্ততীর্থের উদ্ধার ।
বৃন্দাবনে কৈল শ্রীমূর্তি-সেবার প্রচার ॥ ৯০ ॥

śāstra-dṛṣṭye kaila lupta-tīrthera uddhāra
vṛndāvane kaila śrīmūrti-sevāra pracāra

SYNONYMS

śāstra-dṛṣṭye—according to the directions of revealed scriptures; *kaila*—did; *lupta*—forgotten; *tīrthera*—place of pilgrimage; *uddhāra*—excavation; *vṛndāvane*—in Vṛndāvana; *kaila*—did; *śrī-mūrti*—Deity; *sevāra*—of worship; *pracāra*—propagation.

TRANSLATION

In accordance with the directions of the revealed scriptures, both Gosvāmīs excavated the lost places of pilgrimage and inaugurated the worship of Deities in Vṛndāvana.

PURPORT

The spot where we now find Śrī Rādhākuṇḍa was an agricultural field during the time of Caitanya Mahāprabhu. A small reservoir of water was there, and Śrī Caitanya Mahāprabhu bathed in that water and pointed out that originally Rādhā-kuṇḍa existed in that location. Following His directions, Śrīla Rūpa Gosvāmī and Sanātana Gosvāmī renovated Rādhākuṇḍa. This is one of the brilliant examples of how the Gosvāmīs excavated lost places of pilgrimage. Similarly, it is through the the endeavor of the Gosvāmīs that all the important temples at Vṛndāvana were established. Originally there were seven important Gauḍīya Vaiṣṇava temples established in Vṛndāvana, namely, the Madana-mohana temple, Govinda temple, Gopīnātha temple, Śrī Rādhāramaṇa temple, Rādhā-Śyāmasundara temple, Rādhā-Dāmodara temple and Gokulānanda temple.

TEXT 91

মহাপ্রভুর প্রিয় ভৃত্য—রঘুনাথদাস ।
সর্ব ত্যজি' কৈল প্রভুর পদতলে বাস ॥ ৯১ ॥

mahāprabhura priya bhṛtya—raghunātha-dāsa
sarva tyaji' kaila prabhura pada-tale vāsa

SYNONYMS

mahāprabhura—of Lord Caitanya Mahāprabhu; *priya*—very dear; *bhṛtya*—servant; *raghunātha-dāsa*—Raghunātha dāsa Gosvāmī; *sarva tyaji'*—renouncing everything; *kaila*—did; *prabhura*—of the Lord; *pada-tale*—under the shelter of the lotus feet; *vāsa*—habitation.

TRANSLATION

Śrīla Raghunātha dāsa Gosvāmī, the forty-sixth branch of the tree, was one of the most dear servants of Lord Caitanya Mahāprabhu. He left all his material possessions to surrender completely unto the Lord and live at His lotus feet.

PURPORT

Śrīla Raghunātha dāsa Gosvāmī was most probably born in the year 1416 *śakābda* in a *kāyastha* family as the son of Govardhana Majumdāra, who was the younger brother of the then Zamindar Hiraṇya Majumdāra. The village where he took birth is known as Śrī Kṛṣṇapura. On the railway line between Calcutta and Burdwan is a station named Triśābaghā, and about one and a half miles away is the village of Śrī Kṛṣṇapura, where the parental home of Śrī Raghunātha dāsa Gosvāmī was situated. A temple of Śrī Śrī Rādhā-Govinda is still there. In front of the temple is a large open area but no large hall for meetings. However, a rich Calcutta gentleman named Haricaraṇa Ghosh who resided in the Simlā quarter recently repaired the temple. The entire temple compound is surrounded by walls, and in a small room just to the side of the temple is a small platform on which Raghunātha dāsa Gosvāmī used to worship the Deity. By the side of the temple is the dying River Sarasvatī.

The forefathers of Śrīla Raghunātha dāsa Gosvāmī were all Vaiṣṇavas and were very rich men. His spiritual master at home was Yadunandana Ācārya. Although Raghunātha dāsa was a family man, he had no attachment for his estate and wife. Seeing his tendency to leave home, his father and uncle engaged special bodyguards to watch over him, but nevertheless he managed to escape their vigilance and went away to Jagannātha Purī to meet Śrī Caitanya Mahāprabhu. This incident took place in the year 1439 *śakābda.* Raghunātha dāsa Gosvāmī compiled three books named *Stava-mālā* or *Stavāvalī, Dāna-carita* and *Muktācarita.* He lived for a long duration of life. For most of his life he resided at Rādhākuṇḍa. The place where Raghunātha dāsa Gosvāmī performed his devotional service still exists by Rādhā-kuṇḍa. He almost completely gave up eating, and therefore he was very skinny and of weak health. His only concern was to chant the holy name of the Lord. He gradually reduced his sleeping until he was almost not sleeping at all. It is said that his eyes were always full of tears. When Śrīnivāsa Ācārya went to see Raghunātha dāsa Gosvāmī, the Gosvāmī blessed him by embracing him. Śrīnivāsa Ācārya requested his blessings for preaching in Bengal, and Śrīla Raghunātha dāsa Gosvāmī granted them. In the *Gaura-gaṇoddeśa-dīpikā* (186) it is stated that Śrīla Raghunātha dāsa Gosvāmī was formerly the *gopī* named Rasa-mañjarī. Sometimes it is said that he was Rati-mañjarī.

TEXT 92

প্রভু সমর্পিল তাঁরে স্বরূপের হাতে ।
প্রভুর গুপ্তসেবা কৈল স্বরূপের সাথে ॥ ৯২ ॥

prabhu samarpila tāṅre svarūpera hāte
prabhura gupta-sevā kaila svarūpera sāthe

SYNONYMS

prabhu—Lord Caitanya Mahāprabhu; *samarpila*—handed over; *tāṅre*—him; *svarūpera*—Svarūpa Dāmodara; *hāte*—to the hand; *prabhura*—of the Lord; *gupta-sevā*—confidential service; *kaila*—did; *svarūpera*—Svarūpa Dāmodara; *sāthe*—with.

TRANSLATION

When Raghunātha dāsa Gosvāmī approached Śrī Caitanya Mahāprabhu at Jagannātha Purī, the Lord entrusted him to the care of Svarūpa Dāmodara, His secretary. Thus they both engaged in the confidential service of the Lord.

PURPORT

This confidential service was the personal care of the Lord. Svarūpa Dāmodara, acting as His secretary, attended to the Lord's baths, meals, rest and massages, and Raghunātha dāsa Gosvāmī assisted him. In effect, Raghunātha dāsa Gosvāmī acted as the assistant secretary of the Lord.

TEXT 93

ষোড়শ বৎসর কৈল অন্তরঙ্গ-সেবন ।
স্বরূপের অন্তর্ধানে আইলা বৃন্দাবন ॥ ৯৩ ॥

ṣoḍaśa vatsara kaila antaraṅga-sevana
svarūpera antardhāne āilā vṛndāvana

SYNONYMS

ṣoḍaśa—sixteen; *vatsara*—years; *kaila*—did; *antaraṅga*—confidential; *sevana*—service; *svarūpera*—of Svarūpa Dāmodara; *antardhāne*—disappearance; *āilā*—came; *vṛndāvana*—to Vṛndāvana.

TRANSLATION

He rendered confidential service to the Lord for sixteen years at Jagannātha Purī, and after the disappearance of both the Lord and Svarūpa Dāmodara, he left Jagannātha Purī and went to Vṛndāvana.

TEXT 94

বৃন্দাবনে দুই ভাইর চরণ দেখিয়া ।
গোবর্ধনে ত্যজিব দেহ ভৃগুপাত করিয়া ॥ ৯৪ ॥

vṛndāvane dui bhāira caraṇa dekhiyā
govardhane tyajiba deha bhṛgupāta kariyā

SYNONYMS

vṛndāvane—at Vṛndāvana; *dui bhāira*—the two brothers (Rūpa and Sanātana); *caraṇa*—feet; *dekhiyā*—after seeing; *govardhane*—on the hill of Govardhana; *tyajiba*—will give up; *deha*—this body; *bhṛgupāta*—falling down; *kariyā*—doing so.

TRANSLATION

Śrīla Raghunātha dāsa Gosvāmī intended to go to Vṛndāvana to see the lotus feet of Rūpa and Sanātana and then give up his life by jumping from Govardhana Hill.

PURPORT

Jumping from the top of Govardhana Hill is a system of suicide especially performed by saintly persons. After the disappearance of Lord Caitanya and Svarūpa Dāmodara, Raghunātha dāsa Gosvāmī keenly felt the separation of these two exalted personalities and therefore decided to give up his life by jumping from Govardhana Hill in Vṛndāvana. Before doing so, however, he wanted to see the lotus feet of Śrīla Rūpa Gosvāmī and Sanātana Gosvāmī.

TEXT 95

এই ত' নিশ্চয় করি' আইল বৃন্দাবনে ।
আসি' রূপ-সনাতনের বন্দিল চরণে ॥ ৯৫ ॥

ei ta' niścaya kari' āila vṛndāvane
āsi' rūpa-sanātanera vandila caraṇe

SYNONYMS

ei ta'—thus; *niścaya kari'*—having decided; *āila*—came; *vṛndāvane*—to Vṛndāvana; *āsi'*—coming there; *rūpa-sanātanera*—of Śrīla Rūpa Gosvāmī and Sanātana Gosvāmī; *vandila*—offered respects; *caraṇe*—at the lotus feet.

TRANSLATION

Thus Śrīla Raghunātha dāsa Gosvāmī came to Vṛndāvana, visited Śrīla Rūpa Gosvāmī and Sanātana Gosvāmī and offered them his obeisances.

TEXT 96

তবে দুই ভাই তাঁরে মরিতে না দিল ।
নিজ তৃতীয় ভাই করি' নিকটে রাখিল ॥ ৯৬ ॥

tabe dui bhāi tāṅre marite nā dila
nija tṛtīya bhāi kari' nikaṭe rākhila

SYNONYMS

tabe—at that time; *dui bhāi*—the two brothers (Śrīla Rūpa and Sanātana); *tāṅre*—him; *marite*—to die; *nā dila*—did not allow; *nija*—own; *tṛtīya*—third; *bhāi*—brother; *kari'*—accepting; *nikaṭe*—near; *rākhila*—kept him.

TRANSLATION

These two brothers, however, did not allow him to die. They accepted him as their third brother and kept him in their company.

TEXT 97

মহাপ্রভুর লীলা যত বাহির-অন্তর ।
দুই ভাই তাঁর মুখে শুনে নিরন্তর ॥ ৯৭ ॥

mahāprabhura līlā yata bāhira-antara
dui bhāi tāṅra mukhe śune nirantara

SYNONYMS

mahāprabhura—of Lord Śrī Caitanya Mahāprabhu; *līlā*—pastimes; *yata*—all; *bāhira*—external; *antara*—internal; *dui bhāi*—the two brothers; *tāṅra*—his; *mukhe*—in the mouth; *śune*—hear; *nirantara*—always.

TRANSLATION

Because Raghunātha dāsa Gosvāmī was an assistant to Svarūpa Dāmodara, he knew much about the external and internal features of the pastimes of Lord Caitanya. Thus the two brothers Rūpa and Sanātana always used to hear of this from him.

TEXT 98

অন্ন-জল ত্যাগ কৈল অন্য-কথন ।
পল দুই-তিন মাঠা করেন ভক্ষণ ॥ ৯৮ ॥

anna-jala tyāga kaila anya-kathana
pala dui-tina māṭhā karena bhakṣaṇa

SYNONYMS

anna-jala—food and drink; *tyāga*—renunciation; *kaila*—did; *anya-kathana*—talking of other things; *pala dui-tina*—a few drops of; *māṭhā*—sour milk; *karena*—does; *bhakṣaṇa*—eat.

TRANSLATION

Raghunātha dāsa Gosvāmī gradually gave up all food and drink but a few drops of buttermilk.

TEXT 99

সহস্র দণ্ডবৎ করে, লয় লক্ষ নাম ।
দুই সহস্র বৈষ্ণবেরে নিত্য পরণাম ॥ ৯৯ ॥

sahasra daṇḍavat kare, laya lakṣa nāma
dui sahasra vaiṣṇavere nitya paraṇāma

SYNONYMS

sahasra—thousand; *daṇḍavat*—obeisances; *kare*—does; *laya*—takes; *lakṣa*—one hundred thousand; *nāma*—holy names; *dui*—two; *sahasra*—thousand; *vaiṣṇavere*—unto the devotees; *nitya*—daily; *paraṇāma*—obeisances.

TRANSLATION

As a daily duty, he regularly offered one thousand obeisances to the Lord, chanted at least one hundred thousand holy names and offered obeisances to two thousand Vaiṣṇavas.

TEXT 100

রাত্রিদিনে রাধাকৃষ্ণের মানস সেবন ।
প্রহরেক মহাপ্রভুর চরিত্র-কথন ॥ ১০০ ॥

rātri-dine rādhā-kṛṣṇera mānasa sevana
prahareka mahāprabhura caritra-kathana

SYNONYMS

rātri-dine—day and night; *rādhā-kṛṣṇera*—of Rādhā and Kṛṣṇa; *mānasa*—within the mind; *sevana*—service; *prahareka*—about three hours; *mahāprabhura*—of Lord Caitanya; *caritra*—character; *kathana*—discussing.

TRANSLATION

Day and night he rendered service within his mind to Rādhā-Kṛṣṇa, and for three hours a day he discoursed about the character of Lord Caitanya Mahāprabhu.

PURPORT

We have many things to learn about *bhajana,* or worship of the Lord, by following in the footsteps of Raghunātha dāsa Gosvāmī. All the Gosvāmīs engaged in such transcendental activities, as described by Śrīnivāsa Ācārya in his poem about them *(kṛṣṇotkīrtana-gāna-nartana-parau premāmṛtāmbho-nidhī).* Following in the footsteps of Raghunātha dāsa Gosvāmī, Śrīla Rūpa Gosvāmī and Sanātana Gosvāmī, one has to execute devotional service very strictly, specifically by chanting the holy name of the Lord.

TEXT 101

তিন সন্ধ্যা রাধাকুণ্ডে অপতিত স্নান ।
ব্রজবাসী বৈষ্ণবে করে আলিঙ্গন মান ॥ ১০১ ॥

tina sandhyā rādhā-kuṇḍe apatita snāna
vraja-vāsī vaiṣṇave kare āliṅgana māna

SYNONYMS

tina sandhyā—three times, namely morning, evening and noon; *rādhā-kuṇḍe*—in the lake of Rādhākuṇḍa; *apatita*—without failure; *snāna*—taking bath; *vraja-vāsī*—inhabitants of Vrajabhūmi; *vaiṣṇave*—all devotees; *kare*—does; *āliṅgana*—embracing; *māna*—and offering respect.

TRANSLATION

Śrī Raghunātha dāsa Gosvāmī took three baths daily in the Rādhākuṇḍa lake. As soon as he found a Vaiṣṇava residing in Vṛndāvana, he would embrace him and give him all respect.

TEXT 102

সার্ধ সপ্তপ্রহর করে ভক্তির সাধনে।
চারি দণ্ড নিদ্রা, সেহ নহে কোনদিনে ॥ ১০২ ।

sārdha sapta-prahara kare bhaktira sādhane
cāri daṇḍa nidrā, seha nahe kona-dine

SYNONYMS

sārdha—one and a half hours; *sapta-prahara*—seven *praharas* (twenty-one hours); *kare*—does; *bhaktira*—of devotional service; *sādhane*—in execution; *cāri daṇḍa*—about two hours; *nidrā*—sleeping; *seha*—that also; *nahe*—not; *kona-dine*—some days.

TRANSLATION

He engaged himself in devotional service for more than twenty-two and a half hours a day, and for less than two hours he slept, although on some days that also was not possible.

TEXT 103

তাঁহার সাধনরীতি শুনিতে চমৎকার।
সেই রূপ-রঘুনাথ প্রভু যে আমার ॥ ১০৩ ॥

tāṅhāra sādhana-rīti śunite camatkāra
sei rūpa-raghunātha prabhu ye āmāra

SYNONYMS

tāṅhāra—his; *sādhana-rīti*—process of devotional service; *śunite*—to hear; *camatkāra*—wonderful; *sei*—that; *rūpa*—Śrī Rūpa Gosvāmī; *raghunātha*—Raghunātha dāsa Gosvāmī; *prabhu*—lord; *ye*—that; *āmāra*—my.

TRANSLATION

I am struck with wonder when I hear about the devotional service he executed. I accept Śrīla Rūpa Gosvāmī and Raghunātha dāsa Gosvāmī as my guides.

PURPORT

Śrīla Kṛṣṇadāsa Kavirāja Gosvāmī accepted Raghunātha dāsa Gosvāmī as his special guide. Therefore at the end of every chapter he says, *śrī-rūpa-raghunātha-pade yāra āśa caitanya-caritāmṛta kahe kṛṣṇadāsa.* Sometimes it is misunderstood that by using the word *raghunātha* he wanted to offer his respectful obeisances to Raghunātha Bhaṭṭa Gosvāmī, for it is sometimes stated that Raghunātha Bhaṭṭa Gosvāmī was his initiator spiritual master. Śrīla Bhaktisiddhānta Sarasvatī Gosvāmī does not approve of this statement; he does not accept Raghunātha Bhaṭṭa Gosvāmī as the spiritual master of Śrīla Kṛṣṇadāsa Kavirāja Gosvāmī.

TEXT 104

ইঁহা-সবার যৈছে হৈল প্রভুর মিলন।
আগে বিস্তারিয়া তাহা করিব বর্ণন ॥ ১০৪ ॥

iṅhā-sabāra yaiche haila prabhura milana
āge vistāriyā tāhā kariba varṇana

SYNONYMS

iṅhā—of them; *sabāra*—all; *yaiche*—as; *haila*—became; *prabhura*—of Śrī Caitanya Mahāprabhu; *milana*—meeting; *āge*—later on; *vistāriyā*—expanding; *tāhā*—that; *kariba*—I shall do; *varṇana*—description.

TRANSLATION

I shall later explain very elaborately how all these devotees met Śrī Caitanya Mahāprabhu.

TEXT 105

শ্রীগোপাল ভট্ট এক শাখা সর্বোত্তম।
রূপ-সনাতন-সঙ্গে যাঁর প্রেম-আলাপন ॥ ১০৫

śrī-gopāla bhaṭṭa eka śākhā sarvottama
rūpa-sanātana-saṅge yāṅra prema-ālāpana

SYNONYMS

śrī-gopāla bhaṭṭa—of the name Śrī Gopāla Bhaṭṭa; *eka*—one; *śākhā*—branch; *sarvottama*—very exalted; *rūpa*—of the name Rūpa; *sanātana*—of the name Sanātana; *saṅge*—company; *yāṅra*—whose; *prema*—love of Godhead; *ālāpana*—discussion.

TRANSLATION

Śrī Gopāla Bhaṭṭa Gosvāmī, the forty-seventh branch, was one of the great and exalted branches of the tree. He always engaged in discourses about love of Godhead in the company of Rūpa Gosvāmī and Sanātana Gosvāmī.

PURPORT

Śrī Gopāla Bhaṭṭa Gosvāmī was the son of Veṅkata Bhaṭṭa, a resident of Śrīraṅgam. Gopāla Bhaṭṭa formerly belonged to the disciplic succession of the Rāmānuja-sampradāya but later became part of the Gauḍīya-sampradāya. In the year 1433 *śakābda,* when Lord Caitanya Mahāprabhu was touring South India, He stayed for four months during the period of Cāturmāsya at the house of Veṅkata Bhaṭṭa, who then got the opportunity to serve the Lord to his heart's content. Gopāla Bhaṭṭa also got the opportunity to serve the Lord at this time. Śrī Gopāla Bhaṭṭa Gosvāmī was later initiated by his uncle, the great *sannyāsī* Prabodhānanda Sarasvatī. Both the father and mother of Gopāla Bhaṭṭa Gosvāmī were extremely fortunate, for they dedicated their entire lives to the service of Lord Caitanya Mahāprabhu. They allowed Gopāla Bhaṭṭa Gosvāmī to go to Vṛndāvana, and they gave up their lives thinking of Śrī Caitanya Mahāprabhu. When Lord Caitanya was later informed that Gopāla Bhaṭṭa Gosvāmī had gone to Vṛndāvana and met Śrī Rūpa and Sanātana Gosvāmī, He was very pleased, and He advised Śrī Rūpa and Sanātana to accept Gopāla Bhaṭṭa Gosvāmī as their younger brother and take care of him. Śrī Sanātana Gosvāmī, out of his great affection for Gopāla Bhaṭṭa Gosvāmī, compiled the Vaiṣṇava *smṛti* named *Hari-bhakti-vilāsa* and published it under his name. Under the instruction of Śrīla Rūpa and Sanātana, Gopāla Bhaṭṭa Gosvāmī installed one of the seven principal Deities of Vṛndāvana, the Rādhāramaṇa Deity. The *sevāits* (priests) of the Rādhāramaṇa temple belong to the Gauḍīya-sampradāya.

When Kṛṣṇadāsa Kavirāja Gosvāmī took permission from all the Vaiṣṇavas before writing *Caitanya-caritāmṛta,* Gopāla Bhaṭṭa Gosvāmī also gave him his blessings, but he requested him not to mention his name in the book. Therefore Kṛṣṇadāsa Kavirāja Gosvāmī has mentioned Gopāla Bhaṭṭa Gosvāmī only very cautiously in one or two passages of *Caitanya-caritāmṛta.* Śrīla Jīva Gosvāmī has written in the beginning of his *Tattva-sandarbha,* "A devotee from southern India who was born of a *brāhmaṇa* family and was a very intimate friend of Rūpa Gosvāmī and Sanātana Gosvāmī has written a book that he has not compiled chronologically. Therefore I, a tiny living entity known as *jīva,* am trying to assort the events of the book chronologically, consulting the direction of great personalities like Madhvācārya, Śrīdhara Svāmī, Rāmānujācārya and other senior Vaiṣṇavas in the disciplic succession." In the beginning of the *Bhagavat-sandarbha* there are similar statements by Śrīla Jīva Gosvāmī. Śrīla Gopāla Bhaṭṭa Gosvāmī compiled a book called *Sat-kriyā-sāra-dīpikā,* edited the *Hari-bhakti-vilāsa,* wrote a forward to the *Ṣaṭ-sandarbha* and a commentary on the *Kṛṣṇa-karṇāmṛta,* and installed the Rādhāramaṇa Deity in Vṛndāvana. In the *Gaura-gaṇoddeśa-dīpikā,* verse 184, it is mentioned that his previous name in the pastimes of Lord Kṛṣṇa was Anaṅga-mañjarī. Sometimes he is also said to have been an incarnation of Guṇa-mañjarī. Śrīnivāsa Ācārya and Gopīnātha Pūjārī were two of his disciples.

TEXT 106

শঙ্করারণ্য – আচার্য-বৃক্ষের এক শাখা ।
মুকুন্দ, কাশীনাথ, রুদ্র, – উপশাখা লেখা ॥ ১০৬ ॥

śaṅkarāraṇya——ācārya-vṛkṣera eka śākhā
mukunda, kāśīnātha, rudra——upaśākhā lekhā

SYNONYMS

śaṅkarāraṇya—of the name Śaṅkarāraṇya; *ācārya-vṛkṣera*—of the tree of *ācāryas; eka*—one; *śākhā*—branch; *mukunda*—of the name Mukunda; *kāśīnātha*—of the name Kāśīnātha; *rudra*—of the name Rudra; *upaśākhā lekhā*—they are known as sub-branches.

TRANSLATION

The ācārya Śaṅkarāraṇya was considered the forty-eighth branch of the original tree. From him proceeded sub-branches known as Mukunda, Kāśīnātha and Rudra.

PURPORT

It is said that Śaṅkarāraṇya was the *sannyāsa* name of Śrīla Viśvarūpa, who was the elder brother of Viśvambhara (the original name of Śrī Caitanya Mahāprabhu). Śaṅkarāraṇya expired in 1432 *śakābda* at Śolāpura, where there is a place of pilgrimage known as Pāṇḍerapura. This is referred to in the *Madhya-līlā,* Chapter Nine, verses 299 and 300.

Lord Caitanya Mahāprabhu opened a primary school in the house of Mukunda, or Mukunda Sañjaya, and Mukunda's son, whose name was Puruṣottama, became the Lord's student. Kāśīnātha arranged the marriage of Lord Caitanya in His previous *āśrama,* when His name was Viśvambhara. He induced the court *paṇḍita,* Sanātana, to offer Viśvambhara his daughter. In the *Gaura-gaṇoddeśa-dīpikā,* verse 50, it is mentioned that Kāśīnātha was an incarnation of Satrājit, who arranged the marriage of Kṛṣṇa and Satyā, and it is mentioned in verse 135 that Rudra, or Śrī Rudrarāma Paṇḍita, was formerly a friend of Lord Kṛṣṇa named Varūthapa. Śrī Rudrarāma Paṇḍita constructed a big temple at Vallabhapura, which is one mile north of Māheśa, for the Deities named Rādhāvallabha. The descendants of his brother, Yadunandana Bandyopādhyāya, are known as Cakravartī Ṭhākuras, and they are in charge of the maintenance of this temple as *sevāits.* Formerly the Jagannātha Deity used to come to the temple of Rādhāvallabha from Māheśa during the Rathayātrā festival, but in the Bengali year 1262, due to a misunderstanding between the priests of the two temples, the Jagannātha Deity stopped coming.

TEXT 107

শ্রীনাথ পণ্ডিত—প্রভুর কৃপার ভাজন ।
যাঁর কৃষ্ণসেবা দেখি' বশ ত্রিভুবন ॥ ১০৭ ॥

śrīnātha paṇḍita—prabhura kṛpāra bhājana
yāṅra kṛṣṇa-sevā dekhi' vaśa tri-bhuvana

SYNONYMS

śrīnātha paṇḍita—of the name Śrīnātha Paṇḍita; *prabhura*—of the Lord; *kṛpāra*—of mercy; *bhājana*—receiver; *yāṅra*—whose; *kṛṣṇa-sevā*—worship of Lord Kṛṣṇa; *dekhi'*—seeing; *vaśa*—subjugated; *tri-bhuvana*—all the three worlds.

TRANSLATION

Śrīnātha Paṇḍita, the forty-ninth branch, was the beloved recipient of all the mercy of Śrī Caitanya Mahāprabhu. Everyone in the three worlds was astonished to see how he worshiped Lord Kṛṣṇa.

PURPORT

About one and a half miles away from Kumārahaṭṭa, or Kāmarhaṭṭi, which is a few miles from Calcutta, is a village known as Kāṅcaḍāpāḍā which was the home of Śrī Śivānanda Sena. There he constructed a temple of Śrī Gaura-gopāla. Another temple was established there with Śrī Rādhā-Kṛṣṇa *mūrtis* by Śrīnātha Paṇḍita. The Deity of that temple is named Śrī Kṛṣṇa Rāya. The temple of Kṛṣṇa Rāya, which was constructed in the year 1708 *śakābda* by a prominent Zamindar named Nimāi Mullik of Pāthuriyā-ghāṭa in Calcutta, is very large. There is a big courtyard in front of the temple, and there are residential quarters for visitors and good arrangements for cooking *prasāda.* The entire courtyard is surrounded by very high boundary walls, and the temple is almost as big as the Māheśa temple. Inscribed on a tablet are the names of Śrīnātha Paṇḍita and his father and grandfather and the date of construction of the temple. Śrīnātha Paṇḍita, one of the disciples of Advaita Prabhu, was the spiritual master of the third son of Śivānanda Sena, who was known as Paramānanda Kavikarṇapūra. It is supposed to be during the time of Kavikarṇapūra that the Kṛṣṇa Rāya Deity was installed. According to hearsay, Vīrabhadra Prabhu, the son of Nityānanda Prabhu, brought a big stone from Murśidābād from which three Deities were carved—namely, the Rādhāvallabha *vigraha* of Vallabhapura, the Śyāmasundara *vigraha* of Khaḍadaha and the Śrī Kṛṣṇa Rāya *vigraha* of Kāṅcaḍāpāḍā. The home of Śivānanda Sena was situated on the bank of the Ganges near an almost ruined temple. It is said that the same Nimāi Mullik of Calcutta saw this broken-down temple of Kṛṣṇa Rāya while he was going to Benares and thereafter constructed the present temple.

TEXT 108

জগন্নাথ আচার্য প্রভুর প্রিয় দাস।
প্রভুর আজ্ঞাতে তেঁহো কৈল গঙ্গাবাস ॥ ১০৮ ॥

jagannātha ācārya prabhura priya dāsa
prabhura ājñāte teṅho kaila gaṅgā-vāsa

SYNONYMS

jagannātha ācārya—of the name Jagannātha Ācārya; *prabhura*—of the Lord; *priya dāsa*—very dear servant; *prabhura ājñāte*—by the order of the Lord; *teṅho*—he; *kaila*—agreed; *gaṅgā-vāsa*—living on the bank of the Ganges.

TRANSLATION

Jagannātha Ācārya, the fiftieth branch of the Caitanya tree, was an extremely dear servant of the Lord, by whose order he decided to live on the bank of the Ganges.

PURPORT

Jagannātha Ācārya is stated in the *Gaura-gaṇoddeśa-dīpikā* (111) to have formerly been Durvāsā of Nidhuvana.

TEXT 109

কৃষ্ণদাস বৈদ্য, আর পণ্ডিত-শেখর ।
কবিচন্দ্র, আর কীর্তনীয়া ষষ্ঠীবর ॥ ১০৯ ॥

kṛṣṇadāsa vaidya, āra paṇḍita-śekhara
kavicandra, āra kīrtanīyā ṣaṣṭhīvara

SYNONYMS

kṛṣṇadāsa vaidya—of the name Kṛṣṇadāsa Vaidya; *āra*—and; *paṇḍita-śekhara*—of the name Paṇḍita Śekhara; *kavicandra*—of the name Kavicandra; *āra*—and; *kīrtanīyā*—*kīrtana* performer; *ṣaṣṭhīvara*—of the name Ṣaṣṭhīvara.

TRANSLATION

The fifty-first branch of the Caitanya tree was Kṛṣṇadāsa Vaidya, the fifty-second was Paṇḍita Śekhara, the fifty-third was Kavicandra, and the fifty-fourth was Ṣaṣṭhīvara, who was a great saṅkīrtana performer.

PURPORT

In the *Gaura-gaṇoddeśa-dīpikā* (171) it is mentioned that Śrīnātha Miśra was Citrāṅgī and Kavicandra was Manoharā-gopī.

TEXT 110

শ্রীনাথ মিশ্র, শুভানন্দ, শ্রীরাম, ঈশান ।
শ্রীনিধি, শ্রীগোপীকান্ত, মিশ্র ভগবান্ ॥ ১১০ ॥

śrīnātha miśra, śubhānanda, śrīrāma, īśāna
śrīnidhi, śrīgopīkānta, miśra bhagavān

SYNONYMS

śrīnātha miśra—of the name Śrīnātha Miśra; *śubhānanda*—of the name Śubhānanda; *śrīrāma*—of the name Śrīrāma; *īśāna*—of the name Īśāna; *śrīnidhi*—of the name Śrīnidhi; *śrī-gopīkānta*—of the name Śrī Gopīkānta; *miśra bhagavān*—of the name Miśra Bhagavān.

TRANSLATION

The fifty-fifth branch was Śrīnātha Miśra, the fifty-sixth was Śubhānanda; the fifty-seventh was Śrīrāma, the fifty-eighth was Īśāna, the fifty-ninth was Śrīnidhi, the sixtieth was Śrī Gopīkānta, and the sixty-first was Miśra Bhagavān.

PURPORT

Śubhānanda, who formerly lived in Vṛndāvana as Mālatī, was one of the *kīrtana* performers who danced in front of the Rathayātrā car during the Jagannātha festival. It is said that he ate the foam that came out of the mouth of the Lord while He danced before the Rathayātrā car. Īśāna was a personal servant of Śrīmatī Śacīdevī, who showed her great mercy upon him. He was also very dear to Lord Caitanya Mahāprabhu.

TEXT 111

সুবুদ্ধি মিশ্র, হৃদয়ানন্দ, কমলনয়ন ।
মহেশ পণ্ডিত, শ্রীকর, শ্রীমধুসূদন ॥ ১১১ ॥

subuddhi miśra, hṛdayānanda, kamala-nayana
maheśa paṇḍita, śrīkara, śrī-madhusūdana

SYNONYMS

subuddhi miśra—of the name Subuddhi Miśra; *hṛdayānanda*—of the name Hṛdayānanda; *kamala-nayana*—of the name Kamala-nayana; *maheśa paṇḍita*—of the name Maheśa Paṇḍita; *śrīkara*—of the name Śrīkara; *śrī-madhusūdana*—of the name Śrī Madhusūdana.

TRANSLATION

The sixty-second branch of the tree was Subuddhi Miśra, the sixty-third was Hṛdayānanda, the sixty-fourth is Kamala-nayana, the sixty-fifth was Maheśa Paṇḍita, the sixty-sixth was Śrīkara, and the sixty-seventh was Śrī Madhusūdana.

PURPORT

Subuddhi Miśra, who was formerly Guṇacūḍā in Vṛndāvana, installed Gaura-Nityānanda Deities in a temple in the village known as Belagān, which is about three miles away from Śrīkhaṇḍa. His present descendant is known as Govindacandra Gosvāmī.

TEXT 112

**পুরুষোত্তম, শ্রীগালীম, জগন্নাথদাস।
শ্রীচন্দ্রশেখর বৈদ্য, দ্বিজ হরিদাস ॥ ১১২ ॥**

*puruṣottama, śrī-gālīma, jagannātha-dāsa
śrī-candraśekhara vaidya, dvija haridāsa*

SYNONYMS

puruṣottama—of the name Puruṣottama; *śrī-gālīma*—of the name Śrī Gālīma; *jagannātha-dāsa*—of the name Jagannātha dāsa; *śrī-candreśekhara vaidya*—of the name Śrī Candraśekhara Vaidya; *dvija haridāsa*—of the name Dvija Haridāsa.

TRANSLATION

The sixty-eighth branch of the original tree was Puruṣottama, the sixty-ninth was Śrī Gālīma, the seventieth was Jagannātha dāsa, the seventy-first was Śrī Candraśekhara Vaidya, and the seventy-second was Dvija Haridāsa.

PURPORT

There is some question about whether Dvija Haridāsa was the author of *Aṣṭottara-śata-nāma.* He had two sons named Śrīdāma and Gokulānanda who were disciples of Śrī Advaita Ācārya. Their village, Kāñcana-gaḍiyā, is situated within five miles of the Bājārasāu station, the fifth station from Ājīmagañja in the district of Murśidābād, West Bengal.

TEXT 113

**রামদাস, কবিচন্দ্র, শ্রীগোপালদাস।
ভাগবতাচার্য, ঠাকুর সারঙ্গদাস ॥ ১১৩ ॥**

*rāmadāsa, kavicandra, śrī-gopāladāsa
bhāgavatācārya, ṭhākura sāraṅgadāsa*

SYNONYMS

rāmadāsa—of the name Rāmadāsa; *kavicandra*—of the name Kavicandra; *śrī-gopāladāsa*—of the name Śrī Gopāla dāsa; *bhāgavatācārya*—of the name Bhāgavatācārya; *ṭhākura sāraṅgadāsa*—of the name Ṭhākura Sāraṅga dāsa.

TRANSLATION

The seventy-third branch of the original tree was Rāmadāsa, the seventy-fourth was Kavicandra, the seventy-fifth was Śrī Gopāla dāsa, the seventy-sixth was Bhāgavatācārya, and the seventy-seventh was Ṭhākura Sāraṅga dāsa.

PURPORT

In the *Gaura-gaṇoddeśa-dīpikā* (203) it is said, "Bhāgavatācārya compiled a book entitled *Kṛṣṇa-prema-taraṅgiṇī,* and he was the most beloved devotee of Lord Caitanya Mahāprabhu." When Lord Śrī Caitanya Mahāprabhu visited Varāhanagara, a suburb of Calcutta, He stayed in the house of a most fortunate *brāhmaṇa* who was a very learned scholar in *Bhāgavata* literature. As soon as this *brāhmaṇa* saw Lord Caitanya Mahāprabhu, he began to read *Śrīmad-Bhāgavatam.* When Mahāprabhu heard his explanation, which expounded *bhakti-yoga,* He immediately became unconscious in ecstasy. Lord Caitanya later said, "I have never heard such a nice explanation of *Śrīmad-Bhāgavatam.* I therefore designate you Bhāgavatācārya. Your only duty is to recite *Śrīmad-Bhāgavatam.* That is My injunction." His real name was Raghunātha. His monastery, which is situated in Varāhanagara, about three and a half miles north of Calcutta on the bank of the Ganges, still exists, and it is managed by the initiated disciples of the late Śrī Rāmadāsa Bābājī. Presently, however, it is not as well managed as in the presence of Bābājī Mahārāja.

Another name of Ṭhākura Sāraṅga dāsa was Sārṅga Ṭhākura. Sometimes he was also called Sārṅgapāṇi or Sārṅgadhara. He was a resident of Navadvīpa in the neighborhood known as Modadruma-dvīpa, and he used to worship the Supreme Lord in a secluded place on the bank of the Ganges. He did not accept disciples, but he was repeatedly inspired from within by the Supreme Personality of Godhead to do so. Thus one morning he decided, "Whomever I see I shall make my disciple." When he went to the bank of the Ganges to take his bath, by chance he saw a dead body floating in the water, and he touched it with his feet. This immediately brought the body to life, and Ṭhākura Sāraṅga dāsa accepted him as his disciple. This disciple later became famous as Ṭhākura Murāri, and his name is always associated with that of Śrī Sāraṅga. His disciplic succession still inhabits the village of Śar. There is a temple at Māmagācchi that is supposed to have been started by Sārṅga Ṭhākura. Not long ago, a new temple building was erected in front of a *bakula* tree there, and it is now being managed by the members of the Gauḍīya Maṭha. It is said that the management of the temple is now far better than before. In the *Gaura-gaṇoddeśa-dīpikā* (172) it is stated that Sārṅga Ṭhākura was formerly a *gopī* named Nāndīmukhī. Some devotees say that he was formerly Prahlāda Mahārāja, but Śrī Kavikarṇapūra says that his father, Śivānanda Sena, does not accept this proposition.

TEXT 114

জগন্নাথ তীর্থ, বিপ্র শ্রীজানকীনাথ ।
গোপাল আচার্য, আর বিপ্র বাণীনাথ ॥ ১১৪ ॥

jagannātha tīrtha, vipra śrī-jānakīnātha
gopāla ācārya, āra vipra vāṇīnātha

SYNONYMS

jagannātha tīrtha—of the name Jagannātha Tīrtha; *vipra*—*brāhmaṇa;* *śrī-jānakīnātha*—of the name Śrī Jānakīnātha; *gopāla ācārya*—of the name

Gopāla Ācārya; *āra*—and; *vipra vāṇīnātha*—the *brāhmaṇa* of the name Vāṇīnātha.

TRANSLATION

The seventy-eighth branch of the original tree was Jagannātha Tīrtha, the seventy-ninth was the brāhmaṇa Śrī Jānakīnātha, the eightieth was Gopāla Ācārya, and the eighty-first was the brāhmaṇa Vāṇīnātha.

PURPORT

Jagannātha Tīrtha was one of the nine principal *sannyāsīs* who were Lord Caitanya's associates. Vāṇīnātha Vipra was a resident of Cāṅpāhāṭi, a village in the district of Burdwan near the town of Navadvīpa, the police station of Pūrvasthalī and the post office of Samudragaḍa. The temple there was very much neglected, but it was renovated in the Bengali year 1328 by Śrī Paramānanda Brahmacārī, one of Śrī Bhaktisiddhānta Sarasvatī Ṭhākura's disciples, who reorganized the *sevā-pūjā* (worship in the temple) and placed the temple under the management of the Śrī Caitanya Maṭha of Śrī Māyāpur. In the temple as it now exists, the Deity of Śrī Gaura-Gadādhara is worshiped strictly according to the principles of the revealed scriptures. Cāṅpāhāṭi is two miles away from both Samudragaḍa and the Navadvīpa station of the eastern railway.

TEXT 115

গোবিন্দ, মাধব, বাসুদেব,—তিন ভাই ।
যাঁ-সবার কীর্তনে নাচে চৈতন্য-নিতাই ॥ ১১৫ ॥

govinda, mādhava, vāsudeva—tina bhāi
yāṅ-sabāra kīrtane nāce caitanya-nitāi

SYNONYMS

govinda—of the name Govinda; *mādhava*—of the name Mādhava; *vāsudeva*—of the name Vāsudeva; *tina bhāi*—three brothers; *yāṅ-sabāra*—all of whom; *kīrtane*—in the performance of *saṅkīrtana; nāce*—dance; *caitanya-nitāi*—Lord Caitanya and Nityānanda Prabhu.

TRANSLATION

The three brothers Govinda, Mādhava and Vāsudeva were the eighty-second, eighty-third and eighty-fourth branches of the tree. Lord Caitanya and Nityānanda used to dance in their kīrtana performances.

PURPORT

The three brothers Govinda, Mādhava and Vāsudeva Ghosh all belonged to a *kāyastha* family. Govinda established the Gopīnātha temple in Agradvīpa, where he resided. Mādhava Ghosh was expert in performing *kīrtana.* No one within this world could compete with him. He was known as the singer of Vṛndāvana and was very dear to Śrī Nityānanda Prabhu. It is said that when the three brothers performed *saṅkīrtana,* immediately Lord Caitanya and Nityānanda would dance in ecstasy. According to the *Gaura-gaṇoddeśa-dīpikā* (188), the three brothers were formerly Kalāvatī, Rasollāsā and Guṇatuṅgā, who recited the songs composed by Śrī Viśākhā-gopī. The three brothers were among one of the seven parties that performed *kīrtana* when Lord Śrī Caitanya Mahāprabhu attended the Rathayātrā festival at Jagannātha Purī. Vakreśvara Paṇḍita was the chief dancer in their party. This is vividly described in the *Madhya-līlā,* Chapter Thirteen, verses 42 and 43.

TEXT 116

রামদাস অভিরাম—সখ্য-প্রেমরাশি ।
ষোলসাঙ্গের কাষ্ঠ তুলি' যে করিল বাঁশী ॥ ১১৬ ॥

rāmadāsa abhirāma—sakhya-premarāśi
ṣolasāṅgera kāṣṭha tuli' ye karila vāṅśī

SYNONYMS

rāmadāsa abhirāma—of the name Rāmadāsa Abhirāma; *sakhya-prema*—friendship; *rāśi*—great volume; *ṣola-sāṅgera*—of sixteen knots; *kāṣṭha*—wood; *tuli'*—lifting; *ye*—one who; *karila*—made; *vāṅśī*—flute.

TRANSLATION

Rāmadāsa Abhirāma was fully absorbed in the mellow of friendship. He made a flute of a bamboo stick with sixteen knots.

PURPORT

Abhirāma was an inhabitant of Khānākulakṛṣṇa-nagara.

TEXT 117

প্রভুর আজ্ঞায় নিত্যানন্দ গৌড়ে চলিলা ।
তাঁর সঙ্গে তিনজন প্রভু-আজ্ঞায় আইলা ॥ ১১৭ ॥

prabhura ājñāya nityānanda gauḍe calilā
tāṅra saṅge tina-jana prabhu-ājñāya āilā

SYNONYMS

prabhura ājñāya—under the order of Lord Caitanya Mahāprabhu; *nityānanda*—Lord Nityānanda; *gauḍe*—to Bengal; *calilā*—went back; *tāṅra saṅge*—in His company; *tina-jana*—three men; *prabhu-ājñāya*—under the order of the Lord; *āilā*—went.

TRANSLATION

By the order of Śrī Caitanya Mahāprabhu, three devotees accompanied Lord Nityānanda Prabhu when He returned to Bengal to preach.

TEXT 118

রামদাস, মাধব, আর বাসুদেব ঘোষ ।
প্রভু-সঙ্গে রহে গোবিন্দ পাইয়া সন্তোষ ॥ ১১৮ ॥

rāmadāsa, mādhava, āra vāsudeva ghoṣa
prabhu-saṅge rahe govinda pāiyā santoṣa

SYNONYMS

rāmadāsa—of the name Rāmadāsa; *mādhava*—of the name Mādhava; *āra*—and; *vāsudeva ghoṣa*—of the name Vāsudeva Ghosh; *prabhu-saṅge*—in the company of Lord Caitanya Mahāprabhu; *rahe*—remained; *govinda*—of the name Govinda; *pāiyā*—feeling; *santoṣa*—great satisfaction.

TRANSLATION

These three were Rāmadāsa, Mādhava and Vāsudeva Ghosh. Govinda Ghosh, however, remained with Śrī Caitanya Mahāprabhu at Jagannātha Purī and thus felt great satisfaction.

TEXT 119

ভাগবতাচার্য, চিরঞ্জীব, শ্রীরঘুনন্দন ।
মাধবাচার্য, কমলাকান্ত, শ্রীযদুনন্দন ॥ ১১৯ ॥

bhāgavatācārya, cirañjīva śrī-raghunandana
mādhavācārya, kamalākānta, śrī-yadunandana

SYNONYMS

bhāgavatācārya—of the name Bhāgavatācārya; *cirañjīva*—of the name Cirañjīva; *śrī-raghunandana*—of the name Śrī Raghunandana; *mādhavācārya*—of the name Mādhavācārya; *kamalākānta*—of the name Kamalākānta; *śrī-yadunandana*—of the name Śrī Yadunandana.

TRANSLATION

Bhāgavatācārya, Cirañjīva, Śrī Raghunandana, Mādhavācārya, Kamalākānta and Śrī Yadunandana were all among the branches of the Caitanya tree.

PURPORT

Śrī Mādhavācārya was the husband of Lord Nityānanda's daughter, Gaṅgādevī. He took initiation from Puruṣottama, a branch of Nityānanda Prabhu. It is said that when Nityānanda Prabhu's daughter married Mādhavācārya, the Lord gave him the village named Pāñjinagara as a dowry. His temple is situated near the Jīrāṭ railway station on the eastern railway. According to *Gaura-gaṇoddeśa-dīpikā* (169) Srī Mādhavācārya was formerly the *gopī* named Mādhavī. Kamalākānta belonged to the branch of Śrī Advaita Prabhu. His full name was Kamalākānta Viśvāsa.

TEXT 120

মহা-কৃপাপাত্র প্রভুর জগাই, মাধাই ।
'পতিতপাবন' নামের সাক্ষী দুই ভাই ॥ ১২০ ॥

mahā-kṛpā-pātra prabhura jagāi, mādhāi
'patita-pāvana' nāmera sākṣī dui bhāi

SYNONYMS

mahā-kṛpā-pātra—object of very great mercy; *prabhura*—of the Lord; *jagāi mādhāi*—the two brothers Jagāi and Mādhāi; *patita-pāvana*—deliverer of the fallen; *nāmera*—of this name; *sākṣī*—witness; *dui bhāi*—these two brothers.

TRANSLATION

Jagāi and Mādhāi, the eighty-ninth and nintieth branches of the tree, were the greatest recipients of Lord Caitanya's mercy. These two brothers were the witnesses who proved that Lord Caitanya was rightly named Patita-pāvana, "the deliverer of the fallen souls."

PURPORT

In the *Gaura-gaṇoddeśa-dīpikā* (115) it is said that the two brothers Jagāi and Mādhāi were formerly the doorkeepers named Jaya and Vijaya, who later became Hiraṇyākṣa and Hiraṇyakaśipu. Jagāi and Mādhāi were born in respectable *brāhmaṇa* families, but they adopted the professions of thieves and rogues and thus became implicated in all kinds of undesirable activities, especially woman hunting, intoxication and gambling. Later, by the grace of Lord Caitanya Mahāprabhu and Śrī Nityānanda Prabhu, they were initiated, and they got the chance to chant the Hare Kṛṣṇa *mahā-mantra.* As a result of chanting, both brothers later became exalted devotees of Lord Caitanya Mahāprabhu. The descendants of Mādhāi still exist, and they are respectable *brāhmaṇas.* The tombs of these two brothers, Jagāi and Mādhāi, are in a place known as Ghoṣahāṭa, or Mādhāitalā-grāma, which is situated about one mile south of Katwa. It is said that Śrī Gopīcaraṇa dāsa Bābājī established a temple of Nitāi-Gaura at this place about 200 years ago.

TEXT 121

গৌড়দেশ-ভক্তের কৈল সংক্ষেপ কথন ।
অনন্ত চৈতন্যভক্ত না যায় গণন ॥ ১২১ ॥

gauḍa-deśa-bhaktera kaila saṅkṣepa kathana
ananta caitanya-bhakta nā yāya gaṇana

SYNONYMS

gauḍa-deśa—in Bengal; *bhaktera*—of the devotees; *kaila*—I have described; *saṅkṣepa*—in brief; *kathana*—narration; *ananta*—unlimited; *caitanya-bhakta*—devotees of Lord Caitanya; *nā*—not; *yāya*—can be; *gaṇana*—counted.

TRANSLATION

I have given a brief description of the devotees of Lord Caitanya in Bengal. Actually His devotees are innumerable.

TEXT 122

নীলাচলে এই সব ভক্ত প্রভুসঙ্গে ।
দুই স্থানে প্রভু-সেবা কৈল নানা-রঙ্গে ॥ ১২২ ॥

nīlācale ei saba bhakta prabhu-saṅge
dui sthāne prabhu-sevā kaila nānā-raṅge

SYNONYMS

nīlācale—at Jagannātha Purī; *ei*—these; *saba*—all; *bhakta*—devotees; *prabhu-saṅge*—in the company of Lord Caitanya; *dui sthāne*—in two places; *prabhu-sevā*—service of the Lord; *kaila*—executed; *nānā-raṅge*—in different ways.

TRANSLATION

I have especially mentioned all these devotees because they accompanied Lord Caitanya Mahāprabhu in Bengal and Orissa and served Him in many ways.

PURPORT

Most of the devotees of Lord Caitanya lived in Bengal and Orissa. Thus they are celebrated as *oriyās* and *gauḍīyas.* At present, however, by the grace of Lord Caitanya Mahāprabhu, His cult is being propagated all over the world, and it is most probable that in the future history of Lord Caitanya's movement, Europeans, Americans, Canadians, Australians, South Americans, Asians and people from all over the world will be celebrated as devotees of Lord Caitanya. The International Society for Krishna Consciousness has already constructed a big temple at Māyāpur, Navadvīpa, which is being visited by devotees from all parts of the world, as foretold by Lord Caitanya Mahāprabhu and anticipated by Śrī Bhaktivinoda Ṭhākura.

TEXT 123

কেবল নীলাচলে প্রভুর যে যে ভক্তগণ ।
সংক্ষেপে করিয়ে কিছু সে সব কথন ॥ ১২৩ ॥

kevala nīlācale prabhura ye ye bhakta-gaṇa
saṅkṣepe kariye kichu se saba kathana

SYNONYMS

kevala—only; *nīlācale*—in Jagannātha Purī; *prabhura*—of the Lord; *ye ye*—all those; *bhakta-gaṇa*—devotees; *saṅkṣepe*—in brief; *kariye*—I do; *kichu*—some; *se saba*—all those; *kathana*—narration.

TRANSLATION

Let me briefly describe some of the devotees of Lord Caitanya Mahāprabhu in Jagannātha Purī.

TEXTS 124-126

নীলাচলে প্রভুসঙ্গে যত ভক্তগণ ।
সবার অধ্যক্ষ প্রভুর মর্ম দুইজন ॥ ১২৪ ॥
পরমানন্দপুরী, আর স্বরূপ-দামোদর ।
গদাধর, জগদানন্দ, শঙ্কর, বক্রেশ্বর ॥ ১২৫ ॥
দামোদর পণ্ডিত, ঠাকুর হরিদাস ।
রঘুনাথ বৈদ্য, আর রঘুনাথদাস ॥ ১২৬ ॥

nīlācale prabhu-saṅge yata bhakta-gaṇa
sabāra adhyakṣa prabhura marma dui-jana

paramānanda-purī, āra svarūpa-dāmodara
gadādhara, jagadānanda, śaṅkara, vakreśvara

dāmodara paṇḍita, ṭhākura haridāsa
raghunātha vaidya, āra raghunātha-dāsa

SYNONYMS

nīlācale—in Jagannātha Purī; *prabhu-saṅge*—in the company of Lord Caitanya; *yata*—all; *bhakta-gaṇa*—devotees; *sabāra*—of all of them; *adhyakṣa*—the chief; *prabhura*—of the Lord; *marma*—heart and soul; *dui-jana*—two persons; *paramānanda purī*—of the name Paramānanda Purī; *āra*—and; *svarūpa-dāmodara*—of the name Svarūpa Dāmodara; *gadādhara*—of the name Gadādhara; *jagadānanda*—of the name Jagadānanda; *śaṅkara*—of the name Śaṅkara; *vakreśvara*—of the name Vakreśvara; *dāmodara paṇḍita*—of the name Dāmodara Paṇḍita; *ṭhākura haridāsa*—of the name Ṭhākura Haridāsa; *raghunātha vaidya*—of the name Raghunātha Vaidya; *āra*—and; *raghunātha-dāsa*—of the name Raghunātha dāsa.

TRANSLATION

Among the devotees who accompanied the Lord in Jagannātha Purī, two of them—Paramānanda Purī and Svarūpa Dāmodara—were the heart and soul of the Lord. Among the other devotees were Gadādhara, Jagadānanda, Śaṅkara, Vakreśvara, Dāmodara Paṇḍita, Ṭhākura Haridāsa, Raghunātha Vaidya and Raghunātha dāsa.

PURPORT

The *Caitanya-bhāgavata, Antya-līlā,* Chapter Five, states that Raghunātha Vaidya came to see Śrī Caitanya Mahāprabhu when the Lord was staying at Pāṇihāṭi. He was a great devotee and had all good qualities. According to the *Caitanya-bhāgavata,* he was formerly Revatī, the wife of Balarāma. Anyone he glanced upon would immediately attain Kṛṣṇa consciousness. He lived on the seashore at Jagannātha Purī and compiled a book of the name *Sthāna-nirūpaṇa.*

TEXT 127

ইত্যাদিক পূর্বসঙ্গী বড় ভক্তগণ ।
নীলাচলে রহি' করে প্রভুর সেবন ॥ ১২৭ ॥

ityādika pūrva-saṅgī baḍa bhakta-gaṇa
nīlācale rahi' kare prabhura sevana

SYNONYMS

ityādika—all these and others; *pūrva-saṅgī*—former associates; *baḍa*—very much; *bhakta-gaṇa*—great devotees; *nīlācale*—at Jagannātha Purī; *rahi'*—remaining; *kare*—do; *prabhura*—of the Lord; *sevana*—service.

TRANSLATION

All these devotees were associates of the Lord from the very beginning, and when the Lord took up residence in Jagannātha Purī they remained there to serve Him faithfully.

TEXT 128

আর যত ভক্তগণ গৌড়দেশবাসী ।
প্রত্যব্দে প্রভুরে দেখে নীলাচলে আসি' ॥ ১২৮ ॥

āra yata bhakta-gaṇa gauḍa-deśa-vāsī
pratyabde prabhure dekhe nīlācale āsi'

SYNONYMS

āra—others; *yata*—all; *bhakta-gaṇa*—devotees; *gauḍa-deśa-vāsī*—residents of Bengal; *pratyabde*—each year; *prabhure*—the Lord; *dekhe*—see; *nīlācale*—in Jagannātha Purī; *āsi'*—coming there.

TRANSLATION

All the devotees who resided in Bengal used to visit Jagannātha Purī to see the Lord.

TEXT 129

নীলাচলে প্রভুসহ প্রথম মিলন ।
সেই ভক্তগণের এবে করিয়ে গণন ॥ ১২৯ ॥

nīlācale prabhu-saha prathama milana
sei bhakta-gaṇera ebe kariye gaṇana

SYNONYMS

nīlācale—at Jagannātha Purī; *prabhu-saha*—with the Lord; *prathama*—first; *milana*—meeting; *sei*—that; *bhakta-gaṇera*—of the devotees; *ebe*—now; *kariye*—I do; *gaṇana*—count.

TRANSLATION

Now let me enumerate the devotees of Bengal who first came to see the Lord at Jagannātha Purī.

TEXT 130

বড়শাখা এক,—সার্বভৌম ভট্টাচার্য ।
তাঁর ভগ্নীপতি শ্রীগোপীনাথাচার্য ॥ ১৩০ ॥

baḍa-śākhā eka,—sārvabhauma bhaṭṭācārya
tāṅra bhagnī-pati śrī-gopīnāthācārya

SYNONYMS

baḍa-śākhā eka—one of the biggest branches; *sārvabhauma bhaṭṭācārya*—of the name Sārvabhauma Bhaṭṭācārya; *tāṅra bhagnī-pati*—his brother-in-law (the husband of Sārvabhauma's sister); *śrī-gopīnāthācārya*—of the name Śrī Gopīnāthācārya.

TRANSLATION

There was Sārvabhauma Bhaṭṭācārya, one of the biggest branches of the tree of the Lord, and his sister's husband, Śrī Gopīnāthācārya.

PURPORT

The original name of Sārvabhauma Bhaṭṭācārya was Vāsudeva Bhaṭṭācārya. His place of birth, which is known as Vidyānagara, is about two and a half miles away from the Navadvīpa railway station, or Cāṅpāhāṭī railway station. His father was a very celebrated man of the name Maheśvara Viśārada. It is said that Sārvabhauma Bhaṭṭācārya was the greatest logician of his time in India. At Mithilā in Bihar he became a student of a great professor named Pakṣadhara Miśra, who did not allow any student to note down his explanations of logic. Sārvabhauma Bhaṭṭācārya was so talented, however, that he learned the explanations by heart, and when he later returned to Navadvīpa he established a school for the study of logic, thus diminishing the importance of Mithilā. Students from various parts of India still come to Navadvīpa to study logic. According to some authoritative opinions, the celebrated logician Raghunātha Śiromaṇi was also a student of Sārvabhauma Bhaṭṭācārya. In effect, Sārvabhauma Bhaṭṭācārya became the leader of all students of logic. Although he was a *gṛhastha* (householder), he even taught many *sannyāsīs* in the knowledge of logic. He started a school at Jagannātha Purī for the study of Vedānta philosophy, of which he was a great scholar. When Sārvabhauma Bhaṭṭācārya met Śrī Caitanya Mahāprabhu, he advised the Lord to learn Vedānta philosophy from him, but later he became a student of Lord Caitanya Mahāprabhu to understand the real meaning of Vedānta. Sārvabhauma Bhaṭṭācārya was so fortunate as to see the six-armed form of Lord Caitanya known as Ṣaḍbhuja. A Ṣaḍbhuja Deity is still situated at one end of the Jagannātha temple. Daily *saṅkīrtana* performances take place in this part of the temple. The meeting of Sārvabhauma Bhaṭṭācārya with Lord Caitanya Mahāprabhu is vividly described in the *Madhya-līlā,* Chapter Six. Sārvabhauma Bhaṭṭācārya wrote a book named *Caitanya-śataka.* Of the 100 verses of this book, two verses, beginning with the words *vairāgya-vidyā-nijabhaktiyoga,* are very famous among Gauḍīya Vaiṣṇavas. The *Gaura-gaṇoddeśa-dīpikā* (119) states that Sārvabhauma Bhaṭṭācārya was an incarnation of Bṛhaspati, the learned scholar from the celestial planets.

Gopīnātha Ācārya, who belonged to a respectable *brāhmaṇa* family, was also an inhabitant of Navadvīpa and constant companion of the Lord. He was the husband of Sārvabhauma Bhaṭṭācārya's sister. In the *Gaura-gaṇoddeśa-dīpikā* (178) it is described that he was formerly the *gopī* named Ratnāvalī. According to the opinion of others, he was an incarnation of Brahmā.

TEXT 131

কাশীমিশ্র, প্রদ্যুম্নমিশ্র, রায় ভবানন্দ ।
যাঁহার মিলনে প্রভু পাইলা আনন্দ ॥ ১৩১ ॥

kāśī-miśra, pradyumna-miśra, rāya bhavānanda
yāṅhāra milane prabhu pāilā ānanda

SYNONYMS

kāśī-miśra—of the name Kāśī Miśra; *pradyumna-miśra*—of the name Pradyumna Miśra; *rāya bhavānanda*—of the name Bhavānanda Rāya; *yāṅhāra*—of whom; *milane*—meeting; *prabhu*—the Lord; *pāilā*—got; *ānanda*—great pleasure.

TRANSLATION

In the list of devotees at Jagannātha Purī [which begins with Paramānanda Purī, Svarūpa Dāmodara, Sārvabhauma Bhaṭṭācārya and Gopīnātha Ācārya], Kāśī Miśra

was the fifth, Pradyumna Miśra the sixth and Bhavānanda Rāya the seventh. Lord Caitanya took great pleasure in meeting with them.

PURPORT

In Jagannātha Purī Lord Caitanya lived at the house of Kāśī Miśra, who was the priest of the king. Later this house was inherited by Vakreśvara Paṇḍita and then by his disciple Gopālaguru Gosvāmī, who established there a Deity of Rādhākānta. The *Gaura-gaṇoddeśa-dīpikā* (193) states that Kāśī Miśra was formerly the *gopī* in Vṛndāvana named Kṛṣṇavallabhā. Pradyumna Miśra, an inhabitant of Orissa, was a great devotee of Lord Caitanya Mahāprabhu. Pradyumna Miśra was born of a *brāhmaṇa* family and Rāmānanda Rāya of a non-*brāhmaṇa* family, yet Lord Caitanya Mahāprabhu advised Pradyumna Miśra to take instruction from Rāmānanda Rāya. This incident is described in the *Antya-līlā*, Chapter Five.

Bhavānanda Rāya was the father of Śrī Rāmānanda Rāya. His residence was in Ālālanātha (Brahmagiri), which is about twelve miles west of Jagannātha Purī. By caste he belonged to the *karaṇa* community of Orissa, whose members were sometimes known as *kāyasthas* and sometimes as *śūdras,* but he was the governor of Madras under the control of King Pratāparudra of Jagannātha Purī.

TEXT 132

আলিঙ্গন করি' তাঁরে বলিল বচন।
তুমি পাণ্ডু, পঞ্চপাণ্ডব –তোমার নন্দন ॥ ১৩২ ॥

āliṅgana kari' tāṅre balila vacana
tumi pāṇḍu, pañca-pāṇḍava—tomāra nandana

SYNONYMS

āliṅgana kari'—embracing; *tāṅre*—unto him; *balila*—said; *vacana*—those words; *tumi*—you; *pāṇḍu*—were Pāṇḍu; *pañca*—five; *pāṇḍava*—the Pāṇḍavas; *tomāra*—your; *nandana*—sons.

TRANSLATION

Embracing Rāya Bhavānanda, the Lord declared to him: "You formerly appeared as Pāṇḍu, and your five sons appeared as the five Pāṇḍavas."

TEXT 133

রামানন্দ রায়, পট্টনায়ক গোপীনাথ।
কলানিধি, সুধানিধি, নায়ক বাণীনাথ ॥ ১৩৩ ॥

rāmānanda rāya, paṭṭanāyaka gopīnātha
kalānidhi, sudhānidhi, nāyaka vāṇīnātha

SYNONYMS

rāmānanda rāya—of the name Rāmānanda Rāya; *paṭṭanāyaka gopīnātha*—of the name Paṭṭanāyaka Gopīnātha; *kalānidhi*—of the name Kalānidhi; *sudhānidhi*—of the name Sudhānidhi; *nāyaka vāṇīnātha*—of the name Nāyaka Vāṇīnātha.

TRANSLATION

The five sons of Bhavānanda Rāya were Rāmānanda Rāya, Paṭṭanāyaka Gopīnātha, Kalānidhi, Sudhānidhi and Nāyaka Vāṇīnātha.

TEXT 134

এই পঞ্চ পুত্র তোমার মোর প্রিয়পাত্র।
রামানন্দ সহ মোর দেহ-ভেদ মাত্র ॥ ১৩৪ ॥

ei pañca putra tomāra mora priyapātra
rāmānanda saha mora deha-bheda mātra

SYNONYMS

ei—these; *pañca*—five; *putra*—sons; *tomāra*—your; *mora*—Mine; *priyapātra*—very dear; *rāmānanda saha*—with Śrī Rāmānanda Rāya; *mora*—Mine; *deha-bheda*—bodily difference; *mātra*—only.

TRANSLATION

Śrī Caitanya Mahāprabhu told Bhavānanda Rāya, "Your five sons are all My dear devotees. Rāmānanda Rāya and I are one, although our bodies are different."

PURPORT

The *Gaura-gaṇoddeśa-dīpikā* (120-124) states that Rāmānanda Rāya was formerly Arjuna. He is also considered to have been an incarnation of the *gopī* Lalitā, although in the opinion of others he was an incarnation of Viśākhādevī. He was a most confidential devotee of Lord Caitanya Mahāprabhu. Śrī Caitanya Mahāprabhu said, "Although I am a *sannyāsī,* My mind is sometimes perturbed when I see a woman. But Rāmānanda Rāya is greater than Me, for he is always undisturbed, even when he touches a woman." Only Rāmānanda Rāya was endowed with the prerogative to touch a woman in this way; no one should imitate him. Unfortunately, there are rascals who imitate the activities of Rāmānanda Rāya. We need not discuss them further.

In Lord Caitanya Mahāprabhu's final pastimes, both Rāmānanda Rāya and Svarūpa Dāmodara always engaged in reciting suitable verses from *Śrīmad-Bhāgavatam* to pacify the Lord's ecstatic feelings of separation from Kṛṣṇa. It is said that when Lord Caitanya went to southern India, Sārvabhauma Bhaṭṭācārya advised Him to meet Rāmānanda Rāya, for he declared that there was no devotee as advanced in understanding the conjugal love of Kṛṣṇa and the *gopīs.* While touring South India,

Lord Caitanya met Rāmānanda Rāya by the bank of the Godāvarī, and in their long discourses the Lord took the position of a student, and Rāmānanda Rāya instructed Him. Caitanya Mahāprabhu concluded these discourses by saying, "My dear Rāmānanda Rāya, both you and I are madmen, and therefore we met intimately on an equal level." Lord Caitanya advised Rāmānanda Rāya to resign from his government post and come back to Jagannātha Purī to live with Him. Although Śrī Caitanya Mahāprabhu refused to see Mahārāja Pratāparudra because he was a king, Rāmānanda Rāya, by a Vaiṣṇava scheme, arranged a meeting between the Lord and the King. This is described in the *Madhya-līlā,* Chapter Twelve, verses 41-57. Śrī Rāmānanda Rāya was present during the water sports of the Lord after the Ratha-yātrā festival.

Lord Śrī Caitanya Mahāprabhu considered Śrī Rāmānanda Rāya and Śrī Sanātana Gosvāmī to be equal in their renunciation, for although Śrī Rāmānanda Rāya was a *gṛhastha* engaged in government service and Śrī Sanātana Gosvāmī was in the renounced order of complete detachment from material activities, they were both servants of the Supreme Personality of Godhead who kept Kṛṣṇa in the center of all their activities. Śrī Rāmānanda Rāya was one of the three and a half personalities with whom Śrī Caitanya Mahāprabhu discussed the most confidential topics of Kṛṣṇa consciousness. Lord Caitanya Mahāprabhu advised Pradyumna Miśra to learn the science of Kṛṣṇa from Śrī Rāmānanda Rāya. As Subala always assisted Kṛṣṇa in His dealings with Rādhārāṇī in *kṛṣṇa-līlā,* so Rāmānanda Rāya assisted Lord Caitanya Mahāprabhu in His feelings of separation from Kṛṣṇa. Śrī Rāmānanda Rāya was the author of *Jagannātha-vallabha-nāṭaka.*

TEXTS 135-136

প্রতাপরুদ্র রাজা, আর ওড্র কৃষ্ণানন্দ ।
পরমানন্দ মহাপাত্র, ওড্র শিবানন্দ ॥ ১৩৫ ॥
ভগবান্ আচার্য, ব্রহ্মানন্দাখ্য ভারতী ।
শ্রীশিখি মাহিতি, আর মুরারি মাহিতি ॥ ১৩৬ ॥

pratāparudra rājā, āra oḍhra kṛṣṇānanda
paramānanda mahāpātra, oḍhra śivānanda

bhagavān ācārya, brahmānandākhya bhāratī
śrī-śikhi māhiti, āra murāri māhiti

SYNONYMS

pratāparudra rājā—King Pratāparudra of Orissa; *āra*—and; *oḍhra kṛṣṇānanda*—Kṛṣṇānanda, an Oriya devotee; *paramānanda mahāpātra*—of the name Paramānanda Mahāpātra; *oḍhra śivānanda*—the Oriya Śivānanda; *bhagavān ācārya*—of the name Bhagavān Ācārya; *brahmānanda-ākhya bhāratī*—of the name Brahmānanda Bhāratī; *śrī-śikhi māhiti*—of the name Śrī Śikhi Māhiti; *āra*—and; *murāri māhiti*—of the name Murāri Māhiti.

TRANSLATION

King Pratāparudra of Orissa, the Oriyā devotees Kṛṣṇānanda and Śivānanda, Paramānanda Mahāpātra, Bhagavān Ācārya, Brahmānanda Bhāratī, Śrī Śikhi Māhiti and Murāri Māhiti constantly associated with Caitanya Mahāprabhu while He resided in Jagannātha Purī.

PURPORT

Pratāparudra Mahārāja, who belonged to the dynasty of the Gaṅgā kings and whose capital was in Cuttak, was the Emperor of Orissa and a great devotee of Lord Caitanya Mahāprabhu. It was by the arrangement of Rāmānanda Rāya and Sārvabhauma Bhaṭṭācārya that he was able to serve Lord Caitanya. In the *Gaura-gaṇoddeśa-dīpikā* (118) it is said that King Indradyumna, who established the temple of Jagannātha thousands of years ago, later took birth again in his own family as Mahārāja Pratāparudra during the time of Śrī Caitanya Mahāprabhu. Mahārāja Pratāparudra was as powerful as King Indra. The drama named *Caitanya-candrodaya* was written under his direction.

In the *Caitanya-bhāgavata, Antya-līlā,* Chapter Five, Paramānanda Mahāpātra is described as follows: "Paramānanda Mahāpātra was among the devotees who took birth in Orissa and accepted Caitanya Mahāprabhu as their only asset. In the ecstasy of conjugal love, he always thought of Caitanya Mahāprabhu." Bhagavān Ācārya, a very learned scholar, was formerly an inhabitant of Hālisahara, but he left everything to live with Caitanya Mahāprabhu in Jagannātha Purī. His relationship with Caitanya Mahāprabhu was friendly, like that of a cowherd boy. He was always friendly to Svarūpa Gosāñi, but he was staunchly devoted to the lotus feet of Lord Caitanya Mahāprabhu. He sometimes invited Caitanya Mahāprabhu to his house.

Bhagavān Ācārya was very liberal and simple. His father, Śatānanda Khāṅ, was completely materialistic, and his younger brother, Gopāla Bhaṭṭācārya, was a staunch Māyāvādī philosopher who had studied very elaborately. When his brother came to Jagannātha Purī, Bhagavān Ācārya wanted to hear from him about Māyāvāda philosophy, but Svarūpa Dāmodara forbade him to do so, and there the matter stopped. Once a friend of Bhagavān Ācārya's from Bengal wanted to recite a drama that he had written that was against the principles of devotional service, and although Bhagavān Ācārya wanted to recite this drama before Lord Caitanya Mahāprabhu, Svarūpa Dāmodara, the Lord's secretary, did not allow him to do so. Later Svarūpa Dāmodara pointed out in the drama many mistakes and disagreements with the conclusion of devotional service, and the author became aware of the faults in his writing and then surrendered to Svarūpa Dāmodara, begging his mercy. This is described in the *Antya-līlā,* Chapter Five, verses 91-166.

In the *Gaura-gaṇoddeśa-dīpikā,* verse 189, it is said that Śikhi Māhiti was formerly an assistant of Śrīmatī Rādhārāṇī named Rāgalekhā. His sister Mādhavī was also an assistant of Śrīmatī Rādhārāṇī and was named Kalākelī. Śikhi Māhiti, Mādhavī and their brother Murāri Māhiti were all unalloyed devotees of Śrī Caitanya Mahāprabhu who could not forget Him for a moment of their lives. There is a book in the Oriyā language called *Caitanya-carita-mahākāvya* in which there are many narrations about Śikhi Māhiti. One narration concerns his seeing an ecstatic dream.

Śikhi Māhiti always engaged in serving the Lord in his mind. One night, while he was rendering such service, he fell asleep, and while he was asleep his brother and sister came to awaken him. At that time he was in full ecstasy because he was having a wonderful dream that Lord Caitanya, while visiting the temple of Jagannātha, was entering and again coming out of the body of Jagannātha and looking at the Jagannātha Deity. Thus as soon as he awakened he embraced his brother and sister and informed them, "My dear brother and sister, I have had a wonderful dream that I shall now explain to you. The activities of Lord Caitanya Mahāprabhu, the son of Mother Śacī, are certainly most wonderful. I saw that Lord Caitanya Mahāprabhu, while visiting the temple of Jagannātha, was entering the body of Jagannātha and again coming out of His body. I am still seeing the same dream. Do you think I have become deranged? I am still seeing the same dream! And the most wonderful thing is that as soon as I came near Caitanya Mahāprabhu, He embraced me with His long arms." As he spoke to his brother and sister in this way, Śikhi Māhiti's voice faltered, and there were tears in his eyes. Thus the brothers and sister went to the temple of Jagannātha, and there they saw Lord Caitanya in Jagamohana, looking at the beauty of Śrī Jagannātha Deity just as in Śikhi Māhiti's dream. The Lord was so magnanimous that immediately He embraced Śikhi Māhiti, exclaiming, "You are the elder brother of Murāri!" Being thus embraced, Śikhi Māhiti felt ecstatic transcendental bliss. Thus he and his brother and sister always engaged in rendering service to the Lord. Murāri Māhiti, the youngest brother of Śikhi Māhiti, is described in the *Madhya-līlā,* Chapter Ten, verse 44.

TEXT 137

মাধবী-দেবী—শিখিমাহিতির ভগিনী ।
শ্রীরাধার দাসীমধ্যে যাঁর নাম গণি ॥ ১৩৭ ॥

mādhavī-devī—śikhi-māhitira bhaginī
śrī-rādhāra dāsī-madhye yāṅra nāma gaṇi

SYNONYMS

mādhavī-devī—of the name Mādhavīdevī; *śikhi-māhitira*—of Śikhi Māhiti; *bhaginī*—sister; *śrī-rādhāra*—of Śrīmatī Rādhārāṇī; *dāsī-madhye*—amongst the maidservants; *yāṅra*—whose; *nāma*—name; *gaṇi*—count.

TRANSLATION

Mādhavīdevī, the seventeenth of the prominent devotees, was the younger sister of Śikhi Māhiti. She is considered to have formerly been a maidservant of Śrīmatī Rādhārāṇī.

PURPORT

In the *Antya-līlā* of *Caitanya-caritāmṛta,* Chapter Two, verses 104-106, there is a description of Mādhavīdevī. Śrī Caitanya Mahāprabhu considered her to be one of the maidservants of Śrīmatī Rādhārāṇī. Within this world, Caitanya Mahāprabhu had three and a half very confidential devotees. The three were Svarūpa Gosāñi, Śrī Rāmānanda Rāya and Śikhi Māhiti, and Śikhi Māhiti's sister, Mādhavīdevī, being a woman, was considered to be the half. Thus it is known that Śrī Caitanya Mahāprabhu had three and a half confidential devotees.

TEXT 138

ঈশ্বরপুরীর শিষ্য – ব্রহ্মচারী কাশীশ্বর ।
শ্রীগোবিন্দ নাম তাঁর প্রিয় অনুচর ॥ ১৩৮ ॥

īśvara-purīra śiṣya—brahmacārī kāśīśvara
śrī-govinda nāma tāṅra priya anucara

SYNONYMS

īśvara-purīra śiṣya—disciple of Īśvara Purī; *brahmacārī kāśīśvara*—of the name Brahmacārī Kāśīśvara; *śrī-govinda*—of the name Śrī Govinda; *nāma*—name; *tāṅra*—his; *priya*—very dear; *anucara*—follower.

TRANSLATION

Brahmacārī Kāśīśvara was a disciple of Īśvara Purī, and Śrī Govinda was another of his dear disciples.

PURPORT

Govinda was the personal servant of Śrī Caitanya Mahāprabhu. In the *Gaura-gaṇoddeśa-dīpikā,* verse 137, it is stated that the servants formerly named Bhṛṅgāra and Bhaṅgura in Vṛndāvana became Kāśīśvara and Govinda in Caitanya Mahāprabhu's pastimes. Govinda always engaged in the service of the Lord, even at great risk.

TEXT 139

তাঁর সিদ্ধিকালে দোঁহে তাঁর আজ্ঞা পাঞা ।
নীলাচলে প্রভুস্থানে মিলিল আসিয়া ॥ ১৩৯ ॥

tāṅra siddhi-kāle doṅhe tāṅra ājñā pāñā
nīlācale prabhu-sthāne milila āsiyā

SYNONYMS

tāṅra siddhi-kāle—at the time of Īśvara Purī's passing away; *doṅhe*—the two of them; *tāṅra*—his; *ājñā*—order; *pāñā*—getting; *nīlācale*—at Jagannātha Purī; *prabhu-sthāne*—at the place of Lord Caitanya Mahāprabhu; *milila*—met; *āsiyā*—coming there.

TRANSLATION

In the list of prominent devotees at Nīlācala [Jagannātha Purī], Kāśīśvara was the eighteenth and Govinda the nineteenth. They both came to see Caitanya Mahāprabhu at Jagannātha Purī, being thus ordered by Īśvara Purī at the time of his passing away.

TEXT 140

গুরুর সম্বন্ধে মান্য কৈল দুঁহাকারে ।
তাঁর আজ্ঞা মানি' সেবা দিলেন দোঁহারে ॥ ১৪০ ॥

gurura sambandhe mānya kaila duṅhākāre
tāṅra ājñā māni' sevā dilena doṅhāre

SYNONYMS

gurura sambandhe—in relationship with his spiritual master; *mānya*—honor; *kaila*—offered; *duṅhākāre*—to both of them; *tāṅra ājñā*—his order; *māni'*—accepting; *sevā*—service; *dilena*—gave them; *doṅhāre*—the two of them.

TRANSLATION

Both Kāśīśvara and Govinda were Godbrothers of Śrī Caitanya Mahāprabhu, and thus the Lord duly honored them as soon as they arrived. But because Īśvara Purī had ordered them to give Caitanya Mahāprabhu personal service, the Lord accepted their service.

TEXT 141

অঙ্গসেবা গোবিন্দেরে দিলেন ঈশ্বর ।
জগন্নাথ দেখিতে চলেন আগে কাশীশ্বর ॥ ১৪১ ॥

aṅga-sevā govindere dilena īśvara
jagannātha dekhite calena āge kāśīśvara

SYNONYMS

aṅga-sevā—taking care of the body; *govindere*—unto Govinda; *dilena*—He gave; *īśvara*—the Supreme Personality of Godhead; *jagannātha*—the Jagannātha Deity; *dekhite*—while going to visit; *calena*—goes; *āge*—in front; *kāśīśvara*—of the name Kāśīśvara.

TRANSLATION

Govinda cared for the body of Śrī Caitanya Mahāprabhu whereas Kāśīśvara went in front of the Lord when He went to see Jagannātha in the temple.

TEXT 142

অপরশ যায় গোসাঞি মনুষ্য-গহনে ।
মনুষ্য ঠেলি' পথ করে কাশী বলবানে ॥ ১৪২ ॥

aparaśa yāya gosāñi manuṣya-gahane
manuṣya ṭheli' patha kare kāśī balavāne

SYNONYMS

aparaśa—untouched; *yāya*—goes; *gosāñi*—Śrī Caitanya Mahāprabhu; *manuṣya-gahane*—in the crowd; *manuṣya ṭheli'*—pushing the crowd of men; *patha kare*—clears the way; *kāśī*—Kāśīśvara; *balavāne*—very strong.

TRANSLATION

When Caitanya Mahāprabhu went to the temple of Jagannātha, Kāśīśvara, being very strong, cleared the crowds aside with his hands so that Caitanya Mahāprabhu could pass untouched.

TEXT 143

রামাই-নন্দাই – দোঁহে প্রভুর কিঙ্কর ।
গোবিন্দের সঙ্গে সেবা করে নিরন্তর ॥ ১৪৩ ॥

rāmāi-nandāi—doṅhe prabhura kiṅkara
govindera saṅge sevā kare nirantara

SYNONYMS

rāmāi-nandāi—of the names Rāmāi and Nandāi; *doṅhe*—both of them; *prabhura*—Lord Caitanya's; *kiṅkara*—servants; *govindera*—with Govinda; *saṅge*—with him; *sevā*—service; *kare*—rendered; *nirantara*—twenty-four hours a day.

TRANSLATION

Rāmāi and Nandāi, the twentieth and twenty-first among the important devotees in Jagannātha Purī, always assisted Govinda twenty-four hours a day in rendering service to the Lord.

TEXT 144

বাইশ ঘড়া জল দিনে ভরেন রামাই ।
গোবিন্দ-আজ্ঞায় সেবা করেন নন্দাই ॥ ১৪৪ ॥

bāiśa ghaḍā jala dine bharena rāmāi
govinda-ājñāya sevā karena nandāi

SYNONYMS

bāiśa—twenty-two; *ghaḍā*—big water pots; *jala*—water; *dine*—daily; *bharena*—fills; *rāmāi*—of the name Rāmāi; *govinda-ājñāya*—by the order of Govinda; *sevā*—service; *karena*—renders; *nandāi*—of the name Nandāi.

TRANSLATION

Every day Rāmāi filled twenty-two big water pots, whereas Nandāi personally assisted Govinda.

PURPORT

In the *Gaura-gaṇoddeśa-dīpikā* (139) it is stated that two servants who formerly supplied milk and water to Lord Kṛṣṇa became Rāmāi and Nandāi in the pastimes of Caitanya Mahāprabhu.

TEXT 145

কৃষ্ণদাস নাম শুদ্ধ কুলীন ব্রাহ্মণ ।
যারে সঙ্গে লৈয়া কৈলা দক্ষিণ গমন ॥ ১৪৫ ॥

kṛṣṇadāsa nāma śuddha kulīna brāhmaṇa
yāre saṅge laiyā kailā dakṣiṇa gamana

SYNONYMS

kṛṣṇadāsa—of the name Kṛṣṇadāsa; *nāma*—name; *śuddha*—pure; *kulīna*—respectable; *brāhmaṇa*—*brāhmaṇa; yāre*—whom; *saṅge*—with; *laiyā*—taking; *kailā*—did; *dakṣiṇa*—southern India; *gamana*—touring.

TRANSLATION

The twenty-second devotee, Kṛṣṇadāsa, was born of a pure and respectable brāhmaṇa family. While touring southern India, Lord Caitanya took Kṛṣṇadāsa with Him.

PURPORT

Kṛṣṇadāsa is described in the *Madhya-līlā,* Chapters Seven and Nine. He went with Śrī Caitanya Mahāprabhu to carry His water pot. In the Malabar state, members of the Bhaṭṭathāri cult tried to captivate Kṛṣṇadāsa by supplying a woman to seduce him, but although Śrī Caitanya Mahāprabhu saved him from being harmed, when they returned to Jagannātha Purī He asked Kṛṣṇadāsa to remain there, for the Lord was never favorably disposed toward an associate who was attracted by a woman. Thus Kṛṣṇadāsa lost the personal association of Lord Caitanya Mahāprabhu.

TEXT 146

বলভদ্র ভট্টাচার্য—ভক্তি অধিকারী ।
মথুরা-গমনে প্রভুর যেঁহো ব্রহ্মচারী ॥ ১৪৬ ॥

balabhadra bhaṭṭācārya—bhakti adhikārī
mathurā-gamane prabhura yeṅho brahmacārī

SYNONYMS

ballabhadra bhaṭṭācārya—of the name Balabhadra Bhaṭṭācārya; *bhakti adhikārī*—bona fide devotee; *mathurā-gamane*—while touring Mathurā; *prabhura*—of the Lord; *yeṅho*—who; *brahmacārī*—acted as a *brahmacārī.*

TRANSLATION

As a bona fide devotee, Balabhadra Bhaṭṭācārya, the twenty-third principal associate, acted as the brahmacārī of Śrī Caitanya Mahāprabhu when He toured Mathurā.

PURPORT

Balabhadra Bhaṭṭācārya acted as a *brahmacārī,* or personal assistant of a *sannyāsī.* A *sannyāsī* is not supposed to cook. Generally a *sannyāsī* takes *prasāda* at the house of a *gṛhastha,* and a *brahmacārī* helps in this connection. A *sannyāsī* is supposed to be a spiritual master and a *brahmacārī* his disciple. Balabhadra Bhaṭṭācārya acted as a *brahmacārī* for Śrī Caitanya Mahāprabhu when the Lord toured Mathurā and Vṛndāvana.

TEXT 147

বড় হরিদাস, আর ছোট হরিদাস ।
দুই কীর্তনীয়া রহে মহাপ্রভুর পাশ ॥ ১৪৭ ॥

baḍa haridāsa, āra choṭa haridāsa
dui kīrtanīyā rahe mahāprabhura pāśa

SYNONYMS

baḍa haridāsa—of the name Baḍa Haridāsa; *āra*—and; *choṭa haridāsa*—of the name Choṭa Haridāsa; *dui kīrtanīyā*—both of them were good singers; *rahe*—stay; *mahāprabhura*—Lord Caitanya Mahāprabhu; *pāśa*—with.

TRANSLATION

Baḍa Haridāsa and Choṭa Haridāsa, the twenty-fourth and twenty-fifth devotees in Nīlācala, were good singers who always accompanied Lord Caitanya.

PURPORT

Choṭa Haridāsa was later banished from the company of Lord Caitanya Mahāprabhu, as stated in the *Antya-līlā,* Chapter Two.

TEXT 148

**রামভদ্রাচার্য, আর ওড্র সিংহেশ্বর ।
তপন আচার্য, আর রঘু, নীলাম্বর ॥ ১৪৮ ॥**

*rāmabhadrācārya, āra oḍhra siṁheśvara
tapana ācārya, āra raghu, nīlāmbara*

SYNONYMS

rāmabhadrācārya—of the name Rāmabhadra Ācārya; *āra*—and; *oḍhra*—resident of Orissa; *siṁheśvara*—of the name Siṁheśvara; *tapana ācārya*—of the name Tapana Ācārya; *āra raghu*—and another Raghunātha; *nīlāmbara*—of the name Nīlāmbara.

TRANSLATION

Among the devotees who lived with Lord Caitanya Mahāprabhu at Jagannātha Purī, Rāmabhadra Ācārya was the twenty-sixth, Siṁheśvara the twenty-seventh, Tapana Ācārya the twenty-eighth, Raghunātha the twenty-ninth and Nīlāmbara the thirtieth.

TEXT 149

**সিঙ্গাভট্ট, কামাভট্ট, দন্তুর শিবানন্দ ।
গৌড়ে পূর্ব ভৃত্য প্রভুর প্রিয় কমলানন্দ ॥ ১৪৯ ॥**

*siṅgābhaṭṭa, kāmābhaṭṭa, dantura śivānanda
gauḍe pūrva bhṛtya prabhura priya kamalānanda*

SYNONYMS

siṅgābhaṭṭa—of the name Siṅgābhaṭṭa; *kāmābhaṭṭa*—of the name Kāmābhaṭṭa; *dantura śivānanda*—of the name Dantura Śivānanda; *gauḍe*—in Bengal; *pūrva*—formerly; *bhṛtya*—servant; *prabhura*—of the Lord; *priya*—very dear; *kamalānanda*—of the name Kamalānanda.

TRANSLATION

Siṅgābhaṭṭa was the thirty-first, Kāmābhaṭṭa the thirty-second, Śivānanda the thirty-third and Kamalānanda the thirty-fourth. They all formerly served Śrī Caitanya Mahāprabhu in Bengal, but later these servants left Bengal to live with the Lord in Jagannātha Purī.

TEXT 150

**অচ্যুতানন্দ—অদ্বৈত-আচার্য-তনয় ।
নীলাচলে রহে প্রভুর চরণ আশ্রয় ॥ ১৫০ ॥**

acyutānanda—advaita-ācārya-tanaya
nīlācale rahe prabhura caraṇa āśraya

SYNONYMS

acyutānanda—of the name Acyutānanda; *advaita-ācārya-tanaya*—the son of Advaita Ācārya; *nīlācale*—at Jagannātha Purī; *rahe*—stays; *prabhura*—of Lord Caitanya Mahāprabhu; *caraṇa*—lotus feet; *āśraya*—taking shelter.

TRANSLATION

Acyutānanda, the thirty-fifth devotee, was the son of Advaita Ācārya. He also lived with Lord Caitanya, taking shelter of His lotus feet at Jagannātha Purī.

PURPORT

There is a statement about Acyutānanda in Chapter Twelve, verse 13, of *Ādi-līlā.*

TEXT 151

নির্লোম গঙ্গাদাস, আর বিষ্ণুদাস ।
এই সবের প্রভুসঙ্গে নীলাচলে বাস ॥ ১৫১ ॥

nirloma gaṅgādāsa, āra viṣṇudāsa
ei sabera prabhu-saṅge nīlācale vāsa

SYNONYMS

nirloma gaṅgādāsa—of the name Nirloma Gaṅgādāsa; *āra*—and; *viṣṇudāsa*—of the name Viṣṇudāsa; *ei sabera*—of all of them; *prabhu-saṅge*—with Lord Caitanya Mahāprabhu; *nīlācale*—at Jagannātha Purī; *vāsa*—residence.

TRANSLATION

Nirloma Gaṅgādāsa and Viṣṇudāsa were the thirty-sixth and thirty-seventh among the devotees who lived at Jagannātha Purī as servants of Śrī Caitanya Mahāprabhu.

TEXTS 152-154

বারাণসী-মধ্যে প্রভুর ভক্ত তিন জন ।
চন্দ্রশেখর বৈদ্য, আর মিশ্র তপন ॥ ১৫২ ॥

রঘুনাথ ভট্টাচার্য—মিশ্রের নন্দন ।
প্রভু যবে কাশী আইলা দেখি' বৃন্দাবন ॥ ১৫৩ ॥

চন্দ্রশেখর-গৃহে কৈল দুই মাস বাস ।
তপন-মিশ্রের ঘরে ভিক্ষা দুই মাস ॥ ১৫৪ ॥

vārāṇasī-madhye prabhura bhakta tina jana
candraśekhara vaidya, āra miśra tapana

raghunātha bhaṭṭācārya—miśrera nandana
prabhu yabe kāśī āilā dekhi' vṛndāvana

candraśekhara-gṛhe kaila dui māsa vāsa
tapana-miśrera ghare bhikṣā dui māsa

SYNONYMS

vārāṇasī-madhye—at Vārāṇasī; *prabhura*—of Lord Caitanya Mahāprabhu; *bhakta*—devotees; *tina jana*—three persons; *candraśekhara vaidya*—the clerk of the name Candraśekhara; *āra*—and; *miśra tapana*—Tapana Miśra; *raghunātha bhaṭṭācārya*—of the name Raghunātha Bhaṭṭācārya; *miśrera nandana*—the son of Tapana Miśra; *prabhu*—Lord Śrī Caitanya Mahāprabhu; *yabe*—when; *kāśī*—Vārāṇasī; *āilā*—came; *dekhi'*—after visiting; *vṛndāvana*—the holy place; *candraśekhara-gṛhe*—in the house of Candraśekhara Vaidya; *kaila*—did; *dui māsa*—for two months; *vāsa*—reside; *tapana-miśrera*—of Tapana Miśra; *ghare*—in the house; *bhikṣā*—accepted *prasāda; dui māsa*—for two months.

TRANSLATION

The prominent devotees at Vārāṇasī were the physician Candraśekhara, Tapana Miśra and Raghunātha Bhaṭṭācārya, Tapana Miśra's son. When Lord Caitanya came to Vārāṇasī after seeing Vṛndāvana, for two months He lived at the residence of Candraśekhara Vaidya and accepted prasāda at the house of Tapana Miśra.

PURPORT

When Śrī Caitanya Mahāprabhu was in Bengal, Tapana Miśra approached Him to discuss spiritual advancement. Thus he was favored by Lord Caitanya Mahāprabhu and received *hari-nāma* initiation. After that, by the order of the Lord, Tapana Miśra resided in Vārāṇasī, and when Lord Caitanya visited Vārāṇasī He stayed at the home of Tapana Miśra.

TEXT 155

রঘুনাথ বাল্যে কৈল প্রভুর সেবন ।
উচ্ছিষ্ট-মার্জন আর পাদ-সম্বাহন ॥ ১৫৫ ॥

raghunātha bālye kaila prabhura sevana
ucchiṣṭa-mārjana āra pāda-saṁvāhana

SYNONYMS

raghunātha—Raghunātha, the son of Tapana Miśra; *bālye*—in his boyhood; *kaila*—did; *prabhura*—of Lord Caitanya; *sevana*—rendering service; *ucchiṣṭa-mārjana*—washing the dishes; *āra*—and; *pāda-saṁvāhana*—massaging the feet.

TRANSLATION

When Śrī Caitanya Mahāprabhu stayed at the house of Tapana Miśra, Raghunātha Bhaṭṭa, who was then a boy, washed His dishes and massaged His legs.

TEXT 156

বড় হৈলে নীলাচলে গেলা প্রভুর স্থানে ।
অষ্টমাস রহিল ভিক্ষা দেন কোন দিনে ॥ ১৫৬ ॥

baḍa haile nīlācale gelā prabhura sthāne
aṣṭa-māsa rahila bhikṣā dena kona dine

SYNONYMS

baḍa haile—when he grew to be a young man; *nīlācale*—at Jagannātha Purī; *gelā*—went; *prabhura*—of Lord Śrī Caitanya Mahāprabhu; *sthāne*—at the place; *aṣṭa-māsa*—eight months; *rahila*—stayed; *bhikṣā*—*prasāda; dena*—gave; *kona dine*—some days.

TRANSLATION

When Raghunātha grew to be a young man, he visited Lord Caitanya Mahāprabhu at Jagannātha Purī and stayed there for eight months. Sometimes he offered prasāda to the Lord.

TEXT 157

প্রভুর আজ্ঞা পাঞা বৃন্দাবনেরে আইলা ।
আসিয়া শ্রীরূপ-গোসাঞির নিকটে রহিলা ॥ ১৫৭ ॥

prabhura ājñā pāñā vṛndāvanere āilā
āsiyā śrī-rūpa-gosāñira nikaṭe rahilā

SYNONYMS

prabhura—of Lord Caitanya Mahāprabhu; *ājñā*—order; *pāñā*—receiving; *vṛndāvanere*—to Vṛndāvana; *āilā*—he came; *āsiyā*—coming there; *śrī-rūpa-gosāñira*—of Śrīla Rūpa Gosvāmī; *nikaṭe*—at his shelter; *rahilā*—remained.

TRANSLATION

Later, by the order of Lord Caitanya, Raghunātha went to Vṛndāvana and remained there under the shelter of Śrīla Rūpa Gosvāmī.

TEXT 158

তাঁর স্থানে রূপ-গোসাঞি শুনেন ভাগবত ।
প্রভুর কৃপায় তেঁহো কৃষ্ণপ্রেমে মত্ত ॥ ১৫৮ ॥

tāṅra sthāne rūpa-gosāñi śunena bhāgavata
prabhura kṛpāya teṅho kṛṣṇa-preme matta

SYNONYMS

tāṅra sthāne—in his place; *rūpa-gosāñi*—Śrīla Rūpa Gosvāmī; *śunena*—heard; *bhāgavata*—the recitation of *Śrīmad-Bhāgavatam; prabhura kṛpāya*—by the mercy of Lord Caitanya; *teṅho*—he; *kṛṣṇa-preme*—in love of Kṛṣṇa; *matta*—always maddened.

TRANSLATION

While he stayed with Śrīla Rūpa Gosvāmī, his engagement was to recite Śrīmad-Bhāgavatam for him to hear. As a result of this Bhāgavatam recitation, he attained perfectional love of Kṛṣṇa, by which he remained always maddened.

PURPORT

Raghunātha Bhaṭṭācārya, or Raghunātha Bhaṭṭa Gosvāmī, one of the six Gosvāmīs, was the son of Tapana Miśra. Born in approximately 1425 *śakābda,* he was expert in reciting *Śrīmad-Bhāgavatam,* and in the *Antya-līlā,* Chapter Thirty, it is stated that he was also expert in cooking; whatever he cooked would be nectarean. Śrī Caitanya Mahāprabhu was greatly pleased to accept the foodstuffs that he cooked, and Raghunātha Bhaṭṭa used to take the remnants of foodstuffs left by Śrī Caitanya Mahāprabhu. Raghunātha Bhaṭṭācārya lived for eight months in Jagannātha Purī, after which Lord Caitanya ordered him to go to Vṛndāvana to join Śrī Rūpa Gosvāmī. Śrī Caitanya Mahāprabhu asked Raghunātha Bhaṭṭācārya not to marry but to remain a *brahmacārī,* and He also ordered him to read *Śrīmad-Bhāgavatam* constantly. Thus he went to Vṛndāvana, where he engaged in reciting *Śrīmad-Bhāgavatam* to Śrīla Rūpa Gosvāmī. He was so expert in reciting *Śrīmad-Bhāgavatam* that he would recite each and every verse in three melodious tunes. While Raghunātha Bhaṭṭa Gosvāmī was living with Śrī Caitanya Mahāprabhu, the Lord blessed him by offering him betel nuts offered to the Jagannātha Deity and a garland of *tulasī* said to be as long as fourteen cubits. The Govinda temple was constructed by Raghunātha Bhaṭṭa Gosvāmī's order to one of his disciples. Raghunātha Bhaṭṭa Gosvāmī supplied all the ornaments of the Govinda Deity. He never talked of nonsense or worldly matters but always engaged in hearing about Kṛṣṇa twenty-four hours a day. He never cared to hear blasphemy of a Vaiṣṇava. Even when there were points to be criticized, he used to say that since all the Vaiṣṇavas were engaged in the service of the Lord, he did not mind their faults. Later Raghunātha Bhaṭṭa Gosvāmī lived by Rādhākuṇḍa in a small cottage. In the *Gaura-gaṇoddeśa-dīpikā,* verse 185, it is said that Raghunātha Bhaṭṭa Gosvāmī was formerly the *gopī* named Rāga-mañjarī.

TEXT 159

এইমত সংখ্যাতীত চৈতন্য-ভক্তগণ ।
দিঙ্মাত্র লিখি, সম্যক্ না যায় কথন ॥ ১৫৯ ॥

ei-mata saṅkhyātīta caitanya-bhakta-gaṇa
diṅmātra likhi, samyak nā yāya kathana

SYNONYMS

ei-mata—in this way; *saṅkhyā-atīta*—innumerable; *caitanya-bhakta-gaṇa*—devotees of Lord Caitanya; *diṅmātra*—only a fractional part; *likhi*—I write; *samyak*—full; *nā*—cannot; *yāya*—be possible; *kathana*—to explain.

TRANSLATION

I list in this way only a portion of the innumerable devotees of Lord Caitanya. To describe them all fully is not possible.

TEXT 160

একৈক-শাখাতে লাগে কোটি কোটি ডাল।
তার শিষ্য-উপশিষ্য, তার উপডাল ॥ ১৬০ ॥

ekaika-śākhāte lāge koṭi koṭi ḍāla
tāra śiṣya-upaśiṣya, tāra upaḍāla

SYNONYMS

ekaika—in each; *śākhāte*—branch; *lāge*—grow; *koṭi koṭi*—hundreds and thousands; *ḍāla*—twigs; *tāra*—his; *śiṣya*—disciple; *upaśiṣya*—sub-disciple; *tāra*—his; *upaḍāla*—sub-branches.

TRANSLATION

From each branch of the tree have grown hundreds and thousands of sub-branches of disciples and grand-disciples.

PURPORT

It was the desire of Lord Caitanya Mahāprabhu that His cult be spread all over the world. Therefore there is a great necessity for many, many disciples of the branches of Śrī Caitanya Mahāprabhu's disciplic succession. His cult should be spread not only in a few villages, or in Bengal, or in India, but all over the world. It is very much regrettable that complacent so-called devotees criticize the members of the International Society for Krishna Consciousness for accepting *sannyāsa* and spreading the cult of Lord Caitanya all over the world. It is not our business to criticize anyone, but because they try to find fault with this movement, the real truth must be stated. Śrī Caitanya Mahāprabhu wanted devotees all over the world, and Śrīla Bhaktisiddhānta Sarasvatī Ṭhākura and Śrīla Bhaktivinoda Ṭhākura also confirmed this. It is in pursuit of their will that the ISKCON movement is spreading all over the world. Genuine devotees of Lord Caitanya Mahāprabhu must take pride in the spread of Kṛṣṇa consciousness movement instead of viciously criticizing its propaganda work.

TEXT 161

সকল ভরিয়া আছে প্রেম-ফুল-ফলে।
ভাসাইল ত্রিজগৎ কৃষ্ণপ্রেম-জলে ॥ ১৬১ ॥

sakala bhariyā āche prema-phula-phale
bhāsāila tri-jagat kṛṣṇa-prema-jale

SYNONYMS

sakala—all; *bhariyā*—filled; *āche*—there is; *prema*—love of Godhead; *phula*—flowers; *phale*—fruits; *bhāsāila*—inundated; *tri-jagat*—the whole world; *kṛṣṇa-prema*—of love of Kṛṣṇa; *jale*—with water.

TRANSLATION

Every branch and sub-branch of the tree is full of innumerable fruits and flowers. They inundate the world with the waters of love of Kṛṣṇa.

TEXT 162

এক এক শাখার শক্তি অনন্ত মহিমা।
'সহস্র বদনে' যার দিতে নারে সীমা ॥ ১৬২ ॥

eka eka śākhāra śakti ananta mahimā
'sahasra vadane' yāra dite nāre sīmā

SYNONYMS

eka eka—of each and every; *śākhāra*—branch; *śakti*—power; *ananta*—unlimited; *mahimā*—glories; *sahasra vadane*—in thousands of mouths; *yāra*—of which; *dite*—to give; *nāre*—becomes unable; *sīmā*—limit.

TRANSLATION

Each and every branch of Śrī Caitanya Mahāprabhu's devotees has unlimited spiritual power and glory. Even if one had thousands of mouths, it would be impossible to describe the limits of their activities.

TEXT 163

সংক্ষেপে কহিল মহাপ্রভুর ভক্তগণ।
সমগ্র বলিতে নারে 'সহস্র-বদন' ॥ ১৬৩ ॥

saṅkṣepe kahila mahāprabhura bhakta-gaṇa
samagra balite nāre 'sahasra-vadana'

SYNONYMS

saṅkṣepe—in brief; *kahila*—described; *mahāprabhura*—of Lord Caitanya Mahāprabhu; *bhakta-gaṇa*—the devotees; *samagra*—all; *balite*—to speak; *nāre*—cannot; *sahasra-vadana*—Lord Śeṣa, who has thousands of mouths.

TRANSLATION

I have briefly described the devotees of Lord Caitanya Mahāprabhu in different places. Even Lord Śeṣa, who has thousands of mouths, could not list them all.

TEXT 164

শ্রীরূপ-রঘুনাথ-পদে যার আশ ।
চৈতন্যচরিতামৃত কহে কৃষ্ণদাস ॥ ১৬৪ ॥

śrī-rūpa-raghunātha-pade yāra āśa
caitanya-caritāmṛta kahe kṛṣṇadāsa

SYNONYMS

śrī-rūpa—Śrīla Rūpa Gosvāmī; *raghunātha*—Śrī Raghunātha dāsa Gosvāmī; *pade*—at the lotus feet; *yāra*—whose; *āśa*—expectation; *caitanya-caritāmṛta*—the book named *Caitanya-caritāmṛta; kahe*—describes; *kṛṣṇadāsa*—Śrīla Kṛṣṇadāsa Gosvāmī.

TRANSLATION

Praying at the lotus feet of Śrī Rūpa and Śrī Raghunātha, always desiring their mercy, I, Kṛṣṇadāsa, narrate Śrī Caitanya-caritāmṛta, following in their footsteps.

Thus end the Bhaktivedanta purports of *Śrī Caitanya-caritāmṛta, Ādi-līlā,* Chapter Ten, in the matter of the Main Trunk of the Caitanya Tree, Its Branches and Its Sub-branches.

Ādi-Līlā

CHAPTER 11

As the branches and sub-branches of Lord Caitanya Mahāprabhu were described in the Tenth Chapter, in this Eleventh Chapter the branches and sub-branches of Śrī Nityānanda Prabhu are similarly listed.

TEXT 1

নিত্যানন্দপদাম্ভোজ-ভৃঙ্গান্ প্রেমমধূন্মদান্ ।
নত্বাখিলান্ তেষু মুখ্যা লিখ্যন্তে কতিচিন্ময়া ॥ ১ ॥

nityānanda-padāmbhoja-bhṛṅgān prema-madhūnmadān
natvākhilān teṣu mukhyā likhyante katicin mayā

SYNONYMS

nityānanda—of Lord Śrī Nityānanda; *pada-ambhoja*—lotus feet; *bhṛṅgān*—the bumblebees; *prema*—of love of Godhead; *madhu*—by the honey; *unmadān*—maddened; *natvā*—offering obeisances; *akhilān*—to all of them; *teṣu*—out of them; *mukhyāḥ*—the chief; *likhyante*—being described; *katicit*—a few of them; *mayā*—by me.

TRANSLATION

After offering my obeisances unto all of the devotees of Śrī Nityānanda Prabhu, who are like bumblebees collecting honey from His lotus feet, I shall try to describe those who are the most prominent.

TEXT 2

জয় জয় মহাপ্রভু শ্রীকৃষ্ণচৈতন্য ।
তাঁহার চরণাশ্রিত যেই, সেই ধন্য ॥ ২ ॥

jaya jaya mahāprabhu śrī-kṛṣṇa-caitanya
tāṅhāra caraṇāśrita yei, sei dhanya

SYNONYMS

jaya jaya—all glories; *mahāprabhu*—unto Lord Śrī Caitanya Mahāprabhu; *śrī-kṛṣṇa-caitanya*—known as Kṛṣṇa Caitanya; *tāṅhāra caraṇa-āśrita*—all who have taken shelter at His lotus feet; *yei*—anyone; *sei*—he is; *dhanya*—glorious.

TRANSLATION

All glories to Śrī Caitanya Mahāprabhu! Anyone who has taken shelter at His lotus feet is glorious.

TEXT 3

জয় জয় শ্রীঅদ্বৈত, জয় নিত্যানন্দ ।
জয় জয় মহাপ্রভুর সর্বভক্তবৃন্দ ॥ ৩ ॥

jaya jaya śrī-advaita, jaya nityānanda
jaya jaya mahāprabhura sarva-bhakta-vṛnda

SYNONYMS

jaya jaya—all glories; *śrī-advaita*—unto Śrī Advaita Ācārya; *jaya*—all glories; *nityānanda*—unto Lord Śrī Nityānanda Prabhu; *jaya jaya*—all glories; *mahāprabhura*—of Lord Śrī Caitanya Mahāprabhu; *sarva*—all; *bhakta-vṛnda*—devotees.

TRANSLATION

All glories to Śrī Advaita Prabhu, Nityānanda Prabhu and all the devotees of Lord Caitanya Mahāprabhu!

TEXT 4

তস্য শ্রীকৃষ্ণচৈতন্য-সৎপ্রেমামরশাখিনঃ ।
ঊর্ধ্বস্কন্ধাবধূতেন্দোঃ শাখারূপান্ গণান্নুমঃ ॥ ৪ ॥

tasya śrī-kṛṣṇa-caitanya-sat-premāmara-śākhinaḥ
ūrdhva-skandhāvadhūtendoḥ śākhā-rūpān gaṇān numaḥ

SYNONYMS

tasya—His; *śrī-kṛṣṇa-caitanya*—Lord Śrī Kṛṣṇa Caitanya Mahāprabhu; *sat-prema*—of eternal love of Godhead; *amara*—indestructible; *śākhinaḥ*—of the tree; *ūrdhva*—very high; *skandha*—branch; *avadhūta-indoḥ*—of Śrī Nityānanda; *śākhā-rūpān*—in the form of different branches; *gaṇān*—to the devotees; *numaḥ*—I offer my respects.

TRANSLATION

Śrī Nityānanda Prabhu is the topmost branch of the indestructible tree of eternal love of Godhead, Śrī Kṛṣṇa Caitanya Mahāprabhu. I offer my respectful obeisances to all the sub-branches of that topmost branch.

TEXT 5

শ্রীনিত্যানন্দ-বৃক্ষের স্কন্ধ গুরুতর ।
তাহাতে জন্মিল শাখা-প্রশাখা বিস্তর ॥ ৫ ॥

śrī-nityānanda-vṛkṣera skandha gurutara
tāhāte janmila śākhā-praśākhā vistara

SYNONYMS

śrī-nityānanda-vṛkṣera—of the tree known as Śrī Nityānanda; *skandha*—main branch; *gurutara*—extremely heavy; *tāhāte*—from that branch; *janmila*—grew; *śākhā*—branches; *praśākhā*—sub-branches; *vistara*—expansively.

TRANSLATION

Śrī Nityānanda Prabhu is an extremely heavy branch of the Śrī Caitanya tree. From that branch grow many branches and sub-branches.

TEXT 6

মালাকারের ইচ্ছা-জলে বাড়ে শাখাগণ ।
প্রেম-ফুল-ফলে ভরি' ছাইল ভুবন ॥ ৬ ॥

mālākārera icchā-jale bāḍe śākhā-gaṇa
prema-phula-phale bhari' chāila bhuvana

SYNONYMS

mālākārera—of Śrī Caitanya Mahāprabhu; *icchā-jale*—by the water of His wish; *bāḍe*—increase; *śākhā-gaṇa*—the branches; *prema*—love of Godhead; *phula-phale*—with flowers and fruits; *bhari'*—filling; *chāila*—covered; *bhuvana*—the whole world.

TRANSLATION

Watered by the desire of Śrī Caitanya Mahāprabhu, these branches and sub-branches have grown unlimitedly and covered the entire world with fruits and flowers.

TEXT 7

অসংখ্য অনন্ত গণ কে করু গণন ।
আপনা শোধিতে কহি মুখ্য মুখ্য জন ॥ ৭ ॥

asaṅkhya ananta gaṇa ke karu gaṇana
āpanā śodhite kahi mukhya mukhya jana

SYNONYMS

asaṅkhya—innumerable; *ananta*—unlimited; *gaṇa*—devotees; *ke*—who; *karu*—can; *gaṇana*—count; *āpanā*—the self; *śodhite*—to purify; *kahi*—I speak; *mukhya mukhya*—only the chief; *jana*—persons.

TRANSLATION

These branches and sub-branches of devotees are innumerable and unlimited. Who could count them? For my personal purification I shall try to enumerate only the most prominent among them.

PURPORT

One should not write books or essays on transcendental subject matter for material name, fame or profit. Transcendental literature must be written under the direction of a superior authority because it is not meant for material purposes. If one tries to write under superior authority, he becomes purified. All Kṛṣṇa conscious activities should be undertaken for personal purification (*āpanā śodhite*), not for material gain.

TEXT 8

শ্রীবীরভদ্র গোসাঞি—স্কন্ধ-মহাশাখা ।
তাঁর উপশাখা যত, অসংখ্য তার লেখা ॥ ৮ ॥

śrī-vīrabhadra gosāñi—skandha-mahāśākhā
tāṅra upaśākhā yata, asaṅkhya tāra lekhā

SYNONYMS

śrī-vīrabhadra gosāñi—of the name Śrī Vīrabhadra Gosāñi; *skandha*—of the trunk; *mahā-śākhā*—the biggest branch; *tāṅra*—his; *upaśākhā*—sub-branches; *yata*—all; *asaṅkhya*—innumerable; *tāra*—of that; *lekhā*—the description.

TRANSLATION

After Nityānanda Prabhu, the greatest branch is Vīrabhadra Gosāñi, who also has innumerable branches and sub-branches. It is not possible to describe them all.

PURPORT

Śrīla Bhaktisiddhānta Sarasvatī Ṭhākura describes Vīrabhadra Gosāñi as the direct son of Śrīla Nityānanda Prabhu and disciple of Jāhnavā-devī. His real mother was Vasudhā. In the *Gaura-gaṇoddeśa-dīpikā,* verse 67, he is mentioned as an incarnation of Kṣīrodakaśāyī Viṣṇu. Therefore Vīrabhadra Gosāñi is nondifferent from Śrī Kṛṣṇa Caitanya Mahāprabhu. In a village of the name Jhāmaṭapura in the district of Hugali, Vīrabhadra Gosāñi had a disciple named Yadunāthācārya, who had two daughters—a real daughter named Śrīmatī and a foster daughter named Nārāyaṇī.

Both these daughters married, and they are mentioned in *Bhakti-ratnākara,* Chapter Thirteen. Vīrabhadra Gosāñi had three disciples who are celebrated as his sons—Gopījana-vallabha, Rāmakṛṣṇa and Rāmacandra. The youngest, Rāmacandra, belonged to the Śāṇḍilya dynasty and had the surname Vaṭavyāla. He established his family at Khaḍadaha, and its members are known as the *gosvāmīs* of Khaḍadaha. The eldest disciple, Gopījana-vallabha, was a resident of a village known as Latā near the Mānakara railway station in the district of Burdwan. The second, Rāma-kṛṣṇa, lived near Māladaha in a village named Gayeśapura. Śrīla Bhaktisiddhānta Sarasvatī Ṭhākura notes that since these three disciples belonged to different *gotras,* or dynasties, and also had different surnames and lived in different places, it is not possible to accept them as real sons of Vīrabhadra Gosāñi. Rāmacandra had four sons, of whom the eldest was Rādhāmādhava, whose third son was named Yādavendra. Yādavendra's son was Nandakiśora, his son was Nidhikṛṣṇa, his son was Caitanyacāṇḍa, his son was Kṛṣṇamohana, his son was Jaganmohana, his son was Vrajanātha, and his son was Śyāmalāla Gosvāmī. This is the genealogical table given by Bhaktisiddhānta Sarasvatī Ṭhākura for the descendants of Vīrabhadra Gosāñi.

TEXT 9

ঈশ্বর হইয়া কহায় মহা-ভাগবত ।
বেদধর্মাতীত হঞা বেদধর্মে রত ॥ ৯ ॥

īśvara ha-iyā kahāya mahā-bhāgavata
veda-dharmātīta hañā veda-dharme rata

SYNONYMS

īśvara—the Supreme Personality of Godhead; *ha-iyā*—being; *kahāya*—calls Himself; *mahā-bhāgavata*—great devotee; *veda-dharma*—the principles of Vedic religion; *atīta*—transcendental; *hañā*—being; *veda-dharme*—in the Vedic system; *rata*—engaged.

TRANSLATION

Although Vīrabhadra Gosāñi was the Supreme Personality of Godhead, He presented Himself as a great devotee. And although the Supreme Godhead is transcendental to all Vedic injunctions, He strictly followed the Vedic rituals.

TEXT 10

অন্তরে ঈশ্বর-চেষ্টা, বাহিরে নির্দম্ভ ।
চৈতন্যভক্তিমণ্ডপে তেঁহো মূলস্তম্ভ ॥ ১০ ॥

antare īśvara-ceṣṭā, bāhire nirdambha
caitanya-bhakti-maṇḍape teṅho mūla-stambha

SYNONYMS

antare—within Himself; *īśvara-ceṣṭā*—the activities of the Supreme Personality of Godhead; *bāhire*—externally; *nirdambha*—without pride; *caitanya-bhakti-maṇḍape*—in the devotional hall of Śrī Caitanya Mahāprabhu; *teṅho*—He is; *mūla-stambha*—the main pillar.

TRANSLATION

He is the main pillar in the hall of devotional service erected by Śrī Caitanya Mahāprabhu. He knew within Himself that He acted as the Supreme Lord Viṣṇu, but externally He was prideless.

TEXT 11

অদ্যাপি যাঁহার কৃপা-মহিমা হইতে ।
চৈতন্য-নিত্যানন্দ গায় সকল জগতে ॥ ১১ ॥

adyāpi yāṅhāra kṛpā-mahimā ha-ite
caitanya-nityānanda gāya sakala jagate

SYNONYMS

adyāpi—until today; *yāṅhāra*—whose; *kṛpā*—mercy; *mahimā*—glorious; *ha-ite*—from; *caitanya-nityānanda*—Śrī Caitanya-Nityānanda; *gāya*—sing; *sakala*—all; *jagate*—in the world.

TRANSLATION

It is by the glorious mercy of Śrī Vīrabhadra Gosāñi that people all over the world now have the chance to chant the names of Caitanya and Nityānanda.

TEXT 12

সেই বীরভদ্র-গোসাঞির লইনু শরণ ।
যাঁহার প্রসাদে হয় অভীষ্ট-পূরণ ॥ ১২ ॥

sei vīrabhadra-gosāñira la-inu śaraṇa
yāṅhāra prasāde haya abhīṣṭa-pūraṇa

SYNONYMS

sei—that; *vīrabhadra-gosāñira*—of Śrī Vīrabhadra Gosāñi; *la-inu*—I take; *śaraṇa*—shelter; *yāṅhāra*—whose; *prasāde*—by mercy; *haya*—it becomes so; *abhīṣṭa-pūraṇa*—fulfillment of desire.

TRANSLATION

I therefore take shelter of the lotus feet of Vīrabhadra Gosāñi so that by His mercy my great desire to write Śrī Caitanya-caritāmṛta will be properly guided.

TEXT 13

শ্রীরামদাস আর, গদাধর দাস ।
চৈতন্য-গোসাঞির ভক্ত রহে তাঁর পাশ ॥ ১৩ ॥

śrī-rāma-dāsa āra, gadādhara dāsa
caitanya-gosāñira bhakta rahe tāṅra pāśa

SYNONYMS

śrī-rāma-dāsa—of the name Śrī Rāmadāsa; *āra*—and; *gadādhara dāsa*—of the name Gadādhara dāsa; *caitanya-gosāñira*—of Lord Śrī Caitanya Mahāprabhu; *bhakta*—devotees; *rahe*—stay; *tāṅra pāśa*—with Him.

TRANSLATION

Two devotees of Lord Caitanya named Śrī Rāmadāsa and Gadādhara dāsa always lived with Śrī Vīrabhadra Gosāñi.

PURPORT

Śrī Rāmadāsa, later known as Abhirāma Ṭhākura, was one of the twelve *gopālas,* cowherd boy friends, of Śrī Nityānanda Prabhu. The *Gaura-gaṇoddeśa-dīpikā,* verse 126, states that Śrī Rāmadāsa was formerly Śrīdāmā. In the *Bhakti-ratnākara,* Chapter Four, there is a description of Śrīla Abhirāma Ṭhākura. By the order of Śrī Nityānanda Prabhu, Abhirāma Ṭhākura became a great *ācārya* and preacher of the Caitanya cult of devotional service. He was a very influential personality, and nondevotees were very much afraid of him. Empowered by Śrī Nityānanda Prabhu, he was always in ecstasy and was extremely kind to all fallen souls. It is said that if he offered obeisances to any stone other than a *śālagrāma-śilā,* it would immediately fracture.

Ten miles southwest of the railway station Cāṅpāḍāṅgā on the narrow gauge railway line from Howrah in Calcutta to Āmtā, a village in the Hugali district, is a small town named Khānākūla-kṛṣṇanagara where the temple of Abhirāma Ṭhākura is situated. During the rainy season, when this area is inundated with water, people must go there by another line, which is now called the southeastern railway. On this line there is a station named Kolāghāṭa, from which one has to go by steamer to Rāṇīcaka. Seven and a half miles north of Rāṇīcaka is Khānākūla. The temple of Abhirāma Ṭhākura is situated in Kṛṣṇanagara, which is near the *kūla* (bank) of the Khānā (Dvārakeśvara River); therefore this place is celebrated as Khānākūla-kṛṣṇanagara. Outside of the temple is a *bakula* tree. This place is known as Siddha-bakula-kuñja. It is said that when Abhirāma Ṭhākura came there, he sat down under this tree. In Khānākūla-kṛṣṇanagara there is a big fair held every year in the month of *caitra* (March-April) on the *kṛṣṇa-saptamī,* the seventh day of the dark moon. Many hundreds and thousands of people gather for this festival. The temple of Abhirāma Ṭhākura has a very old history. The Deity in the temple is known as Gopīnātha. There are many *sevaita* families living near the temple. It is said that

Abhirāma Ṭhākura had a whip and that whoever he touched with it would immediately become an elevated devotee of Kṛṣṇa. Among his many disciples, Śrīmān Śrīnivāsa Ācārya was the most famous and the most dear, but it is doubtful that he was his initiated disciple.

TEXTS 14-15

নিত্যানন্দে আজ্ঞা দিল যবে গৌড়ে যাইতে ।
মহাপ্রভু এই দুই দিলা তাঁর সাথে ॥ ১৪ ॥
অতএব দুইগণে দুঁহার গণন ।
মাধব-বাসুদেব ঘোষেরও এই বিবরণ ॥ ১৫ ॥

nityānande ājñā dila yabe gauḍe yāite
mahāprabhu ei dui dilā tāṅra sāthe

ataeva dui-gaṇe duṅhāra gaṇana
mādhava-vāsudeva ghoṣerao ei vivaraṇa

SYNONYMS

nityānande—unto Lord Nityānanda; *ājñā*—order; *dila*—gave; *yabe*—when; *gauḍe*—to Bengal; *yāite*—to go; *mahāprabhu*—Śrī Caitanya Mahāprabhu; *ei dui*—these two; *dilā*—gave; *tāṅra sāthe*—with Him; *ataeva*—therefore; *dui-gaṇe*—in both the parties; *duṅhāra*—two of them; *gaṇana*—are counted; *mādhava*—of the name Mādhava; *vāsudeva*—of the name Vāsudeva; *ghoṣerao*—of the surname Ghosh; *ei*—this; *vivaraṇa*—description.

TRANSLATION

When Nityānanda Prabhu was ordered to go to Bengal to preach, these two devotees [Śrī Rāmadāsa and Gadādhara dāsa] were ordered to go with Him. Thus they are sometimes counted among the devotees of Lord Caitanya and sometimes among the devotees of Lord Nityānanda. Similarly, Mādhava and Vāsudeva Ghosh belonged to both groups of devotees simultaneously.

PURPORT

There is a place named Dāṅihāṭa near the Agradvīpa railway station and Pāṭuli in the district of Burdwan where the Deity of Śrī Gopīnāthajī is still situated. This Deity accepted Govinda Ghosh as His father. Even until today, the Deity performs the *śrāddha* ceremony on the anniversary of the death of Govinda Ghosh. The temple of this Deity is managed by the *rājavaṁśa* family of Kṛṣṇanagara, whose members are descendants of Rājā Kṛṣṇacandra. Every year in the month of *vaiśākha,* when there is a *bāradola* ceremony, this Gopīnātha Deity is taken to Kṛṣṇanagara. The ceremony is performed with eleven other Deities, and then Śrī Gopīnāthajī is again brought back to the temple in Agradvīpa.

TEXT 16

রামদাস – মুখ্যশাখা, সখ্য-প্রেমরাশি ।
ষোলসাঙ্গের কাষ্ঠ যেই তুলি' কৈল বাঁশী ॥ ১৬ ॥

rāma-dāsa—mukhya-śākhā, sakhya-prema-rāśi
ṣola-sāṅgera kāṣṭha yei tuli' kaila vāṁśī

SYNONYMS

rāma-dāsa—of the name Rāmadāsa; *mukhya-śākhā*—chief branch; *sakhya-prema-rāśi*—full of fraternal love; *ṣola-sāṅgera*—of sixteen knots; *kāṣṭha*—wood; *yei*—that; *tuli'*—raising; *kaila*—made; *vāṁśī*—flute.

TRANSLATION

Rāmadāsa, one of the chief branches, was full of fraternal love of Godhead. He made a flute from a stick with sixteen knots.

TEXT 17

গদাধর দাস গোপীভাবে পূর্ণানন্দ ।
যাঁর ঘরে দানকেলি কৈল নিত্যানন্দ ॥ ১৭ ॥

gadādhara dāsa gopībhāve pūrṇānanda
yāṅra ghare dānakeli kaila nityānanda

SYNONYMS

gadādhara dāsa—of the name Gadādhara dāsa; *gopī-bhāve*—in the ecstasy of the *gopīs; pūrṇa-ānanda*—fully in transcendental bliss; *yāṅra ghare*—in whose house; *dānakeli*—performance of *dānakeli-līlā; kaila*—did; *nityānanda*—Lord Nityānanda Prabhu.

TRANSLATION

Śrīla Gadādhara dāsa was always fully absorbed in ecstasy as a gopī. In his house Lord Nityānanda enacted the drama Dānakeli.

TEXT 18

শ্রীমাধব ঘোষ – মুখ্য কীর্তনীয়াগণে ।
নিত্যানন্দপ্রভু নৃত্য করে যাঁর গানে ॥ ১৮ ॥

śrī-mādhava ghoṣa—mukhya kīrtanīyā-gaṇe
nityānanda-prabhu nṛtya kare yāṅra gāne

SYNONYMS

śrī-mādhava ghoṣa—of the name Śrī Mādhava Ghosh; *mukhya*—chief; *kīrtanīyā-gaṇe*—amongst the performers of *saṅkīrtana; nityānanda-prabhu*—of the name Nityānanda Prabhu; *nṛtya*—dance; *kare*—does; *yāṅra*—whose; *gāne*—in song.

TRANSLATION

Śrī Mādhava Ghosh was a principal performer of kīrtana. While he sang, Nityānanda Prabhu danced.

TEXT 19

বাসুদেব গীতে করে প্রভুর বর্ণনে।
কাষ্ঠ-পাষাণ দ্রবে যাহার শ্রবণে ॥ ১৯ ॥

vāsudeva gīte kare prabhura varṇane
kāṣṭha-pāṣāṇa drave yāhāra śravaṇe

SYNONYMS

vāsudeva—of the name Vāsudeva; *gīte*—while singing; *kare*—does; *prabhura*—of Nityānanda Prabhu and Śrī Caitanya Prabhu; *varṇane*—in description; *kāṣṭha*—wood; *pāṣāṇa*—stone; *drave*—melt; *yāhāra*—whose; *śravaṇe*—by hearing.

TRANSLATION

When Vāsudeva Ghosh performed kīrtana, describing Lord Caitanya and Nityānanda, even wood and stone would melt upon hearing it.

TEXT 20

মুরারি-চৈতন্যদাসের অলৌকিক লীলা।
ব্যাঘ্র-গালে চড় মারে, সর্প-সনে খেলা ॥ ২০ ॥

murāri-caitanya-dāsera alaukika līlā
vyāghra-gāle caḍa māre, sarpa-sane khelā

SYNONYMS

murāri—of the name Murāri; *caitanya-dāsera*—of the servant of Śrī Caitanya Mahāprabhu; *alaukika*—uncommon; *līlā*—pastimes; *vyāghra*—tiger; *gāle*—on the cheek; *caḍa māre*—slaps; *sarpa*—a snake; *sane*—with; *khelā*—playing.

TRANSLATION

There were many extraordinary activities performed by Murāri, a great devotee of Lord Caitanya Mahāprabhu. Sometimes in his ecstasy he would slap the cheek of a tiger, and sometimes he would play with a venomous snake.

PURPORT

Murāri Caitanya dāsa was born in the village of Sarvṛndāvana-pura, which is situated about two miles from the Galaśī station on the Burdwan line. When Murāri Caitanya dāsa came to Navadvīpa, he settled in the village of Modadruma, or Māugāchi-grāma. At that time he became known as Śārṅga or Sāraṅga Murāri Caitanya dāsa. The descendants of his family still reside in Sarer Pāṭa. In the *Caitanya-bhāgavata, Antya-līlā,* Chapter Five, there is the following statement: "Murāri Caitanya dāsa had no material bodily features, for he was completely spiritual. Thus he would sometimes chase after tigers in the jungle and treat them just like cats and dogs. He would slap the cheek of a tiger and take a venomous snake on his lap. He had no fear for his external body, of which he was completely forgetful. He could spend all twenty-four hours of the day chanting the Hare Kṛṣṇa *mahā-mantra* or speaking about Lord Caitanya and Nityānanda. Sometimes he would remain submerged in water for two or three days, but he would feel no bodily inconvenience. Thus he behaved almost like stone or wood, but he always used his energy in chanting the Hare Kṛṣṇa *mahā-mantra.* No one can describe his specific characteristics, but it is understood that wherever Murāri Caitanya dāsa passed, whoever was present would be enlightened in Kṛṣṇa consciousness simply by the atmosphere he created."

TEXT 21

নিত্যানন্দের গণ যত,—সব ব্রজসখা ।
শৃঙ্গ-বেত্র-গোপবেশ, শিরে শিখিপাখা ॥ ২১ ॥

nityānandera gaṇa yata—saba vraja-sakhā
śṛṅga-vetra-gopaveśa, śire śikhi-pākhā

SYNONYMS

nityānandera—of Lord Nityānanda Prabhu; *gaṇa*—followers; *yata*—all; *saba*—all; *vraja-sakhā*—residents of Vṛndāvana; *śṛṅga*—horn; *vetra*—cane stick; *gopa-veśa*—dressed like a cowherd boy; *śire*—on the head; *śikhi-pākhā*—the plume of a peacock.

TRANSLATION

All the associates of Lord Nityānanda were formerly cowherd boys in Vrajabhūmi. Their symbolic representations were the horns and sticks they carried, their cowherd dress and the peacock plumes on their heads.

PURPORT

Jāhnavā-mātā is also within the list of Lord Nityānanda's followers. She is described in the *Gaura-gaṇoddeśa-dīpikā,* verse 66, as Anaṅga-mañjarī of Vṛndāvana. All the devotees who are followers of Jāhnavā-mātā are counted within the list of Śrī Nityānanda Prabhu's devotees.

TEXT 22

রঘুনাথ বৈদ্য উপাধ্যায় মহাশয় ।
যাঁহার দর্শনে কৃষ্ণপ্রেমভক্তি হয় ॥ ২২ ॥

raghunātha vaidya upādhyāya mahāśaya
yāṅhāra darśane kṛṣṇa-prema-bhakti haya

SYNONYMS

raghunātha vaidya—the physician Raghunātha; *upādhyāya mahāśaya*—a great personality with the title "Upādhyāya"; *yāṅhāra*—whose; *darśane*—by visiting; *kṛṣṇa-prema*—love of Kṛṣṇa; *bhakti*—devotional service; *haya*—awakened.

TRANSLATION

The physician Raghunātha, also known as Upādhyāya, was so great a devotee that simply seeing him would awaken one's dormant love of Godhead.

TEXT 23

সুন্দরানন্দ—নিত্যানন্দের শাখা, ভৃত্য মর্ম ।
যাঁর সঙ্গে নিত্যানন্দ করে ব্রজনর্ম ॥ ২৩ ॥

sundarānanda—nityānandera śākhā, bhṛtya marma
yāṅra saṅge nityānanda kare vraja-narma

SYNONYMS

sundarānanda—of the name Sundarānanda; *nityānandera śākhā*—a branch of Nityānanda Prabhu; *bhṛtya marma*—very intimate servant; *yāṅra saṅge*—with whom; *nityānanda*—Lord Nityānanda; *kare*—performs; *vraja-narma*—activities of Vṛndāvana.

TRANSLATION

Sundarānanda, another branch of Śrī Nityānanda Prabhu, was Lord Nityānanda's most intimate servant. Lord Nityānanda Prabhu perceived the life of Vrajabhūmi in his company.

PURPORT

In the *Caitanya-bhāgavata, Antya-līlā,* Chapter Six, it is stated that Sundarānanda was an ocean of love of Godhead and the chief associate of Śrī Nityānanda Prabhu. In the *Gaura-gaṇoddeśa-dīpikā* he is stated to have been Sudāma in *kṛṣṇa-līlā.* Thus he was one of the twelve cowherd boys who came down with Balarāma when He descended as Śrī Nityānanda Prabhu. The holy place where Sundarānanda lived is situated in the village known as Maheśapura, which is about fourteen miles east of the Mājadiyā railway station of the eastern railway from Calcutta to Burdwan. This place is within the district of Jeshore, which is now in Bangladesh. Among the relics of this village, only the old residential house of Sundarānanda still exists. At the end of the village resides a *bāula* (pseudo-Vaiṣṇava), and all the buildings, both the temples and the house, appear to be newly constructed. In Maheśapura there are Deities of Śrī Rādhāvallabha and Śrī Śrī Rādhāramaṇa. Near the temple is a small river of the name Vetravatī.

Sundarānanda Prabhu was a *naiṣṭhika-brahmacārī,* he never married in his life. Therefore he had no direct descendants except his disciples, but the descendants of his family still reside in the village known as Maṅgalaḍihi in the district of Birbhum. In that same village is a temple of Balarāma, and the Deity there is regularly worshiped. The original Deity of Maheśapura, Rādhāvallabha, was taken by the Saidābād Gosvāmīs of Berhampur, and since the present Deities were installed, a Zamindar family of Maheśapura has looked after Their worship. On the full moon day of the month of *māgha* (January-February), the anniversary of Sundarānanda's disappearance is regularly celebrated, and people from the neighboring areas gather together to observe this festival.

TEXT 24

কমলাকর পিপ্পলাই—অলৌকিক রীত ।
অলৌকিক প্রেম তাঁর ভুবনে বিদিত ॥ ২৪ ॥

kamalākara pippalāi—alaukika rīta
alaukika prema tāṅra bhuvane vidita

SYNONYMS

kamalākara pippalāi—of the name Kamalākara Pippalāi; *alaukika*—uncommon; *rīta*—behavior or pastime; *alaukika*—uncommon; *prema*—love of Godhead; *tāṅra*—his; *bhuvane*—in the world; *vidita*—celebrated.

TRANSLATION

Kamalākara Pippalāi is said to have been the third gopāla. His behavior and love of Godhead were uncommon, and thus he is celebrated all over the world.

PURPORT

In the *Gaura-gaṇoddeśa-dīpikā,* verse 128, Kamalākara Pippalāi is described as the third *gopāla.* His former name was Mahābala. The Jagannātha Deity at Māheśa in Śrī Rāmapura was installed by Kamalākara Pippalāi. This village of Māheśa is situated about two and a half miles from the Śrī Rāmapura railway station. The genealogy of the family of Kamalākara Pippalāi is given as follows. Kamalākara Pippalāi had a son named Caturbhuja, who had two sons named Nārāyaṇa and Jagannātha. Nārāyaṇa had one son named Jagadānanda, and his son's name was Rājīvalocana. During the time of Rājīvalocana, there was a scarcity of finances for the worship of the Jagannātha Deity, and it is said that the Nawab of Dacca, whose name was Shah

Sujā, donated 1,185 *bighās* of land in the Bengali year 1060. The land being the possession of Jagannātha, the village was named Jagannātha-pura. It is said that Kamalākara Pippalāi left home, and therefore his younger brother Nidhipati Pippalāi searched for him and in due course of time found him in the village of Māheśa. Nidhipati Pippalāi tried his best to bring his elder brother home, but he would not return. Under these circumstances, Nidhipati Pippalāi, with all his family members, came to Māheśa to reside. The members of this family still reside in the vicinity of the Māheśa village. Their family name is Adhikārī, and they are a *brāhmaṇa* family.

The history of the Jagannātha Temple in Māheśa is as follows. One devotee of the name Dhruvānanda went to see Lord Jagannātha, Balarāma and Subhadrā at Jagannātha Purī, wanting to offer foodstuffs to Jagannāthajī that he had cooked with his own hands. This being his desire, one night Jagannāthajī appeared to him in a dream and asked him to go to Māheśa on the bank of the Ganges and there start worship of Him in a temple. Thus Dhruvānanda went to Māheśa, where he saw the three Deities—Jagannātha, Balarāma and Subhadrā—floating in the Ganges. He picked up all those Deities and installed Them in a small cottage, and with great satisfaction he executed the worship of Lord Jagannātha. When he became old, he was very much anxious to hand over the worship to the charge of someone reliable, and in a dream he got permission from Jagannātha Prabhu to hand it over to a person whom he would meet the next morning. The next morning he met Kamalākara Pippalāi, who was formerly an inhabitant of the village Khālijuli in the Sundaravana Forest area of Bengal and was a pure Vaiṣṇava, a great devotee of Lord Jagannātha; thus he immediately gave him charge of the worship. In this way, Kamalākara Pippalāi became the worshiper of Lord Jagannātha, and since then his family members have been designated as Adhikārī, which means "one who is empowered to worship the Lord." These Adhikārīs belong to a respectable *brāhmaṇa* family. Five types of upper-class *brāhmaṇas* are recognized by the surname Pippalāi.

TEXT 25

সূর্যদাস সরখেল, তাঁর ভাই কৃষ্ণদাস ।
নিত্যানন্দে দৃঢ় বিশ্বাস, প্রেমের নিবাস ॥ ২৫ ॥

sūryadāsa sarakhela, tāṅra bhāi kṛṣṇadāsa
nityānande dṛḍha viśvāsa, premera nivāsa

SYNONYMS

sūryadāsa sarakhela—of the name Sūryadāsa Sarakhela; *tāṅra bhāi*—his brother; *kṛṣṇadāsa*—of the name Kṛṣṇadāsa; *nityānande*—unto Lord Nityānanda; *dṛḍha viśvāsa*—firm faith; *premera nivāsa*—the reservoir of all love of Godhead.

TRANSLATION

Sūryadāsa Sarakhela and his younger brother Kṛṣṇadāsa Sarakhela both possessed firm faith in Nityānanda Prabhu. They were a reservoir of love of Godhead.

PURPORT

In the *Bhakti-ratnākara,* Chapter Twelve, it is stated that a few miles from Navadvīpa is a place called Śāligrāma that was the residence of Sūryadāsa Sarakhela. He was employed as a secretary of the Mohammedan government of that time, and thus he amassed a good fortune. Sūryadāsa had four brothers, all of whom were pure Vaiṣṇavas. Vasudhā and Jāhnavā were two daughters of Sūryadāsa Sarakhela.

TEXT 26

গৌরীদাস পণ্ডিত যাঁর প্রেমোদ্দণ্ডভক্তি ।
কৃষ্ণপ্রেমা দিতে, নিতে, ধরে মহাশক্তি ॥ ২৬ ॥

gaurīdāsa paṇḍita yāṅra premoddaṇḍa-bhakti
kṛṣṇa-premā dite, nite, dhare mahāśakti

SYNONYMS

gaurīdāsa paṇḍita—of the name Gaurīdāsa Paṇḍita; *yāṅra*—whose; *prema-uddaṇḍa-bhakti*—the most elevated in love of Godhead and devotional service; *kṛṣṇa-premā*—love of Kṛṣṇa; *dite*—to deliver; *nite*—and to receive; *dhare*—empowered; *mahāśakti*—great potency.

TRANSLATION

Gaurīdāsa Paṇḍita, the emblem of the most elevated devotional service in love of Godhead, had the greatest potency to receive and deliver such love.

PURPORT

It is said that Gaurīdāsa Paṇḍita was always patronized by King Kṛṣṇadāsa, the son of Harihoḍa. Gaurīdāsa Paṇḍita lived in the village of Śāligrāma, which is situated a few miles from the railway station Muḍāgāchā, and later he came to reside in Ambikā-kālanā. It is stated in the *Gaura-gaṇoddeśa-dīpikā,* verse 128, that formerly he was Subala, one of the cowherd boy friends of Kṛṣṇa and Balarāma in Vṛndāvana. Gaurīdāsa Paṇḍita was the younger brother of Sūryadāsa Sarakhela, and with the permission of his elder brother he shifted his residence to the bank of the Ganges, living there in the town known as Ambikā-kālanā. Some of the names of the descendants of Gaurīdāsa Paṇḍita are as follows: (1) Śrī Nṛsiṁhacaitanya, (2) Kṛṣṇadāsa, (3) Viṣṇudāsa, (4) Baḍa Balarāma dāsa, (5) Govinda, (6) Raghunātha, (7) Baḍu Gaṅgādāsa, (8) Āuliyā Gaṅgārāma, (9) Yādavācārya, (10) Hṛdayacaitanya, (11) Cānda Hāladāra, (12) Maheśa Paṇḍita, (13) Mukuṭa Rāya, (14) Bhātuyā Gaṅgārāma, (15) Āuliyā Caitanya, (16) Kāliyā Kṛṣṇadāsa, (17) Pātuyā Gopāla, (18) Baḍa Jagannātha, (19) Nityānanda, (20) Bhāvi, (21) Jagadīśa, (22) Rāiyā Kṛṣṇadāsa and (22½) Annapūrṇā. The eldest son of Gaurīdāsa Paṇḍita was known as big Balarāma, and the youngest was known as Raghunātha. The sons of Raghunātha were Māheśa Paṇḍita and Govinda. Gaurīdāsa Paṇḍita's daughter was known as Annapūrṇā.

The village Ambikā-kālanā, which is situated just across the River Ganges from Śāntipura, is two miles east of the Kālanākorṭa railway station on the eastern railway. In Ambikā-kālanā there is a temple constructed by the Zamindar of Burdwan. In front of the temple there is a big tamarind tree, and it is said that Gaurīdāsa Paṇḍita and Lord Caitanya Mahāprabhu met underneath this tree. The place where the temple is situated is known as Ambikā, and because it is in the area of Kālanā, the village is known as Ambikā-kālanā. It is said that a copy of *Bhagavad-gītā* written by Śrī Caitanya Mahāprabhu still exists in this temple.

TEXT 27

নিত্যানন্দে সমর্পিল জাতি-কুল-পাঁতি ।
শ্রীচৈতন্য-নিত্যানন্দে করি প্রাণপতি ॥ ২৭ ॥

nityānande samarpila jāti-kula-pān̐ti
śrī-caitanya-nityānande kari prāṇapati

SYNONYMS

nityānande—to Lord Nityānanda; *samarpila*—he offered; *jāti*—caste distinction; *kula*—family; *pān̐ti*—fellowship; *śrī-caitanya*—Lord Caitanya; *nityānande*—in Lord Nityānanda; *kari*—making; *prāṇa-pati*—the Lords of his life.

TRANSLATION

Making Lord Caitanya and Lord Nityānanda the Lords of his life, Gaurīdāsa Paṇḍita sacrificed everything for the service of Lord Nityānanda, even the fellowship of his own family.

TEXT 28

নিত্যানন্দ প্রভুর প্রিয় —পণ্ডিত পুরন্দর ।
প্রেমার্ণব-মধ্যে ফিরে যৈছন মন্দর ॥ ২৮ ॥

nityānanda prabhura priya—paṇḍita purandara
premārṇava-madhye phire yaichana mandara

SYNONYMS

nityānanda—Lord Nityānanda Prabhu; *prabhura*—of the Lord; *priya*—very dear; *paṇḍita purandara*—of the name Paṇḍita Purandara; *prema-arṇava-madhye*—in the ocean of love of Godhead; *phire*—moved; *yaichana*—exactly like; *mandara*—the Mandara Hill.

TRANSLATION

The thirteenth important devotee of Śrī Nityānanda Prabhu was Paṇḍita Purandara, who moved in the ocean of love of Godhead just like the Mandara Hill.

PURPORT

Paṇḍita Purandara met Śrī Nityānanda Prabhu at Khaḍadaha. When Nityānanda Prabhu visited this village, He danced very uncommonly, and His dancing captivated Purandara Paṇḍita. The *paṇḍita* was in the top of a tree, and upon seeing the dancing of Nityānanda he jumped down on the ground proclaiming himself to be Aṅgada, one of the devotees in the camp of Hanumān during the pastimes of Lord Rāmacandra.

TEXT 29

পরমেশ্বরদাস – নিত্যানন্দৈক-শরণ ।
কৃষ্ণভক্তি পায়, তাঁরে যে করে স্মরণ ॥ ২৯ ॥

parameśvara-dāsa—nityānandaika-śaraṇa
kṛṣṇa-bhakti pāya, tāṅre ye kare smaraṇa

SYNONYMS

parameśvara-dāsa—of the name Parameśvara dāsa; *nityānanda-eka-śaraṇa*—completely surrendered to the lotus feet of Nityānanda; *kṛṣṇa-bhakti pāya*—gets love of Kṛṣṇa; *tāṅre*—him; *ye*—anyone; *kare*—does; *smaraṇa*—remembering.

TRANSLATION

Parameśvara dāsa, said to be the fifth gopāla of kṛṣṇa-līlā, completely surrendered to the lotus feet of Nityānanda. Anyone who remembers his name, Parameśvara dāsa, will get love of Kṛṣṇa very easily.

PURPORT

The *Caitanya-bhāgavata* states that Parameśvara dāsa, known sometimes as Parameśvarī dāsa, was the life and soul of Śrī Nityānanda Prabhu. The body of Parameśvara dāsa was the place of Lord Nityānanda's pastimes. Parameśvara dāsa, who lived for some time at Khaḍadaha village, was always filled with the ecstasy of a cowherd boy. Formerly he was Arjuna, a friend of Kṛṣṇa and Balarāma. He was the fifth among the twelve *gopālas.* He accompanied Śrīmatī Jāhnavā-devī when she performed the festival at Kheturi. It is stated in the *Bhakti-ratnākara* that by the order of Śrīmatī Jāhnavā-mātā, he installed Rādhā-Gopīnātha in the temple at Āṭapura in the district of Hugalī. The Āṭapura station is on the narrow gauge railway line between Howrah and Āmatā. Another temple in Āṭapura, established by the Mitra family, is known as the Rādhā-Govinda temple. In front of the temple, in a very attractive place among two *bakula* trees and a *kadamba* tree, is the tomb of Parameśvarī Ṭhākura, and above it is an altar with a *tulasī* bush. It is said that only one flower a year comes out of the *kadamba* tree. It is offered to the Deity.

Parameśvarī Ṭhākura belonged, it is said, to a *vaidya* family. A descendant of his brother is at present a worshiper in the temple. Some of their family members still reside in the district of Hugalī near the post office of Caṇḍītalā. The descendants of

Parameśvarī Ṭhākura took many disciples from *brāhmaṇa* families, but as these descendants gradually took to the profession of physicians, persons from *brāhmaṇa* families ceased becoming their disciples. The family titles of Parameśvarī's descendants are Adhikārī and Gupta. Unfortunately his family members do not worship the Deity directly; they have engaged paid *brāhmaṇas* to worship the Deity. In the temple, Baladeva and Śrī Śrī Rādhā-Gopīnātha are together on the throne. It is supposed that the Deity of Baladeva was installed later because according to transcendental mellow, Baladeva, Kṛṣṇa and Rādhā cannot stay on the same throne. On the full moon day of *vaiśākha* (April-May), the disappearance festival of Parameśvarī Ṭhākura is observed in this temple.

TEXT 30

জগদীশ পণ্ডিত হয় জগৎ-পাবন ।
কৃষ্ণপ্রেমামৃত বর্ষে, যেন বর্ষা ঘন ॥ ৩০ ॥

jagadīśa paṇḍita haya jagat-pāvana
kṛṣṇa-premāmṛta varṣe, yena varṣā ghana

SYNONYMS

jagadīśa paṇḍita—of the name Jagadīśa Paṇḍita; *haya*—becomes; *jagat-pāvana*—the deliverer of the world; *kṛṣṇa-prema-amṛta varṣe*—he always pours torrents of devotional service; *yena*—like; *varṣā*—rainfall; *ghana*—heavy.

TRANSLATION

Jagadīśa Paṇḍita, the fifteenth branch of Lord Nityānanda's followers, was the deliverer of the entire world. Devotional love of Kṛṣṇa showered from him like torrents of rain.

PURPORT

Descriptions of Jagadīśa Paṇḍita are available from *Caitanya-bhāgavata, Ādi-līlā,* Chapter Four, and *Caitanya-caritāmṛta, Ādi-līlā,* Chapter Fourteen. He belonged to the village of Yaśaḍā-grāma in the district of Nadia near the Cākadaha railway station. His father, the son of Bhaṭṭa Nārāyaṇa, was named Kamalākṣa. Both his father and mother were great devotees of Lord Viṣṇu, and after their death, Jagadīśa, with his wife Duḥkhinī and brother Māheśa, left his birthplace and came to Śrī Māyāpur to live in the company of Jagannātha Miśra and other Vaiṣṇavas. Lord Caitanya asked Jagadīśa to go to Jagannātha Purī to preach the *hari-nāma-saṅkīrtana* movement. After returning from Jagannātha Purī, on the order of Lord Jagannātha he established Deities of Jagannātha in the village of Yaśaḍā-grāma. It is said that when Jagadīśa Paṇḍita brought the Deity of Jagannātha to Yaśaḍā-grāma, he tied the heavy Deity to a stick and thus brought Him to the village. The priests of the temple still show the stick used by Jagadīśa Paṇḍita to carry the Jagannātha Deity.

TEXT 31

নিত্যানন্দ-প্রিয়ভৃত্য পণ্ডিত ধনঞ্জয় ।
অত্যন্ত বিরক্ত, সদা কৃষ্ণপ্রেমময় ॥ ৩১ ॥

nityānanda-priyabhṛtya paṇḍita dhanañjaya
atyanta virakta, sadā kṛṣṇa-premamaya

SYNONYMS

nityānanda-priya-bhṛtya—another dear servant of Nityānanda Prabhu; *paṇḍita dhanañjaya*—of the name Paṇḍita Dhanañjaya; *atyanta*—very much; *virakta*—renounced; *sadā*—always; *kṛṣṇa-premamaya*—merged in love of Kṛṣṇa.

TRANSLATION

The sixteenth dear servant of Nityānanda Prabhu was Dhanañjaya Paṇḍita. He was very much renounced and always merged in love of Kṛṣṇa.

PURPORT

Paṇḍita Dhanañjaya was a resident of the village in Katwa named Śītala. He was one of the twelve *gopālas.* His former name, according to *Gaura-gaṇoddeśa-dīpikā,* was Vasudāma. Śītala-grāma is situated near the Maṅgalakoṭa police station and Kaicara post office in the district of Burdwan. On the narrow railway from Burdwan to Katwa is a railway station about nine miles from Kutwa known as Kaicara. One has to go about a mile northeast of this station to reach Śītala. The temple was a thatched house with walls made of dirt. Some time ago, the Zamindars of Bājāravana Kābāśī, the Mulliks, constructed a big house for the purpose of a temple, but for the last sixty-five years the temple has been broken down and abandoned. The foundation of the old temple is still visible. There is a *tulasī* pillar near the temple, and every year during the month of January the disappearance day of Dhanañjaya is observed. It is said that for some time Paṇḍita Dhanañjaya was in a *saṅkīrtana* party under the direction of Śrī Caitanya Mahāprabhu, and then he went to Vṛndāvana. Before going to Vṛndāvana, he lived for some time in a village named Sāṅcaḍāpāṅcaḍā, which is six miles south of the Memārī railway station. Sometimes this village is also known as the "place of Dhanañjaya" (Dhanañjayera Pāṭa). After some time, he left the responsibility for worship with a disciple and went back to Vṛndāvana. After returning from Vṛndāvana to Śītala-grāma, he established a Deity of Gaurasundara in the temple. The descendants of Paṇḍita Dhanañjaya still live in Śītala-grāma and look after the temple worship.

TEXT 32

মহেশ পণ্ডিত —ব্রজের উদার গোপাল ।
ঢক্কাবাদ্যে নৃত্য করে প্রেমে মাতোয়াল ॥ ৩২ ॥

maheśa paṇḍita—vrajera udāra gopāla
ḍhakkā-vādye nṛtya kare preme mātoyāla

SYNONYMS

maheśa paṇḍita—of the name Maheśa Paṇḍita; *vrajera*—of Vṛndāvana; *udāra*—very liberal; *gopāla*—cowherd boy; *ḍhakkā-vādye*—with the beating of a kettledrum; *nṛtya kare*—used to dance; *preme*—in love; *mātoyāla*—as if a madman.

TRANSLATION

Maheśa Paṇḍita, the seventh of the twelve gopālas, was very liberal. In great love of Kṛṣṇa he danced to the beating of a kettledrum like a madman.

PURPORT

The village of Maheśa Paṇḍita, which is known as Pālapāḍā, is situated in the district of Nadia within a forest about one mile south of the Cākadaha railway station. The Ganges flows nearby. It is said that formerly Maheśa Paṇḍita lived on the eastern side of Jirāṭ in the village known as Masipura or Yaśīpura, and when Masipura merged in the riverbed of the Ganges, the Deities there were brought to Pālapāḍā, which is situated in the midst of various villages such as Beleḍāṅgā, Berigrāma, Sukhasāgara, Cānduḍe and Manasāpotā. (There are about fourteen villages, and the entire neighborhood is known as Pāñcanagara Paragaṇa.) It is mentioned that Maheśa Paṇḍita joined the festival performed by Śrī Nityānanda Prabhu at Pāṇihāṭī. Narottama dāsa Ṭhākura also joined in the festival, and Maheśa Paṇḍita saw him on that occasion. In the temple of Maheśa Paṇḍita there are Deities of Gaura-Nityānanda, Śrī Gopīnātha, Śrī Madana-mohana and Rādhā-Govinda as well as a *śālagrāma-śilā*.

TEXT 33

নবদ্বীপে পুরুষোত্তম পণ্ডিত মহাশয় ।
নিত্যানন্দ-নামে যাঁর মহোন্মাদ হয় ॥ ৩৩ ॥

navadvīpe puruṣottama paṇḍita mahāśaya
nityānanda-nāme yāṅra mahonmāda haya

SYNONYMS

navadvīpe puruṣottama—Puruṣottama of Navadvīpa; *paṇḍita mahāśaya*—a very learned scholar; *nityānanda-nāme*—in the name of Lord Nityānanda Prabhu; *yāṅra*—whose; *mahā-unmāda*—great ecstasy; *haya*—becomes.

TRANSLATION

Puruṣottama Paṇḍita, a resident of Navadvīpa, was the eighth gopāla. He would become almost mad as soon as he heard the holy name of Nityānanda Prabhu.

PURPORT

It is stated in the *Caitanya-bhāgavata* that Puruṣottama Paṇḍita was born in Navadvīpa and was a great devotee of Lord Nityānanda Prabhu. As one of the twelve *gopālas,* his former name was Stokakṛṣṇa.

TEXT 34

বলরাম দাস—কৃষ্ণপ্রেমরসাস্বাদী ।
নিত্যানন্দ-নামে হয় পরম উন্মাদী ॥ ৩৪ ॥

balarāma dāsa—kṛṣṇa-prema-rasāsvādī
nityānanda-nāme haya parama unmādī

SYNONYMS

balarāma-dāsa—of the name Balarāma dāsa; *kṛṣṇa-prema-rasa*—the nectar of always merging in love of Kṛṣṇa; *āsvādī*—fully tasting; *nityānanda-nāme*—in the name of Śrī Nityānanda Prabhu; *haya*—becomes; *parama*—greatly; *unmādī*—maddened.

TRANSLATION

Balarāma dāsa always fully tasted the nectar of love of Kṛṣṇa. Upon hearing the name of Nityānanda Prabhu he would become greatly maddened.

TEXT 35

মহাভাগবত যদুনাথ কবিচন্দ্র ।
যাঁহার হৃদয়ে নৃত্য করে নিত্যানন্দ ॥ ৩৫ ॥

mahā-bhāgavata yadunātha kavicandra
yāṅhāra hṛdaye nṛtya kare nityānanda

SYNONYMS

mahā-bhāgavata—a great devotee; *yadunātha kavicandra*—of the name Yadunātha Kavicandra; *yāṅhāra*—whose; *hṛdaye*—in the heart; *nṛtya*—dancing; *kare*—does; *nityānanda*—Lord Nityānanda Prabhu.

TRANSLATION

Yadunātha Kavicandra was a great devotee. Lord Nityānanda Prabhu always danced in his heart.

PURPORT

In the *Caitanya-bhāgavata Madhya-līlā,* Chapter One, it is said that a gentleman known as Ratnagarbha Ācārya was a friend of Śrī Nityānanda Prabhu's father. They were both residents of the same village, known as Ekacakra-grāma. He had four sons—Kṛṣṇapada-makaranda, Kṛṣṇānanda, Jīva and Yadunātha Kavicandra.

TEXT 36

রাঢ়ে যাঁর জন্ম কৃষ্ণদাস দ্বিজবর ।
শ্রীনিত্যানন্দের তেঁহো পরম কিঙ্কর ॥ ৩৬ ॥

rāḍhe yāṅra janma kṛṣṇadāsa dvijavara
śrī-nityānandera teṅho parama kiṅkara

SYNONYMS

rāḍhe—in West Bengal; *yāṅra*—whose; *janma*—birth; *kṛṣṇadāsa*—of the name Kṛṣṇadāsa; *dvijavara*—the best *brāhmaṇa; śrī-nityānandera*—of Nityānanda Prabhu; *teṅho*—he; *parama*—first-class; *kiṅkara*—servant.

TRANSLATION

The twenty-first devotee of Śrī Nityānanda in Bengal was Kṛṣṇadāsa Brāhmaṇa, who was a first-class servant of the Lord.

PURPORT

Rāḍha-deśa refers to the part of Bengal where the Ganges does not flow.

TEXT 37

কালা-কৃষ্ণদাস বড় বৈষ্ণবপ্রধান ।
নিত্যানন্দ-চন্দ্র বিনু নাহি জানে আন ॥ ৩৭ ॥

kālā-kṛṣṇadāsa baḍa vaiṣṇava-pradhāna
nityānanda-candra vinu nāhi jāne āna

SYNONYMS

kālā-kṛṣṇadāsa—of the name Kālā Kṛṣṇadāsa; *baḍa*—great; *vaiṣṇava-pradhāna*—first-class Vaiṣṇava; *nityānanda-candra*—Lord Nityānanda; *vinu*—except; *nāhi jāne*—he did not know; *āna*—of anything else.

TRANSLATION

The twenty-second devotee of Lord Nityānanda Prabhu was Kālā Kṛṣṇadāsa, who was the ninth cowherd boy. He was a first-class Vaiṣṇava and did not know anything beyond Nityānanda Prabhu.

PURPORT

In the *Caitanya-bhāgavata, Antya-khaṇḍa,* Chapter Six, it is said that Kṛṣṇadāsa, who was known as Kāliyā Kṛṣṇadāsa, was formerly a *gopāla* (cowherd boy) of the name Labaṅga. He was one of the twelve cowherd boys. Kāliyā Kṛṣṇadāsa had his headquarters in a village named Ākāihāṭa, which is situated in the district of Burdwan within the jurisdiction of the post office and police station of Katwa. It is situated on the road to Navadvīpa. To reach Ākāihāṭa, one has to go from the Vyāṇḍela junction station to the Katwa railway station and then go about two miles, or one has to get off at the Dāṅihāṭa station and from there go one mile. The village of Ākāihāṭa is very small. In the month of Caitra, on the day of Vāruṇī, there is a festival commemorating the disappearance day of Kālā Kṛṣṇadāsa.

TEXT 38

শ্রীসদাশিব কবিরাজ—বড় মহাশয়।
শ্রীপুরুষোত্তমদাস – তাঁহার তনয় ॥ ৩৮ ॥

śrī-sadāśiva kavirāja—baḍa mahāśaya
śrī-puruṣottama-dāsa—tāṅhāra tanaya

SYNONYMS

śrī-sadāśiva kavirāja—of the name Śrī Sadāśiva Kavirāja; *baḍa*—great; *mahāśaya*—respectable gentleman; *śrī-puruṣottama-dāsa*—of the name Śrī Puruṣottama dāsa; *tāṅhāra tanaya*—his son.

TRANSLATION

The twenty-third and twenty-fourth prominent devotees of Nityānanda Prabhu were Sadāśiva Kavirāja and his son Puruṣottama dāsa, who was the tenth gopāla.

TEXT 39

আজন্ম নিমগ্ন নিত্যানন্দের চরণে।
নিরন্তর বাল্য-লীলা করে কৃষ্ণ-সনে ॥ ৩৯ ॥

ājanma nimagna nityānandera caraṇe
nirantara bālya-līlā kare kṛṣṇa-sane

SYNONYMS

ājanma—since birth; *nimagna*—merged; *nityānandera*—of Lord Nityānanda Prabhu; *caraṇe*—in the lotus feet; *nirantara*—always; *bālya-līlā*—childish play; *kare*—does; *kṛṣṇa-sane*—with Kṛṣṇa.

TRANSLATION

Since birth, Puruṣottama dāsa was merged in the service of the lotus feet of Lord Nityānanda Prabhu, and he always engaged in childish play with Lord Kṛṣṇa.

PURPORT

Sadāśiva Kavirāja and Nāgara Puruṣottama, who were father and son, are described in the *Caitanya-bhāgavata* as *mahā-bhāgyavān,* greatly fortunate. They belonged to the *vaidya* caste of physicians. The *Gaura-gaṇoddeśa-dīpikā,* verse 156, says that Candrāvalī, a most beloved *gopī* of Kṛṣṇa, later took birth as Sadāśiva Kavirāja. It is said that Kaṁsāri Sena, the father of Sadāśiva Kavirāja, was formerly the *gopī* named Ratnāvalī in Kṛṣṇa's pastimes. All the family members of Sadāśiva Kavirāja were great devotees of Lord Caitanya Mahāprabhu. Puruṣottama dāsa Ṭhākura sometimes lived at Sukhasāgara, near the Cākadaha and Śimurāli railway stations. All the Deities installed by Puruṣottama Ṭhākura were formerly situated in Beleḍāṅgā-grāma, but when the temple was destroyed the Deities were brought to Sukhasāgara. When that temple merged in the bed of the Ganges, the Deities were brought with Jāhnavā-mātā's Deity to Sāhebaḍāṅgā Beḍigrāma. Since that place also has been destroyed, all the Deities are now situated in the village named Cānduḍe-grāma, which is situated one mile up from Pālapāḍā, as referred to above.

TEXT 40

তাঁর পুত্র—মহাশয় শ্রীকানু ঠাকুর ।
যাঁর দেহে রহে কৃষ্ণ-প্রেমামৃতপূর ॥ ৪০ ॥

tāṅra putra—mahāśaya śrī-kānu ṭhākura
yāṅra dehe rahe kṛṣṇa-premāmṛta-pūra

SYNONYMS

tāṅra putra—his son; *mahāśaya*—a respectable gentleman; *śrī-kānu ṭhākura*—of the name Śrī Kānu Ṭhākura; *yāṅra*—whose; *dehe*—in the body; *rahe*—remained; *kṛṣṇa-prema-amṛta-pūra*—the nectar of devotional service to Kṛṣṇa.

TRANSLATION

Śrī Kānu Ṭhākura, a very respectable gentleman, was the son of Puruṣottama dāsa Ṭhākura. He was such a great devotee that Lord Kṛṣṇa always lived in his body.

PURPORT

To go to the headquarters of Kānu Ṭhākura, one has to proceed by boat from the Jhikaragāchā-ghāṭa station to the river known as Kapotākṣa. Otherwise, if one goes about two or two and a half miles from the Jhikaragāchā-ghāṭa station, he can see Bodhakhānā, the headquarters of Kānu Ṭhākura. The son of Sadāśiva was Puruṣottama Ṭhākura, and his son was Kānu Ṭhākura. The descendants of Kānu Ṭhākura know him as Nāgara Puruṣottama. He was the cowherd boy named Dāma during *kṛṣṇa-līlā.* It is said that just after the birth of Kānu Ṭhākura, his mother, Jāhnavā, died. When he was about twelve days old, Śrī Nityānanda Prabhu took him to His home at Khaḍadaha. It is ascertained that Kānu Ṭhākura was born some time in the Bengali year 942. It is said that he took birth on the Rathayātrā day. Because he was a great devotee of Lord Kṛṣṇa from the very beginning of his life, Śrī Nityānanda Prabhu gave him the name Śiśu Kṛṣṇadāsa. When he was five years old he went to Vṛndāvana with Jāhnavā-mātā, and upon seeing the ecstatic symptoms of Kānu Ṭhākura, the Gosvāmīs gave him the name Kānāi Ṭhākura.

In the family of Kānu Ṭhākura there is a Rādhā-Kṛṣṇa Deity known as Prāṇavallabha. It is said that his family worshiped this Deity long before the appearance of Lord Caitanya Mahāprabhu. When there was a Mahārāṣṭrian invasion of Bengal, the family of Kānu Ṭhākura was scattered, and after the invasion one Harikṛṣṇa Gosvāmī of that family came back to their original home, Bodhakhānā, and re-established the Prāṇavallabha Deity. The descendants of the family still engage in the service of Prāṇavallabha. Kānu Ṭhākura was present during the Kheṭari-utsava when Jāhnavā-devī and Vīrabhadra Gosvāmī were also present. One of Kānu Ṭhākura's family members, Mādhavācārya, married the daughter of Śrī Nityānanda Prabhu, who was named Gaṅgādevī. Both Puruṣottama Ṭhākura and Kānu Ṭhākura had many disciples from *brāhmaṇa* families. Most of the disciplic descendants of Kānu Ṭhākura now reside in the village named Gaḍabetā by the River Śilāvatī in the Midnapore district.

TEXT 41

মহাভাগবত-শ্রেষ্ঠ দত্ত উদ্ধারণ ।
সর্বভাবে সেবে নিত্যানন্দের চরণ ॥ ৪১ ॥

mahā-bhāgavata-śreṣṭha datta uddhāraṇa
sarva-bhāve seve nityānandera caraṇa

SYNONYMS

mahā-bhāgavata—great devotee; *śreṣṭha*—chief; *datta*—the surname Datta; *uddhāraṇa*—of the name Uddhāraṇa; *sarva-bhāve*—in all respects; *seve*—worships; *nityānandera*—of Lord Nityānanda; *caraṇa*—lotus feet.

TRANSLATION

Uddhāraṇa Datta Ṭhākura, the eleventh among the twelve cowherd boys, was an exalted devotee of Lord Nityānanda Prabhu. He worshiped the lotus feet of Lord Nityānanda in all respects.

PURPORT

The *Gaura-gaṇoddeśa-dīpikā,* verse 129, states that Uddhāraṇa Datta Ṭhākura was formerly the cowherd boy of Vṛndāvana named Subāhu. Uddhāraṇa Datta Ṭhākura, previously known as Śrī Uddhāraṇa Datta, was a resident of Saptagrāma, which is situated on the bank of the Sarasvatī River near the Triśabighā railway station in the district of Hugalī. At the time of Uddhāraṇa Ṭhākura, Saptagrāma was a very big town, encompassing many other places such as Vāsudeva-pura, Bāṅśabeḍiyā, Kṛṣṇapura, Nityānanda-pura, Śivapura, Śaṅkhanagara and Saptagrāma.

Calcutta was developed under British rule by the influential mercantile community and especially by the *suvarṇa-vaṇik* community who came down from Saptagrāma to establish their businesses and homes all over Calcutta. They were known as the Saptagrāmī mercantile community of Calcutta, and most of them belonged to the Mullik and Sil families. More than half of Calcutta belonged to this community, as did Śrīla Uddhāraṇa Ṭhākura. Our paternal family also came from this district and belonged to the same community. The Mulliks of Calcutta are divided into two families, namely, the Sil family and De family. All the Mulliks of the De family originally belong to the same family and *gotra.* We also formerly belonged to the branch of the De family whose members, intimately connected with the Mohammedan rulers, received the title Mullik.

In the *Caitanya-bhāgavata, Antya-khaṇḍa,* Chapter Six, it is said that Uddhāraṇa Datta was an extremely elevated and liberal Vaiṣṇava. He was born with the right to worship Nityānanda Prabhu. It is also stated that Nityānanda Prabhu, after staying for some time in Khaḍadaha, came to Saptagrāma and stayed in the house of Uddhāraṇa Datta. The *suvarṇa-vaṇik* community to which Uddhāraṇa Datta belonged was actually a Vaiṣṇava community. Its members were bankers and gold merchants (*suvarṇa* means "gold," and *vaṇik* means "merchant"). Long ago there was a misunderstanding between Balla Sena and the *suvarṇa-vaṇik* community because of the great banker Gaurī Sena. Balla Sena was taking loans from Gaurī Sena and spending money extravagantly, and therefore Gaurī Sena stopped supplying money. Balla Sena took revenge by instigating a social conspiracy to make the *suvarṇa-vaṇiks* outcastes, and since then they have been ostracized from the higher castes, namely, the *brāhmaṇas, kṣatriyas* and *vaiśyas.* But by the grace of Śrīla Nityānanda Prabhu, the *suvarṇa-vaṇik* community was again elevated. It is said in the *Caitanya-bhāgavata, yateka vaṇik-kula uddhāraṇa haite pavitra ha-ila dvidhā nāhika ihāte:* there is no doubt that all the community members of the *suvarṇa-vaṇik* society were again purified by Śrī Nityānanda Prabhu.

In Saptagrāma there is still a temple with a six-armed Deity of Śrī Caitanya Mahāprabhu that was personally worshiped by Śrīla Uddhāraṇa Datta Ṭhākura. On the right side of Śrī Caitanya Mahāprabhu is a Deity of Śrī Nityānanda Prabhu and on the left side Gadādhara Prabhu. There are also a Rādhā-Govinda *mūrti* and *śālagrāma-śilā,* and below the throne is a picture of Śrī Uddhāraṇa Datta Ṭhākura. In front of the temple there is now a big hall, and in front of the hall is a Mādhavīlatā plant. The temple is in a very shady, cool and nicely situated location. When we returned from America in 1967, the executive committee members of this temple invited us to visit it, and thus we had the opportunity to visit this temple with some American students. Formerly, in our childhood, we visited this temple with our parents because all the members of the *suvarṇa-vaṇik* community enthusiastically take interest in this temple of Uddhāraṇa Datta Ṭhākura. In the Bengali year 1283 one *bābājī* of the name Nitāi dāsa arranged for a donation of twelve *bighās* of land for this temple. The management of the temple later deteriorated, but then in 1306, through the cooperation of the famous Balarāma Mullik of Hugalī, who was a subjudge, and many rich *suvarṇa-vaṇik* community members, the management of the temple improved greatly. Not more than fifty years ago, one of the family members of Uddhāraṇa Datta Ṭhākura named Jagamohana Datta established a wooden Deity of Uddhāraṇa Datta Ṭhākura in the temple, but that Deity is no longer there; at present, a picture of Uddhāraṇa Datta Ṭhākura is worshiped. It is understood, however, that the wooden Deity of Uddhāraṇa Ṭhākura was taken away by Śrī Madana-mohana Datta and is now being worshiped with a *śālagrāma-śilā* by Śrīnātha Datta.

Uddhāraṇa Datta Ṭhākura was the manager of the estate of a big Zamindar in Naihāṭī, about one and a half miles north of Katwa. The relics of this royal family are still visible near the Dāiṅhāṭa station. Since Uddhāraṇa Datta Ṭhākura was the manager of the estate, it was also known as Uddhāraṇa-pura. Uddhāraṇa Datta Ṭhākura installed Nitāi-Gaura Deities that were later brought to the house of the Zamindar, which was known as Vanaoyārībāḍa. Śrīla Uddhāraṇa Datta Ṭhākura remained a householder throughout his life. His father's name was Śrīkara Datta, his mother's name was Bhadrāvatī, and his son's name was Śrīnivāsa Datta.

TEXT 42

আচার্য বৈষ্ণবানন্দ ভক্তি-অধিকারী ।
পূর্বে নাম ছিল যাঁর 'রঘুনাথ পুরী' ॥ ৪২ ॥

ācārya vaiṣṇavānanda bhakti-adhikārī
pūrve nāma chila yāṅra 'raghunātha purī'

SYNONYMS

ācārya—teacher; *vaiṣṇavānanda*—of the name Vaiṣṇavānanda; *bhakti*—devotional service; *adhikārī*—fit candidate; *pūrve*—previously; *nāma*—name; *chila*—was; *yāṅra*—whose; *raghunātha purī*—of the name Raghunātha Purī.

TRANSLATION

The twenty-seventh prominent devotee of Nityānanda Prabhu was Ācārya Vaiṣṇavānanda, a great personality in devotional service. He was formerly known as Raghunātha Purī.

PURPORT

In the *Gaura-gaṇoddeśa-dīpikā,* verse 97, it is said that Raghunātha Purī was previously very powerful in the eight mystic successes. He was an incarnation of one of the successes.

TEXT 43

বিষ্ণুদাস, নন্দন, গঙ্গাদাস,—তিন ভাই ।
পূর্বে যাঁর ঘরে ছিলা ঠাকুর নিতাই ॥ ৪৩ ॥

viṣṇudāsa,nandana, gaṅgādāsa—tina bhāi
pūrve yāṅra ghare chilā ṭhākura nitāi

SYNONYMS

viṣṇudāsa—of the name Viṣṇudāsa; *nandana*—of the name Nandana; *gaṅgādāsa*—of the name Gaṅgādāsa; *tina bhāi*—three brothers; *pūrve*—previously; *yāṅra*—whose; *ghare*—in the house; *chilā*—stayed; *ṭhākura nitāi*—Nityānanda Prabhu.

TRANSLATION

Another important devotee of Lord Nityānanda Prabhu was Viṣṇudāsa, who had two brothers, Nandana and Gaṅgādāsa. Lord Nityānanda Prabhu sometimes stayed at their house.

PURPORT

The three brothers Viṣṇudāsa, Nandana and Gaṅgādāsa were residents of Navadvīpa and belonged to the Bhaṭṭācārya *brāhmaṇa* family. Both Viṣṇudāsa and Gaṅgādāsa stayed for some time with Śrī Caitanya Mahāprabhu at Jagannātha Purī, and the *Caitanya-bhāgavata* states that formerly Nityānanda Prabhu stayed at their house.

TEXT 44

নিত্যানন্দভৃত্য পরমানন্দ উপাধ্যায় ।
শ্রীজীব পণ্ডিত নিত্যানন্দ-গুণ গায় ॥ ৪৪ ॥

nityānanda-bhṛtya—paramānanda upādhyāya
śrī-jīva paṇḍita nityānanda-guṇa gāya

SYNONYMS

nityānanda-bhṛtya—servant of Nityānanda Prabhu; *paramānanda upādhyāya*—of the name Paramānanda Upādhyāya; *śrī-jīva paṇḍita*—of the name Śrī Jīva Paṇḍita; *nityānanda*—Lord Nityānanda Prabhu; *guṇa*—qualities; *gāya*—glorified.

TRANSLATION

Paramānanda Upādhyāya was Nityānanda Prabhu's great servitor. Śrī Jīva Paṇḍita glorified the qualities of Śrī Nityānanda Prabhu.

PURPORT

Śrī Paramānanda Upādhyāya was an advanced devotee. His name is mentioned in the *Caitanya-bhāgavata,* where Śrī Jīva Paṇḍita is also mentioned as the second son of Ratnagarbha Ācārya and a childhood friend of Hāḍāi Ojhā, the father of Nityānanda Prabhu. In the *Gaura-gaṇoddeśa-dīpikā,* verse 169, it is said that Śrī Jīva Paṇḍita was formerly the *gopī* named Indirā.

TEXT 45

পরমানন্দ গুপ্ত—কৃষ্ণভক্ত মহামতি ।
পূর্বে যাঁর ঘরে নিত্যানন্দের বসতি ॥ ৪৫ ॥

paramānanda gupta—kṛṣṇa-bhakta mahāmati
pūrve yāṅra ghare nityānandera vasati

SYNONYMS

paramānanda gupta—of the name Paramānanda Gupta; *kṛṣṇa-bhakta*—a great devotee of Lord Kṛṣṇa; *mahāmati*—advanced in spiritual consciousness; *pūrve*—formerly; *yāṅra*—whose; *ghare*—in the house; *nityānandera*—of Lord Nityānanda Prabhu; *vasati*—residence.

TRANSLATION

The thirty-first devotee of Lord Nityānanda Prabhu was Paramānanda Gupta, who was greatly devoted to Lord Kṛṣṇa and highly advanced in spiritual consciousness. Formerly Nityānanda Prabhu also resided at his house for some time.

PURPORT

Paramānanda Gupta composed a prayer to Lord Kṛṣṇa known as *Kṛṣṇa-stavāvalī*. In the *Gaura-gaṇoddeśa-dīpikā*, verse 194, it is stated that he was formerly the *gopī* named Mañjumedhā.

TEXT 46

নারায়ণ, কৃষ্ণদাস আর মনোহর ।
দেবানন্দ   চারি ভাই নিতাই-কিঙ্কর ॥ ৪৬ ॥

nārāyaṇa, kṛṣṇadāsa āra manohara
devānanda—cāri bhāi nitāi-kiṅkara

SYNONYMS

nārāyaṇa—of the name Nārāyaṇa; *kṛṣṇadāsa*—of the name Kṛṣṇadāsa; *āra*—and; *manohara*—of the name Manohara; *devānanda*—of the name Devānanda; *cāri bhāi*—four brothers; *nitāi-kiṅkara*—servants of Lord Nityānanda Prabhu.

TRANSLATION

The thirty-second, thirty-third, thirty-fourth and thirty-fifth prominent devotees were Nārāyaṇa, Kṛṣṇadāsa, Manohara and Devānanda, who always engaged in the service of Lord Nityānanda.

TEXT 47

হোড় কৃষ্ণদাস - নিত্যানন্দপ্রভু-প্রাণ ।
নিত্যানন্দ-পদ বিনু নাহি জানে আন ॥ ৪৭ ॥

hoḍa kṛṣṇadāsa—nityānanda-prabhu-prāṇa
nityānanda-pada vinu nāhi jāne āna

SYNONYMS

hoḍa kṛṣṇadāsa—of the name Hoḍa Kṛṣṇadāsa; *nityānanda-prabhu*—of Lord Nityānanda; *prāṇa*—life and soul; *nityānanda-pada*—the lotus feet of Lord Nityānanda; *vinu*—except; *nāhi*—does not; *jāne*—know; *āna*—anything else.

TRANSLATION

The thirty-sixth devotee of Lord Nityānanda was Hoḍa Kṛṣṇadāsa, whose life and soul was Nityānanda Prabhu. He was always dedicated to the lotus feet of Nityānanda, and he knew no one else but Him.

PURPORT

The residence of Kṛṣṇadāsa Hoḍa was Baḍagāchi, which is now in Bangladesh.

TEXT 48

নকড়ি, মুকুন্দ, সূর্য, মাধব, শ্রীধর ।
রামানন্দ বসু, জগন্নাথ, মহীধর ॥ ৪৮ ॥

nakaḍi, mukunda, sūrya, mādhava, śrīdhara
rāmānanda vasu, jagannātha, mahīdhara

SYNONYMS

nakaḍi—of the name Nakaḍi; *mukunda*—of the name Mukunda; *sūrya*—of the name Sūrya; *mādhava*—of the name Mādhava; *śrīdhara*—of the name Śrīdhara; *rāmānanda vasu*—of the name Rāmānanda Vasu; *jagannātha*—of the name Jagannātha; *mahīdhara*—of the name Mahīdhara.

TRANSLATION

Among Lord Nityānanda's devotees, Nakaḍi was the thirty-seventh, Mukunda the thirty-eighth, Sūrya the thirty-ninth, Mādhava the fortieth, Śrīdhara the forty-first, Rāmānanda the forty-second, Jagannātha the forty-third and Mahīdhara the forty-fourth.

PURPORT

Śrīdhara was the twelfth *gopāla.*

TEXT 49

শ্রীমন্ত, গোকুলদাস, হরিহরানন্দ ।
শিবাই, নন্দাই, অবধূত পরমানন্দ ॥ ৪৯ ॥

śrī-manta, gokula-dāsa hariharānanda
śivāi, nandāi, avadhūta paramānanda

SYNONYMS

śrī-manta—of the name Śrī Manta; *gokula-dāsa*—of the name Gokula dāsa; *hariharānanda*—of the name Hariharānanda; *śivāi*—of the name Śivāi; *nandāi*—of the name Nandāi; *avadhūta paramānanda*—of the name Avadhūta Paramānanda.

TRANSLATION

Śrī Manta was the forty-fifth, Gokula dāsa the forty-sixth, Hariharānanda the forty-seventh, Śivāi the forty-eighth, Nandāi the forty-ninth and Paramānanda the fiftieth.

TEXT 50

বসন্ত, নবনী হোড়, গোপাল, সনাতন ।
বিষ্ণাই হাজরা, কৃষ্ণানন্দ, সুলোচন ॥ ৫০ ॥

vasanta, navanī hoḍa, gopāla sanātana
viṣṇāi hājarā, kṛṣṇānanda, sulocana

SYNONYMS

vasanta—of the name Vasanta; *navanī hoḍa*—of the name Navanī Hoḍa; *gopāla*—of the name Gopāla; *sanātana*—of the name Sanātana; *viṣṇāi hājarā*—of the name Viṣṇāi Hājarā; *kṛṣṇānanda*—of the name Kṛṣṇānanda; *sulocana*—of the name Sulocana.

TRANSLATION

Vasanta was the fifty-first, Navanī Hoḍa the fifty-second, Gopāla the fifty-third, Sanātana the fifty-fourth, Viṣṇāi the fifty-fifth, Kṛṣṇānanda the fifty-sixth and Sulocana the fifty-seventh.

PURPORT

Navanī Hoḍa appears to have been the same person as Hoḍa Kṛṣṇadāsa, the son of the King of Baḍagāchi. His father's name was Hari Hoḍa. One can visit Baḍagāchi by taking the Lālagolā-ghāṭa railway line. Formerly the Ganges flowed by Baḍagāchi, but now it has become a canal known as the Kālśira Khāl. Near the Muḍāgāchā station is a village known as Śāligrāma in which King Kṛṣṇadāsa arranged for the marriage of Śrī Nityānanda Prabhu, as described in the *Bhakti-ratnākara, Taraṅga* Twelve. It is sometimes said that Navanī Hoḍa was the son of Rāja Kṛṣṇadāsa. His descendants still live in Rukuṇapura, a village near Bahiragāchi. They belong to the *dakṣiṇa rāḍhīya kāyastha* community, but, having been reformed as *brāhmaṇas,* they still initiate all classes of men.

TEXT 51

কংসারি সেন, রামসেন, রামচন্দ্র কবিরাজ ।
গোবিন্দ, শ্রীরঙ্গ, মুকুন্দ, তিন কবিরাজ ॥ ৫১ ॥

kaṁsāri sena, rāmasena, rāmacandra kavirāja
govinda, śrīraṅga, mukunda, tina kavirāja

SYNONYMS

kaṁsāri sena—of the name Kaṁsāri Sena; *rāmasena*—of the name Rāmasena; *rāmacandra kavirāja*—of the name Rāmacandra Kavirāja; *govinda*—of the name Govinda; *śrīraṅga*—of the name Śrīraṅga; *mukunda*—of the name Mukunda; *tina kavirāja*—all three are Kavirājas, or physicians.

TRANSLATION

The fifty-eighth great devotee of Lord Nityānanda Prabhu was Kaṁsāri Sena, the fifty-ninth was Rāmasena, the sixtieth was Rāmacandra Kavirāja, and the sixty-first, sixty-second and sixty-third were Govinda, Śrīraṅga and Mukunda, who were all physicians.

PURPORT

Śrī Rāmacandra Kavirāja, the son of Khaṇḍavāsī Cirañjīva and Sunanda, was a disciple of Śrīnivāsa Ācārya and the most intimate friend of Narottama dāsa Ṭhākura, who prayed several times for his association. His youngest brother was Govinda Kavirāja. Śrīla Jīva Gosvāmī very much appreciated Śrī Rāmacandra Kavirāja's great devotion to Lord Kṛṣṇa and therefore gave him the title *kavirāja.* Śrī Rāmacandra Kavirāja, who was perpetually disinterested in family life, greatly assisted in the preaching work of Śrīnivāsa Ācārya and Narottama dāsa Ṭhākura. He resided at first in Śrīkhaṇḍa but later in the village of Kumāra-nagara on the bank of the Ganges.

Govinda Kavirāja was the brother of Rāmacandra Kavirāja and youngest son of Cirañjīva of Śrīkhaṇḍa. Although at first a *śākta,* or worshiper of goddess Durgā, he was later initiated by Śrīnivāsa Ācārya Prabhu. Govinda Kavirāja also resided first in Śrīkhaṇḍa and then in Kumāra-nagara, but later he moved to the village known as Teliyā Budhari on the southern bank of the River Padmā. Since Govinda Kavirāja, the author of two books, *Saṅgīta-mādhava* and *Gītāmṛta,* was a great Vaiṣṇava *kavi,* or poet, Śrīla Jīva Gosvāmī gave him the title *kavirāja.* He is described in the *Bhakti-ratnākara,* Ninth *Taraṅga.*

Kaṁsāri Sena was formerly Ratnāvalī in Vraja, as described in the *Gaura-gaṇoddeśa-dīpikā,* verses 194 and 200.

TEXT 52

পীতাম্বর, মাধবাচার্য, দাস দামোদর ।
শঙ্কর, মুকুন্দ, জ্ঞানদাস, মনোহর ॥ ৫২ ॥

pītāmbara, mādhavācārya, dāsa dāmodara
śaṅkara, mukunda, jñāna-dāsa, manohara

SYNONYMS

pītāmbara—of the name Pītāmbara; *mādhavācārya*—of the name Mādhavācārya; *dāsa dāmodara*—of the name Dāmodara dāsa; *śaṅkara*—of the name Śaṅkara; *mukunda*—of the name Mukunda; *jñāna-dāsa*—of the name Jñānadāsa; *manohara*—of the name Manohara.

TRANSLATION

Among the devotees of Lord Nityānanda Prabhu, Pītāmbara was the sixty-fourth, Mādhavācārya the sixty-fifth, Dāmodara dāsa the sixty-sixth, Śaṅkara the sixty-seventh, Mukunda the sixty-eighth, Jñānadāsa the sixty-ninth and Manohara the seventieth.

TEXT 53

নর্তক গোপাল, রামভদ্র, গৌরাঙ্গদাস ।
নৃসিংহচৈতন্য, মীনকেতন রামদাস ॥ ৫৩ ॥

nartaka gopāla, rāmabhadra, gaurāṅga-dāsa
nṛsiṁha-caitanya, mīnaketana rāma-dāsa

SYNONYMS

nartaka gopāla—the dancer Gopāla; *rāmabhadra*—of the name Rāmabhadra; *gaurāṅga-dāsa*—of the name Gaurāṅga dāsa; *nṛsiṁha-caitanya*—of the name Nṛsiṁha-caitanya; *mīnaketana rāma-dāsa*—of the name Mīnaketana Rāmadāsa.

TRANSLATION

The dancer Gopāla was the seventy-first, Rāmabhadra the seventy-second, Gaurāṅga dāsa the seventy-third, Nṛsiṁha-caitanya the seventy-fourth and Mīnaketana Rāmadāsa the seventy-fifth.

PURPORT

The *Gaura-gaṇoddeśa-dīpikā*, verse 68, describes Mīnaketana Rāmadāsa as an incarnation of Saṅkarṣaṇa.

TEXT 54

বৃন্দাবনদাস—নারায়ণীর নন্দন ।
'চৈতন্য-মঙ্গল' যেঁহো করিল রচন ॥ ৫৪ ॥

vṛndāvana-dāsa—nārāyaṇīra nandana
'caitanya-maṅgala' yeṅho karila racana

SYNONYMS

vṛndāvana-dāsa—Śrīla Vṛndāvana dāsa Ṭhākura; *nārāyaṇīra nandana*—son of Nārāyaṇī; *caitanya-maṅgala*—the book of the name *Caitanya-maṅgala; yeṅho*—who; *karila*—did; *racana*—composition.

TRANSLATION

Vṛndāvana dāsa Ṭhākura, the son of Śrīmatī Nārāyaṇī, composed Śrī Caitanya-maṅgala [later known as Śrī Caitanya-bhāgavata].

TEXT 55

ভাগবতে কৃষ্ণলীলা বর্ণিলা বেদব্যাস ।
চৈতন্য-লীলাতে ব্যাস—বৃন্দাবন দাস ॥ ৫৫ ॥

bhāgavate kṛṣṇa-līlā varṇilā vedavyāsa
caitanya-līlāte vyāsa—vṛndāvana dāsa

SYNONYMS

bhāgavate—in the *Śrīmad-Bhāgavatam; kṛṣṇa-līlā*—the pastimes of Lord Kṛṣṇa; *varṇilā*—described; *vedavyāsa*—Dvaipāyana Vyāsadeva; *caitanya-līlāte*—in the pastimes of Lord Caitanya; *vyāsa*—Vedavyāsa; *vṛndāvana dāsa*—Śrīla Vṛndāvana dāsa Ṭhākura.

TRANSLATION

Śrīla Vyāsadeva described the pastimes of Kṛṣṇa in the Śrīmad-Bhāgavatam. The Vyāsa of the pastimes of Lord Caitanya Mahāprabhu was Vṛndāvana dāsa.

PURPORT

Śrīla Vṛndāvana dāsa Ṭhākura was an incarnation of Vedavyāsa and also a friendly cowherd boy named Kusumāpīḍa in *kṛṣṇa-līlā*. In other words, the author of *Śrī Caitanya-bhāgavata,* Śrīla Vṛndāvana dāsa Ṭhākura, the son of Śrīvāsa Ṭhākura's niece Nārāyaṇī, was a combined incarnation of Vedavyāsa and the cowherd boy Kusumāpīḍa. There is a descriptive statement by Śrīla Bhaktisiddhānta Sarasvatī Ṭhākura in his commentary on *Śrī Caitanya-bhāgavata* giving the biographical details of the life of Vṛndāvana dāsa Ṭhākura.

TEXT 56

সর্বশাখা-শ্রেষ্ঠ বীরভদ্র গোসাঞি ।
তাঁর উপশাখা যত, তার অন্ত নাই ॥ ৫৬ ॥

sarvaśākhā-śreṣṭha vīrabhadra gosāñi
tāṅra upaśākhā yata, tāra anta nāi

SYNONYMS

sarvaśākhā-śreṣṭha—the best of all the branches; *vīrabhadra gosāñi*—of the name Vīrabhadra Gosāñi; *tāṅra upaśākhā*—His sub-branches; *yata*—all; *tāra*—of them; *anta*—limit; *nāi*—there is not.

TRANSLATION

Among all the branches of Śrī Nityānanda Prabhu, Vīrabhadra Gosāñi was the topmost. His sub-branches were unlimited.

TEXT 57

অনন্ত নিত্যানন্দগণ—কে করু গণন ।
আত্মপবিত্রতা-হেতু লিখিলাঙ কত জন ॥ ৫৭ ॥

ananta nityānanda-gaṇa—ke karu gaṇana
ātma-pavitratā-hetu likhilāṅ kata jana

SYNONYMS

ananta—unlimited; *nityānanda-gaṇa*—followers of Śrī Nityānanda Prabhu; *ke karu*—who can; *gaṇana*—count; *ātma-pavitratā*—of self-purification; *hetu*—for the reason; *likhilāṅ*—I have written; *kata jana*—some of them.

TRANSLATION

No one can count the unlimited followers of Nityānanda Prabhu. I have mentioned some of them just for my self-purification.

TEXT 58

এই সর্বশাখা পূর্ণ-পক্ব প্রেমফলে ।
যারে দেখে, তারে দিয়া ভাসাইল সকলে ॥ ৫৮ ॥

ei sarva-śākhā pūrṇa—pakva prema-phale
yāre dekhe, tāre diyā bhāsāila sakale

SYNONYMS

ei—these; *sarva-śākhā*—all branches; *pūrṇa*—complete; *pakva prema-phale*—with ripened fruits of love of Godhead; *yāre dekhe*—whomever they see; *tāre diyā*—distributing to him; *bhāsāila*—overflooded; *sakale*—all of them.

TRANSLATION

All these branches, the devotees of Lord Nityānanda Prabhu, being full of ripened fruits of love of Kṛṣṇa, distributed these fruits to all they met, flooding them with love of Kṛṣṇa.

TEXT 59

অনর্গল প্রেম সবার, চেষ্টা অনর্গল ।
প্রেম দিতে, কৃষ্ণ দিতে ধরে মহাবল ॥ ৫৯ ॥

anargala prema sabāra, ceṣṭā anargala
prema dite, kṛṣṇa dite dhare mahābala

SYNONYMS

anargala—unchecked; *prema*—love of Kṛṣṇa; *sabāra*—of every one of them; *ceṣṭā*—activity; *anargala*—unchecked; *prema dite*—to give love of Kṛṣṇa; *kṛṣṇa dite*—to deliver Kṛṣṇa; *dhare*—they possess; *mahābala*—great strength.

TRANSLATION

All these devotees had unlimited strength to deliver unobstructed, unceasing love of Kṛṣṇa. By their own strength they could offer anyone Kṛṣṇa and love of Kṛṣṇa.

PURPORT

Śrīla Bhaktivinoda Ṭhākura has sung, *kṛṣṇa se tomāra, kṛṣṇa dite pāra, tomāra śakati āche.* In this song, Bhaktivinoda Ṭhākura describes that a pure Vaiṣṇava, as the proprietor of Kṛṣṇa and love of Kṛṣṇa, can deliver both to anyone and everyone he likes. Therefore to get Kṛṣṇa and love of Kṛṣṇa one must seek the mercy of pure devotees. Śrīla Viśvanātha Cakravartī Ṭhākura also says, *yasya prasādād bhagavat-prasādo yasyāprasādān na gatiḥ kuto 'pi:* "By the mercy of the spiritual master one is benedicted by the mercy of Kṛṣṇa. Without the grace of the spiritual master one cannot make any advancement." By the grace of a Vaiṣṇava or bona fide spiritual master one can get both love of Godhead, Kṛṣṇa, and Kṛṣṇa Himself.

TEXT 60

সংক্ষেপে কহিলাঙ এই নিত্যানন্দগণ ।
যাঁহার অবধি না পায় 'সহস্র-বদন' ॥ ৬০ ॥

saṅkṣepe kahilāṅ ei nityānanda-gaṇa
yāṅhāra avadhi nā pāya 'sahasra-vadana'

SYNONYMS

saṅkṣepe—in brief; *kahilāṅ*—described; *ei*—these; *nityānanda-gaṇa*—devotees of Lord Nityānanda; *yāṅhāra*—of whom; *avadhi*—limitation; *nā*—does not; *pāya*—get; *sahasra-vadana*—the thousand-mouthed Śeṣanāga on whom Lord Viṣṇu lies.

TRANSLATION

I have briefly described only some of the followers and devotees of Lord Nityānanda Prabhu. Even the thousand-mouthed Śeṣanāga cannot describe all of these unlimited devotees.

TEXT 61

শ্রীরূপ-রঘুনাথ-পদে যার আশ ।
চৈতন্যচরিতামৃত কহে কৃষ্ণদাস ॥ ৬১ ॥

śrī-rūpa-raghunātha-pade yāra āśa
caitanya-caritāmṛta kahe kṛṣṇadāsa

SYNONYMS

śrī-rūpa—Śrīla Rūpa Gosvāmī; *raghunātha*—Śrīla Raghunātha dāsa Gosvāmī; *pade*—at the lotus feet; *yāra*—whose; *āśa*—expectation; *caitanya-caritāmṛta*—the book named *Caitanya-caritāmṛta; kahe*—describes; *kṛṣṇa-dāsa*—Śrīla Kṛṣṇadāsa Kavirāja Gosvāmī.

TRANSLATION

With an ardent desire to serve the purpose of Śrī Rūpa and Śrī Raghunātha, I, Kṛṣṇadāsa, narrate Śrī Caitanya-caritāmṛta, following in their footsteps.

Thus end the Bhaktivedanta purports to the Śrī Caitanya-caritāmṛta, Ādi-līlā, *Eleventh Chapter, in the matter of the expansions of Lord Nityānanda.*

References

The statements of *Śri Caitanya-caritāmṛta* are all confirmed by standard Vedic authorities. The following authentic scriptures are quoted in this book on the pages listed. Numerals in bold type refer the reader to *Śrī Caitanya-caritāmṛta's* translations. Numerals in regular type are references to its purports.

Aitareya Upaniṣad
99
Anubhāṣya
15, 20, 52, 57
Bhagavad-gītā
1, 9, 22, 31, 41, 49, 55, 57, 67, 69, 80, 89, 91, 97, 98, 99, 100, 103, 104, 105, 107, 108-109, 109-110, 111, 113, 115, 118, 122, 123, 124, 125, 127, 164, 167, 169, 174, 181, 241, 242, 257
Bhagavat-sandarbha
124
Bhakti-rasāmṛta-sindhu
75, 78-79, 86-87, 169, 242
Bhakti-ratnākara
303, 356-357, 359, 367, 369, 383
Bhakti-sandarbha
62
Brahma-saṁhitā
98
Bṛhad-āraṇyaka Upaniṣad
98, 125, 132
Caitanya-bhāgavata
221-222, 273, 363
Caitanya-carita-mahākāvya
338-339
Caitanya-caritāmṛta
11, 108, 134, 219-220, 247
Chāndogya Upaniṣad
114, 115, 117, 125
Hari-bhakti-sudhodaya
79
Hari-bhakti-vilāsa
36, 189
Īśopaniṣad
118, 132
Kalisantaraṇa Upaniṣad
62
Kaṭha Upaniṣad
8, 99, 125
Kṛṣṇa-karṇāmṛta
138
Mahābhārata
155, 161, 167, 243
Māṇḍūkya Upaniṣad
117-118, 124
Nārada-pañcarātra
62, 124
Padma Purāṇa
94-95, 104, 178
Paramātma-sandarbha
118
Praśna Upaniṣad
99
Ṛg Veda
99, 103
Śiva Purāṇa
95
Skanda Purāṇa
88
Śrīmad-Bhāgavatam
4, 26, 56, 58, 60, 62, 69, 72, 74, 83-84, 97, 100, 102, 124, 134, 136, 137, 139, 140, 163, 170, 171, 172, 174-175, 188, 199, 239, 244, 280
Śvetāśvatara Upaniṣad
98, 99, 115
Taittirīya Upaniṣad
115-116
Upadeśāmṛta
15
Vāyu Purāṇa
88
Vedārtha-saṅgraha
133
Viṣṇu Purāṇa
99, **106**, 109, 113, **241**

Glossary

A

Abhidheya—acting according to one's constitutional relationship with God.
Ācārya—an authorized teacher who instructs by his own example.
Adhama paḍuyās—scholars who consider devotional activities material.
Advaita-vāda—philosophy of monism.
Ajñāta-sukṛti—pious activities that one executes without his knowledge.
Akiñcana—one who possesses nothing in the material world.
Aparā prakṛti—material energy.
Arcana-mārga—Deity worship.
Artha—economic development.
Asuras—demons.
Āveśa—an incarnation of God, partially empowered.

B

Bhāgavata-jīvana—the life of a devotee.
Bhāgavata-saptāka—seven-day readings of *Bhāgavatam.*
Bhajanānandī—devotee who is satisfied to cultivate devotional service for himself.
Bhakta—devotee.
Bhakti-latā—devotional creeper.
Bhāva—the stage of transcendental ecstacy experienced after transcendental affection.
Brahma-bhūta—stage of liberation from material entanglement when one becomes joyous beyond any hankering or lamentation and gains a universal vision.
Brahma-jñāna—knowledge of the Supreme.
Brahmānanda—pleasure derived from impersonal Brahman realization.
Bubhukṣus—those who desire to enjoy the material world.

C

Caitya-guru—the spiritual master within.
Cid-vilāsa—spiritual pleasure.

D

Dharma—religiosity.

G

Godāsa—servant of senses.
Gopīs—cowherd girlfriends of Kṛṣṇa.
Gosāñi—*See Gosvāmī.*

Goṣṭhy-ānandī—devotees who desire to preach glories of holy name.
Gosvāmī—one who has control over mind and senses.

I

Īśa-tattva—the Supreme Lord.
Īśvara—the supreme controller.

J

Jīva—the soul; or atomic living entity.
Jīva-bhūta—*See Jīva*
Jñāna—transcendental knowledge.
Jīva-tattva—*See Jīva*

K

Kāma—sense gratification.
Kaniṣṭha-adhikārī—devotee in lowest stage of Vaiṣṇava life.
Karma-kāṇḍa—fruitive activities.
Karma-niṣṭhas—those who consider devotional service to be fruitive activities.
Kṛpā-siddha—perfection by the mercy of superior authorities.
Kṛṣṇa-līlā—pastimes of Kṛṣṇa.
Kṛṣṇa-premā—love of Godhead.
Kṣetrajña—the living entity.
Kutārkikas—false logicians.

L

Lobha—greed.

M

Mādhurya-bhaktas—devotees engaged only in conjugal love.
Mahā-bhāgavata—*See Uttama-adhikārī.*
Mahāprabhu—supreme master of all masters.
Mahā-vadānyāvatāra—Lord Caitanya, the most magnanimous incarnation.
Madhyama-adhikārī—devotee with firm faith who preaches to innocent and avoids atheists.
Māyā—the external illusory energy of the Lord.
Mokṣa—liberation.
Mumukṣus—those who desire liberation from material world.
Mūḍha—fool, rascal.

N

Nāmāparādha—offense against holy names.
Nindakas—blasphemers.

Nirguṇa—without material qualities.
Nitya-siddha—eternal perfection attained by never forgetting Kṛṣṇa at any time.

P

Pārakīya-rasa—paramour love.
Paramparā—disciplic succession.
Parā-prakṛti—spiritual energy.
Pāṣaṇḍīs—nondevotees who consider devotional activities material.
Patita-pāvana—Lord Caitanya, the deliverer of the fallen souls.
Prabhu—master.
Pradhāna—the chief principle of creation.
Prākṛta-bhaktas—materialistic devotees not advanced in spiritual knowledge.
Prayojana—the ultimate goal of life, to develop love of God.
Preyas—activities which are immediately beneficial and auspicious.

R

Rajo-guṇa—mode of passion.
Rasābhāsa—incompatible mixing of *rasas*.
Rāsādi-vilāsī—the enjoyer of the *rāsa* dance.
Rasas—spiritual humors.

S

Ṣaḍbhuja—six-armed form of Lord Caitanya.
Sādhana-bhakti—the prescribed duties of service to the Lord.
Sādhana-siddhas—perfection attained by executing rules and regulations of devotional service.
Sādhu—a saintly person or Vaiṣṇava.
Sahajiyās—those who do not follow the scriptural injunctions, considering God to be cheap.
Sālokya-mukti—liberation of residing on the same planet as the Lord.
Samādhi—trance, or absorption in the service of the Lord.
Sambandha-jñāna—establishing one's original relationship with the Lord.
Sārṣṭi-mukti—liberation of having equal opulences with the Supreme.
Sārūpya-mukti—liberation of having same bodily features as the Lord.
Sarva-jña—omniscient.
Śāstras—scriptures.
Sattva-guṇa—mode of goodness.
Sāyujya-mukti—liberation of merging in Brahman effulgence.
Śrauta-vākya—acceptance of the words of the spiritual master.
Śravaṇaṁ kirtanam—hearing and chanting.
Śreyas—activities which are ultimately beneficial and auspicious.
Sūtra—a code expressing the essence of all knowledge in minimum words.

T

Tamo-guṇa—mode of ignorance.

U

Uttama-adhikārī—devotee in highest stage of devotional life.

V

Vaikuṇṭha—the spiritual world which is without anxiety.
Vastra-haraṇa-līlā—Kṛṣṇa's pastime of stealing the clothes of the *gopīs.*
Vedāntī—a person who perfectly knows Kṛṣṇa.
Viṣṇu-bhakti—See Bhakti.
Viśvambhara—one who maintains the entire universe; name of Lord Caitanya.
Vivarta—illusion.

Y

Yogeśvara—master of all mystic powers, Kṛṣṇa.

Bengali Pronunciation Guide

BENGALI DIACRITICAL EQUIVALENTS AND PRONUNCIATION

Vowels

অ a   আ ā   ই i   ঈ ī   উ u   ঊ ū   ঋ ṛ

ৠ ṝ   এ e   ঐ ai   ও o   ঔ au

ং ṁ *(anusvāra)*   ঁ ṅ *(candra-bindu)*   ঃ ḥ *(visarga)*

Consonants

Gutterals:	ক ka	খ kha	গ ga	ঘ gha	ঙ ṅa
Palatals:	চ ca	ছ cha	জ ja	ঝ jha	ঞ ña
Cerebrals:	ট ṭa	ঠ ṭha	ড ḍa	ঢ ḍha	ণ ṇa
Dentals:	ত ta	থ tha	দ da	ধ dha	ন na
Labials:	প pa	ফ pha	ব ba	ভ bha	ম ma
Semivowels:	য ya	র ra	ল la	ব va	
Sibilants:	শ śa	ষ ṣa	স sa	হ ha	

Vowel Symbols

The vowels are written as follows after a consonant:

া ā   ি i   ী ī   ু u   ূ ū   ৃ ṛ   ৄ ṝ   ে e   ৈ ai   ো o   ৌ au

For example: কা kā   কি ki   কী kī   কু ku   কূ kū   কৃ kṛ

কৄ kṝ   কে ke   কৈ kai   কো ko   কৌ kau

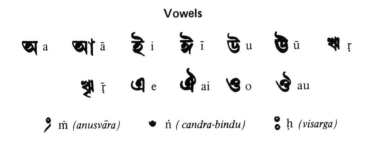

The letter *a* is implied after a consonant with no vowel symbol.

The symbol *virāma* (্) indicates that there is no final vowel. ক্ k

The letters above should be pronounced as follows:

a –like the *o* in h*o*t; sometimes like the *o* in go; final *a* is usually silent.
ā –like the *a* in f*a*r.
i, ī –like the *ee* in m*ee*t.
u, ū –like the *u* in r*u*le.
ṛ –like the *ri* in *ri*m.
ṝ –like the *ree* in *ree*d.
e –like the *ai* in p*ai*n; rarely like *e* in b*e*t.
ai –like the *oi* in b*oi*l.
o –like the *o* in g*o*.
au –like the *ow* in *ow*l.
ṁ –*(anusvāra)* like the *ng* in so*ng*.
ḥ –*(visarga)* a final *h* sound like in Ah.
ṅ –*(candra-bindu)* a nasal *n* sound like in the French word *bon*.
k –like the *k* in *k*ite.
kh –like the *kh* in Ec*kh*art.
g –like the *g* in *g*ot.
gh –like the *gh* in bi*g-h*ouse.
ṅ –like the *n* in ba*n*k.
c –like the *ch* in *ch*alk.
ch –like the *chh* in mu*ch-h*aste.
j –like the *j* in *j*oy.
jh –like the *geh* in colle*ge-h*all.
ñ –like the *n* in bu*n*ch.
ṭ –like the *t* in *t*alk.
ṭh –like the *th* in ho*t-h*ouse.
ḍ –like the *d* in *d*awn.
ḍh –like the *dh* in goo*d-h*ouse.
ṇ –like the *n* in *gn*aw.
t–as in *t*alk but with the tongue against the the teeth.
th–as in ho*t-h*ouse but with the tongue against the teeth.
d–as in *d*awn but with the tongue against the teeth.
dh–as in goo*d-h*ouse but with the tongue against the teeth.
n–as in *n*or but with the tongue against the teeth.
p –like the *p* in *p*ine.
ph –like the *ph* in *ph*ilosopher.
b –like the *b* in *b*ird.
bh –like the *bh* in ru*b-h*ard.
m –like the *m* in *m*other.
y –like the *j* in *j*aw. য
y –like the *y* in *y*ear. য়
r –like the *r* in *r*un.
l –like the *l* in *l*aw.
v –like the *b* in *b*ird or like the *w* in d*w*arf.
ś, ṣ –like the *sh* in *sh*op.
s –like the *s* in *s*un.
h–like the *h* in *h*ome.

Map of Bengal

Indicating the important sites related to
Lord Caitanya and His associates.

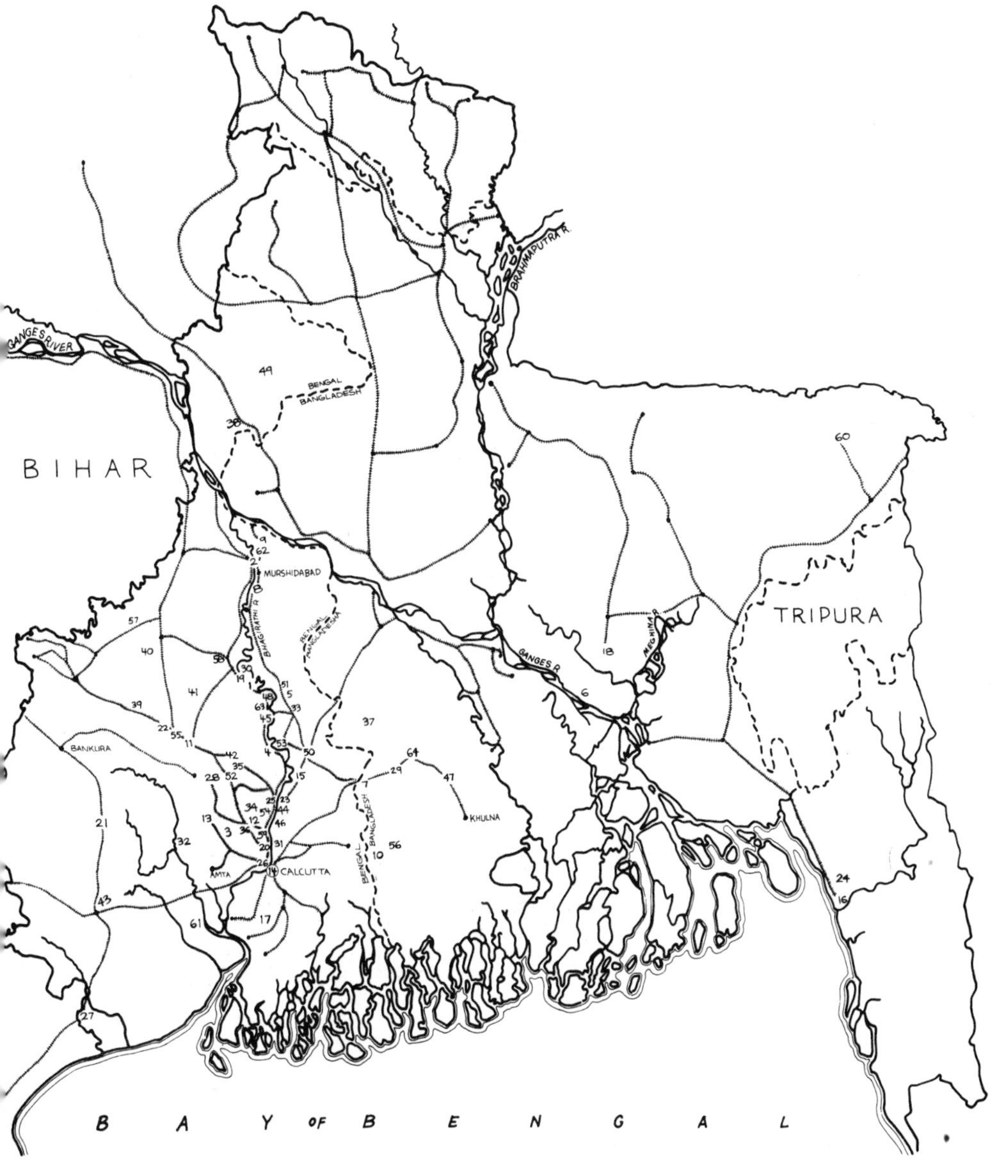

INDEX TO THE MAP OF BENGAL

MAP NO.	NAME of PLACE	PAGE NO.
1.	Ākāihāṭa—*Near Katwa*	375
2.	Ājīmagañja	324
3.	Āṭapura	369
4.	Ambikā-Kālanā	367, 368
5.	Baḍagāchi—*Near Śāligrāma*	382, 383
6.	Bāghiyā	259
7.	Benapola	
8.	Berhampore	
9.	Bhagavangola RRS	384
10.	Bhuḍhana—*Near Sātakṣīrā*	276
11.	Burdwan	
12.	Candītalā	369, 370
13.	Cāṅpāḍāṅgā	359
14.	Calcutta	
15.	Cākadaha	376
16.	Caṭṭagrāma	259
17.	Cattrabhoj	
18.	Dacca	
19.	Dāṅihāṭa	360, 375, 379
20.	Eṅḍiyādaha-Grāma	282, 284
21.	Gaḍabetā	377
22.	Galaśī RRS	363
23.	Hālisahara	220
24.	Hāṭahājāri	259
25.	Hugali	
26.	Howrah	
27.	Jaleśvara	274
28.	Jhāmaṭapura	356
29.	Jhikaragācha	376
30.	Katwa	223, 283
31.	Khaḍadaha	357, 369, 376
32.	Khānākūla-Kṛṣṇanagara	359, 360
33.	Kṛṣṇanagara	
34.	Kṛṣṇapura	312
35.	Kulīna-Grāma	278-279, 300-301
36.	Māheśa	320, 365, 366
37.	Maheśapura	364-365
38.	Maldah	302
39.	Mānakara RRS	357
40.	Maṅgalaḍihi	365
41.	Maṅgalakoṭa	370
42.	Memārī RRS	371
43.	Midnapore	
44.	Naihāṭī	302
45.	Navadvīpa	334
46.	Pāṇihāṭī	265, 332
47.	Phateyābād	302
48.	Pūrvasthalī RRS	275
49.	Rāmakeli	302
50.	Raṇa-ghāṭa	
51.	Śāligrāma	367, 383
52.	Sāṅcaḍāpāṅcaḍā	371
53.	Śāntipura	
54.	Saptagrāma	377, 378
55.	Śar	325
56.	Sātakṣīrā	276
57.	Siuḍi	
58.	Śrīkhaṇḍa	229, 323, 384
59.	Śrīrāmapura	203, 365
60.	Sylhet	
61.	Tamluk	
62.	Teliyā Budharī	384
63.	Vidyānagara	333
64.	Yasohara	302

Index

Numerals in bold type indicate references to *Śrī Caitanya-caritāmṛta's* verses. Numerals in regular type are references to its purports.

A

Abhinnatvān nāma-nāminoḥ
quoted, 125
Abhirāma Ṭhākura
See Rāmadāsa
Abhyutthānam adharmasya
verses quoted, 164
Absolute Truth
beyond reach of imperfect senses, 167
described as person by Vyāsa, 99, 115
full of six opulences, **97**, **131**-**134**
has inconceivable energies, 107, 115, 118, 133
has spiritual body, 100
indicated by *oṁ tat sat,* 123
oṁkāra as, 124
partially understood by devotees, 122
realized by devotional service, 84
understood in three features, 97, 131
Ācāryaratna
See Candraśekhara Ācārya
Ācāryas
accept *oṁkāra* as Absolute Truth, 124
actually independent, 43
break teeth of Māyāvādīs, 123
importance of serving, 161
must understand *Vedānta* philosophy, 83-85
preach according to time and circumstances, 23-24
progress by strictly following, 155
Acintyāḥ khalu ye bhāvā na tāṁs
quoted, 167
Acyutānanda
as devotee of Lord at Jagannātha Purī, **346**
Ādāv ante ca madhye ca hariḥ
verses quoted, 128
Adhītās tena yenoktam
verses quoted, 56
Advaita Ācārya
Acyutānanda as son of, 346
as predominator, **10**-**12**
as trunk of Caitanya tree, **226**
belongs to Viṣṇu category, 5
Caitanya performed dramas with, 258
in form of *bhakta* incarnation, 4, 5, **10**
is very merciful, **158**
rāsas of servitors of, 13
Ahaituky apratihahā
verses quoted, 72
Ahaṁ sarvasya prabhavo
verses quoted, 67, 98
Ahaṅkāra itīyaṁ me
verses quoted, 110
Aho bata śvapaco 'to garīyān
verses quoted, 56
Aikāntikī harer bhaktir
verses quoted, 84, 188
Aitad ātmyam idaṁ sarvam
quoted, 115
Aitareya Upaniṣad
quoted on creation of Viṣṇu, 99
Ajo 'pi sann avyayātmā
verses quoted, 109
A-kāreṇocyate kṛṣṇaḥ
verses quoted, 125
Ākhyāta-candrikā
as book by Rūpa Gosvāmī, 303
Akiñcana-gocara
Lord known as, 2
Akrūra
as Gopīnātha Siṁha, 297
Alaṅkāra-kaustubha
as book by Karṇapūra, 290
Alpākṣaram asandigdham
verses quoted, 88
Amāninā mānadena kīrtanīyaḥ
verses quoted, 39, 52, 168, 307
Amṛta-pravāha-bhāṣya
Chapter Nine of *Caitanya-caritāmṛta* summarized in, 213
Amṛta-pravāha-bhāṣya
summary of Eighth Chapter of *Caitanya-caritāmṛta* in, 157
Ānanda-vṛndāvana-campū
as book by Karṇapūra, 290
Ananta Ācārya
as disciple of Gadādhara Paṇḍita, 200
Anarpita-carīṁ cirāt karuṇayāvatīrṇaḥ
verses quoted, 234
Anarthopaśamaṁ sākṣād
verses quoted, 58
Anāsaktasya viṣayān yathārham
verses quoted, 75
Aniruddha
Vakreśvara Paṇḍita as, 261
Antavanta ime dehā nityasyoktāḥ
verse quoted, 167
Anubhāṣya
cited on appropriate student for *Vedānta* study, 52

Anubhāṣya
cited on seed of material enjoyment, 20
on actual effect of knowledge, 57
quoted on Pañca-tattva, 15
Anupama
as branch of Caitanya tree, **301**-306
as father of Jīva Gosvāmī, 302
Anya-devāśraya nāi, tomāre
verses quoted, 256
Āpani ācari 'bhakti karila
quoted, 247
Apāṇi-pādo javano grahītā
quoted, 99
Apareyam itas tv anyām
verses quoted, 105
Apārthaṁ śruti-vākyānām
verses quoted, 96
Apaśyat puruṣaṁ pūrṇam
verse quoted, 111
Āra kabe nitāicāṅdera karuṇā
verses quoted, 14, 184
Arcanaṁ vandanaṁ dāsyam
verses quoted, 134
Arcye viṣṇau śilādhīr guruṣu
verses quoted, 104
Arjuna
accepted Kṛṣṇa as Supreme Lord, 23
as devotee and friend of Kṛṣṇa, 37
Kṛṣṇa as chariot driver of, 172
Lord became chariot driver of, 138
Arjuna (cowherdboy)
Parameśvara dāsa as, 371
Āruhya kṛcchreṇa paraṁ padam
verses quoted, 60, 102, 136, 172
Āśmarathya
as contemporary of Vyāsadeva, 89
Āśramas
named, 24
Astobhamanavadyaṁ ca sūtram
verses quoted, 88
Ataḥ śrī-kṛṣṇa-nāmādi
verses quoted, 86
Atattvato' nyathā-buddhir vivarta
verses quoted, 118
Athāto brahma-jijñāsā
quoted, 88, 139, 237
Atheists
don't care about next life, 110
those who worship demigods are, 256-257
worship Viṣṇu for material success, 165
Ātmārāma verse
explained to Sanātana Gosvāmī, 305
Ātmā vā idam agra āsīt
quoted, 116
Ātreya Ṛṣi
as contemporary of Vyāsadeva, 89
Auḍulomi
as contemporary of Vyāsadeva, 89
Avadhūta
Nityānanda as, 272
Avaiṣṇava-mukhodgīrṇam
verses quoted, 188
Avajānanti māṁ mūḍhā
verses quoted, 22

B

Baḍa Haridāsa
as devotee of Lord in Jagannātha Purī, **244**
Bādarāyaṇa-sūtra
See Vedānta-sūtra
Bādarī
as contemporary of Vyāsadeva, 89
Bahūnāṁ janmanām ante
verse quoted, 108, 133
Balabhadra Bhaṭṭācārya
as devotee of Lord in Jagannātha Purī, **344**
Balarāma
Caitanya in ecstasy of, **295**, 296
Balarāma dāsa
as branch of Nityānanda, **373**
Bengal
Lord Nityānanda famous in, 153
most devotees of Caitanya lived in Orissa and, 330
Bhagavad-gītā
actual words of Lord found in, 33
as preliminary study of *Bhāgavatam,* 69
cited on appearance of Kṛṣṇa, 9
cited on eternality of soul, 105
cited on Kṛṣṇa as goal of *Vedas,* 57
cited on Kṛṣṇa's energy, 99, 103
cited on only devotee knowing Kṛṣṇa, 122
commented on by rascals, 94
copy of written by Caitanya, 368
describes Kṛṣṇa as energetic, **106**
indirect interpretation of, 121, 126
Māyāvādīs don't accept principles of, 30
one can understand Kṛṣṇa as He is by, 168
quoted on approaching spiritual master, 41
quoted on *Brahma-sūtra,* 89
quoted by Caitanya, **107, 109**
quoted on appearance of Kṛṣṇa, 109-110, 164
quoted on demigod worship, 104, 257
quoted on destinations after death, 241
quoted on developing *bhāva,* 67
quoted on devotees' freedom from sinful life, 181

Bhagavad-gītā
quoted on disciplic succession, 91
quoted on eternality of soul, 167
quoted on fate of envious, 127
quoted on fools who deride Kṛṣṇa's advent, 22
quoted on full surrender to Kṛṣṇa, 69
quoted on glories of *oṁkāra,* 122, 123
quoted on Kṛṣṇa as Absolute Truth, 97
quoted on Kṛṣṇa as compiler of Vedānta, 31
quoted on Kṛṣṇa as goal of *Vedas,* 123
quoted on Kṛṣṇa as knower of *Vedas,* 55
quoted on Kṛṣṇa as origin of everything, 98
quoted on living beings' control of material world, 105
quoted on Lord in heart, 124, 190
quoted on miscreants who don't surrender, 80
quoted on modes of nature, 100
quoted on offering leaf, fruit, etc. to God, 169, 242
quoted on *om,* 125
quoted on principles of miserable life, 1
quoted on purpose of *Vedas,* 49
quoted on separated energy of Lord, 110
quoted on soul as spiritual particle, 118
quoted on spiritual activities of devotional service, 108
quoted on strength of material energy, 104
quoted on superiority of Viṣṇu, 103
quoted on surrender to Kṛṣṇa, 104, 108-109, 111, 133
quoted on transcending modes of nature, 113
quoted on transmigration, 111
quoted on working of material nature, 110
quoted on women etc. approaching Supreme, 174
understood by Arjuna, 37
Bhagavān
Absolute ultimately understood as, 97
Bhagavān Ācārya
as devotee of Lord at Jagannātha Purī, **338**
Bhagavān Paṇḍita
as branch of Caitanya tree, **293**
Bhāgavatācārya
as branch of Caitanya tree, **324**-325, **328**
Bhagavat-sandarbha
as book by Jīva Gosvāmī, 307
cited on glories of *oṁkāra,* 124
Bhagavat-prīti-rūpā
verses quoted, 72
Bhagavaty-uttama-śloke
verses quoted, 174-175
Bhakti
common man can't write books on, 190
Bhakti
considered mental speculation by Māyāvādīs, 83
develops in persuance of Vedānta philosophy, 83-85
devotee's only attachment to Kṛṣṇa in, 136
See also Devotional service
Bhakti-rasāmṛta-sindhu
as book by Rūpa Gosvāmī, 303
cited on auspiciousness of devotional service, 242
Jīva Gosvāmī's commentary on, 306
Kṛṣṇa's qualities described in, 198
quoted on bliss of devotional service, 78-79
quoted on Lord revealing Himself, 86-87
quoted on service of holy name, 169
quoted, 75
taking shelter of, 184
Bhakti-ratnākara
cited, 369
cited, 356-357
cited, 359
cited, 367
cited, 383
quoted on Anupama's devotion to Rāmacandra, 303
Bhakti-sandarbha
as book by Jīva Gosvāmī, 307
quoted on chanting holy names, 62
Bhaktir parasyānubhavo viraktir
quoted, 136, 179
Bhaktisiddhānta Sarasvatī Ṭhākura
cited on actual effect of knowledge, 57
cited on appropriate student for *Vedānta* study, 52
cited on change of heart by chanting, 180,
cited on compilation of *Vedānta,* 89
cited on direct and indirect meanings of *Vedas,* 95
cited on false ecstatic symptoms, 71
cited on genealogical table of Vīrabhadra Gosāñi, 357
cited on hearing from spiritual master, 55
cited on humanitarian activities of Caitanya, 167
cited on Māyāvādīs, 29
cited on players in transcendental dramas, 258
cited on seed of material enjoyment, 20
cited on success in chanting Hare Kṛṣṇa, 168
cited on taking shelter of Caitanya, 184
cited on truth about Pañca-tattva, 5, 12, 15
cited on variegated personal feature of Absolute, 103
cited on worship of Rādhā-Kṛṣṇa, 185

Bhaktisiddhānta Sarasvatī Ṭhākura
established branch at Vrajapattana, 258
explained term "Māyāvādī,"25
his description of Śivānanda Sena, 287-288
his order to his disciples, 77
his paper *Sajjana-toṣaṇī* mentioned, 289
presented philosophy of Jīva Gosvāmī, 83
quoted on fulfillment of spiritual master's mission, 73
quoted on identity of Caitanya, 164
quoted on imitating activities of great devotees, 74-75
quoted on Māyāvādī impersonalism, 82
quoted on message of Caitanya, 165
quoted on symptoms of internal devotees, 13
visited temple at Vallabhapura, 203
Bhaktivinoda Ṭhākura
cited on doctrine of transformation of energy, 117
cited on form of Kṛṣṇa, 98
cited on living beings as energy of Lord, 112
quoted on association of pure devotee, 87
quoted on doctrine of transformation, 114
quoted on mercy of pure devotee, 388
quoted on purpose of *saṅkīrtana,* 233
summarized Chapter Eight of *Caitanya-caritāmṛta,* 157
summarized Chapter Nine of *Caitanya-caritāmṛta,* 213
Bhakti-yoga
based on becoming humble and submissive, 141
everyone attracted to, 21
See also Devotional service
Bhārata-varṣa
See India
Bhāsvān yathāśma-śakaleṣu
verses quoted, 147
Bhāva
development of described, **67**-68
pleasure of, **69**
See also Love of God
Bhavānanda Rāya
as devotee of Lord in Jagannātha Purī, **335**-337
as Pāṇḍu, *335*-337
Bhāvārtha-sūcaka-campū
as book by Jīva Gosvāmī, 306
Bhugarbha Gosāñi
identified, **204**
Bhūmir āpo' nalo vāyuḥ
verses quoted, 110
Bhūtāni yānti bhūtejyā
verses quoted, 241
Bilvamaṅgala Ṭhākura
quoted on insignificance of devotional service, 138
quoted on liberation of devotees, 172
Body, material
subject to destruction, 167
Body, spiritual
after death Vaiṣṇavas get, 53
Brahmā
receives power from Govinda, 147
worshiped by Māyāvādīs, 146-148
Brahmacarya
four divisions of, 26
Brahmajyoti
rests on personal form of Lord, 133
See also Brahman
Brahman
Absolute vaguely understood as, 97
as bodily effulgence of Lord, 84, 133
as expansion of potency of Lord, 131
as original cause, 116, 121
cannot possess energies, 103
defined by Sadānanda Yogīndra, 101
entire world as, 115
indicated by *oṁ-tat-sat,* 123
liberation of merging in, 172-173
Brahmāṇḍa bhramite kona
verses quoted, 81
Brahmānanda Bhāratī
as root of tree of devotional service, **221**, 224, **338**
Brahmānanda Purī
as root of tree of devotional service, **221**, 223
Brahmānando bhaved eṣa
verses quoted, 78
Brāhmaṇas
association of pure devotee makes, 36-37
by qualification not birth, 51
engagements of, 280
Vaiṣṇavas greater than, 18
Brahmaṇaś cāparaṁ rūpam
verses quoted, 94-95
Brāhmaṇās tena vedāś ca
verses quoted, 123
Brahmaṇo hi pratiṣṭhāham
quoted, 125
Brahman realization
insignificant happiness of, 78-79
Brahma-pucchaṁ pratiṣṭhā
quoted
Brahma-saṁhitā
Jīva Gosvāmī's commentary on, 306
quoted on form of Kṛṣṇa, 98

Brahma-saṁhitā
Vaiṣṇavas worship demigods on principles of, 147-148
Brahma satyaṁ jagan-mithyā
quoted, 116
Brahma-sūtra
quoted, 114
See also Vedānta-sūtra, 88
Brahma-sūtra-padaiś caiva
quoted, 89
Brahmā ya eṣa jagadaṇḍa
verses quoted, 147
Brahmeti paramātmeti
verses quoted, 97
Bṛhad-āraṇyaka Upaniṣad
quoted, 125
quoted on six opulences of Lord, 132
quoted on spiritual body of Lord, 98
Bṛhad-vaiṣṇava-toṣaṇī
as book by Sanātana Gosvāmī, 304
Bṛhaspati
Sārvabhauma as incarnation of, 334
Buddhimanta Khān
as branch of Caitanya tree, **296**
Buddhism
Māyāvāda philosophy as covered, 95

C

Caitanya dāsa
identified, 204
wrote commentary on *Kṛṣṇa-karṇāmṛta,* 289
Caitanya Mahāprabhu
accepted direct meaning of *Vedānta,* 95-96
accepted food at house of Tapana Miśra, **35**
appeared as Rāmacandra, 279
appeared as spiritual master of entire world, 176
as form of a devotee, 5
as goal of materially impoverished, **1**-2
as ideal *ācārya,* 27, 45, 65
as Kṛṣṇa Himself, 6, **8**-10, 16, 23, 155
as most magnanimous incarnation, 142-143, 168, 234
as Nārāyaṇa, 86
as only shelter for conditioned souls, 1-2
as predominator, **10-12**
as supreme master of all masters, 2
as tree of love of Kṛṣṇa, **216,** 254
ate Viṣṇu's foodstuffs on Ekādaśī, **294**-295
becomes mad chanting holy name, 63-66
belongs to Viṣṇu category, 5
deprecated misinterpretation, of *Vedas,* 92
devised methods to deliver fallen souls, **28**
Caitanya Mahāprabhu
eternal philanthropic activities of, 167-168
exhibited His Varāha form, 279-280
exhibited mystic powers, **45**
five *tattvas* incarnate with, **3-5**
freely distributed love of God, 168
His body not materially tinged, **8**-9
His gift to human society, **173**-175
inaugurated Kṛṣṇa consciousness movement, 163
in ecstasy of Balarāma, **295**-296
in householder life for twenty-four years, **25**
instructed Sanātana Gosvāmī, 36-38
intolerant of behavior of Jagāi and Mādhāi, 39
introduced Hare Kṛṣṇa *mantra,* 113
known as Gaurasundara, **144, 158, 214**
known as *mahā-vadānyāvatāra,* 4
known as Patita-pāvana, **329**
known as Viśvambhara, **217**
modern so-called followers of, 245
Pañca-tattva important factor in understanding, **154**-155
performed dramas with associates, **258**
presented Himself as number one fool, 54
quoted on duty of Indians, 238
quoted on function of real teacher, 247
quoted on Māyāvādī commentaries, 126
quoted on offenses of Māyāvādīs, 127
quoted on rareness of devotional service, 137
quoted on real identity of living being, 108
quoted on relation of Lord and living being, 89-90, 135
teaches us to be tolerant like trees, **244**
three features of, **285**-288
took position of disciple, 55
recommends *Brahma-saṁhitā,* 147
spoke through writings of Vṛndāvana dāsa Ṭhākura, **189**
stayed at house of Candraśekhara, **34**-35
stressed importance of hearing, 134
three and a half confidential devotees of, 340
took *sannyāsa* in Bhāratī-*sampradāya,* 48
reasons for his descent, 234
visited temple of Viśveśvara, **146**–148
Caitanya-bhāgavata
as book by Vṛndāvana dāsa Ṭhākura, 157
Bhāgavatam quoted in, **188**
cited on Caitanya's arguments with Mukunda Datta, 273
glories of described, **186**-190
originally called *Caitanya-maṅgala,* 186
quoted on Murāri Caitanya dāsa, 363
quoted on Paramānanda Purī, 221-222
Vāsudeva Datta described in, 274-275

Caitanya-candrodaya-nāṭaka
as book by Karṇapūra, 290
written under direction of Pratāparudra, 338
Caitanya-carita
as book by Murāri Gupta, 279
Caitanya dāsa as author of, 289
Caitanya-carita-mahākāvya
cited, 338-339
Caitanya-caritāmṛta
as dictation of Madana-mohana, **209**-210
quoted on function of real teacher, 247
quoted on hearing, 134
quoted on Īśvara purī, 219-220
quoted on only supreme master, 11
quoted on real identity of living being, 108
Caitanyākhyaṁ prakaṭam adhunā
verse quoted, 10
Caitanya-maṅgala
as book by Locana dāsa Ṭhākura, 186
as former name of *Caitanya-bhāgavata,* 186
Caitanya-śataka
as book by Sārvabhauma Bhaṭṭācārya, 334
Candramukha
See Caitanya Mahāprabhu
Candraśekhara Ācārya
as branch of Caitanya tree, **257**-258, **347**
as *kaniṣṭha-adhikārī,* 40
blasphemy of Caitanya intolerable to, **38-41**
Caitanya stayed at house of, **34**-35
Candraśekhara Vaidya
as branch of Caitanya tree, **324**
Candrāvalī
Sadāśiva Kavirāja as, 376
Capitalism
meant for *vaiśyas,* 175
Cārvāka Muni
atheistic theory of, 111
Chāndogya Upaniṣad
quoted, 125
quoted by Śaṅkarācārya, 114
quoted on eternal individuality of soul, 117
quoted on world as Brahman, 115
Choṭa Haridāsa
as devotee of Lord in Jagannātha Purī, **344**
Chāḍiyā vaiṣṇava-sevā nistāra
verse quoted, 161, 170
Cirañjīva
as branch of Caitanya tree, **299, 328**
Civilization, Vedic
considers all aspects of human life, 240
prepares one for next life, 241
Communism
as movement of *śūdras,* 175
Conditioned souls
Caitanya as only shelter for, 1-2
in atmosphere of helplessness, 1
See also Living beings, human beings
Conjugal love
development of devotional service to, 14
devotees in best situated, 13-14
gopīs serve Kṛṣṇa in, 172
Kṛṣṇa accepts form of devotee to relish, **9**-10
tasted by Lord with internal devotees, **15**
tasted even in present life, **137**-138
Creation
as temporary not false, 116
by glance of Lord, 98, 115
none in spiritual world, 105
Cupid
Rāmānanda Rāya vanquished power of, 304

D

Dadāmi buddhi-yogaṁ tam
verse quoted, 190
Daivī hy eṣā guṇamayī mama
verse quoted, 104
Damayantī
as dear maidservant of Caitanya, **265**-266
Dāmodara dāsa
as devotee of Nityānanda, **385**
Dāmodara Paṇḍita
as associate of Lord in Jagannātha Purī, **332**
as branch of Caitanya tree, **268**
noted for objectivity as critic, 304
Damsels of Vraja
Kṛṣṇa as leader of, **7**
See also Gopīs
Dāna-carita
as book by Raghunātha dāsa Gosvāmī, 312
Dānakeli
as drama enacted by Nityānanda, 361
Dāna-keli-kaumudī
as book by Rūpa Gosvāmī, 303
Dāsya-rasa
Kṛṣṇa's servants serve Him in, 172
Death
material possessions can't save one from, 1
remembering *oṁkāra* at, 122
Vaiṣṇavas get spiritual body after, 53
Deity worship
kinds of, 184-185
material devotees attracted to, 85
necessity of, 63
Demigods
as servants of Kṛṣṇa, 148
devotees don't worship, 256-257

Demigods
never equal to Viṣṇu, 178
offense of considering them equal to Lord, 59
Viṣṇu not in category of, 103
worshiped by Māyāvādīs, 143, 146-148, 256-257
worshiped by Vaiṣṇavas on principles of *Brahma-saṁhitā,* 147-148
worshipers of go to planets of, 104, 241
Devānanda
as branch of Nityānanda, **381**
Devānanda Paṇḍita
as branch of Caitanya tree, **298**
Devotional service
above liberation, 2, 137
Absolute Truth realized by, 84
as activity of spirit soul, 108
as cause of love of God, 81, **180**-181
as only means to approach Lord, **134**-135
auspiciousness of, 242-243
bliss of, **78-79**
clearly indicated by *Vedānta,* 102
compared to creeper, 218
considered *māyā* by Māyāvādīs, 25, 30, 82-83
described in *Caitanya-bhāgavata,* **188**
desire tree of brought to earth, **218**
development of to conjugal love, 14
fruits of tree of, **228-230**
functions of tongue in, 169
Lord submissive to devotee due to, **138**
Mādhavendra Purī as storehouse of all, **218-219**
makes one free, 113
mitigates material miseries, 58
nine kinds of, 134, 228
rareness of, **170**-173
Śārīraka-bhāṣya devoid of, 90
test of advancement in, 136
that ignores *Vedas,* 188
transcendental to four goals of life, 69
under direction of spiritual master, **135**-136
Devotees
Absolute Truth partially understood by, 122
as actual followers of *Vedānta,* 56
bodily symptoms of called *āveśa,* 287
compared to bees, **251**
development of *bhāva* in, **67**-68
difference between pure and internal, 15
different types of, 6
don't waste time with Māyāvādīs, 33
don't worship demigods, 256-257
go back to Godhead, 104
imitation of advanced, 74-75
in conjugal love best situated, 13-14
internal potential, 13
Devotees
liberation stands at doorstep of, 172
Lord submissive to, **138**
manifest Kṛṣṇa's qualities, 198-**199**
no distinction between higher and lower, 254
offense of blaspheming, 59
only attachment of is Kṛṣṇa, 136
relate to Lord in five *rasas,* 57-58
should combine to distribute *mahā-mantra,* 232
three classes of, 85
transcendental to social gradations, 24
two classes of unalloyed, 74
Dhanañjaya Paṇḍita
as branch of Nityānanda,
Dharmaḥ projjhita-kaitavo' tra
quoted, 69, 137
Dharmaḥ svanuṣṭhitaḥ puṁsām
verses quoted, 140
Dhaniṣṭhā
Rāghava Paṇḍita formerly the *gopī,* 265
Dharmasya tattvaṁ nihitam
verse quoted, 161
Dhātu-saṅgraha
as book by Jīva Gosvāmī, 306
Dīna-hīna yata chila
verses quoted, 173
Disciplic succession
accepted by Kṛṣṇadāsa Kavirāja, 186
as actually authoritative, 206
supreme science received in, 91
Durgādevī
as shadow of *cit* potency, 147
worshiped by Māyāvādīs, 143, 146-148
Dvāparādau yuge bhūtvā
verses quoted, 95
Dvāparūyair janair viṣṇuḥ
verses quoted, 62
Durvāsā Muni
his disciples satisfied by Kṛṣṇa, 243
Dvāpara-yuga
paramparā honored in, 59
temple worship recommended in, 62
Dvija Haridāsa
as branch of Caitanya tree, **324**

E

Education
faults of modern, 240, 241
Ei chaya gosāñi yāṅra
verses quoted, 161
Ekādaśī
Caitanya ate Viṣṇu's foodstuffs on, **294-295**

Ekadeśa-sthitasyāgner
verses quoted, 113
Ekalā īśvara kṛṣṇa, āra saba
quoted, 148
Eko bahūnāṁ yo vidadhāti kāmān
verses quoted, 99
Enechi auṣadhi māyā nāśibāra
verses quoted, 233
Energy, material
as energy of darkness, 110
as energy of Viṣṇu, 103
deludes conditioned souls, 1
difficult to overcome, 104
eight divisions of, 110
love of God not under jurisdiction of, 72
works as if independent, 110
Energy, transformation of
as proven fact, **118**-119
doctrine of discussed, **114**-122
Evaṁ paramparā-prāptam
verse quoted, 91

F

Faith
in Lord and spiritual master, 38
Form
as spiritual, 98-99, 100
considered material by Māyāvādīs, 25, 80, 82, 102
greater than Brahman and Paramātmā, 133
never deteriorates, 110

G

Gadādhara
as associate of Lord in Jagannātha Purī, **332**
as incarnation of Kṛṣṇa's pleasure potency, **260**
as internal potency of Caitanya, 4, 6
as learned scholar, **158**
as worshiper of three predominators, **12**
devotees headed by, **13**
Puṇḍarīka Vidyānidhi as spiritual master of, 259
Gadādhara dāsa
as branch of Caitanya tree, **282**-284
in ecstasy as *gopī,* **361**
lived with Vīrabhadra Gosāñi, **359**
Gandharvas
as celestial singers, 262
Gaṇeśa
destroys obstacles on path of progress, 147-148
worshiped by Māyāvādīs, 143, 146-148
Gaṅgādāsa Paṇḍita
as branch of Nityānanda, **380**
as branch of Caitanya tree, **267**
Gaṅgādevī
as daughter of Nityānanda, 328-329
Gaṇoddeśa-dīpikā
as book by Rūpa Gosvāmī, 303
Garbhodakaśāyī Viṣṇu
accompanies Lord in *saṅkīrtana,* 15
Garuḍa Paṇḍita
as branch of Caitanya tree, **297**
Gauḍīya-sampradāya
Vedānta commentary in, 57
Gaura-gaṇoddeśa-dīpikā
as book by Karṇapūra, 290
cited on identity of Ananta Ācārya, 200
cited on Bhāgavatācārya, 325
cited on Caitanya's changing name of Pradyumna Brahmacārī, 270
cited on identity of Caitanya dāsa and Rāmadāsa, 289-290
cited on identity of Damayantī, 265
cited on identity of Devānanda Paṇḍita, 298
cited on identity of Dhanañjaya Paṇḍita, 371
cited on identity of Gadādhara, 260
cited on identity of Gadādhara dāsa, 282
cited on identity of Gaurīdāsa Paṇḍita, 367
cited on identity of Ghosh brothers, 327
cited on identity of Gopāla-Bhaṭṭa Gosvāmī, 319
cited on identity of Gopīnātha Siṁha, 297
cited on identity of Jagāi and Mādhāi, 329
cited on identity of Jagannātha Ācārya, 322
cited on identity of Jāhnavā, 363
cited on identity of Jīva Gosvāmī, 306
cited on identity of Jīva Paṇḍita, 380
cited on identity of Kamalākara Pippalāi
cited on identity of Kaṁsāri Sena, 384
cited on identity of Kāśī Miśra, 335
cited on identity of Kāśīnātha and Rudra, 320
cited on identity of Kāśīśvara and Govinda,340
cited on identity of Kāśīśvara Gosāñi, 203
cited on identity of Keśava Bhāratī, 223
cited on identity of Mādhavācārya, 329
cited on identity of Mīnaketana Rāmadāsa, 385
cited on identity of Mukunda dāsa and Cirañjīva, 299
cited on identity of Mukunda Datta and Vāsudeva Datta, 273
cited on prowess of Nakula Brahmacārī, 287
cited on identity of Nārāyaṇī, 191
cited on identity of Paramānanda Gupta, 381
cited on identity of Paramānanda Purī, 222

Gaura-gaṇoddeśa-dīpikā
cited on identity of Pratāparudra and Śikhi Māhiti, 338
cited on identity of Puṇḍarīka Vidyānidhi, 259
cited on identity of Rāghava Paṇḍita, 264
cited on identity of Raghunātha Bhaṭṭa, 349
cited on identity of Raghunātha dāsa Gosvāmī, 312
cited on identity of Rāmāi and Nandāi, 343
cited on identity of Rāmānanda Rāya, 336
cited on identity of Rūpa Gosvāmī, 303
cited on identity of Sadāśiva Kavirāja, 376
cited on identity of Sanātana, 304
cited on identity of Sārṅga Ṭhākura, 325
cited on identity of Sārvabhauma and Gopīnātha Ācārya, 334
cited on identity of Śrīdhara, 293
cited on identity of Śrīkānta Sena, 290
cited on identity of Śrīnātha Miśra and Kavicandra, 322
cited on identity of Śrī Rāmadāsa, 359
cited on identity of Śrīvāsa and Śrī Rāma Paṇḍita, 255
cited on identity of Sundarānanda, 364
cited on identity of Uddhāraṇa Datta Ṭhākura, 377
cited on identity of Vakreśvara Paṇḍita, 261
cited on identity of Vīrabhadra Gosāñi, 356
Gaurahari
Caitanya known as, **214**
Gaura-kṛṣṇodaya
Śrī Govinda dāsa as author of, 261
Gaurāṅga
See Caitanya Mahāprabhu
Gaurāṅga balite ha'be pulaka
verses quoted, 14, 184
Gaurāṅga dāsa
as devotee of Nityānanda, **385**
Gaurasundara
Caitanya known as, **144, 158**
Gaurīdāsa Paṇḍita
as branch of Nityānanda, **367**-368
Gāyatrī-mantra
Jīva Gosvāmī's commentary on, 306
Gītāmṛta
as book by Govinda Kavirāja, 384
Gokula dāsa
as devotee of Nityānanda, **383**
Goloka eva nivasaty akhilātma-bhūto
verse quoted, 113
Golokera prema-dhana
verse quoted, 60
Goodness, mode of
has nothing to do with spiritual varieties, 100
Gopāla
as devotee of Nityānanda, **383**
as seventy-first devotee of Nityānanda, **385**
Gopāla Ācārya
as branch of Caitanya tree, **326**
Gopāla Bhaṭṭa Gosvāmī
as branch of Caitanya tree, **319**
as nephew of Prabodhānanda Sarasvatī, 142
constructed Rādhāramaṇa temple, 152
Gopāla-campū
as book by Jīva Gosvāmī, 307
Gopāla-tāpanī-ṭīkā
as book by Jīva Gosvāmī, 306
Gopāla-virudāvalī
as book by Jīva Gosvāmī, 306
Gopīnātha Ācārya
Īśvara Purī lived in house of, 220
as branch of Caitanya tree, **333**-334
Gopīnātha Siṁha
as branch of Caitanya tree, **297**
Gopīs
as best lovers of God, 15
serve Kṛṣṇa in conjugal love, 172
Gosvāmīs
chanting and dancing of, 17
Kṛṣṇadāsa Kavirāja glorifies, **215**
oṁkāra analyzed by, 125
one must be submissive student of, 185-186
taking shelter of, 184
transcendental activities of, 316
Govinda
as eighty-second branch of Caitanya tree, **326, 328**
Govinda
feeling separation from, 66
See also Kṛṣṇa
Govinda-bhāṣya
as Vaiṣṇava Vedānta commentary, 32, 57
Govinda Datta
as branch of Caitanya tree, **291**
Govinda Gosāñi
identified, **203**
Govinda Kavirāja
as devotee of Nityānanda, **384**
Govindānanda
as branch of Caitanya tree, **291**
Gṛhasthas
four divisions of, 26
must not make livelihood by begging, 280-281
Guru-Gaurāṅga
worship of, 184-185
Guru-kṛṣṇa-prasāde
verses quoted, 81

Gurvaṣṭaka
quoted on mercy of spiritual master, 220

H

Hāḍāi Ojhā
as father of Nityānanda, 380
Haṁsadūta
as book by Rūpa Gosvāmī, 303
Hare Kṛṣṇa *mantra*
always chanted by Svarūpa Dāmodara, 222
as medicine to cure material disease, 281
as reality of all *Vedānta,* 62
attachment to by reading *Bhāgavatam,* 58-59
benefits even lower species of life, 236
chanted by Jagāi and Mādhāi, 329
chanted by sweepers of Kulīna-grāma, **301**
chanted constantly by Murāri Caitanya dāsa, 363
chanted offenselessly, **180**-181
chanting Pañca-tattva *mantra* before chanting, 4
counteracted effects of poison, **297**
ecstatic symptoms while chanting, **67**-68, **72**
even one without money can preach, 243
intoxicating, 246-249
introduced by Caitanya, 113
lotus feet of Lord seen by chanting, **57**-58
ocean of bliss by chanting, **78**-79
offenses while chanting, 4, 157, **177**-179, **183**
one must beg from Lord, 234
perfection by chanting, 165
preaching glories of, 68
real change of heart while chanting, 180
should be chanted fully, 155
success in chanting, 168-169
to be distributed by combined forces, 232
See Holy name
Harer nāma harer nāma
verses quoted, 54, 113
Hari-bhakti-sudhodaya
verse from quoted by Caitanya, **79**
Hari-bhakti-vilāsa
as book by Sanātana Gosvāmī, 304
edited by Gopāla Bhaṭṭa Gosvāmī, 319
quoted on proper initiation of *brāhmaṇas,* 36
quoted on writing of pure devotee, 189
Haridāsa Paṇḍita
qualities of described, **196**-198, **200**-202
Haridāsa Ṭhākura
as associate of Lord in Jagannātha Purī, **332**
as branch of Caitanya tree, **276**-277
cited on potency of *mahā-mantra,* 236
compared to Prahlāda Mahārāja, **277**
Haridāsa Ṭhākura
noted for his forbearance, 304
Hariharānanda
as devotee of Nityānanda, **383**
Hari-nāmāmṛta-vyākaraṇa
as book by Jīva Gosvāmī, 306
Hearing
as most important process, **134**-135
Hindu religion
as philosophical hodge-podge, 257
Hiraṇya Mahāśaya
as branch of Caitanya tree, 294
Hoḍa Kṛṣṇadāsa
as branch of Nityānanda, **382**
Holy name
as essence of Vedic hymns, **54,** 57, **59**-60
as only means of deliverance in Kali-yuga, 54, **61**-63, 287
beyond material contamination, 60
Caitanya becomes mad by chanting, **63**-66
Caitanya blessed Māyāvādī *sannyāsīs* with, **142**
Caitanya taught us to be servants of, 77
called *mahā-mantra,* 68
chanted in humble state of mind, 39
distributed by Pañca-tattva throughout universe, **151**-152
fallen souls delivered by, **73**-75
frees one from material existence, **57**-58
identical with Lord, 56, 57, 59, 60, 68, **122**-126, 169
success in chanting, 168-169
ten offenses against listed, 59
See also Hare Kṛṣṇa *mantra*
Hṛdayānanda
as branch of Caitanya tree, **323**
Human beings
four types of, 84
just like animals, 112
love of God as fifth goal of, **137**
love of God ultimate benediction for, 2
meant for elevation, 241
must be God conscious, 240
questions must arise in hearts of, 139
See also Living beings

I

Icchānurūpam api yasya ca
verses quoted, 147
Idaṁ hi viśvaṁ bhagavān
verses quoted, 124
Ihā haite sarva-siddhi haibe
quoted, 165

Impersonalists
accept Kṛṣṇa as ordinary human, 22
illusioned by material energy, 95
See also Māyāvādīs
Incarnations
described in scripture, 22-23
India
duty of those born in, **237**-239
holy places in, 238
Indirā
as Jīva Paṇḍita, 380
Indradyumna
as Pratāparudra, 338
International Society for Krishna Consciousness
as branch of Caitanya tree, 225
constructed temple at Māyāpur, 330
Īśāna
as branch of Caitanya tree, **323**
Īśopaniṣad
quoted on completeness of God, 118
quoted on six opulences of Lord, 132
Īśvara Purī
as disciple of Mādhavendra Purī, 219-220
as spiritual master of Kāśīśvara, **340-341**
Īśvaraḥ paramaḥ kṛṣṇaḥ
verse quoted, 98
Īśvara-purī kare śrī-pada sevana
verses quoted, 219
Īśvaraḥ sarva-bhūtānām
verses quoted, 124
Iti matvā bhajante mām
verses quoted, 67

J

Jagadānanda Paṇḍita
as associate of Lord in Jagannātha Purī, **332**
as incarnation of Satyabhāmā, **263**-264
Jagadīśa Paṇḍita
as branch of Caitanya tree, **294**
Jagadīśa Paṇḍita
as branch of Nityānanda, **370**
Jagāi and Mādhāi
as branches of Caitanya tree, **329**
converted by Caitanya, 29, **173**-174
Jagannātha
as devotee of Nityānanda, **382**
Jagannātha Ācārya
as branch of Caitanya tree, **322**
Jagannātha dāsa
as branch of Caitanya tree, **324**
Jagannātha Purī
devotees of Caitanya in, **331**-346
Ṣaḍbhuja Deity in temple at, 334
Jagannātha Tīrtha
as branch of Caitanya tree, **326**
Jagannātha-vallabha-nāṭaka
as book by Rāmānanda Rāya, 337
Jāhnavīdevī
as pleasure potency of Nityānanda, 307, 363
Jaimini
as contemporary of Vyāsadeva, 89
Janma-mṛtyu-jarā-vyādhi
verse quoted, 1
Janma sārthaka kari' kara
verse quoted, 238
Janmādy asya yato' nvayād
verse quoted, 94, 103, 107, 121
Jarāsandha
worshiped Viṣṇu, **162**
Jīva Gosvāmī
as greatest philosopher in world, 83
as son of Anupama, 302
as sub-branch of Caitanya tree, **306**-308
cited on Brahman as origin of everything, 121
cited on glories of *oṁkāra,* 124
cited on *oṁkāra* as Absolute Truth, 124
his books listed, 306-307
on association of pure devotee, 37
quoted on chanting holy names, 62-63
quoted on love of God, 72
three accusations against, 307
Jīva-bhūtāṁ mahā-bāho
verses quoted, 105
Jīva Paṇḍita
as branch of Nityānanda, **380**
Jīvera nistāra lāgi' sūtra kaila
verses quoted, 102
Jīvera 'svarūpa' haya-kṛṣṇera
quoted, 89-90, 108, 135
Jñānadāsa
as devotee of Nityānanda, **385**
Jñānena dharmeṇa svarūpam
verses quoted, 133
Jñānīs
are transcendental, 84

K

Kabe hāma bujhaba se yugala-pirīti
verses quoted, 184
Kalau nāsty eva nāsty eva
verses quoted, 54, 113
Kalau śūdra sambhava
quoted, 51
Kalau tu nāma-mātreṇa
verses quoted, 62

Kalisantaraṇa Upaniṣad
quoted on Hare Kṛṣṇa *mantra,* 62
Kāliya Kṛṣṇadāsa
as branch of Nityānanda, **374**-374
Kali-yuga
affects even so-called followers of Caitanya, 245
as age of fools and rascals, 54
atheistic conclusion of, 165
Caitanya descends in, 142-143
holy name to be broadcast in, **59**-60, **61**-63, 287
Jagāi and Mādhāi epitomize population of, 174
material activities expanded in, 110
Śiva appears as Śaṅkara in, 95
Kāmābhaṭṭa
as devotee of Lord in Jagannātha Purī, **345**
Kāmais tais tair hṛta-jñānāḥ
verse quoted, 257
Kamalākānta
as branch of Caitanya tree, **328**-329
Kamalākara Pippalāi
as branch of Nityānanda, **365**-366
Kamala-nayana
as branch of Caitanya tree, **323**
Kaṁsa
Jarāsandha as father-in-law of, **162**
Kaṁsāri Sena
as devotee of Nityānanda, **384**
Kānu Ṭhākura
376-377
Kāraṇodakaśāyī Viṣṇu
accompanies Lord in *saṅkīrtana,* 15
Karmandībhikṣu
discussed *Vedānta* before Vyāsadeva, 89
Karmīs
are materialistic, 84
Karṇapūra
as son of Śivānanda Sena, **289**-290
books of named, 290
Kārṣṇājini
as contemporary of Vyāsadeva, 89
Kāśakṛtsna
as contemporary of Vyāsadeva, 89
Kāśī Miśra
as devotee of Lord at Jagannātha Purī, **334-335**
Kāśīnātha
as sub-branch of Caitanya tree, **320**
Kāśīśvara
as devotee of Lord in Jagannātha Purī, **340-342**
Kāśīśvara Gosāñi
identified, **203**
Kaṭha Upaniṣad
quoted, 125
Kaṭha Upaniṣad
quoted on Absolute Truth as person, 99
quoted on supreme eternal, 8
Kavicandra
as branch of Caitanya tree, **322, 324**
Kavikarṇapūra
as author of *Gaura-gaṇoddeśa-dīpikā,* 191
Keśava Bhāratī
as root of tree of devotional service, **221**, 223
Caitanya accepted *sannyāsa* from, 26
Sāndīpani Muni as, 223
Keśava Purī
as root of tree of devotional service, **221**
Khaṇḍavāsī Mukunda
as branch of Caitanya tree, **299**
Kholāvecā Śrīdhara
See Śrīdhara
Kintu svarūpa-śaktyānanda-rūpā
verses quoted, 72
Kīrtanād eva kṛṣṇasya mukta-
verse quoted, 62, 163
Knowledge
chanting holy name as essence of Vedic, **54**-57
of living beings covered, 111
of Māyāvādīs stolen by Kṛṣṇa, 101
oṁkāra as basic principle of Vedic, 125
real culminates in surrender to Kṛṣṇa, 108-109
scientific must be supported by *śruti* and *smṛti,* 89
spiritual potency full of, **109**-110
useless acquired by material senses, 91
Vedas as source of real, 94
Koṭimukta-madhye 'durlabha'
verse quoted, 137
Krama-sandarbha
as book by Jīva Gosvāmī, 307
Kṛṣṇa
appears as son of Nanda, **7**
as compiler of Vedānta, 31
as energetic, 55, **106**-107
as enjoyer of *rāsa* dance, **7**
as reservoir of all pleasure, **7,** 106
as son of Vasudeva, 75
Caitanya as, 6, **8**-10, 16, 55
demanded one surrender to Him, 16, 168
fully represented by *oṁkāra,* 125
known as *Yogeśvara,* 45
no one equal to or above, 99
presented to Western world as woman hunter, 188
situated in His own abode, 113
storehouse of love came with, **16**
See also Supreme Lord, Caitanya Mahāprabhu

Kṛṣṇa consciousness
as only hope for humanity, 113, 241
based on principle of preaching, 74
benefits even lower species of life, 236
can inundate entire world, 19-**20**
chanting and dancing in, 17
debauchees becoming saints by, 238
doesn't approve demigod worship, 257
following in footsteps of Caitanya, 141, 143, 163
follows injunctions of *Bhāgavatam,* 51
includes consciousness of Caitanya, **162**-163
instructed in *Śikṣāṣṭaka,* 165
meant to make people intelligent, 108
meant to save world from degradation, 126
never under control of Māyāvādīs, 30
only for very fortunate, 81
scarcity of in world, 235
success in by worship of Pañca-tattva, 166
sum and substance of described, 175
supplies proper spiritual medicine and diet, 281
transcendental to material considerations, 18-19
Kṛṣṇa-sandarbha
as book by Jīva Gosvāmī, 307
Kṛṣṇadāsa
identified, **204**
as devotee of Lord in Jagannātha Purī, **343**
as thirty-fourth branch of Nityānanda, **381**
Kṛṣṇadāsa Brāhmaṇa
as branch of Nityānanda, **374**
Kṛṣṇadāsa Kavirāja
accepted disciplic succession, 186
as branch of Caitanya tree, **292**
as Vyāsa of Caitanya's pastimes, 211
his reason for leaving hime, 153
on preaching glories of *mahā-mantra,* 68
Raghunātha dāsa as special guide of, **318**
wrote on order of Madana-mohana, 157
Kṛṣṇadāsa Sarakhela
as branch of Nityānanda, **366**-367
Kṛṣṇadāsa Ṭhākura
sacred thread ceremony performed in family of, 35
Kṛṣṇadāsa Vaidya
as branch of Caitanya tree, **322**
Kṛṣṇa-janma-tithi-vidhi
as book by Rūpa Gosvāmī, 303
Kṛṣṇa-karṇāmṛta
Caitanya dāsa wrote commentary on, 289
Gopāla Bhaṭṭa Gosvāmī wrote commentary on, 319
quoted on insignificance of liberation, 138
Kṛṣṇa-līlāmṛta
recited to Caitanya by Īśvara Purī, 220
Kṛṣṇa-nāma
See Holy name
Kṛṣṇānanda
as devotee of Lord at Jagannātha Purī, **338**
as devotee of Nityānanda, **383**
Kṛṣṇānanda Purī
as root of tree of devotional service, **221**
Kṛṣṇa-prema-taraṅgiṇī
as book by Bhāgavatācārya, 325
Kṛṣṇa-śakti vinā nahe
verse quoted, 68, 178
Kṛṣṇa se tomāra, kṛṣṇa dite
verse quoted, **388**
Kṛṣṇa-stavāvalī
as prayer by Paramānanda Gupta, 381
Kṛṣṇa-varṇaṁ tviṣākṛṣṇam
verses quoted, 4
Kṛṣṇārcā-dīpikā
as book by Jīva Gosvāmī, 306
Kṛṣṇotkīrtana-gāna-nartana
quoted, 17, 316
Kṣatriyas
benefits derived from, 244
engagements of, 280
Kṣipāmy ajasram aśubhān
verses quoted, 127
Kṣīraṁ yathā dadhi vikāra
verses quoted, 147
Kṣīrodakaśāyī Viṣṇu
accompanies Lord in *saṅkīrtana,* 15
Vīrabhadra Gosāñi as, 356-358
Kulīna-grāma
inhabitants of dear to Caitanya, **300-301**
Kurukṣetra
actually exists, 92

L

Labaṅga
Kāliya Kṛṣṇadāsa as, **374**-375
Laghu-bhāgavatāmṛta
as book by Rūpa Gosvāmī, 303
Laghu-toṣaṇī
as book by Sanātana Gosvāmī, 304
Lalita-mādhava
as book by Rūpa Gosvāmī, 303, 304
taking shelter of, 184
Liberation
by offering obeisances to Caitanya, **164**
devotional service above, 137
five kinds of, 172
holy names only way to achieve, 77-78

Liberation
stands at doorstep of devotee, **171**, 172
symptomized by spiritual activities, 108
Life
Caitanya as goal of, **1**
four orders of spiritual, 26
four goals of human, **68**-69
Living beings
as eternally true, 117
as eternal servants of God, 8, 90
as transformations of Lord's energy, 115, **106-107**
compared to sparks of fire, **105**
conditioned by material body, 36
Lord displays pleasure potency as, 106
Kṛṣṇa's qualities minutely present in, 198
should perform welfare activities, **239**-240
subject to bewilderment, **109**
sustain universe, 105, **107**
taken as Lord by Māyāvādīs, **112**-113
transmigration of, 233
very minute in quantity, 8
Locana dāsa Ṭhākura
as author of *Caitanya-maṅgala,* 185
as disciple of Narahari, 299
Lokanātha Gosvāmī
constructed Gokulānanda temple, 152
Lokasyājānato vidvāṁś
verses quoted, 58
Lotus feet of Kṛṣṇa
attachment to, **136**
attained by chanting holy name, **57**-58, 77
greatest offender at, **103**-104
greed to achieve, **70**
held by Gaṇeśa on his head, 147-148
learned think only of, 99
neglected by Māyāvādīs, 102, 127, 135
taking shelter of, 1-**2**
Love
above salvation, 2
as conclusion of all scriptures, **70**
as fifth goal of human life, 2, 58, **68**-69, 137
awakened by talking of Nityānanda, **177**
Bhāgavatam teaches only, 69
bodily symptoms of, **182**
Caitanya as tree of, **216**
causes detachment to everything else, **136**
developed by hearing, 134, 135
devotional service as cause of, 81, **180**-181
distributed freely by Pañca-tattva, 2, 16, **17-21**, 168
induces transcendental symptoms, **70-72**
intoxication of, **245-249**
on favored by fortune attains, **81**
Love
storehouse of increases as distributed, **18**
tasted by chanting and dancing, **17**, 168
Vaiṣṇavas can deliver, 175, **388**
Love, conjugal
See Conjugal love

M

Madana-gopāla
See Madana-mohana
Madana-mohana
worshipers of, 209
Caitanya-caritāmṛta as dictation of, 157, **206-210**
Mādhava
as devotee of Nityānanda, **360, 382**
as principle performer of *kīrtana,* **362**
Mādhava
as eighty-third branch of Caitanya tree, **326, 328**
Mādhavācārya
as branch of Caitanya tree, **328**-329
as devotee of Nityānanda, **385**
Madhvācārya
broke teeth of Māyāvādīs, 123
his philosophy a stumbling block to Māyāvādīs, 95
Mādhavendra Purī in disciplic succession of, 218-219
quoted on holy names, 62
Mādhavendra Purī
as spiritual master of Īśvara Purī, 219-220
as spiritual master of Paramānanda Purī, 221
seed of devotional service first fructified in, **218**-219
Mādhavīdevī
as devotee of Lord in Jagannātha Purī, **339**-340
Mādhurya-rasa
gopīs serve Kṛṣṇa in, 172
Madhyama-adhikārī
must be learned in *Vedānta,* 84
Mahābhārata
only Hari explained in, 128
quoted on following *ācāryas,* 155, 161
quoted on imperfection of logic, 167
story of Durvāsā Muni's disciples in, 243
Mahā-jano yena gataḥ sa
verse quoted, 155
Mahā-mantra
holy name of Kṛṣṇa called, 68
See also Holy name
Mahān prabhur vai puruṣaḥ
quoted, 98

Mahāprabhu śrī-caitanya, rādhā kṛṣṇa
verse quoted, 164
Mahato mahīyān aṇuto' ṇīyān
quoted, 105
Maheśa Paṇḍita
as branch of Caitanya tree, **323**
Maheśa Paṇḍita
as branch of Nityānanda, **372**
Mahīdhara
as devotee of Nityānanda, **382**
Mahīyasāṁpāda-rajo' bhiṣekam
Makaradhvaja Kara
as sub-branch of Caitanya tree, **264**
Mamaivāṁśo jīva-loke
quoted, 118
Māṁ ca yo'vyabhicāreṇa
verses quoted, 108
Mām eva ye prapadyante māyām
verse quoted, 104
Māṁ hi pārtha vyapāśritya
verses quoted, 174
Māṇḍūkya Upaniṣad
cited on expansion of *oṁkāra,* 124
example of mistaking rope for snake in, 117-118
Man-manā bhava mad-bhakto
quoted, 127
Manohara
as branch of Nityānanda, **381**
Manohara
as seventieth devotee of Nityānanda, **385**
Materialists
can't have faith in chanting, 60
inefficient senses of, 91
See also Atheists
Materialism
Māyāvādīs as advocates of utter, 30
Mathurā-mahimā
as book by Rūpa Gosvāmī, 303
Matir na kṛṣṇe parataḥ svato vā
verses quoted, 170
Mattaḥ parataraṁ nānyat
quoted, 97, 103
Māyā
Bhāgavatam relieves one from, 58-59
controlled by Lord, 103
Māyāvādīs consider Kṛṣṇa's body, 82-83
oṁkāra saves one from, 124
saṅkīrtana dispells illusion of, 233
showy display of *Vedānta* study as feature of, 55-56
two potencies of, 101
Mayādhyakṣeṇa prakṛtiḥ
verses quoted, 110
Māyāvāda philosophy
advocates theory of impersonalism, **98**
as covered Buddhism, 95
as mental speculation, 136
takes living beings to be Lord, **112-113**
Māyāvādam asac-chāstram
verses quoted, 94-95
Māyāvādi-bhāṣya śunile haya
verses quoted, 102, **126**
Māyāvādī kṛṣṇe aparādhī
quoted, **30**, 127
Māyāvādīs
accept *Śārīraka-bhāṣya,* 82
address each other as Nārāyaṇa, **53**, 86
as greatest offenders of Lord, **30**, 127
Caitanya devises trick to attract, **23-25**
consider form of Kṛṣṇa material, **25**, **80**, 82-83
consider material world false, 22
consider themselves *jagad-gurus,* 49
don't approve of chanting and dancing, 52, **78**
deny spiritual varieties, 100
differentiate between Lord and His name, 60
equate Lord and living beings, 8
Kāśīra and Saranātha described, 29-30
misinterpret all *śāstras,* 48
moved by hearing Caitanya, **80**
neglect lotus feet of Lord, 135
rāsa dance imitated by, 7
Sadānanda Yogīndra most prominent scholar of, 101
teeth of broken by *ācāryas,* 123
try to defy Vaiṣṇavas, 80
two groups of, 101
worship demigods, 143, 146-148, **256-257**
Māyayāpahṛta-jñānā
verses quoted, 80
Mental speculation
Māyāvāda philosophy is merely, 136
Mercy
of Caitanya necessary to become Kṛṣṇa conscious, 163
of Vaiṣṇavas, 388
perfection attained by spiritual master's, 160, **220**
Mīnaketana Rāmadāsa
as devotee of Nityānanda, **385**
Miśra Bhagavān
as branch of Caitanya tree, **323**
Mitho 'bhipadyeta gṛha-vratānām
verses quoted, 170
Mlecchas
became devotees, **29**
Modes of nature
See Nature, modes of

Mohammedans
converted by Caitanya, 29
Mukhya-vṛttye sei artha
verse quoted, 94
Muktācarita
as book by Raghunātha dāsa Gosvāmī, 312
Muktiḥ svayaṁ mukulitāñjali
verse quoted, 138, 172
Mukunda
as devotee of Nityānanda, **382**
Mukunda
as sixty-third devotee of Nityānanda, **384**
Mukunda
as sixty-eighth devotee of Nityānanda, **385**
Mukunda
as sub-branch of Caitanya tree, **320**
Mukunda Datta
as branch of Caitanya tree, **273**-274
Mukundānanda Cakravartī
identified, **204**
Murāri Caitanya dāsa
slapped tigers, **362**-363
Murāri Gupta
as branch of Caitanya tree, **279**-281
Murāri Māhiti
as devotee of Lord at Jagannātha Purī, **338**-339
Mystic powers
exhibited by Caitanya, **45**
misuse of, 46

N

Naiṣāṁ matis tāvad urukramāṅghrim
verses quoted, 170
Nakaḍi
as devotee of Nityānanda, **382**
Nakula Brahmacārī
Caitanya's appearance in, 285-287
Na māṁ duṣkṛtino mūḍhāḥ
verses quoted, 80
Nāmnām akāri bahudhā
verses quoted, 124
Namo mahā-vadānyāya
verse quoted, 168
Naitat samācarej jātu
verse quoted, 75
Naiti bhakti-sukhāmbhodheḥ
verses quoted, 78
Naivodvije para duratyaya
verses quoted, 74
Nanda
Kṛṣṇa appears as son of, **7**
Nandāi
as devotee of Lord in Jagannātha Purī, **342-343**
Nandāi
as devotee of Nityānanda, **383**
Nandana
as branch of Nityānanda, **380**
Nandana Ācārya
as branch of Caitanya tree, **272**-273
Nanu bhagavan-nāmātmakā
verses quoted, 62
Nārada
accepts *brāhmaṇas* by qualification, 50
Bhāgavatam composed on instruction of, 90
cited on Deity worship, 63
quoted on Kṛṣṇa as servant of devotee, **171**
Śrīvāsa as incarnation of, 255
Nārada-pañcarātra
cited on chanting *aṣṭākṣara*, 124
holy name called *mahā-mantra* in, 68
quoted on Hare Kṛṣṇa *mantra*, 62
Narahari
as branch of Caitanya tree, **299**
Nārāyaṇa
Caitanya appeared as brilliant as, **53**, 86
in form of Vyāsadeva, **88**
Māyāvādī *sannyāsīs* address each other as, 53, 186
Vedas emanate from breathing of, 89
Nārāyaṇa
as branch of Nityānanda, **381**
Nārāyaṇa Paṇḍita
as branch of Caitanya tree, **271**
Nārāyaṇī
Vṛndāvana dāsa Ṭhākura born of, **191**
Narottama dāsa Ṭhākura
inspired by Jīva Gosvāmī, 307
quoted on demigod worship, 256
quoted on development of devotional service, 14
quoted on following Gosvāmīs, 185
quoted on holy name, 60
quoted on service of pure devotees, 161, 170
quoted on story of Jagāi and Mādhāi, 172-173
quoted on taking shelter of Caitanya, 184
Rāmacandra Kavirāja as most intimate friend of, 384
Naṣṭa-prāyeṣv abhadreṣu
verses quoted, 174-175
Nāṭaka-candrikā
as book by Rūpa Gosvāmī, 303
Nature, modes of
can't act in spiritual world, 100

Nature, modes of
effect of associating with, 174
transcended by devotional service, 113
See also Energy, material
Navadvīpa
Caitanya began garden at, **217**
Navadvīpa-śataka
as book by Prabodhānanda Sarasvatī, 142
Navanī Hoḍa
as devotee of Nityānanda, **383**
sacred thread ceremony performed in family of, 35
Nīlācala
See Jagannātha Purī
Nīlāmbara
as devotee of Lord in Jagannātha Purī, **345**
Nirbandhaḥ kṛṣṇa-sambandhe
verses quoted, 75
Nirloma Gaṅgādāsa
as devotee of Lord in Jagannātha Purī, **346**
Nityo-nityānāṁ cetanaś
verse quoted, 8, 99, 125
Nityānanda
as elder brother of Caitanya, 6, **10**
as personified spiritual bliss, 6, **158**
as plenary expansion of Caitanya, 4
as predominator, **10-12**
as son of Hāḍāi Ojhā, 380
as trunk of Caitanya tree, **226, 354**
belongs to Viṣṇu category, 5
broke *sannyāsa* rod of Caitanya, 274
cursed Śivānanda Sena's son to die, 288
devotees of, **353-389**
Gadādhara dāsa as chief assistant of, 283
Gaṅgādevī as daughter of, 328-329
His associates cowherdboys, **363**
in form of devotee's spiritual master, 5
Jāhnavīdevī as pleasure potency of, 307
love of God awakened by talking of, **177**
Mādhava Ghosh dear to, 327
rāsas of servitor of, 13
sent to Bengal, **153**
thief tries to steal jewels of, 294
Vīrabhadra Prabhu as son of, 321, 356
Nondevotees
compared to dogs, **251**
See also Atheists
Notpādayed yadi ratim
verses quoted, 140
Nṛsiṁhānanda Brahmacārī
Pradyumna Brahmacārī's name changed to, **270**
Nṛsiṁha-caitanya
as devotee of Nityānanda, **385**
Nṛsiṁhadeva
manifest in heart of Pradyumna Brahmacārī 270
Nṛsiṁhatīrtha
as root of tree of devotional service, **221**

O

Om ity ekākṣaraṁ brahma
verses quoted, 122, 123
Oṁkāra
analyzed in terms of alphabetical constituents, 125
as resting place of everything, 125
as sound representation of Lord, **122**-126
Bhāgavatam begins with, 124
has all potencies of Lord, 124
Oṁ namo bhagavate vāsudevāya
verse quoted, 94
Oṁ pūrṇam adaḥ pūrṇam idam
verses quoted, 132
Oṁ tad viṣṇoḥ paramaṁ padam
quoted, 103
Oṁ-tat-sad iti nirdeśo
verses quoted, 123
Orissa
most disciples of Caitanya lived in Bengal and, 330
See also Jagannātha Purī

P

Padma Purāṇa
quoted on blaspheming devotees, 178
quoted on offenses of Māyāvādīs, 104
quoted on Śiva as Śaṅkara, 94-95
Padyāvalī
as book by Rūpa Gosvāmī, 303
Pañca-tattva
as important factor in understanding Caitanya, **154**-155
Caitanya descends with, **3-5**
distributed holy name throughout universe, **151**-152
how they distributed love of God, **17-21**
Kṛṣṇadāsa Kavirāja teaches us to offer respect to, 159
one should chant names of full, 4
plundered storehouse of love of Kṛṣṇa, **16**
worship of, 166, 184-185
Pañca-tattva *mahā-mantra*
must be chanted fully, **155**
potency of, 4

Pāñcarātrikī-vidhi
Deity worship stressed in, 63
Pāṇḍavas
Kṛṣṇa's relationship with, 172
Pāṇḍu
Bhavānanda Rāya as, **335**-337
Parābhavas tāvad abodha-jāto
verses quoted, 139
Paramānanda
as fiftieth devotee of Nityānanda, **383**
Paramānanda Gupta
as branch of Nityānanda, **381**
Paramānanda Mahāpātra
as devotee of Lord at Jagannātha Purī, **338**
Paramānanda Purī
as associate of Lord at Jagannātha Purī, **332**
as root of tree of devotional service, **221**-332, 224
Uddhava as, 222-223
Paramānanda Upādhyāya
as branch of Nityānanda, **380**
Paramātma
Absolute partially understood as, 84, 97
as expansion of potency of Lord, 131
Paramātma-sandarbha
as book by Jīva Gosvāmī, 307
quoted on inconceivable potencies of Lord, 118
Paraṁ bhāvam ajānanto
verses quoted, 22
Parameśvara dāsa
as branch of Nityānanda, **371**
Paramparā
instructions in based on *Vedas,* 37
neglected in *Kali-yuga,* 59-60
Pārāśarī
discussed *Vedānta* before Vyāsadeva, 89
Parasya brahmaṇaḥ śaktis
verses quoted, 113
Parāsya śaktir vividhaiva śrūyate
quoted, 5, 6, 98, 109, 115
Parvata Muni
Śrī Rāma Paṇḍita as incarnation of, 255
Paśyanty ātmani cātmānam
verses quoted, 83-84
Patraṁ puṣpaṁ phalaṁ toyam
verses quoted, 169, 242
Patanty adho 'nādṛta-yuṣmad
verses quoted, 60, 102, 136, 172
Patita-pāvana
Caitanya known as, **329**
Peace
found in *saṅkīrtana*
Peace
Kṛṣṇa consciousness only means of, 175
Perfection
by chanting Hare Kṛṣṇa, 165
three ways for, 160
Pitāham asya jagato
verses quoted, 123
Pītāmbara
as devotee of Nityānanda, **385**
Prabha viṣṇave namaḥ
quoted, 37
Prabodhānanda Sarasvatī
belonged to Rāmānuja-sampradāya, 142
cited on influence of Kṛṣṇa consciousness, 21
describes merging as hell, 172
Pradyumna Brahmacārī
as branch of Caitanya tree, **270**
given name Nṛsiṁhānanda Brahmacārī, **286-**287
Pradyumna Miśra
as devotee of Lord in Jagannātha Purī, **335**
Prahlāda Mahārāja
chanted in *saṅkīrtana,* 80
cited on fulfillment of life's mission, 136
Haridāsa Ṭhākura compared to, **277**
his prayer to deliver fallen souls, 74
on serving pure devotee, 170
Prakāśānanda Sarasvatī
belonged to Śaṅkarācārya-sampradāya, 142
converted by Caitanya, 29, 47-143
Prakṛteḥ kriyamāṇāni guṇaiḥ
verse quoted, 174
Prakṛtiṁ svām adhiṣṭhāya
verses quoted, 109
Praṇava
See Oṁkāra
Praṇavaḥ sarva-vedeṣu
quoted, 125
Prāpte sannihite khalu maraṇe
quoted, 48
Prasāda
as diet to cure material disease, 281
importance of taking, 134-135
taken by devotees, 169
Praśna Upaniṣad
quoted on creation of Viṣṇu, 99
Pratāparudra Mahārāja
as devotee of Lord at Jagannātha Purī, **338**
Premā pumartho mahān
quoted, 2, 58, 69
Prīti-sandarbha
as book by Jīva Gosvāmī, 307
love of God explained in, 72

Puṇḍarīka Vidyānidhi
as Rādhārāṇī's father, 259
as spiritual master of Gadādhara Paṇḍita, 259
Purāṇas
only Hari explained in, 128
Purandara Ācārya
as branch of Caitanya tree, **267**-268
Purandara Paṇḍita
as branch of Nityānanda, **368**-369
Pure devotees
association of purifies anyone, 174
becoming *brāhmaṇa* by association with, 36-37
can offer anyone Kṛṣṇa, **388**
cats and dogs liberated by association of, 251-252
don't accept any kind of *mukti,* 172
necessity of approaching, 170
guided by Lord in heart, **210**
headed by Śrīvāsa, **13**
players in transcendental dramas all, 258
transcendental literature written only by, 189-190
Pūrṇam adaḥ pūrṇam idam
verse quoted, 98
Pūrṇasya pūrṇam ādāya
verse quoted, 118, 132
Pūrṇāt pūrṇam udacyate
verse quoted, 115
Puruṣottama
as branch of Caitanya tree, **295**
Puruṣottama
as branch of Caitanya tree, **300**
Puruṣottama
as branch of Caitanya tree, **324**
Puruṣottama Paṇḍita
as branch of Nityānanda, **372**-373

R

Rādhā-Dāmodara temple
established by Jīva Gosvāmī, 307
Rādhā-Kṛṣṇa
worship of Deities of, 184-185
Rādhākuṇḍa
excavated by Gosvāmīs, 311
Raghunātha dāsa resided at, 312
very dear to Kṛṣṇa, 15
Rādhāramaṇa Deities
installed by Gopāla Bhaṭṭa Gosvāmī, 319
Rādhārāṇī
as best of *gopīs,* 15
as pleasure potency of Kṛṣṇa, 125
Caitanya as Kṛṣṇa and, 10, 164
Caitanya tried to taste love of, 234
Rādhārāṇī
Gadādhara dāsa as luster of body of, 282-283
Rādhā-rasa-sudhā-nidhi
as book by Prabodhānanda Sarasvatī, 142
Rādhikā
See Rādhārāṇī
Rāghava Paṇḍita
as branch of Caitanya tree, **264**-266
Raghunandana Ṭhākura
as branch of Caitanya tree, **299**
sacred thread ceremony performed in family of, 35
Raghunātha Bhaṭṭācārya
as devotee of Lord at Vārāṇasī, **347-349**
Raghunātha dāsa Gosvāmī
as associate of Lord in Jagannātha Purī, **332**
as branch of Caitanya tree, **311-318**
as special guide of Kṛṣṇadāsa Kavirāja, **318**
as worshiper of Madana-mohana, 209
Kṛṣṇadāsa Kavirāja prays at feet of, **212**
put in care of Śivānanda Sena, 288
Raghunātha Purī
Vaiṣṇavānanda formerly known as, **379**
Raghunātha (Upādhyāya)
as branch of Nityānanda, **364**
Raghunātha Vaidya
as associate of Lord in Jagannātha Purī, **332**
Rāmabhadra Ācārya
as devotee of Lord in Jagannātha Purī, **345**
Rāmacandra
Anupama's devotion to, 303
Caitanya appeared to Murāri Gupta as, 279
Rāmacandra Kavirāja
as devotee of Nityānanda, **384**
Rāmadāsa
in fraternal love of God, **361**
lived with Vīrabhadra Gosāñi, **359**
Rāmadāsa
as branch of Caitanya tree, **324**
Rāmadāsa
as son of Śivānanda Sena, **289**-290
Rāmadāsa Abhirāma
as branch of Caitanya tree, **327**
Rāmāi
as devotee of Lord at Jagannātha Purī, **342-343**
Rāmānanda Rāya
as branch of Caitanya tree, **300**
as energy of Lord, 6
undisturbed by women, 336
vanquished power of Cupid, 304
Rāmānanda
as devotee of Nityānanda, **382**

Rāmānujācārya
broke teeth of Māyāvādīs, 123
his philosophy a stumbling block to Māyāvādīs, 95
quoted on energies of Absolute, 133
quoted on individuality of soul, 116
Rāmānuja-sampradāya
Prabodhānanda Sarasvatī belonged to, 142
Rāmasena
as devotee of Nityānanda, **384**
Rāmāyaṇa
only Hari explained in, 128
Rāsa dance
imitated by rascals, 7
Kṛṣṇa as enjoyer of, **7**
Rāsas
developed by *gopīs,* 172
devotees relate to Lord in five, 57-58
Rasikānanda-deva
sacred thread ceremony performed in family of, 35
Rasāmṛta-śeṣa
as book by Jīva Gosvāmī, 306
Ratnabāhu
Vijaya dāsa named by Caitanya, **292**
Religion
as first concern of humanity, 240
best described in *Bhāgavatam,* **72**
four principles of, 69
Revatī
Raghunātha Vaidya as incarnation of, 332
Ṛg-veda
quoted on Lord as person, 99
quoted on superiority of Viṣṇu, 103
Ṛg-vedo 'tha yajur-vedaḥ
verses quoted, 56
Rudra
as sub-branch of Caitanya tree, **320**
Rūpa Gosvāmī
addresses Caitanya as most magnanimous incarnation, 142, 168, 234
as branch of Caitanya tree, **301**-306
as worshiper of Madana-mohana, 209
books by, 303-304
cited on auspiciousness of devotional service, 242
constructed Govindajī temple, 152
describes *jagad-guru,* 49
distinguishes between pure and internal devotees, 15
quoted on *bhakti* without reference to *Vedas,* 84
quoted on devotional service ignoring *Vedas,* 188
Rūpa Gosvāmī
quoted on methods of different *ācāryas,* 27
quoted on rareness of devotional service, 81
sent to Vṛndāvana, 152
understood Caitanya as Kṛṣṇa, 16
Rūpa-raghunātha-pade haibe ākuti
verses quoted, 14, 185

S

Śacīdevī
See Śacīmātā
Śacīmātā
Caitanya ate foodstuffs offered at home by, 285
Dāmodara Paṇḍita carried messages from, 268
Īśāna as servant of, 323
Sadānanda Yogīndra
his Māyāvādī philosophy, 82, 101-102
Sadāśiva Kavirāja
as branch of Nityānanda, **377**
Sadāśiva Paṇḍita
as branch of Caitanya tree, **269**
Ṣaḍbhuja
seen by Sārvabhauma, 334
Sa guṇān samatītyaitān brahma
verses quoted, 108
Sakhya-rasa
Kṛṣṇa's cowherd friends serve Him in, 172
Śālagrāma-śilā
worship of, 35
Salvation
devotional service above, 2
See also Liberation
Samādhi
defined, 85
Śambu
See Śiva
Sanātana Gosvāmī
as branch of Caitanya tree, **301**-306
as worshiper of Madana-mohana, 152, 209
books by, 304
preached in western India, **310**
quoted on proper initiation of *brāhmaṇas,* 36
quoted on writing of pure devotee, 189
Rāmānanda Rāya considered equal to by Lord, 337
sent by Caitanya to Vṛndāvana, **150**
taught devotional service by Caitanya, **36-38**
Sanātana
as devotee of Nityānanda, 383
Sāndīpani Muni
as Keśava Bhāratī, 223

Saṅgīta-mādhava
as book by Govinda Kavirāja, 384
Sañjaya
as branch of Caitanya tree, **295**
Saṅgīta-mādhava
as book by Prabodhānanda Sarasvatī, 142
Śaṅkara
as associate of Lord in Jagannātha Purī, **332**
Śaṅkara
as devotee of Nityānanda, **385**
Śaṅkara
as branch of Caitanya tree, **269, 300**
Śaṅkarācārya
accepted *tattvamasi* as *mahā-vākya,* 125-126
as incarnation of Śiva, 94-96, **100,** 148
cheated atheists, 94-96,112
condemned word jugglery, 48, 58
considered Vyāsa mistaken, **114**-117
covers real meaning of *Vedas,* **93-96, 128**
especially stresses Vedānta study, 32
his monist explanations of *Vedānta,* 82
his theory of illusion, 115
Śaṅkara-sampradāya
Keśava Bhāratī belonged to, 26
Prakāśānanda belonged to, 142
Saṅkarṣaṇa
Mīnaketana Rāmadāsa as, 385
Śaṅkarāraṇya
as branch of Caitanya tree, **320**
Saṅkīrtana
as only means of deliverance in modern society, 174
continues despite opponents, 80-81, 143
dispells illusion of *māyā,* 233
everyone intoxicated by, **248-249**
executed by Caitanya, **3-4**
meant to be spread all over world, 245
meant to make people happy, 243
peace found in, 237
propounded with internal devotees, **15**
sannyāsīs necessary to expand, **151**-152
should be preached without discrimination, 230
spiritual master desires disciples to spread, 74
San-mūlāḥ saumyemāḥ prajāḥ
verse quoted, 117
Sannyāsa
accepted by Lord Caitanya, **24-26, 163-164**
four divisions of, 26
Sannyāsīra madhye īśvarera
verses quoted, 221-222
Sannyāsīs
essential for preaching work, 151-152
Śānta-rasa
cows, trees, etc. serve Kṛṣṇa in, 172
Śārīraka
See Vedānta-sūtra
Śārīraka-bhāṣya
accepted by Māyāvādīs as real *Vedānta* commentary, 82
Śārīraka-bhāṣya
as unauthorized commentary, 90, 94
denies doctrine of transformation of energy, 114
one who follows is doomed, 96
rejected by Vaiṣṇavas, 83
Sārvabhauma Bhaṭṭācārya
as branch of Caitanya tree, **333-334**
converted by Caitanya, 29
Sarva-dharmān parityajya
verse quoted, 69, 111
Sarva-karma-paribhraṁśān
verses quoted, 96
Sarvam aṣṭākṣarāntaḥstham
verses quoted, 62
Sarva-vedānta-sārārthaḥ
verses quoted, 62
Sarve vidhi-niṣedhā
verses quoted, 27
Ṣaṣṭhīvara
as branch of Caitanya tree, **322**
Śāstras
Māyāvādīs misinterpret all, 48
See also Scriptures
Satāṁ nindā nāmnaḥ paramam
verses quoted, 177
Sa-tattvato 'nyathā-buddhir
verse quoted, 115
Sat-kriyā-sāra-dīpikā
as book by Gopāla Bhaṭṭa Gosvāmī, 319
Sātvata-pañcarātra
as supplement of *Vedas,* 89
Ṣat-sandarbha
Gopāla Bhaṭṭa Gosvāmī wrote forward to, 319
Satyabhāmā
Jagadānanda Paṇḍita as incarnation of, **263**
Satyarāja
as branch of Caitanya tree, **300**
Satya-yuga
paramparā honored in, 59
Sa vai puṁsāṁ paro dharmo
verses quoted, 72
Sa vṛkṣa-kālākṛtibhiḥ paro 'nyo
verses quoted, 98
Scientists
lack complete knowledge, 91

Scriptures
love of God as conclusion of all, **70**
spiritual master speaks according to, 38
understood from spiritual master, 37-38
Śekhara Paṇḍita
as branch of Caitanya tree, **322**
Senayor ubhayor madhye ratham
verse quoted, 138
Sevonmukhe hi jihvādau svayam
verse quoted, 86, 169
Sense gratification
achieved by pious activities, **170**
Kṛṣṇa immediately delivers to devotee, **171**
Senses
Absolute beyond reach of imperfect, 167
of materialists inefficient, 91
Śikhi Māhiti
as devotee of Lord at Jagannātha Purī, **338-339**
Śikṣāṣṭaka
devotional service instructed in, 165
quoted, 52, 65-66, 307
quoted on chanting holy name, 168-169
quoted on perfectional stage of chanting, 248
Siṁheśvara
as devotee of Lord in Jagannātha Purī, **345**
Sins
committed on strength of chanting, 59
of modern civilization, 244
Siṅgābhaṭṭa
as devotee of Lord in Jagannātha Purī, **345**
Śiva
in form of Śaṅkarācārya, 94-96, **100,** 148
worshiped by Māyāvādīs, 143, 146-148
Śiva Purāṇa
quoted on Śiva's appearance as Śaṅkara, 95
Śivāi
as devotee of Nityānanda, **383**
Śivānanda Cakravartī
identified, 204
Śivānanda Sena
as branch of Caitanya tree, **284-285, 287-290, 338**
experienced three features of Caitanya, **287-**288
his three heroic sons, **289**-290
Skanda Purāṇa
sūtra defined in, 88
Śoce tato vimukha-cetasa
verses quoted, 74
Spirit soul
devotional service as activity of, 108
eternally individual, 116-117, 167
love of God original function of, 69
Spiritual master
as servitor God, 12
becoming *brāhmaṇa* by initiation by,36
desires disciples to preach *saṅkīrtana,* **73-74**
devotional service under direction of, 108,**135-**136
doubts must be referred to, 65
feels obliged to advanced disciple, **73**
hearing from and serving, 37-38, 41, 55
met by grace of Kṛṣṇa, 81
must be *gosvāmī,* 10-11
necessity of faith in, 77
offense of considering him material, 178
offense of neglecting orders of, 59
perfection attained by mercy of, 160, 220, 338
Śravaṇādi-śuddha-citte karaye
verse quoted, 134
Śravaṇaṁ kīrtanaṁ viṣṇoḥ
verses quoted, 134, 228
Śravaṇaṁ naiva kartavyam
verses quoted, 188
Śrīdāmā
Śrī Rāmadāsa formerly, 359
Śrīdhara
as branch of Caitanya tree, **292-293**
as devotee of Nityānanda, **382**
Śrīdhara Svāmī
accepts *brāhmaṇas* by qualification, 51
describes *oṁkāra* as seed of deliverance, 124
Śrī Gālīma
as branch of Caitanya tree, 324
Śrī Gopāla dāsa
as branch of Caitanya tree, 324
Śrī Gopīkānta
as branch of Caitanya tree, **323**
Śrī Govinda dāsa
as devotee of Lord in Jagannātha Purī, **340-341**
Śrī Govinda dāsa
as author of Gaura-kṛṣṇodaya, 261
Śrī Jānakīnātha
as branch of Caitanya tree, **326**
Śrīkānta Sena
as sub-branch of Caitanya tree, **290**
Śrīkara
as branch of Caitanya tree, **323**
Śrī-kṛṣṇa-caitanya rādhā kṛṣṇa nahe anya
verse quoted, 10
Śrīmad-Bhāgavatam
as natural commentary on *Vedānta,* 32, 33, 90, 94, 188
beginning words of, 94
cited on chanting holy name, 56
cited on executing occupational duty, 280

Śrīmad-Bhāgavatam
cited on two kinds of *sannyāsīs,* 26
compiled by Vyāsadeva, 58
first verse of quoted, 121-122
Gītā as preliminary study of, 69
Jīva Gosvāmī fond of from childhood, 306
Kṛṣṇa consciousness follows injunctions of
meant for those aloof from jealousy, 137
professional readers of, 188
quoted in *Caitanya-bhāgavata,* **188**
quoted on acting in knowledge, 136
quoted on best religion, 72
quoted on chanting holy name, 62, 163
quoted on cheating religious systems, 69
quoted on Caitanya, 4
quoted on compilation of Vedic literature, 58
quoted on cosmos as Lord's energy, 124
quoted on development of *bhakti,* 83-84
quoted on effects of associating with modes of nature, 174
quoted on falldown of Māyāvādīs, 102
quoted on falling from *brahmajyoti,* 172
quoted on goal of human life, 139
quoted on good qualities of devotees, **199**
quoted on good qualities of trees, **244**
quoted on instructions of Prahlāda, 170
quoted on Kṛṣṇa as servant of devotee, **171**
quoted on nine kinds of devotional service, 134
quoted on offenses to holy name, 60
quoted on purpose of Vyāsadeva, 102
quoted on Prahlāda's desire to save fallen souls, 74
quoted on promotion to Vaiṣṇava platform, 174-175
quoted on real understanding of *Vedānta,* 140
quoted on real welfare activities, **239**
quoted on spiritual varieties, 100
quoted on superiority of devotional service, 137
quoted on three features of Absolute, 97
recited constantly by Raghunātha Bhaṭṭācārya,
Sanātana Gosvāmī instructed on, **37**-38
349
studied by Sanātana Gosvāmī at home, 304-305
teaches only love of God, 69
verse from quoted by Caitanya, **76**
Śrī Mādhava-mahotsava
as book by Jīva Gosvāmī, 306
Śrī Madhusūdana
as branch of Caitanya tree, **323**
Śrīmān Paṇḍita
as branch of Caitanya tree, **271**
Śrīmān Sena
as branch of Caitanya tree, **282**
Śrī Manta
as devotee of Nityānanda, **383**
Śrīnātha Miśra
as branch of Caitanya tree, **323**
Śrīnātha Paṇḍita
as branch of Caitanya tree, **321**
Śrīnidhi
as branch of Caitanya tree, **255**
Śrīnidhi
as branch of Caitanya tree, **323**
Śrīnivāsa Ācārya
blessed by Raghunātha dāsa, 312
describes six Gosvāmīs, 17, 316
inspired by Jīva Gosvāmī, 307
Śrīpati
as branch of Caitanya tree, **255**
Śrīrāma
as branch of Caitanya tree, **323**
Śrī Rāma Paṇḍita
as incarnation of Parvata Muni, 255
Śrīraṅga
as devotee of Nityānanda, **384**
Śrī Saṅkalpa-kalpavṛkṣa
as book by Jīva Gosvāmī, 306
Śrīvāsa Prabhu
as incarnation of Nārada Muni, 255
as marginal potency of Caitanya, 4
as pure devotee, 5
as worshiper of three predominators, 12
Caitanya performed dramas with, 258
devotees headed by, **13, 215**
dogs in household of liberated, 252
Nārāyaṇa Paṇḍita as associate of, 271
Śṛṇu devi pravakṣyāmi
verses quoted, 96
Sṛṣṭi-sthiti-pralaya-sādhana
verses quoted, 147
Śruti-smṛti-purāṇādi
verses quoted, 84, 187
Sthāna-nirūpaṇa
as book by Raghunātha Vaidya, 332
Stavamālā
as book by Rūpa Gosvāmī, 303
Stavāvalī
as book by Raghunātha dāsa Gosvāmī, 312
Stokakṛṣṇa
Puruṣottama Paṇḍita as, 373
Striyo vaiśyās tathā śūdrās
verses quoted, 174
Sukhānanda Purī
as root of tree of devotional service, **221**

Svarūpa Dāmodara
always chanted Hare Kṛṣṇa, 222
as associate of Lord in Jagannātha Purī, **332**
cited on identity of Caitanya, 10
considers Māyāvādīs insane, 96
Puṇḍarīka Vidyānidhi as friend of, 259
Raghunātha dāsa as assistant of, **313**
Śvetāśvatara Upaniṣad
described Absolute with no hands or legs, 99
quoted on Lord's multifarious energies, 98
quoted on inconceivable energies of Lord, 115
Śyāmakuṇḍa
very dear to Kṛṣṇa, 15
Śyāmānanda Gosvāmī
constructed Śyāmasundara temple, 152
Subāhu
Uddhāraṇa Datta Ṭhākura as, **377**
Subala
Gaurīdāsa Paṇḍita as, 367
Śubhānanda
as branch of Caitanya tree, **323**
Subuddhi Miśra
as branch of Caitanya tree, **323**
Sudāma
Sundarānanda as, 364
Śuddha-bhakata-caraṇa-reṇu
verse quoted, 87
Śūdras
can approach Supreme, 174
communism as movement of, 175
everyone at present born, 51
Śuklāmbara Brahmacārī
as branch of Caitanya tree, **272**
Sulocana
as branch of Caitanya tree, **299**
Sulocana
as devotee of Nityānanda, **383**
Sundarānanda
as branch of Nityānanda, **364**-365
Śūnyāyitaṁ jagat sarvam
verses quoted, 65-66, 248
Supersoul
Lord guides from within as, 210
Supreme Lord
as Parabrahman, 133
compared to blazing fire, **105**
compared to sun, 120-122
compared to touchstone, **120**
full of spiritual potencies, **99**-100
has multifarious energies, 98
identical with His name, 169
known as *Akiñcana-gocara,* 2
opulent in all respects, **119**
Supreme Lord
possesses limited and unlimited energies, 105-106
submissive to devotees, **138**
under influence of transcendental bliss, 72
See also Kṛṣṇa, Caitanya Mahāprabhu
Sūryadāsa Sarakhela
as branch of Nityānanda, **366**-367
Sūtra-mālikā
as book by Jīva Gosvāmī, 306

T

Tac chraddadhānā munayo
verses quoted, 83-84
Tad ahaṁ bhakty-upahṛtam
verses quoted, 169, 242
Tad ananyatvam ārambhaṇa
verse quoted, 114
Tad rajas-tamo-bhāvāḥ kāma
verse quoted, 174-175
Tad evaṁ prīter lakṣaṇam
verses quoted, 72
Tad viddhi praṇipātena
verse quoted, 41
Tad viṣṇoḥ paramaṁ padam
quoted, 99
Tān ahaṁ dviṣataḥ krūrān
verses quoted, 127
Tāṅ-sabāra pada-reṇu mora
verses quoted, 161
Taittirīya Upaniṣad
quoted on Brahman as original cause, 115-116
Tapana Ācārya
as devotee of Lord in Jagannātha Purī, **345**
Tapana Miśra
as devotee of Lord at Vārāṇasī, **347**
as *kaniṣṭha-adhikārī,* 40
blasphemy of Caitanya intolerable to, 39
Caitanya accepted food at house of, **35**
Tasyaite kathitā hy arthāḥ
verses quoted, 38, 77
Tathā dīkṣā-vidhānena
verses quoted, 36
Tatrārpitā niyamitaḥ smaraṇe
verses quoted, 124
Tattvamasi
accepted as *mahā-vākya* by Śaṅkara, 125-126
as partial explanation of *Vedas,* **126-127**
Tattva-sandarbha
as book by Jīva Gosvāmī, 307
Te dvandva-moha-nirmuktā
verses quoted, 180

Tepus tapas te juhuvuḥ
verses quoted, 56
Ṭhākura Sāraṅga dāsa
as branch of Caitanya tree, 324-325
Tirumalaya Bhaṭṭa
as brother of Prabodhānanda Sarasvatī, 142
Traiguṇya-viṣayā vedā
verse quoted, 100
Transcendentalists
three classes of, 84
Transformation of energy
See Energy, transformation of
Transmigration
described in *Gītā*, 111
99.9% of Indians believe in, 237-238
of living beings, 233
understanding science of, 167-168
Trayo vedāḥ ṣaḍ-aṅgāni
verses quoted, 62
Tretā-yuga
paramparā honored in, 59
Tṛṇād api sunīcena
verses quoted, 39, 52, 168, 307
Tulasī
dog has no respect for, 251
Tvayy asta-bhāvād aviśuddha
verses quoted, 100
Tyaktvā dehaṁ punar janma
verses quoted, 241

U

Uddhāraṇa Datta Ṭhākura
as branch of Nityānanda, **377**-379
Uddhava
Paramānanda Purī as, 222-223
Uddhava-sandeśa
as book by Rūpa Gosvāmī, 303
Ujjvala-nīlamaṇi
as book by Rūpa Gosvāmī, 303
Jīva Gosvāmī's commentary on, 306
U-kāreṇocyate rādhā
verses quoted, 125
Upadeśāmṛta
cited on development of devotional service, 15
Upaniṣads
bhakti developed on basis of, 84
explained impersonally by Māyāvādīs, 82
meant to establish personal feature of Absolute, 95
must be understood as they are, **91**-92
108 listed, 92-93
quoted on six opulences of Lord, 132

Uttara-mīmāṁsā
See Vedānta-sūtra, 88

V

Vairāgya-vidyā-nijabhaktiyoga
verse quoted, 334
Vaiṣṇavānanda
as branch of Nityānanda, **379**
Vaiṣṇava-mañjuṣā
cited on Caitanya taking *sannyāsa*, 223
Vaiṣṇavas
as greatest philosophers in world, 83-85
can deliver Kṛṣṇa to everyone, 388
can't tolerate Māyāvāda philosophy, 96
consider creation temporary not false, 116
follow orders of *guru* and Kṛṣṇa, 206-207
get spiritual body after death, 53
greater than *brāhmaṇas*, 18
know how to approach Lord directly, 134
Māyāvādīs try to defy, 80
never accept *sāyujya-mukti*, 172
never see faults of others, **201**
one should not tolerate blasphemy against, 308
only can write transcendental literature, 206-207, 215-216
respectful to everyone, 45
second-class described, 50-51
should be conversant with *Vedānta*, 56-57
tolerant as trees, 39
various philosophies of, 82
worship demigods on principles of *Brahma-saṁhitā*, 147-148
See also Devotees
Vaiṣṇava-toṣaṇī
as book by Sanātana Gosvāmī, 304
Vaiśyas
can approach Supreme, 174
capitalism meant for, 175
engagements of, 280
Vakreśvara
as associate of Lord in Jagannātha Purī, 332
Vakreśvara Paṇḍita
could dance for seventy-two hours, **261-262**
Devānanda Paṇḍita saved by grace of, **298**
Vallabha
as former name of Anupama, 302
Vallabha Sena
as sub-branch of Caitanya tree, **290**
Vanamālī Paṇḍita
as branch of Caitanya tree, **295**-296
Vānaprastha
four divisions of, 26

Vāṇīnātha
as branch of Caitanya tree, **326**
Vāṇīnātha Vasu
as dear servant of Caitanya, **300**
Varāha
Caitanya manifest His form as, 279
Vārāṇasī
Caitanya met with Māyāvādīs at, **34**
devotees of Lord in, **347**-349
impersonalists of, 29
residents of Lord Caitanya, **144**-149
Varṇas
named, 24
Vasanta
as devotee of Nityānanda, **383**
Vasudāma
Dhanañjaya Paṇḍita as, 371
Vasudeva
Kṛṣṇa as son of, 75
Vāsudeva
as full-fledged Absolute Truth, 84
Vāsudeva
as devotee of Nityānanda, **360**
made wood and stone melt, **362**
Vāsudeva
as eighty-fourth branch of Caitanya tree, **326-328**
Vāsudev Datta
as branch of Caitanya tree, **274**-275
Vātsalya-rasa
elderly *gopīs* serve Kṛṣṇa in, 172
Vāyu Purāṇa
sūtra defined in, 88
Vedāham etaṁ puruṣaṁ mahāntam
verse quoted, 98
Vedaiś ca sarvair aham
verse quoted, 31, 49, 123, 126
Vedānta-sūtra
appropriate candidate for study of, 52
as words spoken by Lord in form of Vyāsadeva, **88**
Bhāgavatam as natural commentary on, 90, 94, 188
Caitanya's direct explanation of, 95-96, **131**-140
contents of described, 89-90
different names of, 88
doctrine of transformation of energy in, **114**-117
emanated from breathing of Nārāyaṇa, 89
explained impersonally by Māyāvādīs, 82
fully understood by Vaiṣṇava *ācāryas,* 83-85
Hare Kṛṣṇa *mantra* as reality of all, 62
Kṛṣṇa as compiler of, 31
Vedānta-sūtra
meant to deliver fallen souls, 102
meant to establish personal feature of Absolute, 95
must be understood as it is, **91**-92
no one in Kali-yuga able to study, 55
quoted on doctrine of transformation of energy, 115
quoted on purpose of human life, 237
Vedānta-darśana
See Vedānta-sūtra, 88
Vedānta-sāra
as impersonalist book by Sadānanda Yogīndra, 82, 101
Vedānta-vākyeṣu sadā
verse quoted, 32
Vedānta tu mahā-śāstre
verses quoted, 94-95
Vadanti tat tattva-vidas
verses quoted, 97
Vedānto nāma upaniṣat
text quoted, 82
Vedārtha-saṅgraha
quoted on diverse energies of Absolute, 133
Vedas
emanate from breathing of Nārāyaṇa, 89
Kṛṣṇa known by and knower of, 31, 49, 55, 123
misinterpretation of deprecated by Caitanya, 92
offense of minimizing authority of, 59
person who chants *Ha-ri* has already studied, 56
quoted on faith in spiritual master, 38, 77
quoted on varieties of Lord's energies, 5
Śaṅkara's indirect explanation of, **128**-129
Vede rāmāyaṇe caiva purāṇe
verses quoted, 128
Vedic hymns
holy name essence of, **54,** 59, **59**-60
Vedic literature
as source of real knowledge, 94
blasphemy of, 178
compiled by Vyāsadeva, 58
describes Kṛṣṇa as energetic, **106**
devotional service that ignores, 188
explained impersonally by Māyāvādīs, 82
indirectly described by Śaṅkara, **93-96**
madhyama-adhikārī must be learned in, 84
oṁkāra as principal word in, **122**-126
only Hari explained in, 128
Supreme Lord as goal of, **132**
thousands of references to Viṣṇu's energy in, 103

Vedic literature
understood only in disciplic succession, 37-38
Vedyaṁ pavitram oṁkāra
verses quoted, 123
Vedyaṁ vāstavam atra vastu
verses quoted, 137
Vicitra-śaktiḥ puruṣaḥ purāṇaḥ
verse quoted, 98
Vidagdha-mādhava
as book by Rūpa Gosvāmī, 303, 304
taking shelter of, 184
Vidyānanda
as branch of Caitanya tree, **300**
Vijaya dāsa
as branch of Caitanya tree, **291**-292
Vīrabhadra Gosāñi
as branch of Nityānanda Prabhu, **356**-359
as son of Nityānanda Prabhu, 321
as topmost branch of Nityānanda, **387**
Viṣaya chāḍiyā kabe' śuddha
verses quoted, 14, 184
Viṣṇāi
as devotee of Nityānanda, **383**
Viṣṇu
as maintainer of universe, 56
as predominator, 5
as supreme living force, 8
changes body of devotee, 37
considered product of ignorance by Sadānanda Yogīndra, 101
demigods never equal to, 103, 178
learned think only of, 99
not product of material energy, 103-104
oṁkāra as good as, 124-125
three categories of His potency, **109**-112
worshiped by Jarāsandha, **162**
worshiped for material success by atheists, 143, 146-148, 165
Viṣṇudāsa
as branch of Nityānanda, **380**
Viṣṇupriyā
as wife of Caitanya, 296
Viṣṇu Purāṇa
cited on two energies of Lord, 99
describes Kṛṣṇa as energetic, **106**
quoted on energies of Viṣṇu, 109
quoted on expansion of Lord's energies, 113
quoted on welfare work for all, **241**
Viṣṇu-Purī
as root of tree of devotional service, **221**
Viṣṇu-tattva
Caitanya in ecstasy as, 294-295
Viśvambhara
Caitanya known as, **217**
Viṣṇusvāmī
Māyāvādīs took advantage of his philosophy, 95
Viśvanātha
quoted on mercy of spiritual master, 220
Viśvanātha Cakravartī Ṭhākura
cited on accepting words of spiritual master, 55
quoted on mercy of Vaiṣṇavas, 388
Viśvarūpa
as elder brother of Caitanya, 320
Vṛndāvana
devotee attracted to residents of, 172
Govinda worshiped in, **195-196**
mission of Rūpa and Sanātana in, **311**
Rūpa and Sanātana sent by Caitanya to, **150, 152**
seen by purified mind, 184
Vṛndāvana dāsa Ṭhākura
as author of *Caitanya-bhāgavata,* 157, 186
as incarnation of Vyāsa, **386**
as son of Nārāyaṇī, 190
depicted pastimes of Caitanya, **187**
Vṛndāvana-śataka
as book by Prabodhānanda Sarasvatī, 142
Vṛndāvaneśvarī
See Rādhārāṇī
Vyāsadeva
as compiler of Vedic literature, 58
his doctrine of transformation of energy, **114-**117
Nārāyaṇa in form of as author of *Vedānta,* **88**
saw separated energy of Lord, 111
Vṛndāvana dāsa as incarnation of, **386**
wrote to deliver fallen souls, 102
Vyāsa-sūtra
See Vedānta-sūtra, 88
Vyeṅkaṭa Bhaṭṭa
as brother of Prabodhānanda Sarasvatī, 142

W

Women
can approach Supreme, 174
World, material
actually no scarcity in, 235
as Brahman, 115
as eternally true, 117
as reflection of spiritual world, 108
chanting and dancing not of, 17
considered false by Māyāvādīs, 22
created by glance of Lord, 115
everyone's body temporary in, 98
everything limited in, 105

World, material
extinguishes fiery quality of soul, 105
Supreme Lord beyond, 98
tree of *bhakti* not of, 228
Viṣṇu's name all-auspicious in, 178
World, spiritual
as expansion of potency of *oṁkāra,* 124
considered void by Māyāvādīs, 29
material world as reflection of, 108
no creation in, 105
soul retains identity in, 116
spiritual potency manifested in, 109
spiritual varieties in, **5**
storehouse of love never depleted in, 18
tree of *bhakti* grows in, 228
Viṣṇu belongs to, 104

Y

Yac cakṣur eṣa savitā sakala
verses quoted, 148
Yādavācārya Gosvāmī
identified, 203
Yadā yadā hi dharmasya
verses quoted, **111**, 164
Yadunandana
as branch of Caitanya tree, **328**
Yadunandana Ācārya
initiated by Vāsudeva Datta, 275
Yadunātha
as branch of Caitanya tree, **300**
Yadunātha Kavicandra
as branch of Nityānanda, **373**
Yaḥ prayāti tyajan deham
verses quoted, 122, 123
Yaḥ śambhutām api tathā
verses quoted, 147
Yaḥ sarva-jñaḥ sarva-vit
quoted, 133
Yajñaiḥ saṅkīrtana-prāyair
verses quoted, 4
Yānti deva-vratā devān
quoted, 104, **241**
Yaśodā
Kṛṣṇa appears as son of, 7
Yasya deve parā bhaktir
verses quoted, 38, **77**
Yasyājñay bhramati sambhṛta
verses quoted, 148
Yasya prasādād bhagavat-prasādo
verses quoted, 220, 388
Yataḥ khyātiṁ yātaṁ katham
verses quoted, 177
Yathā kāñcanatāṁ yāti
verses quoted, 36
Yato vā imāni bhūtāni jāyante
verses quoted, **115**, 116
Yavanas
became devotees, **29**
Yāvam na jijñāsata ātma-tattvam
verses quoted, 139
Yayā sammohito jīva ātmānam
quoted, 111
Yena tena prakāreṇa
verses quoted, 27
Ye 'nye' ravindākṣa vimukta
verses quoted, 100
Yeṣāṁ tv anta-gatam
verses quoted, 180
Yoga
as imperfect means of realizing Absolute, 84
Yogasārastava
Jīva Gosvāmī's commentary on, 306
Yogīs
as transcendental, 84
Yudhiṣṭhira
Kṛṣṇa acted as order-carrier of, **171**
Yugāyitaṁ nimeṣeṇa cakṣuṣā
verses quoted, 65-66, **248**